W9-BRL-902

WILLIAM RUFUS

Curtis A. Sumpter

WILLIAM RUFUS

Frank Barlow

Fellow of the British Academy
Emeritus Professor of History in the University of Exeter

UNIVERSITY OF CALIFORNIA PRESS
BERKELEY AND LOS ANGELES

First published 1983
©*1983 Frank Barlow*

University of California Press
Berkeley and Los Angeles, California

Library of Congress Cataloging in Publication Data

Barlow, Frank.
  William Rufus.

  (English monarchs)
  Bibliography: p.
  Includes index.
  1. William II, King of England, 1056?–1100.
  2. Great Britain – History – William II, Rufus,
  1087–1100. 3. Great Britain – Kings and rulers -
  Biography. I. Title. II. Series: English
  monarchs (University of California Press)
  DA197.5.B37 1983   942.02'2'0924 [B] 82–45902
  ISBN 0–520–04936–5

Printed in Great Britain

Tamb. And ride in triumph through *Persepolis*?
 Is it not brave to be a King, *Techelles*?
 Vsumcasane and *Theridamas*,
 Is it not passing brave to be a King,
 And ride in triumph through *Persepolis*?
Tech. O my Lord, tis sweet and full of pompe.
Vsum. To be a King, is halfe to be a God.
Ther. A God is not so glorious as a King:
 I thinke the pleasure they enjoy in heaven
 Can not compare with kingly joyes in earth.
 To weare a Crowne enchac'd with pearle and golde,
 Whose vertues carie with it life and death,
 To aske, and have: commaund and be obeyed:
 When looks breed love, with lookes to gaine the prize.
 Such power attractive shines in princes eyes.

       MARLOWE, *Tamburlaine*, lines 755–69

CONTENTS

ILLUSTRATIONS

PLATES

MAPS

GENEALOGICAL TABLES *pages* 466 *to* 470

Acknowledgements and thanks for permission to reproduce photographs are due to the Archives Départementales de la Seine-Maritime, Rouen, for plate 1a; to the Provost and Fellows of Eton College for plate 1b; to the British Museum for plates 2a, 2b, 2c, 2d, 2e and 4b; to the British Library for plates 3a and 3b; to the Dean and Chapter of Durham for plates 5a, 5b and 14b; to the Bodleian Library, Oxford, for plates 6a and 6b; to the Public Record Office for plate 7; to the National Monuments Record for plates 8a, 8b, 9a, 10, 13b and 14a; to Aerofilms Ltd for plates 9b and 13a; to the Courtauld Institute of Art for plate 11; to the Dean and Chapter of Westminster for plate 12; and to the Phaidon Picture Archive for plates 15a, 15b, 16a and 16b.

The maps and genealogical tables were re-drawn from the author's roughs by Neil Hyslop.

PREFACE

When I was teaching at the University of Exeter, I offered the Reign of William Rufus a few times as a 'Special Subject' and followed my usual method of devoting the seminars to the reading and exposition of the main literary texts. It is, of course, the typical medieval *modus operandi*, and is particularly useful with medieval sources which were not intended to present historical truth as we understand it today. To get even a shadowy understanding of men and women of the distant past is exceptionally difficult and is certainly not a task for the faint-hearted; but close attention to recorded actions and the views of their recorders puts at least the outward behaviour of the actors on display; and most of us think, with the canonists, that there is usually some relationship between *exteriora* and *interiora*.

Although I do not believe we ever made great discoveries in class, I was always surprised by the views of my pupils, who were mostly girls and often religiously inclined. Without exception they disliked Anselm and almost without exception they liked Rufus. Medieval piety has lost most of its savour while medieval panache still strikes a chord. I think they would have liked William of Malmesbury more had they been better equipped to tackle his difficult Latin; but they revelled in Orderic Vitalis. He brought history alive; and they enjoyed particularly his dramatisations. It was no doubt salutary for me to have to appear as Anselm's advocate and to preach the virtues of chroniclers more sober than the monk of St Evroul. All the same, the modern historian should not be too puritanical. He knows – or should know – that he is only commenting on and refashioning the fictions of the past; and to exclude all the best yarns serves no good purpose. They are often the closest we can get to the truth of the matter, metaphors which provide authentic local colour.

In 1955 I wrote (*The Feudal Kingdom of England*, p. 170), 'William Rufus is a controversial figure; but the events of his reign speak for themselves. He confirmed the royal power in England and he restored the ducal rights in Normandy, yet never made a sad labour of his humdrum task. He was a buffoon with a purpose, a jester who accepted his father's mantle but spread it in extravagant caprice.' Although I might express it a little differently now, I am not surprised by my more juvenile conceits. Only the legendary can convey Rufus's true achievement.

I wish to thank my colleagues George Greenaway and Robert Higham, C. Warren Hollister and the general editor of this series for reading my manuscript and making valuable corrections and suggestions for improvement. I am also grateful to my friends and well-wishers, Gabriella Barlow, David Bates, Marjorie Chibnall, Pierre Chaplais, John Fox, John Higgitt, Derek Keene, Arthur T. Lloyd, Henry Loyn, Jeffrey West and George Zarnecki, who have done me kind and useful services.

Frank Barlow
Kenton, Exeter
July 1983

ABBREVIATED REFERENCES

Acta Lanfranci	in *ASC* (text), *q.v.*, 271–5
Act. Pont. Cen.	*Actus Pontificum Cenomannis in urbe degentium*, ed. G. Busson and A. Ledru (Archives historiques du Maine, 2, Le Mans, 1901)
Ann. Winton.	in *Annales Monastici*, ii, ed. H.R. Luard (Rolls ser., 1865)
Anselm, *Letters*	in *S. Anselmi Opera Omnia*, ed. F.S. Schmitt, iii–iv (1946, 1949)
Arnulf of Lisieux, *Letters*	*The Letters of Arnulf of Lisieux*, ed. F. Barlow (RHS, Camden, 3rd ser., lxi, 1939)
ASC	*Anglo-Saxon Chronicle*: text, *Two of the Saxon Chronicles parallel*, ed. J. Earle (1865); commentary and index, C. Plummer (1899); *The Peterborough Chronicle, 1070–1154*, ed. C. Clark (2nd edn, 1970); translation, D. Whitelock with D.C. Douglas and S.I. Tucker, in *English Historical Documents*, ii (1955), ed. D.C. Douglas and G.W. Greenaway (2nd edn, 1981), and independently (1961)
ASS	*Acta Sanctorum*, ed. J. Bollandus, G. Henschenius, etc. (1734–)
Barlow, *EC 1000–1066, 1066–1154*	F. Barlow, *The English Church, 1000–1066* (2nd edn, 1979), *1066–1154* (1979)
Bates, *Normandy before 1066*	David Bates, *Normandy before 1066* (1982)
Battle, I, II, III, IV	*Proceedings of the Battle Conference on Anglo-Norman Studies*, ed. R.A. Brown, I (1978), II (1979), III (1980), IV (1981) (published 1979–82)
Baudri de Bourgueil	*Les oeuvres poétiques de Baudri de Bourgueil*, ed. Phyllis Abrahams (Paris 1926)

Brevis Relatio	in *Scriptores rerum gestarum Willelmi Conquestoris*, ed. J.A. Giles (Caxton Soc., 1845)
CDF	J.H. Round, *Calendar of Documents preserved in France* (1899)
Chron. Abingdon	*Chronicon Monasterii de Abingdon*, ed. J. Stevenson (Rolls ser., 1858)
Chron. Battle	*The Chronicle of Battle Abbey*, ed. and trans. E. Searle (Oxford Medieval Texts, 1980)
Chron. mon. de Hida	in *Liber Monasterii de Hyda*, ed. E. Edwards (Rolls ser., 1866)
Constitutio (domus regis)	in *Dialogus, q.v.*
Craster	H.H.E. Craster, 'A contemporary record of the pontificate of Ranulf Flambard', *Archaeologia Æliana*, 4th ser., vii (1930)
David, *RC*	C.W. David, *Robert Curthose, duke of Normandy* (Cambridge, Mass., 1920)
DB	*Domesday Book, seu liber censualis* . . . , ed. A. Farley (Record Commission, 1783) (the columns in vol. i are indicated by a–d)
De Injusta Vexatione	in Simeon, *Opera, q.v.*, i, 170–95
De obitu Willelmi	in *GND, q.v.*
Dialogus (de Scaccario)	ed. and trans. C. Johnson (1950)
DNB	*Dictionary of National Biography*
Domesday Gazetteer	compiled by H.C. Darby and G.R. Versey (1975)
Domesday Monachorum	D.C. Douglas, *The Domesday Monachorum of Christ Church Canterbury* (1944)
Douglas, *WC*	D.C. Douglas, *William the Conqueror* (1964)
Dugdale, *Monasticon*	W. Dugdale, *Monasticon Anglicanum*, ed. J. Caley, H. Ellis, B. Bandinel (1817–30)
Duncombe, 'Feudal Tenure'	G.R. Duncombe, 'Feudal tenure in eleventh-century England: the Norman Conquest of Kent' (unpublished Exeter MA thesis, 1967)

Eadmer, *HN*   *Historia Novorum in Anglia*, ed. M. Rule (Rolls ser., 1884)

Eadmer, *VA*   *The Life of St Anselm by Eadmer*, ed. and trans. R.W.
                       Southern (1962)

EHR   *English Historical Review*

Facsimiles (of royal T.A.M. Bishop and P. Chaplais, *Facsimiles of English*
  writs)   *royal writs to A.D. 1100* (Galbraith *Festschrift*, 1957)

Farrer, *Honors and*   W. Farrer, *Honors and knights' fees* (3 vols, 1923–5)
  knights' fees

Fauroux, *Recueil*   *Recueil des actes des ducs de Normandie (911–1066)*, ed.
                       Marie Fauroux (Mém. Soc. Ant. Norm., xxxi, Caen, 1961)

Fliche, *Philippe I*   A. Fliche, *Le Règne de Philippe I, roi de France*
                       (1060–1108) (Paris 1912)

Florence   Florence of Worcester, *Chronicon ex chronicis*, ed. B.
                       Thorpe (Eng. Hist. Soc., 1848–9)

FNC   E.A. Freeman, *The History of the Norman Conquest of*
                       England (I, II, 2nd edn, 1870; III–V, 1st edn, 1869–75)

Foreville   *Guillaume de Poitiers: Histoire de Guillaume le Conquérant*
                       [GG], ed. Raymonde Foreville (Paris 1952)

FWR   E.A. Freeman, *The Reign of William Rufus* (1882)

Gaimar   *Lestorie des Engles*, ed. T.D. Hardy and C.T. Martin
                       (Rolls ser., 1888–9)

Gallia Christiana   *Gallia Christiana in provinciis ecclesiasticis distributa*, XI, ed.
                       monks of St Maur (Paris 1759)

Gawain   *Sir Gawain and the Green Knight*, trans. B. Stone (1959)

GEC   G.E.C[okayne], *The Complete Peerage of England, Scotland,*
                       Ireland, Great Britain and the United Kingdom (rev. edn,
                       1910–59)

GG   William of Poitiers, *Gesta Guillelmi*, *see* Foreville

Gilbert Crispin   J.A. Robinson, *Gilbert Crispin abbot of Westminster* (Notes
                       and Docs. relating to Westminster Abbey, no. 3, 1911)

GND   *Guillaume de Jumièges: Gesta Normannorum Ducum*, ed. J.
                       Marx (Soc. de l'Histoire de Normandie, 1914)

GP   William of Malmesbury, *De Gestis pontificum Anglorum*,
                       ed. N.E.S.A. Hamilton (Rolls ser., 1870)

GR	William of Malmesbury, *De Gestis regum Anglorum*, ed. W. Stubbs (Rolls ser., 1887–9)
Greenway, *Mowbray Charters*	D.E. Greenway, *Charters of the Honour of Mowbray* (British Academy, Records of Social and Economic History, n.s. I, 1972)
Halphen, *Anjou*	L. Halphen, *Le comté d'Anjou au XIe siècle* (Paris 1906)
Haskins, *NI*	C.H. Haskins, *Norman Institutions* (New York 1918, 1967)
HBC	*Handbook of British Chronology*, ed. F.M. Powicke and E.B. Fryde (2nd edn, 1961)
HCY	*see* Hugh
Herbert (of Norwich), *Letters*	*Epistolae Herberti de Losinga, Osberti de Clara, et Elmeri*, ed. R. Anstruther (Brussels 1846)
HH	*Henrici Huntendunensis historia Anglorum*, ed. T. Arnold (Rolls ser., 1879)
Hist. mon. Gloucest.	*Historia et cartularium monasterii Gloucestriae*, ed. W.H. Hart (Rolls ser., 1863–7)
Hist. Nov.	William of Malmesbury, *Historia Novella*, ed. and trans. K.R. Potter (1955)
HN	*see* Eadmer
HRH	*The Heads of Religious Houses, England and Wales, 942–1216*, ed. D. Knowles, C.N.L. Brooke, V. London (1972)
Hugh, *HCY*	*Hugh the Chantor: the History of the Church of York, 1066–1127*, ed. and trans. C. Johnson (1961)
Hugh of Flavigny, *Chronicon*	in *Monumenta Germaniae Historica, script.*, viii, ed. G.H. Pertz (Hannover 1759)
Ivo of Chartres, *Letters*	in Migne *PL*, *q.v.*, clxii
JEH	*Journal of Ecclesiastical History*
John of Salisbury, *Letters*	*The Letters of John of Salisbury*, i, ed. W.J. Millor, H.E. Butler and C.N.L. Brooke (1955); ii, ed. Millor and Brooke (1979)
John of Salisbury, *Policraticus*	*Iohannis Saresberiensis episcopi Carnotensis Policraticus*, ed. C.C.J. Webb (1909)

Lanfranc, *Letters*   *The Letters of Lanfranc archbishop of Canterbury*, ed. and trans. Helen Clover and Margaret Gibson (1979)

Latouche, *Maine*   R. Latouche, *Histoire du comté du Maine pendant le Xe et le XIe siècle* (Bibl. de l'école des Hautes Etudes . . . Sciences historiques et philologiques, Paris 1910)

Leges Henrici Primi   ed. L.J. Downer (1972)

Le Patourel, *Norman Empire*   J. Le Patourel, *The Norman Empire* (1976)

le Prévost   *Orderici Vitalis ecclesiasticae historiae libri tredecim*, ed. A. le Prévost (Soc. de l'Histoire de France, Paris, 1838–55)

Liber Eliensis   ed. E.O. Blake (RHS, Camden, 3rd ser., xcii, 1962)

Liber Vitae   *Liber Vitae ecclesiae Dunelmensis*, ed. W.H. Stevenson (Surtees Soc., xiii, 1841)

Liebermann, *Gesetze*   F. Liebermann, *Die Gesetze der Angelsachsen* (Halle 1903)

Lloyd, *History of Wales*   J.E. Lloyd, *A History of Wales*, ii (3rd edn, 1939)

Loyd, *Families*   L.C. Loyd, *The origins of some Anglo-Norman families*, ed. C.T. Clay and D.C. Douglas (Harleian Soc., ciii, 1951)

Luchaire, *Louis VI*   A. Luchaire, *Louis VI le Gros: Annales de sa Vie et de son Règne* (Paris 1890)

Mason, 'Roger de Montgomery and his sons'   J.E.A. Mason, in *TRHS*, 5th ser., xiii (1963), 1 ff.

Migne *PL*   *Patrologia Latina*, ed. J.P. Migne

Morris, *Med. Eng. Sheriff*   W.A. Morris, *The Medieval English Sheriff to 1300* (1927)

Neustria Pia   *Neustria Pia seu de omnibus et singulis abbatiis et prioratibus totius Normanniae*, ed. A du Monstier (Rouen 1663)

Offler, *Durham Episc. Charters*   H.S. Offler, *Durham Episcopal Charters, 1071–1152* (Surtees Soc., clxxix, 1968)

OV   *The Ecclesiastical History of Orderic Vitalis*, ed. and trans. Marjorie Chibnall (1969–81)

OV, *Interpolation* (in *GND*)   see *GND*

Plummer, *Two Saxon Chronicles* *see ASC*

Poole, *The Exchequer* R.L. Poole, *The Exchequer in the Twelfth Century* (1912)

PR 31 H.I *The Pipe Roll of 31 Henry I*, ed. J. Hunter (1833, 1929)

Regesta *Regesta Regum Anglo-Normannorum, 1066–1154*, i, ed. H.W.C. Davis and R.J. Whitwell (1913); ii, ed. Davis, C. Johnson and H.A. Cronne (1956)

Reuter, *Medieval Nobility* T. Reuter, *The Medieval Nobility* (Europe in the Middle Ages, Selected Studies, xiv, 1978)

RHF M. Bouquet, *Recueil des Historiens des Gaules et de la France* (Paris 1738–1876)

RHS Royal Historical Society

Richardson and Sayles H.G. Richardson and G.O. Sayles, *The Governance of Medieval England* (1963)

Round, *FE* J.H. Round, *Feudal England* (1895)

Round, *King's Serjeants* J.H. Round, *The King's Serjeants and Officers of State* (1911)

Sanders, *Baronies* I.J. Sanders, *English Baronies . . . 1086–1327* (1960)

Simeon, *Opera* *Symeon of Durham, Historical Works*, ed. T. Arnold (Rolls ser., 1882–5)

  HDE *Historia Ecclesiae Dunelmensis*, in vol. i

  HR *Historia Regum*, in vol. ii

Song of Roland trans. Dorothy L. Sayers (1957)

SSC W. Stubbs, *Select Charters and other Illustrations of English Constitutional History*, 9th edn, revised by H.W.C. Davis (1921)

Stenton, *English Feudalism* F.M. Stenton, *The first century of English Feudalism, 1066–1166* (1932)

Suger, *Vie de Louis VI* Suger, *Vie de Louis VI le Gros*, ed. and trans. H. Waquet (Paris 1929, 1964)

The Master of Game *by Edward, second duke of York*, ed. W.A. and F. Baillie-Grohman (1909)

Tillmann	H. Tillmann, *Die päpstlichen Legaten in England bis zur Beendigung der Legation Gualas, 1218* (Bonn 1926)
Torigny, *Interpolation* (in *GND*)	*see GND*
TRHS	*Transactions of the Royal Historical Society*
Tristan	Beroul, *The Romance of Tristan*: text, ed. A. Ewert (1967), cited by ll.; trans., A.S. Fedrick (1970), cited by pp.
VA	*see* Eadmer
VCH	*Victoria County History*
VEdR	*Vita Ædwardi Regis*, ed. and trans. F. Barlow (1962)
Vinogradoff, *English Society*	P. Vinogradoff, *English Society in the Eleventh Century* (1908)
Vita S. Godrici	*Libellus de Vita et Miraculis S. Godrici*, ed. J. Stevenson (Surtees Soc., xx, 1847)
Vita Oswini	in *Miscellanea Biographia*, ed. J. Raine (Surtees Soc., viii, 1838)
Vita B. Simonis	in Migne *PL*, q.v., clvi
Vita Wulfstani	*The Vita Wulfstani of William of Malmesbury*, ed. R.R. Darlington (RHS, Camden, xl, 1928)
Wace	*Le Roman de Rou de Wace*, ii–iii, ed. A.J. Holden (Paris 1971–3)
White, 'The Household'	G.H. White, 'The household of the Norman kings', *TRHS*, 4th ser., xxx (1948), 127
Wightman, *The Lacy Family*	W.E. Wightman, *The Lacy Family in England and Normandy 1066–1194* (1966)
Winton Domesday	F. Barlow, M. Biddle, O. von Feilitzen, D.J. Keene, *Winchester in the early Middle Ages* (Winchester Studies, ed. Biddle, I, 1976)
Wright, *Satirical Poets*	*The Anglo-Latin Satirical Poets and Epigrammatists of the Twelfth Century*, ed. T. Wright (Rolls ser., 1872), ii

WILLIAM RUFUS

Chapter 1

BACKGROUND AND YOUTH

William Rufus had a remarkable career, even for the late eleventh century, when opportunities for the adventurous and talented were plentiful. Born into the middle ranks of the French aristocracy, and only a younger son, he rose first through the achievements of his father, William 'the Conqueror', duke of Normandy, and then through the misfortunes of his elder brothers. Still a landless knight-bachelor when his father died in 1087, he took whatever chances came his way, and by the time of his own premature death thirteen years later had become a king of great renown. He was acclaimed by soldiers for his chivalry and magnanimity; and the flaws in his character proved to be no hindrance to success. For Hugh archbishop of Lyons in 1099 he was 'the most victorious king of the English . . . the conqueror of the nations'. Even for his detractors he was a prince who, if he could have corrected his moral faults, would have served as a model for all. But with his violent death in the New Forest on 2 August 1100 perished also his reputation. From being the most fortunate he had become the unluckiest of kings.

William the Red (Rufus) was born in, or just before, 1060,[1] the third son of the duke of Normandy, ruler of one of those semi-independent principalities into which the kingdom of France was divided. By that time the disruption of the larger political units in Europe to the advantage of the nobility and even lower ranks, such as castellans and soldiers of fortune, had been halted.

The Carolingian empire at its peak had extended from the River Elbe in the north to Barcelona and beyond Rome in the south, and from the sea coast in the west to the kingdoms of the Slavs and the Avars in the east. In the ninth century it began to break up. It split first into its component kingdoms; these collapsed into principalities,[2] duchies,

---

[1] *GR*, ii, 379, where it is stated that his death (2 August 1100) occurred when he was above the age of forty: 'major quadragenario'. Cf. Cicero, *Oratio pro Sex. Roscio Amerino*, XIV, 39: 'annos natus major quadraginta'. A more general sense, that he was no longer a young man, is just possible.

[2] A non-committal expression. East of the Rhine were the stem-duchies with ethnic foundations, each representing a distinct *gens*, e.g. Saxony. The position to the west has been variously interpreted; but there have always been some historians who identify duchies such as Aquitaine, Burgundy, Brittany and Normandy with *gentes*; and the

marquisates and groups of counties; and finally, in the eleventh century, some of these began to disintegrate into individual counties, viscounties, castellanies and even smaller lordships.[3] The kingdoms in Britain were never within the Carolingian empire, and, in contrast, the united kingdom of the English was created while the empire fell to pieces.

There was also some reconstruction on the Continent.[4] A few duchies, such as Aquitaine and Brittany, which represented Carolingian sub-kingdoms, managed to survive, even if in an anarchic condition. Within these and out of the ruins of other duchies, noble families created important new principalities: for example, the counties of Blois-Tours, Maine and Anjou were assembled out of the debris of the dissolved Robertine duchy after the death of Hugh the Great, marquis of Neustria and duke of the Franks, in 956; and when his son, Hugh Capet, became king in 987 their rulers claimed ducal rights. Although many of these eleventh-century principalities can be viewed as the private empires of new dynasties, they were also surviving fragments of the Carolingian state, often ruled by descendants of Carolingian nobles and officials. The prince usually exercised all or some of the powers which had once been royal. Whether this authority was the result of usurpation or of lawful devolution hardly matters. The ruler's possession of the former royal domain (fisc) in his territories, his quasi-royal jurisdictional, financial, and military rights, his issue of coinage and his control over the church were not disputed by any higher authority. Kings looked like princes, and princes like kings.[5] And those princes who reconstructed a coherent duchy or county created models for the national states of the twelfth and thirteenth centuries.

Although in the eleventh century there was more order in the north

---

contrast between the structures of early medieval Germany and France is probably less strong than is sometimes depicted. Cf. W. Kienast, *Der Herzogstitel in Frankreich und Deutschland (9. bis 12. Jahrhundert)* (Munich and Vienna 1968). England, too, in the late Anglo-Saxon period can be regarded as composed of stem-duchies, e.g. Wessex, Mercia etc. For the Normans as a *gens*, see G.A. Loud, 'The *Gens Normannorum* – myth or reality?', *Battle IV*, 104.

[3] It has become common among English historians for the first two and the last to be given in their French form, *comté, vicomté* and *seigneurie*, and treated as technical terms. A useful essay on the subject, with a full bibliography, is P. Feuchère, 'Essai sur l'évolution territoriale des principautés françaises (X^e–XIIIe siècle): Etude de géographie historique', *Le Moyen Age*, lviii (1952), 85.

[4] Cf. J. Dhont, *Etudes sur la naissance des principautés territoriales en France (IXe–Xe siècle)* (Bruges 1948); K.F. Werner, 'Kingdom and principality in twelfth-century France' (1968), Reuter, *Medieval Nobility*, 243–90, with a useful bibliography, 231 ff.; Elizabeth M. Hallam, 'The king and the princes in 11th-century France', *Bulletin of the Institute of Historical Research*, liii (1980), 143.

[5] Elizabeth M. Hallam, *loc. cit.*, 155.

than in the south of France, even here there was much diversity in the political structures. Picardy remained completely fragmented into castellanies; and most of the principalities had many of the features of lordships composed of feudal fiefs, assembled by inheritance, marriage, attraction and conquest, and held together by the bonds of homage and fealty. Boundaries fluctuated. Counties like Flanders, Champagne, Blois and Anjou, to name some of Normandy's neighbours, did not possess fixed and continuous limits. They were relatively recent and artificial creations and rested on no historical frontiers. The French royal demesne was in a similar condition. Only the church, feudalized though it might be, preserved in its provinces and dioceses, and occasionally in its subordinate units, the imperial divisions. The others, even if not writ in water, cartographically considered, changed like marbled papers, each pull different from the last.

Normandy, a late arrival on the scene and ruled by barbarian newcomers, was one of the most stable in the area and most centralized in government.[6] It was a *gens*, a nation, and was legitimized by grants of territory made by kings of the Franks to Viking invaders before the Carolingian *pagi* (counties) had completely broken up. The major concessions were made between 911 and 933; in the establishment of its limits the effective range of Scandinavian conquest and geographical features may also have played their part; and by 1050 the principality consisted of twelve more or less entire *pagi* and the western parts of the Vexin and Méresais. It also corresponded roughly with the ecclesiastical province of Rouen, the ancient *Lugdunensis Secunda*, and its seven dioceses.[7] As a result of these several factors, the dominions of the Northmen had continuous and recognizable frontiers which the rulers made indelible by keeping them intact. Even if they should be regarded more as marches than as a sharp line, and although the southern marches were relatively unstable, the boundaries as a whole were better defined than most. Before the end of the tenth century, Normandy's rulers claimed to be dukes and exercised all ducal (royal) rights. Hence the county or duchy retained its internal structure of Carolingian origins which contributed to its cohesion as a political unit. Even the growth of feudalism in the eleventh century did not destroy the ancient institutions.

Beyond its frontiers, the principalities were more typical of the region and age. A good example of one of the more artificial creations, and one

[6] The latest evaluation of the evidence and literature is in Bates, *Normandy before 1066*, where the predominant view among modern French scholars – that there was great institutional continuity from the Carolingian age – is strongly supported. See also Le Patourel, *Norman Empire*, 3 ff.

[7] See the map, with the various types of boundary marked, *ibid.*, 387.

of the less familiar, is Amiens-Valois-Vexin on its north-east boundary
and lying between the Rivers Somme and Seine.[8] Ralf IV of Crépy, a
descendant of the Carolingian royal family, at the time of his death in
1074 held directly seven *comtés* – Amiens, Vexin, Valois, Tardenois,
Montdidier, Vitry and Bar-sur-Aube; received the homage of seven
others – Corbie, Vermandois, Péronne, Meulan, Montfort, Dammartin
and Soissons; and possessed the advocacy of five great monasteries – St
Arnulf at Crépy, Jumièges and St Wandrille in Normandy, Holy Father
at Chartres in the Champagne bloc and St Denis in France. Not only
had these units been obtained in a variety of ways since the early tenth
century, when the family is first observed, but they were also held of
different lords. Ralf held only one of the three major units, Valois,
immediately of the king of France; Amiens he held of the bishop of the
city; and the French Vexin of the abbot of St Denis. This principality
was no more and no less a physical or economic entity than, say,
Flanders, Normandy or Anjou had been two generations before.
Geographically, it was fairly compact (only the Beauvaisis intruded), for
all rulers aimed at concentration; but what held it, like the others,
together was its ruling family: it was essentially a political unit. It was, of
course, surrounded by similar 'states', by Flanders, Champagne, France
(the royal demesne) and Normandy. All such principalities pushed
against their neighbours as a very condition of their existence: sometimes
the alignment of forces produced equilibrium, sometimes extreme
tension; and when the Valois dynasty became extinct in 1077, with
Ralf's childless heir, Simon, entering a monastery, the principality
collapsed. All its neighbours snatched, or tried to snatch, the pieces they
coveted. The several *comtés* were mostly absorbed into other groupings:
the pattern between Seine and Somme had changed. It would not have
been impossible for a similar fate to befall Normandy: it had almost
happened during the minority of Richard I (mid tenth century), in
Robert I's reign (1027–35) and while the Conqueror was a child
(1035–47); and under the rule of William Rufus's elder brother, Robert
Curthose (1087–96), the duchy again disintegrated.

This bald account of the rise and fall of a feudal principality
suppresses the incessant, and to us bewildering, diplomacy and military
campaigns which were necessary for its continuing existence. Each ruler

---

[8] For the origin of this aggregation, see P. Grierson, 'L'origine des comtés d'Amiens,
Valois et Vexin', *Le Moyen Age*, xlix (1939), 81. Ralf de Gouy, who obtained the three
counties by marriage about 923, was a great-grandson of the emperor Louis the Pious.
For its later history, see P. Feuchère, 'Une tentative manquée de concentration
territoriale entre Somme et Seine: la principauté d'Amiens-Valois au XIᵉ siècle', *ibid.*, lx
(1954), 1, with an extensive bibliography.

competed with the others to construct a superior network of alliances.[9] Princes sought for patrons among the greater powers, including the pope,[10] and tried to attract lesser powers into their vassalage. Among equals they married. They had also to make or threaten war against rebels and rivals: there was no court to which they could effectively appeal for the protection of their property.[11] We can identify some of the propitious conditions and special qualities which favoured survival in this fierce struggle for life. Economic wealth was important, for the cost of the enterprise had to be borne by the farmers, fishermen and merchants. The absence of implacably hostile and aggressive neighbours was a help. There had to be sufficient aggravation to maintain the fighting spirit and the sense of unity, but an unremitting feud or a geographical situation which was a standing obstacle or threat to a more powerful neighbour was weakening. Continuity of the princely family, preferably from father to adult son, was almost essential, for a minority always brought trouble, and with the failure of the direct male line there was the tendency for the dominions to be divided among heiresses or distant kinsmen. No less important were the personal qualities of the rulers. The most favoured in this struggle were those who combined martial ability and intelligence with the attractive virtues of open-handedness and loyalty – often referred to as *magnanimitas* – and could keep the respect and help of the church despite the crimes which had to be committed for reasons of state. The art lay in confining the display of repulsive features to enemies. The difficulty lay in knowing who were one's friends.

In the eleventh century the new nations were creating their myths. Of all generalizations, racial characteristics are the most arbitrary; yet every people at every time has given a character to its neighbours. The author of the *Quadripartitus*, an attempt to declare in 1114 the *laga Eadwardi*, the good old laws of Edward the Confessor, wrote of the flippancy of the French, the pugnacity of the Normans, the rages of the Bretons, the ostentation of the men of Maine, the vanity of the Flemish, the splendour of the Germans, the perfidy of Ponthieu, the perjury of Anjou, the theatricality of the Poitevins, the threats of the Danes, and

[9] Cf., for example, Barlow, 'Edward the Confessor's early life, character and attitudes', *EHR*, lxxx (1965), 225. See further Bates, *Normandy before 1066*, 46 ff.

[10] Simon of Crépy (1074–7) appealed to Gregory VII for help against Philip I of France: *Vita B. Simonis*, cols 1212–13.

[11] Simon of Crépy's struggle against the French king was settled by a *conventus nobilium*, at which the wise men gave judgment that the *hereditas* should be restored to Simon: *ibid.*, col. 1214; but we are concerned here more with peace negotiations to settle a war than with purely legal proceedings.

the barbarity of Ireland.[12] The English observer gave his own people no label. The Normans, however, were still unassimilated in 1114, and their traditional reputation has been not only for bellicosity, but also for hardness, capability and cunning.

William Rufus's father, William the Bastard, was the seventh count or duke of Normandy, his mother, Matilda, a daughter of Baldwin V, count of Flanders. The couple had been married about 1052,[13] when the husband was twenty-four and the bride in her teens.[14] The dates of the births of the two eldest sons, Robert and Richard, are uncertain; a fourth son, Henry, was born in 1068. There were even more daughters. Cecily (*Cecilia*), Constance and Adela became well known, the first as abbess of Holy Trinity, Caen, the second as the wife of Alan Fergant, count of Brittany, and the third as the wife of Stephen-Henry count of Blois and the mother of famous sons. Two other daughters, Adelaide (*Adeliza* or *Adelidis*) and Matilda, both probably among the older girls and the former much sought and offered in marriage, died young. A sixth, Agatha, although provided with a history by the Anglo-Norman chronicler Orderic Vitalis, is probably Adelaide under another name. It is likely, therefore, that William and Matilda in the first sixteen years of their marriage raised a family of nine, four boys and five girls, and that William junior was just about in the middle.[15]

These children were of very mixed blood, and such a typically large family provided much room for variation. The Norman counts, of Scandinavian, perhaps Norwegian, origin, had mostly married local noblewomen of similar stock; but Richard II, the young William's great-grandfather, had married a Breton, and the racial background of his grandmother, Herleva, the tanner's daughter from Falaise, is unknown. Although Pope Leo IX in 1049 denounced the proposed

---

[12] Liebermann, *Gesetze*, i, 534. Bates, *Normandy before 1066*, 245, argues that the Normans' reputation for military prowess was simply part of the twelfth-century 'Norman myth'.

[13] The marriage occurred between its prohibition at the council of Rheims (October 1049) and Matilda's witness to two charters in 1053: Fauroux, *Recueil*, nos 130–1. Raymonde Foreville, *GG*, 46 n. 1, and 66 n. 1, suggested 1050–1. Douglas, *WC*, 391, agreed, and changed it to 1051–2. See also Barlow, 'Edward the Confessor's early life, character and attitudes', *loc. cit.*, 247. R.H.C. Davis, 'William of Jumièges, Robert Curthose and the Norman Succession', *EHR*, xcv (1980), 603–4, when arguing that Robert was probably made duke when he came of age, suggests that the marriage took place in 1051. If it could be proved that Robert was made duke in 1067, it would also have to be shown at what age this would be possible. Davis posits sixteen; but fourteen should be considered; and 1053 plus fourteen equals 1067. For the marriage and its circumstances, see further Bates, *Normandy before 1066*, 199 ff.

[14] There is no doubt that William was born in 1027–8; Matilda was, apparently, born after 1031–2: Douglas, *WC*, app. A and p. 392.

[15] See below, app. A.

marriage between William and Matilda as incestuous, the precise impediment, whether of consanguinity or of affinity, has never been established with certainty,[16] and the marriage seems to have been substantially exogamous. The bride's family was much more distinguished than her husband's. The counts of Flanders were members of the high nobility of Europe. In the 1070s William of Poitiers, the Conqueror's encomiast, wrote that Matilda's father, Baldwin V, 'marquis' of Flanders, who ruled in the marches of France and Germany, was not only descended from the counts of the *Morini*,[17] later known as Flemish, but also from the kings of the two neighbouring countries, and was related to the nobility of Constantinople.[18] He was a vassal (*miles*) of the Roman empire and a statesman of the greatest influence.[19] Matilda's mother was Adela, the daughter of Robert II 'the Pious', king of France, and Constance, daughter of William count of Toulouse. Among Adela's brothers were Henry I, king of France (1031–60), and Robert I, duke of Burgundy (1032–75). Hence the children of the Conqueror had through their mother not only distinguished uncles and cousins but also connexions with most of the great nobility of France.

One of the difficulties in making a genealogical tree, however, is ignorance over which persons were considered part of the family. Obviously within a great network of relationships only a smaller group had much practical significance. Almost all historical genealogical charts are constructed on an agnatic principle and demonstrate the leading male line. Although such a family structure will have only a limited correspondence with reality, it is difficult to be sure what should be substituted.[20] Entries in monastic memorial books, requests for prayers by the monks for a listed family group, have been used to show

---

[16] *FNC*, iii, 645 ff.; Douglas, *WC*, 391 ff. For the subject in general, see Constance C. Bouchard, 'Consanguinity and noble marriages in the tenth and eleventh centuries', *Speculum*, lvi (1981), 268.

[17] The ship in which William sailed to England in 1066, a present from the duchess, was called the *Mora*, possibly an allusion to her ancestry: *Brevis relatio*, 22.

[18] Although this claim cannot be substantiated, there is no reason to doubt it: cf. Reuter, *Medieval Nobility*, 6 ff., on such beliefs.

[19] *GG*, 46 ff. Her family was also commemorated, and her connexion with the French monarchy emphasized, in the epitaph on her tomb in Holy Trinity, Caen, and in Godfrey of Amiens's historical epigram: OV, iv, 44 and 46 n. Wright, *Satirical Poets*, ii, 150.

[20] Cf. K. Schmid, 'The structure of the nobility in the earlier middle ages', Reuter, *Medieval Nobility*, 42 ff.; Werner, *op. cit., ibid.*, 149 ff. J.C. Holt, 'Feudal Society and the Family in Early Medieval England: I. The Revolution of 1066', *TRHS*, 5th ser., xxxii (1982), 193.

actual kinship units: and on this type of evidence the English royal family in the eleventh century was quite small. William Rufus, although childless, made benefactions for the souls only of himself and of his parents: he neglected his brothers and sisters and their children; and later Henry I restricted his interest to himself, his wife and legitimate children, his parents and his predecessor as king.[21] Another approach is to detect groups through their use of common ('leading') names; and it will hardly be doubted that the names given to children of a marriage indicate their parents' closest kinship ties and identifications.

The names which William and Matilda gave their children indicate a selective combination of two traditions, with an increasing inclination towards the maternal. Female was quite as important at the time as male kin, and when the wife's family was more distinguished than the husband's, it was usual to take at least some of the characteristic names of her group.[22] The first three boys, Robert, Richard and William, were given the only names which ran in the ducal family: Robert I (1027-35), Richard I, II, III (942-1027) and William Longsword (927-42). The names probably define their order of precedence. But Robert also commemorated the boy's maternal great-uncle and great-grandfather. Adelaide may well have been named after her father's sister; but, after that, the mother's stock of names was favoured, although again from the maternal side: Matilda, her own name, Adela, her mother's, Constance, her grandmother's, and Henry, her uncle's. Cecily, which could be the name the girl took when given as an oblate to Holy Trinity, Caen, or on her profession as a nun, was one of the names (the other was Constance) which Matilda's cousin, Philip I of France, gave to his daughters. In this series Agatha has no place, for it has no obvious source. Orderic Vitalis, the intimate chronicler of this world, who unlike some of his fellow writers was not shy with names, in the whole of his voluminous history mentions only one other Agatha, the possibly third-century virgin and martyr commemorated at Catania in Sicily, whose relics, he claims, were removed to Constantinople by 'Maniaces',[23] presumably in 1042-3. The isolation of this name weighs heavily against it. One significant feature of this list of names which should not be overlooked is the absence of Baldwin, the leading name in the Flemish comital family. The fourth son was called Henry, even though the friendly brother-in-law, Baldwin VI, had succeeded his father in the previous year. It would seem that while the duke was anxious to proclaim his connexion with the

---

[21] In Durham's *Liber Vitae*, 2a–b, in the list of kings to be commemorated no family beyond the wife is mentioned. For references to the royal donor's family in grants of land, cf. *Regesta*, nos 338a, 348a, 372c, 404, and below, 432.

[22] Werner, quoting Schmid, *op. cit.*, 151.

[23] OV, iii, 86; cf. *GR*, ii, 413.

French royal dynasty, he was no less concerned to avoid any suggestion that he was a client of the counts of Flanders.

Robert and William junior were given nicknames in their own times. William of Malmesbury and Orderic, both writing about 1125 but not necessarily in complete independence, agree that Robert was small and stout and was once called by his father in derision *Brevis-ocrea*,[24] literally 'short-boot', but usually given in the French form, 'Curthose'. Orderic, who delighted in such matters, adds that he was also called *Gambaron*, which is probably likewise concerned with his legs (*jambes*), and could possibly refer, as with the Italian form, *gambaro*, a lobster, to some crustacean feature.

According to the Miracles of St Edmund, a good contemporary witness, William was known as 'Longsword',[25] like his great-great-great-grandfather. But this name has been displaced by Orderic's insistence that he was called *Rufus*. The earliest authority for the name seems to be Guibert, abbot of Nogent-sous-Coucy, an abbey not far from Laon and on the English pilgrim route to Rome. In his autobiography written between 1114 and his death in 1124, he tells a discreditable story about the English king, who, he says, was called Rufus because he was one.[26] Bynames like *ruffus*, *rosellus*, *blundus*, *brunus* and *niger*, which describe a person's appearance and were in very common use (there are many Rufuses in Orderic's History), refer primarily to the colour of the hair but also to the related colour of the complexion.[27] If William junior was called *Le ros* or *Le rossel* in childhood – he would, of course, have been named in French, not in Latin – most likely he was a redhead. Guibert's authority has some weight. He was of noble birth, and reporting on a contemporary about whom he should have known the facts; but he was a rather credulous person, and the name is unknown to other early writers. In the *Anglo-Saxon Chronicle* it is plain King William. Eadmer, the Canterbury monk who wrote much about him and is the main authority for his famous oath, never used Rufus, although it would have suited his picture of the tyrant to make him a red king like the devil. As, however, on the one occasion that he mentions the king's most hated servant, it is Ranulf, not Flambard,[28] it is possible that he disdained to

[24] *GR*, ii, 459–60; OV, ii, 365; iv, 114; v, 208.

[25] *Heremanni archidiaconi miracula S. Eadmundi*, in *Ungedruckte Anglo-normannische Geschichtsquellen*, ed. F. Liebermann (Strasbourg 1879), 266.

[26] 'qui Rufus, quod et erat, cognominabatur', Guibert, *De Vita sua libri tres*, I, xxiii; Migne *PL*, clvi, 887.

[27] Olof von Feilitzen, on the bynames of the citizens of Winchester in the surveys of *c.* 1110 and 1148, *Winton Domesday*, 205 ff., *s.v. Bel, Blundus, Brun(us), Galne, Gule, Hwit, Niger, Rosellus, Ruffus, Rust*, and p. 220.

[28] *HN*, 41.

use nicknames for such odious creatures. We come closer to it in William of Malmesbury, who wrote after Eadmer in 1118–24. In *Gesta Regum*, the heading to Book IV is, 'Here begins the fourth book about King William Rufus, the son of King William I', and the next section is headed, 'How King Rufus conquered his enemies'.[29] There can be no certainty, however, that these titles are from the author's pen, especially since in the text the king is never called Rufus: usually he is the king, sometimes William. Much later in Book IV occurs a suggestive passage in a physical description of the king: 'He had a rufous complexion and yellow hair.'[30] It is possible that by middle age the colour of the king's hair had faded and his complexion taken on a fiery hue, but the Malmesbury monk is not a good witness to William's nickname. The Anglo-Norman clerk, Geoffrey de Gaimar, writing shortly before 1140 and possibly elaborating William of Malmesbury, describes the king as having a red beard and blond hair, so that he was surnamed 'le Rus Rei';[31] and Wace, one of Henry II's clerks, in his *Roman de Rou* called him 'Guillelme le Ros'.[32] For Florence, whose sources included the *Chronicle*, Eadmer and William of Malmesbury, he was, when necessary, William junior.

Orderic, however, from start to finish calls him almost always William Rufus or King Rufus.[33] He had a keen nose for the intimate detail of the historical scene (it is he who called the battle of Hastings 'Senlac'), but, although he may have picked up Rufus from a sound source or tradition, possibly from Guibert's book, or William of Malmesbury's, there is little to suggest that William junior was generally and habitually called Rufus in his own lifetime or during the next reign. It is Orderic's enthusiastic propagation of the name which has given it general currency. Nevertheless, the name has been so widely accepted in modern times and is, in the presence of so many Williams, so useful, that it would be inconvenient as well as pedantic to reject it completely. Hence Rufus is used in these pages in order to avoid confusion and is gradually abandoned after William became king.

The byname of the youngest son, Henry *Beauclerk*, can be treated more drastically. It seems to be a fourteenth-century elaboration of the

---

[29] *GR*, ii, 359, 360.

[30] 'colore rufo, crine subflavo', *ibid.*, ii, 374.

[31] 'Barbe aveit russe e crine bloie / . . . Il out le surnun del Rus Rei', Gaimar, ll. 6246–8. The author of *Vita Oswini*, a monk of Tynemouth, who had come from the mother house, St Albans, by way of the cell of Wymondham (Norfolk), and perhaps was Nigel, considered the first prior of this cell (*HRH*, 97–8), and writing at roughly the same time as Gaimar, Florence and OV, called the king both *junior* (p. 21) and *flavus* (p. 22), both of which he could have taken from *GR*.

[32] Wace, l. 9349; cf. 9365, 9699, 'Li reis Ros'.

[33] OV, ii, 120, 186; iv, 126, 148.

clericus bestowed on him in the late thirteenth century.[34] There is nothing to suggest that it was a petname in the family or had any contemporary currency, and is best forgotten.

William Rufus was born into a healthy family. There may have been miscarriages and infant deaths during Matilda's child-bearing period of sixteen years, but the survival of at least nine children into adolescence, and of all but two of these into maturity, is a good record, all the more since she seems to have been a midget, no more than 4 feet 2 inches (1.27m) tall.[35] The Conqueror died in his sixtieth year, his wife probably in her early fifties. At least four of the children improved on that. Robert, who died in 1134, probably reached eighty, Adela, the last to die (1137), her seventies, and Cecily (1127) and Henry (1135) their late sixties. Three of the daughters did less well: Constance (1090) was under thirty when she died, but of poison it was rumoured;[36] Matilda does not seem to have lived long after maturity; and Adelaide (or Agatha) died on reaching marriageable age, perhaps between fourteen and sixteen. Richard and William Rufus died in hunting accidents, the former before he had been dubbed a knight, and so under twenty-two,[37] the latter in 1100, when he was over forty. Only three of the children are known to have had offspring.

This was not an unusual pattern at the time. Although some men and women had a large number of children, others had few or none. Fertility was much reduced by the celibacy prescribed for monks and clerks in major orders, by homosexual practices, by natural incapacity and by

---

[34] C.W. David, 'The claims of Henry I to be called learned', *Anniversary Essays in mediaeval history by students of C.H. Haskins* (Boston and New York 1929), 45; V.H. Galbraith, *The Literacy of the medieval English kings* (Raleigh Lecture on History, British Academy, 1935), 13 ff.

[35] See Douglas, *WC*, 369–70.

[36] *GR*, ii, 333.

[37] Richard witnesses royal charters 1066–9 (*Regesta*, nos 4, 6a, 26), but by 1074 his place had been taken by William Rufus (*ibid.*, nos 73, 75). *GR*, ii, 332 and OV, iii, 114 agree that he died as a boy before he had been dubbed a knight. Cf. Torigny, *Interpolation* in *GND*, 251, 279, and the historical epigram of Godfrey prior of Winchester (Wright, *Satirical Poets*, ii, 152), where he is described as of tender age (*tenera flos*) and learning to hunt. The death occurred some good time before 1086. A dispute over the ownership of Tewin (Herts), on the fief of Peter of Valognes, reveals that a king's thegn named Aldene claimed that it had been confirmed to him and his mother by the Conqueror, 'for the soul of Richard his son' – and could show the royal writ: *DB*, i, 141b–c. If Richard was born about 1055, his death in 1069–74 would fit the evidence. According to Prior Godfrey it occurred on the Ides (13) of September under the sign of the Virgin. *GR* and OV agree that he died while hunting in the New Forest, near Winchester, but differ on the details. According to the former, he met his death in a cloud of poisonous gas, which may mean that he died of a fever rather than by accident; in the latter, followed by Torigny, he was crushed between the bough of a tree and the pommel of his saddle.

the reluctance of some women to remarry after the premature deaths of their husbands. Most of these features can be illustrated from the marital history of the parents of Guibert of Nogent. His father, Everard, apparently a vassal of Raynald count of Clermont in the Beauvaisis, and his beautiful mother, whom Guibert loved and admired but does not name in his autobiography, were married by arrangement of their kinsmen about 1044, when both were adolescent, even perhaps sexually immature, and the union remained unconsummated for seven years.[38] Although Everard's impotence was attributed to sorcery, he was persuaded to experiment with other women, and had a child, which died unbaptized, by one of these. When the spell was finally removed through the help of a wise old woman, the couple had several children, of whom Guibert was the last before his father's untimely death in one of William the Bastard's prisons after the battle of Mortemer in 1054. The widow, who had declined to divorce her husband during his impotence and had rejected the advances of other suitors, refused to remarry, and twelve years after Guibert's birth, when she considered that he was old enough to fend for himself, became a religious recluse. Guibert, who became a monk and abbot, had no children.

The Norman ducal family was intelligent as well as healthy. The three sons and three daughters of William and Matilda who obtained important offices were clearly of at least average ability. William Rufus may not have been quite as sharp as Robert and Henry, but he was no fool and had other qualities. William of Malmesbury, writing about twenty years after the king's death, considered that he was imbued with ambition and purpose;[39] he also thought that Richard, 'a pretty lad', was of high promise.[40] Cecily was a good scholar and Adela became a formidable countess. William of Poitiers, archdeacon of Lisieux, claimed in the usual way of panegyrists that the duke their father was a kind parent who had the best interests of his children at heart.[41] In particular he provided for their religious education[42] and planned profitable marriages.

The six ages of man were defined by Isidore archbishop of Seville (who died in 636) in his popular encyclopaedia, *Etymologiae*, XII, ii.

[38] Guibert, *De Vita sua libri tres*, Migne *PL*, clvi, 856, 859, 877.

[39] *GR*, ii, 359.

[40] *GR*, ii, 332. In Prior Godfrey's flattering poem (see above, n. 37), he is called the most promising of William's sons.

[41] *GG*, 92; cf. *GR*, ii, 359. For William of Poitiers, see R.H.C. Davis, 'William of Poitiers and his History of William the Conqueror', in *The Writing of History in the Middle Ages* (Southern *Festschrift*), ed. Davis, J.M. Wallace-Hadrill (1981), 71 ff.

[42] *GG*, 120. The chapter owes something to Einhard's *Vita Caroli Magni*, cap. 26: ed. and trans. L. Halphen (Paris, 3rd edn, 1947), 76.

Infancy lasted until seven, childhood (*pueritia*) until fourteen, adolescence until twenty-eight, youth (*juventus*), perhaps manhood is better, until fifty, dignity (*gravitas*) until seventy; and old age (*senectus*) closed the series. This scheme, known to most educated clerics, appears to have had some influence on medieval attitudes and educational practices.

It seems to have been usual among the nobility for babies to be given to wet-nurses. Robert is said to have lost his wife, Sibyl of Conversano, shortly after she gave birth to their only child, William (Clito), because the midwife had her breasts bound too tightly on account of the abundance of milk she was producing.[43] This practice would have allowed conception to occur more often than in poorer families where the mother suckled her own babies. There was also much interchange of children of all ages at all levels of society. After the wet-nurse or foster-mother, the aim of most parents was to place their child advantageously in another family so that he could be educated to a higher station; and the households of kings and nobles usually contained some children of their vassals and friends who were being educated with their own offspring.[44] The one boy known to have been educated when a child at Duke William's court with his elder children is Simon of Crépy, born before 1053, one of the elder sons and eventual heir of Ralf IV of Amiens-Valois-Vexin and Adela/Adelaide of Soissons Bar.[45] More would have joined the court later for their military training.

A tradition which persisted through the early Middle Ages was that the children of noblemen should have some sort of a literary education before their training in useful skills. The chapter that Einhard, the biographer of Charlemagne, wrote on the emperor's children is heavily indebted to Suetonius's account of the care that the Emperor Augustus took with the education of his children and grandchildren,[46] and Asser's treatment of the subject in his *Life of Alfred* follows the same line. Einhard says that when the king was at home, the children always dined with him, and when he travelled they always went along, the boys riding at his side, the girls following at the rear of the column protected by some of the bodyguards. Both the boys and the girls were given instruction in

[43] *GR*, ii, 461.

[44] Cf. Dorothy L. Sayers, 'Nurture and companionage', *Song of Roland*, 37.

[45] His biographer states that William and Matilda had fostered (*nutrio*) him: *Vita B. Simonis*, cols 1215, 1219, 1222. Simon's mother was dead by 1053 and his father remarried twice; but the exact reason and date for handing over the child are unknown. For the family and their lands, see above, 5–6. The words *nutrio* and *nutricius* cover a wide range of relationships between a dependant and a surrogate father: they can refer to a foster-parent, a tutor or governor, or, more widely, to a protector. For the last sense, see *VEdR*, 30, 42, 79. See also below, nn. 65, 77, 89.

[46] *Vita Karoli Magni*, cap. 19, 58–62.

the liberal arts (which implies lessons in reading, if not in writing, and the first steps in Latin), and as soon as the boys were ready for it they were taught to ride, handle arms and hunt, while the girls learnt to spin wool with spindle and distaff. Asser's account of Alfred's education is basically the same: instruction in literature and then in hunting.[47] The former consisted of learning to recite poems in the vernacular, psalms and the usual prayers. Asser makes it clear that it was oral education and that Alfred was still illiterate at twelve when he would have been put to more manly occupations. There was also a tradition throughout the Middle Ages that princes should be instructed in moral principles (ethics) and political wisdom.[48] This too probably took the form of learning by heart a number of maxims read out by the tutor.

Among the nobility only two careers were open to sons, the chivalrous and the clerical. The group of male elders who decided family policy were anxious both that the line should be continued and that the patrimony should be maintained intact and preferably enlarged. One or two of the elder sons had, therefore, to be given a military education and for the eldest an advantageous marriage found. These boys passed through the stages of infancy and childhood before being dubbed a knight between the years of thirteen and twenty-two. They then became knights bachelor (*juvenes*: young men), and remained so until they came into a landed inheritance, married and started a family.[49] There was a strong prejudice against arranging a marriage for sons other than the eldest, as provision had to be made out of the estate for at least the counter-gift to the bride, the dower lands (*dos*), which served both as security for the return of the bride's marriage portion, if need be, and as an endowment for the wife, especially in widowhood.[50] There were also the difficulties caused by the church's prohibition of marriage within seven degrees of kinship. Finding a suitable and lawful spouse was not all that easy. And it was harder for the parents of girls. Because of the small number of marriageable males and the relative abundance of girls on offer, the tendency was for the brides to be superior to the grooms in social standing (within, of course, close limits), beauty and education.[51]

[47] *Vita Alfredi*, caps 22, 24: *Asser's Life of King Alfred*, ed. W.H. Stevenson (1904), 19 ff.

[48] Cf. Gerald of Wales, *De Principis Instructione Liber*, ed. G.F. Warner (Rolls ser., 1891).

[49] G. Duby, 'Dans la France du Nord-Ouest au XIIᵉ siècle: les "jeunes" dans la sociéte aristocratique', *Annales E.S.C.*, xix (1964), 855. J. Flori, 'Les origines de l'adoubement chevaleresque: étude des remises d'armes et du vocabulaire qui les exprime dans les sources historiques latines jusqu'au début du XIIIᵉ siècle', *Traditio*, xxxv (1979), 209.

[50] Cf. Coronation charter of Henry I, caps 3–4, Articles of the Barons, cap. 4, Magna Carta, cap. 7, *SSC*, 118, 286, 294. W.S. Holdsworth, *A History of English Law*, iii, 95–6, 157.

[51] Cf. G. Duby, 'Le mariage dans la société du haut moyen âge', *Il matrimonio nella*

If there were a number of sons of a marriage, it was not unusual to select one or two for the church, either those unsuited by physique for the life of a soldier or younger children for whom no lands could be spared or found. Accordingly it must be borne in mind that William and Matilda could have viewed William Rufus and Henry as prospective bishops. But whereas they might easily have offered a handicapped son as a monastic oblate, there was no need with the healthy to take an irrevocable decision in early childhood, and it was prudent to defer a decision for as long as possible. Casualties among those bred to arms – in play, exercises and hunting as well as in warfare – were so heavy that parents had to keep some sons in reserve; and even if these, after being dubbed knight, were not provided with a wife and apanage, and had to make their fortune outside the patrimony, this was a recognized vocation and could produce great prizes. We can see in the case of Guibert of Nogent, his parents' youngest son, how the options were kept open. Although he was put to school as a child, his widowed mother said that if he should want to become a knight when he reached the age of decision, apparently twelve, she would provide for it; and once, when she saw how savagely he had been beaten by his schoolmaster, she suggested that he gave up his studies. But he persevered and eventually became abbot of Nogent sous Coucy.[52] In the case of William Rufus and Henry, changed circumstances as well as their obvious pugnacity and fitness for the chivalrous life may have served to spare them the tonsure.

For female children it was either marriage or a nunnery. It is likely that women suffered from chronic anaemia, caused by protein and iron deficiencies in the diet, and, especially if they bore children, had a shorter expectation of life than men.[53] According to standard Salernitan medical teaching, women were by nature of a cold and wet 'complexion' (complementary to a man's hot and dry disposition), and reached menarche between the ages of twelve and fourteen. Boys, slower to develop, reached sexual maturity at fifteen.[54] But no precise definition of

---

società altomedievale, Centro Italiano di Studi sull' Alto Medioevo, Spoleto, Settimana xxiv, 1976; Spoleto, 1977, 15; C.C. Bouchard, 'Consanguinity and noble marriages in the tenth and eleventh centuries', Speculum, lvi (1981). Since, however, there was no feminine of miles, a woman of even that rank had to be described as nobilis.

[52] Guibert, op. cit., cols 847 ff.

[53] Vera Bullough and C. Campbell, 'Female longevity and diet in the Middle Ages', Speculum, lv (1980), 317.

[54] The Prose Salernitan Questions, ed. Brian Lawn (1979), 196 (qu. 115), 233 4 (qu. 74); 92 (qu. 174), cf. 6(qu. 9). The Salernitan doctors put the menopause at fifty and men's inability to produce sperm at sixty. For girls, see also Bullough and Campbell, loc. cit., 322–5.

legal puberty, or the age of consent, or the minimum age at which a valid betrothal or marriage could be contracted is to be found in either secular or ecclesiastical law in the early Middle Ages. It was a matter for social custom; and it would seem that noble families usually aimed at marrying off as many girls as possible as early as could be. In return for the provision of a marriage portion (*maritagium*, our 'dowry'), which was preferably paid in goods or money, the girl's claim on the patrimony was extinguished and a useful alliance secured. But because few suitable husbands were on offer, many girls were forced to remain celibate. All the same, as with the boys, there was no need to rush the matter. Although a girl considered quite unsuited to matrimony could be given as an oblate, the others could try their luck in the marriage market and take the veil only if they lost. The effect of these social customs on the birth-rate was considerable. In the case of William and Matilda's children, only two of their four sons married, Robert, although betrothed as a child, not until he was in his late forties, and Henry twice, first at thirty-two and then at fifty-three. On the female side, only two of the five or more daughters married, Adela at about sixteen, Constance at about twenty-four. Adelaide, although betrothed at least three times, died a virgin. Moreover, the number of legitimate children who survived infancy produced by this generation was not many – one to Robert, two to Henry, and four to Adela; and only three of these had legitimate issue. Even worse, from a dynastic point of view, the male line ended in 1135 with Henry I, their youngest son.

In the eleventh century, as at most times, it was the father, step-father, or some other adult male relation who was responsible for the safety and education of the boys in the family. In exceptional circumstances, and perhaps more usually in the very highest society, the office was delegated to a guardian, governor (*tutor*) or master. The fatherless William the Bastard was entrusted first to a kinsman, Alan III, count of Brittany,[55] and then to a slightly more distant relative, Gilbert count of Brionne.[56] Osbern, the steward (*dapifer*) of the ducal household, another kinsman, also seems to have had some responsibility for the boy's safety.[57] All were killed during the duke's boyhood by rival factions. At a lower social level some forty years later, the fatherless Guibert of Nogent was put between the years of six and twelve under a clerk, who, he explains in his autobiography, was both his master and his tutor.[58] We meet at this

[55] OV, ii, 86, 88; iv, 76, called *tutor*.
[56] *GG*, 116, cf. Orderic's interpolation, 155–6; OV, iii, 88, called *tutor*.
[57] *GG*, 116, Orderic's interpolation, 156; OV, iii, 88. The inclusion of Thurkell of Neufmarché in this list, cf. Douglas, *WC*, 37, seems to be a mistake caused by OV: see below, n. 65.
[58] 'cum solo paedogogo meo qui et magister fuerat', *De Vita sua*, col. 862, cf. 859, 865.

time, however, with no governor or master in Duke William's household, and it is possible that he usually took the boys with him on his ceaseless travels around his dominions. But Henry, who was brought up in England, detached from the royal court, must have been provided with a surrogate parent.

Much lower in social standing than a governor or master was the *paedogogus*, or tutor, who was responsible for the literary and religious education of the children. A hired clerk, he had no assured path to high preferment in the church. Guibert, born at Clermont-en-Beauvais, just to the east of the duchy, on 2 April 1054 and so a contemporary of William and Matilda's elder children, tells us how difficult it was at that time, owing to the shortage of competent grammarians, to find a good tutor. His own teacher was a clerk who had learnt grammar only in old age, and for six years he suffered under this ignorant and severe, although well-meaning, man.[59] It can hardly have been better in Normandy. Lanfranc of Pavia set up as a schoolmaster at Avranches about 1039 mainly because of the great opportunities, but by 1042 had entered Bec as a monk.[60] Although the Norman dukes had not Charlemagne's or Alfred's love of learning, they were in general religious men and benefactors of monasteries, and those members of the family who entered the church were often patrons of the arts and in their different ways reformers. Robert the Magnificent's brother, Mauger, archbishop of Rouen 1037–55, may have been educated in William of Dijon's abbey at Fécamp,[61] and his cousin, Hugh bishop of Lisieux 1049–77, received a great tribute from his archdeacon, William of Poitiers.[62] William the Bastard's half-brother, Odo, became a patron of scholars at Bayeux and supplied many clerks to serve the king-duke in his household and then as bishops;[63] and John, a more distant kinsman, bishop of Avranches 1060–67 and archbishop of Rouen 1067–87, was a scholar of some note.[64] The duchess Matilda also had probably received a better education than was available in Normandy.

The names of several of William the Bastard's tutors are recorded, Ralf the Monk, William and Turold,[65] but the conditions were most

[59] *Ibid.*, col. 844.

[60] Barlow, 'A view of Archbishop Lanfranc', *JEH*, xvi (1965), 167 ff.; Margaret Gibson, *Lanfranc of Bec* (1978), 15 ff.

[61] Heinrich Böhmer, *Kirche und Staat in England und in der Normandie im XI. und XII. Jahrhundert* (Leipzig 1899), 11.

[62] *GG*, 136 ff.

[63] Cf. Barlow, *EC 1066–1154*, 58.

[64] *GG*, 136. See also D.C. Douglas, 'Les évêques de Normandie, 1035–1066', *Annales de Normandie*, iii, 88.

[65] For Ralf, see Fauroux, *Recueil*, 220, 259; for a master William, *ibid.*, 262; for Turold or Thorold, *GG*, 116. This last clerk seems to have been given a fictitious identity by

unpropitious. The duke never revealed any signs of a literary education and, although he was not hostile to clerical ideals – indeed in his patronage of church reform and his adoption of the Truce of God as a means to pacify the duchy was closely involved in their application – it is unlikely that he would have considered it necessary or desirable that boys who were going to be knights should be educated as clerks. As tutor to his eldest son Robert, he appointed a certain Ilger,[66] a clerk of no distinction. But it seems that as his fortunes rose he paid more attention to the matter. Even though we cannot believe that anyone dared quote in his presence the proverb, '*rex illiteratus asinus coronatus*' – an illiterate king is a crowned ass[67] – his coronation may have changed his views considerably. In the case of the youngest son, Henry, although we are not told the names of his masters or tutors, we are assured by two contemporary, but not necessarily completely independent, chroniclers that he had received the thorough rudiments of a literary education. William of Malmesbury in an extremely flattering and rather extravagant tribute, which, however, on close inspection, is found to commit him to little, informs us that the prince absorbed in childhood the nourishment of books so deeply within him that no later distractions could drive them from his memory, and when he became a ruler he put to good use the philosophy he had imbibed. And although in adult life he did not often read in public or sing except in a low voice, his literary education had well furnished him with political science.[68] Orderic, who greatly admired Henry as king, is a little more specific: he had been put to letters and instructed in both secular and religious knowledge.[69] In short, both writers believed that Henry had benefited from his studies and was a better ruler because of them, but neither seriously claimed that he was literate.[70]

Some of the daughters may have had an even better education. One

---

Orderic. The basic source for the name is the list in *GG* of those supporters of the boy duke who were killed during his minority. When Orderic interpolated *GG* he accepted Turoldus *pedagogus, ibid.*, 156; but when he reproduced the list in the annals which form Book I of *Hist. Eccles.*, the item has become *Turchetillus pedagogus* (OV, i, 158). In Book V he turned this into *Turchetillus de Novomercato* (OV, iii, 88), who becomes *Turchetillus nutricius meus* in Book VII (OV, iv, 82). Thurkell lord of Neufmarché-en-Lyons could not have been a pedagogue, and is unlikely to have been the duke's *nutricius*. Orderic made a slip and then elaborated. Cf. the case of 'Agatha', the duke's daughter: below, app. A, 441 ff.

[66] Fauroux, *Recueil*, 438; cf. 391, 392, all dated 1066 or thereabouts.

[67] His son Henry's engaging habit, according to *GR*, ii, 467.

[68] *GR*, ii, 467–8.

[69] OV, ii, 214; iv, 120: 'tam naturalis quam doctrinalis scientia'. Cf. also the very tall story of Henry reading a letter, OV, vi, 50: 'Litteratus vero rex . . .'

[70] For the debunking of Henry 'Beauclerk', see above, n. 34.

had connexions with Bayeux;[71] but it was Caen which the duke turned into almost a capital residence.[72] It was there that he and the duchess after 1059 founded the monastic communities of Holy Trinity for women and St Stephen's for men as a penance for their illegal marriage; it was to the nunnery that in 1066 they gave their daughter Cecily as an additional sacrifice;[73] and it was in their respective churches that they chose to be buried. In 1063, the duke appointed Lanfranc prior of Bec as first abbot of St Stephen's, Caen,[74] and probably some years later he and the duchess recruited Arnulf of Chocques, the son of a priest in south Flanders, to serve as chaplain and schoolmaster to the nuns.[75] Arnulf was well regarded by contemporaries for his learning and taught Cecily the arts subjects (the *trivium*), Latin grammar, rhetoric and logic. Later he threw in his lot with the Norman branch of the family, became Duke Robert's chaplain, accompanied him and Odo of Bayeux on the First Crusade, receiving a generous bequest from the bishop when he died *en route* in Sicily, and in 1099 after the capture of Jerusalem was elected patriarch of the city.

William Rufus's upbringing lay apparently somewhere between the methods chosen for Robert and Cecily. He would have learned from his mother and nurse to talk in French and to recite nursery rhymes, the Lord's Prayer and perhaps some other simple devotional exercises. Later he would have been taught by a clerical tutor the elements of the Christian religion, the Creed, the ritual and possibly how to recite some of the psalms in Latin. He would not, however, unless he was originally intended for the church, be taught to read or write or the rudiments of Latin grammar. The Conqueror's great-grandson, Henry Plantagenet, was the first king among his descendants to be literate.[76] The boy would also be instructed in the rules of worldly wisdom and of moral behaviour, although these may have made less impression on him than the conventions of his society which he would acquire by imitation from his parents and kinsmen and the nobles at court. And, like all children brought up in large country households, he would have learned much from the servants, both indoor and outdoor, about the lower and grosser aspects of life.

[71] See below, app. A, 444.
[72] For references, see Margaret Gibson, *Lanfranc of Bec*, 99, and Bates, *Normandy before 1066*, 178.
[73] See below, app. A, 444.
[74] Gibson, *op. cit.*, 98 ff.
[75] David, *RC*, 217 ff.; Haskins, *NI*, 74–5; Chibnall, *OV*, v, 176.
[76] Galbraith, *Literacy*, 15–16. Cf. also J.T. Rosenthal, 'The education of the early Capetians', *Traditio*, xxv (1969), 372–3. There is no good evidence for the literacy of Philip I or Louis VI.

As Arnulf of Chocques lived until 1118, he was probably too young to have been involved also in the education of William Rufus; but there is a tradition that Lanfranc took a part. William of Malmesbury believed that it was this prelate who brought him up, made him a knight, secured for him the English throne and kept his bad qualities in check.[77] As the dubbing would have taken place after 1076, the chronicler was thinking particularly of the period after 1070, when Lanfranc was archbishop of Canterbury; but it is just possible that the boy's acquaintance with the monk and religion went further back. He was of about the same age as Cecily, and as she was their parents' oblation at Holy Trinity, Caen, William Rufus, a third son for whom at the time there was no obvious future, may have been chosen for the twin foundation of St Stephen's. He could have been placed there under Lanfranc in 1065–6 on reaching the age of five.[78] Not only is there a nice pattern in this hypothesis, it also suits the duke's state of mind in 1066 as depicted by William of Poitiers: everything possible was done to enlist God's help in the conquest of England.[79] On 18 June 1066 a document associated with the consecration of Holy Trinity and confirming the oblation of Cecily was witnessed by the Countess Matilda and Robert, Richard and William, all three described as sons of the count.[80] But even if the boy was sent to Caen, his father's acquisition of a new realm and the accidental death of Richard, as well as the boy's obvious unsuitability for the religious life, ensured that he would not stay in the cloister but, like his elder brothers, be bred to arms. Yet William Rufus always took an interest, even if usually a sinister one, in the church, for which an unhappy childhood experience could have been responsible. His homosexuality, of course, may have had other causes.

More to young William's taste than schooling in letters were hunting and the other military exercises, and in this he was completely at one with his father and elder brothers. Princes and barons maintained military households, a *familia*, which performed guard and escort duties in the court, and in time of war could be used as a strike-force or as the nucleus of a larger army. These household knights, who can be distinguished from the more senior military friends of the king, were

[77] *GR*, ii, 360: 'eo quod eum nutrierat et militem fecerat'; 367. For the various meanings of *nutrio*, see above, n. 45. J. Flori, *loc. cit.*, 221, 238, 242, suggests that the chronicler was associating Rufus's reception of arms with his coronation by Lanfranc; but this is unlikely.

[78] For William's love of Lanfranc, see *GG*, 126–8.

[79] *GG*, 146 ff.

[80] L. Musset, *Les Actes de Guillaume le Conquérant et de la Reine Mathilde pour les abbayes Caennaises* (Méms. de la Soc. des Antiquaires de Normandie, Caen, xxxvii, 1967), no. 2, witnesses, p. 57; cf. Fauroux, *Recueil*, no. 231; *Regesta*, no. 4.

normally bachelors, serving until they should inherit an estate or be rewarded by their lord, and were under the immediate command of a constable or marshal.[81] Boys in the household and other recruits no doubt trained in their company and graduated into it.

It seems that twelve was the age at which boys started serious military training,[82] and thereafter the apprenticeship to arms, with breaks for games and sport, would have taken up much of the daylight hours. The biographers of Abbot Hugh of Cluny, writing in 1120–2 about events which occurred about 1037, say that when the future saint reached boyhood, his father forced him to begin his military training, which consisted in riding with comrades of his own age and learning to school his horse, brandish his spear, manage his shield, strike and not be struck, and perform 'all the other idiocies' of cavalry warfare, including the taking of spoils and plunder.[83] Hunting was one of the basic parts of military training, for it perfected horsemanship under conditions very similar to those met on campaign. It taught boys and youths how to move in company across the countryside, instilled in them the arts of scouting and selecting a line of advance, and gave excellent training in arms, the bow against many running animals and the sword and spear against the wild boar.[84] No one seems to mention target practice at archery – perhaps it was taken for granted that boys shot at marks. And the paucity of references to the bow are puzzling, especially as it seems to have been a symbol of authority: both Charlemagne in the *Song of Roland* and King Mark in the romance *Tristan* are described as holding this weapon.[85] With falconry, for which again there is little evidence, we are even more in the dark. Although it was undoubtedly an accomplishment of the Anglo-Saxon nobility, there is little to show that it was the sport of the Norman baronage.[86]

William of Malmesbury, with a glance at Cicero's *De Officiis*, II, 13, wrote that William Rufus was very competitive in military affairs, considering it a pleasure to ride, throw the spear and strive with his elders, but only a duty to contend with youths of his own age. He thought that he lost face on the battlefield if someone took up arms before him, or he was not the first to challenge, or did not overthrow the challenger.[87] He trained, of course, in the best of company. There seems little to choose between the Conqueror, Robert

[81] See below, 151.

[82] Cf. the cases of Alfred (above, 16) and Guibert of Nogent (above, 17–18).

[83] Giles of Paris (ed. A. L'Huillier, Solesmes, 1888), 577, (ed. H.E.J. Cowdrey, *Studi Gregoriani*, xi, 1978), 49. Hildebert of Le Mans, Migne *PL*, clviii, 860.

[84] See below, 119 ff.

[85] *Song of Roland*, line 767, p. 81; *Tristan*, 77.

[86] See below, 121–2.

[87] *GR*, ii, 359.

and William as soldiers; and the youngest son, Henry, was by no means outclassed by those. Moreover, their foster-brother, Simon of Crépy, was an excellent knight.[88] Military training was in its nature a group activity. Orderic twice makes the Conqueror complain that his errant son, Robert, had taken away from him many knights whom he had brought up, trained and equipped,[89] and these seem to be the sons of William's great vassals, like Robert of Bellême and the Grandmesnil boys. In this way the prince's sons were brought up intimately with others who later would be not only their brothers-in-arms but also their *fideles*.

It was usual to have a special friend within the group, like Roland and Oliver in the *Song of Roland*, inseparable comrades on the battlefield and off.[90] This pairing is found in most military societies and is not uncommon in society at large; but, except for slang expressions, has no special terminology in modern English. Kings, however, would be expected to be found more with a group of favourites than with one. It was not only more seemly but also the privilege of their rank and wealth. One further feature of this society should be noticed: the extravagant dress which the youths affected.[91] Sexual awareness, the soldier's love of finery and the shameless ostentation of the rich played their parts.

Military apprenticeship came to an end between the years of sixteen and twenty-two. It was often some extraneous event which determined the occasion. In *Tristan*, King Mark, after he had been reconciled to Queen Yseut, gave a banquet, freed a hundred slaves and gave arms and armour to twenty squires whom he knighted.[92] Sometimes, however, it may have been a feat of arms on the field of battle: William I knighted Robert of Bellême in 1073 at the siege of Fresnay in Maine.[93] And sometimes the time just seemed ripe, as when he dubbed his son Henry in 1086, at the age of seventeen, when he was about to leave England for Normandy, and took the new bachelor with him.[94]

The ceremony of dubbing to knight was still simple even at the time when Orderic was writing. He has Lanfranc dress Henry in a suit of mail, put a helmet on his head and gird him with the belt of knighthood.[95] This description would explain the picture on the Bayeux Tapestry,

[88] *Vita B. Simonis*, cols 1211 ff.
[89] 'tirones quos alui (enutrivi) et militaribus armis decoravi (et quibus arma dedi)', OV, iii, 112; iv, 40.
[90] Cf. Sayers, *Song of Roland*, 37.
[91] Cf. Guibert of Nogent, *De Vita sua*, col. 865.
[92] *Tristan*, 114.
[93] OV, ii, 306.
[94] *ASC*, s.a. 1085 = 1086; *GR*, ii, 468.
[95] OV, iv, 120.

designed about 1077, of 'William giving arms to Harold'.[96] The English earl, already clad in his hauberk and with his long sword prominent, is receiving a helmet from the duke, who holds it by the nasal. The two soldiers stand in the open, on campaign; and Orderic does not describe any formal religious rites. The archbishop, when he saw that the prince had become a young man (*juvenis*), gave him arms 'for the defence of the kingdom', and girded him with the belt 'in the name of the Lord'. Men were still concerned with the bare essentials.

In the twelfth century it was usual to dub a batch of comrades at the same time, at a sort of passing-out parade, in order to form a unit of bachelors who would stay together for a few years. It could be that Robert Curthose and others besides Robert of Bellême were dubbed in 1073. If so, the duke's son was about twenty; and although that may seem rather late for one who had been betrothed to the heiress of Maine when a child and recognized as his father's heir or even as duke in 1067, a princely father had no great inducement to acknowledge that his heir was adult: indeed, it may be thought that he had every reason to keep him in leading strings for as long as possible.

Dubbing could not, however, be deferred until the tiro was truly independent. If the average gap between the generations was thirty years, a typical new knight had a father of fifty, ageing to be sure, but usually far from ready to give up anything to his son. In 1073 the Conqueror was in fact forty-five. There was therefore in chivalrous society a large class of bachelors, trained to arms and initiated into manhood, but denied lands and wife. Usually, at least in the twelfth century, the prince appointed a mentor to his son, often an older bachelor, and sent them off with a group of companions on a grand tour of other princely courts in order to get experience of the world.

The theme of a young man entering royal service abroad, then returning to his family in order to take up an inherited position, is common in epic and romance,[97] and must sometimes have occurred in real life. Beowulf, the Geat, served Hrothgar king of the Danes before becoming king of his own people. Tristan, when a youth, left his father's court in Lyoness for that of his uncle, King Mark of Cornwall, accompanied by Governal, whom his father had appointed his governor or tutor; and the two remained constant companions in the adventures which occurred after Tristan had been knighted by Mark. Later he returned home and served Duke Hoël in Brittany. But in this tragic romance the lover of Yseut was doomed.

[96] Phaidon ed., pl. 27.
[97] Cf. K. Hauck, 'The literature of house and kindred' (1954), Reuter, *Medieval Nobility*, 72 ff.

There is no evidence, however, that William of Normandy let Robert or William Rufus willingly out of his sight. It is possible that he was an unduly possessive father and that some of his trouble with Robert stemmed from that. Contemporary society would have expected Robert and his comrades to sow their wild oats, and in widely scattered fields over a good number of years. In tightly-knit bands, at the height of their physical powers, free from constraints, young ruffians and viewed by the peasants as bandits,[98] bachelors rode off in search of adventure, renown and the prizes of the world. Some came back 'as though through the flames of Sodom',[99] others left bastards behind whom they sometimes acknowledged when they had settled down.[100] Those without sure prospects looked for heiresses or other opportunities.[101] Bachelors were not only fomentors of discord but also the most useful troops on campaign, since they fought as much for reputation as for pay. At the same time they were fickle, and not altogether to be trusted, for they had broken loose from their families and had given no hostages to society.

Family discord and rivalry between sons is a common feature of aristocratic society at this time and in no way peculiar to Normandy. No doubt there were many loving fathers and dutiful sons, close-knit families and affectionate brothers and sisters, but the land law caused rifts in most families, and for any estate and its parcels there were usually several sets of related claimants. Given the chance – and this was afforded by any weak rule – ancient disputes were revived and kinsmen were at each other's throats. We shall see this happening when Robert Curthose was duke. A century later, the professors of the medical school at Salerno, which was interested in the problems of generation and heredity, answered the question, 'How is it that parents love their children more than their children love them?', like this.[102] The son's physical nature is created from the substance of his father and mother, that is to say, from the sperm of both; and the sperm is from the purer material of the blood drawn from the heart and the brain. And since the son derives his being from the substance of his father and mother,

[98] Hugh of Semur, the future abbot of Cluny and saint, compensated a peasant whom his companions had robbed of a cow: Hildebert, *Vita S. Hugonis*, Migne *PL*, clix, 860.
[99] OV, iii, 228, on Roger of Warenne and four knights who abandoned the world to become monks at St Evroul. For the licentious household of Hugh of Avranches, earl of Chester, one of those who interceded with the king for Robert Curthose, see OV, iii, 216, and below, 174.
[100] For Robert Curthose's bastards, born before 1087, whom he later acknowledged, see OV, iv, 182; v, 282.
[101] William of Malmesbury believed that one of Robert's adventures between 1083 and 1087 was to seek the hand of one of the greatest Italian heiresses: see below, 39.
[102] *The Prose Salernitan Questions*, ed. Brian Lawn, 47, qu. 101.

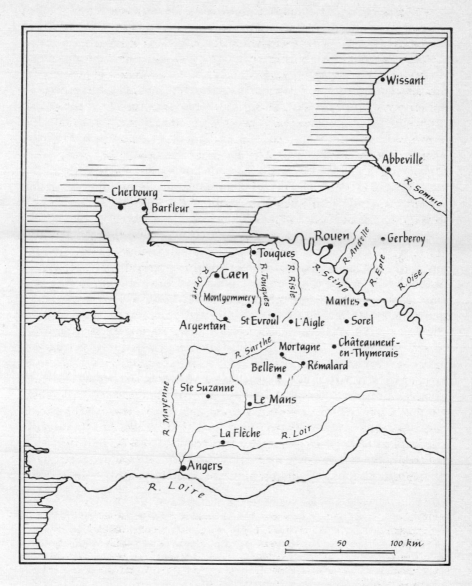

1. Normandy 1077–1087

parents retain their great delight in, and love for, their sons and daughters. But since there is no part of the essence of the children in their parents, the children do not love their parents as much as they are loved by them. The argument may be specious; but the doctors were trying to explain a situation which was taken for granted.

William Rufus was born into a family of martial men and pious women. The duke was religious, too, and not given to sexual excess. He was, however, a prey to other passions – anger, savagery and greed. To judge by his figure he was also a great eater and drinker.[103] We do not know enough about the daughters to characterize them in detail, but they all seem to have been dutiful and good. There was no Mabel of Bellême or Bertrada of Montfort among them, and none, like Charlemagne's daughters, brought shame on her father. In contrast, all the sons were in their different ways immoral. It is hard not to think that Robert was shifty from the start. William Rufus, however, was much steadier. He was thought by William of Malmesbury to have been corrupted not only by the passions of youth but also by the opportunities given by power: some of his outstanding virtues, such as liberality and sociability, deteriorated into vices and were never rectified by old age.[104] All observers agreed that he was a good and faithful son; and the king long before his death preferred him to his firstborn. It seems likely, therefore, that the bond between the two must have been forged in childhood and that the father must have taken some part in his military training despite the many distractions and dangers in the years 1066–72.

In 1077 William Rufus attended with his parents and his elder brother Robert two great ecclesiastical ceremonies, the dedication of his uncle Odo's new cathedral at Bayeux on 14 July and the dedication of St Stephen's, Caen, his father's penitential foundation, on 13 September.[105] He was about seventeen years old, ready to be dubbed a knight, and because of his brother Richard's death he had become a youth of some importance, for he now stood second in succession to his father's dominions. William I's power had reached its peak: since

[103] For his general corpulence and great belly, cf. *GR*, ii, 335. An encomium in the anonymous *De obitu Willelmi*, based on the Astronomer's *Vita Hlodowici imperatoris*, caps 62–4, and Einhard's *Vita Karoli Magni*, caps 8, 22, 24–6, 31, which admits his corpulence, but denies that it was due to gluttony or drunkenness, which he detested, is of little historical value: see L. Engels, 'De obitu Willelmi ducis Normannorum regisque Anglorum: Texte, valeur, et origine', *Mélanges offerts à Mlle Christine Morhmann*, Nouveau recueil (Utrecht-Antwerp 1973). Engels, 245–6, discusses William's great belly and accepts that there is good evidence for it.

[104] *GR*, ii, 366 ff.

[105] OV, ii, 148; *Regesta*, no. 96; L. Musset, *Les Actes de Guillaume le Conquérant et de la reine Mathilde pour les abbayes Caennaises* (Méms. de la Soc. des antiquaires de Normandie, xxxvii, 1967), no. 3; *Regesta*, no. 96.

Rufus's birth he had added to his principality the county of Maine (1063) and the kingdom of England. These acquisitions had also been to the advantage of Robert, for he had been invested with Maine (which he held, in theory at least, of the count of Anjou), and at various times had been recognized as his father's heir, even to the extent, it seems, of having been 'given' the duchy of Normandy. Moreover, King Philip of France (who was fourteen in 1066) had consented to the grant. The occasions on which Robert was acknowledged as duke seem to have been in or before 1066, in 1067 when his father prepared to devote himself for a while to English affairs, and once when the king fell seriously ill at Bonneville.[106] It was exactly as William's own father had done before he set off on his pilgrimage to Jerusalem from which he had not returned. The Conqueror, however, survived the several dangers he had feared, and Robert became in a way duke of Normandy concurrently with his father, probably being regarded during his father's absences in England as the prince-regent on the Continent.

There was nothing in this situation at the time for William Rufus and Henry. As the king had not yet found a wife even for Robert (perhaps not looked for one since the death of Margaret of Mainc), there was no question of marriage for the younger sons; and there is little to suggest that he had it in mind some time to divide up his 'empire' between himself and his sons or, after his death, between his sons alone.[107] Although the father and his firstborn in the decade after 1077 had widely differing views on what rights had been conveyed by these recognitions, the grants had certainly created various legal obligations of great future importance. Two of them should be specially noticed. It is most likely that whenever the Norman barons were required to do homage and swear fealty to Robert, his younger brothers would have been under the same obligation. And it is most unlikely that Philip of France, or his advisers, would have consented to such a transaction unless Robert did homage on the first occasion to him.[108] If both these suppositions are correct, Robert had acquired an outside lord to whom, in his quarrels with his father, he could lawfully turn, and the cadets were firmly shackled in their servitude to their elders. But for the ambitious, while there is death there is hope: Richard had died and so could Robert.

[106] Grant confirmed by the oaths of the magnates and by Philip's consent: *ASC D, s.a.* 1079; ditto and dated pre-Conquest: Florence, ii, 12; cf. OV, ii, 356; iii, 98; iv, 92. Grant in 1067: *GND*, 139, cf. 128, 143–4. Grant at Bonneville: OV, iii, 112. David, *RC*, 11 ff. Davis, as above, 'William of Jumièges', 600 ff. See also below, 36–7, 40 ff.

[107] For a discussion of his attitude, see below, 40 ff.

[108] Cf. C.W. Hollister, 'Normandy, France and the Anglo-Norman *regnum*', *Speculum*, li (1976), 213. Bates, *Normandy before 1066*, 59–62, however, does not believe that William

There was still enough warfare after the final pacification of England in 1071 to keep all but the most ardent knights happy, and it is likely that William Rufus soon joined his father and elder brother on their campaigns. Both sons witness royal charters from 1074 until 18 July 1083, when Robert drops out.[109] Once the king had invaded and intimidated Scotland in 1072, he regarded his kingdom as secure and based himself, no doubt to Robert's disgust and frustration, on the duchy. He entrusted the government of England to a few faithful barons and bishops, including the primate, Lanfranc, and kept with him on the mainland most of the other important Normans whom he had enfeoffed with great estates in the island. Normandy was no longer a pirate lair with the counts outside the society of Christian rulers; William was closely related to most of the neighbouring princes: Robert the Frisian, count of Flanders was Queen Matilda's brother and Philip I of France her first cousin, while Hoël count of Brittany was a kinsman, and later his son, Alan Fergant, became a son-in-law. Only Fulk the Surly (*Richinus*), count of Anjou, was not closely related, and it is also possible that the homage for Maine which Robert had done to his predecessor, Geoffrey the Bearded, about 1063 had not been repeated. But, whether related or not, all these powers were potentially dangerous: they seem to have been jealous of William's success in England; he was not an attractive person; there were in all cases border problems;[110] and some national antipathies and private enmities festered.

Normandy rubbed against Flanders in Boulogne and Ponthieu and against the royal French demesne in the Seine valley (the Vexin) and south of the river in le Méresais at the limit of the diocese of Evreux. Further south, the counts of Mortagne and the lords of Bellême were seldom concerned with ducal interests, while Maine, which lay between Normandy and Anjou, on the whole preferred its southern neighbour. Brittany was sometimes anarchic, a temptation to Angevin as well as Norman interference. The Normans despised the Bretons and hated the Angevins. William had a grudge against Robert the Frisian, who married his step-daughter, Bertha of Holland, to Philip of France and his own daughter to Cnut the Saint of Denmark, thus opening the

---

(the Conqueror) ever did homage to a Capetian king. If this was so, neither would he have allowed Robert to become a vassal. For the homage of younger sons, who received a *comté*, to the duke designate in 996 and 1026, see *ibid.*, 150.

[109] The years represented are 1074, 1077, 1080–3, *Regesta*, nos 73, 75; 96; 124–7; 148; 145–7, 149–50, 159; 182.

[110] For the position on the borders, see J.F. Lemarignier, *Recherches sur l'hommage en marche et les frontières féodales* (Lille 1945), 19 ff.; Le Patourel, *Norman Empire*, index, *s.v.* suzerainty.

Flemish ports again to Danish fleets. Although William's effective military power was a little greater than that of each of his main rivals, their loose alliance against him ensured that he had little pull in the border areas and could expect all his enemies to find a refuge and aid abroad. From 1072, when Fulk of Anjou took the city of Le Mans, the capital of Maine, William was on the defensive, struggling to keep intact what he had inherited and acquired. But Philip of France did not join in the wars against William until 1076, when he reached the age of twenty-four, and the English king was able throughout to prevent hostile incursions into the duchy and confine the fighting to the marches. As the scale of warfare was small, the burden on the duchy and kingdom was not unduly heavy, and for the combatants there was the excitement of the game with its promise of rewards and risk of loss. It was a chancy kind of fighting, but it favoured individual bravery and skill and the virtues of the small band of brothers-in-arms. No soldier could have hoped for anything better.

In 1073 the king recovered Le Mans.[111] In 1074, when Ralf IV, count of Amiens-Valois-Vexin died, his son Simon of Crépy, William's nursling, resisted valiantly Philip of France's attempts to deprive him of his father's conquests and his inheritance, and within a year or two, with papal support, had been confirmed in his titles.[112] In 1075 at Rouen, in the presence of Archbishop John, Queen Matilda and Roger of Beaumont, Simon restored to the patrimony of the cathedral church the vill of Gisors, west of the River Epte, which his father had held on a life-lease. On this site William Rufus was to build a most important frontier castle.[113]

The Conqueror was not personally involved in suppressing the 'rebellion of the earls' in England in 1075, but he had Earl Waltheof executed at Winchester on 21 May 1076, although this seemed to many unjust and to some the beginning of his misfortunes.[114] Later that year, in the belief that the trouble in England had been a Breton conspiracy, he entered Brittany in pursuit of Ralf de Gael, one of the rebels, and was forced to an ignominious retreat by the intervention of Philip of France. Shortly afterwards, Fulk attacked La Flèche in the south of Maine, and the hostilities with Anjou were to continue in a desultory fashion until

---

[111] For these wars and the chronology, see Douglas, *WC*, 401 ff.; Chibnall, OV, iv, xxx ff.; Le Patourel, *Norman Empire*, 74 ff.

[112] *Vita B. Simonis*, cols 1211 ff. For the politics, see Fliche, *Philippe I*, 148–9; Chibnall, 'The Vexin and the frontier with France', OV, iv, xxx ff.; Le Patourel, *Norman Empire*, 16–17.

[113] For the grant see D.R. Bates, 'The origins of the Justiciarship', *Battle IV* (1982), 7; for the castle, see below, 379–81.

[114] OV, ii, 350.

1081. William's eastern flank also was seriously exposed in 1077 when Simon of Crépy, apparently sickened by the fighting and morbidly oppressed by his father's sins, refused the king's offer of a daughter in marriage and abandoned his counties to become a monk.[115] Philip took possession of the eastern, the French, Vexin and thereby pushed the frontier with Normandy back to the River Epte and made himself a close and hostile neighbour.

No less hurtful was the rift which developed between William and his heir.[116] Robert, now about twenty-four and a knight bachelor, was the leader of a band of *juvenes*, mostly the companions of his youth, and was in most unwilling dependence on his father. Orderic Vitalis, a prejudiced observer, considered Robert's company licentious and afflicted with undesirable hangers-on, *jongleurs*, parasites and whores.[117] By parasite he probably meant a male prostitute. Robert himself was shortly to give adequate proof of his heterosexual interests,[118] but sodomy was rife in a society which set much store on single-sex communities, whether in armies or in the *militia Christi*; and a movement to repress it was developing in the church.[119] The king, who was parsimonious and puritanical, cannot have approved of Robert's conduct, but he is unlikely to have tried to keep a soldier son on too tight a rein. Indeed, he seems to have treated the young man with indulgence even if constricted by meanness and laced with mockery;[120] and the queen was fondness itself. Everyone agreed that Robert was a fine soldier, skilful and brave, with a generous nature, winning ways and a plausible tongue; but when he began to demand from his father greater independence, perhaps effective rule over both Maine and Normandy, he only aroused the king's suspicions, anger and utter and stubborn rejection. William had not found a new bride for his heir after Margaret of Maine had died while both were children; he had not even enfeoffed his sons with lands in England,[121] and he was never a victim of charm.

We owe the details of the quarrel to Orderic, who wrote two accounts of the events in 1125–30, half a century later. William of Poitiers, who

[115] *Vita B. Simonis*, cols 1215 ff.
[116] David, *RC*, 18 ff.; Douglas, *WC*, 236 ff.
[117] OV, iii, 102.
[118] See above, n. 100.
[119] See below, 102 ff.
[120] *GR*, ii, 459–60.
[121] Strangely enough, William Rufus had enfeoffed a certain Manasses, presumably a servant, with three virgates of land on the large manor of Stalbridge in north Dorset, which belonged to Sherborne abbey, without the consent of the monks or of the bishop of Salisbury, *DB*, i, 77a. This is, apparently, the only mention of one of the king's sons in that record. He must have done it on one of his visits to the kingdom with his father.

mentions Robert only once in his *History*, and then not by name, tells us nothing; indeed he abandoned the work about 1077, 'hindered by unfavourable circumstances', possibly these very events.[122] Orderic's circumstantial anecdotes and set-pieces are the great ornaments of his *History* and are of course imaginative reconstructions based mostly on oral tradition current in the aristocratic circles from which he drew his information. Not only is some of the detail bound to be fiction but also the presentation is coloured by the attitudes of the closing years of Henry I's reign when the views of high society were much changed. Orderic greatly admired both Henry and William Rufus, with suitable reservations, and strongly disliked the defeated and discredited Robert, and most of Robert's associates, such as Robert of Bellême. In these judgments, which are acceptable to the modern observer, it is, however, likely that he reflected more the views of the 1120s than those of the 1070s and the attitude of the church rather than that of the lay nobility. All the same, his vivid scenes are the closest we can get to the life and times of William the Conqueror and should be gratefully accepted for what they are worth.

In Book IV, Orderic makes the famous quarrel, which must be placed between the dedication of Caen in September 1077 and the siege of Gerberoy in January 1079, and most likely occurred in the campaigning season of 1078, the culmination of a series of attempts by the eldest son to get some independence of his father.[123] This anecdote, concerned with a place only eight miles from St Evroul, Orderic's monastery, and containing details which could not have been invented in 1125, is drawn from local tradition and is probably substantially true. The king, based on L'Aigle just behind the south-east frontier, was preparing to invade the Corbonnais, the Carolingian *pagus* which included the feudal *comtés* of Perche, Mortagne and Bellême.[124] As the lord of Bellême, Roger of Montgomery, was a friend, and his son, Robert of Bellême, was with Robert, the enemy must have been Rotrou I, count of Mortagne and Perche, or one of his vassals or neighbours.[125] The king, as Orderic tells us, was with his two younger sons lodged in the merchant Gunher's house, Robert and his followers in Roger Cauchois's. William Rufus and Henry, who was just ten, paid Robert a visit, went upstairs, began to play dice, 'as soldiers do',[126] made a great shindy, and started to throw

[122] OV, ii, 184; R.H.C. Davis, 'William of Poitiers', 74, 91 ff.

[123] OV, ii, 356 ff.

[124] Le Patourel, *Norman Empire*, map 2.

[125] Chibnall, OV, ii, 360 n. 1, is doubtful whether Rotrou was the enemy. L'Aigle, however, was the obvious base for an invasion of Perche.

[126] It is more likely that OV had forgotten Henry's youth than that he was being satirical.

water down on to the heads of their brother and his friends. Robert, indignant and urged on by his comrades, dashed up the stairs, and the resulting brawl was so fierce that it brought the king on to the scene. He restored order and forced them to make friends. But the next night Robert and his followers decamped and made for Rouen, some sixty miles away, probably one day's forced march, where they attempted to seize the keep. They were prevented by Roger of Ivry, the king's butler, and when William ordered their arrest, fled back through the eastern marches to Hugh of Châteauneuf-en-Thymerais, the brother-in-law of Robert of Bellême.[127] Hugh put his three towns, Châteauneuf, Sorel, north of Dreux, and Rémalard, fifteen miles south-east of Mortagne and on Rotrou's fief, at their disposal; and they chose to base themselves on the last, thirty-three miles south of L'Aigle. They had returned to the war, but on the other side. The king raised troops and with Count Rotrou, whose allegiance he secured and whom he took into his pay, advanced on Rémalard and invested it. During the siege, the rebels were visited by the steward of the king of France, and the castellan, Aylmer of Villeray, was intercepted and killed by some of William's knights. Aylmer's son then made peace with the English king and his guests presumably departed.

Orderic makes William Rufus and Henry friends, and tormentors of their eldest brother whose pretensions they resented. He implies that Robert deserted his father because the king did not punish them for the insult to his dignity. His loss of face before his followers was the last straw. Although there may be some hindsight here and in the words Orderic puts into the mouths of Aubrey and Ivo of Grandmesnil, who urged Robert to cast down his presumptuous younger brothers who had risen above him (symbolized by their occupation of the upper room), the general picture seems true enough. William of Malmesbury also suggests that in the early stages the king did not take Robert's rebelliousness too seriously or tragically. Robin was getting too big for his little boots; but he was a spirited lad, a splendid little fighter.[128]

In Book V, Orderic rewrote his account of the quarrel in the form of imaginary conversations between the king and his heir.[129] Here he is far less trustworthy, and, by confining himself to Robert's basic grievance, his shortage of money and lack of lands which prevented him from rewarding his followers in a proper manner, throws no further light on the relationship between the three brothers. We should notice, however, that William Rufus was content to remain what Robert scorned to be, a

---

[127] Robert of Bellême, the son of Roger of Montgomery and Mabel, inherited all his father's Norman fiefs in 1094. He was a life-long friend of Robert's. For his knighting, see above, 24.

[128] GR, ii, 459–60.

[129] OV, iii, 96 ff.

landless knight in his father's pay, a household retainer, a knight bachelor or, as Orderic has Robert complain, a hireling (*mercennarius*), perhaps mercenary soldier, or vile servant (*mancipium*).[130] When a similar situation developed a century later in Henry II's reign, the younger sons always allied with the eldest against their father. One difference, and perhaps the crucial one, is that whereas Henry's wife encouraged her sons to rebel, William's queen, although to her husband's fury sending money to Robert, was not implicated in the revolt. But we must recognize that William junior had an option in 1077–8: he could have taken Henry to join Robert. Orderic was surely right in making William and Henry loyal to their father by choice and hostile to Robert's irresponsible behaviour.[131] In later years Henry, although often playing for his own hand, joined more readily with William than with Robert.

After Robert left Rémalard, he seems to have gone to his uncle in Flanders,[132] before moving south again to occupy, apparently with the connivance of Philip of France, the fortified town of Gerberoy on the royal demesne in the Beauvaisis on the northern marches of the Norman Vexin.[133] From there he and the soldiers of fortune he recruited and new exiles from Normandy plundered the duchy for booty, and made such a general nuisance of themselves that William was able to enlist Philip in a winter campaign to destroy this robbers' den.[134] Gerberoy was invested in January 1079. In a mêlée before the town, Robert routed the attackers, killing and capturing some of the royal forces and, seemingly with his own hand, unhorsing the king and wounding him in the arm.[135] It was before the days of personal armorial bearings, and knights could not easily be distinguished on the battlefield unless they had announced in advance by what signs they could be identified.[136] In 1091, William II

---

[130] For OV's use of *mercennarius*, see M. Chibnall, 'Feudal Society in Orderic Vitalis', *Battle* I, 43.

[131] Cf. also OV, iii, 115.

[132] *ASC D, s.a.* 1079. OV, iii, 102 ff., has Robert wandering in exile for five years; but this is to confuse or conflate his several separate journeys.

[133] *ASC D, E, s.a.* 1079; *GR*, ii, 316–17; Florence, ii, 12–13; OV, iii, 108 ff.

[134] M. Prou, *Recueil des Actes de Philippe I* (Paris 1908), 242; *Regesta*, no. 115a. Philip's presence at the siege has disconcerted most commentators, and William has been credited with extravagant concessions concerning Robert in order to secure it: see below, n. 180. But William Rufus could always buy Philip off with money: below, 276, 334.

[135] *ASC D, GR*, and Florence say so; *ASC E* evades the point; HH, 207, adds that the king cursed his son. OV surprisingly omits the whole episode.

[136] For example, in 1051–2 at Domfront Geoffrey of Anjou gave notice through a herald what horse he would ride the next day, what shield he would carry and what armour he would wear; and William's representatives reciprocated: *GG*, 40. Such gestures may, of course, have been imaginary epic ornaments.

was unhorsed in a joust by an enemy knight who did not realize that he was the king,[137] but it is hard to believe that in 1079 Robert could not recognize his own father, although one English chronicler gives him that excuse.[138] William Rufus too was wounded in the fight, but the nature of his injury is not recorded. For the Conqueror this was more than a military defeat, it was a personal humiliation; he raised the siege and returned to Rouen. The incident was probably decisive for the future careers of all three sons. It is most unlikely that the king ever completely forgave Robert for what he had done.

The affair was, however, so scandalous that some of the more important Norman barons, whose own sons were involved, set to work to reconcile the two.[139] Even Simon of Crépy, who had left his hermitage to negotiate with King Philip on behalf of Hugh abbot of Cluny, visited the Norman court, helped to restore peace, and had a last and affecting talk with his benefactors before undertaking an even more important diplomatic mission to the Normans in Italy on behalf of the pope. When he died at Rome on 30 September, probably in 1080, Queen Matilda paid for a splendid marble tomb.[140] Yet peace did not come easily in 1079, for the king was determined not to give Robert what he wanted. At last, at Easter (12 April) 1080, William held a great court, perhaps at Rouen.[141] Among his guests were the archbishops of Bourges and of Vienne, Guy count of Ponthieu and several of the northern barons, his half-brother Robert count of Mortain, and his sons Robert and William. Easter was the appointed time for reconciliation, and it looks as though a peace mission, representing perhaps both the king of France and the pope, which had brought back the prodigal son, had been incorporated into the festivities.[142] By 10 May Gregory VII had heard of the reunion and wrote the son a letter of paternal advice.[143] On this occasion all were prepared, publicly at least, to blame the bad counsel of foolish friends who had led the young man astray. Some redefinition of Robert's position must have been made. We are told only that William and the

[137] Below, 284–5.
[138] Florence, ii, 13. He has Robert recognize his vanquished father by his voice.
[139] OV, iii, 110–12.
[140] *Vita B. Simonis*, cols 1219–22. He died on 30 September, after June 1080 (reconciliation between Gregory VII and Robert Guiscard). His visit to Normandy was in either March 1079 or February 1080. See F. Barlow, 'William I's relations with Cluny', *JEH*, xxxii (1981), 137–8.
[141] *Regesta*, no. 123; cf. 125–7.
[142] Cf. OV, iii, 112, who mentions 'legati regis Francorum, nobilesque vicini et amici'.
[143] *Register of Gregory VII*, VII, 27 (ed. Caspar, 508). He wrote at the same time to the king and queen, nos 25–6 (ed. Caspar, 505–7), without, however, mentioning Robert. It was at this time that the pope was trying to get William's vassalage, and would naturally be conciliatory.

barons confirmed Robert's status as heir to Normandy.[144] The county of Maine, which Robert held in theory independently of his father, was not in question. England is not mentioned, but nothing can safely be inferred from that.[145] Everything points to a restoration of the *status quo*.

The family seems to have remained united at least until 18 July 1083.[146] Both Robert and William Rufus attest a number of Norman and English charters and Robert's actions are once noticed by the chroniclers. Malcolm of Scots had invaded the north of England in the late summer of 1079, and in May 1080 Bishop Walker of Durham was killed in a local feud. Bishop Odo, the king's regent, confined his reprisals to Durham;[147] and the king with Robert and probably William junior crossed over to deal with the matter.[148] The king, as a token of confidence in Robert, sent him, probably without his brother,[149] with an English feudal army against Malcolm; and when the troops advanced into Lothian, the king of Scots sued for peace and at Falkirk subjected *Scotia* to the kingdom of England, and gave hostages. If Robert was indeed the godfather of Malcolm and Margaret's daughter, Edith-Matilda, the future wife of Henry I,[150] this must have been the occasion on which it came about. On the way back, Robert founded, or fortified, Newcastle-on-Tyne to improve the defences. According to the Abingdon account, the king was entirely satisfied with what the expedition had achieved and rewarded all who had taken part. Robert, William and Henry were still with the king in England in 1081,[151] and there is no reason to doubt that at least the elder sons accompanied their father in the army he took through South Wales to St David's.[152]

Later that year the king and Robert (and presumably William Rufus) were back in Normandy to deal with the problem of Maine. Fulk the Surly had attacked and burnt La Flèche,[153] and the king in reply

---

[144] OV, iii, 112.

[145] OV's omission could be due to hindsight or carelessness. But, even if he was correct, England could have been regarded as an appendage of the duchy or even as outside the competence of the Norman barons.

[146] *Regesta*, no. 182.

[147] *Chron. Abingdon*, ii, 9. For Odo's expedition, see Simeon, *HDE*, 118. W.E. Kapelle, *The Norman Conquest of the North* (1979), 140–1.

[148] *ASC E, s.a.* 1079; Simeon, *HR*, 211; *Chron. Abingdon*, ii, 9–10. Abbot Adelelm took his contingent in person; hence the Abingdon report. Also Kapelle, *op. cit.*, 141 ff.

[149] There is evidence from the 1091 expedition (below, 293–4) that Robert alone was involved in the peace treaty with Malcolm.

[150] *GR*, ii, 462: 'in baptismo filiola'.

[151] *Regesta*, nos 135, 140.

[152] *ASC, s.a.* 1081; *Chron. Abingdon*, 10. The abbot sent his knights but did not go on this expedition. Lloyd, *History of Wales*, 393–4.

[153] Douglas, *WC*, app. E.

invaded Anjou with a large army.[154] Through the intervention of the church, the peace of Blanchland or Bruyère was made: Fulk recognized Robert as count of Maine and Robert in return did homage to him as a vassal to his lord. Robert's position in Normandy and Maine had been firmly reestablished. But within two years he had quarrelled with his father again, this time irreparably. The new settlements may even have aggravated his sense of grievance, for he seems to have been allowed no more independence than before, and two family tragedies, the disgrace of his uncle Odo and the death of his mother, may have precipitated the break.

William Rufus is noticed in company with his parents and Robert in both Normandy and England in 1082,[155] about the time when Odo was, without warning and for reasons not entirely clear, arrested, condemned and imprisoned. The bishop had been one of his brother's trusted lieutenants in England, with Geoffrey of Coutances and Lanfranc of Canterbury forming not so much an episcopal triumvirate as a group of rivals, each watching over the behaviour of the others. The major discord was between Odo, who was also earl of Kent, and Lanfranc, and there is some evidence that the primate was involved in the other's fall.[156] It was believed that the warlike bishop was raising an army in England from among the king's vassals with the intention of intervening in Italy and perhaps making himself pope. The crime was desertion and seduction of the king's lieges, and twice Orderic Vitalis likens Odo's crime to Robert's.[157] The two may have had other things in common. After the Conqueror's death, they were hand in glove, and although Odo was mostly in England from 1066 until 1082, it would seem that he had not neglected his Norman bishopric and may always have been close to his eldest nephew.

The royal family was still together on 18 July 1083,[158] but after that Robert disappears entirely from view for over four years. Queen Matilda's death on 2 November 1083 probably removed his last friend at court. Robert seems to have travelled widely in Europe: Orderic has

---

[154] OV, ii, 308–10.

[155] *Regesta*, nos 145–6; 147, 149–50, 159. For the last charter and Bishop Odo's presence in Normandy, see D.R. Bates, 'The character and career of Odo, bishop of Bayeux', *Speculum*, l (1975), 4.

[156] OV, iv, 38–44. D.R. Bates, 'Odo bishop of Bayeux 1049–97' (unpublished Exeter PhD thesis, 1970), 247 ff., 'The character and career of Odo', 15 ff.; Chibnall, OV, iv, xxvii ff. See also below, 67, 85 ff. Duncombe, 'Feudal Tenure', 60, 138 ff., argues that Odo only lost his fee *de facto* in 1082 and was never before 1088 condemned by legal process to forfeiture.

[157] OV, iii, 112; iv, 40, in almost identical words.

[158] *Regesta*, no. 182. David, *RC*, 36 n. 86, correctly disposes of no. 199, apparently a later confirmation.

him visiting kinsmen in Flanders, at Trèves, and in Lotharingia, Germany, Aquitaine and Gascony.[159] William of Malmesbury believed that he went to Italy in the hope of marrying Matilda marchioness of Tuscany, a noblewoman of the highest rank and wealth.[160] In September 1087, when the Conqueror died, he was again within reach, perhaps at Abbeville in Ponthieu.[161] He seems always to have been able to get help from Philip of France, whom he now, presumably, recognized as his liege lord. We hear nothing of peace moves this time. Men must have regarded the breach as final: neither father nor son could forgive the wrongs done by the other. Robert and his friends simply waited for the king to die. In 1083 the Conqueror reached his fifty-fifth or fifty-sixth year. Robert was about thirty, William Rufus twenty-three and Henry fifteen.

In the winter of 1083–4, Hubert the *vicomte*, lord of several important fortifications in Maine, rebelled and held out in Ste Suzanne for about two years. After the king had failed to take the stronghold, he left the siege to his captains.[162] He visited England in the spring of 1084 and again late in 1085 when a Danish invasion was threatened, and he was so confident of his security in Normandy that he moved large military forces to the island. At his Christmas court at Gloucester, the Domesday survey was planned, and in the autumn of 1086 he returned to the duchy to celebrate the marriage of his daughter Constance to Count Alan Fergant of Brittany.[163] There is a shortage of authentic dated charters for this period. William Rufus's presence with the king is witnessed only in 1085, probably in England, and in 1086–7;[164] but again there is no reason to think that they were ever separated for long. The son had no fiefs and no office; he remained his father's paid retainer. The position of the youngest brother was quite different. Henry is a witness solely to English charters in 1081–2,[165] and as he was sent to spend the Easter feast in 1084 at Abingdon abbey, 'while his father and brothers were in Normandy', he may have been stationed at Windsor, where Walter fitzOther was constable and the queen sometimes resided.[166] In 1086,

---

[159] OV, iii, 102 ff.

[160] *GR*, ii, 332.

[161] Torigny, interpolation in *GND*, 268.

[162] OV, iv, 46 ff.

[163] OV, ii, 352; iii, 114 and n.

[164] *Regesta*, nos 206, 285.

[165] *Regesta*, nos 135, 147–50; he never witnesses a charter issued in Normandy. According to *Brevis Relatio*, 12, written in Henry I's reign between 1110 and 1120, Henry was 'nutritus in Anglia'.

[166] *Chron. Abingdon*, ii, 12. Henry was accompanied by the diocesan bishop, Osmund of Salisbury, his father's former chancellor, and by Giles Crispin, the lord of Wallingford, while Robert of Oilli, a royal constable and the keeper of Oxford castle, arranged for

probably just before his eighteenth birthday, still in England, he was knighted by his father.[167] Henry had been born in the kingdom and clearly spent much of his youth there; but for what purpose we have no means of knowing. It is just possible that William was grooming him to govern England under an elder brother's tutelage; more likely he was the only member of the family besides the queen and Odo who could be spared to represent William's person in his conquest.

In the summer of 1087, William turned his attention to the Vexin. The garrison of Mantes in the French Vexin had been raiding south across the border into the diocese of Evreux; Philip of France was in the neighbourhood and perhaps Robert as well.[168] In the last week of July, William burst unexpectedly into the town and sacked it as a reprisal. As he rode through the burning streets, he suffered some injury or sickness from which he never recovered. He was taken back to Rouen, and from his bed in lodgings which were prepared for him in the church of St Gervais, a cell of the ducal abbey of Fécamp in the north-western suburbs, he made preparations for his death. He had some five weeks in which to consider his last will and testament.[169]

We know what in the end he decided to do, or allowed to be done; we would also like to know what was the law of inheritance and how he regarded the matter. Was the outcome his original intention, or did he change his mind? There has been considerable interest in these questions in recent years, and although much progress has been made in elucidating the law, William's behaviour has been variously explained.[170] There can be no doubt that the rulers of kingdoms, duchies and counties long before 1087 regarded their dominions as impartible

---

their entertainment at Abingdon. The abbey's knights owed castle-guard service at Windsor castle. For this and Walter fitzOther, see *ibid*., ii, 3, 7, 29. For Queen Matilda in residence at Windsor while the king was in Normandy, ii, 10–11. Windsor, Wallingford, Abingdon, and Oxford were, of course, all on the Thames; and there is a suggestion here of a military command to defend the crossing of the river. For Walter fitzOther, the constable of Windsor and keeper of its forest, see J.H. Round, 'The origin of the Fitzgeralds', *The Ancestor*, i (1902), 119, ii (1902), 91, pedigree, 98. Rufus was often, when king, to be found at Windsor, partly for the hunting, partly because of its strategic situation. Henry's connexion with the abbey later gave him a mistress and a bastard son: *Chron. Abingdon*, ii, 36–7, and below, 142.

[167] *ASC, s.a.* 1085 = 1086.
[168] *ASC, s.a.* 1086 = 1087; *GR*, ii, 336–7, where there is an anecdote about a jest by Philip at William's expense; *OV*, iv, 74 ff.
[169] *OV*, iv, 80 ff.
[170] Among recent commentators are J. Le Patourel, 'The Norman succession, 996–1135', *EHR*, lxxxvi (1971), 225; *Normandy and England, 1066–1144* (The Stenton Lecture, 1970, Reading University, 1971); 'Norman kings or Norman "king-dukes"?', *Droit Privé et Institutions Régionales: Etudes hist. offertes à Jean Yver* (Rouen 1976), 469 ff.

and hereditary possessions, that they formed dynasties and had typical dynastic ambitions. Further it can be seen that the county of Normandy had characteristically descended intact, including all acquisitions, normally to the eldest son (even a bastard) of the late count. The custom must have been strong, for it was maintained by the dying man nominating his successor and making a gift *post obitum*. No testator had broken the rule by bequeathing the county to a brother or younger son or by dividing the inheritance. Provision for cadets and other relatives had been made by giving them an apanage, usually *ante mortem*, for which they owed homage and fealty to the ruling count.

This must have been the policy of the family elders, and it would have been pressed on the dying ruler. On the other hand, it was generally accepted that all members of the family had some claim on the patrimony, and the interest of the beneficiaries varied according to their position in the hierarchy. Although the eldest son probably usually favoured impartibility, his juniors may not have been so dynastically minded. Their first wish was to get as large a share as possible, even if their second was ultimately to dispossess their competitors and reestablish the unity. In the Conqueror's family, however, it would seem that Robert was less ambitious than William and Henry and more ready than they to accept partition. By 1091, Robert and William had agreed that they were both their father's heirs, while Henry considered himself a defrauded heir.[171] None of them ever abandoned his claims on the patrimony, and the cadet, although for long excluded, in the end took it all at the expense of the other surviving kin.

One further complication is the distinction between inheritance or patrimony (*propres*) and acquisitions (*acquêts*), which became of some importance in the twelfth century. Although the rule that 'the firstborn shall have the first fief of the father, but he may give purchases or later acquisitions to whom he prefers' is to be found in *Leges Henrici Primi*, an unofficial lawbook composed early in Henry I's reign to explain the law which ran in the popular courts in England, that is to say, in the shires, hundreds and boroughs, and has been cited in this case, the relevance of this bit of West Saxon customary law to the law of the succession to

Norman Empire, 179 ff. J.C. Holt, 'Politics and Property in early medieval England', *Past and Present*, lvii (1972), 1, and especially 45 ff. J.S. Beckerman, 'Succession in Normandy, 1087, and in England, 1066: the role of testamentary custom', *Speculum*, xlvii (1972), 258 ff. C. Warren Hollister, 'Normandy, France and the Anglo-Norman *Regnum*', *Speculum*, li (1976), 202. R.H.C. Davis, 'William of Jumièges', 597. My own views are, on the whole, closest to Le Patourel's. For noble customary law in England and France (which may not, of course, have applied to kings and princes), see P. Hyams, 'The Common Law and the French Connection', *Battle IV*, 77, and the literature cited.
    171 Below, 85, 281–3.

duchies and kingdoms is not obvious;[172] and we have no evidence that in 1087 it was either a generally accepted principle or one recognized by ruling dynasties. More typical of this period than fragmentation after the death of an acquirer was the creation of larger units by concentrating all types of inheritance and acquisition.[173] What is more, to judge by the struggle of descendants to reassemble separated parts, especially by the 'incestuous' marriage of cousins, division, however caused, was considered a disaster, and was seldom accepted by all the beneficiaries. It can reasonably be presumed, therefore, that a ruler dying in 1087 would be ambitious for his *lignage* and anxious to leave all his dominions to a single son, normally the eldest, and that only special circumstances would induce him to do otherwise.

In William's case the special factor was Robert's desertion, and the only uncertainty is whether the king had decided entirely to disinherit the firstborn in favour of William Rufus (and was dissuaded), or intended to punish Robert merely by confining his inheritance to the patrimony. This problem cannot be solved by analysing the Conqueror's general attitude to his dominions because his mind must have been much influenced by the recent behaviour of his sons, and his intentions could easily have changed from day to day as he thought about the matter. Nor can much reliance be placed on the two extant accounts of the deathbed scenes, the anonymous and deceptive *De obitu Willelmi* and Orderic's theatrical reconstruction. All the same, a brief investigation of these two approaches will help to explain the attitude of the several actors.

Most recent observers of the Anglo-Norman scene have stressed the rulers' sense of unity and autonomy.[174] William's becoming a king

[172] *Leges Henrici Primi*, sec. 70, 21. Chapter 70 is headed 'Consuetudo Westsexe' – the customary law of Wessex. Sections 70, 1–15, deal with wergilds and bots; 70, 16–17, with penances for sinful women; and 70, 20–21a with the laws of inheritance. The enclosing sections to 70, 21, are completely inappropriate to Norman ducal law in 1087: section 70, 20–20a, 'If anyone dies without children, his father or mother shall succeed to the inheritance . . .'; 70, 21a, 'If a person has *bocland* which his kinsmen have given him, he shall not dispose of it outside his kindred.' It may be that 70, 21, is a feudal intrusion into this field where women have almost as much right as men, but, even so, it should not be quoted completely out of context. Douglas, *WC*, 361, believed that the division of 1087 was firmly based on both established law and established Norman practice. Cf. also Hyams, *loc. cit.*, 87–8, where he analyses Glanville, Book VII.

[173] To the examples given by Le Patourel may be added the valuable study of P. Feuchère, 'Essai sur l'évolution', who gives some useful bibliographies.

[174] Le Patourel, by origin a Channel Islander, led the way and invented or popularized the expressions 'cross-Channel empire' and 'king-duke'. (It seems better, however, to call it a kingdom than an empire, for the latter appears mainly in poetry and rhetoric.) Strangely enough, he seems never to have used as illustration the cross-Channel kingdom of the Normans in Apulia and Sicily, apparently because the straits are narrow.

reinforced his desire for independence from the French monarchy, a view shared by the two sons who succeeded him in the kingdom. The Conqueror's tendency to subsume the count-duke in the king, his undifferentiated type of government and his encouragement of the connexion of Normandy and England in so many ways suggest that he was proud that he had made his family great and, in the way of conquerors, hoped that his family would be even greater after him. He was a hard, possessive man, driven by lust for land, money and power, and unwilling to share his property with anyone. There are no signs that he ever felt the urge to arrange for the dissolution of the Norman empire. A county or duchy in France, a county held by his son as a vassal of the count of Anjou, and the kingdom of England may seem disparate entities to us, hardly compatible, but few territorial accumulations are homogeneous in the beginning, and an eleventh-century ruler was accustomed to tenurial heterogeneity. Moreover, it is incredible that most of the inconveniences of a division should not have been immediately obvious to the testator, the barons and, even if less so, the church. It may have needed the events of the next few years to ram the lesson home, but almost every baron concerned in these events must have reflected on how separation would affect him and his family, and been dismayed.

On the other hand, it has been argued that Robert had never been recognized as his father's heir to England.[175] The kingdom, it is implied, was kept in reserve (as an acquisition properly so), and was simply at the king's disposal when the time came for a decision to be taken. If this interpretation is true, it would follow that the king always had it in mind to endow at least two of his sons, or preferred to keep that option open. It is not, however, soundly based on the texts. Orderic makes four references to Robert's recognition as his father's heir, three in connexion with the son's demand that he be given Normandy to govern under his father, who would continue to rule as king of England, and one in connexion with William's eventual grant of the duchy to him in 1087.[176] In none of these cases was a reference to England called for. But we can go even further. Orderic, in his introduction to the quarrel of 1077 and Robert's first desertion, remarks quite generally that 'before Senlac and later when sick' the king nominated Robert as his heir and had homage and fealty performed to him by all the nobles.[177] There is no limitation here to Normandy. Before Senlac, of course, William had only Normandy (and Maine) to bequeath. When sick at Bonneville it was quite another matter; and as the king was still on good terms with

[175] Holt, *op. cit.*, 46 ff. Le Patourel answers him, *Norman Empire*, 183 n.
[176] See above, n. 106.
[177] OV, ii, 356.

Robert it is unlikely that on this occasion he thought to detach England
for Richard (if he was still alive) or for William Rufus, who was only a
youth. And in the settlement which followed the reconciliation in 1080,
William is unlikely to have reduced Robert's prospects. In fact he sent
him immediately to secure the homage of the king of Scots, surely a
significant action. Orderic wrote of Normandy because only Normandy
was in question. His words cannot properly be used as evidence that
Robert was not recognized as William's heir general. It may be that the
cautious Conqueror always kept England in hand, even when he
thought he was dying at Bonneville; but can it seriously be doubted that,
if he had died then, Robert would have taken all, or, if the eldest son had
remained faithful to his father and been his companion and helper to the
end, he would, despite the emergence of two younger brothers, still have
inherited the empire intact? For William Rufus and Henry other
provision would have had to be made. They could have been given
apanages, like the one Henry eventually obtained, or their future left to
chance. It should be noticed that even in 1087, although the one was
twenty-seven and the other nineteen, marriages had been arranged for
neither. Even if the Conqueror after 1083 had left all his options open, he
had given no obvious sign that he proposed to give the younger sons
positions independent of Robert.[178]

Two further factors have to be considered. It was believed that the
king of France had confirmed at least once Robert's status as heir or as
duke.[179] This was a useful precaution and does not imply that the
Conqueror gave the king any active role in determining the descent of
his dominions. The suggestion that William bought Philip's alliance
against Robert in 1079 by agreeing to the permanent separation of
Normandy and England,[180] has little to recommend it. His constant and
successful policy was to deny Philip any active part in the duchy's affairs;
he, too, was a king, and if he had ever granted the duchy to Robert in
any 'real' sense, he must have intended that the king to whom the duke
was subject should be himself. It is obvious that he was not subordinat-

[178] Simon of Crépy's biographer believed that in 1077 William offered Simon, with a
daughter in marriage, 'adoption as a son of his inheritance' ('te haereditatis meae filium
adoptans'), so that they would share their pleasures, friends and enemies. But it cannot
be thought that the king was offering more than a claim to a fief or apanage.

[179] See above, n. 106.

[180] Fliche, *Philippe I*, 280–1, offers as an explanation of why Philip supported William
at Gerberoy against Robert in 1079 (above, 35) that William had promised him that
he would abandon his claim to the Vexin and later surrender Normandy to Robert, a
promise which would lead inevitably to the splitting up of the Anglo-Norman state.
Davis, 'William of Jumièges', 602–3, suggests something similar. It is, of course, pure
supposition. See the judicious remarks of C.W. Hollister, 'Normandy, France and the
Anglo-Norman *regnum*', *Speculum*, li (1976), 212.

ing Robert directly to the king of France, at least in his own lifetime, and unlikely that he was preparing for a future reduction in the virtual autonomy enjoyed by the king-duke in the duchy. Even if both Robert, in his short-term interests, and Philip, in his longer designs, would have construed the acts differently, neither had any direct influence on the decisions taken at Rouen.

The Norman barons may have shared only some of William's views in this business. They were the repository of the law and the upholders of tradition. It can be presumed that they would favour the principles of primogeniture and impartibility in the case of the duchy,[181] and they were aware that they had done homage and sworn fealty on several occasions to Robert as the king's heir or duke, and had entered into engagements with no other son. It is also likely that their view of Robert was much more indulgent than the king's. The problems of heirs were well understood and the wildness of knights bachelor was familiar and tolerable. If Robert had, at his father's bidding, once done homage to Philip of France, he was not necessarily guilty of treason in forsaking the one lord for the other, especially if his father had behaved unreasonably. But the fact is uncertain. Probably more important, the barons themselves had not suffered at Robert's hands and many of their sons were or had been his comrades. It was a time to forget and forgive. Moreover, Robert's personal qualities were attractive to many, and, while the barons did not desire the dismemberment of the empire, they may well have looked forward to the rule of a less tyrannical prince. In the matter of the succession, whatever the royal will might be, to be effective it had to be accepted by them. But there were also limitations on their ability to oppose it. Even if the king was thought to be dying, he might recover and punish the dissidents; and once he was dead there was the sanctity of the bequest, the cogency of the *novissima verba*.[182]

These were the attitudes of those who were involved in the business of the succession to England and Normandy in the autumn of 1087. Attendance at the king's sick-bed would have varied from day to day. Those named as present at the end are Archbishop William of Rouen, Gilbert bishop of Lisieux, the king's doctor John of Tours, his chancellor Gerard, and three members of his family, his half-brother Robert count of Mortain, and the two younger sons, William Rufus and Henry. Odo

[181] Although there was no one generally observed law of inheritance among the Norman nobility, and division of estates was still common, there was a drift towards inequality within the kin group: cf. Bates, *Normandy before 1066*, 118–20.

[182] William of Poitiers was much concerned with impugning the validity of Edward the Confessor's death-bed bequest of the throne to Harold because he regarded it as a real obstacle to the justice of William's actions: *GG*, 172 ff., 208. See further, Beckerman, as above, n. 170.

was in prison and Robert stayed away until it was all over. It is significant – and characteristic – that there was no one there who could in any sense be regarded as representing England; not even the English archbishops had been summoned to attend.[183]

Both the anonymous author of *De obitu Willelmi* and Orderic give some account of what they thought happened at the death-bed. Both were written well after the event, and neither inspires much confidence. The former is usually given pride of place because its brevity and simplicity convey the impression of a factual statement; but it owes these features to its being nothing more than a selective paraphrase of the concluding passages of the Astronomer's *Vita Hlodowici Imperatoris* (Lewis the Pious), written in the mid-ninth century.[184] Its version is that the king ordered his chamberlains to make an inventory of everything in the royal treasury and began to declare how the various items were to be distributed, first to the churches, then to the poor and lastly to the sons. When he allotted the crown, sword and sceptre to William Rufus, the archbishop of Rouen and others present began to fear that he was not going to forgive Robert, and questioned him on the matter. At first the dying man was very bitter about his rebel son, but then he forgave him the sins he had committed against him and granted him the duchy of Normandy which had previously been assigned to him. After this he asked for extreme unction, received it, and died.

The division of the treasure between the three categories, the gift of the crown and sword of state (but not the sceptre) to a son (originally Lothair), the intervention of an archbishop (Drogo) in favour of another son (Lewis), the king's reluctant pardon and the taking of the last sacrament are all borrowed, often word for word, from *Vita Hlodowici*.[185] It is quite possible that the twelfth-century writer was taking suitable detail from the account of Lewis the Pious's death-bed (840) to fill out a story he knew only in outline; but that helps us not at all, for the outline

---

[183] Evidence for the attendance at court in August-September 1087 is not very good. The list in *De obitu Willelmi*, 146 – the first five of the seven names – has little authority, but is not unreasonable. OV assigns active parts to Robert of Mortain and the two sons. Robert of Bellême was on his way when he heard of the king's death, OV, iv, 112; Anselm abbot of Bec was too ill to attend, Eadmer, *HN*, 24. Douglas, *WC*, 359, writes of 'a large company', 'a concourse of magnates', 'an assemblage which was not significantly different from one of the great courts which had supported so many of the decisions of his reign'. But it is difficult to see the evidence for this.

[184] *GND*, 145 ff. For a most important re-evaluation of this piece, see Engels, 'De obitu Willelmi'. Engels convincingly refutes the suggestion that the author was a monk of Caen, 250, 255 n., and suggests 'as a mere hypothesis' that the tract was written in the early decades of the twelfth century in England by someone who had not been personally involved in the events he describes, but had a good knowledge of them, 253.

[185] The texts are printed in parallel by Engels, 223 ff.

is familiar and well attested – it is the detail we lack. Moreover, even this factitious account is ambiguous. The *De obitu Willelmi* does not make it clear either what the king's original intentions were or whether the magnates, led by the archbishop, objected to the apparent grant of England to William Rufus or to the possibility that this also carried Normandy with it, to the complete exclusion of Robert. What is unambiguous is that the archbishop, by urging the king to forgive all his enemies and those who had sinned against him, particularly Robert, before receiving the *viaticum*, secured the duchy for the errant firstborn. On balance it seems that the writer believed that the king intended to disinherit Robert completely in favour of William Rufus. And we must beware of allowing such tainted support to weaken the likelihood that this was indeed so.

Orderic at the end of Book VII devotes to the death-bed one of his most famous set-pieces, a dramatic masterpiece inspired by the historian's view of William's character and reign.[186] Mainer, abbot of St Evroul (1066–89), was at the funeral at Caen,[187] and even in 1130–3, when Orderic was writing, fairly reliable information about the last days of the king must have been in circulation. But to give a factual account of what happened at St Gervais was far from Orderic's purpose: he presented a magnificent balance sheet to which he devoted all his rhetorical gifts. Indeed, he is most uninformative about the matters into which we are inquiring. After the king had denounced one by one those who had injured him, he ordered his treasures to be distributed among the churches and the poor. He then rehearsed his services to the church and commended his interests and projects to his heirs. Turning to these, he recalled that he had granted Normandy to Robert before the battle of Senlac, and as he was the eldest son and had received the homage of almost all the barons of that country, the duchy once given could not be taken away, although he knew that Robert would govern it badly. As England was not an hereditary possession but a conquest, and one obtained and retained at the cost of the murder of thousands of innocent people and every imaginable sin, he was reluctant to bequeath it to anyone but God.[188] Nevertheless he hoped that his son William, who had always been faithful to him, would bring lustre to the kingdom.

[186] OV, iv, 80 ff.

[187] OV, iv, 104.

[188] For a commentary on this passage, see Karl Schnith, 'Normannentum und Mönchtum bei Ordericus Vitalis', in *Secundum Regulam Vivere: Festschrift für P. Norbert Backmund, O. Praem.* (Windberg 1978), 105 ff. It is also possible that William (with OV's hindsight) did not want to be responsible for William Rufus's ill-treatment of the church. It is perhaps a mere coincidence that William II described himself on his seal as 'King of the English by the grace of God', below, 59.

When Henry then asked what was for him, he was told £5,000 of silver, and when he complained that he had no land on which to keep it, his father prophesied that ultimately he would unite all his dominions.

Orderic's account is infused with hindsight and his treatment of the bequest of England coloured by his wish to paint the injustice and evils of the Conquest. It had been a great crime against 'a most beautiful race', and the criminal did not want to make a direct transfer of the guilt to the young William. But, when all the side issues have been stripped away, all that is left is the record of a premeditated division between *propres* and *acquêts*, with not so much as a hint that this was questioned or opposed by anyone present.[189] The final scene is a great dispute on another matter – Robert of Mortain's plea for the release of their brother, Odo of Bayeux, with the other prisoners William had forgiven.

What credence can be given to these two accounts, which may not even be independent,[190] is a matter of opinion. Neither is a reliable witness or adds much of substance to the laconic statement in the *Anglo-Saxon Chronicle*, 'William left behind him three sons. The eldest was called Robert, who was count of Normandy after him, the second William, who wore the crown after him in England, and the third Henry, to whom his father bequeathed incalculable treasures.'[191] All three sources neglect the matters of most interest to us. As the events were determined by the will of Almighty God, there was little temptation to analyse motives or reveal abortive moves. What happened was the Great Plan. It is because of this attitude that we may presume to go behind the accounts given by nearer observers. And at the end of this inquiry we cannot doubt that the king, as a result of Robert's infidelity, was determined that William Rufus should have something, and may well have intended, until the very last minute, that he should take all the lands. It is equally clear, as subsequent events confirm, that the Norman baronage as a whole thought that Robert was the true heir to the patrimony (Normandy) and also, even if less emphatically, to the acquisition (England). What is more, at a death-bed the clergy required that all debts be forgiven, all enemies pardoned, all injustices rectified and all unlawful acquisitions restored before the last rites could be administered.[192] The pressures on William to pardon both Robert and Odo were immense, and in both cases he gave way after a great struggle and with the utmost reluctance.[193] The partial restoration of the

[189] Henry's complaint was that there had not been enough division.

[190] It is likely that *De obitu Willelmi* was written before OV, but any resemblance may be due to a common source.

[191] *ASC*, s.a. 1087.

[192] Cf. Barlow, *EC 1066–1154*, 26–7.

[193] Cf. *GR*, ii, 337, 'Normanniam invitus et coactus Roberto, Angliam Willelmo, possessiones maternas Henrico delegavit.'

firstborn was not, therefore, a considered settlement based on the law of *propres* and *acquêts*; it was the dismemberment of a great achievement done in anger, bitterness and sorrow. Human passions had torn an empire apart.

But it had not been divided into three; and Henry's exclusion from a share in it has sometimes been taken into account when the law of inheritance and the king's motives have been discussed. It has been asked whether Maine was not as much an *acquêt* as England, and could it not likewise have been detached from the duchy and allotted to a younger son? There are a number of problems here, historical as well as legal; but fortunately they need not be investigated, for there is in this case a simple answer on the grounds of feasibility. Maine could not for geographical reasons have been joined to England; because of its turbulence it was an unsuitable apanage or endowment for a knight bachelor of nineteen; and, moreover, Robert's long-established legal claims to the county could not have been transferred to someone else without the consent of all concerned, Robert himself, the count of Anjou and the rebellious barons. The scheme was so impracticable that there is no reason to think that it was ever considered.

It may also be that Henry had already been provided for. Both William of Malmesbury and Orderic Vitalis, writing in his reign, imagined that he had been his mother's heir. The English monk, when describing the death-bed, says that the king granted Henry his mother's possessions.[194] The Norman monk, in the context of Henry's birth in England, remarked that the queen then made him her heir to all her lands in the kingdom.[195] These statements are not contradictory Matilda had had her marriage portion, which could have been a sum of money rather than estates,[196] and also her enormous dower lands in England.[197] The £5,000 given to Henry in 1087 could, therefore, have been a repayment of Matilda's marriage portion or a redemption of part of her English dower lands. There is no reason why the king at such a time should have defrauded his youngest son. Orderic tells the story that Henry went to England in 1088 to ask the new king for his mother's lands and William agreed to release them.[198] Henry was certainly greedy for an apanage or principality, and indeed bought one from Robert; but the mystery of his claims under his mother's will is insoluble.

The king had spoken, and if he left problems as well as legacies, that,

---

[194] *GR*, ii, 337, cf. 468, where Henry obtains both his maternal inheritance and great treasure.
[195] OV, ii, 214.
[196] Robert's wife, Sibyl of Conversano, brought him in 1100, it was believed, the £7,000 required to redeem Normandy from William.
[197] For the distinction between *maritagium* and *dos*, see above, 6, 8.
[198] OV, iv, 148.

as medieval man was wont to say, 'is the way of the world'; 'man proposes but God disposes'.[199] There were no executors to the will, except those who witnessed the testament, men without the power to enforce its terms. It was each of the legatees for himself.

According to *De obitu Willelmi*, the dying king gave William the English *regalia*;[200] in Orderic's version he gave him a sealed letter addressed to Archbishop Lanfranc, kissed him, and sent him on his way. The son must have been provided with money and an escort, and he was allowed to take some of the English political prisoners.[201] The authority of the king still held, and no hindrance was put in his way. He had already reached the coast when messengers overtook him with the news that his father was dead.[202] To Robert was sent Aubrey, the former earl of Northumberland, with the momentous dispatches.[203] Henry busied himself with the safe custody of the money bequeathed him.

When the king finally breathed his last, all government ceased. Those in attendance scattered, and the faithless servants plundered the corpse and the furnishings down to the bed. Two of the deceased's kinsmen, Odo of Bayeux (newly released from prison) and probably Henry, joined the Norman bishops and abbots for the funeral at St Stephen's, Caen, his foundation and chosen mausoleum.[204] But the atrocious scenes at the burial, with the congregation put to flight by the stench after the

[199] *VEdR*, 17, 72 and n.

[200] St Stephen's, Caen, possessed a set of William I's regalia, including a crown, in the years after 1087; and it would seem that these were treasures bequeathed on the death-bed. The Conqueror may well have possessed several sets; and the grants of land made to the monastery by William II and Henry I in exchange for the crown and regalia may only signify the right to borrow them for crown-wearings in Normandy: *Regesta*, no. 397 (1096–7); charter of Henry I (1101–2) making a grant, 'partim pro corona caeterisque ornamentis eidem coronae adjacentibus quae pater eius moriens praedicto sancto dimiserat', *ibid.*, ii, no. 601, and p. 308.

[201] According to Florence, ii, 20, Wulfnoth, the late King Harold's brother, and Morkere, the former earl of Northumbria. He did not get hold of Siweard Beorn, King Harold's son Ulf, or King Malcolm's son Duncan, all of whom were released by Robert, *ibid.*, ii, 20–21. See further, F. Barlow, *Edward the Confessor*, 301 ff.

[202] According to OV, iv, 96, he was at Wissant. Torigny, interpolation in *GND*, 267, makes him ride in the opposite direction to Touques. See below, 53–5.

[203] OV, iii, 112. Cf. Torigny, interpolation in *GND*, 268: Robert was at Abbeville in Ponthieu. Aubrey was probably a member of the Coucy family, whose castle was to the west, near Laon. Clearly the choice of Aubrey was not at random.

[204] F. Barlow, *William I and the Norman Conquest* (1965), 186 ff. The Norman clergy present are listed in OV, iv, 104. *GR*, ii, 337–8, 468, and Torigny, interpolation in *GND*, 265, believed that Henry was there. But there is no list of the laity, and it is difficult to agree with Douglas, *WC*, 362, that 'the Conqueror was once again surrounded by a Norman court comparable to those which had so often graced his reign'. Such evidence as there is suggests that the baronage had better things to do than attend the funeral. It was the same in 1100: below, 429–30.

swollen corpse had burst during the attempt to force it into a sarcophagus far too small, were not an auspicious start to a dynastic tradition, and all his sons and his one royal grandson were, for one reason or another, laid to rest in England. We cannot doubt, however, that the young William, if he had not been sent to the kingdom, would have taken good care of his father's obsequies. Later he had the goldsmith Otho erect an expensive monument, made of gold and silver and adorned with jewels, over the tomb, and had engraved on it in letters of gold an epitaph composed by Thomas of Bayeux, archbishop of York, chosen, according to Orderic, who clearly thought little of it, because of the author's rank.[205]

The several epitaphs provide further evidence of how William's empire was viewed by contemporaries. The six poems which have survived have in common lists of the peoples whom he ruled, but, as regards titles, whereas half play also on the diversity of styles, half use the single epithet of 'king' (rex). Thomas of York's verses are typical of the latter class:

He ruled the savage Normans; Britain's men[206]
He boldly conquered, kept them in his power,
And bravely beat back swords thrust out from Maine
To hold them subject to his empire's laws.
A great king, William, lies within this little urn:
A small house does for ev'n a mighty lord.
He died when Phoebus had in Virgo's bosom lain
For three full weeks and two additional days.[207]

Thomas is followed by Godfrey of Cambrai, prior of St Swithun's, Winchester, although in the associated 'historical epigram' on Queen Matilda he strings together rex, dux and comes.[208] Likewise in one of the

---

[205] Correctly transmitted by OV, iv, 110–12, and incorrectly by De obitu Willelmi. Engels, op. cit., n. 54 and pp. 230, 248–9, establishes the text. For Otho, see Cecily Clark, 'Women's names in post-Conquest England: observations and speculations', Speculum, liii (1978), 227–8, with a full bibliography. He married a rich Englishwoman, widow of a London citizen.

[206] Chibnall, OV, iv, 111, following FNC, iv, 722, translates Britannos as 'Bretons'. Britanni occur in several of these epitaphs, and it is not always certain who they are. But it is impossible to believe that Thomas of York would have omitted the conquest of England (Britain), and the words used, 'atque Britannos/audacter vicit, fortiter optinuit', are much more appropriate to the English adventure than to Norman-Breton relations. Freeman took the completely opposite view and held that it was 'the tomb rather of the Norman Duke than of the English King', for England was not mentioned.

[207] As Engels has shown, op. cit., 248–9, twenty-three days added to 18 August give 9 September, the best date for the Conqueror's death.

[208] Wright, Satirical Poets, ii, 148 ff., nos 5–6.

anonymous epitaphs, England, the Britons, the Scottish people and the men of Maine all joyfully submitted to William while the Norman race flourished under his rule: he was 'the very famous king of the English'.[209] It will be noticed that both the attributed poems were of English origin.

Baudri of Bourgueil's epitaph, written in Touraine, exemplifies the other class:

> He, as the heavenly comet first foretold,
>   Through thickest carnage England won,
> And ruled as duke the Normans, Caesar there;
>   He poured his wealth as from a spring;
> This William, rich in empire, children, wife,
>   Then died, and left them all behind.[210]

An anonymous epitaph offers, 'He was a duke, what is more a king, more Caesar than Caesar; the duke of the Normans brought the Britons under his yoke.'[211] In an anonymous hymn on his death he is king of the English and duke of Normandy, lord of the land of Maine: 'a count in Maine, duke in Normandy, he changed himself from duke into king, most worthy of the laurels of Rome.'[212]

It was a rhetorical device, hardly to be resisted, to juggle with the titles as well as the peoples and countries, and the restrained use made of it shows that, especially in Anglo-Norman circles, it was considered otiose for a king to use his inferior titles, and, moreover, believed that his royal dignity was imperial: a man who ruled several *regna* was a Caesar. It is by no means impossible that William Rufus chose Thomas's poem as much for the contents as because of the author. Faced with a choice, he could have listened to the competitors in translation or taken advice. The archbishop's verses came out of the kingdom, had a royalist tone and also rehearsed achievements which the new ruler was to emulate. William junior never bore any other title but 'king'.

[209] *Guillelmi Neubrigensis Historia*, ed. T. Hearne (1719), communicated by Ed. Burton from a Lambeth MS, p. 685, no. 1.
[210] Baudri de Bourgueil, no. LXXVII.
[211] *Guillelmi Neubrigensis Historia*, p. 686, no. 3.
[212] J.A. Giles, *Scriptores Rerum Gestarum Willelmi Conquestoris* (Caxton Soc., 1845), 73.

Chapter 2

THE KINGDOM OBTAINED (1087–1088)

William Rufus left his stricken father at Rouen on 7 or 8 September 1087 and set off for England with a small party, probably hastily assembled. The one companion for whom we have a name, Robert Bloet, had a key role.[1] A member of the Ivry family and a trusted chaplain of the Conqueror, he would have been known to the English authorities as the king's man of confidence, and may have carried, besides letters, the great seal or some lesser symbol of authority, such as the king's signet. As to the route which the son followed, Orderic Vitalis as so often gives conflicting information; and it is possible that he simply guessed. In Book VII, where the story properly belongs, he has William sail from the cross-Channel port of Wissant, a harbour in the sand-dunes between Boulogne and Calais.[2] In Book X, written a few years later, when he recorded that Robert Bloet was given the bishopric of Lincoln (in 1093), he observed that it was a reward for his having crossed the sea with William from Touques and carried the Conqueror's letter to Lanfranc.[3] Robert of Torigny, who interpolated William of Jumièges about 1139, also gives Touques,[4] but this is at most a preference rather than a confirmation, for he was familiar with Orderic's *History* and was probably drawing on it here.

Neither Orderic nor Robert was influenced in this matter by the practices of their own day, for Henry I established regular domestic ferry routes, with the English terminal at Southampton–Portsmouth and the Norman terminals at Barfleur in the west and Dieppe in the east, both within the duchy. The two Williams, about whose 'transfretations' we know less, seem to have preferred the shorter crossings, but in William II's case probably only because between 1090 and 1096 his foothold was in the north of the duchy. In 1099, however, he made a famous crossing from the Southampton area to Touques;[5] and it may well be this which

---

[1] OV, v, 202. Robert, soon to be William's chancellor, became later the glorious bishop of Lincoln. For his family, see Raymonde Foreville, in *Studia Anselmiana*, xli (Rome 1957), 21 n. See also Barlow, *EC 1066–1154*, 70–1 and *passim*.
[2] OV, iv, 96.
[3] OV, v, 202.
[4] *GND*, 267.
[5] Le Patourel, *Norman Empire*, 163 ff., diagram, 175–6, 'on the use of oars', 177–8. For

associated him with the place in men's minds. Touques, near the mouth of the river of the same name, and just below the important ducal residence of Bonneville, is now behind the modern seaside resorts of Deauville and Trouville, popular anchorages for English yachts. All the crossings from the Channel ports could have been completed, even in 1087, given suitable tides and wind, in a matter of hours, and although travellers had their adventures, there was regular and probably heavy traffic between the various harbours.

If William's purpose in September 1087 was to meet Lanfranc as quickly as possible, the most obvious route (unless it was known that the archbishop was not in Kent) lay north to Wissant by way of Neufchâtel and Abbeville, about 113 miles, two days' hard ride for a small body of determined men leading remounts and requisitioning horses whenever they could.[6] In favourable conditions, Dover could have been reached on the third day and Canterbury on the fourth. But if, as Orderic relates, William was overtaken at Wissant with news of his father's death, he would still have been there at nightfall on 10 September, and, unless he crossed the Channel overnight and then continued without a rest, could not have reached Canterbury before Sunday the 12th. Although this seems the most obvious route and the one most likely to appeal to William, considering his directness of purpose and disregard of danger, there are obvious reasons why it may not have been taken. It is possible that Robert was at Abbeville in Ponthieu, the main crossing over the Seine, and Wissant was subject to Eustace of Boulogne, who was to join the elder brother. It may have been thought that the quicker William got off the mainland the better, and Touques, by way of Pont-Audemer and Pont-l'Evêque, a distance of less than fifty miles, was a comfortable day's ride and entirely under the king's control. If Rufus embarked at night he would reach the Hampshire or Sussex coast the following afternoon. He could have been at Winchester on the third day and London on the fourth or fifth. As regards distance and time there was little difference between the two itineraries.

There is also some independent evidence which favours the western

---

William's crossing in 1099, see below, 403. In the twelfth century, Abbot Lambert of St Nicholas, Angers, sailed from Barfleur at dawn and made Southampton at None, a duration of 9–10 hours: Samson, 'De Miraculis S. Ædmundi', *Memorials of St Edmund's Abbey*, ed. T. Arnold, i (Rolls ser., 1890), 176–7.

[6] For riding speeds and stages, see F.M. Stenton, 'The road system of medieval England', *Ec. Hist. Rev.*, vii (1936–7), 16 ff., where he suggests that an average stage was closer to 20 than 30 miles a day. But see also D. Grinnell-Milne, *The Killing of William Rufus* (1968), 35–6, 134–5, for travellers in a hurry. The best pace of a percheron was a walk of 8 m.p.h.; a trot or canter could not be maintained. This authority allows 11 hours (including 2 hours for rests) for the 72 miles from Winchester to Westminster.

route. Eadmer, a Canterbury monk, who claims to have been with Lanfranc when they first heard of the Conqueror's death, does not say that William brought the news.[7] William of Malmesbury places William's acquisition of the royal treasure at Winchester before the coronation, and ascribes his success largely to this.[8] And Florence of Worcester states that when William arrived at Winchester, en route for his coronation at Westminster, he put the English hostages he had brought with him once more into prison.[9] This support, although not over-whelming, just tips the balance in favour of Touques.

The choice of route, even if influenced by geographical and political factors, is a clue to the nature and purpose of the journey. To have travelled direct to Canterbury, by way of Wissant, with his father's letter to the archbishop notifying him that William was his heir and requiring him to crown him king, would be consistent with the view that a straightforward and legal act was properly executed without demur or question by those concerned.[10] To have aimed first at the treasury at Winchester would put him in company with those who seized the throne in irregular circumstances. It was, of course, whatever the situation, the most sensible thing to do. All worldly men would have thought that he had got his priorities right. At Winchester he would have found at least some royal officials preparing for the Michaelmas audit, and if he was able to put Morkere and Wulfnoth into safe keeping there, most likely in the gaol from which Earl Waltheof had been taken to his execution ten years before, he must have come to an understanding with the sheriff, Hugh de Port, the treasury officials, Henry, Herbert and William Mauduit (I),[11] and other servants of the crown. It was not, however, until after his coronation that he distributed his father's treasures; and it may be that all engagements were provisional on Lanfranc's acceptance of the Conqueror's will.

The kingdom was indeed for the moment virtually in the archbishop's gift. It was generally accepted that no one could become a lawful king without coronation and unction, and that the right to crown the king pertained to the archbishop of Canterbury. Moreover, since both Odo

---

[7] HN, 25. But neither does he say who did.

[8] GR, ii, 359–60.

[9] Florence, ii, 20.

[10] It is significant that neither the original letter nor its tenor was preserved at Canterbury. It would have been sensible for Lanfranc to file this important mandate, but whoever collected and published his correspondence omitted it, and Eadmer passes it over in silence. If indeed a letter ever existed, it could have been suppressed because of its unfortunate consequences for the church. We can compare Anselm's refusal to deposit in the Christ Church archives a letter which Henry I sent to the pope in 1105 about investitures: Anselm, Letters, no. 379; Barlow, EC 1066–1154, 301.

[11] See below, 149.

of Bayeux and Geoffrey of Coutances were at the Conqueror's funeral at Caen,[12] the primate was the most distinguished and influential person in the kingdom. It does not seem that he was regent or that there was a regular regency council:[13] the king ruled England directly from wherever he was; but the archbishop was accustomed to receiving orders from the king, and always carried them out. This mandate, however, was out of the ordinary, and its author was dead. Although Lanfranc was the Conqueror's friend and there was a great bond of trust between them, it cannot be assumed that he was his confidant. He had not been summoned to the death-bed to pay his last respects and receive instructions; and, if we take into account the dying man's uncertainty, it is quite likely that William's arrival in England with the news, quickly confirmed by way of all the ports, that his father was dead, compelled the authorities to make decisions for which they were not adequately prepared. Clearly the candidate could not take the kingdom by force, and it is difficult to see what ready-made supporters he had in the country. If Lanfranc had refused to accept the testament and preferred to wait until he could consult the great Norman barons, he could probably have preserved the empire intact for Robert. But he was a dutiful man, and if he declared boldly for the younger brother there would be many who would accept his judgment and follow his lead.

It is not known when or where William first met the primate. Eadmer reports that Lanfranc was shocked almost to his own death when he heard that the king had died, and also that he was most reluctant to crown the son in his place.[14] The monk is a biased witness, for William was the villain of his story; but we can believe that the prudent archbishop gave no immediate reply. He would have needed both to confirm the genuineness of the testament and to sound out English opinion. But it cannot be doubted, once he had established what was the Conqueror's will and the feasibility of crowning the younger son, that he would carry out his duty. His loyalty to his dead lord was absolute; he saw a rival in Odo of Bayeux and perhaps also in Geoffrey of Coutances; he was an archbishop, not a baron, an Italian, not a Norman, and probably had no great sympathy with baronial ambitions; and it is most unlikely that he preferred Robert to William. He knew the candidate's strengths and weaknesses, and believed he could manage him. No doubt he gave him some instruction in the office and obtained from him assurances of good government before taking the irrevocable step.[15] Nor

[12] OV, iv, 104.

[13] For his position, cf. Margaret Gibson, *Lanfranc of Bec*, 157 ff.

[14] *HN*, 25.

[15] Eadmer, *ibid.*, says that the prince, to overcome Lanfranc's reluctance, promised on oath that, 'justitiam, misericordiam, et aequitatem se per totum regnum si rex foret in

should the postulant's name be overlooked in this context: it was *nomen et omen*. Orderic Vitalis was aware of this, for he makes William, when claiming Normandy in 1090, point out to the barons that he bore his father's name and crown, and that the responsibilities of William *magnus* had devolved on him.[16] About a fortnight elapsed between Rufus's appearance on the scene and his coronation, time enough for all important men in the kingdom to have their say, but insufficient for the organization of cross-Channel leagues in favour of Robert. Clearly Lanfranc steered the right course between an indecorous and private coronation, which could have been challenged as unlawful,[17] and unnecessary and hazardous delay.

The coronation took place in Westminster abbey on Sunday 26 September.[18] It would have been possible for all the bishops and other magnates present in England to have been summoned, and Lanfranc would have assembled his spiritual colleagues. As we have no record of who attended the ceremony and the new king issued no formal charter of liberties, it is impossible to identify the participants. Indeed, dated charters with lists of witnesses are not available before the following Easter, by which time we also have schedules of the supporters of the two brothers. The version of the Anglo-Saxon Chronicle (*E*) which may have been written at St Augustine's, Canterbury, records that Lanfranc performed the ceremony.[19] There was no time, and there would have been no wish, to revise the coronation order, and what had done for the Conqueror in 1066 and at subsequent crown-wearings would have been suitable in 1087.[20] William was, therefore, crowned according to Anglo-

---

omni negotio servaturum; pacem, libertatem, et securitatem ecclesiarum contra omnes defensurum, necne praeceptis atque consiliis ejus per omnia et in omnibus obtemperaturum.' Here the primate was following tradition in requiring the king-elect to agree to take him as his chief counsellor (the Conqueror promised this to Archbishop Stigand), and rehearsing him in the promises of good government which he would make at his coronation. Eadmer was, however, writing with an eye on Anselm's attempts to get similar assurances from the king: see below, 306–7. For similar promises made by Kings Harold and William I, see Florence, i, 224–5, 229.

[16] OV, iv, 180. A practical advantage was that the name or initial did not have to be changed on the coinage and writs.

[17] Cf. William of Poitiers on Harold's hasty coronation: *GG*, 146.

[18] 26 September: *ASC E*, Florence, *De Injusta Vexatione*, 171; 27 September: *GR*, ii, 360.

[19] *ASC E*, 165–6. Cf. *Acta Lanfranci*, 273: 'Lanfrancus in regem elegit et in ecclesia B. Petri in occidentali parte Lundoniae sita sacravit et coronavit.'

[20] Janet L. Nelson, 'The rites of the Conqueror', *Battle IV*, 117, argues plausibly that the Third English Coronation Order, called by Schramm the Anselm-Ordo, a thorough revision after a German model, was the work of Archbishop Ealdred in the 1050s and was used for both coronations in 1066. If, however, she is wrong and Order III is in fact post-Conquest, it should not be associated with either Anselm or Lanfranc, who had no German connexions, but must be put after 1110, when Henry I sent his daughter to marry Henry V and German influence on England became quite strong.

Saxon liturgy in the abbey where his distant kinsman Edward the Confessor was buried and where the 'usurper' Harold and his father had been crowned before him.[21]

If he had indeed brought his father's regalia with him,[22] these could have been used advantageously at Westminster; but there would have been other sets in the English treasuries. The coronation was an initiation ceremony rich in symbolism and replete with meaning, an ecclesiastical ritual conducted in Latin, but incorporating some more secular rites, both old and new, performed in the vernacular.[23] First the new king was 'elected' by the clergy and people, and in return promised that he would protect the church, secure good justice for the people, and abolish all evil laws and customs.[24] The promises were made in French so that they could be fully understood by the congregation. He was then, like Saul and Solomon, anointed by the priests with holy oil and invested with the crown and other insignia. Finally, after the announcement of his royal estate, he took homage from the magnates. According to the Anglo-Saxon Chronicle, 'all the men in England bowed themselves before him and swore oaths' to the crowned prince. He had become the lord king. He was also, as his Great Seal proclaimed, king by the grace of God.

The question at what moment in September 1087 William legally became king, whether it was at the time of his father's gift, when his father died, when Lanfranc accepted him, when he received enough support from the baronage to allow his coronation to take place, or in that ceremony itself, is of some constitutional interest, but can hardly be investigated, let alone answered.[25] Nor can it be said whether there was technically a disputed succession. In the unfolding, however, of what could be regarded as a *coup d'état* (and was so viewed by Robert), it was the coronation which mattered. William had become undisputedly king of England and, perhaps, of other regions too.

Once crowned, he came immediately into all his royal rights, and after so long a servitude it would have been natural for him to have kicked over the traces; but nothing shows more clearly the power of his sponsors, his own respect for his father, and his keen appreciation of the

---

[21] For the importance of such continuities, see Kurt-Ulrich Jäschke, *Wilhelm der Eroberer, sein doppelter Herrschaftsantritt im Jahre 1066* (Sigmaringen 1977), 68 ff.

[22] See above, 50.

[23] For the details of Edward's coronation, see F. Barlow, *Edward the Confessor*, 60 ff.

[24] H.G. Richardson, 'The coronation in medieval England: the evolution of the office and the oath', *Traditio*, xvi (1960), 161 ff., especially 171.

[25] For discussions of the subject, see Karl Schnith, 'Die Wende der englischen Geschichte im 11. Jahrhundert', *Historisches Jahrbuch*, lxxvi (1966), 4 ff.; Barlow, *op. cit.*, 54 ff.; Jäschke, *op. cit.*

circumstances, than the lack of upheaval. William I's sheriffs remained in office, and some continued undisturbed for long, a few into the next reign.[26] Gerard, precentor of Rouen, the Conqueror's chancellor, joined the new king and was confirmed in his office.[27] The iconography of William's 'first' seal is the same as that of his father's:[28] on the obverse the king is shown enthroned in majesty, sitting on a throne without a back; on his head is a crown of five points on which are crosses or trefoils, and from which hang two pendants;[29] he wears a short mantle fastened at the throat over an undercoat with tight sleeves and skirts which reach below the knees; he holds in his right hand an upright sword and in his left an orb surmounted by a cross; and in the field on each side of the king are circular six-leaved ornaments. On the reverse the king is shown on horseback galloping to the right; he wears a hauberk of mail and a conical helmet and holds in his right hand a lance with three streamers and in the left a kite-shaped shield of which the inner side is shown. The inscription, however, was necessarily changed. William I's carried two hexameters, one signalling him as duke of the Normans, the other as king of the English: 'HOC NORMANNORUM WILLELMUM NOSCE PATRONUM; SI[30]/HOC ANGLIS REGEM SIGNO FATEARIS EUNDEM' – 'With this seal recognize William, patron of the Normans; or with this acknowledge him as king of the English'. As the couplet starts on the 'knightly' side, that is presumably the obverse. The seal of the son, however, bore on both sides an identical inscription: 'WILLELMUS D(E)I GRATIA REX ANGLORUM' – 'William by the grace of God king of the English'.

[26] See below, 188.

[27] V.H. Galbraith, 'Girard the Chancellor', *EHR*, xlvi (1931), 77. He witnesses *Regesta*, ii, no. 335a. The dates of his office are 1085(?)– *ante* 27 January 1091. He was replaced by Robert Bloet.

[28] William II's genuine seal is illustrated, *Facsimiles of Royal Writs*, pl. xxx, cf. viiia. It is described by A.B. and A. Wyon, *The Great Seals of England* (1887), 7 (illustrated, pl. II, 15–16). William I's 'second' seal (the only genuine one) is shown in *Facsimiles*, pl. xxviii, and described Wyon, 5 (illustrated, pl. II, 13–14). There are slight differences between the designs in the crown (William I's has 3 points, on which are fleurs-de-lys, and no pendants), the cross of the orb and possibly in the coronation robes. The son introduces the stars in the field, the pendants to the crown and the ornaments on the horse's chest-strap. But most of these are stock features to be found on some of the English coins of the period: pendants (cf. William I, type 2) and stars (cf. William I, type 5, II, type 3).

[29] Also called *prependulia*, they are featured on Byzantine coins: cf. J.P.C. Kent, 'From Roman Britain to Saxon England', *Anglo-Saxon Coins* (Stenton *Festschrift*, 1961), 14; cf. pl. II, 15, III, 5. Wyon, 7, interpreted them as chin-straps. See also last note.

[30] 'Si', the last word on the obverse, must be the first word of the second hexameter on the reverse. Although it can be elided with 'hoc', it is otiose both metrically and grammatically, and may be a mistake.

The son does not qualify his name with *junior* or a number.[31] Likewise with the coinage. It is only possible to establish the order of the thirteen issues of silver pennies inscribed 'William' from the evidence of mules (coins struck in error from an old and a new die); and they have been attributed, eight to William I and five to William II, according to 'proportional distribution'.[32] It may be significant that on the ninth issue the portrait bust, which had usually faced front, was turned right (like William I, type 7), before returning for the rest of the reign to a facing view.[33] But there was no significant change in the inscription: on all thirteen issues it is WILLELM (or variants) REX, with sometimes an abbreviation, often quite summary, of ANGLORUM. From this evidence it is clear that the son never had the wish to dissociate himself from his predecessor or to proclaim the start of a new and better age. That is probably why, unlike his successor, his brother Henry, he did not issue a charter of liberties at his coronation.

The new king took William of St Calais, bishop of Durham, as his closest adviser, and Roger Bigot witnesses many of his early writs. Both were his father's men. The bishop, who had been educated under Odo in the chapter of Bayeux, became monk and prior of St Calais in Maine and then abbot of St Vincent-des-Prés, outside the walls of Le Mans, before receiving his perilous bishopric in 1080, apparently as a reward for his diplomatic missions on behalf of the Conqueror.[34] When in Maine he operated in a sensitive frontier area, and this may have helped him to get Durham. A good scholar and a monk of blameless life, he reformed his northern see and earned nothing but praise from his monks. William Rufus, who was rather tongue-tied, seems always to have been attracted to the good talker. Both William of St Calais and his successor at Durham, Ranulf Flambard, although very different in some ways, were clever, talkative and amusing, full of ideas. Bishop William was reputed to be not only resourceful but wise as well, and it was the former quality which rescued him when the latter was wanting. He was more of the

[31] He is called *junior* or *minor* by those writers who wanted to distinguish him from his father (*magnus* = senior): cf. *Vita Wulfstani*, 61; *De Injusta Vexatione*, 171; Hugh, *HCY*, 34; *Hist. mon. Gloucest.*, i, 68, 102, 109, 115.

[32] George C. Brooke, *English Coins* (1932), 81 ff. Excellent photographs are in *Sylloge of Coins of the British Isles* (British Academy), e.g. R.P. Mack, *R.P. Mack Collection*, xx (1973), pl. XLVI ff. See here, pl. 2.

[33] On the other hand, Henry I, although he wished to dissociate himself from his brother's 'tyranny', modelled his first issue on his predecessor's last (both facing busts), and waited until his second issue (profile/cross fleury) to turn the bust to face left. It is, therefore, not impossible that Rufus kept William I, type 8 ('Paxs') in currency for a time, say until Michaelmas 1088. There was indeed no time between the coronation and Michaelmas 1087 for a general change of dies.

[34] For William, see Barlow, *EC 1066–1154*, 64, 281 ff., and *passim*.

king's age and at first probably more to his taste than Archbishop Lanfranc. According to the Anglo-Saxon Chronicle, 'The king treated the bishop so well that all England went by his counsel and did exactly as he wished.'[35] Rufus here was too trusting.

Roger Bigot also proved to be fallible. This family from Calvados, under-tenants of the bishop of Bayeux and of minor importance in the duchy, prospered through the patronage of Bishop Odo and royal service.[36] Roger founded a great baronial dynasty in England, in 1086 holding a large honour directly of the king in East Anglia. He had benefited from the deposition of Archbishop Stigand and his brother Æthelmaer bishop of Elmham in 1070 and from the forfeiture of Ralf de Gael, earl of Norfolk, in 1075. He married after 1088 Alice, the heiress of the Domesday lord of Belvoir in Leicestershire, and was given by Henry I, whom he served in turn, the honour of Framlingham in Suffolk. He died in 1107, and when his son William was lost in the White Ship disaster of 1120, his younger son Hugh, the future earl of Norfolk, inherited the family estates. Another Hugh Bigot, perhaps Roger's brother, held land in the Bessin of the church of Bayeux in Bishop Odo's time (ante 1097),[37] and there is a reference to a brother William who came to England with Geoffrey Ridel (also drowned in 1120) from Apulia some time between 1075 and 1086.[38] Roger was so commonly known by his byname Bigot, meaning perhaps a pickaxe,[39] that he was never distinguished in the records by any ministerial title. He acted as

---

[35] ASC, 166; GR, ii, 360; Florence, ii, 22. Plummer, Two Saxon Chronicles, 276. The language of ASC has caused confusion about who was trusted, Bishop William or Odo: 'At the head of this plot [in 1088] was Bishop Odo with Bishop Geoffrey and William bishop of Durham. The king trusted the bishop so well that all England went by his counsel and did exactly as he wished; and he thought to treat him just as Judas Iscariot did our Lord.' Since Odo is the principal subject, it is most likely that he is also the one treated well and the prime traitor – and so ASC, 166n. But both GR and Florence, loc. cit., when giving a Latin version of the passage, make William the trusted bishop, and GR even attributes Odo's rebellion to his anger at that. Although they are not completely independent sources (cf. Barlow, EC 1066–1154, 19 n.), it is likely that here they convey the correct meaning of what is garbled in ASC. HH, 211, however, embroiders ASC to make Odo 'justitiarius et princeps totius Angliae', and Simeon, HR, 216, at the end of his derivative account of the rebellion, describes Odo as, 'qui fere fuit secundus rex Angliae'. All writers may have had in mind Odo's position in the kingdom before 1082.

[36] For Roger, see GEC, ix, 568–96; Loyd, Families, 14–15; Morris, Med. Eng. Sheriff, 46 n. 47; Sanders, Baronies, 12, 46–7. For his estates, DB, ii, 87–8 (Essex), 173–90 (Norfolk) and 330b–345b (Suffolk); for their character, VCH Norfolk, ii, 19, Suffolk, i, 396–7.

[37] J.H. Round, Family Origins (1930), 213. The fiefs were about 30 km south of Bayeux at Les Loges (south of Caumont) and Courvaudon (north-east of Aunay).

[38] DB, ii, 180, re Sutton, nr Stalham, Norfolk. Geoffrey became a royal justice: DNB, xlviii, 274; Richardson and Sayles, 174 ff.

[39] Or some other double-headed instrument. The spelling seems to be invariably Bigot in DB and royal documents. Once, DB, ii, 337, Roger is simply called by his byname.

one of the king's justices in 1076–9,[40] and was sheriff of Norfolk and Suffolk, probably for the second time, in 1086.[41] In William II's reign, when in more exalted company, he normally witnesses among sheriffs and stewards, and never has precedence over Eudo *dapifer*. Usually in attendance on the king in his itinerant household, and possibly serving as a steward, he was a factotum who got things done for his master. He was much involved in the issue of writs, orders to the shire courts; but he could also be sent out of the royal court, usually to East Anglia, to act as a royal justice or commissioner. His record of service to three kings is most impressive. He was a member of that high ministerial nobility, the successor to the Old-English thegnage, on which the Anglo-Norman monarchs depended so much.[42] We know nothing about his character beyond what can be inferred from his career. He was at least conventionally religious, granting a church to Rochester cathedral and land to the new cathedral at Norwich. The first may well have been in atonement for the part he had played in the rebellion of 1088. The king confirmed both grants.[43]

Two royal writs from the first months of the reign supply the names of some of the household officials and adherents of the new king. One, addressed to Hugh of Beauchamp, a landowner in Bedfordshire who would seem to be sheriff of Buckinghamshire, informed him that Gilbert Crispin, abbot of Westminster, had established his right to two estates given him by the Conqueror after a hearing before the bishops of Durham and Winchester, Eudo the steward (*dapifer*), Ivo Taillebois (another steward), and Robert the dispenser, all described as 'the king's barons'. The two bishops witness the document.[44] Although in its present form it may not be authentic – it contains *dei gratia* in the address – there is nothing suspicious about the contents. The other writ, issued at Winchester, again in favour of the abbot of Westminster, and addressed to Bishop Maurice of London, Geoffrey de Mandeville (perhaps keeper of the Tower or local justiciar), the sheriff and all the barons of London, French and English, was witnessed by Geoffrey bishop of Coutances, the bishop of Durham, and Roger Bigot.[45]

[40] Round, *FE*, 329.

[41] *Regesta*, no. 138, cf. 122; 373, cf. 385. Round, *VCH Essex*, i, 420; C. Johnson, *VCH Norfolk*, ii, 19; B.A. Lees, *VCH Suffolk*, i, 389–90; Morris, *Med. Eng. Sheriff*, see index. It does not seem, however, that he was sheriff under William II; see below, 447.

[42] See below, 156 ff.

[43] *Regesta*, no. 452, cf. *DB*, ii, 173 (church of East Walton, Norfolk); no. 482, cf. *DB*, ii, 116b, 201b. Roger's chaplain, Ansketil, is noted *DB*, ii, 334b.

[44] *Gilbert Crispin*, 136, no. 9. For Hugh of Beauchamp, see Sanders, *Baronies*, 10. For the household servants, see below, 136 ff. Ivo Taillebois had recently abandoned Duke Robert: see below, 68.

[45] *Gilbert Crispin*, 137, no. 10.

The first action of the new king was to take full possession of the royal treasury at Winchester.[46] He could have been there for the customary final audit of the accounts at Michaelmas (29 September), and, according to the Anglo-Saxon Chronicler, he found it overflowing with the most astonishing treasures, gold and silver, jewels, costly robes and other precious objects, in fact the Aladdin's Cave of a life-long robber baron, most of the plate clearly stolen from churches. Part of this, in accordance with his father's instructions, he distributed for the salvation of the soul of the deceased, which he may have hoped had stuck in Purgatory. To minsters (collegiate churches) were given either 10 marks of gold or 6,[47] to country churches 60d apiece;[48] to every shire was sent £100 to be spent in alms to the poor; and, Florence adds, to the more worthy churches and minsters was sent a share of the church ornaments, the crosses, (portable) altars, shrines, books (or ornamental bindings), candelabra, vases, cruets and other valuables.

The Abingdon monks believed that, although the king had entrusted the whole distribution to their abbot, Reginald, who had been a chaplain of his father, they themselves had done badly. They had received only an excellent text of the Gospels, a silver bucket for the carrying of water for exorcism, a rough piece of silk and an ivory censer shaped like a boat.[49] Nor was the Conqueror's own church of St Martin at Battle fully satisfied with the fate of its share.[50] It recorded that the dying king had ordered his son to give the monastery a manor worth 40 marks of silver (£26 13s 4d), his royal mantle adorned with gold and most precious jewels, and 300 gold and silver reliquaries, most with gold or silver chains, containing the relics of innumerable saints, together with a shrine in the form of an altar, on which he was accustomed to have mass celebrated when on campaign. Many of these things, acquired with the kingdom from his English predecessors, the monks thought, were kept in the royal treasury; and William II carried out his father's wishes and had the goods delivered on 25 October. He also gave the abbey the manor of Bromham in Wiltshire worth £40.[51] However,

[46] *ASC*, 166; Florence, ii, 21. According to HH, 211, who is quite reckless with figures, there were 60,000 lb of silver, besides the precious objects, in the treasury.

[47] Florence divides this category into three: some received 10, some 6, and some less.

[48] *ASC* (ed. Earle, 223) distinguishes between *mynstre* and *cyrcean uppeland*. Florence translates these as *principales ecclesiae* and *ecclesiae in civitatibus vel villis suis* (HH, 211: *ecclesia villae*). The latter should not be translated as 'churches in the cities and villages', as in *ASC*, 166 n. 1, but as 'churches in *his* cities/towns and manors'.

[49] *Chron. Abingdon*, ii, 41.

[50] *Chron. Battle*, 96, 102 ff.

[51] *DB*, i, 65b: a manor which had belonged to Earl Harold, when it had been worth £20. *Regesta*, ii, nos 290a, 314a, 348a. For William's gift of churches in 1094, see below, 328.

as often happened in this reign, the monastery was unable to retain all its acquisitions. In 1097 the king was so harassed by a monk of St Germer de Fly in the French Vexin, to which he had rashly promised a rich chasuble, that while on his Welsh expedition he had given the monk a writ to the abbot of Battle ordering him to pay the bearer 10 marks; and when protests were of no avail, the abbot had to melt down the reliquaries in order to find the silver which enabled the French monk to buy a suitable piece of cloth.[52]

With regard to the alms distributed by the king in money, we can do some very rough sums. If the minsters which received at least 6 marks (48 oz) of gold were the cathedrals and more important monasteries, we have to count 2 metropolitan sees, 13 bishoprics and about 25 convents; and on this basis there would have been paid out at least 300 marks (2,400 oz) of gold, which, at 15s the oz, was worth £1,800.[53] The doles to the 34 shires would cost a further £3,400. This leaves the country churches, for which the grant was 5s, or ¼lb. If we follow Florence in interpreting this category as other churches on the royal demesne (and it is inconceivable that the king would have given money to churches which were not his very own), it would not be unreasonable to posit a similar amount, allowing an average of 400 demesne churches per shire, which is probably on the generous side. The grand total, not counting the gifts of church ornaments, is £8,600.

A sum of this order causes no problems at all. It is rather more than the Conqueror bequeathed to Henry (£5,000) and William paid to take Normandy in pawn for three years (£6,666), but less than the net yield of a land-tax (geld) at 4s the hide,[54] and very much less than the sums which, according to the Anglo-Saxon Chronicler, had been paid to the Vikings as Danegeld, for example £16,000 in 994, £24,000 in 1002, £36,000 in 1007, £48,000 in 1012, £21,000 in 1014, and £82,000 in 1018. Nor can the propriety of the action be questioned. Although his successor in similar circumstances gave no money away in 'charities',[55] William not only behaved like a good son but also improved his position. He disarmed rumours that he was an irreligious libertine, acquired the valuable gratitude of the church and created among the people a

[52] Later God showed his anger at the spoliation of St Martin's by striking the chasuble with lightning. As a result, Abbot Odo of St Germer and the monk-collector Richard travelled to Battle and asked the monks' pardon for the offence: *Chron. Battle*, 106.

[53] The ratio was fairly steady at 9:1 in England between 1104 and 1278, and similar in most other countries in Western Europe: A.M. Watson, 'Back to Gold – and Silver', *Ec. Hist. Rev.*, 2nd ser., xx (1967), 23, table 1. In *PR 31 Hen. I* (Michaelmas 1130), 1 mark of gold is valued at £6, whereas 1 mark of silver is 13s 4d; 1 oz of gold was equivalent to 15s: see below, 216–17. In the case of silver, it makes no matter whether the sums are expressed in lbs or £s.

[54] See below, 238 ff., 259.

[55] OV. v, 292; see below, 429.

general sense of the coming of happier days. It is possible that the country had to pay for this initial liberality by greater contributions to the royal coffers in the future. But there can be no balance-sheet here; and in any case the king's ostentatious generosity was, after this first explosion, mostly directed towards other, more worldly purposes.

One act of chivalrous generosity, however, William denied himself in 1087: the release of the political prisoners, Wulfnoth and Morkere – one the last survivor of the six sons of Earl Godwin of Wessex and his wife Gytha, the Danish princess, the other the last of King Edward's earls of Northumbria. This is surprising. It was, apparently, his father's will; Robert set free and honoured those who fell into his hands; and William was always compassionate to captives acquired in honourable circumstances.[56] Political necessity alone could have forced him to act so much out of character; and although the possible threat to his position from King Harold's brother and earl may seem minimal to us, it must have loomed larger to him, especially when he was threatened by a serious rebellion. Perhaps he remembered Earl Waltheof and the story that in 1075, only twelve years before, the aggrieved Norman-Breton earls had thought of making the Englishman king.[57] Be that as it may, the two remained in custody. Nothing is known of Morkere's fate. Wulfnoth, a harmless old man, incapable after thirty-six years of imprisonment of maintaining himself in the outside world, and probably dead by 1094, seems eventually to have been entrusted to the cloister at Winchester cathedral, for the prior, Godfrey of Cambrai, wrote a highly flattering epitaph:[58]

[56] Cf. his behaviour at Ballon in 1098: OV, v, 244, and below, 386.

[57] F. Barlow, *William I*, 160–2.

[58] Wright, *Satirical Poets*, ii, 148. Wulfnoth is no. 12 in the list of 19 notables, ranging from Cnut to William of Rots, abbot of Fécamp, celebrated by Godfrey in his *Epigrammatica historica*. GR, i, 245 and OV, ii, 179, not necessarily independently, have Wulfnoth imprisoned and die in chains at Salisbury, presumably in the castle. His name, however, turns up in some unlikely places. His 'signature' appears after the earls in a royal charter dated at Hastings, probably in January 1091, confirming Osmund of Salisbury's reorganization of his church; and it would seem that the captive had been produced by the bishop both to testify to some matter and to accompany the king abroad as a security measure: *Regesta*, no. 319. Also, near the end of a long list of notables purporting to witness a forged charter of Bishop William of Durham in 1082, appears 'Wlnoto Haroldi regis germano': Offler, *Durham Episc. Charters*, 20 (indexed under 'Harold II, Ulnoth his *germanus*'). There must have been some tradition that Wulfnoth was normally in honourable captivity; and it would not seem that he was usually 'kept in chains'. Although Salisbury was not more than a day's ride from Winchester, Godfrey's knowledge and interest seem based on closer acquaintance; and it may be that the prisoner was moved around and finished his days in Winchester priory. If the 'earl' was born about 1036, he would have been 15 when given as a hostage to the Conqueror in 1051 and 51 in 1087. His treatment may easily have caused him to appear an old man when he fell into Rufus's hands.

The nobility of his forbears, his simple manners,
   His sound views and honourable judgments,
The strength of his body and the fire of his intellect,
   All these glorify Earl Wulfnoth.
Exile, prison, darkness, inclosure, chains
   Receive the boy and forsake the old man.
Caught up in human bonds he bore them patiently,
   Bound even more closely in service to God.
In spring while the Fishes were warmed by the February sun
   The ninth day under Hermes was the last for him.[59]

William spent the Christmas festival not surprisingly at London instead of the more usual Gloucester:[60] he needed to be at hand and Wales could wait. His first steps can hardly be faulted. He had established excellent relations with the powerful English church, taken one of the cleverest of its bishops as his adviser, retained his father's chancellor who happened also to be the nephew of the bishop of Winchester and the abbot of Ely, and shown in many ways that he intended things to go on much as before. Although the hopes of many for a less oppressive government would have been disappointed, their fears of immediate revolution and disorder would likewise have been unfulfilled. Henry of Huntingdon, who like William of Malmesbury and Florence based himself on a version of the vernacular Chronicle and also like them incorporated material garnered elsewhere, records the bishops present at the Christmas court:[61] Lanfranc of Canterbury, Thomas I of York, Maurice of London, Walkelin of Winchester, Osbern[62] of Exeter, Wulfstan[63] of Worcester, William of Beaufai of Thetford, Robert of Limesy of Chester, William of Durham, Odo of Bayeux, and Remigius of Lincoln. This is a very likely list: the bishops are recorded almost in

---

[59] If the dating couplet (after correcting *Nono* to *Nona*) means that Wulfnoth died on the ninth day of the sun's sojourn in Pisces, the date is 22 February, which also gives an agreement between the poem's 'ver erat' and the usual entry in the calendars for 8 Kal. Mart., 'ver oritur' and variations. If 'under Hermes', which is equivalent to 'under Mercury', means that 22 February was a Wednesday, the year would have been 1088, 1090 or 1094. As the next four epigrams celebrate men who died in 1093, 1095, 1095 and 1093, the year of Wulfnoth's death can only be expressed as 1088 × 94. On the other hand, if 'sub Herme' is a mistake for 'sub Marte', which is more in accordance with Godfrey's usual practice, Wulfnoth died on 9 March in an unidentifiable year.

[60] *ASC*; *Chron. Battle*, 40; *GR*, ii, 360: 'reliquo hyemis quiete et favorabiliter vixit'.

[61] HH, 211.

[62] *Gaufridus* in the printed text. At some stage an 'O' has been misread for 'G', an easy mistake.

[63] *Wlnod* in the printed text.

their proper order;[64] two of those omitted were probably mortally ill (Giso of Wells and Herman of Salisbury); and the see of Chichester was vacant. Unaccounted for are Robert Losinga of Hereford (the astrologer, who this time could have been misinformed),[65] and Gundulf of Rochester. The last, who was to be closely involved with the king, could have been left in Kent to supervise the defences. The allegiance of neither of the missing prelates is in doubt, and it is clear that the king had all the bishops, both the old guard and the new, in his camp.

Within four months of his release from prison, Odo of Bayeux had recovered not only his honours in Normandy but also those in England. He is noticed at Canterbury in company with Lanfranc on 22 December.[66] As the two had been rivals in Kent and the archbishop had been implicated in the bishop's arrest in 1082,[67] Odo must have made overtures which Lanfranc could not decently refuse, and taken this step because a reconciliation with Lanfranc was a necessary preliminary to the recovery of his old position. It is hardly likely that Lanfranc was deceived by the bishop's moves or that the king was overjoyed to see his uncle again. But Odo had been the patron of some of the prelates and barons, he had done no wrong to his nephew, who was looking for friends, and it would have been difficult for the king to appear less generous than the duke. In these circumstances William restored to Odo his English estates and his earldom. An ambiguity in the Anglo-Saxon Chronicle makes it possible to infer that William's welcome was as warm as Robert's and that he made their uncle 'justiciar and ruler of the whole of England', to use Henry of Huntingdon's words. Although this is most likely a mistake,[68] the uncertainty over favour and allegiance reveals

---

[64] Cf. Barlow, EC 1066–1154, 47. Wulfstan should have preceded Osbern. Remigius, a senior bishop, is put last only because HH wanted to insert a paragraph about him.

[65] He did not set off for the dedication of Lincoln cathedral in 1095 because the stars foretold (correctly) that it would not take place: GP, 313.

[66] He helped Lanfranc to install Guy as abbot of St Augustine's: Acta Lanfranci, 273; see also Plummer, Two Saxon Chronicles, 316. The event occurred in Lanfranc's 18th year (August 1087–August 1088), and the consecration is dated 21 December 1087 in Chron. Guill. Thorne . . . de gestibus abbatum S. Aug. Cant., in Twysden, Historiae Anglicanae Scriptores X (1652), col. 1793. The king notified Odo and his lieges in Kent that the new abbot was to have seizin of his lands; and William bishop of Durham witnesses: Regesta, no. 304. This writ may have been issued at the Christmas court. The other chronicles, ASC, 166, GR, ii, 360, Florence, ii, 21 and OV, iv, 124, are less precise about the date of Odo's return and ASC is confused (see above, 61 n. 35). The bishop's English honour had been specially administered and not dispersed during his imprisonment; but it would have taken him a little time to recover possession of all the parts.

[67] GR, ii, 360–1; cf. De Injusta Vexatione, 184; Chron. Abingdon, ii, 9; and above, 38. For Odo's position in Kent, see Douglas, Domesday Monachorum, 27 ff. Odo made a point of ravaging Lanfranc's manors during the rebellion.

[68] See above, 61 n. 35.

how volatile the situation was. In both England and Normandy there must have been a general uncertainty about how things would develop, what form the pattern of lordship would take, which of the brothers would come out on top; and each man of importance would have wondered how to play the game. A few had already taken sides; most probably accepted the situation in which they found themselves, but were not committed irrevocably. They would wait and see.

Meanwhile Robert had been accepted as duke of Normandy and count of Maine without demur. He had taken over the Conqueror's Norman treasury (depleted by Henry's bequest) and, like his brother, distributed much of it for his father's soul.[69] Dukes of Normandy were not in this period invested with their office in a public or ecclesiastical ceremony; the king of France had already acknowledged that Robert was his father's heir, and was his recent ally; so that Robert's entry was domestic and informal. Most of the barons had previously done him homage, and he probably took it again whenever the opportunity occurred. Orderic Vitalis, in a famous passage,[70] recalls how in September 1087 Robert of Bellême on his way to court heard at Brionne that the Conqueror was dead, immediately turned his horse, and returning unexpectedly to his lands drove the ducal guards out of Alençon, Bellême and his other castles. Other magnates, such as William count of Evreux, William of Breteuil and Ralf of Conches, did likewise. There was a sudden collapse of ducal government assisted by Robert's prodigality and thoughtlessness. Everyone knew that he was a weaker man than his father. Conditions in England and Normandy were, of course, quite different. The kingdom had been systematically denuded of leaders, whether native or French, and the new settlers looked to a strong monarchy for their safety. In 1087 it was in the duchy that most of the greater Anglo-Norman barons were congregated, the men who had most suffered from the Conqueror's 'tyranny', for example the prohibition of private war and his insistence on his right to garrison private castles when danger threatened or when he chose; and Robert probably sympathized with them as they liberated themselves from the hated restraints.

Immediately after Robert's accession one of his charters was witnessed by his half-uncle, Robert count of Mortain, the brothers Robert count of Meulan and Henry of Beaumont, and a steward, Ivo Taillebois.[71] All these left shortly for England, and the only one who

---

[69] Florence, ii, 21; OV, iv, 110 ff.; Torigny, *Interpolation*, 268.

[70] OV, iv, 112 ff.

[71] Haskins, *NI*, 285. Robert's charters are calendared, 66–70, and the following statistics are based on this calendar and the printed versions.

returned and, despite a quarrel with the duke,[72] became one of his closest companions was Robert of Meulan. This count in the French Vexin, who was greatly valued as a counsellor, managed to keep the trust of both king and duke, and seems to have been the only magnate who could move freely between the two courts. It was in 1087–8 that the highest nobility chose their lord, and the number of those who witness the charters of both brothers is relatively small. Besides those already mentioned are the third brother, Henry, Odo of Bayeux, William bishop of Durham and Richard of Courcy. The most frequent witnesses to Robert's charters between 1088 and 1095, who clearly formed a close and constant group, were Robert of Meulan (8), William of Durham, during his exile 1089–92 (5), the constable Robert (I) of Montfort (-sur-Risle) (5), Odo of Bayeux (4), William count of Evreux (4), William of Breteuil (4), Ingilram fitzIlbert (4), William Bertram (3), Ralf of Mortemer (2) and two members of the Crispin family, hereditary *vicomtes* of the Norman Vexin, William (II) and Gilbert (2).[73] It is also of interest that five of the last twelve, Count Henry, William of Evreux, Ingilram, William Bertram and Richard of Courcy, were among those listed by the nuns of Holy Trinity, Caen, as their despoilers after the death of the Conqueror.[74]

The new duke took his uncle Odo of Bayeux as one of his counsellors,[75] and Henry chose to stay in Normandy.[76] William had become the odd man out. Henry's position is curious. He seems to have been brought up in England and had usually been closer to Rufus than to Robert; but after the death of their father self-interest alone seems to have directed his steps. His immediate and constant ambition was to acquire land. Although he had a true or invented claim on his mother's estates in England, he considered that he stood more chance of getting a fief from Robert; he may also have thought that he would have much more freedom of action in the duchy than in the kingdom. His interest lay in playing off one brother against the other and in avoiding becoming completely identified with either. He was to learn fairly soon and at heavy cost what a difficult game it was to play. At first, however, he did well. For £3,000 of his inheritance he bought from Robert (or took in

---

[72] For his movements in 1087–95, see below, 266 n. 12.

[73] William (II) was the brother of Gilbert Crispin, monk of Bec and abbot of Westminster; but it is not clear who this Gilbert was. For the family, see *Gilbert Crispin*, 14–15.

[74] List printed by Haskins, *NI*, 63–4.

[75] OV, iv, 114, followed by a judicious tribute to the bishop.

[76] Cf. *GR*, ii, 468: 'inclinatior porro Roberto pro mansuetudine'. Henry seems never to have borne Odo any ill will, and he took his son, John of Bayeux, into his service as a clerk: OV, iv, 116 and n.

pledge for the loan) the *pagi* and bishoprics of Coutances and Avranches, otherwise the Cotentin and Avranchin, and assumed the title of count. This transfer involved the mediatization of Hugh *vicomte* of Avranches and earl of Chester and his whole Norman fief, of the great Geoffrey of Mowbray, bishop of Coutances, Michael bishop of Avranches, and the abbey of Mont St Michel.[77] Earl Hugh does not seem to have been particularly pleased; Bishop Michael accepted the demotion; but Geoffrey of Coutances successfully resisted. According to a history of the church of Coutances, written just after Geoffrey's death in 1093, the proud prelate refused to be under any lord except the duke of Normandy, and, as a result, suffered damage from Henry and other local barons.[78] As for Henry, since he would have been Robert's vassal for this honour, while owing nothing to Rufus, he was for the moment firmly in the ducal camp.

Although Robert considered himself defrauded of England by his brother, there is nothing to suggest that he made of his own accord serious attempts to dispossess him. Robert of Torigny tells the story that when the new duke's vassals urged him to dislodge the usurper immediately by force of arms, he replied with his usual simplicity and almost foolishness, 'By God's angels, even if I were in Alexandria the English would wait for me and would not dare to make a king for themselves before my arrival. Nor would my brother William, for fear of his head, dare to do what you say he has done without my permission.' When, however, he was better informed about events in England, he felt not a little resentment.[79] In this matter, of course, he would have received no encouragement from his old ally, Philip of France, who would have been happy with the dismemberment of the rival kingdom.

The real leader of the rebellion against the king was their half-uncle Odo of Bayeux. He did not necessarily join William at Christmas 1087 with the sole and precise purpose of dethroning him. His first object was to recover his own lands and castles in the kingdom; and although these would serve as a beach-head for a Norman invasion, he needed time to evaluate his reception, sort the political situation out, estimate the king's strength and make soundings among his connections. He would not, however, have gone to England without Robert's consent and acceptance of his schemes, for he would not have jeopardized his bishopric for the mere chance of an earldom; and he must have believed that he could

[77] Contemporary Coutances chronicle: *Gallia Christiana*, xi, instr. col. 221; HH, 211; OV, iv, 118–20; Torigny, *Interpolation*, 269. Le Patourel, *Norman Empire*, 342–4. Fliche, *Philippe I*, 290, thinks the inclusion of Mont St Michel a mistake.

[78] *Loc. cit.*, cols 221–4. Haskins, *NI*, 76, observes that Michael never, and Geoffrey rarely, witnessed a charter of Duke Robert.

[79] Torigny, *Interpolation*, 268. 'Per dei angelos' could be a pun.

draw the duke into any war he might start by the enticement of the crown.[80] Even if there was a true reconciliation at Christmas, this itself created problems. The newcomer resented the favour which the king was showing to William of St Calais,[81] who had once been his protégé, and disliked Lanfranc, who had been the architect of his downfall. He must soon have decided that there would be no great future for him and his friends under William and that the king must be overthrown. He had been accompanied to England, or joined soon after, by his main supporters, his brother Robert of Mortain, Roger of Montgomery, earl of Shrewsbury and Geoffrey bishop of Coutances. The plan they hatched was to make Kent the main base, to appeal to old loyalties, to incite the garrisons of important castles, such as the Tower of London, to declare for Robert, to fortify ports in Kent and Sussex through which reinforcements from Normandy could be channelled, and to organize as many scattered diversions as possible. It seems that Odo took fealty, perhaps on behalf of Robert, from those who joined the conspiracy;[82] and he must have assumed that Robert would intervene with the ducal forces at the right moment.[83]

William of Malmesbury was of the opinion that the bishop, when canvassing Robert's cause, drew attention to his milder nature and greater maturity, whereas William, who had been indulgently brought up – spoilt – showed by his ferocious countenance the ferocity of his character. He would act entirely against right and justice, and soon they would all be deprived of the honours they had so laboriously acquired. Nothing would have been gained by the Conqueror's death if those whom he had fettered William Rufus slaughtered.[84] Orderic put it a little differently. He too thought that the conspirators were protesting against the loss of their wealth and power under the crippling rule of the old king, but also against the added burden – indeed, impossibility – of having now to serve two masters. Only by rejoining the parts could the inconvenience be remedied, and the only possible ruler of the united dominions was Robert, the eldest son and rightful heir.[85] These interpretations are not without merit; the Conqueror's harsh rule had provoked a baronial liberation movement which saw more hope of success under Robert than William. It could have been argued that the

---

[80] According to the chronicle written at Hyde abbey, Winchester, after 1120, but apparently before 1135, Robert sent his two uncles to England in order to dethrone his brother: *Chron. mon. de Hida*, 298.

[81] *GR*, ii, 361. See also above, 61 n. 35.

[82] *De Injusta Vexatione*, 174, 189.

[83] Cf. OV, iv, 124.

[84] *GR*, ii, 360.

[85] OV, iv, 120–4.

division of the kingdom and the rivalry between the brothers would have been advantageous to the barons; but there can be little doubt that it was the difficulties they caused which were uppermost in men's minds. And behind the general malaise were the individual ambitions and grievances of the several participants, although some were drawn into the conspiracy simply by family ties or feudal allegiance.

The Anglo-Saxon Chronicler emphasizes that the rebels were French and that the natives remained loyal.[86] It is the first time since 1066 that he had struck a patriotic note. Against the men of the duke of Normandy stood the English under their English king and won great victories. This attitude also appealed to the twelfth-century chroniclers, William of Malmesbury, Florence and Orderic. But they were stressing the obvious. More notable was the loyalty to the crowned king shown by most of the French settlers in England. Only a very small number of Norman and Anglo-Norman barons, together with some of their vassals and friends, were actively involved in the succession dispute; and William, as king, was able to bring most of his royal resources against them. Robert, on the other hand, never committed his ducal, or indeed any other, army. The main key to the king's security may have been the general loyalty of the sheriffs. These officials not only had custody of the county town and castle and controlled the military forces of their bailiwick, but also were due to pay an instalment of the royal revenues into the treasury at Easter. Their wholesale defection would have made it very difficult for the king. In fact only Roger Bigot in East Anglia, Hugh of Grandmesnil in Leicestershire, and perhaps Geoffrey de Mandeville in London and Middlesex seem to have wavered. In most of the vulnerable areas, Yorkshire (Ralf Pagnell),[87] Gloucestershire (Durand), and Worcestershire (Urse of Abetot), the sheriffs remained loyal. The ministerial nobility had ranged themselves with the bishops behind the new king. Their interest lay in continuity, and by backing the winner and holding on to their offices, and sometimes transmitting them to their heirs, they began to create true English dynasties.

The crucial zones proved to be Kent and Sussex, the south-eastern arc which the Conqueror had divided into castleries entrusted to his closest kinsmen and vassals. The restoration of Odo to his earldom after five years of abeyance was disturbing to a county which was settling down after the great spoliation of church lands by Earl Godwin and his family, particularly in the 1030s and 1040s, and the Norman colonization, which together led to much litigation.[88] Although he was not the robber

[86] *ASC*, 166.
[87] *De Injusta Vexatione*, 172–3, 179. But either just before or, less likely, just after these events he witnesses a charter of Duke Robert: *Regesta*, no. 299.
[88] D.R. Bates, 'The land pleas of William I's reign: Penenden Heath revisited', *Bull. of*

earl of Canterbury tradition,[89] his reinstatement raised problems for several important barons who had some of their lands in Kent and held parcels of both the earl and the churches. A good example is Richard of Tonbridge, the son of Gilbert count of Brionne and the ancestor of the Clares, who had been present at the trial on Penenden Heath and was a vassal of all three powers as well as of the king. In 1088 he retired to a monastery and was succeeded in his English honours of Tonbridge and Clare by his son, Gilbert fitzRichard.[90] Other men, both great and small, were affected by Odo's return, for example, the sheriff of Kent, Haimo, and his son Robert, who seems already to have become a close friend of the king. Although Haimo's actions in 1088 are not noticed by the chroniclers, he clearly had not joined Robert's party, and the loyalty of the two Kentish bishops and the sheriff was probably decisive in that theatre.[91]

In Sussex, which was divided into five longitudinal strips called rapes, and each a castlery,[92] the two central units, Lewes and the Adur Valley (later Bramber), held respectively by the royalists, William of Warenne and William of Briouze, separated the eastern pair, Hastings (William of Eu, son of the count of Eu) and Pevensey (Robert of Mortain), from the most western member, Arundel, belonging to Earl Roger of Montgomery. The position was nicely balanced, and the king encouraged William of Warenne in his loyalty by creating him earl of Surrey.[93]

In the Welsh marches, to oppose the power of the Montgomery family and its satellites, including Welsh allies, William had to rely on the sheriffs and bishops and lesser barons. The abeyance of the earldom of Hereford may or may not have been a help. In the Scottish marches the situation was rather different. The king of Scots, despite his close ties with Robert and the apparent weakness of the English frontier defences, unsettled by much recent reorganization, did not invade. It would seem that after the Danish invasion scare of 1085 the Conqueror had made

---

the *Inst. of Hist. Research*, li, no 123 (1978), especially pp. 17–18. He gives references to the others who have considered these problems.

[89] Bates is better disposed towards Odo than is usually the case: see also his, 'The character and career of Odo, bishop of Bayeux', *Speculum*, l (1975), 8 ff., 16.

[90] Torigny, *Interpolation*, 326; *Domesday Monachorum*, 39–41; GEC, iii, 242–3; R. Mortimer, 'The beginnings of the honour of Clare', *Battle III*, 119. Gilbert fitzRichard was also a vassal of Bishop Gundulf of Rochester: *Textus Roffensis*, ed. T. Hearne 1720), 149; Barlow, *EC 1066–1154*, 174. Richard and his brother Baldwin of Meules were seen on 1 January 1091 by the priest of St Aubin-de-Bonneval condemned for their sins riding with 'Hellequin's Hunt', one of Purgatory's squadrons: OV, iv, 242.

[91] For Haimo and Robert see GEC, v, 683; Douglas, *Domesday Monachorum*, 55 6.

[92] J.H. Round, *VCH Sussex*, i, 354; J.F.A. Mason, 'The Rapes of Sussex and the Norman Conquest', *Sussex Arch. Coll.*, cii (1964), 68–93.

[93] OV, iv, 180. GEC, xii (1), 493–5.

drastic changes in the north, removing Roger of Poitou from Lancashire and in Northumberland replacing Aubrey of Coucy by Robert of Mowbray.[94] In 1088, however, the last, who had probably not secured the new king's recognition of his office, was with his uncle Geoffrey of Coutances at Bristol; and the bishop of Durham was also in the south. Defence against the Scots had fallen to the marcher barons and the sheriff of Yorkshire. These would have had no truck with the Scots; and the Norman rebels may have shrunk from inciting the Scots to invade: certainly the bishop of Durham, friend though he was of Malcolm,[95] would not have stooped to treason of that sort; and in the event the military commands south of the Cheviots were not tested, except by the bishop's own ravaging of his enemies' lands.[96]

The rebellion took place in the spring and summer of 1088; but the detailed chronology and exact sequence of some of the events is uncertain.[97] The Anglo-Saxon Chronicle and its derivatives state that the conspiracy was hatched in Lent (after 1 March), the rebels started ravaging at Easter (16 April), and the king then raised an army and campaigned against them. This report may, however, compress the preliminary stages. According to a miracle story of Fécamp abbey,[98] Robert immediately decided to dislodge his brother, looked round for allies, and recruited 'those guardians of the sea called pirates', requiring them to capture ships sailing from England and turn them over to him, probably to furnish him with an invasion fleet. The pirate ship which comes into the story, although later found to be manned by Flemish sailors and merely in passage, was first thought to be English, for an English-speaking monk was chosen to parley with the crew. By the summer the king too had 'pirates' under his command, and the phrase 'guardians of the sea' strongly suggests the duty squadrons of what later were known as the Cinque Ports.[99] These towns made much of their

---

[94] V.H. Galbraith, *The Making of Domesday Book* (1961), 187–8, and below, 161.

[95] *De Injusta Vexatione*, 195: below, 309.

[96] For the military commands, see W.E. Kapelle, *The Norman Conquest of the North*, 125 ff. For the bishop's ravaging, see *ASC E*, *s.a.*, 167.

[97] *ASC*, 166; *GR*, ii, 360; Florence, ii, 22. OV, iv, 125, 'after Christmas'. The accounts in these chronicles, and also in Simeon, *HR* and HH, are interconnected and go back ultimately to *ASC* or a related set of annals. Cf. the diagram in Barlow, *EC 1066–1154*, 318. Each writer interpolates and modifies his source, and the exact relationship cannot always be elucidated. The position of OV is the most uncertain. Since he wrote Book VII between 1130 and 1133, he could have read any of the others, and in view of the concordances it seems most unlikely that he relied exclusively on oral sources and his own memory.

[98] L'abbé Sauvage, 'Des Miracles advenus en l'église de Fécamp', *Soc. de l'Hist. de Normandie*, mélanges 2 (Rouen 1893), no. 21, pp. 29 ff.

[99] Below, 80. Although these *piratae* were not pirates in the modern sense, the word

1a. Writ of William Rufus, addressed to Ranulf (Flambard) bishop of Durham, Haimo *dapifer* and Urse of Abetot, in favour of Fécamp Abbey, and witnessed at Lillebonne by the count of Meulan. To be dated July–September 1099. (See *Facsimiles of Royal Writs*, pl. XII, and here, 187, 407.)

1b. William Rufus's seal, obverse and reverse, in white (natural) wax, without any varnish. To be dated August 1091–May 1092. Eton College Library. (See *Facsimiles of Royal Writs*, pl. XXX, and here, 59.)

a. Type 1,
Profile
(North, 851).
Minted at Wallingford.

b. Type 2,
Cross in quatrefoil
(North, 852).
Minted at Colchester.

c. Type 3,
Cross voided
(North, 853).
Minted at Canterbury.

d. Type 4,
Cross patée and fleury
(North, 855).
Minted at Sandwich.

e. Type 5,
Cross fleury and piles
(North, 856).
Minted at Shrewsbury.

2. William Rufus's coinage: the five types of silver penny, obverse and reverse. (See
J.J. North, *English Hammered Coinage* (1963), and here, 60.)

living out of cross-Channel traffic and might well have been inclined towards Robert's side. The Fécamp anecdote is good evidence that the duke recruited shipping from England and also provides us with a rough date. The story goes that the abbey's ship, which regularly sailed from England at this time with a cargo of meat, presumably salted carcasses from the abbey's Sussex estates, after a prosperous voyage anchored in the Seine (probably at Harfleur), and was left in charge of a watchman while the brethren and sailors went to a neighbouring town (possibly Montivilliers) to get a meal and the comfort of a fire, for it was winter.[100] In their absence the ship was seized by the pirates and was eventually recovered with the help of a miracle. Winter no doubt lasted until March; but it would have been more usual to procure salted meat between Martinmas (11 November) and Christmas.

Further evidence for an early outbreak of hostilities comes from the *libellus* drawn up to justify the conduct of the bishop of Durham during 1088. From this we learn that rebellions at Dover, Hastings and London had already collapsed before the bishop was charged with treason and disseised of his lands on 12 March.[101] According to the bishop's case it was he who informed the king of the plot, and if he knew the details because he had been approached and drawn some way into it, his subsequent behaviour is understandable. He had started his career in Odo's chapter at Bayeux and was to attach himself to Robert after his disgrace in England. At his trial after the end of the hostilities, the charge made against him was that when the king heard that his vassals, the bishop of Bayeux and Earl Roger of Montgomery and many more, had rebelled and sought to take the crown from him, and, on Bishop William's advice, was riding against them, he ordered the bishop to accompany him. But the bishop, after agreeing that he would go with the seven household knights he had as escort and send to his castle for more, suddenly, and without permission, fled from court with some of his men, and so failed the king in his time of need. Henry of Beaumont, soon to be created earl of Warwick, who laid the charge, affirmed that he had been present when the king had given the order.[102]

In the course of the trial the bishop never denied the fact of the

---

probably denotes sailors trained to fight. For the Channel fleets, see Barlow, *Edward the Confessor*, 172–3; for Fécamp and Sussex, *ibid.*, 39, 205. In 1087–8, just as in 1066, there seems to have been more shipping in the English than the Norman ports.

[100] For the port of Harfleur, which predated Le Havre, and its owner, the nunnery of Montivilliers, see E. Hall and J.R. Sweeney, 'The "licentia de nam" of the abbess of Montivilliers and the origins of the port of Harfleur', *Bulletin of the Institute of Historical Research*, lii (1979), 1.

[101] *De Injusta Vexatione*, 171: the preface to the *libellus*.

[102] *Ibid.*, 181.

desertion, only its significance, and he never explained or excused it. What he constantly denied was that he had been guilty of a crime or of perjury, which in this context probably means renunciation of his fealty to the king and taking an oath to his adversaries, that is to say, treason. His statement of exculpation after he had been found guilty, which takes the form of how he would have pleaded if he had been allowed a 'just', canonical trial, throws some light on the earliest stage of the war.[103] He had never done wittingly, nor attempted to do, any harm in any way to the king as regards his body, land or honour; and in connexion with the rebellion he had not done fealty to, or received it from anyone. He also explained what he had done to help the king. He had told him about the plans of his enemies at the first opportunity after he had learned of them, kept him posted with news until the moment he left the court, and helped him faithfully against all his foes. He would prove that nothing he had done was unlawful. And he would also show that he had kept the loyalty of Dover and Hastings which the king had almost lost, and of London, which had already rebelled. He had himself taken twelve of the leading citizens of that town to the king so that he could use them to give more courage to the rest.

The information about Dover, Hastings and London, even if exaggerated, is unlikely to be invented. Dover was part of Odo's earldom;[104] the castlery of Hastings was held by William of Eu, one of the conspirators;[105] and the Tower of London was probably under the control of Geoffrey (I) de Mandeville, who was based on Essex and whose grandson of the same name played some part in a later war of succession.[106] From this story it would appear that the king, apprised of the plot, reconnoitred the situation in south-east England with only household troops and the escorts of his entourage, and made preventive strikes against the garrisons in some key places before they could take over the towns. If Bishop William's desertion, by alerting the

---

[103] *Ibid.*, 188–9, cf. 174.

[104] *DB*, i, 1a.

[105] *FWR*, i, 33, knew that William of Eu was the son of Robert count of Eu and Lescelina; but since then there has been much argument on whether William of Eu and William count of Eu were separate persons. Cf. Douglas, *Domesday Monachorum*, 64 ff., who would separate, and Chibnall, *OV*, iv, 284 n., who would amalgamate. The latter position seems much the better. In *DB* the count of Eu (i.e. Robert) holds lands in some shires, while in others lands are held by William of Eu, listed among the barons. This is presumably the son, and as both never hold in the same shire, it would seem that the original honour had been divided between father and son. William succeeded to his father's county and title about 1090: see below, 324. Gaimar, l. 6140 (*s.a.* 1095) calls William *Neel*, i.e. *nigellus*, the Black. For the castlery of Hastings, see *DB*, i, 18b; Stenton, *English Feudalism*, 193, and above, 73 n. 92.

[106] Stenton, *English Feudalism*, 222–3.

conspirators, prevented the king from catching the major figures by surprise, the royal fury at his behaviour is as understandable as the bishop's injured innocence.

The next four or five weeks were spent by both sides in organizing their forces. The rebels were not yet ready to come out into the open and the king was in no position to launch a major campaign, especially as he had little to go on except rumours and suspicions. Easter was clearly a critical point, and it is likely that the conspirators failed to attend the king's solemn court.[107] They had fortified and provisioned their castles and sent to Robert for aid. The duke had dispatched Eustace III, count of Boulogne, and three sons of Earl Roger of Montgomery – Robert of Bellême, and two of the younger sons, Hugh of Montgomery, Roger of Poitou – and Arnulf, with a force of knights, including Flemings, as an advance party.[108] Although the king may have put some of his men on the alert earlier, it was probably at Easter that it was decided to mobilize an army and set up headquarters at London. His major supporters are named as Archbishop Lanfranc, Hugh of Avranches, earl of Chester (perhaps annoyed at having been sold to Count Henry),[109] William of Warenne and Robert fitzHaimo.[110] Another influential adherent was Henry of Beaumont, the younger son of Roger, lord of Pont-Audemer and Beaumont-le-Roger in Normandy, and Adeline, sister of the count of Meulan in the French Vexin.[111]

It would not be unreasonable to allow at least a fortnight for assembling a royal expeditionary force in the fields outside London. The English chronicles have the king sending for 'the Englishmen', and later for 'the French and the English';[112] and it was remembered at Ely that

[107] Florence, ii, 22.

[108] ASC, 167; GR, ii, 362; Florence, ii, 22; Simeon, HR, 216; OV, iv, 132. All but OV call Eustace 'the Young', and it is more likely that Eustace III, rather than the one who fought at Hastings, was engaged in this adventure. Florence mentions only Robert of Bellême of the sons of the earl. For these brothers, see Mason, 'Roger de Montgomery and his sons', 13 ff., who points out that the two brothers with Robert were not necessarily Hugh and Roger. Arnulf certainly had a good reputation as a soldier: OV, iv, 302.

[109] It may be that Robert of Rhuddlan was with Hugh rather than the Grandmesnils: see below, 81 n. 140.

[110] OV, iv, 128. Robert fitzHaimo and his brother Haimo were the sons of Haimo, sheriff of Kent, and grandsons of Haimo dentatus. It was Robert's heiress who passed on her father's and uncle's lands to Robert earl of Gloucester, Henry I's bastard: Douglas, Domesday Monachorum, 55–6.

[111] If we correct the Hugh of the printed text to Henry, he was present when the king ordered the bishop of Durham to ride with him against his enemies: De Injusta Vexatione, 181. For the family, see OV, iv, 302–4; GEC, vii, 521–6, xii (2), 357–60, and genealogical table, and below, 266.

[112] ASC, 166; GR, ii, 361; Florence, ii, 22–3; OV, iv, 124–6.

he required the abbey to provide him with the full quota of eighty knights which his father had imposed on the monastery for the defence of the Isle.[113] Clearly the king mobilized all the forces he could, relying on military obligations of all kinds. He also, probably on Lanfranc's advice, made promises to the assembled troops of good government which amplified his engagements at the coronation and set a precedent for general charters of liberties. He undertook to restore to the people the best laws they had ever had, to abolish unjust taxes, and to give back to the people their forests and hunting rights.[114] The results cannot have fallen much below his expectations, and he managed to detach Roger of Montgomery from the rebels (possibly by making extravagant, but insincere, promises), and keep him in his company.[115] His removal of the earl from Arundel, a Sussex port which also dominated Chichester harbour, was a great political success.

Odo had established his headquarters at Rochester, where the Roman Watling Street crosses the Medway by a bridge on its route from Dover by way of Canterbury to London. The episcopal see was a walled city, which was further protected by a post-Conquest motte-and-bailey castle, probably on Boley Hill, outside the South Gate, and thus controlling the entry to the town and bridge.[116] It is clear from what happened later that Odo was in possession of both the fortified city and the castle; but he must have treated the cathedral church, which was in the south-west sector, the key military area, and was damaged during the hostilities, with respect, for during the king's siege of the city Gundulf was allowed free passage by both sides.[117]

Odo chose Rochester as his headquarters, we are told, because of its central position from which both London and Canterbury could be attacked, and because it could be reinforced from the Continent by water by way of the Thames and Medway. It was there that he placed the reinforcements he received from Robert, and by the summer the garrison was supposed to be 500 knights.[118] Some twenty miles south, Gilbert fitzRichard had put Tonbridge castle on a war footing, and still further to the south, on the Sussex coast, Robert of Mortain held Pevensey. A number of subsidiary revolts also broke out. The most destructive, but of least strategic importance, were those in the Welsh marches. More potentially dangerous, but seemingly more half-hearted,

[113] *Liber Eliensis*, 218.
[114] *ASC*, 167; *GR*, ii, 361; Florence, ii, 23; Simeon, *HR*, 215.
[115] *GR*, ii, 361–2. All the chroniclers make him the chief conspirator after Odo.
[116] R.A. Brown, H.M. Colvin, A.J. Taylor, *The History of the King's Works*, ii (1963), 806–7; R.A. Brown, *Rochester Castle* (HMSO, 1969), 5–7.
[117] *Vita Gundulfi* in *Anglia Sacra*, ii, 284.
[118] OV, iv, 126.

was the suspicious behaviour of the Grandmesnils in the East Midlands and of Roger Bigot in East Anglia; and the record may be incomplete.[119]

In April Odo started raiding, treating the archiepiscopal estates with especial severity, and took the booty back to Rochester.[120] The main weakness in his local position was that the peninsula to the east of Rochester, Tonbridge and Pevensey could not be held by such a weak screen when there was no general support for the rebels. The king, who lacked neither prudence nor good fortune,[121] correctly recognized Odo as his main adversary and left all the side-shows to local commanders. He was probably ready to move by the end of April, and with his army of cavalry and foot[122] marched into Kent. His simple plan, to seek out and destroy the main enemy, must have heartened his junior officers, and his determined conduct of the campaign would have confirmed their trust. But no commander would have considered attacking Rochester by forcing a crossing of the tidal River Medway under the shadow of the walls: it had to be reached by looping south by way of the fords between Cuxton and Aylesford. The king therefore chose to protect his rear by first knocking out Tonbridge, where Gilbert fitzRichard and his brother Roger[123] were in command. The town was stormed, Gilbert wounded, and on the second day the castle surrendered.[124] At one stroke the impetuous general had cut the communications between north and south and proved his metal. He then turned against Rochester, but when he heard that Odo, persuaded perhaps by the news that Robert was sending reinforcements to Pevensey, had joined his brother there, he marched south and invested the fortified port by land and sea. The siege lasted for six weeks, and the king, who had the archbishop with him, refused to be distracted by raids from Rochester.[125] In the land operations William of Warenne was seriously wounded in the leg by an arrow and was taken to the Cluniac priory he had founded at Lewes,

[119] *Chron. Abingdon*, ii, 17, records that while the king was besieging Rochester the men of Seacourt, near Oxford, broke the abbey's watercourse at Botley. This may be an example of lawlessness encouraged by the civil war.

[120] *ASC*, 166; *GR*, ii, 360–1, Florence, ii, 22. The last, p. 23, seems to put the raids from Rochester on Canterbury and London during the siege of Pevensey: see below, n. 125. Doubtless the garrison made several sorties.

[121] *GR*, ii, 361.

[122] Mostly English and a smallish (*mediocris*) force: Florence, ii, 23; 30,000 men: OV, iv, 126.

[123] Roger, probably the elder son, had inherited his father's Norman estates of Orbec and Bienfaite: Torigny, *Interpolation*, 326. According to OV, iii, 100, he had been one of Duke Robert's companions during his rebellion against the Conqueror. Cf. also OV, v, 208.

[124] *ASC*, 167; *GR*, ii, 362; Florence, ii, 23. Captured in Easter week: OV, v, 208.

[125] See above, n. 120.

where he died on 24 June.[126] At sea the relieving force sent by Robert was intercepted by the king's 'pirates',[127] presumably a blockading fleet from the Cinque Ports, and destroyed with great loss to the enemy.[128] Finally, lack of food caused the garrison to ask for a truce and, when no succour came, to surrender, probably in the second week of June.[129] Robert of Mortain submitted and may have been pardoned.[130] Odo was captured and offered his freedom on two conditions: that he would secure the surrender of Rochester, and that he would leave England, never to return uninvited.

The royal army then returned with its prisoners to Rochester.[131] But when William sent Odo ahead with a small and unarmed escort to negotiate the surrender, the garrison burst out, captured the whole party and continued the war. There was no certainty at the time whether Odo connived or condoned; but William had been tricked.[132] He had also lost some of his gains; but not all: Sussex and most of Kent had been cleared and all his main adversaries were now cooped up together at a convenient place. With Odo, Eustace, the three Montgomery brothers and, according to the Anglo-Saxon Chronicle probably written at nearby Canterbury, 'all the highest-born men in England and Normandy', together with their troops, in the town and castle, there were too many for comfort. Rochester was even more difficult to relieve by sea than Pevensey; spring was turning to summer; and in hot weather the advantages lay with the besiegers, especially against an overcrowded fortress.

William was a relentless, if chivalrous, commander. He called up more troops to relieve those presently serving,[133] under threat of being dishonoured as *nithing* if they failed his summons.[134] For a siege he needed labourers of various kinds, and it is likely that he had summoned, besides French and English soldiers, all those who under Anglo-Saxon law owed 'works' to the king.[135] With their aid he built two counter-

[126] *Chron. mon. de Hida*, 299; OV, iv, 128.

[127] Simeon, *HR*, ii, 216. For Robert's fleet, see above, 74–5. William was much concerned with possible naval desertions to Robert: cf. *De Injusta Vexatione*, 190.

[128] *ASC*, 167; vivid reconstruction in *GR*, ii, 362–3.

[129] Counting six weeks from the beginning of May. OV, iv, 126, who omits here the earlier stages of the war, puts the siege of Rochester in May.

[130] OV, v, 208, for Robert of Mortain's unwilling defiance, by Odo's persuasion, easy surrender, and restoration to royal favour. Pardons granted during a campaign were, however, insecure.

[131] *ASC*, 167; *GR*, ii, 362; OV, iv, 126 ff. Not in Florence.

[132] As he recalled bitterly at William of St Calais's trial: *De Injusta Vexatione*, 191.

[133] *ASC*, 167–8; *GR*, ii, 362.

[134] Cf. *ASC C, s.a.* 1049, 114.

[135] For these, see F. Barlow, *Edward the Confessor*, 150–1, 169 n. 4; and for the king's later use of them, see below, 372.

castles,[136] and blockaded the town rigorously. Orderic paints a vivid picture of the increasing distress of the garrison, the deaths of men and horses from disease, and the terrible plague of flies.[137] The swarms were so thick that men had to take it in turns to eat while their comrades brushed the flies away. Negotiations for the surrender began. At first the rebels asked for their lands as well as their lives and permission to serve the king. This was refused. Roger of Montgomery and other barons with the king interceded for the leaders, and Orderic describes a great debate in which William and the barons contended with Biblical texts. In the end the king allowed the rebels a semi-honourable surrender.[138] They were to have their lives, but not their lands, and they could come out with their horses and arms. But William also had his victory sounded on the shrill trumpets as the crestfallen leaders emerged, and the English jeered and called for the hangman's noose as they passed. It is likely that Rochester surrendered in July. Robert had left his intervention too late. On 8 July he granted a charter to the abbey of Fécamp on the Norman coast and added to the dating clause, 'on the day when I should have crossed to England'.[139] Perhaps Rochester had not held out as long as he had expected. But it was his failure to send effective help to Pevensey and then Rochester which allowed the garrisons to surrender without breach of duty.

Meanwhile the other insurrections had either collapsed or been contained. There is little information about what the Grandmesnils, Hugh the sheriff and his nephew, that great soldier Robert of Rhuddlan, had been doing in Leicestershire and Northampton,[140] and not much more about the activities of Roger Bigot, who had strong Bayeux ties, in East Anglia.[141] According to a Bury St Edmunds miracle story there was indeed a baronial insurrection in Norfolk, and Robert of Curcun,

[136] OV, iv, 126; v, 210.

[137] OV, iv, 128 ff.

[138] OV, who rehearses the terms (iv, 132; v, 210), calls it a dishonourable surrender, 'cum dedecore'.

[139] David, RC, 51 n. 52, 'quando in Angliam transire debui', which is not quite 'about to cross to England', as Chibnall, OV, iv, 134 n.

[140] For a family tree of the Grandmesnils, see Chibnall, OV, ii, 370. For Robert, see also F. Barlow, *Edward the Confessor*, 191. Although OV, iv, 124, names Robert as one of Odo's supporters, it would seem more likely that he was with his cousin and liege-lord, Hugh of Chester, in the royal camp. A few pages later, 136, the chronicler refers to Robert as 'de obsidione Rofensi rediens', words which suggest more a besieger than a besieged.

[141] ASC, 167; GR, ii, 361; Simeon, HR, 215; OV, iv, 125, but not Florence, name Roger as a rebel. Apparently he 'took' Norwich castle. His family were vassals of the church of Bayeux and it is most likely that he was approached. But how far he went in it is difficult to say. His holding the castle may have been connected with his service as sheriff, and he was certainly restored to what looks like full favour by the autumn.

who held of Roger Bigot the manors of Bridge, Brampton and Uggleshall in north-west Suffolk, tried to seize with his lord's connivance the abbey's neighbouring manor of Southwold for the grazing of his horses. The saint, however, frustrated the evil designs of him and his men.[142]

The rebellions in the West are better recorded. From Bristol, Bishop Geoffrey of Coutances, Odo's old colleague, and his nephew, Robert of Mowbray, raided east and burnt Bath and Berkeley and ravaged around, but failed to take Ilchester in Wiltshire, [143] while William of Eu, lord of Hastings, rode north into Gloucestershire against the royal manor of Berkeley.[144] From the Montgomery lands in the Welsh marches, a major invasion was launched.[145] Three Herefordshire barons, Osbern fitzRichard, son of Richard fitzScrob, lord of Richard's castle and a well-known character in those parts,[146] Roger of Lassy (Lacy), lord of Weobley, who had inherited his honour only three years before, and Ralf of Mortemer, lord of Wigmore,[147] together with Osbern's son-in-law Bernard of Neufmarché, the future conqueror of Brecknock, raised an army of Normans, English and Welsh from Herefordshire, Shropshire and the hinterland, and took Hereford, burnt Gloucester[148] and ravaged Worcestershire. When news came that they were approaching the city, the venerable English bishop Wulfstan took over command of the royal castle while a field army made up of the garrison, the bishop's household troops and bands of citizens crossed the bridge over the Severn, which earlier they had broken, and advanced westwards to meet them. So great a faith had they in their bishop that by a miracle they caught the enemy unawares while destroying the episcopal estates and drove them off, killing 500 of the infantry and capturing some of the knights.

In the north, the bishop of Durham probably remained on the defensive while Ralf Pagnell, the sheriff of Yorkshire, confiscated his

---

[142] 'Heremanni archidiaconi miracula S. Eadmundi', *Ungedruckte Anglo-Normannorum Geschichtsquellen*, ed. F. Liebermann (Strasbourg 1879), 268–9. *DB*, ii, 331b, 371b.

[143] *ASC*, 166; *GR*, ii, 360–1, Florence, ii, 21, 24.

[144] Florence, ii, 24. By 1086 William had succeeded Ralf de Limesy as a vassal of the earl of Hereford: J.H. Round, 'The family of Ballon', *Studies in Peerage and Family History*, 186–7. At Berkeley, Earl William (fitzOsbern) of Hereford had built 'a little castle', *DB*, i, 163b.

[145] *ASC*, 166–7; *GR*, ii, 361; longer accounts in Florence, ii, 24 and Simeon, *HR*, 215; *OV*, iv, 124; *Regesta*, no. 300. *GR* makes Roger of Montgomery the ultimate commander.

[146] For Osbern and Richard, and their relations with the church of Worcester, see Barlow, *EC 1000–1066*, 174–5, *Edward the Confessor*, 94, 125.

[147] Ralf, son of Roger Mortemer, together with the duke and Count Henry, witnessed a Norman charter dated 30 March 1088, probably at Jumièges: Haskins, *NI*, 291.

[148] See also *Hist. mon. Gloucest.*, i, 80.

outlying estates and harried his vassals and tenants.[149] William of St Calais's first action after reaching safety in March was to protest rather insolently to the king, in a letter written in impeccable chancery style, about the wrongs inflicted on him:

> To William king of the English, his lord, William bishop of Durham sends greetings and loyal service.
>
> Know lord that your men of York and Lincoln have arrested my men, seized my lands, and even tried to capture me; and they say that it is on your orders that they have done all these things. I therefore require you, as my lord, to ensure that my men and lands with their chattels are returned to me, your loyal man, whom you have not (formally) charged with any crime and who has never refused to do you justice. If indeed you do charge me later with some crime, I shall be ready to do you justice in your court at a suitable time on receipt of a safe conduct. And I earnestly beseech you to stop treating me so basely and dishonourably and depriving me unjustly of my lands on the advice of my enemies. Not all men, however, have the right to judge bishops, and I offer to you justice (only) in accordance with the laws of my Order. And if in the meantime you would like to have the service of me and my men, I offer it you at your pleasure.

The king's answer to this was to divide the bishop's lands in Yorkshire, mainly Howden and Welton, between Count Odo of Champagne, lord of Holderness, the third husband of his Aunt Adelaide, and Count Alan Rufus, the Breton lord of Richmond. He also agreed that the bishop could visit him under a safe-conduct. But the bishop began to impose so many conditions before he would stand trial — prior restoration of his confiscated lands, damages for his losses, a trial according to canon law, a safe-conduct to and from the court – that negotiations, conducted on the king's side by Guy, the new abbot of St Augustine's and a confidant of Lanfranc's, dragged on for months,[150] while the sheriff of York tried to bring pressure to bear on the rebel. When the bishop finally arrived at the royal court, possibly in July, he was sent away almost immediately because the king refused him permission to purge himself of the charges brought against him by affirming his innocence on his own unsupported oath, and there was total disagreement on how a formal trial should be conducted. The accused demanded trial as a bishop according to the law of the church; the king, supported by his two archbishops, insisted

---

[149] *De Injusta Vexatione*, 171 ff., 179–80. At his trial he claimed that he had stood by with 100 knights while three royal serjeants robbed him of his lands and chattels, p. 186. For this *libellus*, see Barlow, *EC 1066–1154*, 281 ff.

[150] An exact timetable between 12 March and 8 September cannot be constructed from *De Injusta Vexatione*. It would seem likely, however, for several reasons that the bishop came to the royal court after the fall of Rochester in July.

that he be tried as a vassal according to secular law and also that he renounce his safe-conduct.

When the bishop, after his return to Durham, offered only minor concessions while elaborating his basic demands, the king imprisoned the monk who had brought the letter and sent an army against the rebel.[151] This force the Anglo-Saxon Chronicle calls a *here*, which once had meant a Viking army. In command was Roger of Poitou, the third son of Earl Roger of Shrewsbury,[152] supported by Alan Rufus and Odo of Champagne. Although they seem to have entered the city they were unable to take the castle,[153] and on 8 September on behalf of the king made with the bishop an elaborate covenant which guaranteed him a safe return from the royal court if the king refused him a trial 'according to the law appropriate to a bishop by such judges as ought legally to try a bishop'. Why the king should agree in September to terms which he had indignantly refused in the summer is not clear; but it would seem that his clerical advisers were staking everything on the outcome of the first stage of the trial – the proof judgment – by which the court would announce how and where the case should be heard, who would furnish the proof, and the nature of this. They confidently expected that the court would declare that what the king was offering was 'full justice', a just and lawful trial, and hoped that the accused would bow to necessity. It was agreed in the treaty that the case should be heard before Michaelmas, but, although the bishop left his see on 11 September,[154] the trial was postponed until 2 November at Salisbury.

The king allowed the bishop's treason to go so long unpunished because he was busy settling affairs in the south. With the fall of Rochester the situation had been clarified rather more quickly than most men could have expected. By July almost all involved must have realized that William would remain king of England, and although some may have foreseen that this might undermine Robert's position in Normandy, few could have expected that it would cave in as quickly as it did. A new feature which had to be taken into consideration was that henceforth the king would ordinarily reside in England, a change which

[151] *De Injusta Vexatione*, 176 ff., 180. The entry in *ASC*, 168, abbreviated even further in *GR*, ii, 362, is, 'Then the king sent an army [*here*] to Durham and had siege laid to the castle; and the bishop made a truce and rendered up the castle, and relinquished his bishopric and went to Normandy' – a good example of how severe the compression could be in the annals.

[152] Reading *Pictavensis* for the *Putavensis* of the printed text. For Roger, see below, 91.

[153] The castle remained in the hands of the bishop's men until he surrendered it on 14 December after his trial. But he complained that the royal army under earls and barons had forced him for a time to 'abjure' his see, by which he probably meant his city: *De Injusta Vexatione*, 180, cf. 188.

[154] For the date 11 September, see below, 294 and n. 136.

made Normandy more attractive to the wilder men. It was, therefore, a time when not only the rebels and combatants but also those barons who held or claimed lands on both sides of the Channel had to take a decision about their allegiance. If they wanted to keep their lands in England they had to do homage to the king. It was a sign of the times that in July Count Henry, who was apparently about to invade England with Robert, crossed alone and asked for his mother's lands.[155] William granted them instead to Robert fitzHaimo,[156] and Henry returned angrily to Normandy in company with Robert of Bellême.

On 2 November William of St Calais, bishop of Durham, duly attended the royal court meeting at (Old) Salisbury and was received by Urse of Abetot, sheriff of Worcester, acting no doubt as constable[157] and captain of the guard. The treason trial, which lasted less than one winter's day, was held in either the castle or the adjoining cathedral, probably, in view of the king's attitude, in the secular building.[158] Present at the trial, according to the accused, was the might and wisdom of the whole kingdom,[159] by which he meant the earls and barons and the bishops and abbots; but the only names we have are, on the ecclesiastical side, Archbishops Lanfranc and Thomas and Bishop Geoffrey of Coutances, and, on the lay side, the three earls, Roger,[160] Alan and Odo, who had made the covenant with the bishop, and the barons Henry of Beaumont, Roger Bigot, Ralf Pagnell and Ranulf Peverel, lord of Hatfield Peverel in Essex. It is clear from incidental information that a good number of bishops and abbots were there, and the accused complained of the sheriffs, reeves, huntsmen and other officials among the laity. The king and his advisers regarded the whole

[155] Henry witnesses Robert's charter to Fécamp on 7 July (see above, 81 n. 139). *GR*, ii, 468, claims that Robert, while waiting for a favourable wind for the invasion forces, sent Henry to Britain. Cf. OV, iv, 148. Henry witnesses William's grant to Rochester to repair damage done by the king to the cathedral when fighting against his enemies there: *Regesta*, no. 301.

[156] OV, iv, 220, where it is said that the king disseised Henry of these lands.

[157] See below, 151–2.

[158] *De Injusta Vexatione*, 179 ff. For a detailed account of the proceedings, see Barlow, *EC 1066–1154*, 283 ff. For the site, see here, pl. 13a.

[159] *De Injusta Vexatione*, 184.

[160] Roger of Poitou, alone of the three negotiators with the bishop, is not given the title of *comes* in the early pages of the *libellus*, 176–8; but later, 186–7, they are collectively called *comites*. Although this may be a stylistic simplification, Mason's view, 'Roger de Montgomery and his sons', 16 n. 4, that the Roger *comes* on p. 181 must be the father, the earl of Shrewsbury, is surely wrong. Mason knew that the use of the title at this time was chancy. Roger of Poitou may well have been holding what was in effect the county of Lancaster, and in any case by 1091 was a *comes* in France. Earl Roger senior, of course, may also have been present at the trial, but, wiser than some, may have preferred to keep quiet.

body, less perhaps the menials, as the court and the judges of the accused. The charge was put on behalf of the king by Henry of Beaumont, who was an eyewitness of the offence; and, although the king presided, it was the archbishops who usually spoke for him. Barons, as well as the bishop of Coutances, gave their opinion and in company with the prelates declared the judgments as the case proceeded.

Bishop William appeared under a safe-conduct and subject to the terms of the covenant. He had spent some of his enforced leisure that summer in studying the volume of canon law that Lanfranc had compiled and recommended to his suffragans,[161] had decided to argue on its authority that as a bishop he could be tried only by his fellow bishops, according to ecclesiastical law in a canonical place,[162] and intended, if this plea was refused, to appeal from the royal court to the pope for a canonical trial at Rome. This was a particularly offensive move, for neither the king nor the English church had as yet recognized a successor to Pope Gregory VII.[163]. He therefore consistently refused to acknowledge the jurisdiction of the king's court as constituted, challenged the participation of the laity, declined to plead to the charge, refused to accept any of the judgments pronounced, and confined his arguments to procedural issues.

This conflict of laws when expressed so clearly and pushed so uncompromisingly was a most unwelcome innovation, and the bishop's attitude exasperated or infuriated almost every member of the court. All were agreed that the king was offering the bishop a proper trial according to precedent (Odo in 1082) and the law of the land, and following the procedure appropriate to his rank and the nature of the charge. He stood accused of breaking his fealty to the king while on a military campaign, that is to say treason,[164] and it was his fief and castle,

---

[161] Towards the end of the proceedings, the bishop had the book in his hands, presumably Peterhouse, Cambridge, MS no. 74: *De Injusta Vexatione*, 188. For Lanfranc's Collection, see Barlow, *EC 1066–1154*, 145–6.

[162] On one occasion, p. 184, when he protested against the nature of the trial, he claimed that he had not been canonically summoned, but was forced by royal power to attend, and was compelled to speak, when despoiled of his bishopric, outside his province, and in the absence of his 'fellow provincials', in a secular court. This flight of rhetoric shows how theoretical his argument was. Who were the *conprovinciales* who should have attended his canonical trial in the province of York? He was the only effective suffragan of the northern metropolitan, and his archbishop took a part at Salisbury.

[163] See below, 338 ff.

[164] For *periurii reatum* as treason, cf. OV, vi, 352. In 1075 Roger earl of Hereford was accused of *periurium vel fraus*: Lanfranc, *Letters*, no. 32, p. 120. Cf. M. Chibnall, 'Feudal Society in Orderic Vitalis', *Battle I*, 41–2: 'At its simplest, treason was betrayal of one's lord.'

not his bishopric, which were in jeopardy. The court saw no difficulty at all in distinguishing between the vassal (who was on trial) and the bishop (who was not); and, as with Odo, no attempt was ever made to depose him from his office.

William of St Calais's attitude was opportunist: he was defending himself as best he could against an almost certain condemnation; and his brilliance as a pleader comes out clearly in the account of the trial, drawn up it would seem by one of his suite. On the evidence of his behaviour later towards Archbishop Anselm, it is unlikely that he was a convinced Gregorian reformer,[165] but he was a good and learned bishop and was not necessarily insincere in adopting a Gregorian position in order to save his skin. If that was the law of the church, he had every right to invoke it; and there was a little satisfaction to be gained in forcing Lanfranc to renounce his own handbook of the law. The archbishop, however, was not really put out. With a consistency equal to the bishop's, he held from beginning to end that the traitor should be tried according to another book of rules. He was after all a logician of the highest reputation.

The royal court therefore rejected every procedural plea the bishop made, from his demand that the judges be robed in full canonicals to his appeal from an unlawful court to the papal curia. In the end, Henry of Beaumont pronounced the final judgment of the court: forfeiture of his fief (including his castle); and when the bishop refused to accept this, like all the other judgments, he was adjudged under the terms of the covenant to have forfeited his safe-conduct, and, if he did not surrender the castle (the rest of his fief was in the king's hands), to be liable to arrest and imprisonment. The condemned bishop then disputed this interpretation of the covenant and appealed to its three guarantors. Everything hinged on whether the king had offered the bishop a trial which, in his character as bishop, he could not lawfully refuse. If the bishop could lawfully refuse, he had to be taken back to his castle; but if he had no lawful grounds for rejecting it and still refused to plead, he was to be allowed to go abroad after the surrender of his castle.[166] The earls asked that they should not be put in a dishonourable position. Great pressure therefore was put on the bishop by the king and the primate to force him to acknowledge that the court had made a just judgment which he had refused. Finally the bishop, in fear of arrest and imprisonment (and again there was the precedent of Odo in 1082), refused the judgment and again appealed to Rome.

Although this was not entirely what the court required, and the

---

[165] Below, 340 ff.
[166] De Injusta Vexatione, 176–8, 187.

appeal to Rome reiterated the claim that the trial had been unlawful, it was the bishop's formula for accepting defeat and was good enough to satisfy the three earls. His surrender was due to a final loss of nerve or will, not to his legal discomfiture. He bowed to *force majeure*, partly no doubt because now there was little to be gained by returning to his isolated and beleaguered castle. He may even have been sincere in his professed intention to take his case to Rome. His complete ostracism must have been a strain on even so bold a man. By betraying the conspirators and then deserting the king he had offended all. By refusing to submit and throw himself on the king's mercy he outraged the conventional. And by grudgingly admitting defeat while still defying the king he made his position as bad as possible. He would know that once he had been condemned and lost his safe-conduct other enemies would attack; and his main concern became to get out of England as quickly as he could.

The court then turned its attention to these matters, and discussion of them was interspersed with final attempts to find a compromise solution honourable to both sides.[167] Lanfranc made several suggestions which were unacceptable to the bishop because they required him to acknowledge his guilt and ask for mercy.[168] To the end he maintained his innocence. But Lanfranc, however much provoked, prevented Geoffrey of Coutances from bringing against him a charge of cattle-stealing during the siege of Durham. He may have thought it distasteful that another traitor should now join in the attack.

In the later stages of the trial, the king's voice began to be heard more frequently. He had probably listened with amazement and impatience to the skilful pleading of his former friend and had been content to take advice on the procedure; but he was determined that he should not again be defrauded of a castle, and was at all stages vindictive against one whom he now regarded as a personal enemy. Some of the remarks attributed to him have the characteristic note which other recorders of his sayings also convey.[169] In the opening proceedings William observed, 'I thought that the bishop was first going to reply to the charges I have made against him, and I'm amazed that he wants something else.' Later, when the bishop asked permission of the court to consult with his fellow prelates, the king answered typically, 'Consult your own men, you shan't have advice from mine.' When it came to the question of the surrender of the castle, the king was adamant: 'As you won't accept the

---

[167] *Ibid.*, 188 ff.

[168] Cf. Lanfranc's advice to Abbot Thurstan in the previous reign: *Letters*, no. 57, p. 172.

[169] *De Injusta Vexatione*, 181, 184, 185, 186, 190.

judgment of my court, you must now surrender your castle'; then, 'By the face of Lucca, you'll never escape from my hands before I have the castle'; again, 'Believe me, bishop, you're not going back to Durham, and your men aren't going to stay at Durham, and you're not going free, until you release the castle'; and finally, 'You're getting no safe-conduct, and you'll stay at Wilton, until I know that the castle is in my power; and then you can have ships and a safe-conduct.'

William of St Calais chose to sail from Southampton and was held in honourable custody at Wilton by Robert of Conteville, a royal serjeant, until the castle should be surrendered and ships found. The castle was handed over on 14 November to the king's emissaries, his steward Ivo Taillebois and Erneis de Burun, lord of Hunsingore in Yorkshire, the sheriffs or former sheriffs of Lincolnshire and Yorkshire, accompanied by Helpo, the king's crossbowman or engineer;[170] and a week later the bishop asked for ships so that he could travel with Robert of Mowbray.[171] It was stipulated in the covenant that he and his men should have a safe-conduct and be allowed to take with them gold and silver, horses, clothing, armour, hounds and hawks, and 'everything which should be carried from land'.[172] But the king was reluctant to furnish ships which might be seized by Duke Robert, and the bishop was harassed by the sheriff and his minions.[173] Moreover, on 1 December he received a first summons through Bishop Osmund of Salisbury and two royal serjeants to be at the Christmas court at London to make answer to a charge brought against one of his monks, and later a second summons served by Bishop Walkelin of Winchester, Hugh of Port, sheriff of Hampshire, and Geoffrey of Trailley. But a last appeal to the guarantors of the covenant was successful, and at an unspecified date the bishop was allowed to sail to Normandy. As some compensation for his tribulations, his welcome by Robert was so warm that he decided to stay as one of his advisers.[174] If he pursued his appeal to Rome it must have been by letter.

In respect of the enemy combatants William acted with excellent judgment or was very well advised. It was necessary, in order to instil fear, that some should be severely punished, and the king's fanaticism in matters of honour and great sense of dignity ensured that this would be

[170] For the sheriffs, see below, 447–8.

[171] *De Injusta Vexatione*, 192. *Rogerus* in the printed text.

[172] *Ibid.*, 177.

[173] Sheriff Gilbert, whom *FWR*, 114, identified as Gilbert of Bretteville, whom he thought was sheriff of Hampshire or Wiltshire. He held land in Wiltshire, but was most likely sheriff of Berkshire: see below, 189, 446; and, if so, the royal court may already have been on the move from Salisbury to Windsor or London.

[174] For Simeon, *HR*'s erroneous statement, ii, 216–17, that Odo, and not William, was entrusted by Robert with the administration of the duchy, see David, *RC*, 213 ff.

done. On the other hand, there was the need to recruit vassals and make friends, to make a fresh start amid general good will, and William's magnanimity inclined him in that direction. Orderic in his reconstruction of the scene before the surrender of Rochester rehearses the pleas for mercy entered by the king's entourage for the 'arrogant bachelors and the old men blinded by avarice' who were within.[175] All had learnt their lesson; the seniors had stood by his father in times of peril and were important men whose friendship would be of great use to him; and there were many excellent bachelors present whom he could take into his service. In reply, William complained that he had been execrably treated by men to whom he had restored their estates and been a good lord, and that there were dangers to public order in sparing perjurers and robbers. Examples should be made. Nevertheless, the chronicler believed that the king heeded the advice. Elsewhere he wrote that William took what immediate vengeance he could and, in the case of some others, merely bided his time, but that he also prudently overlooked some injuries, especially from the older men, for he remembered their loyal service to his father, rightly considered that they would not misbehave again, and realized that in any case they would soon be dead.[176] In this category we can place Robert of Mortain, Roger of Montgomery, the Grandmesnils and probably Roger Bigot.

One important point neglected by Orderic, probably because at the time it was self evident, is that the combatants fell into different classes. Those who followed their liege-lord in a quarrel incurred little blame according to the standards of the day. And this points to a fundamental distinction: some of the enemy were vassals or allies of Duke Robert, with no obligations at all to William. These could be held prisoner or released for ransom,[177] but they had done nothing dishonourable or illegal. In this class were Eustace of Boulogne, Robert of Bellême and his brother Hugh, if he was indeed at Rochester. It seems that the king allowed such as these either to enter into service or engagements with him or to return to the Continent. Robert of Bellême and Eustace crossed to France. The former, who had no English lands, suffered no penalty; the latter, however, was probably disseized of his great English honour.[178] It would obviously have suited William to make an alliance

[175] OV, iv, 128–32.

[176] OV, iv, 134.

[177] Guibert of Nogent's father, Everard, probably in the service of his lord, Raynald I, count of Clermont in the Beauvaisis, was captured by Duke William at the battle of Mortemer in February 1054, when Raynald escaped (*GG*, 68–74), and died in captivity six or eight months later. Guibert says expressly that it was not the duke's custom to release prisoners for ransom: *De vita sua libri tres*, Migne *PL*, clvi, 860, cf. 843.

[178] In March 1101, when King Henry made a treaty with Count Robert of Flanders,

with the lord of Boulogne, a convenient ferry port in an area of strategic importance to him; but Eustace seems to have been an old friend of Robert Curthose – in 1096 they were to go on crusade together – and William was probably forced to make the best of a bad job. There is no evidence that the two princes were ever in contact again.

The case of the third Montgomery son, Roger of Poitou, is more obscure. William I had endowed him, probably not long before 1086, with a large honour in England, but resumed it while the Domesday survey was being carried out. Some dereliction of duty during the threat of the Danish invasion, an involvement with the errant Robert Curthose, or his marriage, on the advice of his father, to the heiress of the county of La Marche are possible causes of his disgrace. The situation would make his presence among the garrison of Rochester understandable and his easy transfer to William Rufus's allegiance explicable: he made his peace with the new king in order to recover his English estates. By the summer, as we have seen, he was entrusted by William with a military command against the bishop of Durham, and he is found to be in possession of an honour, not exactly the same as before, but equally valuable, which included the whole of modern Lancashire. In 1091 he became count of La Marche in the right of his wife.[179] William probably regarded him as a victim of circumstances.

The criminals were those who had become William's vassals or subjects of him as king of England and had deserted without good excuse to the enemy. They were guilty of treason.[180] But some of these, such as Roger Bigot, had a good excuse: they were from the Bessin and were Odo's vassals or beneficiaries. The Anglo-Saxon Chronicler believed that many Frenchmen gave up their estates and went abroad, and that the king rewarded his loyal subjects with their lands.[181] Orderic thought that William punished some of the rebels with most severe penalties.[182] And the treaty made between the king and duke in February 1091 stipulated the reinstatement of all those who had lost land in England for Robert's sake.[183] But the only victims who are named in the context of

the count of Boulogne was still his enemy: see below, 325. But by the Treaty of Alton in July, Henry restored to Eustace his father's lands in England: ASC, s.a., 177. See also Regesta, ii, no. 556. Cf. C.W. Hollister, 'Magnates and "Curiales" in early Norman England', Viator, viii (1977), 69. For the value of his honour, which ranked equal sixth among the English lay barons, see ibid., 65. For the honour, see J.H. Round, 'The counts of Boulogne as English lords', Studies in Peerage and Family History (1901), 147 ff.

[179] This reconstruction simplifies Mason's in 'Roger de Montgomery and his sons', 14–17. For Roger, see also Sanders, Baronies, 126, and above, 84, 85 n. 160.

[180] See above, 86 n. 164.

[181] ASC, 168.

[182] OV, iv, 134.

[183] See below, 281–2.

1088 are the two bishops, Odo and William.[184] The former was disinherited, banished, and never pardoned. The latter, as we have seen, only escaped summary punishment because the king could not lay hands on him. It would also seem that the Mowbrays were punished. The bishop of Coutances, who witnessed a royal charter which seems to antedate the rebellion,[185] and had made war on the king, had reappeared at court as bold as brass for the trial of the bishop of Durham in November. But his nephew was expected to travel abroad with Durham after the latter's condemnation,[186] and Geoffrey seems to have been mostly in Normandy until his death at Coutances on 2 February 1093,[187] when William allowed the earl of Northumberland to inherit his uncle's English honour. Maybe it was only at this point that Robert of Mowbray returned to England. It is possible that William, because of his anti-clerical feelings, set higher standards for bishops than for lay barons, and in this he would have been encouraged by Lanfranc, who would have no truck with traitors.

Most of the other noble rebels were treated far more leniently. Robert count of Mortain, Odo's brother and a very great landowner in England, witnessed a royal charter which may be dated to the winter of 1087–8,[188] and so could have been regarded as a traitor; and, although Orderic thought him a reluctant rebel, led astray by the more forceful Odo, and a recipient of the royal pardon, he disappears from the English scene. As he was buried in the family abbey at Grestain after his death on

---

[184] Remigius of Lincoln is possibly another. Henry of Huntingdon, archdeacon in that church and in an excellent position to know, claims that he was once accused of treason and was cleared by a servant taking the ordeal of hot iron: HH, 212. Cf. Lanfranc, *Letters* (to Remigius), no. 37. It is possible, however, that the occasion was the 'Rebellion of the earls' in 1075.

[185] He witnesses, with the bishop of Durham, *Regesta*, no. 306; the dating of 345 is more doubtful.

[186] OV, iv, 128, has him with the king at the siege of Rochester. This may easily be a mistake. In any case the reconciliation was short-lived: *De Injusta Vexatione*, 192, where he is shown as due to travel abroad from Southampton on 21 November 1088. See also below, 167–9.

[187] He witnesses a royal charter, *Regesta*, no. 315, given at Hastings at the beginning of 1091, and presumably accompanied the king to Normandy: see below, 278. The contemporary historian of the church of Coutances, who greatly admired Geoffrey, pictures the bishop mostly in his diocese in this period, withstanding Henry's lordship and finishing the rebuilding of his cathedral and palace. On 2 November 1091 he was in his hall when an earthquake damaged the church. The following August he contracted a terminal illness; he was still in Normandy after 15 September 1092, and died on 2 February 1093: *Gallia Christiana*, xi, instr. 221–4. He also probably attended the Council of Rouen in June 1091: below, 286. Cf. J.H. Le Patourel, 'Geoffrey of Montbray, bishop of Coutances, 1049–93', *EHR*, lix (1944), 146 ff.

[188] *Regesta*, no. 296.

8 December 1090, it looks as though he had withdrawn to Mortain.[189] On the other hand, Roger Bigot, like Geoffrey of Coutances present at the trial of the bishop of Durham, was completely restored to favour, and the Grandmesnils seem to have suffered little or nothing. Gilbert fitzRichard of Tonbridge was pardoned, probably because of his wounds, youth and inexperience, but the Clares never gained William's full favour, and their loyalty was always suspect.[190] The effects on the baronage of the rebellion and its suppression were not, therefore, cataclysmic.[191] Even Odo only lost again what he had forfeited in 1082.

For those who went down, others came up. Possibly to hold the Clares in check, Robert fitzHaimo, the son of the sheriff of Kent, was given not only the lands of Queen Matilda but also the honour of Gloucester and a daughter of Earl Roger of Montgomery in marriage.[192] William of Warenne had been created first earl of Surrey before he died of his wounds on 24 June, and was succeeded by his son of the same name.[193] Henry of Beaumont was made first earl of Warwick, probably in the next year.[194] Simon of St Liz (I), the son-in-law of the executed Earl Waltheof, was recognized as earl of Huntingdon and Northampton before 1091.[195] It is also possible that some time in the reign Walter Giffard was created earl of Buckingham.[196] William Rufus was famed for his generosity and no doubt paid all his debts of gratitude in full.

Also in this period he made his first ecclesiastical appointments. To Chichester, vacant by the death of the not very distinguished Stigand, he nominated a clerk even more obscure, a certain Godfrey who died

---

[189] See above, 80 n. 130. He witnesses *Regesta*, nos 325, 451, which may be dated to the pacification immediately after the rebellion. *Regesta*, no. 328, dated 1090, which he witnesses, has other unsatisfactory features; and the entry may be a mistake for Robert of Meulan: see below, 278 n. 64. His witness to nos. 323 (a strange witness list), 325 (? Robert of Meulan) and 451 cannot be used to prove that he was at the royal court after 1087–8. For his burial, see *Neustria Pia*, 529.

[190] As he witnesses a writ probably to be dated 1087, *Regesta*, no. 290, he had probably done homage to the king, and he reappears as witness to a writ which can be dated July 1088, no. 301. After 1091, no. 319, he does not witness again.

[191] For closer investigations of this matter, see below, 167 ff.

[192] OV, iv, 182, 220; *DNB*; Sanders, *Baronies*, 6.

[193] OV, iv, 180 and n.

[194] GEC, xii (2), 358 and appendix A. See also below, 169–70.

[195] GEC, vi, 640–1, xi, 663, *HBC*, 432. His background is extremely obscure, and it seems that he was a royal favourite provided with an heiress: see below, 172–3.

[196] The date of Walter's promotion is uncertain. GEC, ii, 386, inclines towards 1097, while *HBC* favours Henry I's coronation, 1100. In fact in the witness list to the coronation charter he appears untitled after two earls each given a Christian name and title; but his double-barrelled name could have been considered an equivalent identification: *SSC*, 119. Nevertheless, the suspicion remains that he owed his promotion to William: cf. Chibnall, OV, v, 214 n. 2, 296 n. 2.

within a year. But Wells, vacant by the death of the Lotharingian Giso, one of Edward the Confessor's appointments, he gave to his father's doctor, John *de Villula,* or of Tours, so rewarding an old and in some ways distinguished servant of the crown. John was consecrated by Lanfranc in July 1088.[197] Two abbacies also were filled. The appointment of Guy, a monk of St Augustine's, Canterbury, to rule that house was the work of Lanfranc and caused much trouble.[198] The choice of Herbert Losinga, prior of Fécamp, to succeed the last Anglo-Saxon abbot of Ramsey was probably the king's. Herbert's reputation was to suffer from his willingness to buy preferment from his royal master, but in most respects he was an admirable abbot and then bishop.[199]

An unusual feature of the Anglo-Norman political scene in 1087–8 is that neither of the new rulers started with an established clientèle of weight and distinction: both had been landless, and while Robert had been an exile William had been without assured expectations. In 1087 the elder brother was the better placed to assemble a following. He had his bachelor companions-in-arms and the associates of his youth, men like Robert of Bellême and William of Breteuil, sons of great barons, and a strong claim on the allegiance of the conservative elements in Norman society; and he was in a position to take over the dead king's household and canvass those barons and captains who had been with the Conqueror on his last campaign. William Rufus, who had never been the lord of vassals and was a virtual stranger in England, succeeded wonderfully well in his take-over of the kingdom and managed to prevent it appearing as something amputated from the Norman empire. He had lost most of his father's great household servants,[200] and seems to have been without many important baronial friends in his first years as king. The landless Robert fitzHaimo and Henry of Beaumont seem to have been closest to him. Indeed, as his father's household knight, he was probably as accustomed as Robert to raffish company. But his growing sense of importance ensured that he would not be content to be surrounded on all occasions solely by boon-companions, libertines and ruffians. Loyal servants could be recruited; great barons would want to attend his court.

A handful of witnessed writs and charters which can be ascribed to 1088–9 reveal the names of some of those in attendance on the king.[201] At one time or another all the counts and earls with English titles or strong

[197] *Acta Lanfranci,* 273; Barlow, *EC 1066–1154,* 66–7.
[198] M. Gibson, *Lanfranc of Bec,* 189.
[199] Barlow, *EC 1066–1154,* 68–9.
[200] See below, 138.
[201] *Regesta,* nos 289–90, 292–4, 296, 298a, 301–2, 305–6, 314a–c, 325, 370; cf. 383, 431, 442, 446. *De Injusta Vexatione, passim.*

English connexions put in an appearance: Roger of Shrewsbury, Robert of Mortain, Henry of Beaumont, the new earl of Warwick, Alan of Richmond, Hugh of Chester and William (II) of Warenne. The earldoms of Hereford, Huntingdon and Northampton, and now Kent were in abeyance. Among the major barons were Walter Giffard, soon to be created earl of Buckingham, Earl Roger's son, Roger of Poitou, Roger Bigot and Henry of Ferrers, whose sons were to become earls, Roger (I) of Bully (Bouilli), lord of Tickhill (Blythe) in Yorkshire and a relation of Robert of Bellême, Ralf Pagnell, another great Yorkshire baron and sheriff of that county, who spoke at the trial of the bishop of Durham,[202] William Peverel (I) of Nottingham,[203] Walter (I) of Aincourt, lord of Blankney in Lincolnshire, and Bernard of Neufmarché from the Welsh marches. The north Midlands seem to be exceptionally well represented, and all these men, except for some of the greatest, represent those Conquest dynasties which had sunk roots in the kingdom. It is unlikely that most of them were much inconvenienced by the split between England and Normandy; it is probable that they considered that their first loyalty lay to the king of England, whoever he might be; and they knew that there were still lands in the west and especially the north which the king might choose to distribute among loyal and warlike men. It was the steadfastness of such barons that secured the crown for William Rufus.

The bishops and abbots freely attended William's courts and there is no evidence that any held aloof or were kept at bay. It is to be noticed that Thomas I 'of Bayeux', archbishop of York, was, despite his connexion with Odo, as loyal as Lanfranc to the new king, and was with him during the campaigns of 1088. Among the household servants are found the stewards, Ivo Taillebois and Eudo *dapifer*, and the constables, Urse of Abetot, sheriff of Worcester, Hugh (II or III) of Montfort (-sur-Risle), and Robert (I) of Oilli, keepers of the castles of Worcester, Dover and Saltwood in Kent, and Oxford respectively; while one early writ is

---

[202] *De Injusta Vexatione*, 190, where it is Reginald in the printed text. He witnesses a charter of Duke Robert dated 1088: *Regesta*, no. 299, and is believed to have founded Holy Trinity, York, as a cell of Marmoutier, near Tours, in the following year.

[203] There were two, apparently unrelated, William Peverels, one 'of Nottingham', the other 'of Dover'. For the former, a powerful Domesday baron who had custody of Nottingham castle and died in 1114, see GEC, iv, appendix I, 761. The latter, a son or brother of Gilbert Maminot, bishop of Lisieux, who was probably given the lands in Kent of Hugh, nephew of Herbert, by William Rufus (Duncombe, 'Feudal Tenure', 134, 72) and became a favourite of Henry I, was still alive about 1128. When this man (after 1095) and his brothers, Haimo and Pain, witnessed royal writs, they were usually differentiated by 'of Dover'. Accordingly, the plain witness of William Peverel in William's reign is always understood as referring to the older and more important Midland baron.

authorized by William Warelwast,[204] a clerk who was to have a distinguished career in the reigns of the two brothers, specializing in ecclesiastical diplomacy, particularly at the papal curia, and finished as bishop of Exeter. One unexpectedly rare witness to royal documents is Gerard, the chancellor.[205] There is no reason to think that he ever fell foul of the new king. He was the nephew of Bishop Walkelin of Winchester, always in high favour, and of Simeon abbot of Ely. In 1095, when described as a clerk in the royal chapel, he was sent by the king in company with William Warelwast on an important diplomatic mission to the pope,[206] and, perhaps because of this service, was given the bishopric of Hereford in the following year. It is possible that his interest in law, science and even more hermetic branches of knowledge may have caused him voluntarily to resign his office;[207] but all that we know is that by January 1091 he had been succeeded by Robert Bloet, a member of the baronial family of Ivry and likewise a close relation of great prelates.[208]

No record was kept of the king's Christmas court which he intended to hold at London, and the turbulence of 1088 was followed by a year of peace in England. In the summer of 1089, possibly as a thanksgiving for his victory, possibly also to reward a supporter, he joined with Ailwin Cild, a London citizen of native birth, in the foundation of the Cluniac priory of Bermondsey, outside the city on the south bank of the Thames; and one of his soldier friends, Winebald of Ballon, was also involved. Bermondsey was a daughter house of La Charité-sur-Loire, and Winebald could have had some influence there.[209] With this religious foundation, to which he contributed the land, William was taking root in England. He may also in that year have reviewed his military defences in the kingdom. In London the 'White Tower', which his father had commissioned to replace the first castle thrown up in the south-east corner of the Roman wall in 1066–7, was still under construction; and this massive stone keep, for which there was no precedent in England since Roman days, and was surpassed in the kingdom only by that at Colchester, which was also in progress, set a high standard for the new king. His first commission, however, was more modest. He employed Gundulf bishop of Rochester, a skilled mason or architect who had some responsibility for the Tower of London, to build a castle in his cathedral

---

[204] *Regesta*, no. 305.
[205] See above, 59 n. 27.
[206] *HN*, 69–70, and below, 342.
[207] Barlow, *EC 1066–1154*, 72, 257, 259.
[208] *Ibid.*, 70–1, and below, 146.
[209] *Regesta*, no. 398. *HRH*, 114; Brooke and Keir, *London 800–1216* (1975), 312–14; Brian Golding, 'The coming of the Cluniacs', *Battle III*, 75; below, 171 n. 66.

city so as to strengthen the fortifications which had been damaged in the recent hostilities and improve on the little castle outside the walls. This he was to do instead of paying £100 to William for a grant of the manor of Haddenham (Bucks), worth £40 a year, which Lanfranc and then he had had on a life-tenancy. Robert fitzHaimo and Henry of Beaumont told the less than enthusiastic bishop that something costing £40 would satisfy the king. In the event, Gundulf constructed the fortified enclosure in the south-west angle of the city ramparts, the curtain walls and ditch which still confine the twelfth-century keep, at the cost of some £60.[210]

The one event noticed by the chroniclers in 1089 is the death of Lanfranc on 28 May. He had been the most distinguished incumbent of the see of Canterbury since St Dunstan in the tenth century. A monk of unsullied reputation, a renowned master of the arts, a theologian of some note, and a renovator of Canterbury's claim to be 'the mother church of England, Scotland, Ireland and the neighbouring isles', primate of the whole of Britain,[211] his death, however, did not inspire Godfrey prior of Winchester to one of his better obituary poems.[212] The primate, he thought, had lived wisely and justly, a poor man amid great wealth. His birth had done honour to Italy, his teaching to France. He had done much for the Latin arts.

Dwelling on earth your mind sought out the Heavens;
Released from earth you fly up to the stars.

Perhaps he had become in his old age too associated with royal government to be greatly loved by those who had suffered from it. His death was thought by William of Malmesbury to mark the end of the king's tutelage.[213] Rufus had obtained the throne and also held on to the kingdom by the archbishop's help. Now with his enemies defeated and his patron dead, he was free to go his own way.

The disorder in England was so transient that it is easy to overlook the young king's achievement. It should be viewed in the light of what was beginning to happen in Normandy and the permanent foothold which he himself was able to establish in the duchy by turning the tables on his brother. The temptation to think that whereas the duchy had a tradition of disturbance, the kingdom had a sense of unity, should be resisted, for the duchy had never been divided before, while partition had been the usual fate of England. Moreover, the duchy, once William the Bastard

[210] T. Hearne, *Textus Roffensis* (1720), 145–8; *DB*, i, 143d, previously owned by Earl Tostig; Brown, Colvin, Taylor, *The History of the King's Works* (1963), i, 28–31; Brown, *Rochester Castle*, 7–10. For the White Tower and Colchester, see here, pls 8, 9a.

[211] Barlow, *EC 1066–1154*, 39 ff.

[212] Wright, *Satirical Poets*, ii, 150.

[213] *GR*, ii, 367.

had reestablished his father's position, had been at least as orderly as England in the same period. The failure of Stephen in similar circumstances half a century later, with Brian fitzCount able to hold Wallingford, in the heart of the kingdom, in the Angevin interest until his death late in the reign, also puts William II's success into perspective. Both kings were involved in 'more than civil war',[214] the challenge from another member of the family. These feuds were a feature of the medieval scene. Only the strong and resolute came through them unscathed.

[214] Lucan, *Pharsalia*, I, 1–2, a phrase popular with medieval writers.

Chapter 3

THE BACHELOR KING AND HIS DOMESTIC SERVANTS

William Rufus had great physical presence. Although a small man, he was dangerous, like an animal. Archbishop Anselm once likened him to a wild bull.[1] The only portrait is from the pen of William of Malmesbury, who is unlikely to have seen him in the flesh;[2] but even if it is second hand and also based on the medical system of 'complexions', it represents how this vivid actor was remembered. There was a twelfth-century proverb, 'Whoever knew a tall man who was wise, a redhead who was faithful, or a small man who was humble?' The professors of the medical school at Salerno provided an explanation.[3] In the first case, the vital spirits had too far to travel from the heart and brain. In the second, the cause of redness was a choleric complexion (constitution or temperament). Choler was a swift and impetuous 'humour', and the agility it gave a man made him changeable, unstable and ready for anything. This led to infidelity. As for small men, they possessed pride, which was a sort of anger. Anger was a warmth of the heart which passed from the interior to the outside when the mind wanted to carry out the vengeance it had conceived in answer to injuries suffered. Because of the smallness of the man, the erupting heat was constricted and hence fiercer in its action.

William of Malmesbury was interested in medicine and was probably affected by such beliefs. He describes the king as thick-set and muscular with a protruding belly; a dandy dressed in the height of fashion, however outrageous, he wore his blond hair long, parted in the centre and off the face so that his forehead was bare;[4] and in his red, choleric

[1] *HN*, 36. Cf. *EC 1066 1154*, 287 8.

[2] *GR*, ii, 374. The chronicler was born probably early in the reign and given as an oblate to Malmesbury abbey towards the end. There seems to be no literary model for the description, and Abbot Godfrey, who probably came from Jumièges via Ely, must have known the king. In any case, many men in the Malmesbury area would have seen him. For a 13th-century 'portrait', see here, pl. 3.

[3] *The Prose Salernitan Questions*, ed. Brian Lawn, 134, qu. 280; cf. 219, qu. 33.

[4] 'fronte fenestrata' – an open forehead, like a window. Cf. Goscelin of St Bertin, *Vita S. Augustini*, in *ASS*, May, vi, 394 B: 'Facies amabilis . . ., frons mediante coma suis columnis resultabat fenestrata'. To uncover the forehead was probably considered immodest. Orderic, below, 104, condemns centre partings and foreheads shaved like thieves'. On the Bayeux Tapestry almost all men, English as well as Norman, are shown with their hair worn low on the forehead, often to the eyebrows.

face were lively eyes of changeable colour, speckled with flecks of light.[5]
In private with his boon-companions he was easy-going. He cracked
jokes as he dealt with the business of the day, and was never so facetious
as when he was doing wrong, for he hoped that the witticism would dispel
the stigma. In public, however, his lack of eloquence was noticeable, and
when angry he was reduced to stuttering incoherence. He was apt to
assume a ferocious manner, and with his haughty, inflamed face,
threatening eyes, and loud, hectoring voice sought to intimidate the
company.[6] We may infer that the young king, whose high sense of
importance and of the reverence due to the crown was not matched by
natural dignity or suitable powers of expression, was driven to this
boorish, bullying behaviour as a substitute. But although he easily took
offence and was not slow to pay back an imagined insult with interest, he
appreciated boldness in others and was easily pacified. Magnanimity
was one of his virtues. Orderic Vitalis viewed him in much the same way:
he was every inch a soldier, at times violent and swollen with anger, but
in his dealings with soldiers of noble birth always courteous, jovial and
bountiful.[7]

Despite his reluctance to enrich his followers at the expense of the
royal demesne he had inherited from his father,[8] he was renowned for his
generosity, a truly royal virtue. It seems that he knew the difference
between capital assets and revenue, and was lavish only with the latter.
The Malmesbury monk, perhaps for this very reason, considered his
extravagance culpable prodigality and told disapproving stories about
it.[9] Although his condemnation of the king's great rewards to the fine
soldiers he recruited may seem a little unfair, he was thinking of the
hardships caused by raising the money and of the contrasting meanness
to the church. In his ridicule of William's ostentation and confusion of
price and value, he was at one with satirists of all times. Once, when one
of his chamberlains produced a new pair of shoes for him, William asked
what they had cost. 'Three shillings!' he exclaimed. 'You son of a whore!
Since when has a king got to wear shoes as cheap as that? Go and buy me
some for a mark of silver [13s 4d].' So the servant came back with an
even cheaper pair which he falsely claimed had cost a mark; and the king
said, 'Now these are more fitted to our royal majesty.' This unkind story

[5] 'oculo vario, quibusdam intermicantibus guttis distincto'. The writer stresses the
vivacity of the eyes at the expense of hazarding a colour. They were presumably of a light
hue. Some of the epithets are conventional: cf. John of Salisbury on 'Lanuvius': 'turgidus
venter, tumida facies et rubicunda', *Policraticus*, I, prol. (ed. Webb), i, 16.

[6] See also *GP*, 79 and n.5, for his alternation between anger and jesting.

[7] OV, v, 238.

[8] See below, 231–3.

[9] *GR*, ii, 368.

is also a reminder of the finery which soldiers love to put on.[10]

Yet if the king had most of the weaknesses characteristic of soldiers, he had as well most of the virtues. His courage was famous. The only trouble was that he had a little too much. As William of Malmesbury observed, he could have done with rather more fear of God. He was also a lucky commander, a quality much appreciated by subordinates. The English monk thought that only in Wales, where the conditions were exceptionally unfavourable, was he other than successful.[11] Although, unlike his father and brothers, he fought no pitched battles and seldom rolled up the opposing forces completely, he never suffered a disaster or even a serious reverse, and was generally regarded as a victorious king.[12] Such a reputation greatly profited its possessor.

In 1087, when he became king, he was still a knight bachelor. However normal that may have been, it was unusual for a king, whatever his sexual tastes or personal unattractiveness, not to marry. In the eleventh century he needed a wife for the alliance and dowry she brought, for the children she bore, and for her acting as a surrogate during his absence or incapacity. It was a wife's role to rule his household, arrange the ceremonial aspects of his court,[13] look after the guests, distribute alms, maintain the piety of the household and mother the other children being educated at court. Some kings also married for love or came to enjoy their wife's company.[14] Because monkish chroniclers were inclined to think that all active women were evil, the importance of women in early medieval society is often underrated. Orderic, who, although wary of the other sex, was too accurate an observer of his times entirely to ignore it, describes the activities of the bellicose Mabel of Bellême and Isabel of Montfort-Tosny and of the great *femme fatale* of the period, Isabel's half-sister, Bertrada of Montfort. He also shows in some of his vignettes the social role of the lady in her lord's court. For example, he tells of Isabel of Tosny in the hall of the castle at Conches sitting in the company of some of their knights who were gaming and chatting about all sorts of things 'as men do'. Among the things they discussed were their dreams and their meaning.[15] The lord's wife also had her place at ceremonial feasts; and in an age when

[10] Cf. above, 24.
[11] *GR*, ii, 365 6.
[12] See below, 396–7.
[13] Cf. *VEdR*, 41.
[14] Cf. Baldwin III of Jerusalem's happy marriage in 1158 to the twelve-year-old Theodora, after living a dissolute life, and other cases in that kingdom: Bernard Hamilton, 'Queens of Jerusalem', in *Medieval Women*, Studies in Church History, subsidia 1 (Rosalind Hill *Festschrift*), ed. Derek Baker (1978), 158 and *passim*.
[15] OV, iv, 216–18.

hospitality and the rites of the table were so important, the absence of her services would have had a marked effect on the tone.

A court without a lady, and her ladies, would have been considered by many men barbarous and uninteresting, and there would have been a good deal of social pressure on a king to marry. Moreover, in periods when the descent of the crown was not automatically according to strict rules of primogeniture, the magnates who had supported a successful claimant wanted to be rewarded with at least the hope that their families would not have to suffer from a counter-revolution. Those barons who had just put William on the throne at Robert's expense had no desire to see him succeeded by his elder brother or nephew.[16] In any case, most rulers harboured some dynastic ambitions, and even the most libertine or perverse recognized that eventually a wife was a necessary adjunct.

There were, however, counter-pressures. Little encouragement to early marriage was given in intensely militaristic societies, as marriage often preceded retirement from the soldier's life; and the extreme misogamy of some pious clerks[17] could have caused many a bachelor to hesitate before taking so important a step. The Crusaders in 1099 elected as first Christian ruler of Jerusalem the bachelor Godfrey of Bouillon; his successor, his brother Baldwin I, was often without a consort; and the important part which queens were to play in the history of that kingdom was a rather strange result of disorderly matrimonial arrangements.[18] Some soldier kings and dukes postponed marriage rather riskily. Robert of Normandy did not marry until he had returned from the Crusade when he was about forty-seven, and Henry I, possibly in rivalry, married at the same time at the age of thirty-two. Both marriages are typical. Robert had to raise cash for the redemption of Normandy and a dowry was the easiest way of getting it. Henry contracted a useful alliance at the earliest opportunity after his irregular succession to the throne and thereby gave notice that he had become a serious family man, that his time of wandering was over, and that he intended to found a dynasty in rivalry with Robert's. He also proclaimed his difference from William Rufus.

Three chroniclers, Eadmer of Canterbury, William of Malmesbury and Orderic Vitalis, considered that Rufus was dissolute in his private life, and connected his immorality with irreligion and his oppression of the church. They associated him with homosexuals and suspected him of practising that vice. They also believed, Orderic strongest of all, that a

---

[16] For loyalty to Henry I and the revolution after his death, cf. R.W. Southern, 'The place of Henry I in English history', *Proc. of the Br. Acad.*, xlviii (1962–3), 142 ff.

[17] Cf. the diatribe of John of Salisbury, *Policraticus*, VIII, xi (ed. Webb), ii, 748 ff.

[18] Hamilton, 'Queens of Jerusalem', *loc. cit.*

general corruption of morals had occurred during the king's reign, manifested in the extravagant new fashions in men's clothes and hair-styles. The three writers were celibate moralists and defenders of the church, and there are several strands in their charges which have to be disentangled.

Eadmer, the earliest of these writers, was, as Archbishop Anselm's chaplain, although in a good position to know what went on at court, also, through his championship of his master, an extremely hostile witness. It is noticeable that he tells us much more about the king's profanity and hostility to the church than about his dissipation; but he has two anecdotes of great importance. In his *Life of Anselm* he recounts that when the abbot of Bec came to England in 1092 and visited the royal court early in September, he was very warmly greeted not only by the barons but also by the king, who paid him every honour. Yet the abbot asked for a private audience so that he could raise and investigate matters which were the subject of widespread rumour. Stories which did great harm to the king's reputation were in general circulation, and Anselm thought William much to blame.[19]

Eadmer on this occasion tells us nothing more. The second reference to the king's morals is in the *History*.[20] In February 1094, William, when about to cross to Normandy, summoned a large court, including Anselm, by then archbishop, to Hastings. At that time, Eadmer claims, almost all the young men at court grew their hair like girls and, freshly combed, with roving eyes and irreligious gestures, they minced around with girlish steps. It was probably on these words that other writers were to build. Eadmer then informs us that on Ash Wednesday the archbishop directed his sermon against this fashion and brought a good many courtiers to repentance; and those who would not have their hair cut he debarred from the distribution of the ashes and receiving absolution from their sins. Shortly afterwards he raised the matter of sodomy with the king in person and asked that they should combine their forces in a general council of the church in order to prevent the whole land from becoming like the city of the plain (*Genesis* 19). But William was offended and declined to help. Anselm had to wait until Henry's accession, when he was allowed, perhaps encouraged, by the king to mount an attack on sodomy in all ranks of society.[21]

William of Malmesbury knew Eadmer's *History*, and in his *Gesta Regum*, in connexion with the king's employment of Ranulf Flambard and oppression of the church, he describes the extravagant fashions and

[19] *VA*, 63–4. For William of Malmesbury's version of this, see *GP*, 79.
[20] *HN*, 47–9; see also below, 329.
[21] *EC 1066 1154*, 129.

effeminacy of the courtiers.[22] Hair was worn long, clothes were luxurious and shoes had pointed and curled toes. Young men rivalled women in the softness of their bodies, walked with mincing steps and as they moved revealed their thighs. They chose to remain weak and effeminate, and, conquerors of the chastity of others, they took little care of their own. A band of effeminates and a flock of harlots (*ganeae*) followed the court, so that the court of the king of England was more a brothel of catamites than a house of majesty. Later, when listing Henry I's reforms, William of Malmesbury notices that he expelled the effeminates from court and restored the use of lamps at night, a custom which had been suspended during his brother's reign.[23]

Orderic, writing about a decade later, built on these foundations. In Book VIII he first accuses the king of lust,[24] then, lamenting that the lamp of true holiness was growing dim in the world and that all men were doing the deeds of darkness, claimed that the youthful king was shameless and lascivious. He also inserted two great denunciations of the immorality of the time. In the first,[25] devoted to Normandy, he described how sodomitical love, lascivious with its allurements, befouled unpunished those effeminates who were condemned to be burnt in hell, while adultery openly defiled the marriage bed. In the second,[26] on the text of the special shoes with long points like scorpions' tails designed to hide the bunions on Count Fulk of Anjou's feet, he denounced the extravagant fashions of the age. A clown (*nebulo*) at William's court named Robert had begun to stuff the points of such shoes with tow so that they could be curled back like a ram's horn, and because of that was nicknamed Horner (*cornadus*). Other highly improper fashions were long and tight-fitting shirts and tunics, and long robes and mantles with voluminous sleeves. Nobles grew little beards, wore their hair long at the back like whores, and with a centre parting bared their foreheads like thieves. Their abundant locks were carefully tended, sometimes curled with tongs and either caught back in a headband or covered with a cap. Hardly a knight now went uncovered indoors. These fashions were set by effeminates; and catamites practised sodomy. They spent the night in revelry and dicing, and slept all day. Their fashions proclaimed that like stinking goats they delighted in the filth of lust.

Finally, in Book X, written in 1135, when Orderic came to describe

[22] *GR*, ii, 369–70.
[23] *GR*, ii, 470. He imagines the king on the night before his death sleeping in an unlit room: below, 427.
[24] *OV*, iv, 110.
[25] *OV*, iv, 146.
[26] *OV*, iv, 186 ff., cf. 268, where it is said that the fashions soon spread to the lower classes.

William's death and view the victim against the background of eternity and the Last Judgment, he took an even more severe, indeed pitiless, tone. The king was not only expiating the sins of the Norman conquerors and the creation of the New Forest, but also being punished for his own vile life. Near the beginning of the Book he writes that William never had a lawful wife but devoted himself insatiably to obscene fornication and incessant adultery, and, stained by his passions, set a damnable example of foul lewdness to his subjects.[27] Towards the end he refers as well to the rule of effeminates. It was in company with his 'parasites' that the king met his death, and he was mourned only by the mercenary knights, lechers and common harlots who had lost their paymaster.[28] Henry of Huntingdon, about the same time, wrote of the king's insolent flaunting of his sexual excesses.[29]

We can distinguish three matters: the change in men's fashions, the spread of sodomy and the king's private life. The change in fashion is well attested. Orderic claims that before the deaths of Pope Gregory VII and William the Bastard the Normans wore decent clothes, suited in length to the body, and were an athletic race.[30] On the Bayeux Tapestry (c. 1077) they are shown with hair short (or shaven) at the back and sides and low on the forehead, and with clean-shaven faces. In contrast, the English have hair on the neck and sometimes covering the ears, and wear long moustaches.[31] William of Poitiers, writing about 1077, records that at Easter 1067 those present at the ceremonies at Fécamp looked with amazement at the English hostages – 'the long-haired sons of the northern world . . . as beautiful as girls'.[32] And it is likely that the Norman nobility were not only affected by the wealth they acquired after the Conquest but also influenced by English fashions. A 'Merry Jest' type of story told by Geoffrey de Gaimar concerning William Rufus's kinsman, Giffard the Poitevin 'of Barbastre'[33] at a royal court, which, if correctly placed in the new hall at Westminster, can be dated at Whitsun 1099 or 1100, sheds a curious light on this fashion.[34] Walter

---

[27] OV, v, 202.

[28] OV, v, 286–90.

[29] HH, 232 3, a largely derivative passage.

[30] OV, iv, 188.

[31] Cf. Earl Harold and the French and Normans on plates 15–18.

[32] GG, 260. Bishop Wulfstan of Worcester also denounced the fashion of long hair: *Vita Wulfstani*, 23.

[33] Although this seems a strange and mostly incomprehensible description of Walter Giffard (II), lord of Long Crendon (Bucks) and Longueville-en-Caux (Normandy), earl of Buckingham, it is hard to think of another Giffard who might have had 30 squires for knighting.

[34] Gaimar, ll. 6077 ff. Although the story follows an account of the campaign in Maine in 1098, it precedes the news of Malcolm's death (1093) and the rebellion of 1095.

wanted to have thirty of his 'valets' (squires) dubbed knight by the king, but after he had been kept waiting a month for the ceremony he had the hair of himself and all his men cut short. 'They were the first valets ever to have their locks shorn.' When they eventually appeared before the king, he burst into mocking laughter at the strange sight; but when he took it in good part and accepted it as a *courtoisie*, some of his own squires imitated them, and in the end more than three hundred of those present had their heads shorn – and kept them so even after they had left the court.

Such a 'repentance' would have pleased the moralists who were denouncing the new luxury. Their own locks were mutilated by the tonsure – an unpopular disfiguration – and for a variety of reasons they considered hairiness in men of noble rank particularly degenerate. The provincial council of Rouen, held in February 1096 to promulgate the canons of the papal council of Clermont (November 1095), added an injunction that no man should wear his hair long, but should have a proper Christian cut: offenders should be excluded from the church and its sacraments, including Christian burial.[35] Anselm legislated against the outrage in Henry I's reign,[36] but although that king's somewhat selective puritanism may have restrained the new exuberance a little, it is clear that he himself followed some of the new fashions and that they had come to stay. In 1105 an unnamed English prelate wrote to Anselm complaining of the sad moral state of England during his exile.[37] Among other things he said that the laity, and above all the nobility, nearly always married a close relation,[38] and did this secretly; that the sodomites, whom Anselm had excommunicated in his great council (London, 1102), and the long-haired men, whom the following Easter, clad in pontificals, he had publicly debarred from entering the church, were now unmolested, for there was no one in the kingdom who dared act on Anselm's behalf and denounce all these things which were contrary to the law of God; and that the moral climate was now worse than ever. The king also was of this opinion.

Orderic 'reports' a great sermon preached to Henry and his court by the venerable Serlo, bishop of Sées, at Carentan in west Normandy, at Easter 1105, soon after the king had crossed to the duchy in order to wrest it from his brother.[39] The bishop opened with a lament on the miseries of the church under Robert's misgovernment and painted a grotesque picture of the duke's disorderly bachelor court (Sibyl had

[35] OV, v, 22.

[36] Westminster (1102), cap. 25. See *EC 1066–1154*, 129.

[37] Anselm, *Letters*, no. 365.

[38] The purpose was to reunite dispersed family estates, and, although the union was 'incestuous' and eugenically undesirable, it was widely practised.

[39] OV, vi, 60 ff.

3. Coloured miniatures
from British Library,
MS. Cotton Claud.
B VI (13th C.):

a. William the Conqueror
(fo. 119 verso)

b. William Rufus
(fo. 124).

4a. *Il volto santo*, The Holy Face of Lucca, in the cathedral church of St Martin, Lucca. (See here, 116–17.)

4b. *Il volto santo* on the reverse of a thirteenth-fourteenth-century silver grosso of Lucca. Inscription: +. S . VVLTVS . DE LVCA. (See *Corpus Nummorum Italicorum: Tuscania*, xi (Rome 1929), 73–4, types 7 ff.)

been dead two years). Robert relied on unworthy favourites; he wasted his substance on jesters[40] and harlots; and these, while he lay snoring in drunken sleep, even stole his clothes, so that when at last he awoke he had neither bread nor stockings, shoes or drawers, and had to remain naked in bed, unable to go to church.

The bishop then remarked in sorrow that he saw signs of degeneracy even in the congregation before him, for they were all wearing their hair long like women. That sin had been condemned by St Paul (1 *Corinthians* 11:14). Uncut hair was a penance enjoined on the sinful, and by imitating women they forfeited their manly strength. Long beards made them look like he-goats; and it was with filthy, goat-like lust that fornicators and catamites were vilely stained. They looked more like Saracens than Christians. They grew beards so that they would not prick the faces of their mistresses when they kissed them. In short, they had converted the squalor of penance into an instrument of lechery. They also wore the tails of scorpions on their feet, so that they were not only effeminate but also like poisonous snakes. They were too like those locusts described by St John in *Revelations* 9:7–10, who had the hair of women and the tails of scorpions. The bishop begged the king to set a good example, and, when he agreed, produced a pair of scissors and cut the locks of the king, the count of Meulan and most of the nobles. The rest of the royal household followed suit.

Nevertheless, the nobility continued to wear their hair long. Orderic tells how in 1124 the rebel Norman baron William Lovel, when captured in the battle of Bourgthéroulde, had his hair cut so that he could pass himself off as a squire and escape,[41] and relates that when Henry's nephew, Count William Clito, used to visit his young mistress she also washed his hair.[42] In 1128 all the count's knights cut off their locks at Oudenburg in Flanders before the battle of Axspoele, apparently as a sacrifice to God for victory.[43] William of Malmesbury, in his last historical work, *Historia Novella*, mentions that about 1130 a knight living near Malmesbury dreamt that someone was strangling him with his own tresses, and as a result cut them off. The fashion for short hair spread for a time among other knights, but a year later all courtiers were wearing it long again, just like women, and even wore a wig when necessary.[44] There can be no doubt, therefore, that in the late eleventh century long hair, beards and a new luxury in dress came into

---

[40] *Scurrae*: perhaps 'parasites'. For the various medieval meanings, see J.D.A. Ogilvy, 'Mimi, Scurrae, Histriones: Entertainers in the Early Middle Ages', *Speculum*, xxxviii (1963), 607–8 and ff.

[41] OV, vi, 352.

[42] OV, vi, 375.

[43] Galbert of Bruges, *Vita S. Caroli* in *ASS*, March, i, 216 E; Migne *PL*, clxvi, 1038 *ad fin*.

[44] *Hist. Nov.*, 6.

fashion in England and France. This could be regarded as degeneracy from the more austere habits of the Conqueror's court, but it was not directly connected, or indissolubly linked, with sodomy, as even its denouncers accepted. Some men dressed stylishly in order to please women, some to please themselves, some simply because it was the fashion.

It is difficult to know whether in the eleventh century there was an increase in the number of homosexuals or a greater effort on the part of the church to eradicate the sin. Medieval society, with its fostering of single-sex communities, especially the army and the monastic order, and the church with its insistence on celibacy and disgust at the 'animality' of women, produced conditions particularly favourable to homosexuality. The alarm, insofar as the church was concerned, was raised by the eremitical monk, St Peter Damian, in a tract, *Liber Gomorrhianus*, addressed to Pope Leo IX (1048–54).[45] He defined four kinds of sodomitical practice, from solitary masturbation to buggery, and claimed that they had all become widespread among the clergy and were being punished far too leniently (chapters 1 and 22). Sodomy, he declared, was contrary to the law of nature (chapter 14). 'Consider, wretched man, what darkness assails your heart, what dense cloud of blindness encloses you. Does the madness of lust drive you to the male sex? Does the fury of desire incite you towards your own kind, I mean man towards man? Does a he-goat driven by desire ever leap a he-goat? Does a ram lust madly for another ram? Surely a stallion grazing calmly and peacefully in the paddock with another stallion is not aroused until he sees a mare? Never does a bull seek to cover another bull; never does an ass bray with desire for another ass. And so these lost men do not fear to perpetrate what the most brutish animals shrink from with horror' (chapter 17). Sodomy, he declared (chapter 6), was worse than bestiality.

Peter could quote the Bible extensively in condemnation of the sin, but he was in some difficulty when he turned to its proper punishment. The Old Testament had prescribed stoning to death, but the councils, Fathers and popes had little to say on the matter, and the one class of canonical literature which pronounced in detail on this sin, the penitentials, was, in Peter's view, unauthentic and irrational, and completely beneath contempt. He cited the Penitential of Egbert, an English guide to confessors, only in order to point out all its faults (chapters 10 ff.).[46] In his judgment, clerks guilty of any of the forms of sodomy he defined should be deprived of their holy orders. But he asked

[45] Migne *PL*, cxlv, 159.
[46] Cf. *EC 1000–1066*, 269.

the pope to declare the correct penalties. Leo, in a reply prefaced to the tract, agreed that all clerks guilty of any of the varieties of sodomy should be degraded from their orders. But for mercy's sake those guilty of the less heinous forms, if they had been only infrequent sinners, gave up the practice, and repented, could be re-admitted to their former orders.

Peter Damian did not concern himself with the laity or consider any associated features, such as effeminacy in dress. Indeed, he made such uninhibited use of Samson and his locks (chapter 23) that he must have written before the changes in fashion. Anselm, however, was convinced that the vice was rampant at the English and Norman courts, and his view was shared by other observers. For example, Hugh abbot of Flavigny, who came on a papal mission to William II's court in 1096, told a nasty story about a clerk in the chapel royal.[47]

It is hard to believe that William's court could have been a hotbed of homosexuality without his connivance. But the near-contemporary charges against him are far from specific. He was accused of debauchery in general, and if the court harboured catamites, it was also thronged with harlots. Some thought him guilty of adultery, and the Welsh annals record that Henry was able to succeed his brother because Rufus had made use of concubines, and as a result had died childless.[48] Nevertheless, unlike the cases of Robert and Henry, no bastard children are mentioned in any of the sources; and this negative evidence cannot be disregarded. Since no one thought the king impotent, it is likely that he was either sterile or homosexual. Yet, on the other hand, no 'favourites' are named, and his baronial friends and companions were mostly married men. His faithful servant, Ranulf Flambard, who is usually associated by chroniclers with the king's misdeeds, was ostentatiously heterosexual. On the whole the evidence points to the king's bisexuality.[49] In his youth, like Robert, instead of contracting an honest marriage, he had recourse to prostitutes of all kinds; but, unlike his elder brother, he never changed his ways: he had no need to. It is indeed possible that when he fell seriously ill in 1093 and searched desperately

<hr />

[47] See below, 409.

[48] Annales Cambriae, ed. John Williams ab Ithel (Rolls ser., 1860), 30; Brut y Tywysogion, ed. the same (Rolls ser., 1860), 64–6. The words adulterium and adulter had, however, much wider meanings than their modern English derivatives.

[49] Cf. Wace's 'blue' story of William entering the two rivers of Cul and Con: below, p 403 n. 269. Emma Mason, 'William Rufus: myth and reality', Journal of Medieval History, iii (1977), 3, with a reference to C.N.L. Brooke, asserts that there is no positive evidence that the king was a homosexual. But this is special pleading; the chroniclers were in no doubt, and, although they are hostile and biased witnesses, there seems no reason why they should have invented this particular charge. J.S.P. Tatlock, The Legendary History of Britain (1950), 353–5, suggested that Geoffrey of Monmouth's homosexual kings, Mempricius and Malgo, were based on William.

for a remedy, Anselm, as part of his 'penance', suggested or imposed marriage, and that the patient accepted this with the other stipulations. If so, it was another of the promises he found it impossible to honour for the time being.[50] But Robert's case is monitory. Had William not been killed, he might have answered his older rival by taking a bride himself.

All the chroniclers charged William also with ill-treating the church, and there was a general belief that he was irreligious and profane. Once again the stories start with Eadmer. Anselm clearly disliked the king's company and suffered in several ways from his behaviour; and Eadmer reports various disputes between them in a manner intended to discredit the king. He makes the most of William's profanity. He reports that when Gundulf, the saintly bishop of Rochester, admonished the king in 1093 to continue to live a good life even though he had recovered from his near-fatal illness, William, inverting *Romans* 12:17, shouted, 'By the holy face of Lucca, I will not repay God with good for the evil he has done to me.'[51]

Eadmer also suggested that the king was sympathetic to Jews. He tells as hearsay the story, which he clearly did not believe, that William at Rouen accepted money from the local Jews to force some apostates to Christianity to return to their faith, and partly succeeded in his undertaking.[52] He adds the even more preposterous story of the young Jew who, after being accosted by the protomartyr Stephen, a converted Jew, and urged to follow his example and become a Christian, went to a priest, related the vision and was baptized. The youth's father then approached the king, who, when offered sixty marks (£40), agreed to order his son to return to him. When the youth was brought into the royal presence, these exchanges occurred:

> William: 'Your father complains that you have become a Christian without his consent. If this is so, I order you to return to his obedience without more ado and become a Jew again immediately.'
> The youth: 'You are surely joking, my lord king!'
> William: 'Me joke with you, son of filth? Get out of my sight right quick and carry out my order immediately, or, by the face of Lucca, I will have your eyes torn out.'
> The youth: 'No way will I do it. You know very well that if you were a good Christian you would never say things like that. It is the duty of a Christian to join to Christ those who are separated from him by unbelief, not to separate from him those who are joined to him through faith.'

[50] See below, 310 ff.
[51] *HN*, 39.
[52] *HN*, 99–101.

Whereupon the king, discomfited, loaded the youth with insults and had him thrown out. After the waiting father had been contemptuously repudiated by his son, he was ushered again into the king's presence. William said, 'I have done what you asked, now pay me what you promised.' The Jew protested that the king had done no more than confirm his son even more strongly in his apostasy, and said that he would only pay on results. The king retorted that he had done his best, and although he had not been successful, he wanted to be paid for his labour. And in the end the parties settled for half the agreed fee.

The Canterbury monk goes on to report,[53] again as hearsay, that the king at this time was so carried away by self-importance – elation of mind – that he could not bear that anything he ordered to be done should be qualified with 'God willing', for he wanted everything to be ascribed to his own action.[54] Such was his exaltation, it was said, that he believed, and said publicly, that no saint had any influence over God, and that therefore he had no wish, and no one in his senses would want, to call on St Peter or any other saint to come to his aid. With the growth of this confidence in himself he even came to disbelieve in God's judgment (the judicial ordeals), and, claiming that they were unjust, went so far as to maintain that God either knew nothing of what men did, or did not want to pass a verdict on them. As an example, Eadmer, possibly with Lot's fifty righteous men of Sodom (*Genesis* 18:24) at the back of his mind, told the story of how about fifty Englishmen of modest wealth, accused of having killed and eaten the king's deer (maybe on their own estates), were, when they denied the charge, through God's merciful judgment found innocent by the ordeal of hot iron. (Had they failed the ordeal they would have been at least blinded and castrated, perhaps even executed as a penalty.)[55] But when the king was told of their escape, he is said to have exclaimed angrily, 'What's this? God's a just judge? Damn him I say who believes that after this! I swear by — and — [Eadmer suppresses the oaths] that from now on things that can be bent at any man's nod shall be brought before my court, not God's.' Although belief in the pliability of God's judgment, supported by countless miracle stories, was widespread and certainly not heretical,[56] it was, Eadmer concludes, such stories and even worse ones, told of William by various men of by no means despicable reputation, which

---

[53] *HN*, 101–2.

[54] Cf. Gerald of Wales's story, possibly based on this, below, 324.

[55] *GR*, ii, 372. C. Petit-Dutaillis, *Studies and notes supplementary to Stubbs' Constitutional History*, ii (1915), 176–7, 191–5. See also below, 120.

[56] Cf. Gottfried von Strassburg (died *c.*1210), quoted by A.T. Hatto, *Tristan*, 248, 'Christ in his great virtue is pliant as a windblown sleeve. . . . He is at the beck of every heart for honest deeds or fraud.'

gave Anselm the desire to resign his archbishopric, for he knew that there could be no harmony between his way of life and the king's.

Eadmer scrupulously distances himself from the stories of the Jews and the forest offenders. He insists, however, that such anecdotes were current and were regarded by Anselm as at least characteristic. A man about whom such things were related could not have been religiously minded. William of Malmesbury included the story of the poachers in the first edition of *Gesta Pontificum*, but cut it out of the second and omitted it entirely from *Gesta Regum*. Nor did he make over much of William and the Jews.[57] In the first edition of *Gesta Regum* he omitted William's dealings with the Jews of Rouen and substituted a story concerning the Hebrew community in London, which the Conqueror had brought over from Rouen. On some feast day they presented Rufus with gifts, and he was so gratified by these that he even dared to incite the Jews to a contest with some Christians, declaring by the face of Lucca that if they won he would go over to their sect. In the second edition he introduced the Rouen episode, reduced to fifteen words, and expanded a little the London business. The king was only playful, he thought, in his threat to become a Jew. The Christians were some bishops and clerks, who entered the contest with trepidation, but they completely routed the Jews, although these claimed that they had been overcome more by partisanship (*factio*) than by rational arguments.

If the Malmesbury monk progressively weakened the impact of Eadmer's charge of irreligion, Orderic deprived it of its more colourful ornaments. As he delighted in good stories, this must have gone against the grain; but he thought William II such an improvement on Robert in Normandy, especially in his dealings with the church, that he gave no space to lampoons. All the same, he repeated the basic reproaches. He echoed William of Malmesbury in claiming that the son tried to imitate his father in some worldly directions:[58] for example, he pursued military valour and worldly splendour enthusiastically and gave himself too much to pride, lust and other vices. But as regards God, attendance at church and divine worship he showed no ardour at all. Orderic also made no secret of the king's oppression of the English church.[59]

Although it is likely that Eadmer's view of the king's treatment of Anselm is at the base of the whole legend of William's irreligion and that some of the monk's more vivid stories are merely *ben trovato*, it cannot be doubted that the pious considered the king guilty of various offences against the church, financial exploitation, neglect of his religious duties,

[57] *GR*, ii, 371; *GP*, 104–5 n.
[58] OV, iv, 110; cf. *GR*, ii, 359.
[59] For example, OV, v, 200 ff.

irreverence and addiction to profanity. But much of this was little more than the small change of the military world, and even if William was more than averagely spendthrift, he was not abnormal. '*Clericis laicos*' begins a famous bull of Boniface VIII issued in 1296: 'Laymen are notoriously hostile to clerks.' But we notice that William was on excellent terms with bishops of the highest reputation and was shunned by no one but Anselm. He would not have been the only man to be amazed at some of the acquittals secured by trial by ordeal; and in 1215 the church forbade the clergy to take any part in these procedures.[60]

Any suggestion that he was a pagan, a rationalist, or even a sceptic, is clearly absurd.[61] Although he was probably capable of most of the mockery enshrined in the Ruba'iyat of his contemporary, Omar Khayyam (1048–1131), the mathematician and poet from Nishnapur in north-east Persia, his pose was more bravado than cultured hedonism and disbelief. He seems always to have attended the great religious festivals for his crown-wearing. His behaviour in 1093, when he thought he was dying, shows that he intended to make a conventional Christian end; and at Christmas, probably in that year, when he had completely recovered, he made a generous grant to his recent enemy, William bishop of Durham, 'for the sake of his father's soul and his own'.[62] He had in fact since 1087 made several grants to monasteries for this purpose.[63] He was undoubtedly a long-standing patron and benefactor of Battle. He was remembered with gratitude at Rochester for his generosity to the church and his favour to Bishop Gundulf. He contributed in 1089 to the foundation of Bermondsey.[64] His doctor, Baldwin abbot of Bury St Edmunds, made grants for the salvation of his soul.[65] And William performed so great a service to Westminster that his deed was commemorated on a capital which was originally probably in an arcade in the cloister, one of the monastic offices which were under construction during the reign. Two of the three surviving sculptured scenes feature a parchment roll or panchart, in one scene held by Abbot Gilbert Crispin and two monks, in the other by the king, sitting uncrowned on an X-shaped throne and attended by the abbot and

[60] *EC 1066–1154*, 163–4.

[61] The most extreme position is in Hugh Ross Williamson, *The Arrow and the Sword* (1947).

[62] Craster, charter no. I.

[63] *Regesta, passim*. It is likely, however, that most gifts were sold.

[64] For Battle, see above, 63 n. 51, and below, 328. For Rochester, see *Vita Gundulfi* in *Anglia Sacra*, ii, 283–4. For Bermondsey, see above, 96.

[65] D.C. Douglas, *Feudal Documents from the Abbey of Bury St Edmunds* (1932), nos 103, 105.

another monk. In the third scene the abbot is officiating, with the text, 'Ego sum [? pastor bonus]' (*John* 10:11), visible on the service book.[66] It may be that William, as in the next case discussed, confirmed to Westminster a long string of earlier benefactions and that the carving commemorated some sort of 'founders day'.

William also showed considerable interest in St Peter's, Gloucester, a frontier establishment where Serlo, who had been a canon of Avranches and then a monk at Mont St Michel, was abbot throughout the reign. When William was lying ill there in 1093 he gave the monastery the church of St Gundley, Newport, and, probably on other occasions, other estates and privileges.[67] In 1095 he compelled Thomas of York to disgorge those estates which Archbishop Ealdred had taken from Gloucester before the Conquest. And in 1096, when he was squeezing the English church to raise the money for taking Normandy in pawn, he issued a splendid charter of the old type to the abbey, in which he confirmed a miscellany of grants made by him and his barons. These benefactors include Helias Giffard, Roger of Berkeley, Odo fitzGamelin, Winebald of Ballon, Bernard of Neufmarché, Geri and Gunnhildr of

---

[66] The capital, with one side 'chopped off', was discovered in 1807, re-used as a building stone in a wall surviving from an entrance gate to the Old Palace at Westminster, apparently built in 1484. It was sold to a collector, lost by 1831, and is known today only from the woodcuts made from William Capon's drawings and published in *The Graphic and Historical Illustrator* (1834), ed. E.W. Brayley, 87, and in Brayley and J. Britton, *The History of the Ancient Palace . . . at Westminster* (1836), 416, 445–6, pl. xxxv. See also here, pl. 12. For the history of the stone and commentaries, see *Gentleman's Magazine* (1831), i, 545; *The Graphic . . . Illustrator*, 87–8; Brayley and Britton, 446; R. Pierpoint, *Notes and Queries* (3 September 1910), 181; *Gilbert Crispin*, 35; W.R. Lethaby, *Westminster Abbey re-examined* (1925), 34–5. For the monastic offices, with a reconstruction by W.T. Ball, see R.D.H. Gem, 'The Romanesque rebuilding of Westminster Abbey', *Battle III*, and for the sculpture of the period, G. Zarnecki, 'Romanesque sculpture in Normandy and England in the eleventh century', *Battle I*. The capital can be dated to *c.* 1100 and put with others, about one cubic foot in size, which have been discovered in the abbey (Lethaby, figs 17–20), including one showing the Judgment of Solomon. The iconography of the scenes featuring the parchment roll can be compared with the picture in B.L. Cotton. MS Tiberius A 3, fol. 2b (dated *c.* 1050) of King Edgar granting the *Regularis Concordia*: reproduced in T. Symons's edition (Nelson's Medieval Texts, 1953) and elsewhere. The inscription on the capital has been read (*Gentleman's Magazine*) as: E: CLAUSTRU(M) ET REFE . . . . U(M) SUB ABB(AT)E GISLEB(ERTO) . . . . . . R[EG]E WILLELMO SECUN(DO), and considered to refer to the building of the cloister and refectory. Another possibility (my own suggestion), and one which has more relevance to the iconography, is: . . LAUS FU(N)[DATORIBUS] ET RELI(QUIIS)/[SANCTOR]U(M) SUB ABB(AT)E GISLE(BERTO)/[ET REGE] WILLELMO SECUN(DO). It is possible, of course, that one quarter of the original inscription is lost, at the beginning or end or after the first section. For help with the dating of the capital and other matters concerning it I am much indebted to George Zarnecki and Jeffrey West.

[67] *Hist. mon. Gloucest.*, i, 68, 102, 109, 115 (ii, 293), 123, 238–40; ii, 217.

Loges, Patrick *de Cadurcis*, Hugh of Port, Robert fitzHaimo, Ranulf Peverel (of Hatfield Peverel), Roger of Bully, Walter (sheriff) of Gloucester, Ernulf of Hesdin, Nigel of Oilli, Hugh of Lacy, William d'Aubigny and Roger Bigot.[68] Here the king is entirely identified with the well-being of this marcher abbey and joins with his men in its enrichment. If this type of record could safely be extended to other monasteries with fewer archives, we would get a very different picture of William's religious life. We should also notice that even if one of his protégés, Simon of St Liz (I), made his mark on the church only by being the father of St Waldef,[69] his closest friend, Robert fitzHaimo, was not only a benefactor of St Peter's, Gloucester, but also, with his wife, rebuilt Tewkesbury abbey in all its grandeur.[70]

This would seem a very respectable tally for thirteen years as king. Even a prudent man would not have considered it necessary, or even advisable, to make before the age of fifty special religious preparations for his own death. The Conqueror had founded St Stephen's, Caen, and Battle as imposed penitential duties. Henry I was to found Reading abbey at the age of fifty-three, after reigning for twenty one years, and Stephen Faversham abbey in 1148 when about fifty and in the thirteenth year of his reign. That William Rufus had made no major religious foundation at the age of forty is no proof that, given more time, he would not have done at least as much as his father.

The small trickle of Jews which followed the Normans from Rouen to London seems to have had no effect on the English money market or the royal finances before 1100. There is no evidence that either William used their credit facilities, and the immigrants had apparently not even reached Winchester by 1100.[71] As their safety depended entirely on the king, William Rufus would have had some financial dealings with them; and it is not impossible that he, like some others, could have been curious about their outlandish customs. The arrival of a few non-Christians aroused some theological interest, and their medical and magical lore exerted all the fascination of the forbidden and arcane. William's abbot of Westminster, Gilbert Crispin, wrote a tract on the subject, and his chancellor and bishop, Gerard of Hereford, was more criminally involved.[72] It is possible that the king discouraged proselytism, for he

---

[68] *Regesta*, no. LXIa, ii, 410. For Bernard of Neufmarché, whose gifts are omitted from the charter, see *Hist. mon. Gloucest.*, i, 80, 122, 124. He made a grant in 2 William II, possibly as reparation for his part in the western rebellion of 1088 and the burning of the abbey. For the other barons, see also *ibid.*, i, 63 ff., 122 ff.

[69] Barlow, *EC 1066–1154*, 209–11.

[70] *VCH Gloucester*, ii, 62.

[71] They are first noticed in Survey II (1148): *Winton Domesday*, 438.

[72] Barlow, *EC 1066–1154*, 247–8, 259–60.

would have been paid to protect the community from harassment; but to go further is to improve on Eadmer's credulity.

Eadmer, and those who followed him, reported the king's habitual oath, 'By God's face', or 'By the (holy) face of Lucca',[73] in neutral terms, and it should not be regarded as exceptionally outrageous. Oaths of this sort were in general use among the nobility. The Conqueror swore by God's resurrection or splendour,[74] Robert Curthose by the marvels of God,[75] Henry I by the death of Our Lord,[76] and Stephen by God's birth.[77] There were, it is true, bishops, and perhaps others, who avoided this profanity by using such expressions as 'Believe me';[78] but the laity were hard swearers. *Il volto santo, le seint Voult*, the holy face of Lucca, *le vo de Luche*,[79] was a wooden image of Christ in the cathedral church of St Martin at Lucca about which many marvellous stories were told.[80] It was supposed to have been carved by Nicodemus, who met Joseph of Arimathaea at Jesus's tomb (*John* 19:39), but with the face carved by an angel while Nicodemus slept – hence its name. Bought in the Holy Land by a Piedmontese bishop, and dispatched to Europe for reasons of secrecy in an unmanned boat, it made its own way to the port of Luna in Tuscany, where the bishop of Lucca, forewarned by a vision, was there to receive it on Good Friday 782. The bishop of Luna, who put in his own claim to this valuable wreck, was bought off with one of the two ampoules of the Sacred Blood which were hidden in the neck of the statue. This vial was transferred to nearby Sarzana in 1204, where it is still preserved in the chapel 'of the Sacred Blood'. The crucifix and the other ampoule were put in the church of St Frediano at Lucca and later moved to the cathedral of St Martin, where the statue is now housed in a free-standing eight-sided shrine of white marble, the work of Matteo Civitali in 1482–4, in the left aisle of the nave. It was shown on the coins of the commune of Lucca from the time of the Emperor Otto IV (early thirteenth century) onwards, and is mentioned by Dante (*Inf.* xxi, 48).[81]

The oak cross, more than 4 metres high, bears the 2.5-metre figure of

[73] 'Per vultum dei', *HN*, 116; *GP*, 104 n. 'Per vultum de Luca', *HN*, 101; *GR*, ii, 364, 373; *GP*, 83 n. 'Per sanctum vultum de Luca', *HN*, 39; *GP*, 80. The second form is also witnessed to in *De Injusta Vexatione*, 186, probably independently of the others.

[74] *GR*, ii, 336, 460; *Chron. Battle*, 27.

[75] 'De libertate Beccensis monasterii', J. Mabillon, *Annales Ordinis S. Benedicti*, v (Paris 1713), 636–7.

[76] *GR*, ii, 478.

[77] *Hist. Nov.*, 22, 39; *Vita S. Waldefi*, in *ASS*, August, i, 259 F.

[78] 'Crede mihi', e.g. Wulfstan, bishop of Worcester: *Vita Wulfstani*, 26, cf. 46, 61.

[79] Wace, l.9801.

[80] René Herval, 'En marge de la légende du Précieux-Sang – Lucques – Fécamp – Glastonbury', in *L'abbaye Bénédictine de Fécamp* (1959).

[81] See pl. 4.

Christ, dressed in a long robe with full sleeves, carved in cedar of Lebanon, and is now blackened with the smoke of candles. Its true origin is uncertain,[82] but it was an influential model. Luna and Lucca were on the route to Rome followed by generations of English and then Norman pilgrims.[83] Among the visitors were two abbots of Bury St Edmunds, Leofstan (1044–65) and his successor, Baldwin, the royal doctor, in 1070; and one result, it was believed, was the copying of the Holy Face for the rood-cross which surmounted the altar of St Peter in the Suffolk monastery.[84]

A possible clue to William's adoption of the oath is the correspondence between his father and Anselm (II) bishop of Lucca (1073–86), the celebrated canonist and Gregorian reformer, which occurred after Gregory VII's partial loss of Rome in 1083 and probably after Anselm's expulsion from Lucca. In a letter begging the Conqueror to come to Italy and help liberate Rome from the foreigners, the bishop thanked him for some service already rendered and offered to repay it as far as he could *secundum deum*.[85] After the loss of his see, Anselm had become spiritual director to the Countess Matilda of Tuscany, whom Robert Curthose apparently sought in marriage in the period 1083–7; and it is not impossible that the correspondence had arisen out of that business. It would also be in character for the king to have asked the bishop for a drop of the Holy Blood.

William Rufus's interest in the Lucchese relics could have been aroused by this diplomacy. However that may be, there is no great mystery or significance in the oath. For those who reported his words, the piquancy was in the contrast between the holiness of the object sworn upon and the profanity of the remark. No one, however, suggested that the king had deliberately chosen such a sacred and

---

[82] It has often been thought to have been of oriental origin, in accordance with the legend. But David Talbot Rice, 'The Iconography of the Langford Rood', *Mélanges offerts à René Crozet* (Poitiers 1966), i, 169–70, considers that, although the style of a long-sleeved robe, belted at the waist, may derive ultimately from Syria, the Lucca rood is unlikely to be earlier than the eleventh century. Since St Martin's was in ruins before Bishop Anselm I (1057–61) restored it, and, as Pope Alexander II, on 6 October 1070, rededicated it, the cross may have been provided by him, if only from St Frediano's. For the consecration and Abbot Baldwin's possible attendance, see A. Gransden, 'Baldwin, abbot of Bury St Edmunds, 1065–1097', *Battle IV*, 76.

[83] *EC 1000–1066*, 292, and map, 12–13. E. Mâle, *L'art religieux du XIIe siècle en France* (Paris 1922), 255 and figs 169–70, suggests that the diffusion of the style was through lead medallions taken home by pilgrims.

[84] *EC 1000–1066*, 21. For Baldwin and Lucca, see above, n. 82.

[85] Letter printed H. Sudendorf, *Berengarius Turonensis* (Hamburg and Gotha 1850), appendix, no. III, p. 237. It should be noticed that Odo of Bayeux was believed to be preparing to intervene in Italy in 1082: see above, 38. For Robert and Matilda of Tuscany, see above, 39.

revered object on which to swear in order to indulge in deliberate blasphemy. He was following the usual custom, although in an individual way. Perhaps even more mysterious is the oath that Eadmer always reduced to 'By this and that'. According to William of Malmesbury, in a passage he later suppressed, it was 'By the mountains and valleys', presumably a coarse *double entendre*.[86]

The pithy remarks of this soldier king were eagerly collected by contemporaries and passed around. It is just like that other great soldier, the duke of Wellington, in the nineteenth century. Both were plain speakers whose common sense sometimes seemed extraordinary to their hearers. The frankness of the king's egocentricity, his avoidance of cant and his uninhibited sallies could deeply shock. Anselm, another plain speaker, found them most distasteful. But they could also delight. Orderic Vitalis, in the several 'imaginary conversations' he devoted to the king, always gave him the best lines, even when William was engaged in repartee with the black and hirsute Helias of la Flèche, count of Maine, whom the chronicler admired so much. William, because he always did what he pleased and spoke what first came into his head, was full of surprises. This is one of the reasons why some of the monastic chroniclers who should have condemned his *mores* could not entirely conceal the fascination he exerted over them.

Plain speakers are not necessarily plain dealers; and William seems to have distinguished between different types of obligation. While Robert was considered faithless, because weak and pliable, William was renowned for his knightly word. Unquestionably he always observed safe-conducts, and it is likely that on campaign he could be relied on to behave honourably. He was outraged when tricked by others, as at Rochester in 1088, and although it could be argued that at the trial of the bishop of Durham in that year he himself came near to sharp practice against a trickster, the lawfulness of his behaviour was endorsed by the most distinguished arbiters of legality in the kingdom. He undoubtedly played a part in developing the knightly code of behaviour which became known as chivalry. In the observance of what may be called political engagements, however, he seems to have been less scrupulous. For example in 1093–4 he disregarded many of the promises he had made when close to death and was accused by both Malcolm king of Scots and Robert of being in breach of treaty obligations. But he was in a particularly defiant mood at that time, for he thought that he had been injured by God.[87]

Monastic chroniclers, however susceptible they might be to William's

---

[86] *GP*, 104 n., col. 2. Cf. *Ezzech*, 35:8, 36:4, 6.
[87] See below, 298.

attraction, also viewed him and his court with reservations. As well as the sexual excesses, there were the gaming and hunting. By the late eleventh century the church officially disapproved of both. Dicing was considered frivolous and time-consuming, and was associated with drinking and lechery. Hunting led to even greater evils. William was not unusual in his gambling or in his passion for the chase: Edward the Confessor, the Conqueror and Henry I were all mighty hunters; and hardly anyone thought it wrong to kill animals, even as sport. But the church disliked the harsh forest laws which preserved for the king the noble beasts of the chase and the vegetation which harboured them. The creation of the New Forest in Hampshire by William I was considered to have been oppressive and to have involved the depopulation of villages and the destruction of churches.[88] Besides, in a society which was rapidly becoming less barbarous, hunting was thought to be a low pursuit, unbecoming a philosopher king. Moreover, not completely without influence on the clerical attitude, was the fact that, although hunting was forbidden to clerks by canon law and bishops and abbots often found that their episcopal estates had been arbitrarily converted into royal forest,[89] clerks enjoyed no immunity from the forest law. In these circumstances it is not surprising that it was a common superstition that it was most unlucky to meet a clerk when on the way to the hunt. And it was said that there were huntsmen who taught their hounds to bark at collecting boxes (*truncus*) as though they were beasts of the chase.[90] The lay nobility naturally did not share all these ecclesiastical attitudes: they too had wild animals killed and hunted whenever they could; but they found the royal forest restrictive and oppressive, and Henry I, when he needed to curry favour with the magnates, renounced in his coronation charter all his brother's afforestations.[91]

John of Salisbury in his *Policraticus*, a book on the Commonwealth and its rulers written two generations later (completed in 1159), denounces both dicing and hunting when considering the pastimes of courtiers (*de nugis curialium*), and reveals the new attitude of the church. He was not

[88] This was largely a myth: cf. J.H. Round, *VCH Hants*, i (1900), 411–13. For the royal forest and its laws, see Petit-Dutaillis, *op. cit.*, and below, 230–1.

[89] For example, Abingdon abbey lost 4 hides of the village of Winkfield for the extension of Windsor forest: *Chron. Abingdon*, ii, 7. On the other hand, William II granted Malmesbury abbey custody of its own forests and decreed that no royal forester was to meddle in them: *Cartae Antiquae*, PR Soc. xxx (1960), no. 618, cf. 482–3. The abbot of Ramsey was allowed a more restricted privilege: no royal forester was to meddle in his wood except concerning the beasts and assarts: *Regesta*, no. 332.

[90] Hincmar of Rheims, *De divortio Lotharii et Tetburgae*, Migne *PL*, cxxv, 719.

[91] Cap.10, *SSC*, 119. He phrased it, however, in a positive form: by the common consent of his barons he was retaining his forests just as his father had had them.

excessively severe on the former.[92] An art in which the more skilful the performer, the greater his wickedness, was surely to be shunned. But if it relieved the heavy burden of the cares of state and provided a merry interlude without leading to other vices, it could be allowed. Hunting, however, he condemned root and branch, at length, and with every type of invective.[93] Some of the points he made were that huntsmen were half beasts, like centaurs, and with more than half of their humanity discarded, they behaved like monsters. Rarely were they modest, serious or chaste, and never sober. Would it not be shameful for a huntsman to aspire to rule a kingdom or a bishopric? And was it not therefore even more shameful for kings and bishops to lower themselves to the butchery and squalor of the huntsman? Who had ever heard of a holy hunter? Had the Augustines, the Jeromes, the Laurences or the Vincents ever been involved in this insanity? In history all huntsmen from Nimrod onwards had come to sticky ends. In our own time God's anger had struck down in a miraculous way several nobles when out hunting; and those who had chosen to live in a bestial manner had often found a bestial exit from this life. Nor had the hand of God even spared kings, but had taken condign and renowned vengeance for their evil doing. Their names, however, John thought it advisable to withhold.

He was equally severe on the forest laws. There were presumptuous men who dared, even in the sight of God, to claim as their private property and enclose within their own encircling net things that were by nature wild and should belong to all possessors of land. Even more remarkable, it had become a crime punishable by loss of property or of limbs, or even of life, to set snares for birds, knot nooses, entice by music,[94] or lay any sort of trap. Even the bees were forbidden to visit the flowers within the forest. There were men who, to avenge a wild beast and for the sake of an animal, subjected those made in the likeness of God to exquisite tortures, and did not shrink from shedding the blood of one whom the Only-begotten Son had redeemed with his own precious blood. John of Salisbury was engaged in a rhetorical exercise, and, although real indignation shines through his elaborate essay, his attitude has little in common with that of modern animal lovers or preservationists. Few men doubted that God had put wild animals on earth as food for man or that it was proper to destroy predators like foxes and wolves. John's diatribe was against the king's participation in butchery and his monopoly of this degrading and childish business, both of which had evil consequences.

[92] I, v (ed. Webb), i, 398 ff.

[93] I, iv (ed. Webb), i, 390 ff. Cf. F. Barlow, 'Hunting in the Middle Ages', *Trans. Devonshire Assoc.*, cxiii (1981), 1.

[94] Cato, *Disticha* (a standard school text), i, 27: 'the pipes play sweetly while the fowler lulls the bird'; cf. John of Salisbury, *Letters*, ii, 626–7.

Missing, however, from the moralist's indictment is much detailed information about what actually went on; and indeed there are no eleventh- or twelfth-century treatises on hunting and few pictorial illustrations which inspire confidence. This in itself suggests that hunting was still essentially for the pot and that the methods were basic and little affected by sophisticated ritual. But while there were many methods of killing wild animals, only some were considered suitable for noble hunters.

The flying of hawks against other birds and suitable prey was among the noble sports because of the cost of the falcons and the difficulties involved in their training and maintenance. The late Anglo-Saxon kings were devotees: Edward the Confessor delighted in hawks as well as in hounds,[95] and on the Bayeux Tapestry Earl Harold of Wessex is shown at the start of his mission to the Norman court riding with a hawk on his left hand.[96] In the late eleventh-century *Chanson de Roland*, an epic admired by the Normans,[97] the Muslim king Marsilion sent to Charlemagne among other rich gifts a thousand mewed (moulted) falcons, as well as leashes of greyhounds.[98] Falconers are mentioned in Domesday Book, and some shires had the duty of providing the king with birds, the value put on a hawk being £10, as against £1 for a packhorse.[99] Since some of the best birds were imported through the Wash from Iceland and Norway it was a sport which made an impression on the royal financial accounts.[100] The Angevin kings loved the sport, and under them existed a royal marshal of the hawks and a keeper of the falcons.[101] By that time the pastime was popular. In 1164 John of Salisbury met Philip of Alsace, count of Amiens and Vermandois, south of Douai, 'like all rich men' scouring the rivers, ponds and marshes with his hawk;[102] and in the twelfth-century romance *Tristan*, King Mark of Cornwall went hawking

[95] *VEdR*, 40.

[96] Bayeux Tapestry, pls 2, 5, 10, and here, pl. 16a.

[97] It was recited, or referred to, before the battle of Hastings, 'so that those about to fight should be animated by the military prowess of that man': *GR*, ii, 302.

[98] *Song of Roland*, lines 30–1, 128–9, pp. 52, 55.

[99] Falconers: Bernard, *DB*, i, 636; Eric, ii, 272; Godwin, 50d; Osbern, 49c. Renders, for example: Wiltshire, 64c; Worcestershire (a Norwegian bird), 172a; Leicestershire, 230a; Northamptonshire (£42 for hounds, £1 for a packhorse, £10 for a hawk, £1 for a hunter), 219a. These, of course, were traditional, not newly imposed, renders.

[100] Cf. the entries in the Pipe Roll of 1129–30 under Lincolnshire: Outi of Lincoln had undertaken to provide the king with 100 Norwegian falcons (4 to be white) and 100 gerfalcons (6 to be white); he had produced 8 grey Norwegian falcons and 25 grey gerfalcons, and owed the rest: *PR 31 H.I*, 111. Ralf fitzDreux owed the king 3 hawks and 4 gerfalcons as a relief for his father's land: *ibid.*, 121.

[101] Round, *King's Serjeants*, 303 ff. For Henry II's interest in hawking, cf. Arnulf of Lisieux, *Letters*, no. 15, p. 20.

[102] John of Salisbury, *Letters*, no. 136, ii, 2–4.

for cranes.[103] But there is a curious lack of evidence for the interest of the Norman kings. Their practice of the sport seems never to be mentioned; nor are the royal mews and its servants listed in the *Establishment of the King's Household*, a schedule of the officers and their pay drawn up for Stephen of Blois at the beginning of his reign (1135), which takes us back at least to the early years of Henry I's government.[104] Perhaps hawking was an English taste which had less appeal to the rougher Norman nobility.

Kings employed huntsmen, foresters and parkers to manage their forests. These produced venison for the king's larder and for distribution to royal friends, servants and charities, and exploited the vert, the timber and the other products and resources of woodland. They caught animals by the most efficient methods available, using traps, snares, nets, pits and other enclosures into which the game blundered or was driven by dogs, and then killed, usually with the knife. In Ælfric's *Colloquy*, written about 1000, the king's huntsman explains that he hunted various kinds of deer, wild boars and occasionally hares in two different ways. In the first, his hounds drove the animals into nets which he had set up and where he cut their throats. In the second, he just pursued the quarry with swift dogs. Boars, however, were driven up to him by his hounds, and he killed them in an unspecified but courageous way. All the game he caught he delivered to the king, who in return fed and clothed him and from time to time gave him a horse or a piece of jewelry.[105] In the romance *Tristan*, the hero, when banished from King Mark's court at Tintagel and living as an outlaw in the forests and moorlands, was secretly provided with food by the royal forester, Orri, who caught wild boars and sows in his nets, and in his enclosures (*haie*) trapped all kinds of deer.[106] While Queen Yseut (Isolde), Mark's wife, had been with him, he himself had hunted deer for their food, like a poacher tracking his prey on foot with his dog, Husdant, a brachet or bercelet,[107] who followed by scent and whom he taught to hunt without giving tongue (as was required of a lymer).[108] Tristan shot the

[103] *Tristan*, 156.

[104] *Constitutio*, 129 ff. A translation in Hubert Hall, *Court Life under the Plantagenets* (1890), 242 ff., is even less reliable. For further commentaries, see Round, *King's Serjeants*, 268 ff., and White, 'The household', 127. Hall, 249, translated *mueta regis* (the king's pack of hounds) as 'the king's mews', which would indeed explain the 8d a day it received. *Muta* (mew) and *mota/mueta* are easily confused; but it appears unlikely that the mews should appear in the list in the middle of the hunt.

[105] *Ælfric's Colloquy*, ed. G.N. Garmonsway (1939), 23–6.

[106] *Tristan*, 114, ll. 3019–3022.

[107] Husdant is usually called a brachet, e.g. ll. 1440, 1457, 1501, 1539, 1541, 2696; but twice he is called a bercelet, ll. 1551, 2697.

[108] For which, see below, 127.

harboured animal with his bow and arrow; but rarely was the first strike fatal, and the wounded animal had to be followed, sometimes for hours.[109]

Hunting as practised by royalty, the nobility and the military aristocracy, although it also had some utilitarian and economic aspects, was regulated by different sets of conventions. Three main types of hunting may be distinguished: the training of boys in military field-craft[110] instilled the life-long habit of casual hunting whenever the opportunity occurred; the formal hunt, which consisted in following on horseback a pack of hounds; and the even more elaborate 'stable', shooting dismounted at butts with bows and arrows at driven deer.

It was usual when travelling or on the march for the king and his friends, and probably for other small parties, perhaps each man taking his own hunting dogs, to go in pursuit of whatever game was put up;[111] and it was a common recreation for garrison and household troops to go riding in the forest with similar intent. Once men of Bishop Ranulf Flambard's household, when out hunting in his forest of Finchale by the River Wear, in which he had established the hermit Godric, sighted a superb stag, uncoupled their hounds, and set off in pursuit, only to find that the stricken deer had taken refuge in Godric's hut and have it denied to them by the hermit.[112] One of the Conqueror's elder sons, Richard, was killed while riding in the New Forest and 'perforating stags', possibly through collision with the low branch of a tree;[113] and his grandson, another Richard, Duke Robert's son, died in the same forest, either shot through the neck by an arrow or caught by the throat by an overhanging branch.[114] On some of these occasions it may have been left to the hounds to pull the deer down, even if the huntsman gave the *coup de grâce*. On others the hunters shot at the beasts with their bows. William the Conqueror is said to have had such powerful arms and shoulders that he could draw a bow which no one else could bend while spurring on his steed.[115] Shooting from the back of a fast-moving horse, even though the saddle and stirrups were designed to keep the rider in place, was the most difficult and probably most dangerous kind of hunting. On the evidence of the Bayeux Tapestry, the reins were never released when fighting with spear or sword.

[109] *Tristan*, 76 ff. He also invented a mechanical bow, called 'Fail-not', which was 'triggered' by the deer, 87.

[110] For which, see above, 23.

[111] Cf. Anselm's boys chasing a hare: *VA*, 89; below, 373.

[112] *Vita S. Godrici*, 365–6, cf. 66. For Henry I's confirmation of Ranulf Flambard's hunting rights in Northumberland and Durham, Craster, no. XXV, 52.

[113] See above, 13.

[114] *GR*, ii, 332–3.

[115] *GR*, ii, 335.

There were also more organized hunting expeditions using established packs of hounds and an elaborate structure of servants. In
England in this period we know only of the royal hunt, and it is unlikely
that even all the earls had similar hunting establishments. In a satirical
passage, John of Salisbury ridiculed the deployment of great armies of
men and dogs against poor little creatures like the timid leveret: 'and if
their endeavour should earn the glittering prize of a more illustrious
prey, perchance a stag or a wild boar, there is a quite intolerable
hullabaloo: the hunters go mad with joy; the head of the victim and
other appointed spoils are borne before the conquerors; and you would
think it was the king of Cappadocia who had been captured'.[116] In the
fourteenth-century poem, Sir Gawain and the Green Knight, of the three
hunts which are described, the pursuit of the wild boar and of the fox is
made in this way.[117] The animals protected by the royal forest laws were
the red deer (hart and hind), fallow deer (buck and doe), roe deer and
the wild boar.[118] The Norman kings appear to have preferred to hunt
stags of the red deer and it would seem unlikely that they chased hares,
foxes, wild cat or other small beasts except on informal occasions.
Although almost all these animals produced in season valuable pelts and
useful 'grease', and were certainly not despised as game,[119] kings
probably thought that they should normally be concerned only with the
noblest beasts. Nor is there much evidence about actual boar hunts,
although the wild pig was the fiercest quarry available in England and,
since it was dispatched by the dismounted hunter with spear or sword,
provided a true test of courage. Tristan was wounded in the leg, and
incapacitated for some time, by a large tusker,[120] but he was a hero of
romance.

In Edward duke of York's treatise on the royal hunt, written at the
beginning of the fifteenth century and largely translated from Count
Gaston de Foix's Livre de Chasse, this following of hounds by mounted
men is called 'hunting by, or with, strength'; and in an original chapter,
based obviously on his own experience, he describes the organization in
detail.[121] Although the royal hunt in the fifteenth century was probably

[116] Policraticus, I, iv (ed. Webb), i, 22–3. Cf. Horace, Epist., I, vi, 39.
[117] Gawain, 74 ff., 84 ff. In Alexander Neckam, De Naturis Rerum, ed. T. Wright (Rolls
ser. 1863), 204–5, the wiles of the hunted fox are described.
[118] C.R. Young, The Royal Forests in Medieval England (1979), 4. See further, J.C. Cox,
The Royal Forests of England (The Antiquary's Books, 1905); O. Rackham, Ancient
Woodland (1980).
[119] Gaston de Foix in his Livre de Chasse, started in 1387, followed by Edward duke of
York in his The Master of Game, included the hare, wolf, fox, grey badger, wild cat and
otter, as well as the reindeer, chamoix, ibex, bear and rabbit, which Edward omitted.
[120] Tristan, 63.
[121] The Master of Game, cap. xxxv.

much more elaborately arranged than it had been in the eleventh, it contained the same types of hound and servant, usually with the same names, and can be employed with caution to elucidate the brief inventory of hunt servants and hounds contained in the *Establishment of the King's Household* of 1135, which is not without its difficulties and has been variously interpreted.[122]

There is no mention in the *Establishment* or in Domesday Book of a Chief Huntsman or anyone equivalent to the Master of Game. And although it is possible that the most important of the huntsmen entered as landholders in the Survey could have been such an official, these seem to have been primarily local servants.[123] On the evidence of the *Establishment*, it looks more likely that in 1135 the hunt attached to the court was under the command of the constable or of the marshalsea.[124] The other hunt servants in 1135 were knight huntsmen at 8d a day (the normal pay for a knight), whippers-in[125] at 5d, huntsmen of the harriers at 3d, mounted huntsmen of the wolfhounds at an unspecified rate, twenty serjeants at 1d a head and four horn-blowers at 3d each. By the fifteenth century there was an elaborate ritual of hunting calls,[126] some of which may have gone back to much earlier times. There were also in 1135 an unspecified number of men who carried the king's bow, paid 5d a man per day; some other archers at the same rate; and Bernard, Ralf

[122] See above, 122 n. 104.

[123] Chetel (his father served King Edward), *DB*, i, 36d; Cola, 50b, ? 63c, ? 73d (his father's land); Croch, 49a, 74c; Edward, 84d; Edwin, 50c (given him by King Edward); Godric, 74a; Godwin, 84b; ? Harding (held T.R.E.), 74a; Siward, 160d; Turbert, 51c, 74c; Ulric (his father served King Edward), 50d, 74a–b, 84b; Ulviet, 50c, 52c, 74b, 84b; Waleran, 48b, 51c, 72a, 82b; Wulfwi (held T.R.E.), 36c. Waleran and Ulviet were well endowed and could have been chief huntsmen. The latter was dead by 1130 leaving an heir under age. The sheriff of Hampshire owed £118 for the custody of his heir: *PR 31 H I*, 37. For Waleran, see also Round, *VCH Hants*, i, 424. Croc witnessed royal charters.

[124] For which, see below, 151.

[125] *Revised Medieval Latin Word List* (Latham), following Ducange, who followed Hearne, explain *catator* as 'cat-hunter *or* ? hunter'. Johnson (*Dialogus*) thought, possibly correctly, that it was a back formation from *chasseur*, and rendered it 'huntsman'. In *Gawain*, l. 1139, *cacheres* coupled their hounds in the kennels, called them out, and blew on their horns: Tolkien and Gordon, 51, translated it as 'kennel-men', Stone, 46, as 'hunters'. In *The Master of Game*, however, grooms called *chacechiens* (dog-chasers) help the berners to bring up the hart-hounds, 248, cf. 177, and, as they seem to be the subordinates of the berners, would have been connected with the harriers or main pack. Baillie-Grohman does not explain the term in either the appendix or the glossary. 'Whipper-in' would seem to be the modern equivalent.

[126] Edward of York did not honour his promise (p. 170) to devote a chapter to 'blowing', but he describes the horn, cap. xxii, and mentions *passim* the hunting calls: see *The Master of Game*, appendix, *s.v.* Horns, Hunting music, and cf. Hunting cries. Roland's famous horn was called *Olifant* (*Song of Roland*, ll. 1059, 1070, etc.), which signifies a horn made of an elephant's tusk.

the Robber, and their fellows, each paid 3d a day for undefined services.
The reference here is to the ordinary bow (*arcus, archearius*), not the
crossbow. William II had crossbowmen at court: in 1088 Helpo went
with the steward Ivo Taillebois to receive the surrender of Durham
castle;[127] and *arbalistarii*, who may have been garrison, rather than
household, troops, are listed in Domesday Book.[128] Nevertheless, the
terms usually used by the chroniclers of this period when mentioning the
chase make it quite clear that hunters, whether mounted or on foot, used
exclusively the bow drawn by the arm.[129] King Mark and Tristan
had bows made of tough laburnum wood, and the knight, when on the
alert, usually carried two arrows in his hand.[130]

Henry I seems to have had three distinct packs of hounds at court:[131]
the king's pack; the untitled main pack, which may have been known as
the harriers; and the wolfhounds.[132] The last was fixed at twenty-four
running dogs and eight greyhounds; and the livery for the whole section
was 20d a day, with £6 a year (£8 was claimed) for the purchase of horses.
If the hounds were allowed 10d a day, that left only as much for the men,
which seems a small allowance for the six or eight servants envisaged.
But since the wolf-hunt had a short history in England owing to the
extinction of its quarry, it cannot be discussed in the light of later
evidence.

Although there are ambiguities, it would seem that there were at least
four categories of hunting dog in the royal kennels in 1135. These were

[127] See above, 89.

[128] (*ar*)*balistarius* covers a wide range of technicians, from the workers of siege engines
to the handlers of a crossbow. Some other terms used in *DB*, e.g. *ingania*, i, 160c, 207b,
219a (Richard and William), *ingeniator*, Waldin, 365c, *machinator*, 52a (Thurstin), and
artifex, ii, 269b (Rabel), may designate different skills; but these men often occur in
conjunction with crossbowmen. For these, see Berner, ii, 267b–268b; Gilbert, ii, 268b,
444–444b; Nicholas, i, 117b, 238a, 244b; Odard, 36d; Odo, 298b, 329d, 365d; Rainald,
ii, 97b; Ralf, ii, 269, 445; Robert, ii, 269; Walter, i, 169a; and Warin, 74d. Odo was the
most important of these: Sanders, *Baronies*, 78. He was dead by 1115–18, leaving no heir
of his body; his lands passed to Amfrey (I) de Chancy, who may have been a nephew.

[129] It is only OV, with his use of *catapulta* as an elegant variation for *sagitta*, who
confuses the matter: cf. v, 282, 288, where *sagitta* is interlined.

[130] *Tristan*, 77, 147.

[131] The hunt described was certainly part of the court, but whether it was fully
itinerant or was moved from time to time to convenient centres where kennels were
ready, is not indicated. It is allotted no transport in the *Constitutio*.

[132] The wolf-hunters and their horses, men and dogs are listed separately and cause no
trouble in this respect. The other distinction has not been made before, and depends on
associating the brach-keepers (*braconarii*) with the king's pack (*mueta regis*). The rest of
the servants and hounds, including the huntsmen of the harriers (*venatores del harred*) are
then assigned to the main pack. But even if this construction is correct, the elements may
have been variously assembled according to circumstances.

not distinct breeds, about which almost nothing is known, but divisions according to function. They were the lymer or leash-hound, led by a lymerer; brachets with their brach-keepers; harriers under the charge of berners; and greyhounds looked after by fewterers.[133] The running dogs of the wolf-hunters would have been similar to the harriers and brachets. The main distinction was between greyhounds and the rest. Brachets or bercelets were primarily shooting dogs, which hunted by scent, and were trained to discover and move the game usually for the individual hunter or a small party.[134] In 1135 brach-keepers were paid 3d a day, and if the 8d a day for 'the king's pack'[135] is the allowance made for the keep of the brachets, these would have been the king's personal dogs.

In the main hunt the function of the brachet was divided between the lymer and the harriers. The lymer, a scenting dog held on a long liam or leash (in the fifteenth century three-and-a-half fathoms long), had the task of searching out the game before the hunt moved off at dawn. The dog and its leader tracked a beast to its lair or den, harboured it, and prepared to move it out when the hunt was ready. It could also be used at later stages, whenever its skills were required.[136] In 1135 the lymer was allowed ½d a day and its leader 1d. The pack of hounds which then took up the chase, and likewise followed by scent, were the harriers or running dogs, which later could be called raches and were similar to the brachets.[137] In 1135 there seem to have been great hounds in leashes of four and small hounds in leashes of six,[138] with an allowance of 1d per leash. Edward of York preferred raches coloured brown tan.[139] In the

---

[133] Cf. William's Norman writ, from the latter part of his reign, addressed to F the fewterer and Isenhard the berner, who exact the old Carolingian tax, bernage, and were, no doubt, the kennelmen in charge of the greyhounds and harriers respectively: Haskins, *NI*, 82. For the tax, see Bates, *Normandy before 1066*, 153.

[134] *The Master of Game*, appendix, 204, *s.v.* Bercelet. For useful references, see *Dict. of Med. Latin from British Sources*, *s.v. bersellettus, brachettus, braconarius*.

[135] On the assumption that *mueta regis* means this, and not the royal mews: see above, 122.

[136] *The Master of Game*, caps xv, xxiii, xxvi, xxxiv, and *passim*; appendix, *s.v.* Limer. At the trial of Bishop William of Durham in 1088 the admiring barons called Lanfranc, 'vetulus ligaminarius': see above, 87, and *EC 1066–1154*, 286.

[137] *The Master of Game*, cap. xiv and *passim*; appendix, *s.v.* Rache and Running hounds. In the *Constitutio* they are referred to as [hounds] *del harred*, which Hall translated 'hart'. Johnson, 135 n. 6, seems to have regarded *harred* as a variant of *harde*, a cord or leash, and so a trained pack of hounds on leash. Round, *King's Serjeants*, 284 ff., successfully associated it with 'harrier', which lexicographers derive, with some hesitation, from 'hare', although Baillie-Grohman would derive it from O.E. *hergian*, to ravage or harry.

[138] This, I think, is how Round, *op. cit.*, 288, understood the passage. Hall, 249, gave, (the huntsmen) 'of the great hart and of the small hart'. Johnson preferred, although he did not refer to Round, 'the great leash . . . and the small leash'.

[139] *The Master of Game*, cap. xiv, 105–6, for a physical description.

later Middle Ages these were in the charge of berners,[140] and berners duly appear in the *Constitution* with a livery of 3d a day.

Finally there were the greyhounds, the noblest dogs and usually to be found in the company and thoughts of kings and nobles.[141] They, of course, hunted by sight, and in the medieval hunt were usually released in relays of two or three couple, posted in advance along the expected line of the chase and slipped when the quarry and the hounds already chasing it had passed.[142] As they were required to kill or hold the fiercest and strongest game, they were probably, although of mixed kinds, in general closer to the rough Irish wolfhound or Scottish deerhound than to the smooth and more elegant courser. Even if their name in English is not derived from grey (in Latin and French it is associated with the hare), hounds of a light colour were the most prized, although Gaston de Foix preferred those coloured red fallow with a black muzzle.[143] Their handlers, the fewterers, in 1135 received 3d a day for themselves, 2d for each of their men and $\frac{1}{2}$d for each of their hounds.

There are a few scenes from the sporting life on the Bayeux Tapestry, designed in the 1070s, which give us a view of hunting, but seemingly only in its more informal and professional aspects. Earl Harold is shown riding to Bosham not only carrying a hawk but also with hounds running ahead, first a couple of small dark dogs (probably brachets), then three larger lighter-coloured ones, wearing collars with prominent leash rings (probably greyhounds) (plates 2, II).[144] When the party embarks, two nobles, one perhaps Harold, carry hounds, again wearing collars, in their arms through the water to the ship (plate 5). Scenes from the hunt also occur in the margins, but with less detail because of the smaller scale. In a wolf-hunt, two men on foot, with batons in both hands, follow two couple of free running dogs, their heads raised, and so perhaps greyhounds (plate 8). In a stag-hunt two large hounds, one with

[140] *The Master of Game*, 148, 177, where there is mention of yeomen berners on foot and grooms called *chacechiens* (see above, 125 n. 125). For the development of the word from bran, out of which dog-biscuits were made, see appendix, *s.v.* Berner. There are also some useful references, *s.v. bernagium, bernarius, bernator*, in *Dict. of Med. Latin from British Sources*. For bernage, see above, 127 n. 133. Round, *op. cit.*, 271, regarded the berner as in charge of the 'ordinary' hounds, by which he meant the harriers: Johnson, however, preferred to regard him as a 'feeder of hounds'.

[141] *The Master of Game*, cap. xv and *passim*; appendix, *s.v.* Greyhound. For their special esteem, cf. *Song of Roland*, 55, 79, 149; *Tristan*, 146, l. 4372: a baron riding with two large greyhounds (*levriers*).

[142] *The Master of Game*, cap. xxxiv and *passim*; appendix, *s.v.* Relays.

[143] *Ibid.*, 113.

[144] Here, pl. 16a. Round, *op. cit.*, 269, saw a couple of running dogs (i.e. harriers) followed by a leash of the great hounds, by which he meant here greyhounds (*leporarii*), 'distinguished by their long legs, their powerful hindquarters and the collars about their necks'.

a collar, pull down the quarry while a dismounted huntsman, with a couple of smaller dogs on leash and a similar couple in front, blows his horn (plate 14). Again none of the dogs has his nose to the ground; but only the first couple are undoubted greyhounds.

Besides the chase 'in strength', the other main method of hunting in vogue among the nobility throughout the Middle Ages was the shooting of driven and sometimes coralled animals. In eleventh- and twelfth-century documents concerning forests and hunting, the words *deorhege* and *saete*, or, in Latin, *haia* and *stabilatio* (with variants), are frequently found in association. The former means a (deer)-hedge, and, by extention, an area enclosed by hedges, the latter a camp or enclosed place. In the eleventh century in many contexts the two seem to be synonymous or very alike. The main difference between them would appear to lie in the former being a permanent compound created by growing trees which had to be lopped once a year, while the latter was built of timber, constructed out of nets, or even largely composed of human beaters converging to make a closed circle, and was as much an occasion as a fixed place.[145] In Edward of York's treatise, however, *stabilatio*, translated as 'stable', is either one of those stations, usually on the boundaries of the area being hunted, where men and hounds were placed for driving the game towards the archers and preventing it escaping, or one of the stands or trysts where the noble archers were posted.[146]

The eleventh-century usage is well illustrated. In 1086 on the manor of Lingen in Herefordshire there were three 'hedges for catching the roebuck', and in neighbouring Lye two.[147] At Kington in Worcestershire was a hedge in which wild animals were caught,[148] and at Corfton in Shropshire a hedge for catching roebuck.[149] Some of these were very large, perhaps entire woods. For example at *Donnelie* in Warwickshire, perhaps in Hatton, was a hedge half a league square.[150] And men sometimes claimed a part of a hedge: for instance at Marston Moretaine in Bedfordshire, Erfast claimed half a hedge (*sepes*) which had pertained to the manor in his predecessor's time.[151] There may be a difference here between the customs of the east and west Midlands. The larger hays can

---

[145] Vinogradoff, *English Society*, 292, regarded the *haia* as the permanent hedges round a wood and the *stabilatura* as temporary hedges built during the hunting season for drives. Cf. also above, 122.

[146] *The Master of Game*, cap. xxxvi and appendix, *s.v.* Stable.

[147] *DB*, i, 260b. There is a useful map of forest and hays in Young, *op. cit.*, 9.

[148] *DB*, i, 176c.

[149] *DB*, i, 256c.

[150] *DB*, i, 240a. Vinogradoff for the location.

[151] *DB*, i, 211c.

be likened to whole woods which had been enclosed, as at Shell in Worcestershire and at Windsor in Berkshire.[152] But in the Welsh marches they were clearly only a part of a wood. At Rushock in Herefordshire, which Earl Harold had held, was a *haia* within a large wood.[153] And not entirely dissimilar was the park for wild animals at Hollow Court, Worcestershire, which was but a fraction of the wood.[154]

Two eleventh-century Anglo-Saxon treatises associated with the diocese of Worcester list the duties of thegns, geneats, cottiers and the reeve towards the maintenance of royal deer-hedges. These had to be pruned after Christmas, and the geneat had also to build and maintain *saete*.[155] In Domesday Book it is recorded that some thegns in South Lancashire had duties just like villeins at the king's residences and their appurtenancies, such as fishponds and, in the woods, *haiae* and *stabiliturae*.[156]

Some communities also had duties at these enclosures when the king arrived to hunt. Twelve of the better burgesses of Shrewsbury provided the watch when the king slept in the city, and burgesses who owned horses guarded him when he went hunting. Also the sheriff sent thirty-six footmen to the enclosure for as long as the king was there, but to the park at Marsley, some eight miles south-west of the town, the same number for eight days only.[157] It was the custom at Hereford when the king went to hunt for one man from each household to go to the enclosure in the wood.[158] Perhaps this duty was much more widespread, and it is the Domesday record which is defective, for among the customs of Berkshire is included the 50s penalty owed to the king for neglect of a summons to the enclosure for the hunt (or venison),[159] and the *Laws of Henry I* include non-attendance at enclosures as one of the pleas of the forest.[160]

On this evidence it must have been a common method of hunting to have deer driven into an artificial enclosure of some sort so that they could there be killed (the battue). Henry I about 1115 granted by

[152] *DB*, i, 176b, 56d. Cf. below, 131 n. 161.
[153] *DB*, i, 185c.
[154] *DB*, i, 180c.
[155] *Rectitudines*, caps. 1,1; 2; 3,4; *Gerefa*, cap. 12: Liebermann, *Gesetze*, i, 444–6, 453. Cf. also Bishop Oswald of Worcester's *Indiculum Libertatis*, printed B. Thorpe, *Diplomatarium Anglicum* (1865), 263, for the vassals' duty of finding men to build the bishop's *venationis sepes* and, on request, sending their own *venabula* (? hunt-servants or hounds) to the bishop's hunt.
[156] *DB*, i, 269d.
[157] *DB*, i, 252a (*stabilatio*).
[158] *DB*, i, 179a (*stabilitio*).
[159] *DB*, i, 56c (*stabilitio*).
[160] *Leges Henrici Primi*, cap. 17, 2, p. 120 (*stabilita*).

charter to the church of Salisbury the tithe of venison in certain forests, except that which was taken in enclosures in the forest of Windsor;[161] and a probably apocryphal story told by William of Malmesbury about Edward the Confessor throws further light on the subject. The king was enraged one day when out hunting to discover that a rustic had disturbed those enclosures in which deer were driven into nets (casses) – but confined his anger to swearing.[162] When King Arthur visited King Mark of Cornwall the knightly guests either went jousting or pursued stags in the meadows, beasts which would seem to have been coralled for their sport.[163] On another occasion King Mark waited on horseback on the moor near Tintagel at a clearing which peasants had burnt for him, and listened to his hounds giving tongue in the distance, but left before they and the huntsmen appeared.[164] Presumably he was stationed to shoot at the deer they were driving before them into the clearing. In Reginald of Durham's *Life of St Godric* is a description of a large glade or circus near Finchale in the bishop's forest north of the city which teemed with wild animals. It was called 'the royal enclosure' (saepes regia) because it was in the form of a crown encircled on every side by woods, and, as befitted a king, lay reclining at ease, watching without any hindrance all the serious business of the sportsmen displayed before its eyes. Hence anyone wishing to see the conduct of the hunt could in that place without any exertion at all follow with his eyes all the tracks of the wild animals and clearly observe the rapid movements of the hounds.[165]

The first day's sport in *Sir Gawain and the Green Knight* provides an elaborate description of this kind of hunt, and although of the fourteenth century, seems to do no more than round off the earlier evidence.[166] It was Christmas, which was in the close season for male deer,[167] the

---

[161] *Register of St Osmund*, ed. W.H. Rich Jones (Rolls ser. 1883), i, 201; papal confirmation, *Sarum Charters and Documents*, ed. the same (Rolls ser. 1891), 12 (*stabilia*). Cf. also above, 130 n. 152.

[162] *GR*, i, 236 (*stabulata*).

[163] *Tristan*, 139.

[164] *Ibid.*, 115–17.

[165] *Vita S. Godrici*, 63.

[166] *Gawain*, 64 ff., 71–2. Edward of York devoted his last chapter to 'Of the ordinance and the manner of hunting when the king will hunt in forests or in parks for the hart with bows and greyhounds and stable': *The Master of Game*, cap. xxxvi and appendix, s.v. Reseeyvour, Stables, Tryst.

[167] John of Salisbury, *Policraticus*, I, iv (ed. Webb), i, 23, seemed to think that, although there was hunting all the year round, there was no blowing of horns from the eighth degree of Capricorn until Gemini (? January until June), unless a wolf, or perchance a lion, tiger or leopard was the prey, which, thank God!, were rare in our parts. According to later rules, the close season for male deer was 14 September to 24 June, while females were hunted from 14 September to 2 February: Stone, *Gawain*, 177. Baillie-Grohman, *The Master of Game*, appendix, s.v. Seasons of Hunting, gives a more elaborate calendar.

company was, as usual, up before dawn, and the lord, like Edward the Confessor long before him,[168] heard Mass and then breakfasted while the kennelmen and huntsmen made preparations to drive the hinds. Fewterers and their leashes of greyhounds went with the beaters to their stations on the hill tops (Edward of York's 'stables') in order to drive down and keep in position the deer which brachets and raches (both hunting by scent) chased up the valley. The noble hunters were stationed at bends in the glades (Edward of York's 'trysts') and shot with bows and arrows at the beasts as they were driven past. Those animals which were only wounded were hunted by greyhounds into *resayts*, 'receiving stations', where they were slaughtered.[169] Finally the carcasses were cleaned, skinned and butchered. The offal with bread soaked in blood was fed to the hounds; the rest was taken back to the castle with much blowing of horns.

William Rufus did not live much indoors. He was mostly in the saddle, travelling, hunting or on campaign, or in any combination of these. His life-style, except for the military aspect, was probably quite close to that of an eighteenth-century squire, as shown, for example, in Fielding's *Tom Jones* or even the later Surtee's 'Jorrocks' novels. But although Arthur, Charlemagne, Mark and other such heroes 'loved the active life and cared little for lying down for long or lolling on a seat',[170] they all possessed fine residences, Arthur at Camelot, Charlemagne at Aix and Mark at Tintagel, to which they retired at the proper times, for only in them could the pleasures of entertaining and feasting be enjoyed to the full. William, who with his new palace at Westminster tried to rival, even to surpass them, like them and his Germanic ancestors lived with his men in a hall, in essentials not all that different from Heorot, built by Hrothgar, king of the Danes, at Leire in Zeeland, described in the poem *Beowulf* some three centuries before. Attached to the great hall, besides the chapel, were the kitchens and the other domestic offices, and, usually reached by a door behind the dais, was the king's chamber, comprising not only his bedroom but also his private living quarters and business rooms.[171] In the courtyard were the stables, the kennels and the mews.

[168] *VEdR*, 40.

[169] 'toraced and rent at the resayt', *Gawain*, l. 1168, translated by Stone, 65, as 'dragged down and met death at the dog-bases', and by Tolkien and Gordon, 52, as 'pulled down and killed at the resayts', i.e. 'receipts', or receiving stations. These 'lothe trysteres' (low-lying trysts or stations) as they were also called, l. 1170, where strong greyhounds killed the escaped or wounded deer, are contrasted with the 'trystors' (l. 1146) on the hills, where the fewterers with their greyhounds were based. See also above, 131 n. 166.

[170] *Gawain*, ll. 87–8.

[171] *EC 1000–1066*, 119–20, for the palace in *VEdR* and its servants.

Medieval kings were itinerant; but wherever the king stayed, whether in palace, castle, hunting lodge or in the field, the basic pattern of the hall and its attachments was set out. The Norman kings inherited from their English predecessors houses (*domus*), sometimes more grandly called 'palaces', in Winchester and Westminster. The Conqueror rebuilt and extended the former,[172] William II built a new hall for the latter.[173] They probably had other permanent lodgings in the areas they often visited,[174] although castles would serve for shelter.

As the Conqueror had been a widower since 1083 and the last of his daughters was married in 1086, the succession of a bachelor king caused no upheaval in the household. There was no complication of a dowager queen and no problem of setting up a new establishment for a queen consort and her ladies and servants. Although William Rufus had two brothers and three sisters still living, besides two half-uncles and many cousins, he does not give the impression, despite his loyalty to his father, of having been a great family man. His brother Henry sometimes joined him and seems usually to have been made welcome; but there are no signs of a close attachment to his sisters. During his short reign the only nephew to seek his patronage was Robert's bastard, Richard, who joined his court possibly when his father went on Crusade.[175] This is in sharp contrast to the court of his successor, where the queens, the king's children, both legitimate and bastard, nephews and other kin played a prominent part. With William so hospitable and generous, the isolation from kinsmen could have been caused more by their relative scarcity and the dislike which some of them had for him than by any deliberate policy of estrangement on his part. It is more than likely that the tone of his court was not to the taste of all. All the same, his court had its domestic side. An epitaph once in Lincoln cathedral records that William of Aincourt, son of Walter (I), Domesday lord of Blankney, south-east of the city, a kinsman both of Bishop Remigius who built the church and of the king, had died while he was being brought up (*aleretur*)

---

[172] *Winton Domesday*, 289 ff.

[173] See below, 371–2.

[174] The 'palace site' at Cheddar seems to have had a continuous history until the thirteenth century: P. Rahtz, "The Saxon and Medieval Palaces at Cheddar, Somerset', *Medieval Archaeology*, vi–vii (1962–3), 53. There were also royal palaces held by earls which sometimes reverted. At York was the palace where, in the chamber, Earl Tostig had had two noblemen murdered, and where, in the centre of the hall, in March 1065, Countess Judith, his wife, had had a great fire kindled in order to test the incorruptibility of some hairs from the recently discovered corpse of St Oswi, king and martyr: Florence, i, 222; *Vita S. Oswini*, 14–15, 19. Archbishop Lanfranc had fine stone and timber houses built for him in the archiepiscopal vills for the use of him and his successors when travelling round their estates: *HN*, 16.

[175] See below, 419.

in William's court.[176] William I of Eton, the eldest son and heir of Walter fitzOther, constable of Windsor, testified in old age, when, after a distinguished career in the world, he had become a canon of Llanthony Secunda in Gloucestershire, that he remembered hearing as a boy in William's household, perhaps in 1095, a pre-Conquest story about Ealdred of York and Gloucester abbey.[177] Rufus is also described as the 'gossip' of William of Aldrie,[178] which may mean that he was the Godfather of that minor baron's child. It is, therefore, possible that not a few of the children of his barons were educated in his household. With this king the sources tend to conceal not the secrets of the court but its more ordinary features.

A man of quality was never unaccompanied,[179] and kings lived publicly in a large entourage. At the centre of the royal court was the body of household servants which an heir was supposed to take over from his father, or retire on pension.[180] The scheme described in the *Establishment*, a schedule of the entitlements to wages, food and other liveries of the royal household servants drawn up about 1135, appears to go back in most of its features at least to the court of the new king's elder uncle, and in essentials to its English and Norman prototypes.[181] The document takes us through the servants of the chapel, the stewards' department, the dispensary, pantry, larder, kitchen and buttery, the chamber, the constabulary and marshalsea, and out into the courtyard for the huntsmen and their hounds. This is typical of the establishment of any great house in the Middle Ages and for long afterwards; but it must be borne in mind that since the household, like the king, was itinerant, it had some of the characteristics of the headquarters company of a general officer in the field, a unit which could pack up at a minute's notice and load all its equipment on to sumpter horses or carts,[182] and which was

---

[176] Quoted by Stenton, *English Feudalism*, p. 32 n.

[177] *Hist. mon. Gloucest.*, ii, 112: 'qui regi Willelmo secundo collateralis puer audivit' – he was serving as a page. For the case, see above, 114. For the family, see genealogical table, no. 12.

[178] See below, 357–8.

[179] *Dialogus de Scaccario*, 44.

[180] *Ibid.*, 95.

[181] For King Edward's court and household, see Barlow, *Edward the Confessor*, 162 ff.; cf. *EC 1000–1066*, 115 ff. The service *per vicem*, in rotation, of the dispensers and chamberlains (and perhaps others) in the Anglo-Norman household is typical of O.E. thegn service at the royal court. For the court of the Norman dukes, see Douglas *WC*, 144 ff. Wide reforms of the court were attributed to Henry I: White, 'The household', 130–1; but Walter Map (see n. 196) is not a very trustworthy witness.

[182] H. Hall, *Court Life under the Plantagenets*, 141, imagined the train of packhorses and ox-wains waiting in the yard to convey the king's treasure from Westminster to Winchester; but the *Constitutio* only mentions horses, and it is possible that the household managed to dispense with the stronger but slower draught animals.

equipped to go under canvas.[183] Furniture and equipment, with all its joints, in the absence of glue, pegged or clamped, was collapsible and easily portable; and most departments had on their strength their own means of transport. The porter of the king's bed had three halfpence a day for his man and a sumpter horse with its livery;[184] and when the king was itinerant the usher (door-keeper) of the chamber was entitled to 4d in respect of the royal bed.[185]

The progresses of the king's court had also some of the features of an army on the march through enemy territory. Anselm's biographer, Eadmer, when reporting reforms made by Henry I about 1108, gives a terrible account of the depredations of William Rufus's servants and military household.[186] The multitude which accompanied the king was subject to no discipline and completely devastated the country through which it passed. Many were so evil that when they left the lodgings on which they had been forcibly quartered they carried off or destroyed everything that they had been unable to consume, taking some things to sell in the market and setting fire to the rest, or, if it was drink, washing their horses' legs with it before pouring it away. Only modesty prevented Eadmer from telling what wrongs they did to the householders and what indecencies they offered their wives and daughters. As a result, whenever people heard that the king was on his way they fled from their homes with everything they could remove and took refuge in woods and other places of safety. Henry, the monk asserts, ordered all this lawlessness to stop on pain of blinding or amputation of hands, feet or other members. What is more, the edict was enforced and secured a reformation of the court's behaviour. Eadmer is a very prejudiced witness, but here it is more likely that he exaggerated Henry's benevolence than William's carelessness. The Anglo-Saxon Chronicler blamed Henry as well as William, and it was one of the evils of the age.[187]

[183] The tent-keeper (cortinarius) is listed under the marshalsea (p. 135). Cortina also meant a curtain or hanging, while tenta, tentorium and similar words were used for marquees. There is room for doubt here, although White, 'The household', 154, brushes it aside. There can be no doubt, however, that tents were carried on progresses and campaigns: cf. Song of Roland, ll. 159–61, 671, pp. 57, 77; and they were used for ceremonies and receptions: cf. Tristan, 94, 109, 130, 139.

[184] 133. Hall, 247, makes him 'the porter of the king's litter'.

[185] 135 (under the marshalsea).

[186] HN, 192–3. Cf. a similar reference to the depredations of William's fewterers, falconers and riff-raff in the eulogy on Henry contained in the prologue to the lawbook, Quadripartitus, written about 1115, ed. Liebermann, Gesetze, i, 534, where decurionum torciae (? the torches of the tax-gatherers) could be an allusion to Ranulf Flambard.

[187] For the court's ravaging in 1097, see below, 376. For Henry's depredations in 1104, see ASC, s.a., 179: 'and always wherever the king went there was complete ravaging of his wretched people caused by his court, and in the course of it often there were burnings and killings; All this was to anger God/And these wretched folk to vex.' For Earl Hugh of Chester's destructive court, see below, 174.

The *Establishment*, however, presents a more civilized, indeed homely, picture. All court servants when on duty were entitled to eat in the 'house', and the upper servants received special daily allowances of bread and wine, presumably so that they could entertain, candles and candle-ends for lighting, and wages as well. There is no reference to the livery of robes. As the allowance of wine was either one sextary, or a half, according to rank, and the sextary was probably four gallons,[188] the upper servants either did much entertaining or had a good number of dependants. There were six grades of pay for those of knightly status and above:

5s a day	*3s 6d*	*2s*
	(5s when eating out of the household)	(2s 10d when eating out)
chancellor	chief constables stewards master-butler master-chamberlain treasurer	(?) master-dispenser of bread and wine[189] master-dispenser of bread master-dispenser of the larder master-dispenser of the buttery

		2s
		clerk of the spence of bread and wine chamberlains, serving in rotation

1s 2d	*10d*	*8d*
(2s when eating out)	(1s 7d when eating out)	chamberlain of the chandlery
master-marshal	dispensers of bread, serving in rotation[190]	under-marshals (when out of court
under-constables	dispensers of the larder, serving in rotation	
1s 2d		
treasurer of the chamber	dispensers of the buttery, serving in rotation	

	10d	
	master of the writing office	

---

[188] As gallons and half sextaries are listed, the sextary should be at least three gallons, and four is neater.

The richest livery, as well as the largest salary, was the chancellor's: he received a daily allowance of one royal (*dominicus*) and two salt simnels (superior bread), one sextary of claret and one of household wine, one large candle and forty candle-ends. At the lower end, the master of the writing office received one salt simnel, half a sextary of household wine, one large candle and twelve candle-ends, and the chamberlain of the chandlery just half a sextary of household wine. With the other upper servants of the household, account was taken both of their rank and of the requirements of their office. Beneath those already listed there was a large social gap. The lower servants earned from 1d to 3d a day.

This grading is intelligible and important. There were six offices of the highest rank, all headships of departments; but missing from the list are a master-pantler, the head of the pantry, the bread office, and a master-larderer, and it would seem that the offices were non-existent at that time.[191] Nor is there a master-huntsman. In the second rank (2s a day) were the master-dispensers, those who issued the commodities produced by their departments, and presumably kept the accounts. The one anomaly is that the servants of the chamber, the chamberlains who served in rotation, are raised a grade into this class, probably because of their proximity to the king. The third grade (1s 2d and below) consisted

---

[189] There are problems with the dispensers. In the MSS of the *Constitutio* the clerk of the spence of bread and wine and the dispensers of bread are listed after the chancellor and chapel; but Johnson imitated White in moving them down to follow the stewards. The clerk, although not called a master, is paid 2s a day. The next listed is the master-dispenser of bread, who receives the same liveries as the clerk and more money (2s 10d), but only if he eats out. Then the master-dispensers of the larder and of the buttery are equated with the master-dispenser of bread and wine, who does not occur. There is similar confusion with the dispensers who serve in rotation: those of the larder are equated with the rotating dispensers of bread and wine (a class which in this combined form does not occur), and those of the buttery with the rotating dispensers of the spence (which again cannot be identified). It is possible that the clerk of the spence of bread and wine was in fact (as his pay suggests) a master and had under him dispensers who served in rotation, but have been omitted from the list. Alternatively, a whole section has fallen out.

[190] See previous note.

[191] Round, *King's Serjeants*, 197 ff., devoted a section to the pantler, but, although he had found an interesting charter concerning the pantler at Rouen, he could not demonstrate the existence of the office in England before the coronation roll of 1286. He was reduced to making the absurd suggestion, p. 219, that the *computator panis*, a servant who received nothing beyond his rations, was the pantler. Nor did he draw attention, when discussing the king's larderer, pp. 233 ff., to the fact that that officer likewise was missing from the *Establishment*: the larder was 'staffed on the same principle as the others', p. 234. In general, Round paid insufficient attention to the rates of pay as a guide to rank. White, 'The household', 139, although much interested in the pay and allowances, followed Round's suggestion about the pantler.

largely of dispensers who served in rotation and the subordinates of officers of the highest rank.

The arrangements were not immutable. An event which probably caused long-standing malformation of the household was the separation of England from Normandy. Some of the Conqueror's servants must have preferred to transfer to Duke Robert and remain in the duchy. The butlers Hugh and Roger of Ivry appear to be a case in point, and the defection led to a split between the English and Norman offices which later led to trouble.[192] Other changes are noticed in the *Establishment*. Henry I had more than doubled the wages and liveries of Robert *de Sigillo*, his master of the writing office;[193] some officials appear in the list by name rather than by office, which suggests that either they had not been established or there was some anomaly in their case; and the wolf-huntsmen were claiming £8 a year instead of £6 for buying horses. It also seems that the court treasurer was an innovation of Henry's. But the general impression is one of stability.

Most of the officers with a title who were not in holy orders were what the secretariat of the Domesday survey classed as *ministri* or *servientes regis*, royal servants or serjeants, or sometimes, usually when they were of English birth, as *taini regis*, the king's thegns. They were listed in the record usually in groups after the king's barons because they were enfeoffed servants, owing their duties, as dispenser, cook, huntsman or whatever, in return for their land, a tenure distinct from holding by barony or knight service, and known later as serjeanty. Their offices and lands were, like other fiefs, hereditary, although subject to the payment of a relief (succession duty) by the heir. On the Pipe Roll of 1130 are many examples of men paying a relief 'for the land and office [*ministerium*] of their father.'[194] It is impossible, however, to trace back to the Conquest most of the families which held serjeanties in the thirteenth century, or even some of the twelfth-century holders, and it is sometimes unsafe to identify the Domesday tenant of their manors as their predecessor in the office.[195] Within a structural stability there was much casual change. Hence few of William II's servants can be named.

The king paid his servants well. The upper echelons had not only profitable estates, free board and lodgings at court, valuable liveries and generous pay, but also in some cases the perquisites of their office. They

---

[192] Round, *op. cit.*, 140 ff.; *Domesday Monachorum*, 56–7; *Regesta*, i, xxvii; and see below, 145.

[193] *Constitutio*, 129.

[194] See below, 257–8.

[195] Richardson and Sayles, 422 ff., are highly critical of Round's assumption that all offices in the household were from the beginning serjeanties. But Round is defended by C. Warren Hollister, 'The origins of the English treasury', *EHR*, xciii (1978), 269.

were not supposed to charge their fellow servants, who, for example, got their writs sealed free.[196] But they closed their ranks against outsiders; and when a chancellor could proffer the king probably 5,000 marks for his seal (exactly half the sum William paid for the revenues of the duchy of Normandy for five years), there were obviously rich takings from the chapel, and with the royal court the goal of so many suitors, there were pagoda trees for most servants to shake. In this way they recouped the cost of buying their office.

When we turn to the functional organization of the household, the *Establishment* fails us in some respects. The marked differentials in pay and allowances must indicate a hierarchy of rank, but do not necessarily disclose a chain of command. Certainly the highest paid of the servants, the chancellor, was not in overall charge of the household. It is possible that the stewards were in control of most of the servants of the hall, and it would be reasonable to think that those servants with the title of master were in charge of their departments. But the pantry and larder had no masters even in 1135, and the king should not be pushed too far out of sight. All these men were his domestics with whom he was in daily contact; and he was directly concerned in any dispute between them.[197]

Although the chancellor heads the list of the *Establishment*, let us pass him by for the present and start with the departments which served the mundane requirements of the house. The stewards (or sewers) were the highest paid servants in the hall.[198] It was their office to serve the dishes, and their English predecessors had been called 'plate-thegns'.[199] When Archbishop Anselm was a boy at Aosta he had a vision of God's house (*aula*) which he imagined to be at the top of the mountain. After he had climbed up to it and entered the royal hall he found God alone with his steward, for all the other servants were busy with the harvest; and God, after some pleasant conversation, ordered his steward to place the whitest of bread before his guest, and Anselm partook of it.[200] In romances the seneschal, which is an alternative name for steward, is usually portrayed as a nobleman's chief servant. Kay was King Arthur's seneschal, and Jesus was a kind steward at the marriage in Cana when

[196] See the entertaining story told by Walter Map of the dispute between the dispenser, Thurstin fitzSimon, and the keeper of the seal, Adam of Yarmouth, in Henry II's reign: *Gualteri Mapes de Nugis Curialium*, ed. T. Wright (Camden Soc., 1850), 231–2; Round, *op. cit.*, 192–3.

[197] As in the case of the quarrel described in the previous note.

[198] They occur in the MSS of the *Constitutio*, probably by mistake, after the dispensers of bread. At William I's court the steward (William fitzOsbern) was the most important official: Douglas, *WC*, 145–6, 148. See also Stenton, *English Feudalism*, 73 ff.

[199] Round, *op. cit.*, 68 ff.

[200] *VA*, 4–5.

he changed the water into wine.[201] We are told nothing in the *Establishment*, or elsewhere, about the stewards' terms of service at the English court, how many had to be on duty at one time and whether there was a roster; but it has been suggested that in Henry I's reign a team of four stewards served in rotation.[202]

The *dapifer* who made the greatest impression on Domesday Book under that description was Eudo fitzHubert (de Rie or Ryes), who had been enfeoffed with a large honour in ten counties, mostly in the east Midlands, East Anglia, Essex and London, where he may have owned a stone house. In Normandy he held the castle and honour of Préaux. He married about 1088 Rohese, daughter of Richard fitzGilbert of Tonbridge (Clare) and Rohese daughter of Walter Giffard, and died, apparently childless, in 1120, when his honour escheated to the crown. Although he preserved the name of his father, his family circumstances are unknown.[203] Others described as stewards in the Survey are Haimo sheriff of Kent – or his son of the same name, possibly both[204] – and a certain Godric who held lands in East Anglia.[205] From charter and chronicle evidence we can add the names of Ralf of Montpinçon, a great friend of the abbey of St Evroul, Roger Bigot, who also acted sometimes as sheriff, Ivo Taillebois, who died about 1094, William, who occurs in 1091, and a Gilbert, perhaps Rohese's brother.[206] Although there is no reason to doubt that such men were not too grand to place a dish before the king, there must have been other waiters in the hall who are not listed in the *Establishment*. It is, indeed, possible that the steward on duty was also in general charge of the catering side of the hall, supervising the pantry, larder and kitchens; and, as there is provision for extra pay

[201] Cf. *Tristan*, 43, 71, 120, 159.
[202] *Regesta*, ii, xi, where the four in 1100 are identified as Eudo, Haimo, Roger Bigot and Ralf (de Montpinçon).
[203] *DB*, i, 61c, 132b, 139a, 197c, 205d, 212b, 227a, 336d; ii, 48b ff., 239b ff., 402b ff. See also Round *FE*, 469 ff., pedigree chart, opposite p. 472, 'The legend of Eudo dapifer', *EHR*, xxxvii (1922), 1; W. Farrer, *Honors and Knights' Fees*, iii (1925), 164 ff.; N. Denholm-Young, 'Eudo Dapifer's honour of Walbrook', *EHR*, xlvi (1931), 623; Loyd, *Families*, 40; Sanders, *Baronies*, 92; Richardson and Sayles, 217–19. His brother, Adam fitzHubert, who died in 1098, held in Kent of the bishop of Bayeux and the archbishop of Canterbury.
[204] *DB*, i, 14b (Kent), 36c (Surrey), ii, 54b–56b (Essex), where Haimo dapifer has a quite substantial estate. Haimo *dentatus*, killed in 1047, was the father of sheriff Haimo, who had two sons, Haimo and Robert fitzHaimo. See further, Douglas, *Domesday Monachorum*, 55–6, Morris, *Med. Eng. Sheriff*, 44 n. 29, 46 n. 47.
[205] *DB*, ii, 202–205b (Norfolk) and 335b (Suffolk).
[206] For Ralf, see OV, iii, 164; Loyd, *Families*, 69. For Roger, see above, 61–2. For Ivo, who married Lucy, an heiress who after his death *c.* 1094 married Roger fitzGerold of Roumare, see Sanders, *Baronies*, 17–18, and above, 68. For William see below, 279. See also *Regesta*, i, xxiii–xxiv; *HBC*, 71–2.

when stewards ate out, outside duties were envisaged, for example, at the treasury.[207] Stewards also served as sheriffs.

Next is listed, possibly as a connecting link with the following departments, the clerk of the spence of bread and wine.[208] The dispensary with its dispensers was the issue-department, and this clerk of the dispensary, as he was paid on the same scale (2s a day) as the several master-dispensers, must have been of the same rank, and may have received from them, and then reissued, the provisions for the hall. Only one family of royal dispensers is well known at this time, and it had very modest origins as tenants of the Tancarvilles (chamberlains) in Normandy. Robert fitzThurstin, the brother of Urse of Abetot, one of the king's marshals and a substantial landowner and sheriff in the west Midlands,[209] held in 1086 land in chief of the king in Oxfordshire, Gloucestershire, Leicestershire, Warwickshire and Lincolnshire, and was also, like his brother, a tenant of the bishop of Worcester.[210] When, at some point before 1098, he restored several estates to Westminster abbey, he named among the witnesses five of his fellow officials, his brother Urse, Herbert the king's chamberlain at Winchester, Ivo Taillebois (steward), William chamberlain (of London), perhaps William Mauduit, and the goldsmith Otho.[211] Robert was clearly a man of parts, for Orderic Vitalis remembered that it was he who so resented the king's chaplain Ranulf throwing his weight about in the hall and ordering important persons about as though he spoke for the king, that he called him, prophetically, *Flambard*, a devouring flame.[212] It is, perhaps, a mere coincidence that a neighbour of his in the manor of Ludwell in Oxfordshire was another royal servant named Ranulf.[213]

Many of Robert's lands and possibly his dispensership seem to have been inherited by his brother, whence their combined lands and offices passed to the husbands of Urse's daughters, Roger Marmion and Walter

[207] For Eudo's duties at the treasury, see Richardson and Sayles, *loc. cit.* For his witness of a royal writ of a financial nature, see below, 235.

[208] *Constitutio*, 130. See also above, 137 n. 189. White, 'The household', 137, would explain his presence here as due to his clerical status which made him subject to the chancellor, and his office as dispensing bread and wine for the whole household.

[209] *DNB*, lviii, 52; Sanders, *Baronies*, 75; Emma Mason, 'Magnates, Curiales, and the Wheel of Fortune', *Battle II*, 135 ff., on Urse and Robert. Loyd, *Families*, 1–2, considered that in Normandy the family was of no importance.

[210] *DB*, i, 160c, 168b, 230b, 234d–235a, 375b–c; 172d–173a. Needless to say he was not required to pay a relief in 1095 when the other episcopal barons were assessed: see below, 235–6. It is possible, however, as J. Armitage Robinson suggested, *Gilbert Crispin*, 147, that he was dead by then.

[211] *Gilbert Crispin*, 146, charter 27.

[212] *OV*, iv, 172.

[213] *DB*, i, 160c.

(I) of Beauchamp.[214] Nevertheless, a royal dispenser, Thurstin, who became a vassal of Abingdon abbey in a rather interesting way, may have been a son, albeit illegitimate, of Robert's. According to the monastery's chronicle,[215] William II, acting on malicious information, imprisoned and starved to death one of its knights, Anskil, dispossessed his widow and son William, and bestowed his estate at Sparsholt (Berks) on Thurstin, who was in turn succeeded by his son Hugh. There were other, even less expected, consequences of Anskil's disgrace. His widow was so assiduous in entreating the help of the king's brother, Henry, who had boyhood connexions with the abbey,[216] that she had a child by him, whom she named Richard; and Henry in return looked after her interests. It was probably in his reign that William, her son by Anskil, married a niece of Abbot Faricius and the sister of another royal dispenser, Simon.[217] The ramifications of the royal court were both wide and also closely knit. Courtiers, *curiales*, were indeed a family group.

No other servants of the hall are listed in the *Establishment* at this point. The policing and door-keeping services and the stoking of the fires were performed by men under the command of the constable and marshal, and will be noticed when we reach those officers. The chief constable, although paid the same as the stewards, received superior liveries and was certainly not subordinate to them. Another of this 'outdoors' group may be mentioned here. In a passage interpolated by Ælfric Bata into Ælfric's *Colloquy*, the king's hunter is made to say, 'I have the chief place in the hall';[218] and although this does not seem to be true of the Anglo-Norman court, it is unlikely that so important an official was confined to the yard.

The pantry, as we have noticed, was not headed by a master-pantler, but by the dispensers of bread, the men who distributed the baked loaves. There was a master-dispenser, who, although a permanent official, could eat out, and dispensers who served in turn, an usher (door-keeper) of the spence, and an accountant, who received rations but not apparently a wage. This man, *computator panis*, was probably the tally-man of the dispensary who received the loaves from the bakers.[219]

---

[214] Sanders, *Baronies*, 75, 145. Urse's son and successor, Robert, was banished for a crime by Henry I, thus fulfilling Wulfstan's curse and prophecy; *GP*, 253, and below, 152. For Walter of Beauchamp, see Emma Mason, *loc. cit.*, 138.

[215] *Chron. Abingdon*, ii, 36–7.

[216] Above, 39.

[217] Simon held properties in Winchester *c* 1100: *Winton Domesday*, I, 283, cf. 114; II, 1069. As his son and successor as dispenser was named Thurstin (see above, 139 n. 196), there may well have been a relationship also with the family in which that name ran.

[218] Edward Schröder, 'Colloquium Ælfrici', *Zeitschrift für Deutsches Altertum und Deutsche Litteratur*, xli (1897), 288; *Ælfric's Colloquy*, ed. Garmonsway, 26. For the Colloquy, see *EC 1000–1066*, 281.

[219] Wrongly identified by Round with the pantler: see above, 137 n. 191.

Also listed under the dispensers of bread are the nappers or napiers, who were in charge of the table linen and had a man and a packhorse on their charge. A keeper of the tables (*bordarius*) with his packhorse was possibly responsible for the transport of the king's table (a board mounted on trestles); and the bearer of the alms-bowl was the one who begged at meals or collected the remains of the food. Perhaps it was he who distributed the crumbs from the table to the poor at the gate. About 1110, Oin the napier owned a tenement in High Street, Winchester;[220] and other napiers are mentioned on the Pipe Roll of 1130.[221]

The bakery was staffed by four bakers who were divided into pairs. While one of these was on duty the others went ahead to the next place of call and took with them 40d to buy a quarter (*modius Rothamagensis*) of flour. From this they were to bake 40 royal and 150 ordinary (salt) simnels, and 260 baker's loaves. The royal simnels were to be enough for four men, the salt simnels for two and the common loaves for one.[222] Two royal bakers are mentioned in Domesday Book, Osmund under Dorset and Erchenger under Cambridge; both had very modest estates.[223] Also in the bakery was a waferer, who likewise received only his food. He was the confectioner who made wafers, which are probably better described by another modern form of the word, waffles. The serjeanty was, at least later, associated with the tenure of Liston Overall in Essex.[224]

The larder, which provided the meat, had a staff similar to the pantry's in that it was without a master-larderer or lardiner at its head; but larderers who served in rotation are mentioned. There was a master-dispenser and other dispensers who served in rotation, an usher, and slaughtermen or butchers; the carter of the larder and the serjeant who received the venison (and other game) are listed after the servants of the kitchens. One of William II's larderers was Hugh, whose son Henry succeeded him in the office. Both held land in Winchester, Henry near the end of the king's kitchen at the palace.[225] Humphrey took land from Ramsey abbey about 1091-2,[226] John, who had a son, John the clerk,

[220] *Winton Domesday*, I, 6. For his wife or widow, see *PR 31 H I*, 143. For napery service, see Round, *King's Serjeants*, 222 ff.

[221] Michael *naparius*, 86, 102 (excused danegeld); Torel, 56, 59.

[222] If the last sentence refers simply to the size of the loaves, bread sufficient to issue to 450 persons was catered for; if it means that the simnels were to be divided up before issue, provision was made for 720 persons.

[223] *DB*, i, 85a, 202c. For the king's baker, see Round, *op. cit.*, 232-3.

[224] Round, *op. cit.*, 227 ff. The 1086 tenant was probably Ilbod, who is listed among men of the royal servant class: *DB*, ii, 95b.

[225] *Regesta*, ii, nos 803-4; *Winton Domesday*, I, 16, 18, 59. Hugh's grant of a tenement to the church of Winchester for the good of his soul was confirmed by the king in September 1096: V.H. Galbraith, 'Royal Charters to Winchester', *EHR*, xxv (1920), no. XI, *Regesta*, ii, no. 377a.

[226] *Regesta*, no. 413.

gave a messuage in York to Whitby abbey,[227] and a royal larderer in
1102 was Roger, a clerk, whom Henry I in his careless way appointed
bishop of Hereford.[228]

Two kitchens are described, the king's kitchen (*dominica coquina*) and
the great kitchen.[229] In the first were two cooks: the cook of the king's
kitchen and the cook of the king's privy servants (*privati*) and the
dispensers.[230] Their emoluments beyond their food are not mentioned,
but each had 1½d for his man. There was also an usher and his man, a
scullion in charge of the dishes, who had a man and a packhorse, a
sumpter-man and a serjeant. The great kitchen was in charge of a
named official not given a title and staffed likewise by two cooks, several
serjeants, an usher of the roasting house and his man, a turn-spit, a
scullion with a packhorse and a carter with his horse. At least seven royal
cooks are noticed in Domesday Book, all with small estates. Ansgar was
the best rewarded, and was given an individual rubric under Essex. He
held land in Wiltshire worth £3 10s a year, in Somerset £5, and in Essex
10s.[231]

The buttery, the department which provided the drink, was differently organized, for there was a master-butler as well as a master-
dispenser, together with dispensers who served in turn.[232] There were
also an usher and his man, cellarmen (*hosarii*) and their men, a cooper
(*buttarius*)[233] and his men, several labourers and a serjeant with a man
and two packhorses. Also under the butler were cup-bearers, four
serving at a time but only two eating in the house, each with a man, the
mazer-keeper (the guardian of the cup of maple wood), fruiterers and
their men, and a carter and his horses. Little, however, can be
discovered about the buttery from Domesday Book. A butler named

[227] *Cartularium Abbathiae de Whiteby*, ed. J.C. Atkinson (Surtees Soc., lxix, 1879), 6.
[228] *EC 1066–1154*, 80.
[229] *Constitutio*, 131–2. For kitchen serjeanties, see Round, *op. cit.*, 243 ff.
[230] White, 'The household', 140, reads, 'cocus . . . et dispensator(es)', and therefore
translates it as, 'the cook and the dispenser(s) of the king's private household'. It is true
that otherwise no dispensers of the kitchen are listed; but the dispensers of the larder may
have sufficed. The OFr equivalent of *privati* was *privez* (cf. Gaimar, l. 5789), which can be
translated 'household'.
[231] Alric, *DB*, i, 153a; Ansgar, 73c, 98c, ii, 97; Gilbert, i, 229b; Humfrey, 170a; wife
(widow) of Manasses, 98d; Tezelin, 36d; Walter, ii, 95. Perhaps Aubrey *de Coci*, i, 58b,
329d, should be included. For Theoderic the king's cook, a T.R.E. tenant at Winchester
who was dead by *c.* 1110, see *Winton Domesday*, I, 185.
[232] *Constitutio*, 132–3. For buttery serjeanties, see Round, *op. cit.*, 140 ff.
[233] White, 'The household', 142–3, translates it as 'keeper of the butts', and thought
that he looked after the wine stored in the cellar in butts, while the *hosarii* saw to its
transport. But it may be that the wine was mostly on the move and the cellar was usually
a cart.

Hugh, although given his own rubric, held only two very modest estates, together worth £2 1s a year, in Bedfordshire.[234] William d'Aubigny (I), who was styled butler in 1101, and about 1110 held two messuages in Winchester, among a colony of other serjeants, one of which he sublet to Herbert the chamberlain, held land in Norfolk of William Rufus and may have served him too in the office.[235] In 1113 itinerant canons of Laon cured at Winchester a retired royal butler named Ralf Buarius, also described as a knight, who had been blind for eight years and was succeeded in his post by his sons, but nothing more is known of this family.[236] A serjeanty of the hose (wine vessels shaped like a boot) was later attached to the manor of Cresswell in Bray on Thames, and the holder of this tenement in 1086 was Alwin son of Cheping.[237] An usher of the buttery before 1130 was Hugh of Kivelli.[238] On this evidence it would seem unlikely that the buttery at the beginning of William II's reign had priority over the pantry and larder or was headed by anyone comparable in status with the stewards, or the master-dispenser or master-chamberlain of later reigns. A possible reason for this has already been suggested.[239] The rise of the Aubigny family was, however, dramatic, for William I's younger brother, Nigel, was among the most favoured of Henry I's 'new men',[240] and his son, William II, usually called pincerna to distinguish him from a third namesake, Brito, married King Henry I's widow, Adela, and was created an earl by Stephen.[241]

At this point it is convenient to consider two departments of the household which had a role in the royal administration and government of the kingdom, the chapel and the chamber. The chapel royal, staffed by royal priests and clerks and responsible not only for the religious services in the court but also for the conservation of the relics and other royal treasures of a spiritual, artistic or literary nature, was of considerable antiquity in England, although not under that Frankish

---

[234] DB, i, 216a. This may be Hugh of Ivry, who was William I's butler and probably accompanied him to England in 1066: White, 'The household', 141, and see above, 138. If so, an Oxfordshire estate, DB, i, 157d, must be added.

[235] He witnesses Henry I's treaty with Robert of Flanders in 1101 (see below, 325 n. 265) as pincerna. See also Winton Domesday, I, 14, 33; Regesta, no. 373. He was a beneficiary of Odo of Bayeux's disgrace as well as of the king's generosity in Norfolk: Dorothy M. Owen, 'Bishop's Lynn', Battle II, 143, 149–50. He died in 1139.

[236] Herman, 'De miraculis S. Mariae Laudunensis', Migne PL, clvi, 978. Poole, The Exchequer, 55, argues for the date 1123. A 'Radulfus pincerna' in Durham's Liber Vitae, 53, col. 3, may be the butler of the earl of Warwick, whom he follows.

[237] DB, i, 63c. In c. 1110 Chiping son of Alwin held two properties in Winchester: Winton Domesday, I, 135, 241.

[238] Round, op. cit., 183–5.

[239] Above, 138.

[240] Greenway, Mowbray Charters, 17 ff.

[241] Farrer, Honors and Knights' Fees, iii, 7.

name.[242] It had probably always provided a secretariat for the king when required, and by the eleventh century was producing those royal letters, known as writs, which were notifications of grants of lands or of rights, addressed to a shire court and authenticated by the royal seal. It is generally accepted that the Conqueror took over the Old-English chapel and *scriptorium*, with its staff and traditions, and that Edward the Confessor's clerk, Regenbald, may have been his first chancellor, a title which was introduced by the Normans. After about 1070, writs began to be written in Latin and also to be used for a wide variety of administrative orders.[243] How the duties of dictating, writing and sealing the writs and performing the religious services were organized in the late Anglo-Saxon and early Norman period is, however, unknown.

The *Establishment* mentions only three officials:[244] the chancellor with his exceptionally high emoluments; the master of the writing office (*scriptorium*), originally paid only 10d a day; and the chaplain in charge of the chapel and relics. It may be inferred that the chancellor, who after 1070 was usually rewarded with a bishopric on retirement, was in charge of the department and that he drafted and dictated the writs. The master of the writing office, presumably his deputy in this work, was also the keeper of the king's seal, for one of the best-known holders of the office, Robert, who became bishop of London in 1141, was known as *de Sigillo*.[245] Although the master must surely have had some scribes and other clerks and servants under him, they are not mentioned in the *Establishment*, possibly because they were paid either by him or the chancellor. The third official, the chaplain-custodian, is allowed some underlings, if not colleagues. He had food for two men, and four serjeants of the chapel had double rations apiece. The two packhorses had a livery of 1d a day and 1d a month for shoeing. For the religious services the chaplain had four wax candles a week, for a light before the relics one each night, and thirty candle-ends; for mass he had one gallon of claret, for the ceremonial washing of the altar on Maunday Thursday one gallon of household wine, and for Easter Sunday, when all the faithful were supposed to communicate, one sextary of best claret and one of the common sort.

William II's chancellors were Gerard, whom he appointed in 1096 bishop of Hereford and whom Henry I translated to York;[246] Robert Bloet, who in 1093-4 obtained Lincoln;[247] and William Giffard, who at

---

[242] *EC 1000–1066*, 115 ff., especially 124 ff.; Barlow, *Edward the Confessor*, 164 ff.
[243] *Facsimiles of Royal Writs*, ix ff.
[244] *Constitutio*, 129.
[245] *Ibid. EC 1066–1154*, 96.
[246] Above, 59.
[247] Below, 328.

the beginning of Henry's reign was promoted to Winchester.[248] Robert was in office by 27 January 1091 and ceased to act about the time of his consecration in February 1094.[249] The keeper of the seal at the beginning of the reign was Ranulf Flambard, who may also have been master of the *scriptorium*;[250] and it is possible that Richard *de Capella*, who became bishop of Hereford in 1121,[251] may go back to the previous reign. Three of the scribes of the *scriptorium* have been distinguished by their hands; and of these the second is thought to have been a Norman, the third English. The second has earned the compliment of being 'as accomplished a calligrapher as ever worked in the chancery'.[252] A good number of royal chaplains with relatively small endowments are listed in Domesday Book, but not all necessarily served in the household chapel. Of Edward the Confessor's clerks, Regenbald, Albert the Lotharingian and some others were still alive and holding their, sometimes rich, benefices.[253] A more recent beneficiary of royal bounty was Ranulf (Ralf) Flamme or Flambard, who held smallish parcels of land, including two churches, of a total value of about £30 a year in seven counties.[254] Two of Ranulf's brothers, Fulcher and Osbern, were likewise in the chapel royal.[255] Chaplains promoted to bishoprics by William II were Godfrey (Chichester), John of Tours (Wells), Ralf Luffa (Chichester), Hervey (Bangor), Samson (Worcester) and Ranulf Flambard (Durham). Peter, the brother of chancellor Gerard, was another of his chaplains.[256] Thurstin, from the church of Bayeux, 'one of William's favourite clerks', was made archbishop of York by Henry in

[248] Barlow, *EC 1066–1154*, 78–9.

[249] He witnesses as chancellor in January 1091 (*Regesta*, nos 315, 319) and in 1091–2 (*ibid.*, nos 328*, 329–32). He was appointed bishop in March 1093, and in September and at Christmas witnessed under that title (*ibid.*, nos 337–8). A royal notification to the officials in Kent, which, if the inclusion in the copy of an unnamed archbishop means that Anselm had been invested, can be dated after 25 September, confirms a grant made by 'Robert my chancellor, that is to say the bishop of Lincoln' (*ibid.*, no. 340, LIII). It is possible, therefore, that Robert continued to act as chancellor until his delayed consecration at Hastings in February 1094 (*HN*, 47–8) or even until 19 March, when the king sailed for Normandy and left him behind. William Giffard is probably the chaplain William of *Regesta*, no. 315 (January 1091). Since he witnesses as chancellor no. 350, dated at Eu and addressed to Robert Bloet most likely at the beginning of his episcopate, it is probable that he was appointed before 19 March 1094. He also witnesses no. 349, which must be earlier than Easter 1095.

[250] See below, 195.

[251] *EC 1066–1154*, 84.

[252] *Facsimiles of Royal Writs*, xvi–xix.

[253] *EC 1000–1066*, 156–8.

[254] See below, 200 n. 163.

[255] See below, 193 ff. Fulcher witnesses *Regesta*, i, nos 464, 480.

[256] *EC 1066–1154*, 66 ff. For Peter, see below, 409.

1114.[257] Most of these were men of outstanding ability. Scribes are not much featured in Domesday Book; but Gisulf, the king's scribe, had a tenement in Winchester about 1110,[258] and a little later Bernard assembled a decent estate in the West Country.[259]

Just as the chapel royal was developing into an 'office of state', so too was the chamber. As it was the closest to the source of power, it was the chief financial office and the great spending department.[260] In his private apartments the king not only kept such money as he required at hand, perhaps still in a box under his bed, but also transacted most of the business in which he was involved. We should not, however, imagine that there was always a suite of separate rooms. In the romance *Tristan* the hero was banished from the chamber of King Mark because he was suspected of adultery with Queen Yseut; and we are given several glimpses of the overcrowding and complete lack of privacy in that area. Less than a spear's length from the king's bed, in which the queen also lay, was placed Tristan's bed; and at his feet slept Yseut's squire, Perinis. Among others who slept in the room was the hunchback dwarf, Frocin. No wonder that Tristan sometimes strayed into the royal bed – once by leaping from the one to the other, so as not to leave a trace on the floor – or that everyone knew what was going on.[261] We are told that in William II's court no lamps were lit at night,[262] an invitation to complete disorder. With such promiscuity in even respectable chambers it is unlikely that the domestic and business functions were separately located. There may, however, have been some specialization of personnel. For specifically financial matters the king required at the minimum someone to look after the household treasury and act as his financial adviser and agent, and another to liaise with or control the main treasury at Winchester – both equally, it must be clearly understood, 'privy purses'. According to the *Establishment*, under the master-chamberlain there was a treasurer, who was often out of court, and William Mauduit (II), a man who is known to have been in turn treasurer of the chamber and chamberlain of the treasury,[263] the two basic offices we have postulated.

[257] Hugh, *HCY*, 34; Barlow, *EC 1066–1154*, 83.
[258] *Winton Domesday*, I, 223; II, 680. J.H. Round, 'Bernard the king's scribe', *EHR*, xiv (1899), 422, 428.
[259] *Ibid.*, 417 ff.
[260] For this difficult and contentious subject, see *inter alios*, G.H. White, 'Financial administration under Henry I', *TRHS*, 4th ser., viii (1925), 56, 'The household', 130–1; H.G. Richardson, 'The Chamber under Henry II', *EHR*, lxix (1954), 596; Richardson and Sayles, 216 ff.; C. Warren Hollister, 'The origins of the English treasury', *EHR*, xciii (1978), 262.
[261] *Tristan*, 60–65.
[262] Above, 104.
[263] Richardson and Sayles, 423, 428 ff.

It does not seem that William Rufus had a master-chamberlain; and there can be little doubt that the financial administration, concerned as it was with the king's personal money and valuables stored in various repositories, was still flexible, and that the titles treasurer and chamberlain were to some extent interchangeable, especially in non-technical contexts. There must have been a permanent or rotating staff at Winchester and probably in London; but there was also a good deal of cross-posting and *ad hoc* movement of personnel. They were all the king's servants, and he used them as he pleased. It is possible that the 'court treasurer', whose successors in the office can be listed from the reign of Henry I, was a creation of that king;[264] but this, it would seem, hardly changed the system. The most important servants at Winchester in William's reign were Henry the treasurer and the chamberlain (of the treasury), Herbert. The former, perhaps a married clerk, had a small local estate which is listed in Domesday Book and the Winton Domesday.[265] His office may have been that which later was styled 'guardian [*custos*] of the treasury'. Herbert, undoubtedly a married clerk, was in 1086 a much richer man, a large mesne tenant as well as holding in chief, and owning much property in the city. He became Henry I's treasurer, and if it was he who was involved in the assassination attempt on that king in 1118, he was blinded and castrated as punishment.[266] His son, Herbert fitzHerbert, likewise a chamberlain, paid a relief of over 353 marks, perhaps 500, for inheriting his father's land, a few years before 1130.[267] Another 'Winchester' chamberlainship was probably held by William Mauduit (I), who held Porchester castle and harbour, useful for the export of treasure to Normandy.[268] In London there was William the chamberlain, who may be the same man.[269] In the itinerant court itself there must have been someone under the king who exercised general supervision over the royal finances. As there seems to be in

[264] Most recently, Hollister, *op. cit.*

[265] Richardson and Sayles, 219-20; Hollister, *op. cit. DB*, i, 49a, from which it appears that he obtained this Hampshire estate from the Conqueror. An under-tenant of his was Geoffrey the marshal. In Winchester, however, he held his land before 1066. *Winton Domesday*, I, 184; his widow was in possession *c.* 1110.

[266] Suger, *Vie de Louis VI*, 190. Hollister, *op. cit.*, 267.

[267] *Winton Domesday*, I, preface. Richardson and Sayles, 217 ff., 426-7. The Abingdon Chronicle, reporting business done with Herbert during the vacancy of the abbey in 1097-1100, describes him as the king's chamberlain (*cubicularius*) and treasurer: *Chron. Abingdon*, ii, 43.

[268] Round, *VCH Hants*, i, 432; Hollister, *op. cit.*, 264-5; Emma Mason, 'Magnates, curiales and the Wheel of Fortune', *Battle II*, 131 ff.

[269] A royal writ, to be dated 1081-5, is addressed to him after Geoffrey de Mandeville (probably keeper of the Tower of London) and the sheriff: *Gilbert Crispin*, 129, doc. no. 4. In 1086 he held an estate of the bishop: *DB*, i, 127c. Mason, *loc. cit.*, 131. See also below, 151 n. 277.

William II's reign no specific office with that duty, it is possible that there were informal arrangements and that one of the stewards, such as Eudo, or a chaplain, like Ranulf Flambard, acted in this capacity and so pointed the way to the 'court' treasurer of Henry I.[270]

The king also used chamberlains as sheriffs, just as he did stewards.[271] Such household officials were accustomed to financial administration and could be posted out of court either because it was necessary to put a loyal man in charge of local affairs or because a rescue operation to set the rent and tax gathering in order had to be mounted. The sheriff was the all-purpose royal official in the shire, with military and judicial duties as well as financial. A man who had served as sheriff could also act as a judge. We have already seen how at the very beginning of the reign the stewards Eudo and Ivo Taillebois and Robert the dispenser, under the presidency of the bishops of Durham and Winchester, heard a case concerning land.[272]

Other royal chamberlains were, of course, engaged in more domestic duties – like buying the king's boots[273] – and under the master-chamberlain were, according to the *Establishment*, the chamberlains who served in turn, the chamberlain of the chandlery, who was concerned with the candles, the king's tailor, and the ewer,[274] whose principal responsibility was to provide the king's water, but also got 1d for drying the king's clothes when he was on his travels and 4d for providing the king's bath, except at the three great festivals, Christmas, Easter and Whitsunday, when the king wore his crown and the fees went to the church where the festivities took place. It is likely that William Rufus lived before fashion set high standards of personal hygiene for noblemen; but it is difficult to be sure. On 2 December 1077 Mabel of Bellême, countess of Shrewsbury, was murdered in her chamber, relaxing in bed, it was rumoured, after taking a bath;[275] and there was no more cruel amazon than she. Within half a century of William's death even knights were taking baths. Tristan made a habit of it, and once when in that

[270] Hollister, *op. cit.*, 272.

[271] Morris, *Med. Eng. Sheriff*, 46–7, 73, puts it the opposite way: a few favoured sheriffs held, or were given, great household offices at court. But in some cases at least the family had held the household office before 1066, and in any case it would seem more likely for a household officer to be posted to a shire than for a sheriff to be recuited for the household. The principal feature, however, is the interchangeability and lack of undue specialization in the royal service.

[272] Above, 62.

[273] Above, 100.

[274] For the king's tailor, see Round, *King's Serjeants*, 257 ff., and for the ewer, 214 ff. Ranulf Flambard escaped from the Tower of London in 1101 by means of a rope smuggled in by *minister aquae bajulus* in his water pot: *GR*, ii, 471.

[275] OV, iii, 134–6, 160.

defenceless state was visited by a very angry Yseut.[276]

The laundry receives scant attention, and it is not clear how clothes were washed at court. All we are told in the *Establishment* is that the wages of the laundress were not known, or perhaps in dispute.

At least thirteen royal chamberlains are noticed in Domesday Book.[277] The most important of these were the brothers Humphrey and Aiulf, the latter also described as sheriff (possibly of Somerset). Humphrey was quite a substantial landowner, holding in Surrey, Hampshire, Southampton, Berkshire, Wiltshire, Dorset, Somerset, Gloucestershire, Leicestershire and Suffolk, and may likewise have acted as sheriff.[278] Another important man, Robert Malet, Domesday lord of Eye, a large landowner in Suffolk and a sheriff of that county, although not given the title of chamberlain in Domesday Book, is thought on other grounds to have held that office; but he was out of William Rufus's favour and witnessed none of his writs and charters.[279] Five royal chamberlains, besides Herbert, held tenements in Winchester about 1110. Three of these, Aubrey, Geoffrey and William of Houghton, are possibly identical with the Domesday tenants bearing those names. William Mauduit (I) had been succeeded by his son, Robert Mauduit; and William of Pont-de-l'Arche, also a sheriff, who may have been too young to have served William Rufus, makes his appearance.[280] There are at least three important ministerial dynasties here, and on the whole chamberlains did well out of royal service.

Finally we reach the officers of the guard, police and the hunt. Three constables are listed in the *Establishment* by name, and as the first was paid on a higher scale than the others – indeed, only a little less than the chancellor – we have in effect one master and two under-constables. By the twelfth century there were three hereditary constableships held in the families of Montfort (-sur-Risle), Oilli and Abetot;[281] and Hugh

---

[276] *Tristan*, 43, 160, cf. 122, 134.

[277] Aiulf, *DB*, i, 52a, 63a, 73a, 82d (sheriff, in index, 75a); Alberic (Aubrey), 49c, 63d (the queen's chamberlain), 74d *bis*; Alwold, 58a, 63d; Bernard, 51c; Geoffrey (see below, 442), 49b; Gundwin, ii, 436b; Herbert, i, 48d; Hervey (*cubicularius*), 85a; Humfrey, 36c, 49a, 52a, 63a, 73a, 83a, 99b, 170a, 230c, 236a, ii, 433–4; Odin, i, 74d; Siric, 50a; Thurstin, 48a, 52a, 74d, 216c; William, 127a (a vineyard in London), 127c, 151b, 167a, 209b (a church), 216b (the successor to a priest).

[278] *Regesta*, i, nos 395, 448–9.

[279] Henry I made him master-chamberlain before 1105: GEC, x, appendix F, 51, supplemented by C.W. Hollister, 'Henry I and Robert Malet', *Viator*, iv (1973), 115. He was a favourite of both William I and Henry, but not, apparently, of Rufus.

[280] Herbert, *Winton Domesday*, I, preface; Alberic (Aubrey), I, 102; Geoffrey, I, 246; Robert Mauduit and his father William, I, 45; William of Houghton and son, I, 196; William of Pont-de-l'Arche, I, preface.

[281] White, 'The household', 150–2; cf. also *Regesta*, ii, xv–xvii.

(III) of Montfort, who had inherited the English lands,[282] Robert (I) of Oilli, a big tenant-in-chief in Oxfordshire who died about 1093 and was succeeded by his brother Nigel, and Urse of Abetot seem to have served William II in the office. Those three families were also constables of the royal castles at Dover, Oxford and Worcester respectively. Robert of Oilli, who was at first an oppressor of neighbouring Abingdon abbey and took from it a meadow, across the river from the castle, for the use of his knights (he also built the north bridge), at the end of his life contributed much to the rebuilding of the abbey church in which he and his wife were later buried.[283] Urse, who built a castle 'almost down the throats' of the monks of Worcester, and was cursed in famous words by the diocesan bishop Wulfstan – 'Hattest thu Urs, have thu Godes kurs' – seems to have made his fortune in England entirely through his military talents.[284] Hugh Oillard, who held lands in Winchester about 1110 and who had been succeeded in his lands and office before 1130 by his son William, may likewise have been a constable.[285] The Domesday ancestors of the two under-constables named in the *Establishment* were Odo fitzGamelin, the father of William fitzOdo, and Ralf de Pomeroy, the grandfather of Henry, both Devonshire barons.[286] Roger (de Pîtres) was the father of Walter, a constable under Henry I.[287] But none of these men was given the title of constable in the Survey, and their descendants may simply have held temporary appointments.

The constable, who took his name from the stables, was essentially a military officer and, under the king, in command of those household knights whom William Rufus recruited so eagerly and rewarded so generously. This was the *familia*, the military household, which is not covered in detail by the *Establishment*.[288] Archbishop Anselm, an aristocrat who loved feudal and military imagery, was fond of likening the kingdom of God to the royal court.[289] Towards the end of October 1097, when about to go into exile, partly because of trouble over the

[282] For this family and the problems of its pedigree, see Douglas, *Domesday Monachorum*, 65 ff. See also, below, 387, for Robert I, Hugh's elder brother, who inherited the Norman lands.

[283] *Chron. Abingdon*, ii, 7–8, 12–15, 24–5. Sanders, *Baronies*, 54.

[284] *GP*, 253. Loyd, *Families*, 1–2. And see above, 141–2.

[285] *Winton Domesday*, I, 8. Round, *King's Serjeants*, 6.

[286] OV, vi, 346; Sanders, *Baronies*, 48, 106–7; White, 'The household', 151–2; Round *FE*, 486–7, 'Bernard the king's scribe', 426; Loyd, *Families*, 78.

[287] Round, *King's Serjeants*, 79 ff.; *Regesta*, i, xxvi.

[288] Cf. *GR*, 368–9, for the number and depredations of the king's household knights. For the *familia*, see J.O. Prestwich, 'The Military Household of the Norman kings', *EHR*, xcvi (1981), 1. For constables, see also Stenton, *Feudal England*, 78 ff.

[289] *VA*, 93–6; 'Dicta Anselmi', *Memorials of Saint Anselm*, ed. R.W. Southern and F.S. Schmitt (1969), 150–1; 'De humanis moribus', caps 38, 80, *ibid.*, 52, 70.

soldiers he had provided the king for the Welsh campaign, he visited Canterbury and called his monks together to hear his farewell charge. By using the analogy of the courts of temporal princes, he reminded them of the service they owed to God. The prince had various kinds of knights in his court or palace: some were performing their duties in return for the lands which they held of him; some were serving for pay; and others bent themselves to his will in order to recover their inheritance which had been lost through their parents' fault. Those in the first category were well established and stable, and were secure as long as they obeyed their lord; the second, however, the mercenaries serving for worldly gain, were more restless, and often became dissatisfied with their pay and conditions, and dropped out; but the third, provided they had a firm purpose to recover their inheritance, would suffer with patience every possible burden and insult in pursuit of that end. His monks, therefore, should try not to be like the mercenary knights, but rather like those who, despite the sin of their father Adam, strove manfully to recover the heavenly kingdom which was theirs by inheritance.

The master-constable was probably also responsible for the general policing of the court, the production of guards, door-keepers (*ostiarii*, ushers), and those marshals who kept order in the hall and preserved the king's privacy. According to the *Establishment*, there were in the household a master-marshal and four under-marshals.[290] As the master was paid on the scale of the under-constables it would seem that the marshalsea was subordinate to the constabulary.[291] One of the tasks of the master-marshal was to keep the tallies which recorded all payments made out of the king's treasury and chamber, which suggests that he was responsible for the security of the treasures and accountable for them.[292] But marshals were associated particularly with horses, and their duties included messenger service and probably supervision of the hunt.[293] It is said that the under-marshals served the household servants, especially in finding billets (harbinger service), when the court was on the move, and performed other outside business for the king. When thus engaged they were paid 8d a day, and their serjeants 3d. Also on the strength of the

[290] *Constitutio*, 134.

[291] Round reached this view on other grounds and seemingly with great reluctance: *King's Serjeants*, 63, 82, and the prefatory *addenda et corrigenda*. Stenton, *Feudal England*, 70, stresses the original low status of the marshal – a horse-breaker. See also GEC, x, appendix G, 'The rise of the marshal', xi, appendix E, 'Marshals under the Conqueror'.

[292] Prestwich, however, *loc. cit.*, 7, suggests that the *dona et liberationes* were payments to the household knights, who, he believes, received retainers of at least £5 a year and wages, when on duty, of 1s a day, that is to say, more than the going rate of 8d.

[293] For the servants of the hunt, with which the *Constitutio* concludes, see above, 126–9.

marshalsea were ushers, some of whom were knights, watchmen and their men, and a stoker of the fires who, from Michaelmas to Easter, received 4d a day for the fuel. With the watchmen we reach the lowest level of rations, baker's loaves and ale. Later there was a marshal of the whores of the king's house; and the custody of whores was associated with the ushers.[294] But none of this appears in the *Establishment*, and writers about William II's licentious court allege that the policing was reduced and all standards relaxed.[295]

Gilbert, the ancestor of a famous family of marshals, may have served that king, and it has been suggested that Robert the marshal, a Domesday tenant, was his father.[296] Another Domesday landowner, Geoffrey the marshal, has been identified as the son of Miles and the ancestor of Robert de Venoix, who also held the office.[297] Of the marshals Roger and Gerond nothing more is known.[298] At least four porters (ushers) occur in the Survey,[299] and two royal serjeants held tenements in Winchester about 1110.[300]

William employed some of his household servants, notably stewards, chamberlains and constables, as we have seen, as sheriffs and perhaps as itinerant justices.[301] The best known, the most infamous, in many ways the most interesting, and certainly one of the most important of his servants was his chaplain Ranulf Flambard, who operated largely out of court, involved in the royal administration at large. His person and career are discussed in the next chapter, in connexion with the king's government.[302] As with Ranulf, so with his master and with the court as a whole, there is a contrast between personal weaknesses and governmental strength and efficiency. A rather disreputable court was staffed by obviously loyal servants of proved ability. Anselm may have thought privately that the household was ruled by Satan and served by devils: it was a far cry from the house of God he had visited in his dreams at the

---

[294] Round, *op. cit.*, 97–8, 103–4.

[295] Above, 102 ff.

[296] *DB*, i, 73b. Round, *op. cit.*, 89; *Regesta*, i, xxvi–xxvii. GEC, xi, 125, disagrees. Gilbert's son, John, appears as master-marshal in the *Constitutio*, 134.

[297] *DB*, i, 49a,b. Round, *King's Serjeants*, 89–90, *VCH Hants*, i, 430; GEC, xi, 122–4; Loyd, *Families*, 109. GEC, xi, 125. Geoffrey was in 1086 a sub-tenant of Henry the treasurer, and presumably had duties at the Winchester treasury.

[298] *DB*, ii, 94, 438b. GEC, xi, 125.

[299] John *hostiarius*, *DB*, i, 74c, 98c; Miles *portarius*, 49c; Robert *hostiarius*, 235a; William *porto'*, *hostiarius*, 117c, 292a. Round, *VCH Hants*, i, 431, identifies Miles as door-keeper at the royal gaol or castle at Winchester.

[300] Erchembald, *Winton Domesday*, I, 107; Herfrid, 44.

[301] Cf. Stenton, *English Feudalism*, 78. The services of all a lord's ministers were at his disposal for the administration of his fee, and it was for him to choose whom he would send on a particular errand.

[302] Below, 193 ff.

summit of the Alpine peak. But for the domestics, sweet were the fruits of office and glorious was it to be so close to even such a king as William Rufus. These mandarins were more likely to echo the Psalmist (Psalm 84), 'My soul longeth, yea, even fainteth for the courts of the Lord. . . . Blessed are they that dwell in thy house . . . for a day in thy courts is better than a thousand on earth. I would rather be a doorkeeper in the house of my God than to dwell in the tents of wickedness.'

Chapter 4

THE NOBILITY AND HIGHER CLERGY AND THE ROYAL GOVERNMENT

That there was an upper class in England after the Conquest, as before, and that this was in a special relationship to the monarchy, goes without saying. Although there is no need to discuss here whether either was in origin a nobility by birth or through service, the post-Conquest aristocracy was in its detailed composition doubly recent. Not only was it a completely new creation in the kingdom but also a selection out of those families which the Conqueror had particularly favoured in the duchy. In the half century after 1042, with initial instability followed by exceptional opportunities for advancement, some new men, mostly soldiers, vassals of the Norman baronage, were able greatly to improve their economic and social position and enter the upper class. Orderic Vitalis wrote that William I transformed the humblest of his clients into rich tribunes and centurions in England, and that these *nouveaux riches* themselves had clients in England far richer and more powerful than their own fathers had been in Normandy.[1] There is, however, an element of exaggeration here, and exceptions should not be stressed at the expense of the overall picture. The general situation was that members of an existing aristocracy were transplanted to the kingdom and soon assumed their customary position.

It was not, however, exactly the same position which the previous nobility had enjoyed. The Anglo-Danish thegns were a class recognized and defined by the law, a class with boundaries, surmountable only by legal process, clear cut and obvious to all. Their successors were referred to by the king as his barons, a word which meant a man, or vassal.[2] As barons were also part of the larger class of *fideles*, those who had sworn fealty to the king, and the almost identical category of tenants-in-chief, strictly speaking *baro* denoted not a rank but a relationship. This is even more obvious when we observe that the king's barons had their own barons (as Orderic pointed out), often called by historians 'honorial

---

[1] OV, ii, 260, 264. For the Norman nobility, see L. Musset, 'L'aristocratie normande au XIᶜ siècle', in *La Noblesse au Moyen Age*, ed. P. Contamine (Paris 1976), 71; Bates, *Normandy before 1066*, 34–5, 99 ff.

[2] *Dictionary of Medieval Latin*, ed. R.E. Latham, *s.v. baro*. I.J. Sanders, *Feudal Military Service in England* (1956), 1 ff.

barons'.[3] But just as *comes*, which originally meant a companion, became a rank (count), so could *baro*.

There was, however, no precise and comprehensive definition of baronage in this period. Although barons typically had the duty of providing a quota of knights to the royal army, and those with a *servitium debitum* of ten or more could have been considered barons *par excellence*,[4] this does not cover all cases. We notice occasional attempts to distinguish them from the wider category of the tenants-in-chief and royal servants in general. Eadmer wrote that the Conqueror limited the bishops' power to excommunicate his barons and servants (*ministri*);[5] and Henry I in his coronation charter distinguished between his barons, counts/earls and other tenants.[6] But the king and others normally referred to important royal officials, such as major domestic servants, sheriffs, judges, Domesday commissioners and members of the Exchequer board, as barons. The Westminster memorandum recording a transaction between Abbot Gilbert and Thurstin, the royal dispenser, lists as witnesses, first, Bishop Walkelin of Winchester, Urse of Abetot (Thurstin's brother), Herbert the king's chamberlain at Winchester, Ivo Taillebois (a royal steward) and three vassals (*homines*) of Robert, then, 'among other of the king's barons', Hugh of Beauchamp, William Baynard, Peter of Valognes, William the chamberlain (? Mauduit), Hugh of Buckland, Otho the goldsmith, 'and many other clerks and laymen'.[7] The 'other barons' are mostly sheriffs, but include two important finance officers, a chamberlain and the king's goldsmith who was probably also Master of the Mint. It would seem that the transaction took place at the meeting of some royal finance committee.

Nor was an exact definition of the baronage achieved soon after the Norman period. The language of the preamble and conclusion to Henry II's Constitutions of Clarendon (1164) is revealing in its diversity.

---

[3] For these see Stenton, *English Feudalism*, cap. 3. For the honorial barons on the Lacy honour of Weobley, see W.E. Wightman, *The Lacy Family in England and Normandy* (1966), 152 ff.

[4] For the quotas in 1166 see Round, *FE*, 225 ff. This is, however, a very controversial subject. As Duncombe, 'Feudal Tenure', 229–30, pointed out, most of Round's baronies were created after 1086, largely by amalgamations. See also R. Mortimer, 'The beginnings of the honour of Clare', *Battle III*, 119, 134, on the variability of fiefs and the possible effects of this on the quotas. But Round was defended by C.W. Hollister, 'Military obligation in Late-Saxon and Norman England', *Ordinamenti Militari in Occidente nell'Alto Medioevo*, Centro Italiano di Studi sull'Alto Medioevo, Spoleto, Settimana xv, 1967 (Spoleto 1968), i, 181 ff.

[5] *HN*, 10, *SSC*, 96.

[6] *SSC*, 118, cap. 2.

[7] Ely Inquest, *SSC*, 101, *DB*, i, 2a, 175d; *Dialogus de Scaccario*, 70; and for the Westminster document, above, 141.

Because dissension had arisen between the clergy, the king's judges and
the barons of the kingdom, an inquest had been held in the presence of
the archbishops, bishops and clergy and the earls, barons and magnates
(*proceres*) of the kingdom. But in subsequent definitions the magnates
become the more noble and ancient men in the kingdom. Moreover, the
business was transacted before the witness of ten counts/earls and twenty
mostly ministerial barons, all of whom are named and are described as
some of the magnates and nobles of the kingdom, both clerical and lay,
attending the royal court.[8] It is clear that, although this is a legal
context, *procer* and *nobilis* are hardly technical terms, and no one would
have cared to define *baro*.

Besides the complication of there being two related problems – who
were the baronage; and who were members of the nobility? – it seems
likely that, as is usual with class distinctions in mobile societies, different
views on these matters were in circulation at the same time. One opinion
seems to have been that the baronage was essentially that stratum which
lay between the counts and the officials; and those holding that view
would no doubt include in the nobility only the counts/earls and barons.
But two complementary maxims – royal office ennobles, and nobles
receive royal offices – worked powerfully at this time to rank *ministri* with
fideles. Both were ennobled because of their closeness to the king. This,
however, would hardly have been the opinion of the more ancient
nobility by blood; and society at large possibly always made the further
distinction between the major and the minor barons. By the time of the
Dialogus de Scaccario (*c.* 1178), the barons of the Exchequer divided
tenants-in-chief between those who held greater or smaller baronies;[9]
and when the baronage in the thirteenth century began to claim the
right to advise the king, this classification, although it seems never to
have been based on fixed rules, became of importance.[10]

There is little to suggest that the new landowners considered
themselves to have inherited the social and legal privileges of the thegns:
on the evidence of Domesday Book the rank had been devalued and was
being used for knights and lower royal officials.[11] More probably, most
of those who held land or office directly of the king aspired to nobility

---

[8] *SSC*, 163–4, 167.

[9] 'Quidam enim de rege tenent in capite que ad coronam pertinent, baronias scilicet
maiores seu minores': *Dialogus*, 96.

[10] Cf. Assize of Clarendon (1166), cap. 1, 'statuit praedictus rex Henricus de consilio
omnium baronum suorum', *SSC*, 170. According to Magna Carta, cap. 14, in order to
obtain the common counsel of the realm, archbishops, bishops, abbots, earls and major
barons shall be summoned by individual writ; all others who hold of the king in chief
shall be summoned generally through the royal sheriffs and bailiffs: *SSC*, 295.

[11] Even so, one of William II's writs was addressed to the sheriff and his servants and
all the thegns, instead of the more usual barons and/or lieges: *Regesta*, ii, no. 335a.

and were, indeed, accorded respect by humbler people. But medieval society was very hierarchically minded, and long-standing territorial dynasties would not have cared to be ranked with poorer and more recent families or with upstart royal domestics. Another complication was that, whereas many of the tenants-in-chief of the crown held small estates, there were at the next step down the feudal ladder, among those variously called honorial barons or rear- or mesne-tenants, not a few rich and important men. There was also the problem of the status of this class of feudal vassal in the escheated earldoms of Hereford and Kent. The Conqueror recognized the situation in August 1086, possibly as a result of the Domesday Survey, when at Salisbury he took fealty from all the important mesne tenants, the honorial barons, and so brought them into an immediate relationship with the crown.[12] This measure, possibly a special security expedient, and its repetitions may have created an ambiguous position. The characteristics of European nobility in general were direct subordination and access to the ruling prince; possession of jurisdiction over one's own subordinates; ownership of a fortified centre to one's estates, after which the dynasty was named; the right to hunt noble beasts on one's lands; and freedom from general taxation and common duties.[13] On this criterion, if we disregard the royal forest laws, the major, if not the minor and honorial, English barons would qualify.

Orderic describes how the Conqueror gave great honours in England to counts and magnates (*comites et optimates*), whom the chronicler also calls noblemen.[14] In his list of those whom he considered the most important he starts with five French or Norman counts – Eustace of Boulogne, Robert of Mortain, William of Evreux, Robert of Eu and Geoffrey son of Rotrou count of Mortagne[15] – and continues with nine magnates (and their own main barons), to whom he claimed William gave English counties: his steward William fitzOsbern (with Walter of Lacy), Hugh of Avranches (with Robert of Rhuddlan and Robert of Malpas), Roger of Montgomery (with Warin the Bald, William Pantulf, Picot and Corbet), Walter Giffard, William of Warenne and his brother-in-law, Odo of Champagne, besides Gerbod of Flanders, Earl Waltheof and Ralf de Gael, who had disappeared from the scene by

---

[12] *ASC, s.a.*, 162. Florence, ii, 19, expresses it differently: the king ordered the archbishops, bishops, abbots, counts/earls, barons and viscounts/sheriffs, in company with their knights (*milites*), to meet him at Salisbury on 1 August, and when they arrived he forced their knights to swear him fealty against all other men. Although the Latin terminology is unexpected, there may be no real conflict here, since *milites* had gone up the social scale by Florence's time. Cf. also Stenton, *op. cit.*, 111 ff.

[13] Cf. L. Genicot, 'Recent research on the medieval Nobility', in Reuter, *Medieval Nobility*, 22, 24.

[14] OV, ii, 260–6.

[15] Geoffrey was not, however, a tenant-in-chief in 1086.

1076. He describes the great powers of bishops Odo of Bayeux and Geoffrey of Coutances, who in their different ways had authority over the others; and he names two castellans, Hugh of Grandmesnil (Leicester) and Henry of Ferrières (Tutbury). In Orderic's eyes these were the main English nobles after 1070; and most of them lived into William II's reign.

The chronicler's views can be checked by Domesday Book, which provides lists of the tenants-in-chief of the king in each county for the year preceding William junior's accession. The arrangement of the entries improves with the successive drafts, and by the time of the Exchequer Domesday some principles governing the order had emerged. After the royal demesne are listed the ecclesiastical tenants, from the archbishops to humble clerks, then the lay tenants, from the counts to endowed domestics. The counts form an unmistakable group at the head of each county survey. But after this the classification is looser. It would seem that there was usually some attempt to rank the tenants, bearing in mind their prestige, the size of their estates and whether or not they held an office of the king. This led to three badly-defined and unsignalled groups: barons without an office; royal officials such as sheriffs, stewards and dispensers; the lesser servants, huntsmen, carpenters, cooks and such like. The boundaries between these categories are usually most uncertain. Although the lowest servants are sometimes grouped under a heading such as 'the lands of the king's thegns' or 'the land of the king's serjeants',[16] under Cambridge the land of two royal carpenters precedes that of Countess Judith and other noble widows.[17] The Domesday commissioners and their clerks were not compiling a social register; and they obviously did not spend much time on the niceties of precedence. It is, therefore, difficult to discover whom they considered a baron or noble. We can disregard here the clerical tenants, for their status was *sui generis*. The problem is where to draw the line after the counts. It would seem that there was a feeling that even major royal servants were socially inferior to large landowners who held no office, and that the nobility consisted of the counts/earls and the major barons, whoever they might be.

In England only a few of the counties (shires) were put under a count (earl), the remainder being in charge of a *vicomte* (viscount, sheriff). Only in Cheshire, Shropshire and Cornwall was the local earl the major landowner (in 1086 the earldoms of Kent and Herefordshire were in the king's hands), but counts held lands in all shires except Herefordshire. In 1086 nine of the English landowners bore the comital title, and five or six of these owed their rank or designation to their continental position. Count Eustace, never given his territorial appellation 'of Boulogne',

<hr>

[16] Cf. Hants, *DB*, i, 53d, Wilts, 74c.   [17] *DB*, i, 202a–b.

presumably because of his eminence,[18] was probably regarded as the most distinguished of them all. The counts of Evreux and of Meulan usually follow him. Count Alan (whether 'of Brittany' or 'of Richmond' is undisclosed) and the counts of Eu and Mortain have more variable positions. The three remaining counts, Roger, Hugh and Aubrey, who owed their title indubitably to their English appointments, are almost invariably ranked in that order and listed as such. This is a very disparate company. The foreign counts were nobles of distinction, although it is noticeable that the count of Mortain, the Conqueror's half-brother, possibly because he was the son of a *vicomte* and a tanner's daughter, was sometimes placed low on the list. Roger of Montgomery, earl of Shrewsbury, although himself *vicomte* of the Hiémois, clearly ranked above Hugh *vicomte* of Avranches and earl of Chester. And Aubrey of Coucy, earl of Northumberland since 1080, usually comes last, possibly because his honour, distributed between five Midland shires, had recently escheated to the crown, evidence that he, although still accorded the title, was no longer in office.[19] The title, in post-Conquest England probably quasi-hereditary from the start, was shared only by the wife, and not by the sons, in the lifetime of the father. In the Domesday Book schedules, William of Eu, the son of the ruling count (Robert),[20] is usually well down the list of tenants-in-chief, as are Harold son of Earl Ralf and Richard son of Count Gilbert; Hugh of Montgomery follows the earls in Staffordshire, and Roger of Poitou, another son of Earl Roger, who had just lost his large honour 'of Lancaster', likewise appears as a simple baron. This seems more restrictive than usual continental usage.

[18] Isidore, *Etymol.*, X, 184, cf. 146: 'nobilis, non vilis, cuius et nomen et genus scitur.'

[19] *HR*, ii, 199, cf. 384, for a history of the earls which is so compressed that it has misled many into thinking that Robert of Mowbray succeeded Aubrey within a year of the latter's appointment (1080). The account of Robert is equally succinct. In *DB*, Aubrey is listed in the county indexes as if he still held the lands, but in each breve – Wilts (i, 69a), Oxon (157c), Northants (224b), Leics (231c–d) and Warwicks (239c) – there is something, either past tense or a special note at the end, to indicate that he was no longer in possession. In the case of Warwickshire, a note that the lands are in the king's hands has been cancelled and 'Geoffrey de Wirce has custody' substituted. Everything points to a recent escheat. See also above, 73–4, and below, 167–8. Round, reviewing *Regesta*, i, in *EHR*, xxix (1914), 355, suggested that Aubrey was that lord of Coucy in Picardy who had been present with William I and Philip of France at the siege of Gerberoy (*Regesta*, no. 115a: see above, 35), and witnessed charters of Duke Robert in 1088 (no. 299) and, as Alberic de Cocceio, in 1095 (no. 384). In September 1087 Aubrey was dispatched by the Norman barons to Abbeville, not far from Coucy-le-Château, to recall Robert to succeed his dead father as duke: see above, 50. But he had lost his lands and castle at Coucy and was captured in bed some time after 1078. The fullest account is in J. Tardif, 'Le procès d'Enguerran de Coucy., *Bibl. de l'Ecole des Chartes*, lxxix (1918), 8ff.

[20] For the difficulties over William (count) of Eu, see above, 76 n. 105.

The Norman rulers, both in the duchy[21] and then in the kingdom, were sparing in their creation of counts and earls and never minded when a title lapsed. They preferred to be served by *vicomtes* or sheriffs, and only two of these – Roger of Montgomery and Hugh of Avranches in the 1070s – were promoted to an earldom during the reign of the Conqueror and his sons. It was not until the 1140s, at the height of the rivalry between Stephen and Matilda, that four descendants of Domesday shrieval families were girded with the belt.[22] But although royal *vicomtes* and sheriffs, as well, of course, as honorial sheriffs, were by their very titles kept firmly below the counts and earls,[23] they had important provincial governorships, ruling counties, sometimes groups of them, with the help of the wardenship of the county towns and castles; and if they could found a dynasty, or, even better, make their office hereditary,[24] they might expect their descendants to rise in the social scale. They undoubtedly enjoyed or acquired membership of the baronage. It is often said that the Norman kings appointed barons to the office.[25] To judge by their place in the witness lists to charters and in the Domesday schedules, it might be better to say that royal sheriffs were regarded as barons of a sort. They were in 1087 a rather miscellaneous lot. Whereas Baldwin sheriff of Devon was the son of Gilbert count of Brionne and great-grandson of Richard I duke of Normandy, had his own castle at Okehampton as well as the custody of Exeter and was certainly a nobleman by birth, most of the others have obscure origins; and the few that are well known, like Haimo sheriff of Kent, the son of Haimo *Dentatus*, lord of Torigny, were clearly ministerial nobility.

Because there was no noble class recognized and defined by the law and baronial tenure and rank had not had time to assume clearly recognizable characteristics, it is impossible to say how many of the tenants-in-chief listed in 1086 after the earls would have been regarded by contemporaries as one or the other, or both. Nor is it clear where honorial barons stood. They were certainly of higher social standing than knights and other free tenants, and they and their holdings are identified in Domesday Book within the baronial fiefs, probably because their demesne farms were, like those of their lord, immune from taxes and service due to the king.[26] Likewise they often had jurisdictional

---

[21] D.C. Douglas, 'The earliest Norman counts', *EHR*, lxi (1946), 129.

[22] Hugh, the second son of Roger Bigot (Norfolk); Miles of Gloucester, grand-nephew of Durand de Pîtres (Hereford); Patrick, grandson of Edward of Salisbury (Salisbury); and Geoffrey de Mandeville, grandson of his namesake (Essex).

[23] Although the Norman *vicomtes* were the deputies of the count/duke of Normandy and could have risen with their master.

[24] See below, 187 ff.

[25] Cf. Morris, *Med. Eng. Sheriff*, 41 ff.

[26] See below, 241.

rights over their own vassals and free tenants.[27] But whatever pretensions to nobility they may have had within their lord's honour, they
would have had no general claim to that status. And even if they became
immediate vassals of the king through the escheat of the honour, it seems
that they stood no great chance of promotion in rank. Few of Odo of
Bayeux's surviving vassals became tenants-in-chief after 1088, the
Douvres family of Chilham and Bishop Gilbert Maminot of Lisieux's son
at West Greenwich being among the exceptions. Most of the baronies
which arose out of the debris were new creations.[28] Promoted by the
forfeiture of Earl Roger of Hereford in 1075, however, was the important
Lacy honour of Weobley.[29]

If honorial barons had an ambiguous status, anything lower was
clearly outside the nobility. By the twelfth century, feudal society in
England was considered to be composed of earls, barons and vavassors.[30]
This last category comprised not only knights but also all enfeoffed
soldiers and any tenant who had any sort of military duty. It is
significant that when royal knights are featured in Domesday Book they
appear at the end of the list among the menials: in the eleventh century
milites and their servants, *armigeri*, squires, seem in most literary contexts
to be little more than common soldiers;[31] knighthood conferred as yet no
social distinction; and the emergence of knights as a distinct and
honourable class did not get under way before Henry I's reign.

By the thirteenth century, some 200 estates, mostly created by the
Norman kings and earls, were considered baronies, and about 130 of
these were held by the king's barons in William II's reign.[32] In Berkshire
in 1086, to take one county as an example, forty of the king's tenants,
including five or six officials, might well have been considered of
baronial standing. That would leave about a score on the wrong side of
the salt. In 1166 there were in the kingdom as a whole perhaps a

[27] Stenton, *English Feudalism*, 99 ff.

[28] Duncombe, 'Feudal Tenure', 131 ff., and see below, 172.

[29] Wightman, *op. cit.*, 117 ff.

[30] Stenton, *op. cit.*, 15 ff.; P.R. Cross, 'Literature and Social Terminology: the
Vavasour in England', in *Social Relations and Ideas* (Hilton *Festschrift*), ed. T.H. Aston *et al.*
(1983), 109.

[31] Knightly status in the eleventh century is a controversial subject. For some views,
see G. Duby, 'Les Origines de la Chevalerie', *Ordinamenti Militari in Occidente nell'Alto
Medioevo*, Centro Italiano di studi sull'Alto Medioevo, Spoleto, Settimana xv, 1967
(Spoleto 1968), ii, 739; P. Van Luyn, 'Les Milites dans la France du XIe siècle', *Le Moyen
Age*, lxxvii (1971), 5, 193; J. Flori, 'Chevaliers et chevalerie au XIe siècle en France et
dans l'Empire germanique', *ibid.*, lxxxii (1976), 125; *idem*, 'Les origines de l'adoubement
chevaleresque', *Traditio*, xxxv (1979), 232–3; Bates, *Normandy before 1066*, 50–5, 109–11.
Cf. also Goscelin of St Bertin's story of the behaviour of an *armiger* in the garrison of
mercenary troops put by William I in Canterbury castle in 1085–6: BL MS Cotton.
Vespas. B xx, fos 184 ff.

[32] Sanders, *Baronies*.

hundred royal tenants who owed quotas of ten knights or more.[33] All we can say, therefore, is that in 1086 there was a relatively small number of landowners beyond the counts/earls, possibly between one and two hundred, whom the king regarded as his barons, and that this body contained men very unequal in wealth and prestige. In that respect they were similar to the much larger class of thegns which they had replaced.

They differed more markedly from the thegnage in their nomenclature.[34] Whereas the earls and thegns of the Anglo-Danish kingdom had normally borne dithematic Germanic names which, when permuted within families, constituted an extensive and significant *onomasticon*, the Anglo-Norman baronage introduced and remained faithful to a restricted list of names, mostly of French origin. Among the major barons of 1086 only Edward of Salisbury and one or two Alfreds[35] and Osberns were reminders of the Germanic past common to both races. William was by far the most popular name, followed by Robert. The third ducal name, Richard, was relatively rare among the baronage. Other popular names were Hugh, Ralf/Ranulf, Geoffrey, Roger, Walter and Gilbert.[36] With ducal names popular in the many families which claimed to be descended from the dukes or their consorts, and the whole pool of fashionable Christian names so small, surnames became a necessity. In Domesday Book the territorial designation, the 'house name', is by far the most common, barons taking their name from the residence to which they were most attached, usually a fortification, the *caput honoris*. This adoption of a territorial name has sometimes been thought to signify the change from an agnatic to a cognatic system of relationships, the evolution of a new backbone, based on stricter hereditary descent, within the traditional amorphous family grouping.[37] As a variation of the territorial name, the patronymic remained popular. And, thirdly, some quite important men had acquired hereditary bynames, for example, Bigot. In Berkshire, after the three counts, we have Henry of Ferrières (–St Hilaire, Eure), William fitzAnsculf and Walter Gif(f)ard, each representing one of these forms.

[33] Round, *FE*, 246 ff. Cf. also above, 157 n. 4.

[34] For 'leading names' cf. K. Schmid, 'The structure of the Nobility in the earlier Middle Ages', in Reuter, *Medieval Nobility*, pp. 39 ff.

[35] E.g. Alfred of Hispania (Epaignes, Eure), lord of Nether Stowey (Somerset). Alfred of Lincoln was a Breton.

[36] In the index to this book, which, of course is not confined to the Anglo-Norman aristocracy, the count is, William (61), Robert (46), Hugh (31), Ralf/Ranulf (28), Geoffrey and Roger (24), Richard (18), Walter (15), Gilbert (14).

[37] Cf. L. Genicot, 'Recent research on the medieval Nobility', in Reuter, *Medieval Nobility*, 27, on the views of 'the Freiburg school'. Since this chapter was written has appeared J.C. Holt, 'Feudal Society and the Family in Early Medieval England: I. The Revolution of 1066', *TRHS*, 5th ser., xxxii (1982), 193.

On a European scale, the social position of the Anglo-Norman nobility would seem to be among the lowest. Not one dynasty could claim sixth-century Roman origins: the nearest family with such pretensions was that of Montfort l'Amaury, on the wrong side of the boundary with France.[38] Few barons were 'international', with estates disregarding the boundaries of other major principalities, few had a wide reputation or played any part on the European stage; none can be numbered among the princes who participated in the First Crusade. An earl of Chester or a count of Mortain, although vassals of a king, were socially far inferior to a count of Blois, who could trace his line back to the seventh-century Burgundian nobility of Frankish origins,[39] and were well below the level of even more recent princely dynasties, such as the counts of Anjou. They were probably the social equals of a count of Ponthieu. The nobility of a count/duke of Normandy, who became a king by conquest, was not automatically and instantaneously raised to the position of that which had been grouped under a pre-Conquest English king or was to be found beneath the kings of France and Germany.[40] Nor, although economic strength is an obvious attribute of medieval nobility, and only in late-Anglo-Saxon England were poor nobles to be found, did new wealth give the Anglo-Norman baronage an immediate entrée into the appropriate social level. Most visitors to the English kingdom for two centuries after the Conquest considered its society provincial and lacking in distinction. The inferiority of the nobility was not only a consequence of the newness of the royal house but also contributed to the continuance of its low standing. Rulers were judged by the rank of those who supported them on solemn occasions. William II was less prestigious than Philip I of France, himself a prince of the lowest reputation, because the Capetian dynasty had a century's start on the Norman, and its nobility up to five centuries. Such a disparity could not be obliterated in a generation. But if William Rufus behaved at times like a parvenu, his younger brother Henry was a little more porphyrogenite. The gap was beginning to narrow.

One of the most important social events determined by class was

---

[38] Bates, *Normandy before 1066*, 34–5, 134, argues that the Norman aristocracy of the eleventh century, like that in other regions of France, was a continuation of the Carolingian. But even if this was so, its members were unaware of the fact: their own genealogies went back only to the period 1020–50 and in the twelfth century they created pedigrees which connected them with the ducal family. See *ibid.*, 106 ff. For the Montfort family, see K.F. Werner, 'Noble families in Charlemagne's kingdom', in Reuter, *Medieval Nobility*, 155 ff.

[39] Werner, 77 and n. 66.

[40] There were, it will be noticed, no dukes (except for the ruling prince) or margraves in either Normandy or England. The Anglo-Saxon earls, however, were called *dux* in Latin documents and had some claim to be Germanic 'stem-dukes'.

marriage. With few exceptions, marriages were contracted within the stratum of social equals. But the nuances are important, and a number of factors affected the exact status of the marriage partner. The recognition by the late eleventh century in France that women could inherit land in the absence of a direct male heir made the heiress a much desired object in feudal society and gave her a certain, and to some extent selective, chance of marriage. It did not, however, always allow her to choose a social superior, for, although there was little danger of her being taken in marriage by a worthless adventurer or by a man of greatly inferior social standing, if her marriage was under the control of her lord, he might be induced to sell it to some useful vassal or servant. And the girl who would have no more than her dowry (*maritagium*) was in an even worse position, for while girls on offer were plentiful, sons allowed to marry were few.[41] Hence in general brides were of a relatively higher social standing than the grooms.

It does not seem that the Norman dukes had discouraged cross-border marriages; indeed, William the Conqueror appears to have regarded them as a means of extending his power. He betrothed his own heir to the heiress of the count of Maine and was ready to marry his daughters to other ruling princes. Roger of Beaumont married a daughter of the count of Meulan, Roger of Montgomery first the heiress to Bellême and second Adelais of Le Puiset, his son Robert of Bellême the heiress to Ponthieu, and William of Evreux a daughter of the count of Nevers. Orderic, in his passage on the new English nobility, mentions that Hugh earl of Chester married the daughter of Hugh of Claremont in the Beauvaisis and William of Warenne married Gerbod of Flanders's sister. But as a rule the Anglo-Norman nobility married among themselves. As a result, the distance between the king and his barons began to widen. Most of the Conqueror's barons, owing to the irregular unions and fecundity of earlier dukes, were related in some distant way to him; and Orderic recalls that he gave his niece Judith to Earl Waltheof and that his sister had married Odo of Champagne, nephew of Count Theobald. The chronicler omitted, as notorious, the king's relationship to Odo of Bayeux and Robert of Mortain. But neither the Conqueror nor William Rufus had bastard daughters to bestow on favoured members of the nobility; and it was not until Henry became king that a new crop of nobles closely related by blood to the king could arise. The lack of royal blood in the Anglo-Norman baronage between 1066 and 1100 could have been another reason for its undistinguished social standing. In that period no baron made a marriage on a par with Tostig Godwinson's to Judith of Flanders in Edward the Confessor's reign.

[41] See above, 18.

The Wheel of Fortune was always in Orderic's mind when he viewed the careers of the nobility.[42] The accession of any new king altered the flow and direction of the stream of patronage, and normally there was a switch of favour to younger men and often to those of less assured standing, to men anxious to rise; and any rebellion produced losers and winners. That William II would make some changes would have been expected. By 1087 the founders of the new kingdom who had survived until Domesday Book were twenty years older, and many were approaching retirement or death. Nor could it be guaranteed that their children would be congenial to the new ruler. The composition of the court would inevitably change. But it was possible for dynasties to survive royal indifference or coldness; not Amurath an Amurath succeeded, and it would not seem that William II's reign was a particularly dangerous or unsettled period. In the early years he created several new earls. He quickly restored Roger of Poitou, Roger of Montgomery's third son, to his honour of Lancaster and may have given him the comital title.[43] As a reward for loyal service in 1088 he made William of Warenne earl of Surrey and Henry of Beaumont earl of Warwick.[44] Later he recognized Simon of St Liz (I) as earl of Huntingdon and Northampton and possibly created Walter Giffard first earl of Buckingham.[45] Some time after 1093 he entitled Roger of Montgomery's youngest son, Arnulf, earl of Pembroke, the family's recent conquest in Wales.[46]

Robert of Mowbray's tenure of Northumberland is difficult to unravel. It is usually stated that he was appointed earl in 1080–1 after Aubrey of Coucy had abandoned the office almost immediately after receiving it.[47] But this is based on an arbitrary interpretation of Simeon of Durham's summary history of the earldom, and, as we have seen,[48] Aubrey seems to have departed only shortly before the Domesday Survey of 1086 and was even then still enjoying the title. Indeed, it is tempting to associate his resignation with Roger of Poitou's loss of Lancashire, and associate both with the Danish invasion scare of 1085 and defence measures which the king took in the north. Simeon does say,

[42] Cf. Emma Mason, 'Magnates, curiales and the Wheel of Fortune', *Battle II*, 118. Cf. also K. Schmid, *op. cit.*, 54: 'the leading stratum of the kingdom changed almost with every king'.

[43] See above, 85 n. 160. In 1094, described as Earl Roger called 'of Poitou', he granted the church of Lancaster and other estates to St Martin's, Sées: *CDF*, no. 664.

[44] See above, 77, 93. For Henry of Beaumont, see also Emma Mason, *loc. cit.*, 126 ff.

[45] See above, 93.

[46] See below, 322.

[47] E.g., *HBC*, 441.

[48] Above, 161.

however, that it was the Conqueror who replaced Aubrey with Robert, and on the face of it that would seem likely. Robert was the client of his uncle, Geoffrey bishop of Coutances, and the bishop was William I's, not William II's, friend.[49] The promotion must have been late in the reign, for Robert was still not a tenant-in-chief of the crown in the spring of 1086, unless his lands were confined to Northumberland and Durham, which were not surveyed; and he witnesses as earl no charter of repute before March–December 1094.[50]

It is possible that he was given the frontier earldom when the Conqueror left for Normandy in the summer of 1086. Even so, he does not seem quickly to have established his position there. He was in the duchy some time in the first year after the king's death, for he is listed by the nuns of Holy Trinity, Caen, as one of their despoilers in that period.[51] Moreover, it was from Bristol, in association with his uncle, that he campaigned against the new king, and although the twelfth-century chroniclers William of Malmesbury and Florence style him earl in their accounts of the episode, the more contemporary Anglo-Saxon Chronicle does not.[52] It may be suspected that, although Geoffrey and Robert remained in England while the Conqueror fought his last campaign on the Continent, Robert's earldom was not fully recognized by the next king.

As the uncle was readmitted to court by November 1088,[53] it might be expected that the nephew too would have been pardoned for his support of the duke. It is reported, however, in the account of the trial of the bishop of Durham, that the bishop, after his condemnation, asked for ships to convey him to Normandy on 21 November, as he wished to accompany Robert (in the text, Roger) of Mowbray on his crossing.[54] Although this interesting bit of news does not necessarily mean that Robert was going, like Durham, into enforced exile, or that they had

[49] The twelfth-century *Vita S. Oswini* written at Tynemouth, also implies that Robert was appointed by the Conqueror. Since Robert granted that priory to St Albans in the teeth of Durham's claims, he gets a favourable notice: p. 15. The origins of this family are also obscure. As Geoffrey was related to Nigel (II), *vicomte* of the Cotentin, and 'bought' the local bishopric, he was probably a member of a Cotentin family: cf. Bates, *Normandy before 1066*, 197–8.

[50] *Regesta*, nos 148, 196–7, 286 and 318 are forgeries, and in no. 168, a Norman charter which seems genuine and is earlier than 1084, although he appears as Robert Mowbray *comes*, he is listed after the *vicomtes*. It would seem that this pancart version was updated. The only genuine charters he witnesses indisputedly as earl are 349 (March–December 1094), 363 (1095) and ii, 372c (1093 × 5).

[51] Haskins, *NI*, 63.

[52] *GR*, ii, 360: *comes Humbrensium*; Florence, ii, 21: *comes Northymbriae*, but, p. 24, no title. *ASC*, s.a.

[53] He was present at the trial of the bishop of Durham: see above, 88.

[54] *De Injusta Vexatione*, 192, where he is not styled earl, a title given to the others.

been colleagues in the north, it does at least point in that direction. If he was indeed banished in 1088, the logical time for his return would be September 1091, when the bishop was restored to Durham;[55] but Geoffrey of Coutances remained mostly in Normandy until his death in February 1093,[56] and perhaps it was at that point, when William allowed Robert to inherit his uncle's English honour, that the nephew was restored to the earldom. The bishop and earl soon became enemies,[57] and the scene was set for Robert's rebellion and ruin in 1095.[58]

William II, therefore, continued to leave the earldoms of Kent and Hereford vacant, and resumed the honours of the count of Boulogne and of the earl of Northumberland, but by his recognitions and new creations almost doubled the number of counts and earls with strong English connexions. His appointments were all for good political reasons, strengthening rather than diminishing royal authority, and hardly reducing his revenues, since some, if not all, cost their recipients a large entry fine.[59] Almost all the new earls were from the oldest Norman families and most were promoted in order to give them rank rather than create new military commands. Lancaster and Pembroke were, of course, frontier lordships, but three of the new earls were closely grouped in the Midland shires, and of these probably only Henry of Beaumont had custody of a royal castle (Warwick). The case of William of Warenne is significant. Although his territorial base was in Sussex, he was presumably given the title of Surrey, in which shire he held no land at all, because there were other great lords who held rapes in Sussex, including Earl Roger of Shrewsbury, and they could have felt slighted had their peer, or indeed social inferior, taken his title from that county, although we may be sure that there was never any suggestion that any of them would have been mediatized. Nothing shows more clearly than this how an earldom was becoming little more than a title of honour. With the office went a claim to the 'third-penny', a third part of the profits of the shire court, but seemingly to nothing more.[60]

As a contribution to the changed status, William did not normally add to the existing possessions of his new earls. Exceptionally, the landless Henry, a cadet of a great family and the king's companion in the dark days of 1088, was endowed with the Warwickshire estates of

[55] Below, 294.
[56] See above, 70, 92.
[57] *HDE*, i, 124; *HR*, ii, 261; *Miracles of St Cuthbert, ibid.*, 345–7; *Regesta*, no. 349. See also Offler, *Durham Episcopal Charters*, 3 ff.
[58] Below, 346 ff.
[59] Below, 253 ff.
[60] J.H. Round, *Geoffrey de Mandeville* (1892), 287 ff.

Turchil of Arden, but it was left to his elder brother, Robert of Meulan, who inherited their father's Norman and English honours in 1094, to set him up properly by handing over his own Domesday estates in Warwickshire and Northamptonshire.[61] Indeed, these family arrangements may have been made a condition of Henry's promotion. On the evidence, it would seem that William created earls as cheaply as possible and that in no way were the profits from the forfeitures dissipated by the new creations. His successor was far more lavish, although mostly in his later years.

Changes in the composition of the highest titled stratum of society were less important than the extinction of some of the richest families and the reduction in the influence of some others. In 1086 the ten wealthiest landowners, excluding English prelates, were Odo of Bayeux, his brother Robert of Mortain, Roger of Montgomery, William (I) of Warenne, Alan Rufus of Brittany and Richmond, Hugh of Avranches, earl of Chester, Richard of Clare, Geoffrey of Mowbray, bishop of Coutances, Geoffrey (I) of Mandeville and Eustace II of Boulogne, roughly in that order.[62] Not all these were intimates of the Conqueror at the end of his reign. Odo was in prison and Eustace had fallen away, but the remaining eight were still outstanding members of the Anglo-Norman aristocracy and of the generation which, in the wake of the Conqueror, and in cooperation with him, had created the new order. Of this ten (or their successors), only three, William of Warenne, Alan of Richmond and Hugh of Avranches, were conspicuously loyal to William II. Of the remaining seven, three, Odo, Eustace and the Mowbrays, lost their lands, and a further three, Robert of Mortain and his heir William, Gilbert fitzRichard of Clare and Geoffrey de Mandeville, never recovered the king's full favour. But William did not regard the survivors of the rebellion of 1088 as particularly dangerous. He gave Roger Bigot frequent employment and welcomed him at court; he allowed Geoffrey de Mandeville to retain a key position in London;[63] he encouraged the Montgomery schemes in Wales and became a great admirer of Robert of Bellême; and even if he mistrusted Gilbert of Clare, that baron may have received the Norfolk lands of Rainald

---

[61] Sanders, *Baronies, s.v.* Warwick; C.W. Hollister, 'Magnates and *Curiales* in early Norman England', *Viator*, viii (1977), 71–3; cf. Levi Fox, 'The Honor and earldom of Leicester', *EHR*, xxxiv (1939), 386 ff.

[62] Hollister, *ibid.*, table A, 65; *Battle II*, 185 n. 7.

[63] Stenton, *English Feudalism*, 222–3, considered that custody of the Tower was never lost by the Mandevilles, but that they did not have continuous possession of the shrievalties of London and Middlesex, Essex and Hertfordshire. William confirmed the grant of a manor by Geoffrey and his wife to Westminster abbey: *Regesta*, no. 402.

fitzIvo early in the reign[64] and was in his army in 1091 and 1095. In fact the rebellions and conspiracies of 1088, 1095, 1101, 1102 and 1106, in which several of the wealthiest families were involved, were all failures, a feature which ensured the maiming or destruction of those baronial houses.

Against these important, but hardly revolutionary, changes must, however, be set the massive 'biological' continuity within the middle and lower ranks of the baronage, a stability found also in the household officials and the king's servants in the shires. Of 128 honours which can be identified in Domesday Book and by the thirteenth century had some claim to be baronies, 49 were held throughout William's reign by the same person, 45 passed to a son, 11 to a daughter, 3 to a brother, and 1 to a nephew.[65] That is to say 109, or 85%, remained undisturbed or descended by hereditary right. Nor are all the outstanding cases likely to be exceptions to this rule: in six the relationship between the two holders is unknown, and for thirteen information is simply lacking. For example, Alfred of Marlborough's lands, including Ewyas Harold (Herefordshire), passed to Harold, son of King Edward the Confessor's Earl Ralf; Little Easton (Essex) passed from Walter the Deacon to Robert, younger son of Walter fitzOther, lord of Eton (Buckinghamshire) and castellan of Windsor castle; Thurstin fitzRolf's lands at North Cadbury (Somerset) went to Winebald de Ballon (Maine), lord of Caerleon and brother of Hamelin, whom William put in Abergavenny.[66] Even if the successor was unrelated, and this cannot be proved, William seems to have made no attempt to add such estates to the royal demesne. In the case of the Breton Judhel, whom William expelled from Totnes at the beginning of his reign for an unknown reason, and replaced with Roger (I) de Nonant, a man in his favour, he compensated him in 1095, when Robert of Mowbray lost his honours, by granting him the earl's lands in Devon, the future barony of Barnstaple. Only in a very few cases can the king's arbitrary interference be identified or suspected, and when we consider the natural as well as the military and political hazards to which landed families were exposed, William's reign must be considered a period of exceptional tranquillity.

This is also shown by the small number of established barons and servants who were greatly enriched by the king and by the paucity of

[64] R. Mortimer, 'The beginnings of the honour of Clare', *Battle III*, 119, believes that these estates were acquired 'probably soon after the Domesday Inquest'. For the lands, see *DB*, ii, 230 ff.

[65] The following statistics and illustrations are drawn from Sanders, *Baronies*.

[66] See also J.H. Round, 'The family of Ballon and the conquest of South Wales', *Studies in Peerage and Family History* (1901), 181. Winebald was a founder-benefactor of Bermondsey priory: *Regesta*, no. 398. Hamelin was a benefactor of St Vincent at Le Mans, where his gratitude to William was recorded: *CDF*, no. 1045.

new men who entered the baronage during the reign. The shortage of royal charters and financial records from this period may distort the picture a little; but it is unlikely that many upstarts crept in entirely unnoticed. Eudo *dapifer* received some estates, and no doubt there were pickings for such men as the brothers Urse of Abetot and Robert *dispensator*,[67] but they do not seem to have been heaped with rewards. Nor were many landless men so endowed by the king as to take their place among the greater baronage. Apart from Henry of Beaumont, only Robert fitzHaimo, the son of the sheriff of Kent and a constant companion of the king, can be cited.[68] William took advantage of the forfeiture of Odo of Bayeux's honour to endow some of his own men, but whether before the bishop's death in 1097 cannot be said. In Kent he enfeoffed Geoffrey Talbot (Swanscombe), an anonymous younger son of Haimo *dapifer*, founder of the Crevequer family (Chatham), and William Peverel of Dover.[69] Other baronial families which originated in the reign were largely those whom he planted or confirmed in the frontier areas in order to protect or advance the kingdom. In Wales were the conquests of Philip of Briouze and Bernard of Neufmarché;[70] in Cumbria William enfeoffed Ranulf of Bricquessart and Ivo Taillebois, both discussed more fully below, and in Yorkshire the Rumilly and Balliol families[71] and Geoffrey fitzPain (Warter). The fact that the new men had mostly to be settled on the marginal lands shows how dense and orderly by 1087 was the settlement in the rest.

One of the most useful ways in which William helped his favourites, however, was in providing them with rich or important wives. He gave Lucy of Bolingbroke, a great heiress, perhaps the daughter of Thorold, a post-Conquest sheriff of Lincoln, first to a steward, Ivo Taillebois, whose parentage is unknown, then to Roger fitzGerold, brother of Robert and son of Gerold 'Miles Christi', a seneschal, lord of Roumare (near Rouen) and castellan of Neufmarché, and finally to Ranulf le Meschin (i.e. the young) of Bricquessart, *vicomte* of Bayeux. He thus created families, one of which was to become earls of Lincoln, the other to inherit the earldom of Chester.[72] For Simon of St Liz, a knight of obscure parentage, he

[67] Hollister, 'Magnates and *Curiales*', 71; Emma Mason, 'Magnates, Curiales and the Wheel of Fortune', 135 ff.

[68] See above, 169–70 and Hollister, *ibid*.

[69] Duncombe, 'Feudal Tenure', 133 ff., 72 ff. It is not clear whether it was William or Henry I who created the new baronies of Cogges and Patricksbourne.

[70] See below, 321–2.

[71] See below, 297–8. Robert of Rumilly was grateful to William, making a grant to the Montgomery abbey, St Martin's, Troarn (dioc. Bayeux), for the souls of his lord King William, William's father and mother, himself and his heirs: Bruton priory cartulary, BL MS. Egerton 3772, fo. 115r (transcript kindly provided by Dr D.R. Bates).

[72] Lucy's identity, despite much research, remains uncertain: see *inter alios*, GEC, vii, appendix J, 'The Countess Lucy'; iii, 166; vii, 667: Round, *FE*, 328–31. She was

provided in about 1090 Matilda, a daughter of Earl Waltheof and Judith, his cousin.[73] The earldoms of Huntingdon and Northampton were a great prize for this fine soldier. For Robert fitzHaimo was procured Sibyl, one of the younger daughters of Roger of Montgomery, earl of Shrewsbury,[74] an alliance which, no doubt, helped William's friend to establish himself in Wales. These examples are probably only the most noteworthy of William's common practice, and in all these cases but Ivo's he was rewarding household knights, most of whom would hold important military commands in both his own and his younger brother's reign.[75]

The English Orderic was fascinated by the *mores* of the Norman aristocracy, with its mixture of brutality, lawlessness, greed and piety. He penned many interesting character sketches of the men who thronged his great panorama of Norman history, and those which he devoted to Roger of Montgomery, earl of Shrewsbury, and Hugh of Avranches, earl of Chester, will serve as examples. Of Roger, the patron of his father, Odelerius of Orleans, and the lord of Warin, a patron of St Evroul, both of whom are mentioned, he wrote approvingly:

> He was wise and temperate and a lover of justice, and he loved the company of wise and sober men. He had with him for a long time three wise clerks, Godebald, Odelerius and Herbert, to whose advice he profitably gave heed. To Warin the Bald, small in body but great in heart, he gave his niece Amieria in marriage and made him sheriff of Shrewsbury; and Warin bravely defeated the Welsh and all other enemies and pacified the whole area entrusted to him. To other commands in the shire he appointed William Pantulf, Picot and Corbet and his sons Roger and Robert, and other brave and loyal vassals. And with the help of their intelligence and courage he flourished greatly among the greatest of the magnates.[76]

---

certainly related to Thorold (Turold), probably a Norman, to Robert Malet, lord of Eye, to Alan of Lincoln, a Breton, lord of Thoresway, and possibly to Earl Ælfgar of Mercia. The first, rather than the last, is now more often viewed as her father. As for Roger and Robert fitzGerold, it has been suggested, on evidence unknown, that they were brothers of Edward of Salisbury, lord of Chitterne (Wilts): cf. *CDF*, no. 376; R.W. Eyton, *A Key to Domesday . . . Dorset Survey* (1878), 76.

[73] GEC, vi, 639 n. Judith was the daughter of his aunt Adelaide by her second marriage to Lambert of Lens.

[74] OV, iv, 182; genealogical table, below, no. 6.

[75] Cf. J.O. Prestwich, 'The Military Household of the Norman Kings', *EHR*, xcvi (1981), 10 ff. Prestwich seems to allow the *familia* to include all the king's military companions, whether counts/earls, barons or knights bachelor. But, even though it was a brigade of guards, it would seem unlikely that territorial nobles could have been subordinated to a constable.

[76] OV, ii, 262.

Of Hugh of Chester, however, he was far more critical:

> This man, with the help of many cruel barons, shed much Welsh blood. He was not so much lavish as prodigal; his retinue was more like an army than a household; and in giving and receiving he kept no account. Every day he devastated his own land, and preferred falconers and huntsmen to the cultivators of the soil and ministers of God. He was so much a slave to the gluttony of his belly that, weighed down by a mountain of fat, he could hardly move. He was addicted to lust and from harlots had many children of both sexes, who almost all came to an unfortunate end.[77]

Later Orderic turned again to the subject:

> He loved the world and all its pomps, which he regarded as the chief part of human happiness. He was an active soldier, an extravagant giver, and took great pleasure in gaming and debauchery, and in jesters, horses and hounds, and other such vanities. An enormous household, which resounded with the noise of a crowd of youths, both noble and common, was always in attendance upon him. Some good men, clerks as well as knights, also lived with him, and he gladly gave them a share in both his labours and his wealth. In his chapel was Gerold, a clerk from Avranches, honest, religious and well-educated . . . who tried hard to improve the conduct of the courtiers by setting before them the example of their ancestors. In many of them he perceived, and censured, carnal lust, and he deplored the utter negligence that some showed in the worship of God. He uttered salutary warnings to the chief barons, the simple knights and the noble youths, and made a large collection of stories from the Old Testament and more recent Christian histories of the campaigns of holy knights, in order to serve them as models. He recited excellently the struggles of Demetrius and of George, of Theodore and of Sebastian, of Duke Maurice and the Thebean legion, and of Eustace, the general officer, and his men, all of whom by their martyrdom earned a crown in heaven.[78] And he also told of the holy warrior William [of Gellone], who, after many campaigns, renounced the world, and under the monastic rule fought gloriously for the Lord.[79]

The king and the earls set the tone for feudal society at large; but it can be argued that in the long run it was the honorial barons rather than these who were the main shapers of feudal custom;[80] and it is likely that it

[77] OV, ii, 260–2.
[78] Sts George, Sebastian and Maurice were the martyrs invoked to aid the barons and the army in the *Laudes Regiae* of 1084 × 95: see below, 400.
[79] OV, iii, 216.
[80] Duncombe, 'Feudal Tenure', 51, 95 ff., for the position of the English in Kent after the Conquest. For the position of English women and their influence as wives, mistresses, mothers, nurses, etc., see Cecily Clark, 'Women's names in post-Conquest England; observations and speculations', *Speculum*, liii (1978), 223.

was especially at this level that the landowners were also influenced by English habits. English thegns continued to hold land in most of the honours and there is no suggestion that English women were other than admired. It is, indeed, likely that the Normans' adoption of new 'unseemly' fashions was by way of imitation of the natives.[81]

Not entirely dissimilar to William's treatment of the baronage was his management of the church, despite the differences between the two sectors. Unlike the new lay aristocracy, the clerical possessed an ancient and legally defined hierarchical structure, with ranks and dignities completely independent of the king, and they ruled over coherent units, usually shires or groups of them.[82] In charge of provinces were the two archbishops, with Canterbury, although its legal primacy over York was disputed, undoubtedly the more important. Within the southern province the bishop of London ranked next, thanks to his office of dean, followed by the bishop of Winchester, the sub-dean. The bishop of Rochester was directly subordinate to Canterbury and acted as his vicar-general, but whether this raised or lowered his dignity is not clear. The rest of the bishops ranked according to seniority of ordination. In the province of York, where the bishop of Durham was the only usual suffragan, for the inclusion of the Scottish bishops had little practical effect, there was less organization. Even more unequal was the reputation of the several sees in Christendom at large. Two bishoprics, York and London, had antecedents in Roman Britain and received special recognition in Pope Gregory the Great's letter as transmitted by Bede; but more influential in later times were Bede's witness that Canterbury was the mother church in Britain and the natural weight given to sees located in well-known cities, like London and Winchester. By William II's reign, however, with the removal of several sees from obscure places into cities, some of the more glaring inequalities of the Old English church had been removed.

Nevertheless, despite this formal independence of royal power, bishops and abbots were in some ways even closer to the king than were earls and barons. They were, almost without reservation, his feudal vassals. The king invested them by their episcopal ring and staff or abbatial crozier with their benefice; they did him fealty and homage; and they owed him all the services due from a baron except, perhaps, physical combat in battle. And if, in the shape of the pope, a rival lord lurked in the background, the threat was far less menacing than that posed, in the case of the lay aristocracy, by the duke of Normandy or the king of France. Moreover, bishops and abbots had no honorial barons,

---

[81] Above, 105 ff.
[82] *EC 1000–1066*, 159 ff., *EC 1066–1154*, 29 ff.

laymen or clerks, bound to their cause by ancient family allegiance and prepared to support them against the king. As we have seen, William of St Calais, bishop of Durham, had no personal following when he was recalcitrant in 1088.[83] What is more, and this was beginning to distinguish the higher clergy from the baronage, they had been selected for their office by the king himself, or his father, and owed him and his family gratitude for the gift. Even if William II made them pay for the benefice, most of them were grateful for the opportunity to buy. They did not expect to get a valuable property for nothing. Finally, although they were not bound to the king by the camaraderie of warfare, they had a spiritual association which could be as close. They were responsible for the salvation of the royal family, being entrusted with its tombs, regalia and treasures, and charged with the duty of constant intercession with God for its good fortune on earth and ultimate reception in heaven. To them were attributed not only the keys of St Peter but also hermetic knowledge, special skills and exceptional wisdom.

In Domesday Book, as we have noticed, and in other royal documents, archbishops, bishops and abbots were ranked above counts/earls and other barons and royal officials. This had been the practice in the Anglo-Saxon kingdom, where it had been held that an archbishop had a rank equivalent to that of a royal prince and a bishop to that of an ealdorman (*dux*, or duke).[84] With the change in terminology after the Conquest, prelates dropped a step on the ladder. The usual phrases in use were earls and barons and archbishops and bishops; and that is how it stayed. Abbots ranked after bishops, and in the king's court in 1128, despite their protest, they were called after the barons.[85] Moreover, although in some obvious ways prelates were, or could have been regarded as, the king's barons, they were more correctly his bishops and abbots, as the trial of the bishop of Durham in 1088 shows.[86] In 1082 it seems to have been Lanfranc who suggested that the treasonable bishop of Bayeux should be arrested and tried in his quite distinct and unrelated character of earl of Kent.[87] In 1088 he could have made a similar distinction between the bishop and the baron. But he chose not to, presumably because he considered, reasonably enough, that the situations were not analogous and because he did not want to split a bishop into two separate persons. Instead he made a distinction between the bishop's fief, which was in jeopardy, and his bishopric, which was not. This led to several legal arguments which circled round

[83] Above, 75 ff.
[84] *EC 1000–1066*, 96–7.
[85] *EC 1066–1154*, 85.
[86] For the trial, see above, 85 ff.
[87] See above, 38.

the point without ever identifying it precisely.[88] Throughout the trial, as reported by a clerk of the accused, the pair of contrasting terms – earls and barons and archbishops and bishops – was bandied about, and the accused took every opportunity to stress his episcopal character. He wanted all the bishops to be dressed in canonicals; he claimed that it was his bishopric which had been confiscated and despoiled; and he seems even to have pretended that he did not hold a fief – at least he tried to avoid speaking of it. Lanfranc, however, held fast to both his propositions: a bishop was being tried canonically by his fellow bishops, but he stood to lose only the fief he held of the king. This was a subtle and unduly legalistic distinction, but it helped to preserve the integrity of the episcopal person when it was threatened by the need to punish a bishop for a secular crime.

Bishops and abbots, therefore, despite their valuable attributes and despite their separate order, were very much at the mercy of the king. Although the prelates, no more than the lay nobility, would have conceded that they owed their possessions and liberties simply to ducal or royal grants, princely patronage was in their case more obvious, because better commemorated. Even the strictest churchmen accepted that kings were, or should be, patrons of the church. Above all, the general lack of hereditary succession to the great benefices deprived the prelates of the main protection enjoyed by the baronage. It was, indeed, the eleventh-century reform movements in the church, with their insistence on the celibacy of its ministers and their removal from ordinary family law and society, which made them for a time so helpless against princely power. They were outside the vendetta and the other defences of the kin. Often they had no powerful relations, or none at hand. To whom could Anselm of Aosta turn for help when he was ill-treated by William? He could, of course, turn to his 'order', his spiritual brethren and children and his father in God; and they had spiritual powers, not only the persuasion of moral principles but also the coercion of anathema. But not even a conventionally religious king, like Henry I, any more than a 'wicked' king, like Philip I of France, was easily moved from his purpose by papal threats. William, when in good health, would have shrugged off excommunication without a tremor. Hence, although the reformers had had to break private ownership of benefices before they could substitute the rule of the church's own laws, between the shedding of one carapace and the hardening of the other, all defences were down.

The royal attitude to the English church is made absolutely clear by the instruments of royal government which have survived. The listing in

[88] *De Injusta Vexatione*, 179–86.

Domesday Book of the lands of the clerical aristocracy and the great churches immediately after the royal demesne, although owing something to special honour, owed something also to the king's special interest in them. And this interest is amply confirmed by the purpose and terms of the extant royal writs, most of which were preserved in monastic archives or cartularies. Indeed, although it is usual to portray William II as anti-clerical, his records and business correspondence show him constantly and intimately involved in church affairs. It is true that there is a gross distortion here owing to the loss of most royal instruments issued at the instance of the baronage, but it should not be over-corrected. Bishops and abbots, because of their ambitions as well as their weakness, were probably inclined more than the barons to solicit royal protection and privileges; and because of their ability to pay, and since they posed no threat to royal power, were the more likely to receive them. On the other hand, papal privileges for English churches in this period hardly exist.[89] They were considered of little practical use, all the more since the very identity of the true pope was, at least in the king's view, often in doubt.

Archbishops, bishops and abbots were certainly members of the upper class, and ranked high in that stratum. Their origins, however, seem to have been miscellaneous. William II inherited two archbishops and twelve bishops from his father – nine Normans, two Italians, two Lotharingians and one Englishman. Five were monks and nine clerks, but three of the monks as well as three of the clerks had started their careers as cathedral clergy. The exact family background, however, is unknown except in a very few cases. The Englishman, Wulfstan of Worcester, was the son of a vassal of an earlier bishop of that see and had been educated in the episcopal household. The bishop of Exeter, Osbern fitzOsbern, although the brother of William fitzOsbern, earl of Hereford and the steward and friend of William I, had been educated at Edward the Confessor's court. Giso, the Lotharingian clerk at Wells, was another survivor from Edward's household. Archbishop Lanfranc sprang from the urban patriciate of Pavia, Thomas I of York was the son of a Norman priest. Two clerks with territorial surnames, Robert of Limesy (Chester) and William of Beaufai (Thetford), may have come from baronial families. On this evidence it is abundantly clear that the new bishops in England formed an aristocracy, having reached their high office through service, in many cases originally to another bishop, before being chosen by the king. None was a close relation of the duke-king or even, except in one case, a member of the major baronage; but if we add the

---

[89] None from this reign was found in English archives by W. Holtzmann, *Papsturkunden in England* (3 vols, 1930–52).

two typically noble Norman bishops who were large landowners in England, Odo of Conteville (Bayeux) and Geoffrey of Mowbray (Coutances), the mixture becomes a little closer to what had been the norm in both Anglo-Saxon England and Normandy. All the same, the immediate post Conquest bishops were less connected by birth with the lay nobility and less integrated into local society than had been the case in the past in both countries. The Conqueror had taken the opportunity to promote those whom he considered talented, loyal and useful men.

His son followed dutifully in his wake.[90] Six of his father's men, Thomas I of York, Walkelin of Winchester, Osmund of Salisbury, Osbern fitzOsbern of Exeter, Robert of Limesy of Chester and Maurice of London, continued to hold office throughout all or most of his reign, as did also Gundulf of Rochester, an archiepiscopal appointment. It would have been impossible for the new king to repeat his father's purge in 1070 of an inherited episcopate, and probably he had no wish to do so. Vacancies occurred at Canterbury, Wells, Chichester (twice), Durham, Thetford, Hereford, Lincoln, Worcester, Salisbury and Winchester, and William appointed to all but the last two, which, owing to the exile of the archbishop of Canterbury, had to be left vacant. He also in 1092, as a result of the conquests in North Wales, made an appointment to Bangor. His choice fell on eight royal clerks or chaplains and two monks. Most, if not all, of these had served his father. John de Villula (Wells) had been his doctor and Gerard (Hereford) his chancellor; Anselm abbot of Bec had been summoned to his death-bed.[91] Of the ten, all but three – John de Villula from Tours, Hervey (Bangor) from Brittany and Anselm (Canterbury), ultimately from Aosta in the kingdom of Burgundy – seem to have been of Norman origin. The only undoubted noblemen by birth were Anselm, who was related through his mother to the counts of Savoy,[92] and Robert Bloet (Lincoln) from the Norman baronial family of Ivry. Gerard and Samson (Worcester) came from illustrious clerical dynasties and had been dignitaries in Norman cathedrals.

There was, therefore, in the episcopate, as in the baronage, massive continuity. The only change to be noticed is that the son's appointments were if anything of better quality than his father's. The two monks could hardly have been bettered, and Anselm was a more original metaphysician than his master Lanfranc. The clerks were men of first-rate ability, and, apart from Godfrey of Chichester, who lasted no more than a year and about whom nothing is known, all made their mark. Not only were they skilled administrators, some of them were also well-educated, even scholars. Gerard owned a Hebrew psalter and died while reading 'a

[90] *EC 1066–1154*, 66 ff.
[91] *HN*, 24.
[92] Anselm, *Letters*, no. 262; Eadmer, *VA*, 3.

book of curious arts'. He seems also to have encouraged legal studies.[93] Moreover, Ralf Luffa (Chichester) was regarded by William of Malmesbury as an excellent and most pious bishop.[94]

Most of William's beneficiaries were, however, under a cloud. It was believed that he made them purchase their office, an act which caused both seller and buyer to be guilty of simony. What is more, their reputation suffered in the twelfth century because by then lay investiture and the doing of homage by prelates had been condemned, and also because the standards of respectability and learning were rising fast. Simony, always widespread in some form or other in the church, was probably blatant in William's reign. Herbert Losinga, abbot of Ramsey and a former prior of Fécamp, a distinguished scholar educated under John of Ravenna, paid 1,000 marks in 1091 to get Thetford for himself and the abbey of New Minster (Winchester) for his father.[95] And this sin, considered by other monks unforgiveable in one who should have known better, was probably taken for granted in respect of the clerks. If Ranulf Flambard had to pay for Durham in 1099, it can hardly be doubted that most of the others had done likewise. Such a purchase price was, after all, similar to the relief paid by a baron on succeeding to an honour. But church reformers had been denouncing this sin for at least half a century and by the 1090s everyone knew that it was forbidden. After Christmas 1093 Herbert Losinga, probably at the instigation of the new archbishop, went to Urban II, whom William had not yet recognized as pope, to confess his crime and make amends. Urban accepted his resignation, but then reinstated him. When, however, the returning penitent arrived back at Hastings, where William was waiting to cross to Normandy and quarrelling with Anselm, he was promptly deprived of his bishopric by his irate lord. William presumably resumed the temporalities and anything else he could confiscate. But his anger seems, as usual, despite the enormity of Herbert's behaviour, quickly to have subsided, and soon the bishop was, with the king's help, building a new church and monastery at Norwich, into which he moved his see.[96] These matters too may have cost the bishop much money. At the end of

---

[93] *EC 1066–1154*, 257, 259.

[94] *GP*, 265–7.

[95] *EC 1066–1154*, 68–9, 240 ff.

[96] *ASC E, s.a.* 1094, 171; *GR*, ii, 385–7; *GP*, 151; Florence, ii, 33–4 (in three versions). As Herbert was at Canterbury for Anselm's consecration on 4 December 1093 (*HN*, 42) and at the Christmas court at Gloucester (*Regesta*, no. 338), the journey must have taken place between then and 19 March 1094, when William sailed for Normandy. It was presumably after his visit to the pope that he, together with the Cardinal-archdeacon Roger, was entrusted with a papal legation and disciplinary duties against the archbishops of Rouen and York: *Gallia Christiana*, xi, instr. p. 18, no. XIV; *HCY*, 6–7. This would have compounded his injury to the king. But a complication is that the

the reign, Anselm viewed from exile Ranulf Flambard's method of entry into the episcopate with shocked incredulity; but even he had eventually to swallow this crime.[97] None of William's bishops was deposed, even in the new climate which accompanied the accession of Henry I and the return to authority of the primate.

More unpopular, if less sinful and unlawful, was William's enjoyment of the profits of sees during vacancies.[98] This was analagous to the resumption or wardship of a lay honour. He cannot, however, except in two instances, be considered to have behaved unreasonably. In the cases of Wells and Chichester (1088), Thetford (1091) and Worcester and Hereford (1095), the bishopric was left vacant for less than a year, sometimes much less, and Lincoln (1092) for well under two years. But Durham (1096) remained in royal custody for over three years and Canterbury (1089) for four-and-a-half. The vacancies at Winchester and Salisbury at the end of the reign were not necessarily what William wanted. Since the king normally preferred one of his clerks, he was subjected not only to general ecclesiastical pressure but also to the entreaty of interested claimants to make a substitution. When Walkelin of Winchester died in 1098, his obvious successor was Ranulf Flambard; and it could be that Durham was kept in reserve while attempts were made to see if it was possible to put this through despite Anselm's exile and the opposition in monastic circles which the nomination would have caused.

The long vacancy at Canterbury is, therefore, the one unjustifiable abuse of which William was guilty. His motives were probably mixed: the revenues of the richest bishopric were most welcome, and the removal of the king's traditional chief adviser reduced moral pressure on him and the court. But there may also have been real difficulty in finding a suitable candidate who was acceptable to all the interested parties. He had to be a monk; and with Normandy in Robert's hands there were problems, clearly not unsurmountable, but just sufficient to hamper the business. The way in which Anselm was finally put on show throughout England by his backers throws some light on this aspect.[99] There can be no doubt that because of this hiatus the English church lacked for a time spiritual leadership; but so it might had William secured the translation to Canterbury of, say, Walkelin of Winchester. Herbert Losinga would

---

archdeacon is noticed in Normandy before 11 December 1093: *Regesta*, no. 342. Three royal writs in favour of Herbert are probably associated with his restoration: *Facsimiles*, no. 18, *Regesta*, ii, nos 385a–c. If so, they show that Ranulf Flambard had been administering or 'roughing up' the bishop's fief. See also below, 206–7.

[97] Below, 196.
[98] Below, 234 ff.
[99] Below, 301 ff.

have done quite well, although he was hardly a Lanfranc or an Anselm; but none of the others who got English bishoprics in that period seems up to the mark. As for the small diocese of Canterbury itself, the monks, under their prior Henry, whom William appointed abbot of Battle in 1096, continued to serve the cathedral church, and the saintly Gundulf of Rochester carried out the episcopal functions, a task rendered the easier by the smallness of his own diocese.

William's record in respect of the bishoprics passes muster by the standards of the time, but his hand fell heavier on the royal abbeys.[100] He inherited about twenty-six abbots from his father, of whom about six were natives, the rest predominantly Norman, but including two Frenchmen, one Italian and one Breton. Once again the family background of only a few is known. Gilbert Crispin, abbot of Westminster, a former monk of Bec, came from a most distinguished family,[101] and Geoffrey, abbot of New Minster, Winchester, had the territorial designation of *Mala Terra*. Paul of St Albans was a nephew of Archbishop Lanfranc and Simeon of Ely was the brother of Bishop Walkelin of Winchester. Baldwin of Bury St Edmunds, a former French monk, had been Edward the Confessor's doctor and was still highly regarded for his medical skill. Almost all that we know about the others is that they had been monks in Normandy or thereabouts, and this does not tell us much about the social class into which they were born. The Old English abbots had been for the most part thegns by birth and usually related to the local aristocracy. But with their post-Conquest successors, as with the bishops, not only were the local connexions broken but also, it would seem, often enough men of a lower social class were appointed. Probably not unconnected with these features was the reduction of their importance in the royal court. Abbots had been exceptionally influential in the Old English kingdom. By 1087 the Conqueror's most trusted abbots, Lanfranc and William of St Calais, were bishops, and it is difficult to point to anyone who had replaced them in the royal counsels. Only one of the twenty-six, Herbert Losinga, was to be promoted to the episcopal bench by William II. A change in social and religious attitudes was altering the public roles which abbots were expected to play.

Bath was demoted to a priory when William sold it to the bishop of Wells as his cathedral see.[102] Five of the Conqueror's abbots were not replaced when they died, and seven, including the infamous Thurstin of

---

[100] Dates and biographical information from *HRH*.

[101] His father, William Crispin, was castellan of Neauphle in the French Vexin, and his mother, Eve, was from the far more eminent family of Montfort-l'Amaury: Robinson, *Gilbert Crispin*, 13 ff., and genealogical chart, below, 469, no. 8.

[102] *EC 1066–1154*, 48.

Glastonbury and the excellent Gilbert Crispin of Westminster, continued into Henry I's reign. Only one English abbot, Leofwine (II) of Coventry, is known to have lasted well into William's reign, although there may have been others in the six houses for which names are lacking.[103] William made or sanctioned eleven or more appointments, the last being to St Albans in 1097. Only one of these, apparently an Englishman, was elected from within the house (Aldwin to Ramsey in 1091); to Battle went the prior of Christ Church, Canterbury, to Burton the sacrist of Winchester, to Winchcombe a monk of Gloucester, to Malmesbury a monk from Jumièges, and to St Albans a monk from Lessay. To St Augustine's, Canterbury, William appointed Hugh of Fleury, an old soldier who was not yet in orders; and he sold New Minster to Robert Losinga. At least four of William's abbots – Guy of Pershore, Aldwin of Ramsey, Wimund of Tavistock and the unnamed incumbent of Muchelney – were deposed by Anselm at his inaugural Council of Westminster in 1102, the first three for simony. But it should in fairness be noticed that Anselm also condemned five men who had been elected since 1100.[104]

It can also fairly be said that William had a typical layman's view of monasticism, and one which, however unfashionable it was becoming as the century wore on, he shared with some great monks of his father's time, like Herlwin, Gilbert of Brionne's knight, the founder of Bec, the view that it was holiness and humility, rather than learning and sacerdotal polish, which mattered most. This is well illustrated by the story of his appointment to St Augustine's, which, although related by William Thorne in the fourteenth century, must go back to an earlier account.[105] After Abbot Guy's death in August 1093, the monks asked the king for permission to elect, but he refused on the grounds that he wanted to hold all the abbatial staves in his own hands. At that time any church in England could be bought. As it happened there was in the monastery an old soldier, Hugh of Fleury, who had served both Williams as a knight, and, on a recent visit to Canterbury with the king, had gone into the monastery to pray and had decided to remain. After he had persuaded the abbot to accept him as a conversus, he had gone to Normandy to divest himself of his earthly possessions. As he had neither wife nor son, he gave some of his lands to his kin and some to churches, while other parts he sold in order to raise money to give to the poor. He then returned to Canterbury with not a little cash.

The monastery decided to send Hugh, accompanied by two discreet

---

[103] Abbotsbury, Athelney, Cerne, Milton, Muchelney and Pershore.

[104] *HN*, 141–4; Wilkins, *Concilia*, i, 382; Mansi, *Concilia*, xx, 1149.

[105] *Chronica Guill. Thorne . . . De Gestibus abbatum S. Augustini Cantuariae* in R. Twysden, *Historiae Anglicanae Scriptores X* (1652), coll. 1794–8.

monks, to the king to try to soften his heart by means of prayers or money; and when William saw Hugh, whom he remembered as a proud knight, now serving Christ in monkish garb, he burst into tears and said, 'I grant you this my kinsman as your abbot . . . and if you do not accept him on the spot, I will come and burn your monastery down.'

A completely anonymous story in the Hyde chronicle seems to be another version of this affair.[106] An abbey sent to the king two monks, who had each raised a large sum of money, together with a third, whose only role was to conduct the successful candidate home. After the two had bid against each other, William in his wisdom asked the third what he was doing there. When this man had explained his part and declared that he was not in the auction, the king said, 'Come here then and receive the office of abbot, for you are the only one worthy of the honour.' According to Thorne, Hugh then protested that, as he was both illiterate and untrained, he was a completely unworthy and unsuitable candidate. His objections were, however, overruled, and, the chronicler believed, he did well in the office. He built the chapter house and dormitory at his own expense, erected a pulpit in the church and purchased abroad a bronze Jesse candelabrum for the choir, other furniture, and vestments so marvellously sewn with gold thread and gems that even 'today' they were called, after their donor, *Floriae*. He established an annual commemorative service on 3 July for the souls of all benefactors of the monastery and the souls of the relatives of all the brethren, alive and dead, and ordained that thirty paupers should be fed on his own anniversary. And he also enacted that whenever a monk of the house should die, before the body was buried the abbot should pay five shillings from his own fund, presumably for the welfare of the soul of the departed. We notice that Hugh was not one of the abbots deposed by Anselm.

To the reformed monastic way of thinking, William's behaviour was, however, deplorable. He appointed no abbot of any stature and he gradually allowed the monasteries to become acephalous, so that he could take the abbatial estates into his own hands and enjoy the revenues.[107] The communities, of course, continued to operate under their priors and administer their own lands,[108] and the loss they suffered

[106] *Chron. mon. de Hida*, 299–30. The anecdote of 'William and the honest monk' became part of the posthumous legend of the king: T. Callahan Jr, 'The making of a monster: the historical image of William Rufus', *Journal of Medieval History*, vii (1981), 181–2.

[107] Below, 234 ff. and fig., 261.

[108] Royal writs protecting the monks during a vacancy are quite common. Cf. two in favour of St Albans after the death of Abbot Paul in 1093, both witnessed by Ranulf Flambard: *Regesta*, ii, nos 400a–b.

from the removal of their abbots was not necessarily catastrophic, not even serious. Abbots were tenants-in-chief with many duties, including usually military service. They were already withdrawing a little from the common life of their monks, and William's policy only accelerated the process. Moreover, his interference with the monastic estates must be viewed in the context of the nepotism practised by most of the abbots. For example, he forced Paul of St Albans to enfeof Hugh of Envermeu with a vill in return for homage and service; but Paul's own nepotism, his alienation of land to relatives, is given even more prominence by the annalist.[109] The flowering of Benedictine culture in England during the twelfth century is proof that William had not done the monasteries irreparable harm.

Beyond the household and royal demesne, the king ruled over his barons and prelates, whose behaviour he strictly regulated. Barons required his permission for foreign journeys, building a castle, alienating land, getting married or arranging for the marriage of their children or other dependants; and he forbade private warfare.[110] He was also usually ready to listen to complaints of denial of justice made against them by their vassals. Similarly he controlled his prelates. It is in William II's reign that we first find mention of the ancient or ancestral customs which governed their behaviour; and the reference back must be to the Conqueror's reign and perhaps to ducal regulations. The king claimed that his consent was necessary for all traffic between his dominions and the papal curia: no pope was to be recognized, no papal legates or letters come in, no prelate or legal appeal go out, without his express sanction. Also no prelate could excommunicate a royal baron or servant, and no ecclesiastical council could promulgate laws without his authorization. This type of control was by no means unusual in the eleventh century. The king regarded himself as the lord and master of all his vassals, both lay and clerical. But when in 1098 Count Roger I of Sicily accepted a papal legation from Pope Urban II, it was acknowledged that he enjoyed such authority only by papal grant. As it happened, Anselm, who hated the English regulations and had fallen foul of the king over

---

[109] *Gesta Abbatum monasterii S. Albani*, ed. H.T. Riley (Rolls ser. 1867), i, 54, 64.

[110] For feudal 'incidents', see below, 253 ff. Alienations of land were tightly controlled. For example, William confirmed Earl Roger of Shrewsbury's grant of a manor to Cluny and Marcigny and his endowment of Shrewsbury abbey: *Regesta*, nos 353; 356, cf. 358 Royal control of castle-building at this time in England can only be inferred from Norman and later English evidence: see Caen Inquest of July 1091, Haskins, *NI*, 282, cap. 4; *Leges Henrici Primi*, caps 10,1; 13, 1, pp. 109, 117; *Regesta*, ii, no. 1475.

them, was with the pope at Capua when the concordat was negotiated.[111]

A king was not remote from the nobility and his control was supposed to be paternalistic. His family had, more or less recently – and in the case of the Normans most recently – arisen out of it, and his interests remained closely identified with theirs. Indeed, he could not survive without the cooperation of the nobles, for he had no other basis of power.[112] A rich king could buy the service of mercenary soldiers, and all kings could use a certain number of low-born servants, but if he became isolated from the nobility he would find himself drained of power. In this period no king could rule successfully through hired armies and menial agents. The nobility would not stand for it. Although barons could probably manage fairly well without a king, they never in fact chose to do so: it was beyond their conception. Ailing dynasties and tyrannical kings were always replaced, for even if the nobles aspired to a fair measure of independence, they also valued their closeness to a distinguished monarchy. Royal power was particularly precarious at the beginning of a reign and was threatened whenever the king was incapacitated. William II's political and military achievements in 1087–8 were not only necessary but also remarkable. He made himself quickly the leader of a baronage which initially had little interest in his cause, and there seem to have been no desertions in 1093 when he became seriously ill.

The scope of the king's government was, however, limited. Although in the eleventh century the English kingdom was more centralized than the French, it was similarly composed of largely self-governing lord-ships, and, as in France, the nobility hardly entertained the view that their own governmental power within their honours was delegated or even subject to royal supervision or control. The barons had their own barons and vavassors, their own court and servants, their own castles, their own world. At the same time, under the rather special English conditions, with their scattered honours, their still alien character, and the abiding sense of partnership in a great adventure, there could be no isolation either from each other or from the king. England was so small that only north of the Tyne could an earl skulk and nurture illusions of independence. The Welsh marches, in which William took so much interest, although enjoying special privileges were not far enough away. But in general the nobility tried to reconcile two imperfectly compatible

[111] *EC 1066–1154*, 279–80.
[112] Cf. K.F. Werner, 'Important noble families in the kingdom of Charlemagne', in Reuter, *Medieval Nobility*, 138 ff.: 'the high nobility . . . was at once the main enemy and the only ally of central government. . . . It is the complete dependence of the king on the nobility which needs to be stressed.'

aims: to rule their own honours free from outside interference and to enjoy the kind of royal favour which could be obtained only by frequent attendance at court or presence in the army.

Moreover, since not only were the feudal honours scattered and intermixed with the no less dispersed royal demesnes, but also lay within the more ancient and integral local government units, the shires and hundreds or wapentakes, complete privacy from royal attention was not easy to achieve; and in these circumstances the honorial and shire courts were not so much competing centres of government as complementary and alternative. More than two hundred writs of William II have survived in some form or other, and almost all are addressed, *inter alios*, to the official called a *vicomte* in Latin and French and the shire-reeve in English. Very occasionally a count/earl, sometimes the shire bishop, is added and given precedence, but rarely was the sheriff bypassed; and it is quite clear that he was, as well as the king's estate agent and tax gatherer,[113] his immediate and omnicompetent executive officer. It was not unusual for the king's chancellor, from whose office these writs originated, to add in the address the sheriff's servants or other royal *ministri*. It was also common for the address to conclude with the king's barons in the shire, or his *fideles* (his vassals or lieges), or both, and not unusual for these to be described as both French and English. It is to be inferred that the sheriff would publish the business of the writ in the shire court, where the residual addressees attended, and make use of the court for its implementation. To what extent the honorial barons of the great feudatories were involved in the routine business of the shire court cannot be said, but it is hard to believe that they entirely escaped the net of 'the king's lieges, both French and English'. However that may be, the local importance of the sheriff was considerable, and his position in the royal administration crucial.

No complete list of William II's sheriffs can be compiled; but for most of the thirty-one shires which might be expected to have had, or shared, a royal sheriff, some holder of the office can be identified.[114] Although William I had made enough changes to remind occupants that the office was a ministry which had not been granted in fee, his favourites could have expected a long tenure and would have hoped to have been succeeded by their heir, and there is no clear sign that William II dispelled the ambiguity. He too certainly made changes, and some which were punitive. He seems to have kept Roger Bigot out of the shrievalties of Norfolk and Suffolk;[115] and Geoffrey de Mandeville did

[113] See below, 223 ff.

[114] See list, below, 446. It should be noticed that the Norman *vicecomites* (*vicomtes*) were similarly usually in charge of a *pagus*, the old Carolingian administrative unit

[115] Morris, *Med. Eng. Sheriff*, 47 n.

not have an unbroken tenure of London and Middlesex.[116] Although for most of the shires we have only one name and rarely more than two, this may be caused by the limited and patchy evidence, because in the case of Yorkshire, where there would seem to be no special reason for insecurity, we can identify no fewer than four holders of the office during the reign. We also notice the activities of one of the more professional type of sheriff which Henry I was to favour. Hugh of Buckland held, probably at different times, the shrievalties of Bedfordshire, Essex, Hertfordshire, Middlesex and Berkshire, and was to be greatly patronized and employed by the next king.[117]

On the other hand there was considerable continuity and stability. In ten cases at least – and this could be a great understatement – William took over his father's sheriff, and most of these either retained the office throughout the reign or passed it to their heir. Baldwin fitzGilbert of Exeter was probably succeeded by his three sons, William, Robert and Richard, in turn. Peter of Valognes, who married the sister of Eudo *dapifer*, continued to hold Essex and perhaps Hertfordshire. In Gloucestershire the shrievalty was kept in the hands of the de Pîtres family.[118] Hugh de Port may have been retained in Hampshire and Picot in Cambridgeshire. In Kent, Haimo *dapifer* may have outlived both Williams. In Leicestershire it is possible that Hugh of Grandmesnil survived the disgrace of 1088 and was succeeded by his son Ivo.[119] In Northamptonshire, William de Cahagnes remained undisturbed. In Wiltshire, Edward of Salisbury seems to have lasted into Henry I's reign, although it is possible that his tenure suffered an interruption.[120] In Worcestershire, Urse of Abetot also served the first three Norman kings and appeared to have created an hereditary office. Some of William II's appointments, such as Hugh of Beauchamp in Buckinghamshire and Ranulf brother of Ilger in Huntingdonshire, also had a long tenure.

The social and economic standing of the sheriffs varied a good deal. Probably the only undoubted nobleman in his own right was Baldwin fitzGilbert of Devonshire. Hugh of Grandmesnil ran him close. Some seventeen other holders were probably considered of baronial standing because of the value of the lands they held in chief of the king,[121] and not

---

[116] See above, 170 n. 63.

[117] Morris, *op. cit.*, 52. H.E. Salter, 'A dated charter of Henry I', *EHR*, xxvi (1911), 489–91.

[118] Roger de Pîtres was succeeded by his brother Durand (occ. 1086), and Durand by Roger's son Walter (*c.* 1096): Morris, *op. cit.*, 50 n.

[119] *Ibid.*, 49 n. 58.

[120] *Ibid.*, 47 n.

[121] Gilbert of Bretteville, Hugh of Beauchamp, Henry and Hermer de Ferrers, Aiulf, Peter of Valognes, Hugh de Port, Ranulf brother of Ilger, Haimo *dapifer*, William de Cahagnes, William fitzCorbucio, Edward of Salisbury, Urse of Abetot, Ralf Pagnell, Geoffrey Baynard, Erneis de Burun, Bertram de Verdun.

a few of these, for example the Abetot family, were very obviously *nouveaux riches*. To be included in this group are at least three of the five household officials known to have held the office, the steward Haimo (Kent), the chamberlain Aiulf (Somerset) and the constable Urse (Worcestershire). But the steward Godric (Suffolk) and the chamberlain Humphrey (Norfolk), who in 1086 held only modest estates of the crown, would have earned the title of baron more through their offices than because of their territorial position. The rest fall between the mediocre and the totally obscure. Gilbert of Bretteville, who held land in Berkshire and Wiltshire, established a modest dynasty.[122] But probably he and Peter (Oxfordshire) were overshadowed by Walter fitzOther, castellan of Windsor and ancestor of the Fitzgeralds. Others simply dropped out of record.

An unexpected feature is that ten of William II's sheriffs do not appear in Domesday Book as holding much, or in most cases any, land of the king in the county of which they subsequently became sheriff.[123] William de Cahagnes held but one hide in Northamptonshire worth £1 a year; Godric *dapifer* had a paltry collection of small holdings in Suffolk; and Ranulf brother of Ilger, a large tenant elsewhere, held only one manor in Huntingdonshire. A further two, Aiulf (Somerset) and Bertram de Verdun (Yorkshire) held lands of the king only in other shires; and the remaining five, Turold and Osbert (Lincolnshire), Earnwig (Nottinghamshire), Peter (Oxfordshire) and Geoffrey Baynard (Yorkshire), were not tenants-in-chief of the king in 1086 at all. The absence of a powerful territorial base must have been a reminder of their dependence on the king.

Some of the nonentities, for most of whom we have only a single name, may have been cadet members of well-known families, important honorial barons or rising men endowed with land by the king after 1086. But none can be shown to have founded an important dynasty, and it is clear that, whereas William inherited a number of important sheriffs, and kept some of them in office, he took care not to create a new crop of comparable standing. Not only did he use somewhat meaner tools, he also kept them in the dust. We notice that Hugh of Buckland took advantage of his position in Berkshire to get a retainer from Abingdon abbey,[124] but it was Henry I, not William, who made his fortune. As

---

[122] See also *Chron. Abingdon*, ii, 26, 159, for him and his son Robert. Their place of origin, *Brittewella*, is uncertain. There are several Brettevilles in Normandy and a Brightwell in Berkshire.

[123] Duncombe, 'Feudal Tenure', 32, points out that in several cases a pre-Conquest sheriff was succeeded in his lands by the Norman sheriff of another shire. For example, the lands of Osweard sheriff of Kent passed to Hugh de Port, sheriff of Hampshire. This feature may indicate early post-Conquest switches of office.

[124] *Chron. Abingdon*, ii, 43. Haimo *dapifer* (II) of Kent got an estate in 1111 from St

William was served loyally by his sheriffs, it is likely that he allowed them a fairly free hand. Their profits would have come more from 'farms' and custodies and all the perquisites of authority than from grants in fee from the royal demesne.[125]

Entrusted to the sheriffs was all the routine royal administration in the shires and, in an emergency, the holding of the fort until the other barons and, in the last resort, the king could lend them a hand. Revenue, justice, defence and the execution of many administrative orders must have kept them pretty busy; and the inclusion in the address of many writs of a second name or a reference to shrieval servants or the royal *ministri* is evidence that there may often have been an under- or deputy-sheriff, and that the sheriff could also call on the network of royal reeves, foresters and other servants on the demesne lands. Writs concerning Huntingdonshire were sometimes addressed to Ranulf brother of Ilger and his nephew R.[126] And the usual conclusion to the address not only indicated that much of the business would be carried out in the county court in the presence of many of the most important men of the shire, but was also an appeal from the king to those men to cooperate with his officials in helping them to carry out his duties as their lord and king.

The shire barons must have been able to exert some influence over the sheriff's actions, especially if the royal official was one of themselves. Another check at some times was the existence of a local royal justiciar.[127] Often, perhaps usually in the early Norman period, the sheriff was also justiciar;[128] but the offices could be, and sometimes were, separated. When they were, the justiciar occasionally took precedence of the sheriff. Two writs of William II addressed to Maurice bishop of London, Geoffrey de Mandeville and the sheriff (or R. Delpare), and to all the barons (or all the king's lieges) of London, would seem to mean that Geoffrey was then justiciar of the city,[129] although it is just possible that he was included as keeper of the Tower. Ralf Passelewe was justiciar in East Anglia when Ralf de Beaufai was sheriff;[130] Ralf Pagnell seems to have been justiciar of Yorkshire during the shrievalty of a certain H.[131]

Augustine's in return for the service of 'legal aid' in the shire or royal court against any baron: *The Black Book of St Augustine's*, ed. G.J. Turner and H.E. Salter (1924), ii, 462.

[125] See below, 223 ff.

[126] *Regesta*, nos 413, 447.

[127] H.A. Cronne, 'The office of Local Justiciar in England under the Norman kings', *Univ. of Birmingham Hist. Journ.*, vi (1958), 18. William T. Reedy Jr, 'The origins of the General Eyre in the reign of Henry I', *Speculum*, xli (1966), 688 ff.

[128] Cf. Hugh of Buckland in Berkshire, 'vicecomes et publicarum justiciarius compellationum': *Chron. Abingdon*, ii, 43.

[129] *Regesta*, nos 306, 444.

[130] Cronne, *op. cit.*, 28–9.

[131] *Regesta*, no. 412.

These three men had also been, or were about to be, sheriffs. It would, therefore, seem that, sometimes in order to reduce the workload of the sheriff or to give more men employment or experience, sometimes to act as a control on the other official, William now and then separated the two offices; and this practice was extended by Henry I.

The king's sheriffs and justices, and to some extent his earls, bishops and abbots, formed the standing governmental network in the shires, and they were based particularly on the county cities and boroughs, strongholds which were normally reinforced by a royal castle. This was not a corps of low-born royal agents divorced from local society or working against the interests of the nobility and gentry. It was in any case ultimately government by consent. Moreover, the main class that the king governed, the magnates, were supposed to be his friends, companions and counsellors, members of his court and army, men with whom he shared both the burdens and pleasures of his office. William needed, therefore, at court two different kinds of helper: a body of technical men in his household, advisers, experts, agents, deputies, clerks and other menials, and a set of aristocratic friends and companions who could also serve to keep open his lines of communication with the baronage at large. The first extended to the sheriffs and justices in the shires, the second formed part of that aristocratic connexion which could also exert pressure at the periodical great courts. The two circles, although working cheek by jowl and not mutually exclusive, were distinct. No one would have put Ranulf Flambard in the second or Robert fitzHaimo in the first; but some barons, such as Eudo *dapifer*, clearly bridged the gap.

William, like most of his class, probably had only a limited appetite for routine administration. With his intense interest in his rights, he is unlikely to have been either lazy or irresponsible; and William of Malmesbury could envisage him on the morning of his death engaged in the transaction of serious business which entailed the postponement of hunting until the afternoon.[132] But it is unlikely that he did anything of a business nature that he could safely depute to someone else. Nevertheless, the amount of assistance he needed was not enough to require a formal system or even a significant modification of the traditional household organization.

For identifying the inner group of administrators round the king, the witnesses to the royal writs, the administrative instruments of the court, should serve as a good guide. One hundred and fifty five of these have been analyzed. Seventy eight, just about half, are attested by a single witness, forty-three by two, twenty by three, and five by four. Nine other

---

[132] See below, 421.

writs with a larger number of witnesses have also been counted because, although concerned with grants of land and coming close to charters, they are witnessed by members of the ministerial circle. At least sixty-one different names appear on these instruments; but thirty-one appear only once, nine twice and three thrice; and, with these excluded, we are left with eighteen. Even this group can be usefully subdivided. Four men witness twenty or more writs apiece, and a further five ten or more. The detailed list of these top nine functionaries is Ranulf Flambard, both as chaplain and bishop (35), William Giffard the chancellor (32), Eudo the steward (27), William bishop of Durham (26), Roger Bigot (18), Bishop Walkelin of Winchester (18), Robert Bloet both as chancellor and as bishop (17), Robert fitzHaimo (15) and Urse of Abetot (15). There are five clerks and four laymen. All the clerks were, or were to become, bishops. All the laity were barons and, except for Robert fitzHaimo, who was the son of an official, held a household office.

Before proceeding to a further analysis it is prudent to test the list by reviewing names which on other grounds might have been expected to feature more prominently. The witness of Gerard, William's chancellor immediately after his accession, appears only once.[133] The reason seems to be that in those first insecure years William thought it advisable to have his writs attested by more important men, usually bishops and barons.[134] William's important councillor, Robert count of Meulan, witnesses only six writs, although three as the sole witness: presumably as a great noble he was not usually bothered with such business. Haimo *dapifer* and sheriff of Kent likewise witnesses only six, and never on his own: it is likely that he operated mostly out of court. Similarly Ivo Taillebois, another steward, has only two or three attestations. One seemingly important household official, Robert the dispenser, Urse's brother, witnesses twice, once alone, once with a fellow. Some of these men – and indeed some others with few extant attestations – may be poorly represented owing to the unselective nature of the evidence, but on this test there is no reason to distrust the import of the statistics.

Returning to the top nine, it has already been noticed that half the writs have but a single witness, and that more than three witnesses was exceptional. Most of the regular witnesses appear in all combinations. The exception is Bishop Walkelin, who never witnesses alone. In this he is like Haimo *dapifer*. This feature is not easily explicable. William bishop of Durham witnessed frequently alone (10), and there are other great

---

[133] *Regesta*, ii, no. 335a.

[134] Cf. *Regesta*, nos 289 (Eudo *dapifer*), 290 (Eudo *dapifer*, Roger Bigot, Gilbert fitzRichard), 291 (Roger Bigot), 295 (Earl Roger), 296 (Robert count of Mortain), 304–5 (bishop of Durham), 306 (Geoffrey bishop of Coutances, William bishop of Durham, Roger Bigot), all from 1087–8.

names like Robert count of Meulan and some of the grandees at the very
beginning of the reign which stand by themselves. Apart from this, the
situation is fairly straightforward If we group the witnesses according to
office, the concurrent stewards, Eudo (27), Roger Bigot (18) and Haimo
(6) make a good showing with fifty-one attestations between them.
Eudo's large contribution may reflect his special connexion with royal
finance.[135] The consecutive chancellors, Gerard (1), Robert Bloet (11)
and William Giffard (32), together provide forty-four attestations; and,
although Robert witnessed as often with one or two companions as
alone, William was more often alone or with one other. As he was
chancellor in the years when William was mostly abroad and Ranulf
Flambard was left behind in England, it was possibly this split which
helped to create the tradition that the chancellor was the normal verifier
of a writ. The constables as a class are not prominent in this connexion,
only Urse of Abetot, who was also an active agent out of court, showing
up well; and other royal officials are poorly represented. Ranulf
Flambard's twenty-nine attestations as chaplain and six as bishop,
fifteen unaccompanied, are, of course, outstanding, all the more since he
was a frequent addressee. It cannot be doubted that he became
increasingly the key official and that even if he did not have a special
office beyond his chaplaincy he had a special position.

If Ranulf was pushing seventy when he died in 1128 – and he was
supposed never to have had a day's illness until the last two years before
his death – he would have been born about 1060, an exact contemporary
of William Rufus. He was the son of Thurstin, a village priest in the
diocese of Bayeux, and had at least three brothers, Fulcher, Osbern and
Geoffrey. Thurstin became a monk at St Augustine's, Canterbury,
possibly under Guy (Wido) (1087–93), who was also remembered at
Durham. The mother, whose name was not recorded, seems to have
come to live in London, for the bishop took her back to Normandy when
he fled from Henry's prison in February 1101.[136] Although both William
of Malmesbury and Orderic Vitalis regarded Ranulf's origins as

[135] See above, 150.
[136] *GR*, ii, 368–9; OV, iv, 170–2, v, 310. For his father, see Durham obituary in *Liber
Vitae*, 140: 'Kal. Jan , Turstinus monachus S. Augustini, pater Rannulfi episcopi'. For
his mother, see OV, v, 312, where she is described as a fortune-teller and sorceress
(*sortilega, venefica anus*), who had lost an eye through conversing with the devil. But as her
boat was being robbed by pirates, her incantations are understandable. Fulcher became
a royal chaplain, and Ranulf was using his services in 1100: *Regesta*, no. 464. For their
brother, Osbern, see *Chron. Abingdon*, ii, 23, and C.N.L. Brooke, 'The composition of the
chapter of St Paul's 1086–1163', *Cambridge Hist. Journ.*, x (1951), 130. The best modern
study is R.W. Southern, in *Medieval Humanism and other Studies* (1970), 183, supplemented
by H.S. Offler, 'Rannulph Flambard as bishop of Durham', *Durham University Journal*,
lxiv (1971), 14.

remarkably humble and obscure, they were not completely unlike their own, and a good number of bishops in Normandy and England were the sons of parish priests. All that a talented offspring from such a home required was a benefactor, and the obvious patron was his diocesan bishop, in Ranulf's case Odo of Bayeux. According to Orderic, Ranulf was brought up with shameful parasites among the servants of the court, and by this he seems to mean the royal court. Be that as it may, Odo supplied his brother with many of his clerks,[137] and it would be surprising if the youthful Ranulf was not acquainted with both households.

Orderic attributes to the clerk, on account of the squalor of his upbringing, more acquaintance with cunning tricks and the artful use of words than with literature: he was almost illiterate.[138] But again he denigrates. The various capacities in which Ranulf was employed prove that he had at least a working knowledge of Latin. Royal writs, inventories and accounts were his stock in trade when he was a royal clerk and chaplain. Archbishop Thomas of York, even though he was a compatriot, would not have consecrated a completely unsuitable candidate to the bishopric of Durham.[139] Ranulf attracted scholars to his household; and his monks, no reluctant critics of episcopal short-comings, came to regard him as a worthy pastor. Indeed, he can be viewed as an exemplary bishop by contemporary standards.[140]

He was endowed with most of the qualities necessary for success in the world: good looks, health and strength, intelligence, a ready tongue, courage and boundless ambition. From an examination of his skeleton it seems that he was about 5′ 9″ (1.75 m) tall, short-headed (brachy-cephalic), and with a powerful lower jaw, a sloping forehead and a large occipital protuberance.[141] The bracing winds of poverty sharpened his appetite to overtake his betters. The lower rungs of the ladder of

[137] *EC 1066–1154*, 58.

[138] OV, v, 310; cf. 322, where his brother Fulcher is also *pene illiteratus*.

[139] According, however, to Anselm, writing to the pope in 1101, Thomas confessed in the court of Henry I that he did not regard Ranulf as a brother bishop and that all the promises he made before consecration had been deceitful: Anselm, *Letters*, no. 214, iv, 113. But by 1101 Thomas was dead and times had changed.

[140] Note as well as his translation of St Cuthbert at Durham, a very well-publicized event, his translation of St Oswi, king and martyr, at Tynemouth on 20 August 1110: *Vita S. Oswini*, 15, 24. In the first citation the date should read 'millesimo centesimo [decimo], tercio decimo Kal. Sept.', to agree with the obviously correct dating on p. 24. The Hugh *abbas Salesberiensis*, noted on each occasion as accompanying Ranulf Flambard and Richard d'Aubigny, abbot of St Albans, is presumably the abbot of Selby (W. Yorks) (*Salebi* in *DB*): *HRH*, 69. Ranulf was in confraternity with New Minster, Winchester: below, 235.

[141] J.T. Fowler, 'An account of excavations made on the site of the chapter house of Durham cathedral in 1874', *Archaeologia*, xlv, pt 2 (1880), 386–8.

patronage he climbed are not perfectly clear. According to the York tradition, in the summer of 1086 he was with the royal court on the Isle of Wight, en route for Normandy, and at that time he was a royal chaplain and keeper of the king's seal under Maurice the chancellor.[142] In fact Maurice, archdeacon of Le Mans, had been nominated bishop of London at Christmas 1085 and was consecrated in the following spring, so he may already have been succeeded as chancellor by Gerard. The Durham tradition is similar, although even hazier: Ranulf was in the service of Maurice bishop of London until, taking offence because he was deprived of a deanery, he left him for the king in the hope of greater profit.[143] The York story is much to be preferred, for the chaplain had already earned sizeable rewards from the king by 1086, and it would seem that if Ranulf quarrelled with Maurice over a deanery, this happened after the bishop had left the royal service.

Maurice may have become chancellor in 1078, when Osmund left to become bishop of Salisbury, and Ranulf could have been introduced into the chapel royal about that time. This would give the younger man eight years in which to acquire the important position which Orderic believed he had in the Conqueror's household.[144] Since he was as often called the king's chaplain as his clerk, and Anselm states explicitly that he was a *sacerdos*,[145] it is probable that he was from the start of his royal service in priest's orders; but by the end of the Conqueror's reign his functions had become largely administrative, and it may be that, just as in Henry I's reign, the offices of master of the *scriptorium* and keeper of the seal went together. If Ranulf issued the royal writs, Orderic's stories make good sense: the chaplain's starting actions on his own initiative, bringing charges against many men in the king's hall and giving orders to his superiors as though acting by royal authority.[146] Keepers of the seal seem in general to have regarded themselves as fine fellows, in with the king and a cut above their peers.[147] Orderic tells us that because of the chaplain's unwelcome officiousness a dispenser nicknamed him Flambard. The name appears elsewhere in different forms: Flamme and Flambard (and other minor variations) in Domesday Book, Passeflambard in the *English Chronicle* and Florence.[148] Eadmer and William of

---

[142] Hugh, *HCY*, 5–6, 26.

[143] Simeon, *HDE, cont. I*, i, 135, written after 1144.

[144] OV, iv, 170–2, where *Guillelmus magnus* should be translated 'William senior'.

[145] Anselm, *Letters*, no. 214, iv, 112; cf. Florence, ii, 46.

[146] OV, iv, 172.

[147] Cf. above, 139 n. 196.

[148] For *DB* references, see below, 200 n. 163. *ASC, s.a.* 1128, 194; Florence, ii, 35; 'Flambard' in Anselm, *Letters*, no. 214; 'Flammard' in Ivo of Chartres, *Letters*, Migne *PL*, clxii, 162, cf. *flamigeri filii*, col. 155.

Malmesbury characteristically ignored it, but the latter not through ignorance, for he called him 'the tinder of avarice' and 'the torch of iniquity'.[149] Archbishop Anselm knew that he was called Flambard, and in 1101 told the pope that it was on account of his cruelty, which was like a consuming flame.[150] Orderic repeated this explanation. *Flamma* in the vernacular would have been *flambe*, and in its more extended forms the word may have meant a torch, torch-bearer, scorcher, or something like that. In modern French *flambard* can mean a gay dog, swell or toff (to use Edwardian slang), someone who shows off: the word is pejorative, but not without a touch of envy and admiration.

Ranulf basked in the old king's favour. It is not easy to imagine the Conqueror doting on the young man because of his beauty and graces, but there could have been something of this. Ranulf was a man of many parts and, perhaps, of many faces. He is one of a small number of persons of his period whose character was analyzed with some care by contemporaries, and his stature survives the scrutiny of even hostile witnesses. Strong and handsome, fond of clothes and richly dressed,[151] witty and eloquent, full of ideas and imaginative schemes, ready for great enterprises, he was a born leader. Active and impatient, he was quick to take decisions and to move on to something else. He had a volatile temperament: his mood changed easily between good and bad temper and in his talk there was such a mixture of seriousness and levity that it was often difficult to know exactly what to believe.[152] No one doubted, however, the acuteness of his mind or his loyalty to the king. It was also noticed how generous and faithful he was to his own men, and later how lavish in alms to the poor. He was above all *magnanimus*, like William Rufus. And although, like Thomas Becket as described by John of Salisbury,[153] he was probably 'a mighty trifler in the court, seeming to despise the law and the clergy and imitating the magnates in their low pursuits', no one questioned his religion or charged him with being a hypocrite. As bishop, partly perforce, he devoted himself to his duties in his diocese and city. His episcopal crozier was a comparatively simple staff, probably made in the north and decorated with an attractive zoomorphic design in niello inlay on the silver plating. The finger ring

---

[149] 'fomes cupiditatum', *GR*, ii, 368, cf. 'rapuitque in fomite flammam', Virg. *Aen.*, I, 176; 'nequitiarum faece (abl.)', 470, presumably to be corrected to 'face', for *fax*, a torch, makes better sense than *faex*, dregs.

[150] Anselm, *Letters*, no. 214.

[151] The richness of his clothes when he was abducted is noticed: below, 199; and he gave sets of fine vestments to Durham: Simeon, *HDE, cont. I*, i, 140.

[152] The most elaborate and acute character sketch is in Simeon, *op. cit.*, i, 139–41. Cf. OV, iv, 170. William of Malmesbury, *GR*, ii, 368, follows Eadmer, *HN*, 41.

[153] John of Salisbury, *Letters*, ii, 244.

found in his grave was a plain gold hoop set with an unengraved sapphire [154] He seems to have avoided austerity and ostentation alike. All admired his courage and nerve, indeed panache, perhaps flamboyance. But in his capacity as a royal servant he was arrogant and hectoring towards those with whom he did business, although his loud voice and threatening countenance – playing the king – always seemed a bit of an act put on for the occasion. He made a lot of money in the royal service with which he bought a bishopric, and he used his position, in the usual way, to get lucrative posts for his relatives and sons.

He had a good appetite for sensual pleasure, for food and drink and women, but this did not incur much censure.[155] His wife or mistress before he became bishop was Ælfgifu, a member of a wealthy Anglo-Danish merchant family of Huntingdon and the sister of Beatrice who married a leading member of the merchant guild of that town. She was the mother of some, if not all, of his children, and when he took episcopal orders he found her a suitable husband in Huntingdon and often stayed at her house on his journeys to and from the south. On one of these occasions, about 1114, it is reported that he tried to seduce her niece, Theodora, the future anchorite, Christina of Markyate.[156] William of Malmesbury tells the incredible story that at Durham Ranulf forced monks to eat with him in his hall, and not only served them with prohibited food (presumably meat), but also had it served by beautiful waitresses in tight clothes and with their hair hanging down their backs. Those monks who lowered their eyes he called hypocrites, and those who answered back lacking in respect. Ranulf was the sort of man who, perhaps deservedly, attracted such scabrous anecdotes.[157]

Tales were also told about his resource and bravery – how he foiled an attempt on his life by pirates and how he escaped from the Tower of

---

[154] J.T. Fowler, op. cit., 387–8; T.D. Kendrick (and A.B. Tonnochy), 'Flambard's Crozier', The Antiquaries Journal, xviii (1938), 236 ff. The crozier was cleaned and repaired in 1937 at the British Museum. See here, pl. 5.

[155] OV, iv, 170, mentions gluttony, drunkenness, and lust; OV, v, 312, his jollifications in the Tower of London in 1100–1101, when a prisoner. He also, punning on flamma, calls him corpulentus flamen – a fat priest. In DB Herefordshire, indexed under 'The wife of Ralf the chaplain', a woman and her son Walter held two small estates in chief, worth 16s a year: i, 187c. But this is unlikely to be a wife of Flambard, for Hereford is well off his beat and Walter (although he could be a step-son) does not link. In any case, wives, when listed, were usually widows.

[156] The Life of Christina of Markyate, ed. and trans. C.H. Talbot (1959), 34 ff. Neither Ælfgifu (Alveva) nor her niece Theodora/Christina appear in the Durham necrology or obituaries, unless the latter is 'Christina sanctimonialis de Silva', commemorated on 6 Id. December: Liber Vitae, 147. But a Margaret with her mother Beatrice (both rather unusual names) are listed: 38c.

[157] GP, 274 n. (1st edn). Cf. the story about the bishop's niece and the cardinal-legate John of Crema, Annales Monastici, ii, 47–8; HH, 245–6.

London down a rope at night after Henry I had thrown him into prison.[158] The first story is related by the Durham chronicler after the bishop's death, and can have lost nothing in the repeated telling. Although there is no way of dating the episode except to 1086–99, it is possible, as the chaplain, described as 'the executor of the king's business', seems to have been exercising general authority, that it belongs to 1091 or 1094, when the king was out of the country.[159] The story goes that one of Ranulf's vassals, Gerold, suborned by the chaplain's enemies, hatched a plot to kidnap and kill him. Disembarking from a small boat, probably at London or Westminster, he claimed to have been sent by Maurice bishop of London who was at death's door on his manor on the river – presumably Stepney, where Ranulf himself had an estate – and wanted Ranulf to visit him.[160] Suspecting nothing, Ranulf got on board with his notary and a few other servants, but became suspicious when Gerold steered down the main channel straight for the sea, and held his course until they came up with a larger vessel at anchor which seemed to be waiting their arrival and was full of armed men. Realizing the situation, Ranulf threw his ring overboard and his notary followed suit with his master's seal,[161] to prevent their use by the

[158] Simeon HDE, cont. I, i, 135 ff. ASC, s.a. 1100, 1101; GR, ii, 470–1; Florence, ii, 47–8.

[159] The story is interpolated into an account of Ranulf's episcopate and cannot be dated from its context. If Maurice was, indeed, bishop at the time, the terminus a quo is Christmas 1085 or April 1086, and if Ranulf did, as would be expected, accompany the king to Normandy in August 1086, the kidnapping occurred either in those five or seven months or in William II's reign. The seal which comes into the story does not really help, for neither is it precisely identified, nor do we know when the chaplain ceased to be keeper of the royal seal. The first half of 1086 seems to be a rather unlikely time for such a strike against a royal servant. The Conqueror was at Winchester at Easter, Westminster at Whitsun, and Salisbury on 1 August, before leaving for the Isle of Wight, and the Domesday survey was being carried out. It was a bad year in many ways; but the king, at the height of his powers, was greatly concerned with his security. Nor is it likely that Maurice would have been (falsely) described as close to death immediately after his promotion to the bishopric. Also it would seem that the Durham writer, with his use of the stock epithets for Ranulf's position and his suggestion that the chaplain was acting as regent, thought that the event took place under William II. But he could have been mistaken, and Southern, op. cit., 187, dates the event 1085–7.

[160] The bishop's manors on the north bank (he had none on the south) were Fulham and Stepney, DB, i, 127b–d. Since the boat went downstream, clearly from London or Westminster, the former is ruled out.

[161] 'et notarius suus sigillum illius', i.e. Ranulf's seal. That the chaplain made use of a signet ring is understandable; but it would seem unlikely that he also had a personal seal, inscribed presumably with 'Sigillum Rannulfi Capellani Regis', which he entrusted to a notary or keeper. Much more likely, although this raises important administrative, even 'constitutional' issues, Ranulf had a copy of the king's 'great' seal, like the one later kept at the Exchequer for the use of the chief justiciar. But the problem is difficult, especially since the event cannot be dated.

conspirators and their paymasters to validate writs which would disturb the country, for the seals were known throughout England. Ranulf was then transferred to the sea-going vessel and his companions were put ashore after they had sworn to keep the abduction secret.

The ship sailed out to sea and then took a southerly course (perhaps into the Medway if it had not reached the North Foreland). While the chaplain sat apart in the prow, his captors discussed how they should kill him. Two sailors were chosen to do the deed, either by throwing him overboard or beating his brains out, and were to receive his fine clothes as payment. However, a dispute between them over who should have his mantle held things up until, towards nightfall on the second day, a violent storm blew up from the south and the stricken ship was driven back on its course into the Thames. When it was again proposed to kill the prisoner, the second-in-command offered Ranulf his support, and he, 'great-hearted [*magnanimus*] as always when in danger', called on Gerold to observe the fealty he owed him, and promised him rewards if he would spare his life. In the end, the captain, more terrified by the chaplain's authority than seduced by his promises, agreed, and when the vessel reached port, entertained him in his house overlooking the strand before taking flight and going into permanent exile. Whereupon Ranulf called out all the knights of the district and with a strong bodyguard returned noisily to London, where he was received with amazement, for he was already rumoured dead. After this, the story concludes, Ranulf was even more in the royal confidence and thus able to scotch all the schemes of his rivals and enemies.

At William I's court Ranulf seems to have been employed mostly 'in the house'. As he accompanied the king to Normandy in 1086, even if he played some part in the planning of the Domesday Inquest, a project which would seem to have been within his special field of interest, he could have been little involved in its execution.[162] Nevertheless, the pattern of his own estates revealed by the Survey shows that while the bulk of his honour, the estates in Surrey, Oxfordshire and Hampshire, were derived from the king, and the one piece he held from Osmund bishop of Salisbury may be a payment for looking after the ex-chancellor's interests at court, those held of the bishop of London and the abbeys of Glastonbury and Bath could have been picked up when those institutions were without a pastor, and give a hint that the

---

[162] V.H. Galbraith, who would have liked to have involved Ranulf, if he could, was unable to do so: *The Making of Domesday Book* (1961), *Domesday Book, its place in administrative history* (1974), indexes, *s.v.* Flambard. Sally Harvey, 'Domesday Book and Anglo-Norman governance', *TRHS*, 5th ser., xxv (1975), 190–2, takes the subject up again.

chaplain may already have gained some experience of administering ecclesiastical custodies.[163]

Always an opportunist, he must have joined William II as early as possible, for he was acting for the king in 1088 at the vacant abbeys of Ely, Ramsey and Winchester (New Minster), and in the following year, when Lanfranc died, at Canterbury.[164] He had become a specialist in this field. By 1091 he was authorizing royal writs,[165] and was gaining entry into the highest circle of royal servants. Orderic believed that the chaplain by the use of flattery and other unworthy means became an intimate of the young king;[166] and it cannot be doubted that the two were always on excellent personal terms, although not, of course, companions or anything except master and servant. The earliest observers described Ranulf's activities and functions without attributing to him any formal office. For Eadmer, who saw him in action at Canterbury, he was the principal executive of the royal will.[167] The Anglo-Saxon chronicler, in his notice of the chaplain's promotion to Durham, remarked that he had driven and managed all the king's courts throughout England.[168] For William of Malmesbury, who was familiar with both accounts, Ranulf was the man who, when it was decided to impose the land tax, doubled the rate. He was an invincible pleader in the courts (*causidicus*), and (as Suetonius wrote of Domitian[169]) 'extravagant in both words and deeds'. He raged against suppliants as though they were rebels, while the king laughingly exclaimed that he was the only man in the world to behave in this way, caring nothing at all for men's hatred as long as he pleased his lord. He was the main custodian of ecclesiastical honours and influenced the

[163] Surrey: in Godalming and at Tuesley, *DB*, i, 30d; Oxfordshire: in Oxford town, 154a, Milton under Wychwood, 157a, and see above, 141; Hampshire: Funtley, 49b, *Bile* and Beckly in Ringwood, 51b; Berkshire: in Winterbourne of the bishop of Salisbury, 58b; Middlesex: in Stepney of the bishop of London, 127b; Somerset: *Vudewiche* in Freshford of Bath abbey, 89d, iii, 186b; Wiltshire: in Corston of Glastonbury abbey, 67a. The see of London was vacant in 1085, Glastonbury was without a ruler after 1083 during Thurstin's exile, and Bath may have needed a coadjutor during Ælsige's last years.

[164] See below, 233 ff.

[165] *Regesta*, i, nos 321–2, 390.

[166] OV, iv, 170–4; cf. *HDE, cont. I*, 135, 139.

[167] 'regiae voluntatis maximus executor', Eadmer, *HN*, 41; cf. 'negotiorum totius regni exactor', Florence, ii, 44; 'regalium negotiorum executor', *HDE, cont. I*, 138; 'placitator sed perversor, exactor sed exustor totius regni', HH, 232, cf. n. 5. 'regalium provisor et exactor vectigalium', Samson, 'De Miraculis S. Ædmundi', *Memorials of St Edmund's Abbey*, ed. T. Arnold, i (Rolls ser. 1890), 156.

[168] 'the aeror ealle his gemot ofer eall Engleland draf and bewiste'; the translation is too loose in *ASC*, 175, *s.a.* 1099.

[169] Suet., *Dom.*, 12.

king's patronage.[170] He was regarded at Abingdon abbey as the king's chaplain and justiciar of the kingdom of England.[171] For Archbishop Anselm he was not just a publican (that is to say, a farmer of the royal taxes, and so a sinner), but a very prince of publicans, who was imprisoned by Henry I for embezzling the money which, as a publican, he owed from his offices.[172]

On one occasion the Malmesbury chronicler called Ranulf *procurator* of the whole kingdom, an expression more attractive to stylists than vulgar terms such as *senescallus* or *dapifer* because it was to be found in Cicero and other classical authors.[173] It was later used of and by Roger of Salisbury, Ranulf's successor in this position, and of other royal officials.[174] A *procurator* was essentially the manager or steward of an estate, responsible for its running and profits; and the estate which Ranulf eventually managed was the kingdom of England, or, more specifically, the royal demesne in its widest form. His job was to exploit all the royal rights and to maximize the king's revenue. A steward also usually held his lord's court. This term was taken up by the Durham chronicler and Orderic when they elaborated the points made by their predecessors.[175] Florence, rewriting the Anglo-Saxon Chronicle and taking something from William of Malmesbury, made Ranulf royal justiciar and tax-gatherer of the whole kingdom.[176] Orderic, the legatee of all the others, believed that William gave Ranulf authority over all the royal officials, even over the magnates.[177] Ranulf's wife seems to have

---

[170] *GR*, ii, 368–9, *GP*, 274.

[171] *Chron. Abingdon*, ii, 39–40. The abbey had dealings with him.

[172] Anselm, *Letters*, no. 214, iv, 112–13.

[173] 'totius regni procurator', *GP*, 274, repeated *HDE, cont. I*, 135, 139; 'summus regiarum procurator opum et iusticiarius', OV, v, 310.

[174] In 1123 × 6 Roger styled himself 'R. episcopus Saresb' sub domino nostro rege Henrico regni Angliae procurator', Doris M. Stenton, 'Roger of Salisbury Regni Angliae Procurator', *EHR*, xxxix (1924), 79; cf. 'tempore vestrae procurationis', Bishop Herbert of Norwich, *Letters*, no. 26, p. 50. Richardson and Sayles, 160. Arnulf of Lisieux used the terms *major procurator domus/regis* once to describe Henry II's household steward and once to indicate the seneschal of Normandy: *Letters*, 20, 191. In the *Dialogus de Scaccario* there is mention of the *generalis procurator* of a sheriff, 82; and the classical equivalent of the vulgar *senescallus* is given as *generalis economus*, 117, cf. 116. In Alexander Neckam, *De Naturis Rerum*, 254, *senescallus* is equated to *procurator domus militis*.

[175] See above, 200 n. 166.

[176] 'Placitator ac totius regni exactor', Florence, ii, 46, probably substituting *placitator* for William of Malmesbury's *causidicus* (above, n. 170). Cf. also above, 200 n. 167. This office gave him the power to mulct the rich by taking away their lands and goods, and the poor by imposing frequent, heavy and unjust taxation. The royal 'itinerant' justices, including Ranulf, of Lent 1096 (below, 208) were called by Tavistock abbey *placitatores*.

[177] OV, iv, 170; v, 310.

put it about that he was next after the king and a judge over the whole of England.[178]

These descriptions, when stripped of censure and hyperbole, probably give a correct indication of how Ranulf was employed by William II, and the writers' failure to allot him an office, whether traditional or novel, beyond his chaplaincy, seems equally well-founded. Ranulf certainly acted as a royal judge, and he could well have been one of those 'justiciars of the whole of England', who are more commonly met with in the next reign.[179] But he was hardly the capital or chief justiciar of later times, and in suggesting that he was, and in isolating him and making him the scapegoat for all the oppressive actions of the government, the chroniclers mislead. He is normally, even late in the reign, found acting with colleagues, especially Walkelin bishop of Winchester, the stewards Haimo and Roger Bigot, and the marshal Urse of Abetot. These men were protected both by their respectable backgrounds (except in Urse's case) and, even more cogently, by their offices. Ranulf had no protection of any kind except royal favour, and this informality was found offensive. It is also likely that he was the most active operator in the group, the one who, with Urse, did not mind doing the rough and unpopular jobs.[180]

Because of Ranulf's adventures it is easy to exaggerate his insecurity and rootlessness. In fact he was a dynast. Three or four of his sons are known. Thomas and his unnamed younger brother whom he tried to intrude into the bishopric of Lisieux in 1102, when both were scarce twelve years old,[181] if they were born after 1090 were probably the children of Ælfgifu. Elias, prebendary of St Paul's, London, and of Lincoln, and one of Henry I's clerks,[182] could also have sprung from Huntingdon. Ralf, parson of Middleham, like his father a patron of St Godric of Finchale, prebendary of St Paul's, and after 1138 a member of Archbishop Theobald's household,[183] would seem to be one of the

---

[178] 'totius Angliae iudex, secundus post regem', *The Life of Christina of Markyate*, 40. Cf. the expressions of Ov, above, 201 n. 173, *GR*, n. 170, and Florence, n. 176.

[179] For Ranulf as a judge, on this occasion with his brother, Osbern, see *Chron. Abingdon*, ii, 21. For *iustitiarii totius Angliae*, see Richardson and Sayles, 174 ff.; W.T. Reedy Jr, *loc. cit.*, 694.

[180] J.H. Round, however, considered Bishop Walkelin 'as exacting as the king' in his treatment of his own manors and a fit companion for Ranulf: *VCH Hants*, i, 414–15. But he seems to have had enough of it in the end: see below, 257.

[181] Ivo of Chartres, *Letters*, nos 149, 153–4, 157, Migne *PL*, clxii, 154 ff.; OV, v, 320–2. David, *RC*, 151–2.

[182] *The Registrum Antiquissimum of the Cathedral Church of Lincoln*, ed. C.W. Foster, Lincoln Record Soc., xxvii (1931), i, no. 33, p. 26 = *Regesta*, ii, no. 1104; *ibid.*, no. 1364; below, 203 n. 185. Round, 'Bernard the king's scribe', *EHR*, xiv (1899), 428–9.

[183] Obit, 6 Id. Jan. in calendar in *Liber Vitae*, 141; Reginald of Durham, *Vita S. Godrici*,

5. Ranulf Flambard's pastoral staff (a) and episcopal ring (b), found in his tomb at Durham. (See here, 196–7.)

6a. The Anglo-Saxon Chronicle (E), part of the entry for 1087–8 (the king's accession). (Bodleian Library, MS. Laud. Misc. 636, fo. 66 recto. Translated D. Whitelock, p. 166.)

6b. Anglo-Saxon Chronicle entry for 1099 and part of the entry for 1100. (Ibid, fo. 73 recto. Translated D. Whitelock, pp. 175–6.)

younger children. There were also his nephews. Because he was a more important man than any of his brothers, he may have had additional family responsibilities when Fulcher died on 29 January 1102 after holding the bishopric of Lisieux for only a few months. And by that time there were places in his own diocese. Osbert the sheriff was his secular, Ranulf the archdeacon his spiritual deputy. Robert, Richard and William, all with ducal names, were given fiefs; and there was a niece.[184]

Moreover, although royal service had inherent dangers, the chaplain, with the help of his patron Maurice, quickly established a base for his family in the bishopric of London. It was Maurice who completed the organization of St Paul's and its prebendal system; and prebends were held by Ranulf (Totenhall), by his brothers Fulcher (Ealdstreet) and Osbern (Consumpta-per-Mare), and by his sons Elias and Ralf (both Sneating).[185] It is, therefore, no surprise to find that commemorated in the Durham *Liber Vitae* were Ralf son of Algod and his family, important in both St Paul's and the city,[186] although Bishop Maurice himself does not seem to have been entered. Deans of St Paul's, as they held an unendowed office, commonly were prebendaries of Totenhall; but there is no good evidence that Ranulf was ever dean; indeed his 'deprivation' of a deanery by Maurice in the Durham story may reveal his disappointed hopes;[187] and it is possible that great ambitions in London were only realized in part. But as a whole he did not do too badly. Probably through his connexion with Huntingdon and his familiarity with Robert Bloet he also gained places for himself and his family in the cathedral church of Lincoln; and he acquired benefices in other collegiate churches.[188] By 1099 he was well qualified to become a bishop

---

66; below, n. 185; He witnesses a number of Theobald's charters, sometimes as Ralf of Durham, sometimes as Ralf son of Ralf bishop of Durham: A. Saltman, *Theobald archbishop of Canterbury* (1956), 262, 286, 368, 404, 474, 546.

[184] Offler, 'Rannulf Flambard as bishop of Durham', 21 ff., *Durham Episcopal Charters*, 101, 105, and *passim*. For the niece, see above, 197 n. 157. She was possibly the daughter of Ranulf's brother Geoffrey, for whom see *PR 31 H.I*, 79. Archdeacon Ranulf's obit, 18 Kal. Jan. is in the calender in *Liber Vitae*, 147.

[185] *John le Neve: Fasti Ecclesiae Anglicanae, 1066–1300*, compiled by Diana E. Greenway, I, *St Paul's London* (1968), 43, 47, 77, 79.

[186] *Liber Vitae*, 50, a–b.

[187] Above, 195. C.N.L. Brooke, 'The composition of the Chapter of St Paul's', especially Appendix II, argued that Ranulf was for a time dean; Diana E. Greenway, *op. cit.*, Appendix I, is much more doubtful: it is only an inference from Ranulf's tenure of the prebend of Totenhall. The Durham story seems to be evidence against rather than for the theory.

[188] He was succeeded by his son Elias in a Lincoln prebend: above, 202 n. 182. He also held the deanery of Twynham (Christchurch) (Hants) and prebends in St Martin's, Dover, and Salisbury: *Regesta*, nos 361, ii, 562, 753.

of a certain type. When he died in possession of a great bishopric and fief which he had cherished and adorned, he cannot have considered his career a complete failure.

Moralists viewed Ranulf as the deplorable servant of a deplorable king. Modern historians have been interested in his function and in whether this foreshadowed the chief justiciarship of later times. In the course of the twelfth century it became increasingly necessary for rulers not only to use a deputy, an *alter ego*, but also to formalize the office. English kings began to move hesitantly towards the creation of the post of chief justiciar, although it hardly ever acquired a certain title, bishops to make experiments which led to the appointment of commissaries and vicars-general.[189] Such offices were required because of an increase in the business connected with government and the more frequent absences from duty of the titular rulers. But there is a fully discernible background. William I entrusted his half-brother, Odo of Bayeux, from time to time with considerable viceregal powers in England.[190] Under William Rufus, who had no useful kin, the position of Bishops William of Durham and Walkelin of Winchester has to be considered. William of St Calais operated in the royal council in 1088 and 1091–6; Walkelin seems to have been prominent only after 1092. We know that the former was in the beginning the king's chief counsellor;[191] and clearly after his exile Walkelin became for some years his colleague or rival, and after his death took his place. It seems, too, that the chancellor, Robert Bloet, and Ranulf Flambard not only kept their inner position after promotion to the episcopal bench but also improved it.

The question arises, had these bishops in turn a special position or title at court or outside? This, however, seems unlikely. If the possibilities are reviewed, the only one worthy of consideration would be the chief justiciarship; and it would be hazardous to think that this position, which even in its heyday at the end of the twelfth century was hardly an office,[192] existed as early as this in any shape or form. Nor was Walkelin necessarily a member of the closest circle round the king. He was probably not as intimate as Robert fitzHaimo or Robert of Meulan,

---

[189] F.J. West, *The Justiciarship in England, 1066–1232* (1966). *EC 1066–1154*, 139–40; Irene J. Churchill, *Canterbury Administration*, i (1933), 25 ff., 54 ff.

[190] D.R. Bates, 'The Origins of the Justiciarship', *Battle IV*.

[191] See above, 60–1. In Durham's *Liber Vitae*, presumably through the agency of either William of St Calais or Ranulf Flambard, but, since Henry of Warwick is unmarried, probably the former, appear the Beaumont clan – Roger of Beaumont and his wife Adeline, Robert count of Meulan and his wife Isabel, Earl Henry, Richard the chaplain and Ralf the butler – and the Bigots – Roger and his wife Atheles and their son William: *Liber Vitae*, 53c, 55a.

[192] West, *The Justiciarship in England*, 31 ff. *FWR*, i, 333 and App.T, regarded Ranulf Flambard as the first (chief) justiciar.

possibly even as Ranulf Flambard when chaplain. He was, of course, bishop of Winchester, the seat of the treasury; and it is likely that he was the king's main administrative deputy, a man both of position and of business, on whom the ruler relied to keep royal affairs in good order with the help of a group of assistant justiciars. What prevented him from becoming more than a forerunner of Henry I's Roger of Salisbury was the king's usual residence in England until 1096, which discouraged the growth of the regency function, and the bishop's death soon after the situation changed. He was succeeded in this position by Ranulf Flambard, and in his case future developments were destroyed when his master died. But it would not seem that Roger of Salisbury, although often considered the first royal capital justiciar, advanced much beyond Ranulf's position.

Royal business could be transacted in this rather informal way partly because there was not much of it and partly because of the nature of most of what there was. The increasing volume of administrative orders emanating from the royal court did not entirely signify an increase in purposeful royal government, but rather a new general interest in documentary titles. In most of the transactions on record in writ or charter the king was simply answering a petitioner, probably always at a price. In other words, he was being induced to sell some service. The larger part of William II's instruments are confirmations or protections of rights which the petitioning church claimed already to possess; others were the proof of the purchase of further privileges. What is more, since it is unlikely that the marshals in the royal court did messenger service for anyone but the king,[193] it was presumably the successful petitioner who took the writ, or made his own arrangements for it to be delivered, to the sheriff or other addressee. In considering whether to grant the petition, the king might have needed advice, perhaps even an investigation of the Domesday dossier,[194] or have found it necessary to hold some sort of inquiry, either at court or in the shires. In some cases his own favour or malice towards the petitioner would have been decisive. But in almost all, little was required of him beyond his general view of the matter. And the business was usually concluded by a terse and peremptory order. A royal writ addressed to Durand the sheriff and the barons of Hampshire, and witnessed by the bishop of Durham, is a perfect example. 'See to it [*Facite*] that the monks of St Peter of the bishopric of Winchester hold in peace the land in Hayling Island that Queen Emma gave them, according to the evidence of the royal

[193] See above, 153.

[194] Cf. a writ addressed to the bishop and sheriff of Somerset, and witnessed by William bishop of Durham and Ranulf Flambard, confirming a grant of William I to St Peter's, Winchester, as ascertained by the bishop of Durham from *breves meos*, *Regesta*, ii, 386a.

book.'[195] The royal secretariat wastes no words, and so no parchment.

Sometimes, however, more action was called for. When an important person (only monastic examples have survived) complained to the king of some injustice done to him, the king could order the sheriff or some other trusted agent to take summary action, make an investigation, or hold a trial.[196] For example, by a writ witnessed by Haimo *dapifer* and Hugh of Beauchamp, William ordered Ranulf Flambard and all sheriffs and justiciars to secure the return to Ramsey abbey of all fugitive serfs whom the abbot and his men could locate, and prevent anyone detaining them.[197] Sometimes a trial was held before special royal judges. For example, Gilbert Crispin, abbot of Westminster, won a claim to some land in the presence of Bishop William of Durham, Walkelin bishop of Winchester, Eudo *dapifer*, Ivo Taillebois and Robert *dispensator*.[198] This hearing must surely have taken place in the royal court. Sometimes the king presided in person at a hearing, as at the trial of William of Durham in 1088.[199] When he confirmed Carlisle's subjection to the spiritual jurisdiction of the archdeacon of Durham, perhaps in 1096, he ordered that if anyone else claimed a share in it, the claim was to be made in 'my court' at Easter.[200] At Easter 1100 at Winchester he issued a writ in favour of Walter abbot of Evesham, who had won his case against Bishop Samson of Worcester in the king's presence (*coram rege*); and moreover he decreed that any further attempt by the bishop to question those privileges which his father and he had confirmed to Evesham should likewise come before the king's own court.[201]

The king also on occasion dispatched special commissioners out of court to investigate, hear and determine matters of importance to him. When the monks of St Augustine's, Canterbury, after Lanfranc's death in 1089, rebelled against their abbot, Guy, William sent Bishop Walkelin of Winchester and Gundulf of Rochester with some unnamed barons to Canterbury in order to deal with the matter. And this they did.[202] It might be expected that among the barons was sheriff Haimo. Two documents obtained by Herbert bishop of Thetford, probably after

---

[195] V.H. Galbraith, 'Royal charters to Winchester', *EHR*, xxxv (1920), no. XII; *Regesta*, ii, no. 483a. Cf. *DB*, i, 43a (*Helinghei*), where, however, there is no mention of Queen Emma.

[196] Cf. *Regesta*, nos 383, 420, 426.

[197] *Ibid.*, 419.

[198] *Ibid.*, 370.

[199] Above, 85 ff.

[200] *Regesta*, no. 478, as enlarged in ii, 407. Possible dates are early 1093, 1095, 1096, with the last, following the death of the bishop of Durham, the most likely.

[201] *Regesta*, no. 429; *Monasticon Anglicanum*, ii, 19, no. ix.

[202] *Acta Lanfranci*, 274–5; *EC 1066–1154*, 163.

his restoration to the see in 1095, are particularly interesting.[203] By one writ, witnessed by the bishop of Durham, Ranulf Flambard was ordered to put Herbert into possession of the jurisdiction and all other customs which his predecessors had possessed, and to do him justice in respect of the encroachments and wrongs which he and his vassals had suffered. By the other, witnessed by Ranulf and addressed to the sheriff of Norfolk and Suffolk, the king announced that he had restored to Herbert the lands which were claimed from him and recorded in the *breves* made for the king (a reference to Domesday Book and particularly to the *invasiones*, the illegal occupations, recorded therein, ii, 197b–201b), and, further, that Herbert and his vassals were quit of all the lawsuits which Ranulf had brought against them. Ranulf would seem to have taken advantage of Herbert's disgrace to investigate encroachments on the royal demesne revealed by the Domesday Inquest, a 'persecution' halted by Herbert's recovery of William's favour. Perhaps a little later Bishop Walkelin, Ranulf and Roger Bigot surveyed and allocated the lands which the king had allotted to Herbert for building a new cathedral, monastery and episcopal palace in Norwich. Walkelin and Ranulf witnessed the writ of authorization which was addressed to the sheriffs of Norfolk and Suffolk:[204] they were authorizing their own activities; and it is just possible that the king was abroad.

Herbert, however, did not always have it his own way, particularly in respect of the great monastery of Bury St Edmunds, which claimed to be exempt from the jurisdiction of its diocesan bishop.[205] In 1094 the aged abbot Baldwin, the famous physician who had started as King Edward's doctor, completed the rebuilding of the choir of the monastic church and petitioned the king for permission both to have it dedicated and also to translate into it the body of St Edmund, king and martyr. But when William, after first agreeing to both, later postponed the former, perhaps because of Herbert's objections, and then went abroad (in March), everything was postponed until the following year. The business must have been discussed again at Rockingham in February or at a slightly later court, for the abbey was disturbed by stories that some courtiers were suggesting that the body of the martyr was not in fact present in an incorrupt state at Bury and that the metalwork attached to the shire should be seized in order to pay for soldiers (*ad militare stipendium*). But on 25 April Bishop Walkelin and Ranulf Flambard arrived on an unexpected and, as it turned out, most welcome visit as royal

---

[203] *Regesta*, ii, 385b–c, cf. a. See also above, 180.

[204] *Regesta*, no. 385.

[205] Barlow, *EC 1066–1154*, 172–3. 'Heremanni archidiaconi miracula S. Eadmundi', *Ungedruckte Anglo-Normannorum Geschichtsquellen*, ed. F. Liebermann, 274 ff.; Samson, 'De Miraculis S. Ædmundi', *loc. cit.*, 155–60. For the widespread doubts about the incorruption of the saint's body, see *ibid.*, 168 ff.

commissioners or justices. They announced that they had come to perform the translation of the saint, despite the opposition of the bishop of Thetford, spent the Thursday and Friday in the abbey engaged in unspecified royal business, and on the Saturday prepared for the ceremony, the bishop fasting and abstaining from secular activities. On Sunday 29 April 1095, Walkelin conducted the service for the removal of St Edmund, together with the saints Botulf and Firmin, from the old church to the new, and went out to preach a rousing, but perhaps over-long, homiletic sermon to the people. The miraculous cure of a Northampton knight, who had been injured by the surging crowd, drew the congregation away, but they returned to ask the bishop to intercede with St Edmund to end the long drought which was endangering the crops. The saint's body was brought out of the church, and Walkelin's resumed sermon was this time terminated by a miraculous downpour. It was a great occasion, attended by a large concourse of men and women. Walkelin granted an indulgence to all who visited the shrine, and the monastery was very content.

A good example of a 'localized' judicial eyre comes from 1096, when William dispatched his magnates (*optimates*) Walkelin of Winchester, Ranulf Flambard, William Capra and Harding son of Eadnoth the Staller 'to hear the pleas of the crown in Devon, Cornwall and Exeter'.[206] William Capra, lord of Bradninch and brother of Ralf de Pomeroy, lord of Berry Pomeroy, was a well-known west-country baron; Harding and his father had been important officials of King Edward the Confessor and were the ancestors of the Berkeleys. Even if one of their tasks was to raise money for the taking of Normandy in pledge, they also, no doubt, as was usual at the time, investigated and enforced all royal rights. They certainly inquired into the abbot of Tavistock's claim to Werrington; and, after Wimund had proved his title in the royal court, William granted the manor to the monastery for the souls of his father, mother and himself, and gave Wimund seizin through the gift of an ivory knife, which the abbot prudently preserved within the shrine of St Rumon. The writ was witnessed by Bishop Walkelin, John bishop of Bath and Thurstin abbot of Glastonbury. The king's uncle, Robert of Mortain, had died in 1090, and it is possible that his son and heir,

---

[206] *Monasticon Anglicanum*, ii, 497; *Regesta*, no. 378. *FWR*, ii, 508, was the first correctly to identify Harding. The history of Werrington has been investigated by H.P.R. Finberg, 'The early history of Werrington', *EHR*, lix (1944), 237; *Lucerna* (1964), 171 ff. W.T. Reedy, *loc. cit.*, 693, following Finberg, denies that this was a judicial eyre; but financial and judicial business cannot be separated at this time. For the genealogy of the Berkeleys, see O. Barron, 'Our oldest families: X. The Berkeleys', *The Ancestor*, viii (1904), 73. For their lands, see A. Williams, 'Land and power in the 11th century: the estates of Harold Godwineson', *Battle III*, 181.

William, was still in royal wardship. This would help to explain the mission of royal justices within a great frontier earldom.

The chroniclers are most uninformative about the arrangements which William made for the government of England when he went abroad. Exceptionally, the Winchester annalist recorded that in November 1097 Bishop Walkelin and Ranulf Flambard were left in charge.[207] But there is no reason why the king should have set up a special regency council. In practice, the royal court split when he went abroad. He was accompanied by his baronial friends, Robert of Meulan, Robert fitzHaimo and the rest, and he took his chancellor with him and doubtless some other household officials and personal servants. But ducal officals were awaiting their lord in Normandy. In any case William would not want to denude England of all the men on whom he relied. English bishops rarely if ever went with him to the duchy, nor did Ranulf Flambard. Indeed, on such evidence that exists, it would appear that most of the group of administrators already identified through their regular witness of royal writs stayed at home. And this body of servants, fully accustomed to managing his affairs, he could direct almost as easily from Normandy or Maine as from Gloucester or Carlisle.

In this connexion the writs dispatched from the king's court in Normandy to recipients in England deserve special attention. None can be identified from 1091. In 1094 William sent from Eu an order to his former chancellor, Robert Bloet, bishop of Lincoln.[208] Either in that year, or after he had taken Normandy in pledge (1096–7), he twice directed writs to Bishop Robert, Ranulf Flambard, Haimo *dapifer* and Urse of Abetot.[209] In the autumn of 1097 from the Isle of Wight, en route for Normandy, he sent a notification to Bishop Walkelin, Bishop Samson of Worcester, Ranulf Flambard, the royal justiciars and Walter sheriff of Gloucester. The writ was witnessed by William Giffard the chancellor and Urse.[210] The last named could have taken it back with the king's final instructions. From Foucarmont, between Aumale and Eu, possibly in the autumn of 1098, the king implemented a decision of his court by a writ addressed to 'his justiciars in England', Ralf bishop of Chichester, Ranulf Flambard and Urse of Abetot.[211] Bishop Ralf was included

[207] *Ann. Winton.*, ii, 39.

[208] *Regesta*, no. 350.

[209] *Ibid.*, nos 422, 424, and see below, 224–5, 365. In no. 424 Ralf bishop of Chichester is possibly a mistake for Robert Bishop of Lincoln, for, although Ralf is referred to in no. 459a as one of the king's justiciars in Sussex, he seems never to have been one of the king's justiciars of England. But this writ concerned Sussex.

[210] Liber Eliensis, 207; *Regesta*, no. 389; and see below, 376. Cf. a writ, dated 'Kinver', in favour of Bishop Walkelin, addressed to W. sheriff of the Isle, witnessed by Ranulf Flambard, Urse, and Croc the huntsman. *Regesta*, ii, 412d.

[211] *Regesta*, nos 423–4; see below, 395.

because the matter concerned Sussex. On 12 November, probably 1098, from Pont-de-l'Arche, two writs, witnessed by the chancellor, were sent to England, one addressed to Robert Bloet, the other to all the king's sheriffs and servants in the whole of the kingdom of England.[212] In 1099 from Lillebonne, William addressed Ranulf Flambard, now bishop of Durham, Haimo *dapifer* and Urse.[213] The king could, therefore, address either Bishop Robert Bloet alone, the whole body of sheriffs and other royal servants, or a select group. Since in one of the writs to the small body the king refers to other justiciars, it is possible that all the named addressees also were justices who sometimes or usually had associates of less importance. Indeed, they resemble those groups who in the next reign will be called *justitiarii totius Angliae* – judges, justices or justiciars of the whole of England – in order to distinguish them from the local justiciars.[214] -

It is easy, and probably correct, to think that in the case of the writs addressed to a group of men, the king was sending instructions to an administrative commission he had left behind. At its head was always a trusted and experienced bishop, and included were Ranulf Flambard and usually Haimo *dapifer* and Urse of Abetot, two soldiers. They had no exclusive authority; they were not a vice-regal committee; they may not even have been a strictly limited and formal body. To a large extent they represented the group of royal servants which, even when the king was in England, was often employed at some distance from his person. In some fashion they were an alternative team to that in regular attendance on the king, with Ranulf Flambard substituting for the chancellor. They were, above all, the men on whom William relied completely; and they were also, it should be noticed, one and all his father's men, servants with strong roots in Norman society and, except for Ranulf and Urse, of baronial background. Even Urse by 1094 had achieved respectability as a baron, and when Ranulf obtained a bishopric in 1099, he too had arrived.

The king's officials and ministers were his private servants and in Latin there was only one word (*ministri*) to cover them all. The kind of work they did, certainly in its details, would have been considered by the barons as largely a matter for the king alone. Nor, except for a brief period after the Conquest, when needs must, would the greater landowners have wanted, or have been deemed suitable, to undertake any but the most important royal commissions. For routine administration the king was flying high enough with men of the status of Eudo

[212] See below, 393-4.
[213] *Regesta*, no. 416, *Facsimiles*, no. XII, and see below, 407.
[214] See above, 202 n. 179.

dapifer, Haimo or Urse. There was nothing anti-baronial in this type of government which William had inherited from his father; and there seems little evidence of a split during his reign between, on the one side, ministerial bishops and barons and, on the other, the grandees. A cleavage would come about only if the king perverted the system by refusing to confirm lawful rights, by over-charging for services, or by favouring some section at the expense of another. Such behaviour would have caused discontent and ultimately defiance and rebellion. In 1095 William had to face a revolt, but it did not receive much support, and however onerous and unpopular his government may have been at some times and in some circles, he never alienated the mass of his barons.

To what extent, either in theory or in practice, the king governed with the advice and consent of his magnates, is difficult to say. The most regular meetings of the nobility with the king were at the crown-wearing ceremonies at the great church festivals of Easter, Whitsun and Christmas; and the Anglo-Saxon Chronicler usually noted where William held these assemblies. The tradition was forming that the king visited Winchester at Easter, Westminster at Whitsun and Gloucester at Christmas.[215] His avoidance of Canterbury, the mother church, is remarkable. It was also traditional for some of the most solemn acts of the king to be performed on these occasions, notably the grant of lands in fee and the nomination of bishops. Land charters seem normally to have been provided with a witness list which recorded some of the most important magnates present when the business was transacted.[216] It was believed by Orderic Vitalis that William consulted his barons at Winchester in 1090 before making a claim to Normandy.[217] It seems also that the great aid of 1096, levied to raise the cash for taking Normandy in pawn, was discussed with the magnates.[218]

Exactly who was present on these occasions cannot be established, for royal charters, in their transmitted form, with more than ten witnesses are rare. There seem to be about six with between ten and seventeen, and the only one with more is the exceptional charter issued on 27 January 1091 at Dover for the bishop of Bath with its sixty-two witnesses – fourteen bishops, thirteen abbots, twelve chaplains, eight earls, five stewards, and ten largely ministerial barons.[219] But charters with shorter lists from the periods 1088–9, 1091, 1094–5, 1097 and 1099 probably provide in aggregate a roll-call of the notables who were usually at

[215] Cf. *ASC E, s.a.* 1086 = 1087, 164; *GR*, ii, 335; *Vita Wulfstani*, 34.
[216] Cf. S. Keynes, *The Diplomas of King Æthelred the Unready* (1980), 126 ff., 154 ff.
[217] Below, 273.
[218] Below, 246–7.
[219] *Regesta*, no. 315. Those with between 10 and 17 attestations are nos 301, 325, 326, 338a, 348a, 414a.

court.[220] At all times the bishops seem to have attended in force. Until at least 1091 the counts and earls make a brave show and, together with no fewer than ten major barons, provide a company which could hardly have been improved upon. After 1091 the witness of counts and earls becomes rare, and even the witness of major barons is sparse. But this feature is probably to be explained by the poor survival of witnessed charters from those years, apparently due simply to chance, although possibly to a change of policy in the chancery. From other sources William can be shown to have been frequently in the company of the magnates; when he obtained Normandy he welcomed his brother's most faithful men to his court and camp; and a king engaged almost incessantly in war is unlikely to have distanced himself from his earls and barons. External wars usually gave stability at home and strengthened a prince's hold over the aristocracy.[221]

It does not seem likely, therefore, that even after 1091 William destroyed the traditional community of interest between king and magnates and created a noteworthy split between magnates and curials which it was Henry I's achievement to repair.[222] The decay of the great post-Conquest dynasties was a slow process which had started before 1086 and continued after William II's reign. The men usually at court, the nobles and administrative servants, were obviously largely men of his own choice, but they were a selection from the baronage at large, not a rival group. Inevitably Orderic brought against him the standing charge against kings of replacing dead grandees with inferiors (*degeneres*); but he did not press it as insistently as in the cases of the Conqueror and Henry I.[223] William was, of course, accused of maintaining a licentious court, and although most of his friends and servants were married men and fathers of children, and there is nothing to suggest that only sodomites found his favour or formed a close circle around him, catamites and whores were present, and some barons may have been as fastidious as Anselm and taken their cue from their father in God. William was also much blamed in some, perhaps mainly clerical, circles for employing the low-born Ranulf Flambard in oppressing the church. But in general he hardly behaved very much differently from his

---

[220] Above, 94–6, below, 278–80, 331, 360, 372–3, 400.

[221] Cf. Bates, *Normandy before 1066*, 178–9.

[222] As suggested by C.W. Hollister, 'Magnates and *Curiales* in early Norman England', *Viator*, viii (1977), 63 ff., 'Henry I and the Anglo-Norman Magnates', *Battle II*, 93 ff. Cf. also Emma Mason, 'Magnates, curiales and the Wheel of Fortune', *ibid.*, pp. 118 ff. We should notice that some of the greatest magnates expressed their gratitude to William: cf. Robert of Meulan, *CDF*, 326, *Regesta*, no. 414; Hamelin of Ballon, *CDF*, no. 1045; Robert of Rumilly, lord of Skipton, see above, 172 n. 171.

[223] OV, iv, 202; ii, 260, 264; vi, 16.

father and younger brother, and none of the charges against him, individually or in sum, amounts to an accusation of an anti-baronial policy.

William may well have been unpopular in some church circles. He would have done better if, like his equally severe predecessor and successor, he was married. Edith of Scots would have served him well. All the same, he seems to have got on well enough with his bishops and abbots, apart from Anselm. As for the baronage at large, there is little to suggest that he was unpopular. He shared their main interests and was a man of honour whom they could respect and trust. Above all, he was a competent military commander who took care of his troops, promptly ransomed prisoners, and won sufficient glory to satisfy his subordinates. That the baronage had grievances against him by the end of the reign is evident from the concessions they extorted from his successor. But the true key to this episode is more the initial weakness of Henry I than the intolerable tyranny of the dead man. A king who was generally regarded, even by monastic chroniclers, as *magnanimus* and chivalrous and especially partial to the nobility, remained throughout his life part of the aristocratic society to which he was born and bred. One proof of this is that he was remembered by the poetic romancers of the twelfth century as a second Arthur:[224]

> qui mult est nobles e gentilz . . .
> Li reis Ros fu de grant noblesce,
> proz fu et de mult grant largesce[225]

– most noble, most valiant, most generous. And it is hard to believe that this mirror of knighthood had been polished entirely in base company.

[224] Below, 396–7.
[225] Wace, ll. 9133, 9365, cf. 9699.

Chapter 5

THE SINEWS OF WAR

William II was widely regarded as a spendthrift. As he came suddenly and unprepared into great wealth after years of relative penury in his father's household, it was only to be expected. He spent, even if in some good causes, what his avaricious and miserly father had hoarded, and then looked round eagerly for more. But, probably again because his inheritance was unexpected, he kept a very tight hold on his estates, and, although careless about the succession, increased rather than dissipated the royal demesne. He was accused by chroniclers of oppressing the church and the farmers in order to raise money to lavish on soldiers, courtiers and personal display. His financial agent, Ranulf Flambard, incurred much odium, and the next king had to renounce at the beginning of his reign many of his brother's financial 'illegalities'.

Nevertheless, these charges need critical evaluation. The financial measures of even 'good' kings were unpopular in the circles which they affected, and as it was impossible to introduce completely new methods of raising money except at times of national peril, an ambitious ruler could do no other than seek to maximize the yield from the traditional sources of revenue, a straining of rights which was widely regarded as tyrannical. Richard fitzNeal, in his explanation of the procedures of the Royal Exchequer written in the middle of Henry II's reign, remarked quite frankly, 'I have said once and for all, and it must always be kept in mind, that it is the king's profit which is served in all these matters.'[1] Moreover, although William II and Henry I were big spenders, they also, like their father, left behind them money in their treasuries. This 'superplus', to use the treasury terminology, compounded their cardinal sin of avarice, for moralists were committed to the view that any money surplus to essential needs which was not devoted to the advancement of the church and its ends was either wasted or put to harmful use.

The country's wealth was derived almost entirely from the profits of agriculture,[2] and in the view of the Anglo-Saxon Chronicler the weather

---

[1] *Dialogus*, 38.

[2] *DB*, however, with its omission of the two largest cities, London and Winchester, and its general neglect of towns and the profits of trade and industry, is responsible for a distortion which must be borne in mind. In 1113 a mission from Laon cured at Winchester a usurer named Walter Kiburo, whom the citizens claimed had £3,000 in his treasury: Herman, 'De miraculis S. Mariae Laudunensis', Migne *PL*, clvi, 978.

was unfavourable in this period in about one year out of two. The principal complaints were of heavy rains, high winds and lack of warmth, so that crops ripened late or were spoilt and cattle suffered from plague. Conditions were if anything worse in Henry's reign.[3] Usually the chronicler complained about the weather and the taxes in the same breath, and the connexion is obvious. The king directly exploited agricultural profits in two main ways: he drew rents from his own estates scattered throughout the kingdom (but almost absent from Sussex, Shropshire, Herefordshire and Chester), and he levied a tax, danegeld, on all occupied land irrespective of ownership, but less the many franchises. The unit for all lords was the manor, a seignorial creation which served as an item in the records of both the rent and the tax collectors. In some parts of the kingdom the manor was frequently coincident with the village (although there were often irregularities) and in other parts, notably eastern and northern England, the manor was more artificial and complex. But there can be no doubt that in 1087 – and long before that – there was a 'manorial system' in the kingdom. When the Domesday inquest surveyed the realm, it produced a list of all the manors into which the territory investigated was divided. The royal commissioners and those who instructed them believed that every parcel of agricultural land, and the inhabitants and stock upon it, pertained to some manor, and although they had difficulty in applying the theory in the eastern and northern counties, on the whole it served them well; and if necessary they made it fit.

If we look at the attitude towards their resources taken by William I and his two royal sons, it is clear that, although there are differences due to character and circumstances, there is a basic and wide-reaching similarity. All acknowledged the obligation to share their resources as king and duke with their barons, servants and church. After the Conquest, the king kept only a little over a sixth of the total rental of the rural properties (manors) in the kingdom in his own hands, while assigning roughly a half to his barons and leaving almost a quarter in the possession of the church.[4] Nevertheless his own estates were larger than those of any one baron or closely connected group of vassals, and by contemporary standards he was richly endowed. Although he and some of his descendants, owing to the repeated need to buy support, may have reduced their share of the total landed wealth, they were putting capital to good use and hardly behaving irresponsibly. Their partnership with the barons and church also led to their freeing the home farms of a

[3] Bad weather, famine or disease was recorded in the period 1066–1135 in the following years: 1082, 1086–7, 1089 90, 1095–9, 1105, 1109–12, 1115–19, 1124–5, 1131.

[4] W.J. Corbett, 'The development of the duchy of Normandy and the Norman Conquest of England', *Cambridge Medieval History*, v (1926), 508.

widening circle of vassals and servants from liability to the land tax and some other common burdens, a costly, even if necessary, measure.

It is, however, unlikely that these kings allowed their vassals much interest in the way in which they administered their own resources. They regarded the estates they kept in their own hands – and all their other royal rights – as their very own, and the revenue from them as theirs to spend as they chose. They were answerable for their disbursements to no man or body of men, and in fact we have no record of their expenditure. They would have acknowledged – even William Rufus when seriously ill – that in the last resort they were accountable to God for their earthly stewardship; but while fortune smiled they acted as though the day of reckoning was a long way off. They did their best to make their rent and tax collectors render accounts to the last penny, sometimes halfpenny, for what was owed to them, but they operated without the guidance of any general fiscal planning or accounting. Characteristically there were few running and no grand totals of any kind in Domesday Book or in the audits of the king's revenue, known to us as the Pipe Rolls, which are extant from 1130 and then from 1155 onwards.[5] The king and his advisers knew, of course, roughly what each source of the royal revenue would produce in the current financial year – Michaelmas to Michaelmas – because their yield was fairly stable. But from day to day the kings lived from hand to mouth. In this optimistic and carefree attitude they were at one with all the great *rentiers* in western Christendom.

Auxiliary to this fecklessness was the widespread illiteracy and even more general innumeracy. Laymen needed clerks to keep their accounts, and with the ordinary use of roman numerals all arithmetical processes were difficult.[6] The only coin in currency was the thin silver penny, sterling,[7] at 240 to the pound, either in weight or reckoning. The silver was approximately of a fineness of 925 thousandths. All other monetary expressions were units of account; and the treasury arithmetic was complicated by its use of several different systems of computation. Sums were reckoned in pounds, shillings and pence, marks of silver (13s

---

[5] General audits or a stocktaking of the contents of the Winchester treasury took place, however, in Henry I's reign. In 1128–9 his favourite kinsmen, his eldest bastard, Robert earl of Gloucester, and the Breton Brian fitzCount, both knights, had made such an audit: *PR 31 H.I*, 129–31. References to 'an account of the whole receipt of the kingdom' and 'a general account of the treasury' are in *Dialogus*, 24–5, 32.

[6] R.L. Poole, *The Exchequer in the Twelfth Century* (1912), 75 ff., 82 ff. But laymen were perfectly able to engage in financial transactions, for example merchants and sheriffs; and see n. 1.

[7] P. Grierson, 'Sterling', *Anglo-Saxon Coins* (Stenton *Festschrift*), ed. R.H.M. Dolley (1961), 266. The term first appears about 1078 and was probably connected with the introduction of a heavier penny of 22.5 grains.

4d), or marks of gold (£6), with in both cases 8oz to the mark. Horses, hounds and hawks, and silver or gold rings were sometimes demanded by or proffered to the king, and had a conventional money value for account.[8] As the main rental and tax accounts, together with the treasury receipts — the tallies – were reckoned in pounds, shillings and pence, whereas most other payments were expressed in marks of silver, it is likely that the former represented the practice of the Old-English treasury, and the latter common usage. The mark, like the later guinea, was the currency of gentlemen, and with the princes of commerce it was commonly the mark of gold. Moreover, the treasury had inherited from the pre-Conquest period the complication that some payments had to be made not by counting out the money (by tale), but by weight, or with compensation after an assay. Also, while the ounce of silver normally contained sixteen pence, it was reckoned at twenty pence for the payment of royal rents.[9] Men who could understand all the rules were proud of their expertise. It is not, in fact, particularly difficult to grasp the system behind the Exchequer accounts and to read and understand them. But making totals remains a wearisome (and chancy) business. Some members of William II's court were acquainted with that ancient counting device, the abacus, and it was put to good use at the Exchequer, a new central accounting board established by Henry I early in his reign.[10] It was not, however, an instrument of high finance.

The main administrative office was at the treasury at Winchester, with a subsidiary in London. Political control remained with the king in his itinerant court, where he was advised and aided by chamberlains and other servants. His principal financial factotum, and no doubt adviser, after the first few years of the reign was his chaplain Ranulf Flambard, who with his fellow justices, especially Bishop Walkelin of Winchester and the constable Urse of Abetot, were responsible for seeing that the royal revenues were collected to the last penny. Ranulf and Urse were William's trusted agents, for ever travelling between the court and the regions where the taxes were imposed and collected.[11]

The main financial document available to William II and his ministers was the 'description', the cadastral survey, of the kingdom known as Domesday Book, which his father had commissioned at

[8] Cf. above, 121 n. 99. *PR 31 H.I* provides other examples: cf. below, 259. Richard fitzNeal, *Dialogus*, 121–2, discusses only the proffer of hawks and falcons, 'royal birds'.

[9] Salley Harvey, 'Royal Revenue and Domesday Terminology', *Ec. Hist. Review*, 2nd ser., xx (1967), 221.

[10] Poole, *The Exchequer*, 42 ff.; C.H. Haskins, 'The abacus and the king's curia', *EHR*, xxvii (1912), 101; Gillian R. Evans, 'Schools and Scholars: the study of the abacus in English schools c. 980–c. 1150', *EHR*, xciv (1979), 71.

[11] See above, 148 ff., 199 ff.

Christmas 1085 and had only just been completed.[12] It was kept in the treasury at Winchester. There were as well earlier lists and records, and the Domesday inquest had produced a mass of subsidiary or unusable statistics. It may be that the two basic schedules, a list of the county farms and a list of landowners with the hidage of their estates, remained convenient for reference, especially to clerks used to the old-fashioned ways, but Domesday Book updated them and provided the new information which the king had desired.

The purpose of the survey was not only to satisfy the king's curiosity about the financial and tenurial situation in the kingdom he had conquered, but also to increase his revenue in both the short and the long term.[13] He wanted to know what he had and what he should and could get. In the famous words of the Anglo-Saxon Chronicle:

> [After Christmas] the king had much thought and very deep discussion with his council about this country – how it was occupied and with what sort of people. Then he sent his men all over England into every shire, and had them find out how many hundred hides there were in the shire, and what land and cattle the king himself had in the country and what dues he should have each year from the shire. Also he had a record made of how much land his archbishops had, and his bishops and abbots, and his earls, and – although I write at too great length – what and how much everybody who was occupying land in England had in land and cattle, and how much money it was worth. So very narrowly did he have it investigated that there was not a single hide or virgate of land, nor indeed (it is shameful to tell, but it seemed no shame to him to do) one ox or one cow or one pig which was omitted from the record. And all these records were brought to him afterwards.[14]

According to a document known as the Inquest of Ely (*Inquisitio Eliensis*),[15] the commissioners had the following schedule of questions to put to the local authorities and communities: 1) What is the name of the manor? 2) Who held it in the time of King Edward? 3) Who holds it

[12] V.H. Galbraith, *The Making of Domesday Book* (1961), *Domesday Book* (1974). R. Welldon Finn, *The Domesday Inquest and the making of Domesday Book* (1962), *An Introduction to Domesday Book* (1963), *Domesday Studies: The Liber Exoniensis* (1964), *The Eastern Counties* (1967), *The Norman Conquest and its effect on the Economy, 1066–86* (1971). Recent surveys of the literature and its findings include H.R. Loyn, 'Domesday Book', *Battle I*, 121; Salley Harvey, 'Domesday Book and Anglo-Norman Governance', *TRHS*, 5th ser., xxv (1975), 175, 'Recent Domesday Studies', *EHR*, xcv (1980), 121. An invaluable territorial index is *Domesday Gazetteer*, ed. H.C. Darby and G.R. Versey (1975).

[13] For the financial implications of the term *descriptio*, cf. J.O. Prestwich, 'War and Finance in the Anglo-Norman State', *TRHS*, 5th ser., iv (1954), 26 n.

[14] *ASC*, s.a. 1085, 161–2.

[15] *SSC*, 101. Cf. also *Dialogus*, 63–4; Galbraith, *The Making of Domesday Book*, 60 ff.; and below, 233–4.

now? 4) How many hides does it contain? 5) How many ploughs are there on the demesne (home farm)? 6) How many ploughs are there among the men? 7) How many villeins, cottagers and slaves, freemen and sokemen are there? 8) How much wood? 9) How much meadow? 10) How many mills? 11) How much has been added or taken away? 12) How much was the whole worth, and how much now? 13) How much did each freeman and sokeman have, and how much now? 14) Could more (profit) be had from it than is now obtained? The schedules of questions seem to have varied a little from one set of commissioners to another. The question whether the manor was under-exploited (14) was rarely answered directly to the Ely formulation, and the Ely list omits, probably by mistake, the inquiry into animal population which the Anglo-Saxon Chronicle vouches for, and which produced statistics to be found in the preliminary reports of the inquest, only to be excluded from the final 'Exchequer' version. But otherwise the schedule seems to be correct.

The elaborate inquiry, based partly on existing treasury and other official documents, partly on schedules produced by local stewards, reeves and bailiffs, and with the information checked and counter-checked by juries of local inhabitants and tested and supplemented in every other way available, produced a mass of statistics which had to be arranged for publication. The findings of each commission were processed locally into an area survey, of which the Exon Domesday, covering the counties of Wiltshire, Dorset, Somerset, Devon and Cornwall, is the main surviving example, having been preserved in the archives of the cathedral chapter at Exeter. But these area surveys were found by the central directorate to be defective in arrangement, idiosyncratic in terminology and far too detailed; and in a final revision, which, despite all its errors and faults, does great credit to the secretariat, all the reports, except that for the eastern circuit, were abbreviated, standardized, and edited into one manageable volume. The eastern counties, because of lack of time or the special problems posed by their tenurial complexity, were presented in an incompletely digested form in a second volume (Little Domesday). These two volumes are usually referred to as the Exchequer Domesday.

The Anglo-Saxon Chronicler was impressed by the thoroughness of the scrutiny. But all those who have been engaged in the compiling of statistics know how specious the declared or published figures can be; and the Domesday record is no exception. The neatness of the final draft, the near-standard presentation of the material, the almost unfailing provision of seemingly exact and persuasive figures, sums of money at least to the nearest penny, areas or assessments at least to the virgate (thirty acres) – create an impression of amazing attention to detail and exceptional trustworthiness. But if it is attempted, for example, to reconcile the contemporary tax accounts with Domesday statistics, it is soon discovered that the survey is riddled with omissions, approximations and inaccuracies.[16] Nevertheless, although these failures in detail may baffle those investigators whose questions can only be answered when the figures are accurate to the last fraction, for the investigation of the macro-economy of the kingdom the Domesday statistics are safe enough. The record is not a gigantic fraud. The commissioners of inquiry tried to find the answers to the questions they were instructed to ask, and those questioned could not have got away with completely misleading answers. Some fictions and guesses had to be accepted; some errors were overlooked or were introduced into the record; many assumptions are not explained. And if the modern user of the statistics keeps these features in mind, he too need not hesitate to round off his probably inaccurate totals and ignore most of the fiscal refinements. Although such irreverence would have scandalized the treasury clerks, with figures of this sort a pound or two either way is neither here nor there.

The survey is, in both its preliminary and final forms, a land register. It lists, shire by shire, the manors grouped according to lordship, and hence is also a feodary, a book of fiefs, recording the composition of the estates of the king, his tenants-in-chief and the church. It gives the immediate history of each estate, its value, its machinery and its manpower, but not, in its Exchequer form, its animal population. It also records the rateable value of each estate and divides the assessment between manorial demesne (the home farm) and tenant land. A good number of disputes over ownership were settled by the commissioners at the time; others were recorded for future hearing.

From the survey we learn that the two main ascending units of fiscal administration were the manor and the shire or county, and that the king's principal financial official in the county was the shire-reeve or sheriff. As an example – not quite chosen at random – of a manor, we may take the description in Exon Domesday of Kenton in Devon, a group of settlements, including a village with its church, on the western bank of the estuary of the River Exe, roughly half way between Exeter and the sea coast.[17] The information is given more or less on the basis of the *Inquisitio Eliensis* questionnaire and in its order, but is here rearranged and expanded a little in order to make it more intelligible. In 1086 Kenton was held by the king, having fallen to him with other estates in 1075 on the death of Queen Edith, the Confessor's widow, who had been

[16] Cf. Finn, *Domesday Studies: The Liber Exoniensis*, 103 ff.
[17] *DB*. iii, 94b; cf. i, 100d. See here, pl. 7.

holding it in 1066. It was rated at 3 hides and 1 ferling (a quarter of a virgate, or a sixteenth of a hide), and if fully exploited could have employed 20 ploughs.[18] There was a home farm (demesne), rated at 1 hide, which employed 4 ploughs and 6 slaves. There were also 30 tenant-farmers (*villani*, villeins), probably each with a separate farmstead, and 10 cottagers (*bordarii*), whose land was rated at the remaining 2 hides and 1 ferling, and who made use of 15 ploughs. Also on the manor were 4 swineherds who together paid 20s a year rent, 8 saltpans rented at 20s a year, and one mill rented at 50d a year. Besides the land under arable cultivation there were 10 acres of meadow, 150 acres of pasture and a wood half a league long and 4 furlongs wide. The animal stock was 20 (draft) animals, 200 sheep and 20 goats. The manor was worth (or yielded) £30 a year.

It is a feature of medieval finance that profitable rights were usually leased from their owner by an entrepreneur, known as a farmer, for a fixed annual rent, the farm. The value of Kenton, £30, is what the farmer had agreed to pay for all the lord's rights in that manor. And when we are on the royal estates those rights included not only the rents and services and other payments owed by the tenants and other dependants, and the profits of the manorial court, the halimote, but also sometimes the profits of hundredal jurisdiction, because these were attached to certain manors. The principal farmer of the king's lands in the shire or county, in 1066, 1086 and 1130, was the sheriff, and his farm was known as the county farm, the account which was at the centre of the Exchequer audit.[19] It may be that originally he had answered for all royal rights in his bailiwick, but by 1086, as we shall see, it was usual for some groups of manors, often casual additions, such as escheats or forfeitures, or groups assigned to a special purpose (e.g. dower lands), to be farmed by other royal servants, and this situation had been regularized by 1129. What had been no doubt a very profitable monopoly had been breached and a factor of competition introduced. Once agricultural and urban profits began to recover from the disturbances of 1065–72, the king lost interest in fixed farms and long leases.

[18] W.G. Hoskins, 'The Highland Zone in Domesday Book', *Provincial England* (1965), expounds the Devonshire survey topographically. Besides allocating to every villein a separate farmstead (p. 33), he would also explain 'the number of ploughs which could till a manor' as the number of ploughlands it contained, and equate these with the number of villein farms (pp. 43 ff.). But he runs into difficulty when, as in the case of Kenton, there is land for 20 ploughs and 30 villeins. His solution (p. 44) is 20 farms between 30 villeins. We may add that 15 ploughs and 20 oxen is marvellously equivocal.

[19] For the sheriff, see *Dialogus*, 78 ff. Morris, *Med. Eng. Sheriff*, 62 ff. For his farm, see G.J. Turner, 'The Sheriff's Farm', *TRHS*, n.s. xii (1898), 117.

Domesday Book not only informs us methodically about the value of
manors and their assessment to danegeld and provides a good deal of
other information about the king's financial rights in the shires and
boroughs, it could also be used as the base line for increasing the yield of
all sources of royal revenue. For example, many of the king's feudal
rights, such as the relief, the succession duty and the sale of wardships
and marriages, could henceforth be related more closely to the annual
rental of the honour in question;[20] and here could be one of the causes of
the blame which William II's government incurred. It would also seem
that, even if the commissioners were not themselves involved in
reassessing the manors to the land tax,[21] the information they collected
would enable it to be done.

Domesday Book throws direct light on only some parts of the royal
revenue, and it is not until half a century later, when audits of the royal
income, the Pipe Rolls, become available, that we can get a general
perspective of it. The first extant, the isolated record for 31 Henry I,[22] is
an audit of all sums which were due to be paid (in whole, in part, or
excused) at the royal treasury in Winchester castle[23] in the financial year
ending at Michaelmas 1130, and it would seem to account for the whole
of the royal revenue. It is not concerned with the value of services due to
the king, e.g. military service, but it is difficult to envisage any other
major source of the royal livelihood which bypassed it. To the best of our
knowledge no revenues were paid directly into the king's chamber or
any other treasury or spending department as a rule, or were audited
separately.[24] In 1130 payments to the king in Normandy and similar
irregularities were audited at the English Exchequer, and the circumstances mentioned only because special evidence of receipt was required.
Unfortunately the Pipe Roll of 1130 has suffered physical damage and is

[20] Galbraith, *Domesday Book*, 14.

[21] In 1975 Salley Harvey, 'Domesday Book and Anglo-Norman Governance', 186 ff.,
argued that the ploughland figures – there is land for x ploughs – were a new fiscal
assessment and had the effect of doubling the previous ratable value of the kingdom. The
intention was to replace danegeld based on the hide by a plough tax, a carucage, as was
indeed done in the second half of the twelfth century. But by 1980, 'Recent Domesday
Studies', she had apparently dropped the idea.

[22] In the *Dialogus* are references to 'the old annual rolls of Henry I', 42, cf. 58, which
imply that in 1178 a series for that reign still existed. It is therefore significant that
Richard fitzNeal makes no reference to those from earlier reigns. Presumably the Pipe
Roll was a product of the Exchequer. Some form of audit must, however, have existed
before that court was founded.

[23] The treasury was probably moved from the (old) palace to the (new) castle after the
Conquest: *Winton Domesday*, 304–5.

[24] Judith Green, 'William Rufus, Henry I and the royal demesne', *History*, lxiv (1979),
338, mentions the possibility of money being paid into the chamber, without venturing a
firm opinion on its likelihood.

no longer complete; but for the counties covered we can establish almost to a penny what the total indebtedness to the king was and what money he actually received.

There are obvious dangers in using an audit of 1130 to explain William II's revenue. The reorganization carried out by Henry I and Roger of Salisbury must have left its mark, but the 'charter of liberties' which Henry I granted after his coronation in order to proclaim that the bad old days of his brother had gone for good and that a new day had dawned, serves as a useful control. It lists and abolishes the most unpopular 'bad customs' and 'unjust exactions' of his father and brother and promises to restore most of the laws of King Edward.[25] As almost all these illegalities had been reintroduced by 1129, we can be confident that once Henry felt safe on the throne he reimposed all his ancestral rights. Nothing basic was changed; and indeed a financial system which had come largely unaltered through the Norman Conquest and was to persist in its essentials for centuries more, is unlikely to have been seriously reformed by a king so avid for his prerogatives as Henry I. The Pipe Roll of 1130 can, therefore, be used to throw light on the financial system of the previous reign, provided it is used with proper caution.

These Michaelmas audits are lists of debts and payments on account, arranged mostly according to counties, single or in groups; and the officer whose accounts were audited was for the most part the sheriff, who was at once the chief debtor and the principal debt collector. The only major classification in each set of accounts was the distinction made, after the county farm which always headed the list, between old and new debts.[26] The former were those which had appeared on the previous year's Pipe Roll and had not been totally acquitted; the latter were those contracted during the current financial year and supplied from several extraneous sources. The minimum debt allowed an individual entry was probably one mark of silver (13s 4d) – the sheriff usually answered with a lump sum for smaller debtors – and besides the name of the debtor, the nature of the debt is also indicated. But there is no subject classification, and even the results of a single operation – such as the visit of itinerant justices – are sometimes dispersed. It looks as though all debts, whatever their cause, were on an equal footing as far as the financial administration was concerned. Danegeld, judicial penalties, feudal 'incidents' and all the offerings which later were called 'fines and oblations' appear indiscriminately and in the same way. The heading to the current additions is *Nova placita et novae conventiones*. The former – pleas – refers particularly to judicial matters, but covers the

[25] *SSC*, 116 ff.
[26] The procedures are meticulously explained in *Dialogus*, especially 70 ff.

profits from any sort of case; the latter is the more neutral 'agreement', 'bargain' or 'fine', usually translated 'covenant'. Henry in his coronation charter, although he called them more simply 'pleas and debts', made the same distinction.[27] It would not, however, be easy to divide the entries between the two categories.[28]

There is a lack of discrimination largely because the Pipe Roll is a financial document. Debts are simply debts; and what interested the Barons of the Exchequer was not so much how they had been incurred as who was responsible for their payment. A convenient modern classification would be into (1) the yield of the demesne lands of the crown; (2) danegeld (or other forms of taxation); (3) the profits of justice; (4) the profits of tenure, or feudal incidents; and (5) miscellaneous sales and profits. It is, however, difficult to sort the Pipe Roll entries into categories 3–5 because the description of the debts is not always precise and in practice the boundaries between these categories proves to be vague; and this is a reminder that any modern subdivision of 'pleas and covenants', however necessary, is anachronistic and arbitrary.

The one surviving roll from Henry I's reign provides us with a general picture of royal finance which can be used, with proper caution, for his predecessor's. In this defective record of the audit at the Exchequer at Michaelmas 1130, almost two thousand individual items totalling £67,610 passed under review.[29] If the missing accounts for Herefordshire, Shropshire, Somerset and Worcestershire, and part of the account for Hampshire (including Southampton and Winchester), together with some minor losses, are reckoned at one-eighth of the total, we can raise the figure to £76,060. This sum of the book entries is, however, misleading. It comes as a surprise to discover that only something over £23,000 of the £67,610, that is to say, a little over a third, had been paid in cash into the treasury. Even if we add the £1,880 which had been disbursed by the sheriffs and other accounting officers on behalf of the king in alms, wages, purchases, maintenance of estates and buildings, etc.,[30] the king's net income from the areas reviewed was only £24,912, or 37 per cent of the total. The missing 63 per cent is explained by pardons (mostly of geld and *murdrum* fines on privileged

[27] Cap. 6, *SSC*, 118.

[28] Richard fitzNeal, who treats of these categories in *Dialogus*, 104 ff., makes the distinction that pleas are inescapable penalties, covenants voluntary agreements.

[29] My figure. W. Stubbs, *Gesta Regis Henrici Secundi Benedicti abbatis* (Rolls ser., 1867), ii, p. xcix, reckoned it at £66,593, and held that the figure had dropped to £48,781 by 1189. Jonathan D. Caplan, in an unpublished Univ. of California PhD dissertation, quoted by Hollister, 'Henry I and the Anglo-Norman Magnates', *Battle II*, 186 n. 20, apparently makes £24,200 paid into the treasury, £5,500 exempted and pardoned.

[30] But not in maintenance of the demesne manors, which was taken care of by the farm, and, if neglected, was debited to the sheriff. Cf. below, 228 n. 52.

demesne) totalling £4,760, or 7 per cent, and debts totalling almost £38,000, or 56 per cent. Indebtedness of this order is, however, an ordinary feature of medieval royal finance. It arose because most debtors were allowed to pay by instalment over a good number of years,[31] partly owing to the shortage of money, partly because in the case of the purchase of a lucrative right it was accepted that repayment should be out of the profits. When William II, close to death in 1093, promised to forgive all his debtors he was proposing to give away a sum in excess of his annual revenue and probably four times what he had expended in 1088 in alms for his father's soul.[32] No wonder he protested that no man could keep all his promises.[33]

These figures can be broken down into the major categories. Out of the total amount under review, £67,610, the royal demesne which was farmed by the sheriffs (the county farms) account for £14,897 (22 per cent), other lands and escheats in the king's hands £5,565 (8 per cent), danegeld £5,645 (8 per cent) and the remainder £41,503 (62 per cent). But when we look at the cash revenue produced by these four sources, £23,029, we get a quite different picture. The county farms yielded £7,765 (34 per cent), the other lands and escheats £3,862 (17 per cent), danegeld £2,852 (12 per cent) and the remainder £8,550 (37 per cent). If we also take into account the £1,883 which the sheriffs and other custodians of royal lands had expended on the king's behalf, we see that the royal demesne in 1130 produced more than half (54 per cent) of the net royal revenue.[34]

Let us now look at each of these main categories in turn. First, the royal estates. Those groups of manors which were 'farmed' for the profit of the king are usually called the royal demesne, and although the term is anachronistic for the eleventh and twelfth centuries,[35] there seems no harm in using it provided we do not attribute to it anachronistic features. It was not state land or a fixed and privileged area. Its composition fluctuated; the manors which comprised it were widely scattered and in no significant way distinct from manors under other

[31] In the twelfth century the amount which each debtor had to pay in the current term was fixed by the Barons of the Exchequer before the summonses to attend the next meeting were drawn up: *Dialogus*, 69 ff.

[32] See above, 64

[33] Below, 300.

[34] Sir James H. Ramsay, *A History of the Revenues of the Kings of England, 1066–1399* (1925), i, 53–4, offers the following figures for the net revenue: total paid in or accounted for in respect of county and borough farms, £11,082 9s 8d; ditto for pleas, oblates and covenants, £10,055 5s 2d. Neither of these corresponds exactly with my categories. His figure for the grand total, £25,464 3s, is in excess of mine, £24,912, by 2 per cent. For Caplan's figure of £24,200, see above, 224 n. 29.

[35] B.P. Wolffe, *The Royal Demesne in English History* (1971), 17 ff.

lordship; and it was subject to no special restraints, laws or constitutional theory. We are concerned with the private estates of a king who
had no other 'official' or 'public' endowments.

In the Exchequer Domesday, rationalizing the more disorderly
arrangement in the area surveys, the *terra regis*, the king's land, in each
shire is entered first after the cities and royal boroughs. As each manor is
given a value it is relatively simple to work out by addition the value of
the royal estates in that shire, and, by continuing the process, in the
kingdom at large. There are also sometimes indications of how and by
whom the demesne was farmed. Let us look in some detail at the county
of Devon. In the Exchequer version the demesne is subdivided,
according to the identity of the former owner of the manors, into six
groups: King Edward's lands (called in Exon Domesday the lands
pertaining to the kingdom), Queen Edith's (the Confessor's widow),
Gytha's (Earl Godwin's widow), Earl Harold's (Gytha's son, earl of
Wessex, and king in 1066), Earl Leofwine's (Harold's brother) and
Queen Matilda's (the Conqueror's dead wife, who had held Brihtric's
lands).[36] In Exon Domesday categories 2–5 are lumped together and
referred to as 'the lands of the earls', i.e., the escheated land of the
Godwin family;[37] but the confusion was subsequently sorted out,
presumably because each group had developed an organic unity.
Indeed, we learn from Exon Domesday that some of the groups were
separately farmed. A note at the original end of the royal manors, but
before three which were subsequently discovered and entered, reads,
'Baldwin pays £375 a year as farm to the king for the lands of the earls;
Gotselm pays £108 a year for the lands of Queen Edith; and Reginald
pays £24 to the king's farm for Ordulf's land.'[38]

These totals can be explained with reference to the lists of manors and
their values. The £108 is the correct sum of the four manors which
Queen Edith had held. Ordulf's manor of Broadclyst, which is put at the
end of the 'lands of the earls' in the Exchequer version, was indeed worth
£24. The £375, however, is not quite so simple. It represents the £336
due from the estates of Gytha, Harold and Leofwine, plus £1 from an
estate at Blackpool which had been held by King Edward, plus £38 for
two of the three manors listed in the addendum. The third manor in this
group, Tiverton, is there by mistake (although the entry is not
cancelled), for it reappears word for word, but not with identical
abbreviations, twelve folios later in the list of manors which had been
held by Queen Matilda.[39] In the Exchequer version, however, it is the

[36] *DB*, i, 100 ff.
[37] *DB*, iii, 83 ff., 93 ff., 108 ff.
[38] *DB*, iii, 97b, *ad fin.*
[39] *DB*, iii, 110b.

second entry which is omitted. Despite these confusions, £375, plus £108, plus £24, which is £507, is the correct total for the manors listed in categories 2–5. We can also see from various references in the text of Exon Domesday that category 1, the former lands of King Edward, were being farmed by the sheriff Baldwin, and the lands of Queen Matilda by that Gotselm who also farmed Queen Edith's lands. The values of these groups were £252 and £186. The total value of the royal demesne in Devonshire was reckoned, therefore, at £945. Since one of the obvious purposes of the Domesday inquest was to discover what was due to the king, it would not be over credulous to think that William Rufus at the beginning of his reign was owed almost a thousand pounds a year from his estates in this one county.

Orderic Vitalis put the Conqueror's revenue from the 'just' rents of England, not counting oblations and pleas and many other financial rights, at £1,061 10s 1½d a day.[40] An annual rental of some £387,449 is, of course, absurd; but if Orderic wrote daily by mistake for monthly, he would be near the mark, for a figure of £12,738 12s 6d is close to modern calculations. The total value of the royal estates (including the queen's lands) in the twenty-seven counties surveyed in 1086 has been put at £12,600,[41] or, taking in as well receipts from the boroughs and other customary payments listed, at almost £14,000.[42] Most commentators have regarded this as more or less net revenue.[43] When we turn to the Pipe Roll of 1130, it is clear that considerable changes have occurred. The county farms have been reassessed, apparently quite recently, in order to take account inter alia of the many permanent alienations from royal demesne which had occurred since the last assessment had been made.[44] And there seems to have been no attempt to increase the sources which contributed to the sheriff's farm. These continued to be designated royal manors, most of the cities and boroughs, and the ordinary profits of the hundred and shire courts.[45]

[40] OV, ii, 266.

[41] Corbett, Camb. Med. Hist., v, 508.

[42] Judith Green, loc. cit., 337.

[43] R.W. Southern, 'The place of Henry I in English History', Proc. of the British Academy, xlviii (1962–3), appendix, argues, in order to explain the apparent drop in revenue from the demesne which occurred between 1086 and 1130, that the Domesday values were gross, and the sheriffs' farms always much less than their sums. But this theory seems to be misconceived, and is not accepted, for example, by Judith Green, loc. cit. Richard fitzNeal, Dialogus, 40–1, claimed that until Henry I's reign the royal manors paid no money to the kings, only victuals. But this nonsense is disproved by DB: in 1086 only a few 'farms of a day/night' remained.

[44] Judith Green, loc. cit., 349–50. Richard fitzNeal, Dialogus, 41–2, seems to give a garbled account of the reassessment of the county farms under Henry I.

[45] Cf. Dialogus, 64–5.

The county farms once established by Henry I remained largely unchanged for centuries afterwards; but the king and his ministers were always thinking how they could increase the yield despite the credits they had to allow the sheriffs for land they had taken away, the *terrae datae*. Henry I in his coronation charter denounced the general money tax (*monetagium commune*) which had been imposed on the cities and counties and was an innovation since King Edward's day. In future whoever was caught with false money, whether he was a moneyer or anyone else, should pay the penalty.[46] In other words, the penalty was to be transferred from the community to the individual offender; and although the condemned impost has often been regarded as a mintage tax imposed on moneyers when they changed their dies, it may have been one of a series of schemes to compensate the king for the loss of revenue caused by payment in debased or clipped coinage.[47] From the Pipe Roll of 1130 we see that many sheriffs had agreed to pay an increment or *gersum*, sometimes 100 marks for a five-year tenure of the shire, payable in instalments of 20 marks a year.[48] Larger sums also had been offered. The sheriff of Oxford owed 400 marks[49] and in 1129 two of Henry's most trusted servants, Aubrey de Vere and Richard Basset, had taken over eleven counties from remiss predecessors for a 'surplus' of 1,000 marks, and this they paid off in the first year as well as all the county farms in full.[50] Moreover, sheriffs paid to be relieved of the office;[51] and outgoing sheriffs sometimes had to pay large amounts because the demesne manors were found to be understocked or otherwise run down.[52]

[46] Cap. 5, *SSC*, 118.

[47] Cf. *Dialogus*, 38 ff.; Johnson, *ibid.*, xxxviii ff.

[48] For example, William of Ainsford 100 marks for Essex and Hertford for five years – pardoned the balance of 80 marks because he only held them for one year: *PR 31 H.I*, 52–3. Hugh de Wareville 200 marks for Northamptonshire and Leicestershire – pardoned the balance of 180 marks because he had only held them for half a year: *ibid.*, 85. Cf. Robert of Stanley, who seems to have held Staffordshire for the full term at 20 marks a year: *ibid.*, 73.

[49] *Ibid.*, 2.

[50] *Ibid.*, 43–4, 52–3, 63, 81, 90, 100. Eleven counties for 1,000 marks because Essex and Hertford were charged as one (see n. 48). This *surplus*, entered at the end of the Hertford entry, p. 63, cannot have been the actual surplus received beyond the farms by the two men acting not as farmers but as custodians, as Judith Green suggests, *loc. cit.*, 350. The roundness of the sum would of itself disprove that. They had acquitted it by paying 400 marks into the Winchester treasury and 500 marks in coin and 100 marks in silver plate into the Norman treasury. Another scrap of evidence that they had offered five times more than their predecessors is that Aubrey de Vere owed 100 marks for permission to withdraw from the counties of Essex and Hertford, p. 53.

[51] For example, three men offered six marks of gold (£36), of which they had paid half, to be released from being sheriffs of London: *PR 31 H.I*, 149.

[52] Under Oxfordshire, Restold still owed from 1128–9 £239 15s 2d for the

There were clearly various means by which the yield from the county farms could be kept at a high level. The Norman kings were determined to take what they could of the rising profits from agriculture and trade; and we cannot doubt that William II and Ranulf Flambard exploited all the options open to them. Indeed, they may simply have been following in the footsteps of William I. The Anglo-Saxon Chronicler, probably a monk of St Augustine's, Canterbury, in his savage obituary notice of the Conqueror, wrote that 'he sold his land on very hard terms as hard as he could. Then came someone else who offered more than the other had given, and the king let it go to him. Then came a third, who offered still more, and the king gave it to him, for he did not care how sinfully his reeves had got the money from poor men, or how many unlawful things were done.'[53] It is possible that the chronicler was thinking more of ecclesiastical custodies and escheats or other casual accessions than of the county farms, or was referring to the *gersum*, which was also called an *augmentum* or *crementum* in Domesday Book;[54] but he was drawing attention to a general practice followed by all the Norman kings. Nor, apparently, was there much complaint from the aristocracy about this kind of behaviour, for it hardly affected them; indeed, it was their own practice. When Henry I in his coronation charter renounced his brother's illegalities, he carefully reserved his 'lawful farms' while remitting most judicial penalties and debts owed to William II.[55]

From the Pipe Roll of 1130 we can calculate that the sheriffs should have paid into the treasury something over £7,500 for the farms of the thirty shires recorded; and if we supply the six missing figures from the later twelfth-century rolls, we obtain a total of some £8,700.[56] On this evidence it would seem that the value of the royal demesne had dropped between 1086 and 1130 by 31 per cent, that is to say by an average annual loss of £85. We are not, however, comparing like with like. The £14,000 of 1086 includes the value of all escheats, except the most temporary, while the 1130 figure excludes all escheats, however long-

---

depreciation of the county in respect of grain, houses, barns, mills, fishponds, villeins, bordars, geburs, ploughmen and hay, and land which had not been put to use; £28 0s 4d for the loss of bulls, oxen, cows, pigs and sheep; and £7 10s for the destruction of woods – besides other sums for other malpractices: *ibid.*, 2. In Berkshire William of Pont-de-l'Arche accounted for 48s for the purchase of 16 oxen and £36 8s 4d for 500 sheep, for restocking the manors of the shire: *ibid.*, 122.

[53] *ASC, s.a.* 1087, 163.
[54] For which see Morris, *Med. Eng. Sheriff*, 64.
[55] Cap. 6, *SSC*, 118.
[56] These are my figures. Cf. also Judith Green, *loc. cit.*, 351. W. Stubbs agreed with Gerald of Wales, *De Instructione Principis*, ed. G.F. Warner (Rolls ser., 1891), viii, 316, that Henry II obtained about £8,000 gross from the farm of the counties: *Gesta Benedicti Abbatis* (Rolls ser., 1867), ii, pp. lxxxviii–lxxxix.

standing. The precise book-entry value of all the estates in the king's hands in 1130 outside the county farms cannot be given, but as Henry received from them in that year at least £3,862 (with a further £660 disbursed on his behalf) and was still owed £1,043, their value should have been about £5,600. If we add this sum to the county farms, we get a total of £14,300, which is if anything larger than the 1086 figure; and we have not taken into account the increments paid by the sheriffs or the value of the custodies in the missing portion of the audit.

We can also reconstruct the actual cash revenue received by the king from the complete schedule of estates in his hands in 1130. From the county farms of those shires for which the accounts survive, he received £7,765, with £1,883 expended on his behalf, that is to say, £9,648. If we add the money received from the estates outside the county farms (£3,862 and £660), we reach £14,170. And if we add an eighth to compensate for the lost portion of the accounts, we come to almost £16,000. This, of course, is not strictly comparable with the Domesday values of £14,000. It is the amount of money which the royal farmers paid into the treasury, or spent for the king, in the financial year 1129–30, with no account taken of the year for which it was owed or of the remaining indebtedness. There is nothing (except the addition of one-eighth) theoretical about it. It is very near the actual weight of the silver coin.[57]

The sheriff's farm was concerned with the traditional royal income from land. The forests, which the Norman kings created by reserving to themselves hunting rights over large stretches of the country,[58] although outside the farms, can also be considered to be part of the demesne. They certainly provided the king and his friends with both sport and food; but their economic exploitation has left no great impression on the Pipe Roll of 1130, possibly because of the loss of one of the Hampshire membranes with the accounts of the New Forest. Cesses or rents (census), usually a farm of £5, are sometimes recorded but the new forest in Wiltshire was rented at £25 a year and the forest of Windsor at £26.[59] More

---

[57] These are my figures. As some of the payments were by tale, the actual weight of the coin would have been a little less.

[58] For the royal forests and the position of baronial demesne within them, see Dialogus, 56 ff. The best account of the legal and constitutional history of the royal forest is still C. Petit Dutaillis, Studies and Notes supplementary to Stubbs' Constitutional History, ii (1915), 147 ff. See also, above, 119 ff.

[59] For example, Oxford, 2–3; Wiltshire, 17; Windsor, 127–8. Other forest rents are under Yorks, Hunts, Glos, Northants and Leics, Rutland, Bucks and Beds, and Warwicks. Ten per cent was regularly deducted as tithe. The degree of uniformity suggests that the whole system was relatively new in 1130. Richard fitzNeal, Dialogus, 30–1, explains, very fancifully, why manors had farms and woods had cesses. The cesses of woods and forests are again treated, rather unsatisfactorily, 103–4.

important, however, were the penalties inflicted by the justices of the forest for breaches of the special law.[60] Henry I in his coronation charter with the consent of his barons retained in his own hands his forests as his father had held them.[61] By implication he surrendered his brother's afforestations, and with them the income they brought in. He was soon, however, creating new forests of his own which more than compensated for the loss. Also in 1130 a new component of the royal demesne makes an appearance – the mines royal. In the accounts for Carlisle, William II's conquest, the burgesses of that borough are recorded as having paid into the treasury £5 in respect of the old farm of the silver mines and as owing the whole £40 for the current year.[62]

It is clear from the figures that Henry I, despite his alienations of demesne, was, through forcing sheriffs to pay increments and, more important, exploiting custodies and escheats, receiving at least as much revenue from land as his father. There is no reason to think that 1129–30 was exceptionally rich in windfalls or that Henry had completely transformed the financial system, but he had probably been pushing his fiscal rights hard. Although the Anglo-Saxon Chronicler complained bitterly of William Rufus and Ranulf Flambard at the end of the reign and claimed that the king wanted to be the heir of everyone, both clerk and layman,[63] it was Henry's oppressive taxes and courts that he denounced more regularly. It would seem that Henry was forced into becoming a systematic extorter of casual profits because of his generosity with the inherited demesne. William, in contrast to Henry, did not bring in a large number of 'new men' or 'raise men from the dust'; he created no new 'super-magnates';[64] characteristically he refused to endow Henry in England. He did not have queens, nephews or bastards to endow; and his obligations to the church were kept under close control. He soon repented of his one crisis of conscience and did not live long enough to make careful preparations for the hereafter. On the other hand, for two-thirds of his reign he was without the revenues of Normandy and Maine, so that all rewards had to come from his English resources.

William must have purchased some support while he secured the throne: for example, he reinstated his uncle Odo in his forfeited earldom; but his confiscations after the 1088 rebellion, notably the bishopric of

---

[60] Petit Dutaillis, op. cit., 171 ff. And see above, 120.
[61] Cap. 10, SSC, 119.
[62] PR 31 H.I, 142.
[63] ASC, s.a. 1100, 176.
[64] A phrase of C.W. Hollister, who considers William mean to his barons, unlike the extravagant Henry: 'Magnates and Curiales in early Norman England', Viator, viii (1977), 63 ff., 'Henry I and the Anglo-Norman magnates', Battle II, pp. 93 ff.

Durham and the honours of Odo, Boulogne and Mowbray, more than compensated for the one large new honour he created, that for his friend, Robert fitzHaimo.[65] Nor did his creation of new earls cost him much.[66] The rebellion of 1095 led to the permanent resumption of the earldom of Northumberland and the confiscation of several honours,[67] and the consequent enfeoffments were not extravagant. Moreover, he added Carlisle to the royal demesne.[68]

William and Henry seem to have viewed the demesne differently, and there was room for different attitudes. Alienations from demesne were not necessarily unwise. They were not simply losses. It was necessary to reward men whose services were valued or desired. Moreover, enfeoffments were seldom pure gifts but more in the nature of investments which secured for the donor a large sum of money in return, normally paid by instalment over a number of years, as well as the perpetual service of a vassal together with valuable feudal rights (incidents).

The floating part of the demesne, custodies and escheats, was a most important source of royal revenue and could to some extent be created by the king. In the financial year 1129–30 it yielded almost half the amount received from the county farms.[69] What is more, the king's temporary recovery of an estate and the enjoyment of its revenues was only the beginning of a series of profitable transactions, the feudal incidents, most of which will be considered later.[70] The profit from escheats was seldom in the permanent recovery of the land. There was almost always someone – often a number of persons – who could claim to be the heir of a landowner who died childless; and the gain to the king lay not in denying the claims but in choosing the successor and making him pay an entry fine (relief) assessed not only on the value of the estate but according to the weakness of the claim. The Pipe Roll of 1130 is littered with such bargains. Nor were forfeitures, usually for rebellion, net gains, for there was often an innocent son or brother or other kinsman who was naturally opposed to the destruction of the family's fortune; and in any case the loyal barons expected rewards at the expense of the traitors. Henry I when pardoning in his coronation charter some classes of debt owed to his predecessor excepted bargains made to secure the inheritance of other men or to acquire things which belonged more justly to someone else.[71] To a few reversions the king

[65] Above, 89 ff.
[66] Above, 167–70.
[67] Below, 357–9.
[68] Below, 297–8.
[69] See above, 225.
[70] See below, 253 ff. For purprestures (confiscated encroachments), escheats and custodies/wardships, see *Dialogus*, 92 ff. Cf. *GR*, ii, 369.
[71] Cap. 6, *SSC*, 118. S.E. Thorne, 'Henry I's coronation charter, ch. 6', *EHR*, xciii (1978), 794, would make some textual emendations, e.g. here 'heirs' for 'inheritance'.

clung stubbornly. The traitor Odo of Bayeux, although not childless, had no better heir than his royal half-nephews. His lands in Kent were still being farmed by the sheriff as a separate entity in 1130, thirty-four years after his death. In that financial year they yielded £225 13s 9d, and possibly a further £61 0s 2d, nearly all net revenue.[72] Conversely, in the same year in Northamptonshire Anselm of Ceoches answered for 170 marks, 5 warhorses and 3 palfreys, of which he had paid 20 marks, for recovering his land in England which the sheriff had been farming.[73]

The complete recovery of infeudated estates and their permanent incorporation into royal demesne was rare after the great resumptions which occurred in the wake of the Norman Conquest; but William Rufus had had some success, and there was always plenty of baronial and church land temporarily in the king's hands for one reason or another. Custodies, precisely because they were short-term, were lucrative. When it was guardianship of the under-age heir to a barony or other honour held in chief of the king, the estates could be plundered and the marriage of an heiress, possibly also of an heir, sold to the highest bidder. Henry I allowed in his coronation charter that the custody of the land and of the children should pertain to the widow or another kinsman.[74] But royal custody was still being abused in 1215. The church protested even harder: it did not completely accept the king's right to custody, still less his diversion of the profits to his treasury, and it recorded its complaints in its chronicles. Henry I opened his charter with a promise that the church should be free, and that on the death of an archbishop, bishop or abbot he would take nothing from the demesne of the church or its tenants until the successor was appointed.[75] These, however, were probably more limited concessions than would appear at first sight, and there is nothing to suggest that he ever behaved much differently from his predecessor.[76]

According to the *Dialogus de Scaccario*, when a barony or other large estate fell into the king's hands, he, or whoever was acting for him, sent a party of clerks and laymen to survey it and discover its rental value. A farmer or custodian (keeper) was then appointed.[77] The practice went back at least to William I and Ranulf Flambard. Ely abbey was in the king's hands, at first through the incapacity of Abbot Simeon and after 1093 because of his death, probably from the later years of the Conqueror until the end of his successor's reign.[78] William I, with the consent of the abbot, put Ranulf Flambard in economic control. The

---

[72] *PR 31 H.I*, 63–4.
[73] *Ibid.*, 81, 84.
[74] Cap. 4.
[75] Cap. 1.
[76] Margaret Howell, *Regalian Right in Medieval England* (1962), 16 ff.
[77] *Dialogus*, 123–4.
[78] *Liber Eliensis*, 218 ff., *HRH*, 45.

chaplain decreed what part of the monastery's revenues should go to the monks for their food and clothing, and while investigating the assets broke open a chest of vestments which the prior, Thurstin, had assembled.[79] On Simeon's death the Winchester monks he had introduced left for home with all the precious vestments, reliquaries and other treasures they could lay their hands on, and these were destroyed by fire when they lodged at Guildford on the journey. Such incidents show how necessary, even if sometimes ineffective, royal custody was. Ranulf's administration of the abbey was probably guided by two still extant surveys: a *descriptio* of the goods in the treasury[80] and a *descriptio* of the lands, the *Inquisitio Eliensis*.[81] The first was to prevent peculation and alienations, the second to establish what farm could be demanded or imposed. At Canterbury, which was without a pastor for more than half the reign, immediately after Lanfranc's death royal servants carried out a *descriptio* of all that pertained to the bishopric. Allowance was made for the food of the monks and the remainder was farmed. To make it worse, the farm was renegotiated each year and given to the highest bidder. As a result, the exploitation was severe, and all this happened, according to Eadmer, not only at Canterbury but wherever a prelate died.[82] The *Domesday Monachorum* is probably to be associated with these events or their sequel.[83]

There can be no doubt that William II not only had the custody of vacant bishoprics and abbeys but also took their revenues less the amounts allowed to maintain the chapter or monastic community and other necessary outgoings,[84] and exploited the assets fairly stringently. In 1215 King John promised that his officers holding a custody would take only reasonable revenues, customs and services and would not destroy or waste the tenants or other assets. They would also maintain in good order the buildings, parks, fishponds, mills and all other property.[85] There was the temptation to fell the timber and sell it off, to run down the animal stock and the stores in the barns, and to let the buildings go to rack and ruin. Whether William II disregarded the law and abused his rights it is difficult to say. According to the St Albans

[79] *Liber Eliensis*, 219–20.

[80] *Ibid.*, 223–4.

[81] Galbraith, *The Making of Domesday Book*, 136 ff., especially 141–2. See also above, 218–19.

[82] *HN*, 26–7; cf. *ASC*, s.a. 1100, 176, and the versions of this in *GR*, ii, 369, and Florence, ii, 46. Cf. also OV, iv, 172 ff.; v, 203.

[83] Douglas, *Domesday Monachorum*, 64.

[84] Cf. the writ obtained by the Worcester monks in 1095–6: 'all property appropriated to the maintenance of the monks is to be in the hands of the prior', *Regesta*, no. 388. Complaints, see above, n. 82, were of the meagreness of the allowance.

[85] *Magna Carta*, caps 4–5, *SSC*, 293.

7. Domesday Book, vol. I, fo. 100 verso. The Kenton (Chentone) entry is the fourth item in col. 2. (See here, 220–1.)

8a. The White Tower, Tower of London. (See here, 96, 371–2.)

8b. St John's chapel, in the Tower.

Chronicle, his keepers cut down their woods and taxed their tenants.[86] Eadmer's influential complaints about the treatment of Canterbury lie behind most of the generalized denunciations of the royal behaviour.[87] But although the Winchester annalist regarded the vacancy at New Minster after 1088 and Ranulf Flambard's custody as disastrous (in 1090 the king took a great treasure from the church, but perhaps this was the Old Minster), the monks entered 'Ranulf the king's chaplain' in their *Liber Vitae*,[88] and from Ely, Abingdon and Durham there was nothing more than hardly avoidable grumbles.[89]

Eadmer is specific only on the matter of the archiepiscopal estates, which suggests that the monks were not unfairly treated, and his story manages to make Anselm appear completely intransigent and William almost reasonable.[90] He denounces Ranulf Flambard, who served a writ on the archbishop on the very day of his enthronement, as cruel and menacing, and relates how during the vacancy men with fierce and threatening faces were to be found even in the cloister demanding money for the king. William of Malmesbury thought that especially hurtful were the frequent changes in personnel.[91] These English monks were probably more sensitive than the abbot of Bec, who, from his background and experience, was entirely, even if uncomfortably, at home in the feudal world. And the archbishop-elect stipulated as one of his conditions for accepting the office that the archbishopric should be delivered to him exactly as it had been on the day Lanfranc had died, free from any enfeoffments or other changes made during the vacancy, and also that justice should be done him in the case of those other estates which Lanfranc had claimed but failed to recover. It would have been difficult to ask for more.

The king expected during a vacancy to get, beyond the value of the estates less the outgoings, various feudal profits. In 1095, when the bishopric of Worcester fell into custody on the death of Wulfstan, he directed a writ, witnessed by his chaplain Ranulf (Flambard), Eudo his steward, and Urse of Abetot, his constable and sheriff of Worcester, to all the French and English who held free lands on the bishopric.[92] He announced that the honour had reverted into his hands and listed the

[86] *Gesta Abbatum Mon. S. Albini*, ed. H.T. Riley (Rolls ser., 1867), i, 65.

[87] Cf. above, 234 n. 82.

[88] *Ann. Winton.*, ii, 36; cf. p. 37, *s.a.* 1092, and p. 39, *s.a.* 1097, on Ranulf's spoliation of vacant churches. *Liber Vitae . . . of the New Minster and Hyde Abbey*, ed. W. de Gray Birch, Hants Record Soc., 5 (1892), 67.

[89] *Liber Eliensis, loc. cit.; Chron. Abingdon*, ii, 42–3; Simeon, *HDE, cont. I*, 135.

[90] See below, 306 ff.

[91] *GP*, 77–8.

[92] T. Hearne, *Hemingi Chartularium ecclesiae Wigorniensis* (1723), i, 79–80; reprinted, but without the details, *SSC*, 109.

relief which his barons had assessed on each of those tenants.[93] Thirty-two men were allotted sums ranging from Orderic the steward's £40 to six men who were to pay only £1 a head. Among the tenants were the bishop of Hereford (£10), the abbot of Evesham (£30) and Archdeacon Ailric (£5). The most important baron was Roger of Lacy (£20). About half the tenants, or their fathers, can be identified with their holdings in Domesday Book on the bishop's fee in Worcestershire, Herefordshire and Warwickshire;[94] and there seems to be no exact relationship between the hidage and the tax. Either, therefore, the basis of assessment has been obscured by tenurial changes between 1086 and 1095, or, more likely, as the total demanded comes to £250, it was a round and arbitrary sum. It is noticeable that the bishop's most important vassal by far, Urse of Abetot, was not required to pay anything; and it is noted in Hemming's Cartulary that Roger fitzDurand, assessed at £10, had obtained a royal writ of pardon. Durand, a former sheriff, had held 11 hides 1 virgate of the bishop in 1086.[95] Royal servants had their perquisites. The writ ends with the threat, 'And if there is anyone who will not do this, Urse and Bernard will seize both their lands and their chattels into my hands.' It would seem that these two, the latter perhaps the royal chaplain Bernard fitzOspac, were the royal keepers, and that the tax was in recognition of the change of lordship, a not unusual feudal custom.[96] It would not be surprising if other tenants were tallaged under some euphemistic title, such as gift or aid. In 1128–9 Henry I's keepers of the bishopric of Durham took 'gifts' (dona) from the knights and also from the thegns, drengs and 'small men' of the bishopric.[97]

The king also hoped to get some return, again disguised as an aid or such like, from the incoming prelate. This, according to canon law, was simony, the selling and purchase of a spiritual office; but in 1093–4 even the high-principled Anselm, under pressure from his friends, was prepared, most reluctantly, to pay the king an aid of £500, although he would collect nothing from his vassals, who had suffered enough during the vacancy. He was, however, saved from this imprudent action by the king's contempt for this paltry sum and his wish for at least double, preferably £2,000.[98] In 1090 the learned and more than respectable abbot of Ramsey, Herbert Losinga, to his lasting shame, had bought

---

[93] J.O. Prestwich, 'War and Finance in the Anglo-Norman State', *TRHS*, 5th ser., iv (1954), 30, suggested that these barons were those who in the next reign would be called Barons of the Exchequer, and must have composed some central financial board.

[94] *DB*, i, 172d, 164d, 238c.

[95] Identified as sheriff, *DB*, i, 165a, under the manor of Bishop's Cleeve (Glos).

[96] Howell, *Regalian Right*, 16 ff.

[97] See below, 237, cf. 257.

[98] *HN*, 43 ff., *VA*, 67; and see below, 246–7, 327, 330–1.

New Minster, Winchester, for his father and the bishopric of Thetford for himself at the cost of 1,000 marks;[99] and in 1099 Ranulf Flambard, probably without a qualm, paid £1,000 for the bishopric of Durham.[100] It was, as he had foreseen, an excellent investment.

It is possible to suggest some very approximate figures for the yield of ecclesiastical custodies in William II's reign. Eleven vacancies of more than a few months, involving nine bishoprics, occurred during the reign. A possible yield can be derived from two directions: the value of the episcopal estates (as distinguished from enfeoffed and chapter land), as shown by Domesday Book, and the yield of the custodies entered on the Pipe Rolls of Henry II. On the whole the latter figures are substantially larger than the former. Among the possible explanations are that the episcopal demesne had increased in both size and value between 1086 and the second half of the twelfth century, or that the king, by allowing pitiless exploitation, was able to get a rent from farmers considerably greater than the normal value. Another difficulty is that Domesday Book does not always distinguish clearly between the demesne lands of the bishop and the estates of the chapter, and, moreover, the position may have changed between 1086 and the later twelfth century.

The case of the bishopric of Durham throws some light on the problems. Unfortunately we have no Domesday value for the episcopal estates; but we know that Ranulf Flambard took £300 a year from the bishopric when custodian in 1096–9,[101] and we have the detailed accounts of the custodians from Michaelmas 1128 to Michaelmas 1130 preserved on the Pipe Roll of 31 Henry I.[102] On this occasion the farm seems to have been divided into two parts: Geoffrey Escoland answered for £428 18s a year and Ansketil of Worcester for £220 for the manors of the bishopric, a total of £648 18s a year. Geoffrey also answered for a tax on the animals of the bishopric (cornage) at £110 5s 5d a year, and for an aid or gift of the episcopal knights, probably on a single occasion, worth presumably much more than the £58 6s 8d for which he accounted at Michaelmas 1130. A tax by both keepers on the thegns, drengs and 'small men' in their respective areas was similarly represented by £46 5s 4d and 19 marks. Geoffrey also accounted for 'pleas and conventions' which sede plena would have gone to the bishop. He had paid in £5 10s and 12 marks, and £4 10s and 6 marks were outstanding. The bishopric was, therefore, worth about £780 a year to Henry I, not counting the unknown sum taken from the tenants as an aid. The next figure that can be given is for 1195–6, when Richard I's custodians

[99] Florence, ii, 34, MS L, based on GR, ii, 385–7, GP, 151–2.
[100] GP, MSS BC, 274 n. 3.
[101] Simeon HDE, cont. I, 135.
[102] PR 31 H.I, 128 ff.

answered for £6,280 os 2½d, of which one-third was taxation revenue.[103]

Although this is an isolated case, it certainly gives food for thought. Clearly the three sets of figures are not strictly comparable. Ranulf Flambard's £300 may be no more than the farm, or a part of it. But as this in 1128–30 totalled £649 a year, it can safely be inferred that here, at least, the administration of William II and his chaplain was far from oppressive, and that as a rule, perhaps, their farms were closer to the Domesday values than to those obtained in the later twelfth century. Account has also to be taken of the taxation of the tenants, which may often have added 50 per cent in the opening year. With these considerations in mind, estimates of the farms of the several bishoprics have been made and are used in the following pages;[104] and since no attempt has been made to include aids, tallages and other extras, the figures may be considered to be on the low side.

In addition to the profits of the bishoprics, thirteen royal abbeys were in custody, mostly for very long periods. In their case it is even more uncertain how much of the Domesday values was allocated for the maintenance of the monks. No doubt the proportion varied from house to house and from time to time; but in the following calculations half the annual Domesday value of the estates has been reckoned as net profit to the king, again probably an underestimate.[105]

Although almost all the figures are estimates and may sometimes be seriously wrong, they can be used for comparison with the estimates of revenue from other sources, and they also form a pattern which is likely to be substantially correct and is of considerable interest. With regard to the custody of bishoprics, the vacancies, except those at Canterbury 1089–93 and at Durham 1096–9, were accidental and were not necessarily prolonged by the king for simple financial reasons; and although it is not beyond the bounds of possibility that he engineered Anselm's exile in 1097 in order to enjoy once more the revenues of Canterbury and of those other dioceses which would fall vacant and, because of Anselm's absence, could not be filled, it is unlikely that he was so calculating. It is, however, suspicious that when the revenue from the custody of bishoprics fell off after Canterbury had been filled in 1093, the loss was made good from the profits of vacant abbeys.

In the first half of the reign the income from the bishoprics in custody rose fairly steadily. In the first financial year (to Michaelmas 1088) William drew only £419 from Wells, Chichester and Durham. In the

[103] Howell, *Regalian Right*, 217.

[104] See fig., below, 262.

[105] The *DB* values are taken from Knowles, *The Monastic Order*, 702–3, and the vacancies are calculated from *HRH*. See also the next two notes. In the case of Ely, the net yield is reduced until 1093 because provision had also to be made for the abbot.

next year Canterbury, the greatest plum, replaced Wells, although only for four months, and the income doubled. From Michaelmas 1090 until Michaelmas 1093 the full impact of the Canterbury revenues and the replacement of Durham by Lincoln pushed up the receipts to £1,759, £1,652, £1,485 and finally £1,750. In that same period the only major supplementation from the monasteries was the custody of Ely and New Minster, Winchester, which together produced £445 a year; but in 1092–3, St Augustine's, Canterbury, Chertsey and Malmesbury were added; and in that year the total from ecclesiastical custodies rose, from £767 in 1087–8, to a peak of £2,385. In the four years which followed, 1093–7, when the king was much engaged in warfare and had also to raise the cash with which to buy the revenues of Normandy, the yield from the bishoprics fell catastrophically: £292 in 1093–4, £262 in 1094–5, £598 in 1095–6 and £300 in 1096–7. Relatively short vacancies at Hereford and Worcester were almost over when Durham fell into the king's hands and provided the only diocesan revenue in 1096–7. The situation was, however, saved by a spate of vacancies in the monasteries which produced £1,263, £1,263, £1,320 and £1,813, and which in 1096–7 raised the king's total income from ecclesiastical custodies to £2,113,[106] almost the same as it had been in 1092–3.

In the last three years of the reign, 1097–1100, with Canterbury again in the king's hands and Winchester, the next wealthiest see, falling in, and with the yield from the monasteries pushed up to over £2,000 a year, the total annual revenue rose to £4,358, £4,494 and £4,562, thus doubling the previous peaks.[107] But the king, of course, did not live to enjoy all the revenues which were audited at Michaelmas 1100. This pattern, which does not depend entirely on the arbitrary figures chosen, explains why Anselm complained so bitterly to William in 1094 about the vacant monasteries and why there were so many complaints against the king's rapacity in his last years. From 1092 he plundered about half the wealthiest royal abbeys and after 1096 was able to draw on the bishoprics as well. On the estimated figures, which may well be on the low side, William derived during his whole reign £16,400 from the bishoprics and £14,800 from the monasteries, a total of £31,200, or an average of £2,400 a year. There was also the revenue from lay custodies and escheats, at which not even a guess can be made, although the

---

[106] The Winchester annalist claims that in 1097 Ranulf Flambard, who was with Bishop Walkelin acting as regent, had the custody of sixteen bishoprics and abbeys: *Ann. Monast.*, ii, 39. My own figure for 1096–7 is 1 bishopric and 9 abbeys and for 1097–8 3 bishoprics and 10 abbeys; but as the history of some monasteries is obscure, tha annalist may well have be right.

[107] *ASC, s.a.* 1100, names the three bishoprics and mentions eleven abbeys let out for rent. Again my own figure for the monasteries falls short, this time by two.

honours of Odo of Bayeux, Eustace of Boulogne and Robert of Mowbray should have brought in something like £4,500 a year.[108] The total yield must have more than compensated for any alienations which William II had made from the lands he inherited from his father, and was probably well in excess of the ordinary profits from the land tax. The general picture so far is more of the restless exploitation of feudal rights over vassals and subjects than of a steady income from traditional farms.

So much for the royal demesne. The other big source of royal revenue for which Domesday Book provides statistics is the general land tax, called 'danegeld' in the Pipe Rolls, which in most parts of the country was levied annually on the manors at so many shillings the fiscal hide or its equivalent (carucate or sulung). Doubts have been expressed, however, from as early as the second half of the twelfth century, whether it was indeed an annual custom. Edward the Confessor is said to have abolished it in 1051;[109] and in 1078 Richard fitzNeal claimed that William I and his successors imposed it only in times of war.[110] But this is disproved by the Pipe Roll of 1129–30, from which it is abundantly clear that for some time before 1130 danegeld had been a customary and annual tax. According to *Leges Edwardi Confessoris*, which probably date from Henry I's reign, it was an annual tax at 12d from each hide of the whole country, except that, until 1096, the demesne of all churches was exempt.[111] There is in fact no good evidence for discontinuity, and it is impossible to suggest any good reason why William I or his immediate successors should have foregone this valuable source of revenue, a tax with which the Domesday survey was undoubtedly concerned. Accordingly, we may hold with confidence that during William Rufus's reign geld was levied annually, with only the rate a matter at issue. Although 1s or 2s the hide may have been considered the normal rate, this was often, perhaps usually, exceeded by the Norman kings.

In 1086, while the survey was being carried out, a geld at the extremely high rate of 6s the hide was being collected; and each activity helped the other. Bound up with Exon Domesday is an audit of the collectors' accounts for the five shires of the circuit.[112] One of the purposes of the Domesday survey was to establish and record the assessment to tax of each manor, and we are commonly given three

[108] C.W. Hollister, 'Magnates and *Curiales* in early Norman England', *Viator*, viii (1977), table A, 65.

[109] For the difficulties concerning this, see F. Barlow, *Edward the Confessor*, 106, 155–7.

[110] In an interesting, although historically inaccurate, account of the history and nature of the tax: *Dialogus*, 54 ff., especially 56.

[111] Liebermann, *Gesetze*, i, 634–5, and see below, 246 nn. 138, 139.

[112] V.H. Galbraith argued that the accounts were for 1086, R.R. Darlington held to the traditional ascription to the 'mickle geld' of 1083–4. For some comments on the arguments and an essay on 'Inquisitio Gheldi', see Finn, *The Liber Exoniensis*, 97 ff.

figures (or two from which the third can be calculated): the hidage of the lord's manorial demesne (the 'inland' or home farm), of the tenant farmers, and of the whole manor; and $a + b = c$. The reason for the separation of the manorial demesne is that at some time in the past the home farms of the barons (and this seems to have included the barons of the barons – the 'honorial barons') had been exempted from the geld.[113] In 1100 Henry I in his coronation charter added the manorial demesne of the knights.[114] In William II's reign, therefore, geld was paid by the lands held by the knights and other gentry and the tenant farmers (*villani*).

The audit preserved in Exon Domesday gives us precious information about the mechanics of the collection in the south-western shires.[115] The tax was paid in two instalments, the first due before Christmas, the second before Easter. There were local collectors for each shire, or group of hundreds, called *fedagri*, but sometimes 'hundredsmen', who, in return for their duties, retained the yield from 1 hide or less in each hundred. In Devon the hidage they claimed was 24 hides $2\frac{1}{2}$ virgates from the 31 hundreds listed. At 6s the hide this gave them £7 7s 9d. The local collectors paid their actual receipts to two men, William *Hostiarius* and Ralf de Pomeroy, whose duty it was to convey the money to the king's treasury at Winchester. Ralf, a baron, was the ancestor of a royal constable, and William the door-keeper or usher was a royal serjeant.[116] Perhaps both men had duties at Exeter castle. The Somerset transporters rendered account for £2 for their fee, and for 9s 8d which they had expended on hiring packhorses, buying forels (parchment or leather cases for the money, usually to hold £100) and wax (for sealing them), and hiring a scribe. They also had to account for £2 11s 3d which had gone astray in transit.[117] In 1130 it was the sheriffs who accounted for the tax and therefore had ultimate responsibility for its collection.

In the audit of the 1086 danegeld we are given for each hundred, (1) the number of fiscal hides in it (its rateable value), (2) the net receipt from (3) the number of hides which had paid (these two figures reveal by division the rate), and (4) the reasons why the yield falls short of the total liability of the hundred – the amount of the exempt manorial

---

[113] For a definition of the demesne, see *Dialogus*, 56. J.A. Green, 'The last century of Danegeld', *EHR*, xcvi (1981), 245, discusses exemptions and pardons.

[114] Cap. 11, *SSC*, 119. Writs of *perdono* (pardon), which are noted in the danegeld accounts on the Pipe Rolls, are described in *Dialogus*, 32–3. For the exemption of the Barons of the Exchequer from 'common assizes', murdrum fines, scutage and danegeld, see *ibid.*, 48. The beneficiary was not to exact the amount pardoned from his tenants and pocket it. For some classes there was a statutory exemption, *ibid.*, 49–52.

[115] *DB*, iii, 65 ff.

[116] For these two, see above, 152, 154 n. 299, and cf. 208.

[117] *DB*, iii, 526b–527. For forels, which in 1178 cost 2d each, see *Dialogus*, 8, 12.

demesne of the king and baronage, the hidage claimed by the collectors, the several disputed claims to exemption, and the defaulters. The administration was being criticized at the time and has incurred much modern disparagement, but by eleventh-century standards it more than passes muster. In 1086 geld had been paid in Devon from 613 of its 1,028 hides:[118] 351 were exempt because they were royal or baronial manorial demesne and 24 were the fee of the collectors, which leaves 39 hides of disputed claimants to exemption and defaulters, a temporary failure rate of less than 4 per cent. And since on the evidence of the Pipe Roll of 1130 arrears were usually pardoned by the king, they must have represented justifiable claims to exemption. The geld raised from Devonshire in 1086 was £180 6s net from £187 13s 9d gross. If those who conveyed the money to the treasury at Winchester were paid, like those in Somerset, £2 10s, the total cost of collection would have been under £10, about 5.3 per cent.

The one serious loss of revenue was caused by the exemption of the manorial demesne of the barons and other privileged persons and bodies. In Devon in 1086 it cost £105 3s. In the south-west circuit as a whole, since 30 per cent of the 10,269 hides in the five shires were exempt as demesne, and another $9\frac{1}{2}$ per cent for various reasons had failed to pay, the king had received only about £1,755 net, whereas the total potential yield was some £3,000.[119] F.W. Maitland reckoned that in 1086 the whole of England was rated at some 70,000 hides.[120] Allowing the same wastage as found in the south-west circuit, the total yield would have been some £12,300 when geld was imposed at the rate of 6s the hide.

The first detailed account we have of danegeld collected on a national scale is in the Pipe Roll of 1130. The sheriffs accounted for a tax apparently at 2s the hide and for an aid from the cities and boroughs, presumably in lieu, assessed on each in a round sum. In the case of Devon, the sheriff had paid £62 3s into the treasury, he had pardoned at least eight persons to the tune of something over £20, and what he owed (if anything) is missing.[121] These figures, if multiplied by three, closely match those of 1086. From the accounts of the thirty-one counties listed (the figures for four shires and about six boroughs are missing) we can abstract the following figures: received from the sheriffs, £2,517 (shires) and £335 (boroughs), total £2,852; pardoned, £2,179 and £257, total £2,436; owed by the sheriffs, £322 and £35, total £357. The grand total

[118] It is a typical discrepancy that Maitland, *Domesday Book and Beyond*, 464, should have counted the *DB* hidage of Devonshire to 1119.

[119] Finn, *loc. cit.*, 110.

[120] *Domesday Book and Beyond*, 464–5.

[121] *PR 31 H.I*, 157–8.

is £5,645. If we add to £2,852 one-eighth of that for the missing units, we get £3,209 as the possible net proceeds of the tax in 1129–30.

It also seems that in some shires which had never been assessed to geld in hides or carucates, the pastoral areas of the north, a general tax on animals was imposed as an equivalent to danegeld. The Westmorland account is defective in the Pipe Roll of 1130, but the farmer had paid into the treasury £43 for the 'geld of animals' for the current year.[122] The farmer of Carlisle owed £85 8s 8d a year for this tax, and in 1130 accounted for five years.[123] The keeper of the bishopric of Durham rendered account for 'cornage', a tax on cattle, for two years at £110 5s 5d a year, and had paid in £83 7s 2d and £81 16s 3d.[124] The only exemption mentioned belonged to the canons of St Mary, Carlisle, who were pardoned £1 18s 4d.

After 1130 there is a gap in the series of Pipe Rolls until Henry II's reign. Maitland reckoned that a geld from the mid-twelfth century had a book-entry value of over £5,000, but, with the franchises, was unlikely to yield more than £3,000.[125] As Henry I had added the manorial demesne of the knights to the existing exemptions and the tendency was for franchises to increase rather than diminish, it looks as though William II could easily have received £4,000 from a geld at 2s the hide.[126] This agrees with our earlier figure arrived at by a different route. Nor was this the maximum which could be obtained. The assessment could be varied, the number of exemptions reduced, and the rate could be raised.

It has been thought, not unreasonably, that the Domesday survey was intended to be, among other things, the first step towards complete reassessment of all estates to the land tax. Evidence of earlier re-ratings, sometimes of individual manors, sometimes of wide areas, can be found in the record. Usually the hidage had been reduced, although in the Conqueror's reign it had occasionally been increased.[127] But if that was

---

[122] *Ibid.*, 143.

[123] *Ibid.*, 141.

[124] *Ibid.*, 131.

[125] *Domesday Book and Beyond*, 29–30, 464–5, 545–6.

[126] There was probably between 1086 and 1130, besides Henry I's block concession, a steady erosion of liability through particular exemptions, most of which were probably sold. In *PR 31 H.I*, 104, under Bedfordshire, among those pardoned the tax were Humphrey (*Unfr'*) *villanus*, Walter *bordarius*, and Theobald *clericus* – it would be difficult to go much lower in the social scale.

[127] C. Hart, 'The hidation of Huntingdonshire', *Proc. of the Cambridge Antiqu. Soc.*, lxi (1968), 55, *The hidation of Northamptonshire*, Leicester Univ. Occas. Papers, 2nd ser., iii (1970), *The hidation of Cambridgeshire, ibid.*, vi (1974); Salley Harvey, 'Domesday Book and its predecessors', *EHR*, lxxxvi (1971), 755–60; J.A. Green, 'The last century of Danegeld', 244–5. For reductions in Sussex (Earl Roger and others) see *VCH Sussex*, i, 360–1.

the intention, nothing much came of it. Orderic tells a very muddled story about Ranulf Flambard advising the new king to have the *descriptio* of the whole kingdom revised. There should be a new division of England (? into hundreds and hides)[128] in order to reduce the over-generous assessments of Edward the Confessor.[129] If Orderic is making the chaplain point out that the assessed hidage on which the tax was paid was less than the actual acreage under cultivation, this is exactly what might be expected, for in many cases it was obviously true. But when Orderic adds that Ranulf with the king's permission then carried out a new survey, measured all the ploughlands which are called hides in English with a rope (*funiculo mensus est*), and confiscated all property discovered to be above a certain amount, we must demur.

In the first place the chronicler is quoting from the prophet Amos's prediction of calamities in Israel: 'Thy wife shall be an harlot in the city, and thy sons and thy daughters shall fall by the sword, and thy land shall be divided by line [*funiculo metietur*]; and thou shalt die in a polluted land: and Israel shall surely go into captivity forth of his land' (Amos 7:17). Orderic was thinking of the disasters which had fallen on his enslaved native country and of the iniquities of the king and his servant. And in any case, although a new assessment could have been made on the basis of the values disclosed by the survey or on the estimated ideal capacity of the manors, nothing in fact seems to have been done, at least on the grand scale. Moreover, even if Orderic's reductions and confiscations can be understood to mean that a new ratio between fiscal hidage and arable acreage was introduced, this change left no trace on the later history of the collection of danegeld.[130]

In the later part of the reign, the king in Normandy addressed a writ in favour of Thorney abbey to Bishop R. (probably Robert Bloet of Lincoln), Ranulf (Flambard) the chaplain, H(aimo) the steward, and Urse of Abetot, who, on the evidence of another writ similarly addressed, would seem to be his 'justiciars of England'.[131] He ordered

[128] Cf. *Dialogus*, 64.

[129] OV, iv, 172.

[130] It is possible, however, that Ranulf carried out more realistic surveys of estates which came into royal custody: see above, 234.

[131] *Regesta*, no. 422 (LXXII). In the calendar Bishop R. is identified as Robert of Lincoln, although no. 424, with a similar address, is printed as giving Ralf bishop of Chichester in full. Robert is the more likely in both cases. The writ was issued at *Roseium*, which is identified in the index as Rozoy-en-Brie (S.E. of Paris), corrected, ii, 406, to Rosay (Seine Inf.); but Rosay-sur-Lieurre, south-west of Lyons-la-Forêt (Eure), in a favourite hunting area in the Vexin, is the most likely. The date is as difficult to establish as the place. The witness of William (Giffard) as chancellor makes it after 1093–4 and it is earlier than Ranulf's promotion to bishop in 1099. The king was abroad 19 March–29 December 1094, September 1096–4 April 1097, 11 November 1097–10 April 1099, and

them to assess (*admetior*) the abbey to gelds, scots, military service and all other customs as favourably as any other honour in the whole of England which had the same amount of land. 'And if you have taken anything from the abbey on this occasion [*propter hoc*], give it all back and assess it just as I have ordered.' Obviously Thorney had objected to some tax levied by the regents and the king was offering some relief.[132] But as this seems to be an isolated instance, it is no evidence for a general re-rating, nor does it appear that the justiciars were to do anything beyond considering the justification of Thorney's assessment in the light of the size of the monastery's endowments. The criterion was to be comparison, the commonest yardstick in these matters. There is no suggestion, beyond the use of *admetior*, that they were to carry out a measured survey of the estates.[133]

The point surely is that what the Conqueror might have been able to do had he lived was outside the power of his successor at first. The opportunity for large-scale reform was lost, and William II was probably realistic in opting for maintaining the old system as best he could. In 1088, when he was rallying the people to his standard during the rebellion, he promised them the abolition of 'unright' gelds (such as the Conqueror's tax at 6s the hide).[134] But, wrote the Anglo-Saxon Chronicler, 'it did not last any time'. He accused the king of oppressing the kingdom in 1090, (1094),[135] 1096, 1097 and 1098 with 'manifold' or unjust gelds (*ungylda*), and in the unfavourable notice of his death referred to his oppressive exactions of military service and 'ungelds'.[136] It may be inferred that in the first years of his reign he had been more moderate in his demands; but even in 1096 he was less extortionate than the Conqueror had been on at least two occasions, and it is noticeable that Henry I in his coronation charter did not think it necessary to do more than widen the exemption from geld. He was in fact, as we have

June to September 1099. It would be nice to be able to associate the writ with the 'unbearable geld' of 1096, but that would be a mere guess. See also above, 209, below, 365.

[132] Since Thorney seems never to have had an assessment to knight service (cf. J.H. Round, *FE*, 251), there may have been royal or ministerial pressure in this direction in William II's reign.

[133] Because of the use of *admetior*, the writ has naturally been associated with Orderic's *metior*: cf. Galbraith, *The Making of Domesday Book*, 211. But the more important word in Orderic is *funiculo*, which is absent from the writ. Henry I's writ of 1103 in favour of Ramsey abbey, *Regesta*, ii, 650, brought in here by Galbraith, does not seem to be connected with the re-rating of geld.

[134] *ASC*, 169

[135] *GR*, ii, 376; Florence, ii, 35; omitted from *ASC*.

[136] *ASC*, 174–6.

already seen, frequently blamed by the Anglo-Saxon Chronicler for his severe taxes.

The 1096 exactions, however, made a great stir and were widely reported by the chroniclers. The taxes were imposed to raise the 10,000 marks (£6,666 13s 4d) the king had agreed to lend his brother Robert, on the security of the duchy of Normandy, to enable him to go on the Crusade.[137] Geld was levied at 4s the hide.[138] But a simple doubling of the rate probably brought in only an additional £4,000, which was not enough to meet the exceptional expenditure; and the nature of the resentment aroused by the levy shows that something more than the rate was involved. It is possible that baronial manorial demesne was deprived of its exemption, but more likely that the king took from his barons, both lay and ecclesiastical, an aid in lieu.[139] William of Malmesbury, followed by the Worcester chronicler, believed this, and tells how the earls, barons and sheriffs raised it by taxing their knights and agricultural tenants, while the bishops and abbots melted down the gold and silver ornaments of their churches.[140] The Worcester chronicler embroiders with the story that when the bishops and abbots complained at court about the 'unbearable impost [*pensio*]', the king, driven to his customary fury, ordered them to break up their shrines; which they did.[141] Eadmer explains what Archbishop Anselm did.[142] He was advised by some of his friends that he should give the king an aid (*auxilium*), but, although he accepted that this would be both reasonable and honourable, he had no money to hand. So on the advice of, among others, Bishops Walkelin of Winchester and Gundulf of Rochester, and with the consent of the majority of the members of the chapter, he took 200 marks of silver from the treasury of the church of Canterbury, partly in silver, partly in gold, and he gave this sum, together with what he had been able to raise from his vassals, to the king. Later he granted the monks one of his demesne manors, Petham, five miles south of the city, which was then worth about £30 a year, for seven years as recom-

[137] See below, 362–4.
[138] *Leges Edwardi Confessoris*, in Liebermann, *Gesetze*, i, 636.
[139] H.W.C. Davis, *England under the Normans and Angevins*, 108. Eadmer clearly distinguishes, and Florence implies that there was an aid. A.L. Poole, *From Domesday Book to Magna Carta*, 111, disagreed: the entry in the *Leges Edwardi Confessoris* (see last note) that the barons made the grant and that holy church was not excepted, made the whole operation an aid. For the aid in connexion with the 1094 expedition, see above, 236, and below, 327.
[140] *GR*, ii, 371. The stories of melting down chalices, caskets, crucifixes, book-covers, etc., are reminiscent of those told at the beginning of the century in connexion with geld: *Hemingi chartularium*, ed. T. Hearne (1723), i, 248–9.
[141] Florence, ii, 40.
[142] *HN*, 74–5.

pense.[143] Eadmer gives these details to rebut the slander that Anselm had been guilty of despoiling his church.

Abingdon abbey regarded the geld at 4s the hide as exceptional and intolerable: to meet it the monks had to melt down silver vases and surrender their livestock to the royal collectors.[144] At Malmesbury, where the chronicler was an eye-witness, the otherwise exemplary abbot Godfrey was punished by God with the King's Evil for the measures he took to pay this insupportable tax to the king. Relying on bad counsel, he thought an easy way to meet his own share was to strip twelve copies of the Gospels, eight crosses and as many shrines of their gold and silver, only to be deceived when the yield was no more than 72 marks, that is to say, £48,[145] a sum less than the amount required.

There may also have been some experiments which anticipated the various schemes introduced in the second half of the twelfth century designed to supplement or replace danegeld. What look like novel ways of raising money can be seen in the Pipe Roll of 1130. An 'old aid of knights' is accounted for under Surrey, Essex, Northamptonshire (the abbot of Crowland), Lincolnshire (the bishop), Carmarthen, Devon (including the bishop) and Cornwall.[146] It looks as though a general aid had been taken some years back from the barons, assessed perhaps on knights' fees. There are also references to aid paid by the shires of Yorkshire, Berkshire and Middlesex.[147] Ranulf Flambard would seem to have been more audacious than Roger of Salisbury, and it is possible that such imposts were first devised by him. But in financial matters William Rufus and Ranulf were at heart neither, as Orderic would have it, avenging instruments of the Lord God, nor enlightened fiscal reformers. Their aim was the efficient and, in some directions, immoderate enforcement of existing royal rights to the last farthing.

The final main category of royal revenue is 'pleas and covenants', which we will try to subdivide. Pleas were the profits of jurisdiction. Justice was most profitable in the Middle Ages for it not only brought in

---

[143] Eadmer's *Petteham* is evidently *DB*'s *Titeham*, i, 3c, which was worth £20 a year in 1086 and from which the monks drew a rent of 8s. Poole, *loc. cit.*, wrongly identified it as Peckham, *Pecheham* in *DB*. East Peckham, 4d, was a Christ Church manor (*terra monachorum*) and worth only £8 in 1086, while West Peckham, 7c, which was rented at £12, was on the fief of the bishop of Bayeux.

[144] *Chron. Abingdon*, ii, 38.

[145] *GP*, 432. F. Barlow, 'The King's Evil', *EHR*, xcv (1980), 6.

[146] *PR 31 H.I*, 49, 58, 84, 114, 189, 153-4, 159.

[147] *Ibid.* 26, 124, 151. It is called *preteritum auxilium*, which should refer to the financial year 1128-9. If so, in view of the scarcity of the references, it could hardly have been imposed on the whole kingdom. Cf. also Haskins, 'The abacus', for *assisa communis* and the arithmetical problem of dividing 200 marks between the 2,500 hides of Essex, as posited by Hugh of Buckland.

money but also gave political power. Most kings employed justice as an instrument of government: it was used to punish enemies and, in a negative way, to reward and protect friends. The king had a right to do justice on his vassals and tenants, to hear their disputes as well as to judge their crimes, and he had the right to take the profits from the punishment of certain more heinous crimes, whosoever the perpetrator, offences which became known as the pleas of the crown. He also reserved to himself punishment of all offenders against the forest laws. William I is said to have abolished capital punishment and substituted the milder penalties of blinding and castration.[148] By Henry I's reign, hanging had certainly been reintroduced for thieves.[149] But on the whole the death penalty was for robbers and thieves caught in the act. The land and chattels of such criminals fell to the owner of the jurisdiction. Land was also forfeit for treason and perhaps for some other serious offences. But the usual penalty for a brush with the law was a money fine. One of the largest penalties recorded on the Pipe Roll of 1130 is £2,000 inflicted on the Jews of London 'for killing a sick man',[150] probably an unfortunate patient.

A person who had no defence to a charge or was found by some method of proof guilty, was adjudged to be in the king's mercy; and the amends he had to pay (the amercement) were fixed either by the suitors of the court or, in major affairs, by the king. The practice came close to arbitrary fines assessed according to the circumstances and the seriousness of the crime. It was, of course, liable to abuse; and Henry I in his coronation charter promised a major reform. He conceded that if any of his barons or vassals should be found guilty of an offence (*forisfacere*), he would not be forced to give a pledge which put his money at the king's mercy, as was the custom in the reigns of the two Williams, but should make amends as was the custom before the Conquest, that is to say according to the degree of the transgression.[151] In other words, there would be a return to the system of *bots* and *wites*, fixed and customary penalties as laid down by the law. There is no evidence, however, that this promise was implemented: arbitrary penalties had come to stay. The aim of those subject to them became to secure that they should be reasonable and according to the gravity of the offence.[152]

William II's exploitation of justice was one of the main planks in the charges of misgovernment brought against him. The Anglo-Saxon

[148] 'The laws of William the Conqueror', cap. 10, *SSC*, 99.
[149] In 1124 Ralf Basset and his fellow justices at a session in Leicestershire hanged 44 men and blinded and castrated 6: *ASC*, 191.
[150] *PR 31 H.I*, 149.
[151] Cap. 8, *SSC*, 119.
[152] *Magna Carta*, caps 20–22, *SSC*, 295–6.

Chronicler believed that the king relied increasingly on evil counsellors, of whom Ranulf Flambard was the chief. This chaplain 'drove' and controlled all the king's courts (*gemote*) throughout England, so that justice disappeared and injustice prevailed.[153] William of Malmesbury elaborated. In William's reign no one became wealthy unless he was a money-changer; clerks had to be lawyers and priests rent-collectors ('farmers'). There was not a man so base or so stained with crime that he would not be heard if he appealed to the king's avarice; the rope would be loosed from the very neck of a thief if he promised the king money.[154] The Worcester chronicler repeated the charge more prosaically.[155] From other evidence it appears that Ranulf was one of a group of royal servants who could be called, in contrast to local judges of various kinds, 'justiciars of the whole of England'.[156] They had duties, administrative, financial and judicial, which put them collectively above all other officials, especially when the king was out of the country, and made them the prime agents of royal authority or tyranny. Royal justice was a political as well as a financial tool, and, *pace* the Malmesbury monk, not everything was for sale. In 1096 the king refused large sums of money offered by barons to save the traitor William of Aldrie from execution by hanging.[157]

Despite Henry's promise of reform, the fruits of such a policy are scattered throughout the Pipe Roll of 1130. When the king's justices visited a shire it was as though an avenging force had ripped through it: almost everyone in sight was put in the king's mercy. Apart from the criminals and litigants, there were communities which had concealed offences, suitors, juries and lawmen who had made mistakes or given wrong verdicts, and officials who had let criminals escape.[158] The justices left behind them long schedules of 'pleas' to be collected; and penalties owed by individuals or by the sheriff who had the duty of collecting them appear frequently on the roll, and were paid on the instalment system. It was difficult for anyone to avoid falling foul of the law at some time. No wonder there were conspiracies to get men off. We

---

[153] *ASC, s.a.* 1099, 1100, pp. 175 (where the translation is too weak), 176. Florence, ii, 46, putting this into Latin, makes Ranulf's office 'placitator ac totius regni exactor'.

[154] *GR*, ii, 369.

[155] Florence, ii, 46.

[156] Above, 210.

[157] *Chron. mon. de Hida*, 301. For the case, see below, 357–8.

[158] Richardson and Sayles, 173 ff. A more sceptical view of judicial eyres in the reigns of William II and Henry I is taken by William T. Reedy Jr, 'The origins of the General Eyre in the reign of Henry I', *Speculum*, xli (1966), 688. He argues that under William I and II and until *c.* 1124 the kings used only *ad hoc* commissioners, and that from *c.* 1124 until 1135 localized eyres operated. The general eyre started with the Assize of Clarendon in 1166.

have already seen William's fury at the escape of a number of Englishmen accused of forest offences by surviving what he considered, no doubt rightly, rigged trials by ordeal.[159] All things considered, we cannot doubt that William II got at least as much money as Henry I out of pleas.

Besides the profits of courts, there was a fairly lucrative communal penalty, the *murdrum* fine, which the Conqueror had introduced.[160] It was imposed by the sheriff on the hundred in which a corpse was found which could not be proved to be that of a native Englishman, and for which the slayer could not be produced. The original penalty seems to have been between £30 and £40. Sheriffs rendered account regularly in the Pipe Roll of 1130 for 'murders', often at £10 or 10 marks, sometimes twice as much, and also for the pardons which they had allowed, apparently to the manorial demesne of the barons.

Around the penalties was a penumbra of payments made to the king in connexion with the administration of justice. Even if royal officials shrank from conceding that justice was for sale,[161] it could hardly be denied that there was much which concerned it which could be purchased. In 1129–30 in Buckinghamshire and Bedfordshire Richard fitzAlfred, a royal butler, owed 15 marks for the privilege of sitting with the royal justice, Ralf Basset, when hearing the pleas of the crown.[162] In Yorkshire the judges and jurors of the shire owed £100 for the concession that they need not serve again.[163] In East Anglia the king's serjeant Benjamin had been farming the pleas of the crown as well as lastage (tolls). He had promised to make a profit of 500 marks.[164]

Litigants, especially reluctant litigants, offered money for a variety of services. The routine fee was 10 marks of silver, but for anything exceptional more was expected. Men paid the king (usually by way of his itinerant judges) for having justice in respect of their land, or their father's land (probably for a writ of right which set in motion a proprietory action),[165] for proving their title through the *duellum*, the judicial combat, or for permission to abandon the action.[166] They paid to get the king to give them arbitrary relief or to force their lord to do them justice. Richard, prior of Winchester, owed £80 for the recovery into demesne of land which had been held unjustly by an under-tenant.

[159] Above, 111.

[160] See *Dialogus*, 52–3, where the penalty is put at £36 or £44.

[161] Cf. *ibid.*, 120, where Richard fitzNeal, in his discussion of such offerings, treats the matter with reasonable candour.

[162] *PR 31 H.I*, 101.

[163] *Ibid.*, 34.

[164] *Ibid.*, 91. Richardson and Sayles, 186–7. He had a brother named Joseph.

[165] *PR 31 H.I*, cf. E. de M. and WH. (p. 10), H. de F. (p. 11).

[166] Cf. N. de R. (p. 11), R. fG. (p. 14), W. de A. (p. 42).

H. de G. owed 17 marks for the king's order to Geoffrey de Mandeville to let him have his father's land.[167] Men paid for holding their land in peace, for respite from actions until the king should return from England, or for life.[168] W. de A. owed 100 marks for not having to plead against his vassals re land which his father had held in demesne; but T. fG., apparently one of them, had paid 40 marks to have seizin of his land from W. de A.[169] Men paid to use the royal machinery for the enforcement of debts.[170] They paid for the king's help against a more powerful adversary, for example, W. fE. against the count of Brittany, and the dean of London (20 marks) against his bishop.[171] Vassals of the count of Mortain paid for an agreement negotiated between them and the king's nephew.[172] Men paid to get a judgment enforced.[173] In criminal matters they offered money to vary the mode of proof – for example, G. de NC. owed 20 marks for permission to clear himself by oath instead of by the ordeal of hot iron[174] – and they paid to be released from prison.[175] And if they put out money to gain the king's favour, they put out even more to avert his anger. O. de L. owed 200 marks to abate the king's malevolence towards him and O. his clerk.[176] To have to pay for justice is common practice; that injustice can sometimes be had at a price is the way of the world.

A few examples from the Abingdon chronicle show that the position was similar in William II's reign. All three concern the abbey's knights, who were the cause of many of its troubles, in the time of Abbot Reginald (Rainald), 1084–97. The abbot had a nephew named Robert whom he wanted to endow, and, as there was no 'vavassor-land' available, gave him the village of Dumbleton. The monks objected, for it was a gift of Archbishop Ælfric (995–1005) on condition that it should never be taken away from the brethren. But when the abbot tried to recover the land, Robert refused to give it up, and the case went before the king. The abbot offered William 50 marks and two horses for a writ ordering the land's restitution; Robert then made a counter-offer of 70; and the abbot

[167] Pp. 38, 55; cf. also, H. de MV. (p. 54).
[168] Cf. N. de R. and R. de D. (p. 11), R.B. (p. 14), H. fR. (p. 26), W. fH. (p. 32), A. fR. (p. 113).
[169] Pp. 29, 33.
[170] Cf. W. de C. (p. 39), P. 1. (p. 149).
[171] Pp. 93, 148.
[172] P. 33.
[173] Cf. R. fl. (p. 11).
[174] P. 35.
[175] E.g. Peter chamberlain of the bishop of Winchester (old debt of 844 marks), p. 39; Geoffrey de Burn (2oz of gold), p. 43; three Welshmen in Pembroke (? old debt of £75 4s), p. 137.
[176] P. 82.

had to raise his bid to the same amount. It was, however, an attack of paralysis which finally brought the nephew to surrender the village.[177] On another occasion when the abbey's knight Anskil was disgraced by the king, the abbot had to pay William £60 in order to retain part of the knight's fief.[178]

Even more costly and vexatious to the abbey was a case which seems to have started in 1095 and which concerned the abbot's son-in-law, another Reginald. This knight was threatened, apparently on the evidence of the treasury accounts, with a long term of imprisonment unless he paid the king 500 marks and produced sureties for payment. But hardly had the abbot stood surety for 300 marks and other friends for 200, when the knight fled to Flanders and took refuge with the count. Whereupon the king called upon the sureties to pay up. The abbot in turn resumed the fiefs which the knight had held of the abbey, fourteen hides and a mill, and also took the opportunity to restore one of the estates, the ten hides at Leckhampstead, to the monks.[179] One of the witnesses to this restitution (which proves to have been nominal) was Ranulf Flambard, 'the king's chaplain and justiciar of the kingdom of England', who had arrived to collect the money owed to the king; and the abbot, who had no ready cash, was forced to pawn his manor, which in 1086 had been worth £10 a year, to a certain Hugh de Dun for £20, in order to keep his creditor at bay. The debt of £300 and the heavy danegeld of the next year crippled the abbey financially. A few years later the knight, helped by the count of Flanders, made his peace with the king and recovered his Abingdon estates, less Leckhampstead, which was still in pawn. While the abbey was vacant after Abbot Reginald's death, Hugh de Dun offered the king £20 for a grant of the pawned village in fee, but the royal custodian, a monk, matched the offer and secured its return. Nevertheless, the abbey could not retain possession. It granted the manor to Herbert, 'the king's chamberlain and treasurer', apparently in return for his professional services as well as the knight service due from it, and it was inherited by his son, Herbert fitzHerbert. Another three hides at Hanney were granted to Hugh of Buckland, sheriff of Berkshire and 'royal justiciar'.[180] The king's servants joined in

---

[177] *Chron. Abingdon*, ii, 35–6.

[178] *Ibid.*, ii, 37, cf. 4. See also above, 142.

[179] In 1086 the knight Reginald held 10 hides in Leckhampstead, 1 hide in Tubney and 4 hides in Frilford of the abbey: *DB*, i, 58d. In 1095 the abbot resumed the first two estates, 2 hides in Frilford, 1 hide in Hanney, and a mill. In a list of Abingdon knights from the reign of Henry I, Reginald held Tubney for 1 knight, and 1 hide in Frilford and 12 hides elsewhere for 1½ knights. The 10 hides at Leckhampstead were held by Herbert fitzHerbert; John fitzRobert held in Hanney for ⅕ of a knight. These knights' fees were unstable, but the abbey normally reckoned 10 hides to a knight's fee.

[180] *Chron. Abingdon*, ii, 37–40, 42–3.

to take their pickings when something went wrong.

Not always distinguishable from 'pleas', and also having affinities with 'covenants', are the profits of feudal incidents. These consist of all those profitable rights which a lord had over his vassals and which proceed from the tenure of fiefs. And since they normally arose when the vassal or his family was at a disadvantage, the lord was tempted to abuse them. Henry I in his coronation charter expressly renounced some of his predecessor's actions in this field, only, it seems, to reintroduce most of them himself. They remained the chief frictional points between the monarchy and the baronage, and King John had to make new concessions in Magna Carta. It would appear that feudal law, introduced wholesale, but in a variety of packages, after 1066, never acquired an authority sufficient either to protect the vassal against seigneurial exploitation or the lord against derelictions of duty on the part of his vassals. Some conflict of interest was inherent in the situation and showed itself whenever the balance of power shifted. When the king was weak, as after his seizure of the throne, he had to make concessions to his barons. When he had established his power, he took what he could from them whenever the opportunity arose. The king also profited from the lack of unity among his vassals. It was a very competitive society, and one man's fall usually led to another man's rise. The king had two faces: one radiated his favour and gave promise of lands, offices, perquisites of all kinds and immunity from the lawsuits and machinations of rivals; the other threatened his *ira et malevolentia*, his anger and ill will, and not only proclaimed exclusion from all royal favour but also was the signal for the dogs of envy to close in and start to drag the unprotected vassal down.[181]

The basic seigneurial right was to recover his land permanently or temporarily because of a vassal's inability to perform the services due. Treason led to forfeiture, death without leaving an heir of the body to escheat, incapacity of any sort or the succession of a minor to custody or wardship. These reversions could be profitably exploited. On the Pipe Rolls, major forfeitures and resumptions, because they were administered by royal officials, are usually given a separate entry and heading, and have already been discussed in connexion with the shrinkage and expansion of the royal demesne.[182] Smaller estates were released to kinsmen (at a price) or auctioned to farmers, and the payments and indebtedness of these are recorded at random on the rolls. For example, in Kent the widow and brother of Walter fitzGodwin offered 100 marks to have the custody of the land and sons of the dead

---

[181] Cf. J.E.A. Jolliffe, *Angevin Kingship* (1955).

[182] Above, 231 ff. According to *Dialogus*, 95, the formula varied according to whether the estate was a barony or not. For other kinds of escheats, see *ibid.*, 97-8.

Walter. They had paid 10 marks into the treasury and still owed 80.[183]
In Northamptonshire Geoffrey de Clinton, an important royal servant,
owed 80 marks for the custody of the son of William of Dives and his
land.[184] In Hampshire the sheriff, William of Pont-de-l'Arche, owed
£118 for the custody of the son of William Rufus's huntsman, Ulric,
'until he was capable of holding his land'.[185]

Magna Carta ruled that an heir whose land had been in custody
should not also have to pay a relief (succession duty); in other cases
payment should be according to a fixed tariff.[186] Whatever the practice
of the Norman kings may have been in the former circumstances,[187]
there is no doubt that they used the relief both as a source of revenue and
as a political instrument, being merciful towards favourite families and
severe towards those out of favour. Henry I in his coronation charter
opened the section dealing with his predecessor's 'unjust oppressions and
bad customs towards his barons' with an important promise: in future
on the death of one of his earls, barons or other tenants-in-chief, the heir
would not have to buy back his land, as under William II, but would
recover it with a just and lawful relief. He also, when cancelling some
types of debt owed to his predecessor, remitted all reliefs which had been
agreed for a lawful (perhaps direct) inheritance, and anything which
had been pledged in connexion with such a succession.[188] It is doubtful,
however, whether Henry was less rapacious than his brother. Payments
for having a father's land (not always called a relief) are scattered
throughout the Pipe Roll. At one extreme, in Essex, Geoffrey (II) de
Mandeville was liable for £866 13s 4d (1,300 marks, probably only part
of the original fine) 'for the land of his father' (William I). In 1129–30 he
had paid £133 6s 8d (200 marks) and still owed the balance.[189] The next
entry is in marked contrast: Geoffrey Mauduit was liable for 7 marks as a
relief for the land of his father. He had paid 5 marks and was pardoned
the remainder 'for the love of the earl of Warenne'.[190] Not far away is the
record of the fine which two brothers paid as a relief for their father's
land: Roger and Robert de Raimes each owed £50; both had paid
during the year 25 marks and owned 50 marks. It is not unlikely that
originally they had owed 100 marks apiece.[191]

[183] *PR 31 H.I*, 66.
[184] *Ibid.*, 83.
[185] *Ibid.*, 37. See above, 125 n. 123.
[186] Caps 2–3, *SSC*, 293.
[187] Richard fitzNeal allowed that Henry II sometimes, perhaps usually, took a relief after custody, but could see the injustice in this: *Dialogus*, 94–7.
[188] Cap. 6, *SCC*, 118. Thorne (as above, 232 n. 71) would amend the text and reduce the scope of the concessions. For Henry II's alleged practices, see *Dialogus*, 96–7, 121.
[189] *PR 31 H.I*, 55.
[190] *Ibid.*
[191] *Ibid.*, 54.

The king's treatment of the widows and daughters of his vassals was a frictional point in both 1100 and 1215. It was generally agreed that the lord had a proper interest in the marriage and remarriage of women under his lordship because it disposed of their land. He also had the right to a fine when an agreement was made or land was transferred. He could, of course, be unreasonable and extortionate; and it is quite clear that many widows resented being sold with their land without their consent. Henry I conceded that if one of his barons or vassals wanted to give his daughter, sister, niece or other kinswoman in marriage, he was to consult the king; but the king would not take any fine for giving permission and would not prohibit the marriage unless it was to one of his enemies. The king reserved the right, if the heir was a girl, to give her in marriage with her land after he had taken the advice of his barons; and nothing is said here about her wishes or in condemnation of the usual royal practice of selling this profitable windfall. But he did make concessions in respect of widows. If the baron's widow was childless, she should have her dower lands (*dos*) and marriage portion (*maritagium*), as long as she remained chaste,[192] and he would not give her in marriage except in conformity with her wishes. These provisions were not repeated for the widow with children, for they were subsumed in her guardianship of the children and of the whole fief.[193]

Nevertheless, fines associated with marriage and widowhood are plentiful on the Pipe Roll of 1130 and show how William II could have exploited his rights. Men or parents paid large sums for the marriage of an heiress in the royal custody. In Kent Robert de Vere answered for £315 for his wife and her land. He had paid £80 and owed the balance.[194] In Essex Ralf fitzWilliam owed 10 marks and one warhorse for Juliana, daughter of Richard of Winchester, and her land.[195] In Berkshire William Croc accounted for 200 marks of silver and 2 of gold for the daughter of Herbert the Chamberlain with her marriage portion, and of this he had paid 20 marks of silver.[196]

Widows seem to have been even more in demand. Some paid a fine to avoid a forced marriage. In Norfolk William fitzRichard fitzHermer had offered a sum so that his mother could marry a man of her own

---

[192] The *dos* came from the dead husband's estate; the *maritagium* was what she had brought with her: see above, 16, 18. Richard fitzNeal, following Exodus 21:10, calls the *dos*, 'the price and reward of her chastity': *Dialogus*, 115. Rohese, daughter of Richard fitzGilbert, who married Eudo the steward about 1088 (above, 140), took as *maritagium* her father's demesne manor of Thorncroft in Surrey, worth £7 10s *p.a.* in 1086 (*DB*, i, 35c): W. Farrer, *Honors and Knights' Fees*, iii, 167.

[193] Caps 3–4, *SSC*, 118. See also above, 233.

[194] *PR 31 H.I*, 64.

[195] *Ibid.*, 59.

[196] *Ibid.*, 125.

choice. He had paid 10 marks that year and still owed £5.[197] In Suffolk Wiverona, widow of Evorwac of Ipswich, had made a similar agreement and had paid £2 that year and owed 4 marks.[198] In Lincolnshire Earl Ranulf (de Gernon) of Chester and his mother, Lucy of Bolingbroke, the great heiress, are recorded as being heavily in debt as the result of the death of Earl Ranulf le Meschin. Among other things he owed the king 500 marks for the agreement which the king had made between him and his mother concerning her dower lands. She owed the king 45 marks for the same agreement, and had paid 20 marks of this to the queen on the king's orders. She also accounted for 300 marks for her father's lands (she had paid in 200) and for 500 marks for permission to remain unmarried for five years. This was a *cri de coeur*.[199] In Kent Turgis of Avranches had offered the king 300 marks of silver and 1 of gold and one warhorse for the land and widow of Hugh of Abertiville and to have custody of Hugh's son until he should be twenty years old. He had paid one instalment of £40.[200] Possibly under the general rule that all transfers of land had to be paid for, widows regularly had to pay to get possession of their entitlements. In Norfolk Basilia, widow of Odo of Dammartin, had agreed to pay 60 marks in order to get her dower lands.[201] In Kent Agnes widow of Geoffrey Talbot owed 2 marks of gold for having her dower lands and marriage portion.[202] Under Colchester the royal servant Haimo of St Clare answered for 135 marks, of which he had paid 50, for his wife with her *dos* and *maritagium*.[203]

Orderic Vitalis mentions a few fines demanded by William Rufus, all in connexion with the Montgomery family, into whose household the chronicler had been born. In 1096 the king fined Hugh earl of Shrewsbury £3,000 for implication in the conspiracy of the previous year and required 'enormous sums' from the others involved. In 1098–9, after Hugh's death, he demanded the same amount from Robert of Bellême for his succession to his brother's earldom and 'a great sum of money' for Robert's succession to, or wardship of, the lands of his dead kinsman, Roger of Bully, which included the important castle of Tickhill.[204] William was selling valuable commodities, and Orderic thought that he knew their worth; but in the absence of Pipe Rolls we cannot tell how much cash he collected.

[197] *Ibid.*, 92.
[198] *Ibid.*, 96.
[199] *Ibid.*, 110. For her previous (probably forced) three marriages, apparently without intermission, see above, 172.
[200] *Ibid.*, 67.
[201] *Ibid.*, 94.
[202] *Ibid.*, 67.
[203] *Ibid.*, 139.
[204] OV, iv, 284; v, 224–6.

Lastly under the heading of feudal incidents we come to aids. When regulated by Magna Carta (cap. 12), a distinction was made between the obligatory payments and gracious aids. As William II had no son to dub knight and no daughter to marry, and never had to be ransomed, he had no call except on the generosity of his barons and others. But this probably did not deter him. There is some evidence that in the Norman period the aid (*auxilium*) was both a loose expression and a euphemism. It can hardly be separated from the gift (*donum*), and could be extracted arbitrarily. William II asked the newly consecrated archbishop of Canterbury, Anselm, for an aid, and the prelate, although he thought it might be simoniacal, offered the totally unacceptable sum of £500.[205] The danegeld raised in 1096 to pay Robert for Normandy was in part an aid,[206] and the sums taken from counties and boroughs in Henry I's reign in lieu of danegeld were given the same title.[207] According to the Winchester annalist, who was well placed in respect of financial matters, Ranulf Flambard not only exploited vacant churches on behalf of the king but also took from the others, presumably bishoprics and abbeys, on the average 300–400 marks a year. As this remark occurs under the year 1097, when the chaplain and the bishop of Winchester were acting for the king during his absence abroad, these exactions are probably part of the exceptional measures taken to meet the war expenditure of the latter part of the reign. And the chronicler thought that it was William's demand for the immediate payment of £200, which arrived after the bishop had started to celebrate Mass on Christmas day 1097, that caused Walkelin's death ten days later. For the prelate knew that he could not raise this sum without robbing the poor or despoiling the treasuries of the church, and, weary of such things, he prayed God to release him from his tribulations.[208] How the £200 should be described we cannot say; but it would seem that in the Norman period 'aid' was often extortion in disguise, a tax irregular in incidence and various in its application.

Our last subdivision of 'pleas and covenants' – miscellaneous sales and profits – is composed of little more than the loose ends of those we have already examined. One of the most lucrative components, the sale of offices, is, when it was a freely negotiable bargain, related to *gersums* like those paid by sheriffs for their counties or to the farm of any lucrative royal right, but, when concerned with an office which was considered hereditary, is more akin to a relief, and subject to the same rules or mis-

[205] See below, 327.
[206] See above, 246, and cf. *dona* taken from the tenants of the bishopric of Durham, above, 236.
[207] Richard fitzNeal considers aids and gifts of cities and boroughs, *Dialogus*, 108–9.
[208] *Ann. Winton*, ii, 39.

rule. These quasi-hereditary offices are almost entirely serjeanties, with the ministry attached fairly firmly to the tenure of land.[209] We can again take some examples from the Pipe Roll of 1130; and four purchases of office occur closely together under Wiltshire.[210] Humphrey de Bohun accounts for £22 10s as a relief for his father's land and for 400 marks to be the king's steward. John the Marshal owes £22 13s 4d for his father's office and land. Adam de Port has bought a royal stewardship and still owes £5 13s 4d. And William fitzHerbert of St Valery is still responsible for £2 6s 8d owed for the land and office of his father. As would be expected, it is the non-hereditary and also more profitable offices which fetch the highest prices. In 1130 Geoffrey Rufus, the king's chancellor since 1123 and Ranulf Flambard's successor at Durham (1133), still owed £3,006 13s 4d (4,510 marks) 'for his seal'.[211] But such fines were not always collected in full. As Geoffrey had not paid anything off in 1129–30, it looks as though his debt was in abeyance; and if he had to settle it when he was given his bishopric, no one was guilty of simony.

In 1130 guilds of weavers, fullers and cordwainers were paying the king in ounces or marks of gold for their guilds;[212] and as these were serious debts they formed a useful addition to the royal income. It is not known, however, whether such craft and merchant guilds go back to William II's reign. Beyond this point it is difficult to classify sales; and we can take as an example of miscellaneous purchases those for which Hervey bishop of Ely accounted under Cambridgeshire.[213] He had bought for at least $7\frac{1}{2}$ marks of gold an office for his nephew William; he had made long ago for at least 100 marks of silver an agreement with the king in Normandy; he owed £100 for a lawsuit between him and the abbots of Bury St Edmunds and Ramsey; he had tendered at least £240 so that the knights enfeoffed on the bishopric surplus to the service owed should not be counted for fiscal or service purposes and that Chatteris abbey should be free of wardpenny; he had bought for £1,000 (and actually paid that year £364 on account) the privilege that the episcopal knights should perform castle guard at his own castle on the Isle of Ely instead of at the royal castle at Norwich; and, finally, his nephew Richard paid a fine in respect of land which his uncle had given him.

Among miscellaneous profits, treasure trove,[214] or fines for concealing

[209] See above, 138.
[210] *PR 31 H.I*, 18.
[211] *Ibid.*, 140.
[212] E.g. the weavers and cordwainers of Oxford, *ibid.*, 2, 5; the weavers of Lincoln, 109, 114; the weavers and fullers of Winchester, 37; the weavers of London, 144; and a man fined to become an alderman in the merchant guild of York, 34.
[213] *Ibid.*, 44–5.
[214] Cf. *Dialogus*, 98.

treasure, and wreck occur not infrequently, but do not amount to much. In this area the main feature is the large number of small payments which, although but a fraction of the total indebtedness, together made a sizeable contribution to the royal revenue. The yield could probably have been increased a little if the king had instructed his finance officers to put more pressure on his debtors, but the more spectacular sums were owed by his familiars and servants, men whom he had no wish to harry until they fell from grace. Indeed, at that social level indebtedness was a method of royal control: those who owed him money were very much at his mercy. One false step, and he would begin to distrain on the debtor's chattels, then on his land, and finally on his person, in order to enforce payment.[215] The political manipulation of indebtedness is often regarded as one of the crafty measures of King John, but in fact it seems an ordinary feature of Norman and Angevin kingship.

Although the royal revenue has had to be illustrated mostly from examples taken from 1129–30, there is no reason to doubt that Henry I for the most part followed in his elder brother's footsteps, and, as it is likely that both kings became more rapacious in the later parts of their reigns, that William by 1100 was gathering in at least as much money as Henry received in a period of peace thirty years later. If so, we can estimate his ordinary annual cash revenue at some £29,000, made up of about £15,000 from the estates in his hands, £4,000 (at 2s the hide) from danegeld, and up to £10,000 from 'pleas and covenants'.[216] These are probably minimal figures, and it is quite clear that William in his last four years pushed up his revenue considerably, perhaps at times even doubled it. He was receiving not only greater sums from the English church but also all the Norman ducal revenues, whatever those may have been. Even Maine could have contributed something to the cost of its acquisition. Twenty-nine thousand pounds of silver was the equivalent (at 15s the oz) of 39,000 oz of gold. Perhaps a more useful means of evalution is to look at some prices and wages. In 1130 a warhorse was usually valued by the Exchequer at £2 and a palfrey and riding horse at £1–£1 10s.[217] An ox could be bought for 3s and a sheep for under 5d.[218] The carcass of a grazing ox cost 1s and that of a sheep 4d, while enough

[215] Richard fitzNeal gives much space to the treatment of defaulting debtors and the law of distress: cf. *Dialogus*, 106 ff., 119.

[216] Ramsay, *The Revenues of the Kings of England*, i, 7, thought that William II's income should be placed between that of Henry I, which he estimated at something less than £28,000, and that of William I, which he estimated at under £20,000 (p.3), and came down for £25,000. He did not believe, however, that either of the Williams levied danegeld annually.

[217] Cf. *PR 31 II.I*, 85, 125; 100, 118, 134.

[218] *Ibid.*, 122.

wheat to bake bread for a hundred men could be had for 1s.[219] The daily wage (less livery and maintenance) of the top royal minister, the chancellor, was, as we have seen, 5s a day, and that of the meanest household servants 1d.[220] A cavalry soldier, a knight, could be hired for 8d a day.[221] In these circumstances an unencumbered income of £29,000 a year went quite far, and twice as much was wealth indeed.[222]

The Norman kings of England were very rich, perhaps richer than some of their Angevin successors. Richard fitzNeal in his treatise on the Exchequer was not much concerned with royal expenditure, but in his dedication of the work to Henry II he allowed himself to say that although the government and safety of a kingdom depended on the ruler's wisdom, strength, moderation and justice, money was a necessary instrument of power in both peace and war. In times of peace, worthy objects for the prince's money were the building of churches and the relief of the poor, in wartime the fortification of castles and soldiers' pay. Money was intended not to be hoarded but to be spent – in proper causes and on proper objects. These were the true purposes of a noble mind.[223] William II might have earned only half that encomium, but in his day he was widely considered to be *rex magnanimus*, a king more generous than his peers. The household expenses of such an ostentatious prince were considerable. He had to pay wages to soldiers and subsidies to friends and allies, and meet all the other costs of his military campaigns. Castles had to be maintained, improved and provisioned, horses and arms purchased, and ransoms paid for his captured knights. There were also occasionally great investments or capital expenditures. He took Normandy in pawn and planned to follow suit with Poitou. He had a great hall built for him in the palace at Westminster. There was nothing dishonourable in any of this. On the contrary, it did him great credit. But all could see that the expenditure was not only financed by extortion but also was entirely one-sided, aimed at worldly glory.

[219] *Dialogus*, 41.

[220] See above, 136–7.

[221] *Ibid.*; *Dialogus*, 13; Round *FE*, 271 ff.

[222] M. Pacaut, *Louis VII et son Royaume* (Paris 1964), 155–8, estimates the annual revenue of Louis VII of France (1137–80) at about 200,000 *livres parisis*, that is to say about £62,500 sterling. His figures, however, are not of the same kind as the English net receipts used here and the total appears to be much more speculative. No one, including the early Capetians themselves, seems to have thought that they were wealthier than the Norman kings of England.

[223] *Dialogus*, 1–3.

THE ESTIMATED REVENUE FROM ECCLESIASTICAL CUSTODIES

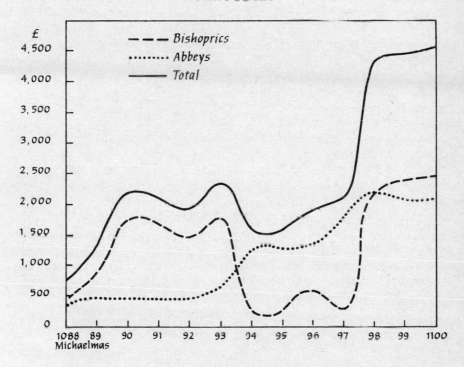

THE FARMS OF THE BISHOPRICS
(all figures are *per annum*)

Diocese	Domesday Value	Typical farm in Henry II's reign[1]	Suggested figure for William II's reign
Canterbury	1,324[2]	1,350	1,350
Chichester[3]	109	240	110
Durham	—	—	300
Hereford[4]	195	270	200
Lincoln[5]	325	900	400
Salisbury	436	410	440
Wells[6]	163	—	180
Winchester[7]	802	1,440	820
Worcester	313	300	320

1. Selected from Margaret Howell's tables, *Regalian Right*, 211 ff.
2. Salley Harvey, 'Domesday Book and Anglo-Norman Governance', 184–5, makes the figure about £1,586.
3. The *DB* figures are unambiguous, but the disparity is awkward.
4. *DB* does not distinguish clearly between the lands of the bishop and those of the canons. Here the disparity is probably due to the devastated state of the lands in 1086.
5. Although there is a large gap, the twelve demesne manors of the bishop mentioned in *DB*, i, 190b, seem to be accounted for.
6. The next bishop added the city and abbey of Bath, so there are no comparable figures.
7. Another case of an inexplicable disparity.

Chapter 6

THE THREE BROTHERS (1088–1095)

Orderic Vitalis wrote that William Rufus never forgave his uncle Odo, for he was so imperious (*magnanimus*), irascible and tenacious of memory that he was loth to forget any injury he had suffered unless he had had his revenge. Bitterly and swelling with anger, he recalled that Odo had dared to raise a rebellion against him.[1] His attitude towards his brother Robert was, however, not so inflexible. Robert too had done him an injury, but he was his elder brother, to whom he had possibly done homage before 1087,[2] and there had been no enormity in his behaviour in 1087 8. It had not been an unexpected and painful betrayal by a friend. The two had never been close: indeed, they had been rivals for years; and the king was prepared to continue on that footing. He would pay Robert back in the same coin when the opportunity arose, and throw in something more for good measure. As for Henry, he was still a cub whose erratic behaviour his brothers tolerated a little impatiently until it became too much to bear, and then they smacked him down. Although there is little to suggest that William loved his brothers, he was always correct in his treatment of social equals. He was innocent alike of the unremitting severity of his father, the faithlessness of Robert and the cruelty of Henry. Given the territorial situation after 1087, for which he himself had little direct responsibility, he played a part which quickly attracted the most support in the Anglo-Norman world. He was, of course, the wealthiest of the brothers.

Their rivalry involved them in the seduction of each other's vassals, a costly business whether in gifts of money or land or in promises, and in general at the expense of princely authority and to the profit of the magnates. Although it might be thought that such activity raised important legal and moral problems both for the seducers and the seduced, there are few signs of these in contemporary literature. Orderic put the issue in the 'debates' of the barons in 1087–8 largely in terms of the suitability of the candidates to rule; at all events, he seems to have thought that after the Conqueror's death the barons were free to choose.[3] Nowhere does he set up the case of an individual baron troubled

[1] OV, iv, 209; repeated and embroidered, v, 208 ff.
[2] See above, 29
[3] See above, 71, 81.

in his conscience by conflicting claims on his loyalty. There is, however, the interesting case of Nivard of Septeuil in 1098–9.[4]

In the sagas and epics, fidelity to a man's lord is regarded as one of the supreme virtues; but in practice a vassal was sometimes in difficulty. Many landholders had several lords and often conflicting duties, and even if there was a doctrine of liege-lordship and homage, it was the relative power of the lords which seems often to have determined the vassal's allegiance in a particular situation. The problem – or opportunity – was greatest for the marcher barons. Contemporary morality was shocked only if there was personal treachery or a man changed sides too often. Henry may have incurred some contempt in 1087–94 for his unprincipled manoeuvres. In general the barons seem to have been able to perform their duties to their several lords without falling completely foul of any; and when it was necessary to make a decisive choice – as between William II and Robert – to have adhered to their decision once made.

Some men, of course, had little choice and were simply the victims of circumstance. Such a one was Edgar Ætheling, the grandson of Edmund Ironside, and, like his father Edward, destined to a life in exile.[5] In 1074 he had crossed from Flanders to his brother-in-law's court in Scotland, then accepted an offer from Philip of France of the town of Montreuil-sur-Mer as a base against the Normans, but, after shipwreck on the voyage out, returned to Scotland and, on the advice of King Malcolm and Queen Margaret, his sister, sued the Conqueror for pardon. When this was granted, he joined the king in Normandy.[6] He is next noticed in 1086, when, with the king's permission, he decided to seek his fortune in Norman Italy and left for Apulia with two hundred knights, whereupon his sister, Christina, entered Romsey abbey in Hampshire.[7] In view of his notorious restlessness it seems unlikely that he had spent the whole of the last twelve years at the royal court, and it is possible that he had attached himself for a time to Robert Curthose, whose contemporary he was, and shared his misadventures, for they were friends later in life. This would explain his breach with the Conqueror. William of Malmesbury, however, in a rather unsympathetic notice,[8] depicts Edgar idling away many shameful years at court and behaving so foolishly that once he surrendered to the king his daily allowance of £1 in return for just one horse. Perhaps the chronicler thought that he should have been more of a patriot. The Ætheling had

---

[4] Below, 394.
[5] For his earlier history, see Barlow, *Edward the Confessor*, 217–18, 244–5.
[6] *ASC D, s.a.*, cf. E.
[7] *ASC, s.a.*; Florence, ii, 19.
[8] *GR*, ii, 309–10.

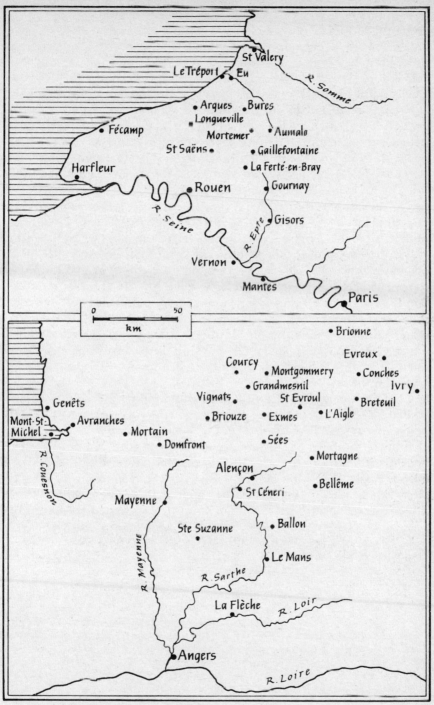

2. Normandy (Upper and Lower) 1087–1091

certainly become a typical boon-companion, and, if he really went to Apulia, he was soon back, for he rejoined Robert shortly after he became duke, and in 1088–9, according to Orderic,[9] was one of his chief counsellors. Later, as we shall see, he flitted between the Norman, English and Scottish courts, obviously always welcome for a time.

Greater men had more independence. The Beaumont family had acquired a great marcher principality.[10] Possessing the lordships of Beaumont-le-Roger and Pont-Audemer in Normandy south of the Seine, the county of Meulan in France and large estates and earldoms in England, but weakened by the enmity of the Tosny family, it tried to solve its problems by dividing its honours within the kin. In 1089–90, when Duke Robert imprisoned Robert count of Meulan, a veteran of the battle of Hastings, who had crossed from England, Roger of Beaumont interceded for his son. Orderic tells how he recalled his own unblemished *fidelitas* to the duke, his father and grandfather; and the duke, acknowledging the old man's constant 'legality', granted him his request. Roger indeed remained loyal to his lord until he retired to the family monastery at Préaux, in preparation for his death.[11] His elder son, Robert count of Meulan, as an 'international' noble, seems to have managed to keep in with both brothers, although it is possible that he did not like William over much; certainly he seems to have preferred Henry I as king.[12] The cadet, Henry of Beaumont, however, attached himself from the beginning to William.

The family of Bellême-Montgomery was similarly placed in the south. William Talvas had possessed a large collection of fiefs strung along the Norman marches from Brittany to the Vexin, held variously of the king of France, the duke of Normandy and the count of Maine. When his heiress, the notorious Mabel Talvas of Bellême, married a great Norman baron, Roger II of Montgomery, *vicomte* of the Hiémois, who after the Conquest received West Sussex and later most of Shropshire with the title of earl (of Shrewsbury), a major dynasty was created.[13] After Mabel

[9] OV, iv, 186; cf. v, 272, where it is also said that Robert was *quasi collactaneus*, almost a foster-brother, which is clearly an exaggeration.

[10] See above, 77 n. 111.

[11] OV, iv, 204 ff., 302.

[12] Robert witnessed charters of Duke Robert in 1087 (Haskins, *NI*, 285), 1088 (*Regesta*, no. 299), 1089 (*ibid.*, no. 310), 1091 (*ibid.*, no. 317), Feb. 1092 (Haskins, p. 68, no. 7), 1091–2 (*ibid.*, no. 8), 1091–5 (*ibid.*, p. 292), and 15 Aug. 1095 (*Regesta*, no. 384). See also below, 282, 286. But he was in England in 1089 (below, 271), 1090–1 (below, 278), in the summer and at Christmas 1093 (below, 306, 326), and probably in Feb. 1095 (below, 341). In 1094 he succeeded to his father's lands in Normandy and England and transferred his own English lands to his younger brother Henry (above, p. 169–70).

[13] For the family, see J. Boussard, 'La seigneurie de Bellême aux Xe et XIe siècles', *Mélanges Louis Halphen* (Paris 1951), 43; Mason, 'Roger de Montgomery and his sons', 1; M. Chibnall, 'The descent and lands of the lords of Bellême', OV, ii, 362 ff.

was murdered in 1077/9, their son, Robert of Bellême, inherited her estates with the castles of Bellême, Alençon and Domfront[14] and the bishopric of Sées; and the Conqueror, who loved this family well, obtained for him a marriage with the heiress to the county of Ponthieu, at the other extremity of the duchy. Robert, who had been one of Robert Curthose's companions in the years before 1087, started by supporting the new duke, but although, after their quarrel in 1088, he played more for his own hand, because of his geographical situation he looked more to the king of France than to the king of England. Orderic, a neighbour at St Evroul, disliked him intensely. He depicts him as a strong and intelligent man, subtle and faithless, and with a plausible tongue; a fine soldier, pre-eminent in the family skills of castle-building and military engineering, but a man of many vices: hostile to the church, insatiable in his avarice and lust, above all horribly cruel, torturing and mutilating those enemies who fell into his clutches.[15]

William Rufus was less pliant than his elder brother and, as a king, less tolerant of changes of allegiance. Orderic makes him in 1088 refer to rebels only as traitors, perjurers and criminals, and imagines those who pleaded for them either using the argument of expediency or drawing attention to their past services.[16] In the eyes of William II, a change of allegiance could not be legalized by a formal renunciation of fealty, the *diffidatio*, justified by an alleged offence on the part of the lord. Those who deserted him in 1088, whatever their excuse, were traitors, although, as we have seen, he did not push the theory very hard except in a few cases. Whereas lords, especially kings, tended to be authoritarian, most vassals inclined in the opposite direction, and in 1087–96 individual Anglo-Norman barons seem to have considered themselves free to choose between the two senior brothers, but normally took no action until the political or military situation made it possible or necessary. Neither ruler punished rebel barons with any penalty more severe than confiscation of fiefs or limited imprisonment before 1096. In that year William was more brutal.[17]

It was in this world of allegiances which shifted according to pressure exerted or inducements offered that the three brothers operated. As soldiers there was little to choose between them, although a case could be made for Henry's superiority. As paymaster, William had no equal. In 1088 it was Henry who came off worst. In July he abandoned the irresolute Robert in favour of the victorious king, was then rebuffed by William, and when he returned to Normandy with Robert of Bellême,

---

[14] These, of course, were only his main fortresses: OV, iv, 300; vi, 398, writes of his 34 very strong *castella*.

[15] OV, iv, 158–60; cf. Mason, *loc. cit.*, 24 ff.

[16] Cf. OV, iv, 120 ff., 128 ff.

[17] Below, 357–8.

one of the captains at Rochester whom the king had released,[18] was with his companion immediately arrested by the duke, probably on the advice of Odo of Bayeux.[19] Robert may well have thought that both had betrayed him by making their peace with William, and he also coveted their lands. He had used up on the unsuccessful English campaign the money he had received from Henry for the Cotentin and Avranchin,[20] and, as Odo wanted him to assert his authority in Maine, the capture of Robert of Bellême opened the way and secured his left flank. On the other hand, the action confirmed the allegiance of Robert's father, Roger earl of Shrewsbury, to William, and provoked the earl with the king's permission to cross to the Montgomery estates in Normandy and fortify his castles so that he could intercede with, or threaten, the duke.[21]

Odo, who was put in charge of the prisoners,[22] also, if Orderic can be trusted, gave the duke some good advice, which the chronicler puts in the form of an amusing speech in the ducal court at Rouen.[23] It is likely that the bishop, now aware that his nephew's rule would be confined to the duchy, was anxious that he should take the opportunity to assert his authority throughout his dominions and so strengthen his position that it could not be challenged by William. Particularly he urged Robert to march on Le Mans, secure Maine, and then attack Roger of Mont-gomery and eradicate him and all his evil seed from the land for ever. Nine strong castles and more were in their hands, and from some of them (including Alençon and Domfront) Robert of Bellême had expelled the ducal garrisons in 1087 on hearing of the Conqueror's death. Odo knew full well that ducal power was weakest in that sector.

In August Robert led an expedition into the southern marches.[24] His commanders were Odo, who owed him the service of twenty knights,[25] William count of Evreux, Ralf II of Tosny or Conches and William of Breteuil. The three nobles came from south-east Normandy, between the rivers Risle and Eure, and were closely related. Ralf of Tosny and William of Evreux were half-brothers, for their mother, Godeheut, had

[18] See above, 90.

[19] OV, iv, 148. Torigny, *Interpolation*, 269, has Robert, 'at the suggestion of wicked men', arrest Henry at Rouen and dispossess him of his lands.

[20] *GR*, ii, 468.

[21] OV, iv, 149.

[22] *GR*, ii, 468–9, has Robert imprison Henry in the castle at Rouen; OV, iv, 148, has Robert entrust both prisoners to Odo, who kept Henry at Bayeux and Robert at Neuilly-l'Evêque. The English chronicler is not well informed on these events, and the Norman is to be preferred.

[23] OV, iv, 150 ff.

[24] OV, iv, 154 ff.

[25] Haskins, *NI*, 8, 15–17. See also Bates, *Normandy before 1066*, 168–9, on the quotas.

married successively Roger I of Tosny and Richard count of Evreux. William of Breteuil, one of the duke's companions in his years of exile, was their nephew, for his father, the great William fitzOsbern, earl of Hereford, had married Ralf's sister.[26] Through both William of Evreux, a great-grandson of Duke Richard I, and William fitzOsbern, they were related to Odo and Robert Curthose. The seniors were also men of great military experience. Odo, William of Evreux and Ralf had fought at Hastings, and Ralf had been in the army at Mortemer in 1054. William of Breteuil's father had had an important command at Hastings. Some of the best veteran captains were prepared to serve the duke, and in August and September 1088 they carried all before them. Robert made a triumphant entry into Le Mans and also received the submission of most of the nobility, including Geoffrey of Mayenne, Robert the Burgundian lord of Craon and Sablé, and Helias of La Flèche. The only two castles which resisted, Ballon in Maine and Robert of Bellême's stronghold of St-Céneri, south-west of Alençon, were forced to surrender; and, to inspire terror, the duke had the castellan of St-Céneri blinded and other defenders mutilated. Orderic believed that as a result the garrisons of Alençon and Bellême were preparing to submit, but the duke, when total victory was within his grasp, not only abandoned the campaign but also made his peace with Roger of Montgomery and released Robert of Bellême from prison. They may have engaged to promote his interests in the region. Henry seems to have been let out some time later.[27]

Robert Curthose's belated show of strength in 1088 was not enough to convince the Norman magnates that he was a changed man, and the next year saw the onset of the anarchy which many had hoped for or feared. South and south-west of St Evroul are the hills and forests which form the watershed between the valley and estuary of the Seine and the valley of the Loire, in the eleventh century an area of frontier lordships with strong castles, and it is to the crescent from Evreux in the east to Vignats in the west that Orderic Vitalis pays the closest attention. But ducal power in the marches of Normandy had diminished even under the Conqueror after 1066, and after his death there was a more general collapse. Barons were able to reactivate all the claims to land which lay

---

[26] See genealogical table, below, 468, no. 7.

[27] OV, iv, 158. William of Malmesbury, *GR*, ii, 468-9, who was not concerned with Robert of Bellême, says that Henry was released *post medium annum*, after six months or after June, then spent more than a year in England before returning to Normandy shortly before February 1091. Nothing firm can be based on this. OV mentions Henry's release, 'at the petition of the magnates', in an undateable context: iv, 164. It would seem that Henry was set free after Robert, but the date and his subsequent movements before 1091 are completely obscure.

dormant in feudal society, and this led to a complex series of feuds and
wars, usually between branches of the same family. There is archaeological evidence for a spate of unlicensed castle building by the magnates at this time.[28] It was this widespread rejection of the *status quo*
which gave an opportunity to the bigger operators, like Robert of
Bellême, Henry and William Rufus, to manipulate the rebelliousness in
their own interests. As chronology is not Orderic's strongest point, and
the events of 1088–92 are particularly difficult to put in order, it is
simpler to sketch the situation on a geographical basis, starting with the
south-west.

Maine was already in revolt by 1089. Duke Robert appealed to his
overlord for the county, the count of Anjou, and the much-married and
dissolute Fulk the Surly named as his price Robert's help in securing the
hand of Bertrada, daughter of Simon the Elder of Montfort (-l'Amaury)
and niece of William count of Evreux, whose wife Helwise was bringing
her up. William for his part demanded the 'return' to himself and his
nephew, William of Breteuil, of a string of estates which he claimed were
theirs by hereditary right but had been retained by the Conqueror.
Robert complied, and Fulk, who married Bertrada before 24 April 1090,
only to lose her in May 1092 to King Philip of France, managed to keep
the Manceaux quiet for the best part of a year.[29]

The dissident barons, however, led by Geoffrey of Mayenne in the
north and the youthful Helias of La Flèche in the south, imprisoned the
pro-Norman bishop of Le Mans, Hoël, expelled the Norman castellans,
and procured a claimant to the comital title in Hugh of Este, younger
son of Azzo marquess of Liguria, a nobleman of high rank, and
Gersendis, sister of Hugh IV of Maine. But Hugh proved unsatisfactory,
and in the summer of 1091 or 1092 sold his title to his cousin, Helias, the
son of Paula, Gersendis's sister, and John of La Flèche.[30] Helias, a man
greatly admired by Orderic, was a claimant with whom the Norman
dukes had to come to terms.

Further to the north-east, Geoffrey II count of Mortagne and Perche,
another who had fought at Hastings,[31] waged war on his kinsman
Robert of Bellême because of a dispute over land.[32] When Duke Robert
gave the castle of Exmes in the marches of Normandy and Bellême to his

[28] Bates, *Normandy before 1066*, 114–15.

[29] OV, iv, 182–6, 260–4. Latouche, *Maine*, 41.

[30] OV, iv, 192–8; *Act. Pont. Cen.*, 393. Latouche, *Maine*, 41 ff. Bishop Hoël took refuge
in England: see below, 278. The date of Helias's purchase was either 1091 or 1092:
Latouche preferred the latter, but may well have been wrong.

[31] *GG*, 196.

[32] OV, iv, 160–2, and see genealogical tables 4, 6. Fliche, *Philippe I*, 40 ff., 226–7, is
sceptical of OV's story about Bertrada.

faithful vassal, Gilbert, son of Engenulf of L'Aigle, on the other side of St Evroul, Robert of Bellême attacked it, and in the following year (1090 or 1091) Gilbert was ambushed and killed. Geoffrey of Mortagne then made an alliance with Gilbert's nephew of the same name and gave him his daughter in marriage.[33]

Further north, the Evrécin was particularly disturbed, and the Norman frontier castle of Ivry-la-Bataille was in frequent dispute. In 1089 its castellan, Ascelin Goel, a vassal of William of Bretcuil, surrendered it to Duke Robert. William bought it back and campaigned against the castellan. He had a success when Amaury III of Montfort, Bertrada's brother, who was supporting the rebel, was killed, but, possibly in February 1091, was defeated in battle and captured by Ascelin, aided by Amaury's brother Richard and some French knights. He had to pay the castellan an enormous ransom, give him his daughter to wife, and abandon Ivry.[34]

Another claimant to that castle was Robert count of Meulan, who, 'puffed up with the gifts and promises of King William', crossed from England probably in the autumn of 1089,[35] to demand its return on the grounds that his father, Roger of Beaumont, had held it. Robert Curthose, however, refused the request, pointing out that Ivry had been exchanged by Roger for Brionne, and, when his visitor repudiated that bargain, had him imprisoned and entrusted Brionne to Robert of Meules, the grandson of Count Gilbert, the founder of the stronghold.[36] But through the crafty intervention of Roger of Beaumont not only was his son released but the duke also agreed to sell Brionne back, and, possibly in June 1090, helped the Beaumonts to take it by storm from the new constable. In the end, Robert of Meules was compensated elsewhere.[37] Bec abbey told a rather different story.[38] Robert of Meulan, after he had guilefully obtained Brionne from the duke, tried to enforce his lordship over Abbot Anselm and the monastery; but the abbot resisted skilfully and the monks indignantly, and in the end the duke, angered by this attempted usurpation, took Brionne back and gave it to the hereditary claimant, Roger de Bienfaite (possibly a mistake for his

[33] OV, iv, 200–202, and see below, genealogical table 4.

[34] OV, iv, 198–202.

[35] J. Yver and M. Chibnall accept OV's date, spring 1090: OV, iv, 204 n. But Robert of Meulan witnessed Duke Robert's charter dated at Eu almost certainly in 1089: below, 273. He was back in England by January 1091: below, 278.

[36] See below, genealogical table 10.

[37] OV, iv, 204 ff.

[38] 'De libertate Beccensis monasterii', J. Mabillon, *Annales Ordinis S. Benedicti*, v (Paris 1713), app. no. xii, pp. 636–7, cf. 245–6. Sally N. Vaughn, 'St Anselm of Canterbury: the philosopher saint as politician', *Journal of Medieval History*, i (1975), 282–3, suggests that Anselm's complaint was the main cause of the count's imprisonment by the duke.

cousin, Robert of Meules). However that may be, it is clear that the count of Meulan, when in possession of Brionne some time between 1088 and the autumn of 1090, came into conflict with Anselm and his monks. Later, as a counsellor of William II and Henry I, he was several times involved in disputes between Anselm, as archbishop of Canterbury, and the king; and the obvious coolness in their relations could easily have originated in this quarrel.

The area was also disturbed by the enmity between the wives of the half-brothers and neighbours, Ralf of Tosny and William count of Evreux. The latter was married to Helwise, daughter of William count of Nevers. The Tosny family had migrated from the French Vexin and Ralf likewise married outside Normandy. He had obtained from Simon the Elder of Montfort his daughter Isabel or Elizabeth as a reward for providing him with William's sister Agnes, his own half-sister, whom he had abducted at night. Agnes became the mother of Amaury III, Richard and Bertrada, whom we have already met. The feuding wives are two of the small number of women to whom Orderic deigns to pay much attention. He says that both ruled their husbands and oppressed their vassals; both were beautiful, talkative and lively, but while Helwise was shrewd, cruel and mean, Isabel was generous, high-spirited and playful, popular with all. Elsewhere he remarks that in widowhood she atoned for the lust to which she was too much addicted in her youth.[39] An Amazon queen, she went on campaign dressed and armed like a knight and always acquitted herself well. Regardless of this, in this war, which Orderic attributes to Helwise's resentment at something said about her by Isabel, the troops of Conches seem to have had the worst of it, for Ralf called on the duke for help. When his plea was disregarded, he turned to the king of England, who ordered his supporters to go to his aid.[40]

The duke himself is noticed mainly in Upper Normandy, north of the Seine, for that, although the traditional main base for ducal power, was also the area most susceptible to the kings of France and England. On 24 April 1089 he was at Vernon, west of the Epte, which was the effective frontier with the French royal demesne, 'about to invade France',[41] and later he besieged the stronghold of the count of Eu on the northern boundary.[42] Also in 1089, this time in alliance with Philip of France, he

[39] OV, iii, 126–8.

[40] OV, iv, 212 ff.

[41] *Regesta*, no. 308, dated with details in the cartulary copy.

[42] *Ibid.*, no. 310, dated with details in the cartulary: 'dum idem Robertus esset ad obsidionem Auci ea die qua idem castrum sibi redditum est.' As the count of Eu seems never to have lost complete control of the *caput* of his county, he may have held the castle when the town (*castrum*) surrendered. The name of the count is not given. According to

attacked La Ferté-en-Bray, a castle of Gerard of Gournay in the north-east, and in return for the king's help granted him the strategic manor of Gisors on the Epte, which belonged to the archbishop of Rouen.[43] As the count of Eu and Gerard were soon to show themselves supporters of William Rufus, Robert may have been making a preventive strike. On the evidence of the witness lists to charters granted at Vernon and Eu, Robert had with him his captains, Odo of Bayeux, William count of Evreux, and William of Breteuil, and his constable, Robert I of Montfort (-sur-Risle), the brother of Hugh III, who was in England.[44] Also in attendance at Eu was Robert count of Meulan, recently arrived from the kingdom;[45] and present at both places were Robert's confiden-tial advisers, William of Arques, monk of Molesme, and the exiled William bishop of Durham. But Edgar Ætheling, another exile in Normandy, does not witness.

By 1090 William Rufus had decided to intervene in Normandy. Orderic imagines him summoning his barons with their knights to Winchester and addressing them on the subject.[46] He advanced two main reasons: the need to avenge himself on his brother and an appeal from the Norman church, which was suffering from the anarchy. His barons approved the project. The plan was to buy the allegiance of barons in Upper Normandy. Among those whom he attached to his side were Walter of St Valery in the county of Ponthieu, who controlled an important harbour on the River Somme; his cousin, Stephen of Aumale on the river Bresle, the son of Odo count of Champagne, who had been his Aunt Adelaide's third husband; Robert count of Eu; Gerard of Gournay, with his three castles (Gournay, La Ferté-en-Bray, Gaillefon-taine) on the high land between the sources of the Bresle and the Epte; Walter Giffard (II) of Longueville-en-Caux and a large landowner in England; and Ralf (I) of Mortemer-sur-Eaulne and lord of Wigmore in the Welsh marches, Stephen of Aumale's present or future father-in-law. What these lords did was to put their castles on a war footing at the

OV, it was the old Robert, who had fought at Mortemer (1054), who went over to King William in 1090, and this would be the last known act of his life. He was succeeded by his son William, already a large landowner in England and one of the conspirators of 1088: see above, 73 ff. According to Torigny, *Interpolation*, 270, the count in 1090 was this William.

[43] For the castle, OV, iv, 182. For the joint attack and the grant of Gisors, dated 1089 in the abbey of Fécamp's account, *Gallia Christiana*, xi, instr. 18, reprinted *RHF*, xiv, 68. Fliche, *Philippe I*, 292-3, 299-301, would correct the date to 1090 or 1091. David, *RC*, 81, accepts 1089. Duke Robert attested a grant of Gerard's to Bec, presumably before this event: Haskins, *NI*, 68, no. 9.

[44] For the family, see Douglas, *Domesday Monachorum*, chart, p. 70.

[45] See above, 271 and n. 35.

[46] OV, iv, 178-80.

king's expense and also garrison them with mercenary knights paid by the king.[47] It was 1088 in reverse, particularly for Ralf of Mortemer.

By the summer of 1090 the marches of Normandy from Maine to the Evrécin were in disorder; William had secured the allegiance of perhaps the greater part of Upper Normandy; and Count Henry was striving to make his apanage independent.[48] He too fortified his castles, looked to his vassals and friends and recruited mercenaries. He had with him Hugh of Avranches, earl of Chester, and Richard (I) of Reviers, later to be rewarded in England with the honour of Plympton and become the ancestor of the earls of Devon.[49] In October William's friends instigated a revolt in Rouen.[50] The merchants of the city were no doubt suffering both from the anarchy in the duchy and the severance of the link with London. The leader of the malcontents was Conan, son of Gilbert Pilatus, the richest and most powerful of the citizens, who had his own military resources and organized a faction. The plan seems to have been that at the beginning of November the royalists in Gournay and other castles should attack the city and be admitted by the 'Pilatians'. But Robert got wind of the plot, summoned William of Evreux, William of Breteuil, Gilbert of L'Aigle[51] and other loyal vassals to his standard, and also Robert of Bellême and Henry. The compliance of the last two is at first sight surprising. Both had been imprisoned by Robert in 1088 and since then had held aloof. It can only be thought that both believed that a crucial point had been reached and decided that they preferred to keep Robert Curthose as duke. And it was almost certainly this decision which saved Robert. It can therefore be said that William's diplomacy had been faulty: that he had aimed too low and had not bought the key allies. But, on the other hand, we do not know if an alliance with Henry and Robert of Bellême could have been obtained at anything less than prohibitive cost. It seems that Henry at this time was incensed more against William than Robert, and that Robert of Bellême could have had no possible interest in William's victory. Moreover both would have been outraged by a bourgeois revolution. This was an issue which served to close knightly ranks.

When the fighting started on 3 November, the duke and Henry were in the castle, situated in the south-east angle of the city's walls, and some royalist troops had found a way into the town and were awaiting the signal. A royalist force of three hundred knights under Reginald, the

---

[47] *ASC, s.a.* 1090; *GR*, ii, 363; Florence, ii, 26, for St Valery and Aumale; OV, iv, 182, for the rest. *GR*'s account of the years 1089–91 is muddled. Fliche, *Philippe I*, 292 ff.

[48] OV, iv, 220.

[49] Sanders, *Baronies*, 137.

[50] OV, iv, 220 ff.

[51] Probably the uncle rather than the nephew: see above, 271.

second son of William of Warenne, first earl of Surrey, arrived at the West Gate just as a relieving force under Gilbert of L'Aigle crossed the bridge over the Seine and tried to enter the South Gate. While the situation was nicely balanced, Robert and Henry burst out of the citadel, and Robert was persuaded to leave by the East Gate lest he die ignobly in the mêlée. He crossed the river by boat and in the suburban priory of Notre-Dame-du-Pré, in company with his adviser, the monk, William of Arques, rather cravenly awaited the outcome.[52] Henry was the only one of the brothers to fight in person. It would seem from Orderic's account that Gilbert of L'Aigle stormed his way in and joined forces with Henry, and that the two then slaughtered the citizens indiscriminately and captured the ringleader, Conan, before Reginald could make much impression. When the insurrection collapsed, the royal forces fled in disorder. Savage reprisals were inflicted by the ducal soldiers. Conan was thrown to his death from the castle tower by the jeering Henry himself,[53] Other captains, including Robert of Bellême and William of Breteuil, were more interested in loot and took citizens captive for ransom. One man, William fitzAnger, was thought to have paid £3,000 to escape from the latter's prison. The pillaging and ransoms no doubt compensated many of the duke's supporters for their campaign expenses, whereas William Rufus had gained little in return for vast disbursements. The Anglo-Saxon Chronicler complained of the unjust gelds the king imposed on England, doubtless as a result.

In the course of the year, Robert took two important counter-measures. He made an alliance with Helias of Saint-Saëns (a stronghold in the centre of Upper Normandy to the south of the arc formed by Longueville – Mortemer – Aumale) and gave him an illegitimate daughter to wife, with Arques and Bures-en-Bray as her *maritagium*.[54] Helias remained faithful to his father-in-law and duke, and his three castles served to cover Rouen to the north. Robert also appealed to his old ally and overlord, the king of France, who proved to be less dependable. It was in Philip's interest that Normandy should remain in the weak hands of Robert and not be joined to England, but he was poor and could not resist English silver. In 1090 he entered Normandy to

---

[52] This church had been built by the Conqueror and his wife on land claimed by Bec, and was granted by Robert to the abbey, together with the tithes from his nearby park, in Feb. 1092 (? *recte* 1091), possibly as a thanksgiving for his escape: *Neustria Pia*, 613. For the date, see below, 281 n. 76. The suburb was called Emendreville (*Hermentrudisvilla*), and seems now to be the parish of St Sever. It was here that Anselm abbot of Bec fell ill when attempting to visit the Conqueror's death-bed: *HN*, 24.

[53] As this episode is also mentioned in *GR*, ii, 469, there is no reason to doubt it.

[54] *OV*, iv, 182.

attack a royalist town, perhaps Aumale, but was bought off.[55]

William celebrated the Christmas festival, as in 1087 and perhaps the intervening years, at Westminster.[56] He had decided to campaign in person in Normandy and must have been encouraged by the news that Robert had been diverted to a new quarry.[57] After the sack of Rouen, Robert of Bellême, who had been expanding north-east across the River Orne, was resisted by Hugh of Grandmesnil and Richard of Courcy with their strongholds to the east of the River Dives. This Giroie clan, which originated in Brittany and had reached the Evrécin by way of Bellême in the first half of the eleventh century, had remained hostile to the other family. A little war, but costly in lives, broke out before Christmas 1090, and Robert of Bellême persuaded the duke to help him capture Courcy. In reply, Hugh and Richard probably appealed to William for help.[58] On the night of 1 January the priest of St-Aubin-de-Bonneval mistook the ghostly squadrons of 'Hellequin's Hunt' for Robert of Bellême's household troops hastening to the attack. Courcy was still under siege on 23 January, when the bishop of Sées, who had attempted to intervene and had been insulted by the duke, died in his cathedral church.

By 27 January William was at Dover, preparing to cross the Channel. We are told that eventually he sailed with a large fleet and a great treasure,[59] but detailed information is entirely lacking. Not only are we ignorant of the actual naval and military arrangements in 1091, we are also in the dark as to the king's rights in these matters and his usual measures. The exact composition of his army is a mystery. We do not know whether his English barons owed him knight service abroad, and, if so, whether it was limited to forty days;[60] the transport duties of the

[55] *ASC, s.a.*; *GR*, ii, 363; Florence, ii, 26–7. The Chronicle and its dependents associate this royal attack on an unnamed place with the beginning of the Norman rebellion and date it firmly 1090. If this is right, a border fortress is more likely. Torigny, *Interpolation*, 270, has Philip help Robert in an attack on Eu shortly before peace was made between the brothers, i.e. Feb. 1091. It seems also that Robert attacked Eu in 1089: above, 272. Although it is quite possible that there is some confusion, it is no less possible that we are concerned with three distinct episodes, and it is tempting to associate the reconciliation between William Rufus and the bishop of Durham with a French attack on a royal garrison in Feb. 1091. If there is confusion, a choice has to be made between the closer in time (*ASC*) and the nearer in place (OV and Torigny). For differing views, see Fliche, *Philippe I*, 292 ff., David, *RC*, 55–60, and Chibnall, OV, iv, 236–7 n. 3.

[56] *ASC, s.a.* 1091, 168.

[57] OV, iv, 228 ff., 238.

[58] See below, 279.

[59] OV, iv, 236, cf. 250.

[60] For the belated development of Norman feudal customs, see Bates, *Normandy before 1066*, 122–8, 133–4, 168–72, 258–9. In the case of England special arrangements were usually made for foreign expeditions. Stenton, *English Feudalism*, 176–7, glances at these matters: he thought that the English barons owed military service across the Channel.

Channel ports are not clear;[61] and there is nothing to show how the military stores were procured and handled. These cross-Channel expeditions, although a feature of the post-Conquest period, were novel, sporadic, and by 1091 hardly customary. The last had occurred in 1086. Almost all had been in the nature of the king simply travelling from one part of his empire to another and would not have involved the shipping of a large army. The king would normally have been accompanied by his household troops and by his baronial friends with their retinues; and, if necessary, this nucleus could be reinforced in various ways from the resources of the region.

It is possible that William's expedition in 1091 was slightly different, in that he was going to operate in a 'foreign' and more hostile area; but it was nothing like that of 1066. He already had the allegiance of much of Upper Normandy, and was intending to rally his supporters, consolidate his acquisitions, and see what further gains could be made. He remained abroad for six months and probably intended to stay longer. In these circumstances it would seem most unlikely that he took with him more than military cadres which would serve if necessary as the command structure for an army, in addition to the large sum of money necessary for the payment of subsidies, the hiring of troops and all the other military expenditure. It is likely that he discussed these matters with his barons at the Christmas court and made arrangements with individuals, sometimes accepting personal service, sometimes other duties or money in lieu.[62] As for stores and transport, these may have been the responsibility of the sheriffs of the maritime shires. Treasure would have been carried under guard from Winchester in the shape of barrels of silver pennies. For his own conveyance across the sea he may have relied on the 'steerman', or master, of the royal yacht. This vessel, perhaps with the traditional designation of *esnecca*, 'sea-snake', was commanded from 1066 to 1086 by a serjeant named Steven fitzAirard. In Domesday Book he is shown as owning houses in Southampton and Warwick, the manor of Padworth in Berkshire worth £4 10s, and four hides of land in Warwickshire worth £4. If he held a naval command it was clearly Southampton and its hinterland. Before 1120 he had been succeeded in his office by his son Thomas, who in the night of 25 November, when drunk, ran his large vessel, *The White Ship*, on to a rock off Barfleur with such tragic and disastrous consequences.[63]

For a recent intervention into the vexed subject of military service, see John Gillingham, 'The Introduction of Knight Service into England', *Battle IV*, 53.

[61] Cf. Le Patourel, *Norman Empire*, 164 ff.

[62] For scutage, which clearly went back to this time, see, *inter alios*, Stenton, *op. cit.*, 178 ff.

[63] OV, vi, 296; *DB*, i, 52a, 63c, 238a, 243d. See also *Calendar of Charter Rolls* (Record

In 1091 the king, because of his northerly destination, intended to sail from Kent or Sussex. A group of charters issued while he assembled his company or awaited a favourable wind shows that all the greatest English magnates, both clerical and lay, were in attendance, although most had come only to wish him God speed.[64] The archbishop of York (Canterbury was vacant) and all twelve English bishops as well as Geoffrey of Coutances and Hoël of Le Mans,[65] together with thirteen abbots of major houses, compose an impressive body of prelates. Two of them, we may note, Wulfstan of Worcester and Baldwin of Bury St Edmunds, had been appointed by Edward the Confessor. Of all these, Geoffrey and Hoël were probably the only ones intending to sail. Robert Bloet, the new chancellor, and eleven chaplains, including Samson, Wulfstan's successor as bishop, and Ranulf Flambard, show that the king was not short of clerks.

Among the laity, the ministerial nobility predominate. The charters list eight earls, about the complete tally of those with large English interests: Roger of Shrewsbury, Robert of Meulan and his brother Henry of Warwick, Simon of Northampton, Hugh of Chester, Alan of Brittany (and of Richmond), Walter Giffard of Buckingham and William (II) of Surrey. The king's cousin and ally, Stephen of Aumale, witnesses one of his charters at about this time.[66] Wulfnoth, probably King Harold's captive brother, and possibly once more taken from custody in order to accompany the king as a hostage appears in one list.[67] It is not known how many of the others, besides Earl Hugh,[68] went to

Publ.), ii, 102, no. 5, cf. nos 7, 15. Cf. Haskins, 'The administration of Normandy under Henry I', *EHR*, xxiv (1909), 230–1; Le Patourel, *op. cit.*, 177–8.

[64] *Regesta*, nos 315 (and ii, 399), 319, 326, 359. Nos 315 and 319 are dated; 326 and 359 have linked witnesses. No. 328, dated 1090 and with a long list of witnesses, most of whom are supported by 315 and 319, is not, however, completely satisfactory. The king is followed by an unnamed archbishop of Canterbury, and count Robert of Mortain heads the earls. But if we disregard the impossible archbishop and change Robert into the more probable count of Meulan, we have what looks like a very credible list of courtiers and one which supplements the others.

[65] Hoël, after a short imprisonment in 1090 and an unsuccessful appeal to Robert for help, crossed to England and joined William, with whom he stayed for about four months. When neither brother invaded Maine, he made his peace with the rebels and recovered his bishopric at the end of June 1091: *Act. Pont. Cen.*, 385–92. David, *RC*, 72–3.

[66] *Regesta*, no. 328. The son of the Conqueror's sister Adelaide by her third husband Odo, he nevertheless probably took his title from her first husband, Enguerrand II, count of Ponthieu and lord of Aumale. This town may have been his mother's *dos*. He married Hawise, daughter of Ralf of Mortemer, lord of Wigmore and of St-Victor-en-Caux. Cf. GEC, i, 352; and see below, genealogical table 1. For his adventures after 1095, see below, 347 ff.

[67] No. 319. See also above, 65–6.

[68] Hugh witnessed a charter in Normandy: *Regesta*, ii, no. 317a.

Normandy: the likeliest are Roger of Montgomery, Robert of Meulan, Alan of Brittany and Stephen of Aumale.

The royal household officials are especially well represented in the witness lists. There are at least five stewards, Eudo, together with his brother, Hubert (I) of Ryes, Ivo Taillebois, Haimo sheriff of Kent, Roger Bigot and William. Aiulf appears among the sheriffs and with that designation. Robert *dispensator* was present, as were the three constables, although not listed as such: Robert's brother, Urse of Abetot, Robert (I) of Oilli, with his brother Guy (Wido),[69] and Hugh (III) of Montfort, the son of the man who had fought at Hastings. William of Aubigni (I) may have been the king's butler. Croc the huntsman also was there, doubtless to arrange sporting distractions for his master while they waited. As well as the sheriffs already mentioned (Haimo, Aiulf and Urse), Hugh of Port (Hampshire) was in attendance. These men were both household officials and barons; but we cannot say in what capacity they were at court, whether as quartermasters, military officers or barons accompanying the king. It would seem likely, however, that the greater number of the sheriffs would stay behind to carry out their duties in the shires.

Most of the other barons listed were probably intending to cross the Channel with the king. There was a small contingent of the great Giroie clan, the sons of Hugh of Grandmesnil, Robert and Ivo, and their brother-in-law, Robert, Richard of Courcy's son, anxious to relieve the pressure on their beleaguered fathers.[70] Rather more of those in attendance on the king had preponderant English interests. Two of the king's closest friends were there, Haimo's son, Robert, and Roger fitzGerold (of Roumare), soldiers who were to win large rewards. Gilbert fitzRichard of Tonbridge (or of Clare) and Ranulf Peverel of Hatfield Peverel were barons from the south-east. Five were centered in the western shires: Ernulf (I) of Hesdin, Humphrey de Lisle (a Robert de Lisle also was present), Roger of Nonant of Totnes,[71] Walter Hosat from Somerset and William fitzBaldwin of Okehampton, Gilbert of Clare's cousin. Eight were from the Midlands and north: Alfred of Lincoln, Henry de Ferrers of Tutbury, Geoffrey de Wirce, a Breton from La Guerche, William (I) Peverel of Nottingham, Roger (I) de Bully of Tickhill, William (I) de Percy of Topcliffe, Yorkshire, and Geoffrey de Stuteville and Ralf Pagnell of the same county. Of these, Gilbert of

---

[69] Guy was the brother of Nigel: *Regesta*, no. 466, cf. 410; and Nigel was the brother and heir of Robert I: Sanders, *Baronies*, 54.

[70] See above, 276. For a genealogical table, see Chibnall, OV, ii, opposite p. 370.

[71] The king while in Normandy confirmed a charter of Roger in favour of Abbot Achard of Angers, the confirmation being witnessed by Earl Hugh of Chester and Robert fitzHaimo: *Regesta*, ii, no. 317a.

Clare, Ernulf of Hesdin, Henry de Ferrers, William Peverel, Roger de
Bully and Ralf Pagnell were among the major barons of the kingdom,
with lands in many shires.

This is the last occasion in the reign which is illuminated by several
elaborate charters of the old type with lengthy witness lists. Either the
demand for solemn confirmations had for the time being been satisfied,
or important beneficiaries were becoming increasingly content with the
authority of a simple royal writ with its minimum of attestation. The list
of courtiers in 1091 is therefore particularly valuable. It enables us to see
that at least half of these earls, officials and barons had also witnessed
royal charters in 1087–8; and there is enough scattered documentary
evidence from the later years of the reign to show that many of those men
continued to frequent the court until the very end. It is clear that by
1091 a group of trusted servants and companions-in-arms had already
formed round the king. How many other barons and knights, omitted
from the witness lists, were in the king's company it is impossible to say;
but if the baronage at large and the feudal host were present en masse,
they left no documentary evidence. Nor can it be shown who, if anyone,
had special responsibility for the government of England while William
was abroad, but, to judge by later occasions, he would have relied on
Bishop Walkelin of Winchester, aided by Haimo *dapifer*, Urse of Abetot
and Ranulf Flambard, to watch over his interests.

On 2 February the king sailed from one of the ferry ports, probably
Dover or Hastings,[72] perhaps aiming for St Valery at the mouth of the
Somme or Le Tréport on the Bresle, and set up his headquarters at
nearby Eu.[73] Orderic believed that he was courted not only by the
Norman barons of the region but also by Frenchmen, Bretons and
Flemings, presumably mercenary knights whom he needed for garrison
and field duties. On receipt of the news, Robert of Bellême and Robert
Curthose abandoned the siege of Courcy, and the duke moved north.
There does not seem to have been much fighting; but the Durham
chronicler tells how the exiled bishop made his peace with the king. One
of the towns (*castellum*) garrisoned by the king's men was besieged and
about to be captured when the bishop intervened and persuaded the
attackers to withdraw; and for this service the king restored him to all his
honours in England.[74] It is possible that we are concerned with King
Philip's attack on Eu, mentioned by a later chronicler;[75] if so, we can also
believe that the bishop, a famous diplomat, was involved in the peace

---

[72] On the charter evidence, above, 279 n. 64.

[73] OV, iv, 236, 250.

[74] Simeon, *HDE*, 128. The event is dated the third year of his exile, i.e. Dec. 1090 –
Dec. 1091.

[75] Above, 276 n. 55.

negotiations. Before the end of the month the king and duke, who may have had Eustace of Boulogne with him, had come to terms.[76]

Several accounts of the treaty 'of Rouen'[77] are extant, one comprehensive, the others selective. The earliest and most detailed statement is in the Anglo-Saxon Chronicle.[78] Robert was to grant William the county of Eu, Fécamp and Cherbourg, and leave in his lordship those barons who had gone over to him. In return, William was to help Robert recover all their father's lands, especially Maine, except those, of course, already mentioned. He was to give Robert lands in England and restore to the duke's supporters what they had lost in the kingdom in 1088. Moreover, each was to be the other's heir: William was to take all Normandy if Robert died without a legitimate son and Robert was to inherit England if William died (here there is no mention of a possible heir of the body). Each party produced twelve guarantors of the treaty. William of Malmesbury repeats some, and Florence most of this, and according to them it was the monastery of Fécamp which was granted, an important ducal abbey, owing the service of ten knights, adjacent to a useful port and with close connexions with England.[79] Orderic, here quite independent of the others, puts it a little differently: Robert granted William the county of Eu, Aumale and all the lands of Gerard of

[76] Through the mediation of barons who held lands of both brothers: *GR*, ii, 363; with the help of Philip of France, present with the duke at the attack on Eu: Torigny, *Interpolation*, 270. At Rouen: OV, iv, 236; at Caen: Torigny, *loc. cit.*, followed by *FWR*, i, 275 and App. M. David, *RC*, 60, sensibly suggests that Torigny was confusing the truce with the Inquest of 18 July. A ducal charter (see above, 275 n. 52), also calendared *Regesta*, no. 327, and Haskins, *NI*, 68, no. 7, and witnessed by, *inter alios*, Archbishop William of Rouen, Eustace of Boulogne, Robert of Montfort, Robert of Meulan and William of Durham, and with a reservation in favour of his brother, William *gratia Dei rex Anglorum*, as well as himself, is dated Feb. 1092, indiction 15. The year and indiction agree, but unless the bishop of Durham returned on an embassy at that time, or his witness is a mistake, the year would have to be 1091. Eustace also witnesses Haskins, no. 10.

[77] Florence, ii, 34 n., MS. C, locates the conference on the treaty in 1094, which took place where the oaths confirming it had been taken in 1091, *in Campo Martio*; and afterwards Robert went to Rouen and William to Eu. In Rome the Campus Martius was the flood plain of the Tiber where army musters and exercises took place, and at Rouen, according to *FWR*, i, 251, it was outside the east gate. It is convenient to refer to the treaty 'of Rouen'.

[78] *ASC*, *s.a.*, 169.

[79] *GR*, ii, 363; Florence, ii, 27. Haskins, *NI*, 8; Barlow, *EC 1066–1154*, 186 ff., 240 ff. At a date shortly after Robert and Philip's attack on La Ferté (? 1089: above, 272–3) and before 1093, Abbot William of Rots of Fécamp was in England: *Gallia Christiana*, xi, instr. 19. But since the abbey and ducal palace were cheek by jowl and protected by the same sub-circular fortifications, and the bourg depended on these, the intention must have been to surrender the whole complex. For the site, see Annie Renoux, 'Fouilles sur le site du château ducal de Fécamp (Xᵉ–XIIᵉ siècle)', *Battle IV*, 133.

Gournay and Ralf of Conches in return for enormous gifts.[80] Later, when summarizing the events of 1090–6, he reckoned that William held more than twenty towns (*castra*) in Normandy, and in addition had the support among others of Robert count of Eu, Stephen of Aumale, Gerard of Gournay, Ralf of Conches, Robert count of Meulan, Walter Giffard, Philip of Briouze (between Domfront and Argentan) and Richard of Courcy.[81]

One of the clauses – William's promise to Robert and his supporters in 1088 of reinstatement or compensation in England – is difficult to take seriously. For example, it is hard to believe that William intended to restore Kent to their half-uncle, Odo of Bayeux, when William of St Calais recovered Durham only as the reward for a specific service.[82] Indeed, Odo kept himself, or was kept, well out of sight during the period of *détente*. It may be suspected that explicit or tacit exceptions to a general amnesty have been omitted from the record. According to Orderic, Henry made legal demands on both brothers for a share of his father's lands and, when refused, recruited mercenaries and fortified his castles.[83] The treaty, in return, envisaged his immediate and permanent disinheritance, for if we consider Robert's grant to William of Cherbourg (and possibly Mont St Michel),[84] both in Henry's possession, in the context of the king's undertaking to help Robert recover all his father's lands and also in the light of future events, it is most likely that they agreed to dispossess the cadet of the apanage he had bought and that William was to get a share of the spoils. Furthermore, Edgar Ætheling was deprived of his Norman lands and had to take refuge once more in Scotland, where he plotted his revenge.[85]

No one explains on what terms Robert granted vassals and their lands to William. Orderic's belief that the king bought the grants with money was probably well founded: it was a type of bargain typical of both parties. William was acquiring an apanage similar to that which Henry had held. It is unlikely that he was to hold it otherwise than as a feudal benefice (perhaps as a money-fief), and if he had done homage to Robert

---

[80] OV, iv, 236. Torigny, *Interpolation*, 270: William was to keep his 'conquests', Fécamp, Eu and the lands of Stephen of Aumale.

[81] OV, v, 26. This is the first appearance in the story of Philip of Briouze, soon to be a conqueror in Wales: below, 322.

[82] OV, when reviewing Odo's later career, observed that the bishop was always a supporter of Robert and an opponent of William, and left on the Crusade in 1096 because he could not bear to submit to the new ruler: OV, v, 220.

[83] OV, iv, 250.

[84] Florence, ii, 27, adds the abbey, possibly because he described Henry's ejection from it.

[85] *ASC*, s.a., 169. Florence, ii, 27–8, puts the confiscation after the campaign against Henry.

before 1087, repetition of the ceremony may not have been required. Robert would know that his brother would be a very independent vassal, but his position would be little different from that, say, of Robert of Bellême. Some light on their relative positions is shed by an inquest which they held at Caen on 18 July into the judicial rights of the Conqueror.[86] Robert, described consistently as count (*comes*) of Normandy, always precedes William, styled king of England; and together they are called the sons and heirs of the King William who acquired the kingdom of England. It is clear that the findings apply only to Normandy, but William's participation and his appearance by name in the clause which safeguards all the rights of the interested parties not recorded in the document, shows that, while Robert remained titular ruler and some form of condominium under his supremacy was envisaged,[87] there had been a true partition of the duchy between the heirs. The third brother is not mentioned. It is difficult to analyze the legal position further and unwise to attempt greater precision. It is possible that there was some ambiguity at the time.

When we consider the treaty as a whole, it seems that, whether or not the parties believed that both would honour it – and, if so, whether they had good grounds for such a belief – the terms were fairly even. If the short-term advantages – the money and the immediate help against Henry, the rebels in Maine and other enemies – were mainly Robert's, and the medium-term benefits – the entry ports and the substantial bridge-head – were William's, the clause regarding the succession to the undivided Norman empire was undoubtedly in Robert's favour. But the last, it will be noticed, was at Henry's, not William's expense. The agreement was shrewdly negotiated and left the game nicely balanced between the king and the duke. In such a violent and changeable world, short-term advantages could often be the more profitable, and the feckless Robert may easily have thought that he had outsmarted William and put Henry out of the running.[88] All the same, William's intervention was an event which set a precedent and impressed contemporaries. A notification of a grant by a certain Erbald to the abbey of Marmoutier at Tours in 1091, through the agency of Robert

---

[86] Printed and edited by Haskins, *NI*, 277 ff.

[87] Robert and William confirmed an exchange made, probably at this time, by the abbot of St Stephen's, Caen, and William de Tournebu: Haskins, *NI*, 69, nos 14–15. Earlier Robert had made a grant to Holy Trinity, Caen, with the consent of his brother Henry: *ibid.*, no. 19.

[88] Although medieval history is littered with succession agreements which failed to materialize, some came to term; and if the sons believed that the English crown had passed by testamentary authority in 1066 (twice) and 1087, another convention was certainly worthwhile. Torigny, *Interpolation*, 270, writing with hindsight, considered the treaty *probrosa atque damnosa* for the duke.

count of Normandy, was dated, 'the very year in which his brother William king of the English, son of the most glorious King William, came to Normandy from overseas in the reign of King Philip of France'.[89]

William's most immediate obligation was to help Robert recover fully his remaining share of the patrimony, and, although they had a campaign against the rebels in Maine in mind, they thought it necessary first to protect their flank by going against Henry.[90] The combined authority of the two brothers compelled Hugh of Avranches and others of Henry's barons and castellans to submit, and the count with his household knights was forced to take refuge in the monastery of Mont St Michel. An assault on this fortress, which rises abruptly out of the treacherous sands and waters at the mouth of the Couesnon, was not inviting, and in March 1091 the brothers mounted a siege, both making their headquarters on the north side of the bay – William in the cathedral city of Avranches, Robert to the west at Genêts.[91] The purpose was clearly to cut Henry off from the Cotentin and possibly to allow him to escape to Brittany if he so chose.

William of Malmesbury tells two stories about the siege, one to illustrate the king's 'magnanimity', the other to show the duke's clemency. One day the king saw from his tent some enemy knights insolently riding past in the distance, and unable to restrain his valour and confident that none of them would dare resist him, dashed off to attack them on his own, riding a horse which that day had cost him £10 – a most expensive animal.[92] But he had been over-confident: he had his horse killed under him, was thrown to the ground and dragged along for a time by the stirrup, and was only saved from serious injury by his armour. The knight who had brought him down was just about to strike with his sword when William, terrified by his danger, called out, 'Stop, you fool! I'm the king of England.' The knights recognized his voice, and with fear and trembling raised him to his feet and brought up another mount. Without waiting for assistance, William vaulted into the saddle and, sharply running his eyes over the group of soldiers, asked who had done it. Amid the general silence the one responsible, aware of his rashness but not afraid to defend himself, called out, 'It was

[89] CDF, no. 1179.

[90] OV, iv, 250 ff. Although omitted from ASC, there are accounts in GR, ii, 363–5, 469–70, and Florence, ii, 27.

[91] Wace, ll. 9535 ff. Although the poet, who was born in Jersey and educated at Caen, could have been drawing on local tradition, his editor, A.J. Holden, suggests that sometimes he supplied appropriate detail in order to improve the story: ibid., iii, 115.

[92] In PR 31 H.I (1129–30) dextrarii are usually valued at £2: cf. pp. 85, 100, 125. Other types of horse, e.g. coursers (fugatorii) and palfreys were valued at £1–£1 10s: pp. 118, 134. Wace, ll. 9545 ff., tells the story rather differently.

me. But I didn't know you were the king. I thought you were only a knight.' The answer amused William, and with sudden affability he replied, 'By the face of Lucca, from now on you'll be my man, and in my service get a proper reward for your courage and spirit.'

The chronicler was very impressed by this example of William's magnanimity and could compare it only with Alexander the Great's treatment of the Persian soldier.[93] The episode also has other lessons. William was utterly confident, and with justification, that no one would dare to harm him once he was identified. But we notice that he could not be recognized by his arms or from his partly concealed face, nor, in this case, from his horse.[94] What we cannot learn from the story is whether the chronicler believed that William owed his immunity to his royalty or to his being Henry's elder brother or lord, or even to his natural authority. Would Robert have been treated in exactly the same way? In any case, it was episodes such as this which earned William the respect of the knightly class, and also, we see, of the monks who chronicled their deeds. It may simply be a matter of chance that William's discomfiture in hand-to-hand fighting was noted on two occasions while none of his outstanding feats of arms went into the record.

The other story is more equivocal, but seems to be told at Robert's expense.[95] When the besieged became short of water, Henry sent envoys to Robert to say that it was wicked to deprive them of something which was provided for all mankind to enjoy, and that Robert should test their valour in other ways, employing the courage of his soldiers rather than the force of the elements. And the duke, because of his pliable nature, ordered his piquets to let water be taken through their lines. When the king learnt of this, he shouted angrily at his brother, 'A fine sort of general you are, sending water to the enemy! How can we possibly conquer them if we provide them with food and drink?' But Robert laughingly replied, 'Do you really think we should condemn our own brother to die of thirst? And what other brother would we have if we lost him?' At this the king, scornful of Robert's weakness, brought the campaign to a premature close[96] and took both brothers with him back to England to deal with Scottish and Welsh affairs.

Although William of Malmesbury, Florence and Robert of Torigny

---

[93] Cf. *The Prose Life of Alexander*, ed. J.S. Westlake, EETS, no. 143 (1913), 40-1. G. Cary, *The Medieval Alexander* (1956), 197, 317-18.

[94] Cf. the events at Gerberoy in 1079, above 35.

[95] *GR*, ii, 365. Wace, ll. 9579 ff., is similar, but improves the story by having Robert send Henry a cask of the best wine.

[96] This may be the source of Florence's statement, ii, 27, that William became bored by the length of the siege and went away *impacatus*, 'unpeacefully' – perhaps 'without having settled the matter', or just 'angrily'.

thought that the king and the duke quarrelled over the conduct of the siege and did not achieve their purpose,[97] their interpretation is less plausible than Orderic's. He believed that Henry asked for an honourable surrender, which his brothers were pleased to allow.[98] In other words, they simply wanted to see the back of him, for a time at least. It was probably early in April 1091 that he was permitted to march out of Mont St Michel with his men and baggage; and as William and Robert seem not to have campaigned against the rebels in Maine and their leader Hugh of Este,[99] they must afterwards have been occupied with the takeover of Henry's lands and the general pacification of the duchy. There was still war in the south-east between Robert of Bellême and Geoffrey II of Mortagne and Perche. In the Evrécin, the war between William of Evreux and Ralf of Tosny was raging late in 1091 or 1092, when the count attacked Conches and Richard of Montfort (-l'Amaury) was killed, and was only concluded when William of Breteuil and others of the count's supporters were captured. It cost the main captive £3,000 to get his freedom, and William of Evreux bought a settlement by nominating as his heir his nephew, Roger, Ralf of Tosny's son.[100] All this was of interest to the king, for Ralf was his vassal. Disturbances probably also continued in other regions of less interest to Orderic. Nevertheless, the new alliance between duke and king must have had a calming effect, and the seriousness of their intentions was shown in the summer. The archbishop of Rouen held a provincial synod after Pentecost (1 June) and on 18 July duke and king held an inquest at Caen into ducal rights. Even though these measures were in Robert's interest, the drive towards strong and orderly government came from the king and his advisers. It was in his passionate desire to restore his father's empire in all its dimensions that William differed most from his elder brother.

Although it is inconceivable that Archbishop William's synod of bishops and abbots, attended by the duke and, among others, seemingly by the bishops of Coutances, Durham, Bayeux and Evreux, and the nobles Gilbert Crispin (? III) and his cousin William Crispin (II), Robert of Montfort (-sur-Risle), Robert count of Meulan and Ralf of Conches (Tosny), did not pass a series of decrees concerned with the disorder of the last four years, they have not been transmitted.[101] The

[97] Torigny, *Interpolation*, 270; see also previous note.

[98] OV, iv, 250.

[99] See above, 270, and OV, iv, 196, where her makes Helias of La Flèche tell Hugh of Este that William and Robert were about to invade Maine.

[100] OV, iv, 214–16; and see above, 270–1.

[101] OV, iv, 252; *Regesta*, ii, no. 317b. Although the chronicler does not mention the attendance of the king, his absence cannot be assumed. The council of Rouen (1096) which preceded Robert's departure on Crusade, re-enacted the Truce of God: see below, 361.

only business recorded is the election, after consultation with the duke, of Serlo abbot of St Evroul to the bishopric of Sées. This was an important political appointment, for the bellicose Robert of Bellême and Geoffrey of Mortagne were among his parishioners. Orderic, whose abbot he was, does not mention consultation with those magnates, and Serlo was to have a rough time, occasionally having to take refuge in England or Italy. The findings of the bishops and barons meeting at Caen six weeks later have survived.[102] Their inquiry was into the judicial rights which the Conqueror had had in the duchy, especially those which had been the most violated, and the schedule produced is complementary to the inquest into the judicial rights of the church which William I had held at Lillebonne in 1080.[103] Attention is drawn to the peace which those going to and from the ducal court or army should enjoy (1–3). The building of private fortifications is controlled, and the duke's right to garrison them and his right to take the son, brother or nephew of one of his barons as a hostage for his fealty are noticed (4–5). Acts of violence, unlawful remedies and private war are forbidden or restricted (6–12, 14). And the ducal monopoly of coinage is reaffirmed and its standard defined (13). It is also recognized that no omission from the record was to prejudice the rights of those concerned, that is to say, Duke Robert, King William and the barons.

On 21 July the monks of St Evroul, deprived of their abbot through his elevation to Sées, met to elect his successor, and when a few days later they went to present their candidate to the duke, they discovered that, to the general surprise, he had decamped and left with the king for England.[104] The great problem is whether their brother Henry had gone with them. William of Malmesbury, as we have seen, believed that he did;[105] and the monks of Durham fabricated, probably in the late twelfth century, a splendid charter of Bishop William of St Calais, which, if genuine, would have to be dated between mid-September and mid-December 1091, and to which they gave as witnesses, among others, the three brothers.[106] With such forgeries there is always the possibility that the terms of a genuine charter have been revised, but also that the

---

[102] Above, 283 n. 86. Cf. Bates, *Normandy before 1066*, 162 ff., where he stresses the continuity from Carolingian notions of authority.

[103] Barlow, *EC 1066–1154*, 148 ff.

[104] OV, iv, 252–4; cf. 250, where he says that William stayed in Normandy until August.

[105] See above, 285.

[106] F. Barlow, *Durham Jurisdictional Peculiars*, 73–4; Offler, *Durham Episc. Charters*, 48 ff., where it is dated 14 Nov. 1091–May 1092. Both these dates are, however, mistaken: the bishop re-entered his see on 11 Sept. (below, 294) and Duke Robert sailed from the Isle of Wight on 23 Dec. It can be agreed that the purported occasion is the army's return from the peace conference with King Malcolm.

forgers constructed a witness list from a variety of sources, in this case William of Malmesbury or his derivatives.

The Malmesbury monk, however, was not well informed about this period or Henry's movements, and Orderic, who was rather better placed, tells a quite different story: Henry went from Mont St Michel through Brittany to 'France' – that is to say, skirted Normandy to the south and east – and lived for something less than two years in the Vexin,[107] presumably under the protection of the French king and put in a position from which he could threaten the duchy. That would take us to about Christmas 1092. In a later passage Orderic writes that in 1092 the rebel citizens of Domfront, one of Robert of Bellême's greatest strongholds, called in Henry to be their lord, and from there he made war on Duke Robert and carved out a large principality. Here we are once more on firm ground.[108] Although there is a somewhat mythical flavour to the exile in the Vexin, Orderic's whole story fits the general situation well. Henry's brothers were still uncompromisingly hostile to him in July 1091, when they made their inquest into judicial customs, just before they left for England, and even had they wished to take him with them to prevent him doing mischief behind their backs, it was probably then too late to think of that. Robert of Torigny offers a third version: after William had returned to England, Henry, with the king's consent and the help of Earl Hugh of Avranches, Richard of Reviers and Roger of Mandeville, recovered the Cotentin and rewarded the earl with the grant of St James on the Breton frontier.[109] As Henry and Hugh travelled together to England in 1094, probably from Cherbourg,[110] Torigny's story may at least be partly true. All that we can be sure of is that by 1092 Henry was living like a robber baron in the southern marches of Normandy, and, as his position was at the expense of Robert of Bellême and his rapine at Duke Robert's, he had become a potential ally of William Rufus.

William and Robert travelled to England in July 1091 because Malcolm Canmore, king of Scots, had invaded in May.[111] According to

[107] OV, iv, 250–2.

[108] OV, iv, 256 ff.; v, 26. Orderic knew one of Henry's prisoners who had a miraculous escape from Domfront, and can hardly be far wrong on this episode. OV, iv, 292 ff., considered that Henry was already raiding from Domfront in 1092.

[109] Torigny, *Interpolation*, 271. He gives this order of events: expulsion from Mont St Michel, entry into Domfront, recovery of the Cotentin. David, *RC,* 79, accepts the story. Wace, ll. 9618 ff., takes Henry to Paris. The Coutances chronicle, written about 1093, does not refer to Henry's disappearance from the region: *Gallia Christiana*, xi, instr. 221–4.

[110] Below, 334.

[111] *ASC, s.a.*, 169; *GR*, ii, 365; Florence, ii, 28; Simeon, *HR*, ii, 218, copies Florence, 221 independent; OV, iv, 268.

William of Malmesbury, the sedition of the Welsh was also a factor and the brothers began with an unsuccessful expedition against them, on which they lost many soldiers and horses – a typical result, for William, who was invariably successful in arms elsewhere, never managed to cope with the mountainous terrain and inclement weather in Wales.[112] It is possible, despite the silence of the other chroniclers, that the king showed the flag in the Welsh marches; but it is most unlikely that he risked substantially weakening his forces while he prepared for a major campaign against Scotland.[113]

No chronicler gives a specific reason for Malcolm's invasion. The general situation was that besides the long history of feuds and warfare in Northumbria, Malcolm, through his marriage to Margaret, regarded himself as representing the Old-English dynasty. He and the Conqueror had made a treaty at Abernethy in 1072, renewed by Robert at Falkirk in 1080, under which Malcolm became William's vassal and gave hostages.[114] The subsidiary clauses have to be inferred, but they must have included an undertaking that each would respect the other's territories and not harbour his enemies. Margaret's brother, Edgar Ætheling, left Scotland after Abernethy. Whether the frontier was defined in detail we cannot say, but as William in 1072 exercised little authority north of the Humber, it seems unlikely. When the Conqueror died, the treaty presumably lapsed, for it was an engagement not between states but between persons; and if Malcolm had any personal obligations to the Conqueror's sons they were to Robert, who was not only a friend of Edgar Ætheling but probably Godfather to Malcolm and Margaret's daughter, Edith-Matilda. Although Malcolm, who was getting old, had not interfered in England in 1087–91, not even when the new king was in great difficulty and the bishop of Durham was beleaguered in his city, he seems to have kept aloof from the English court and entered into no engagements with the new king.

His hands were, therefore, free. And if, as surely was the case, Edgar complained to him that it was on William Rufus's insistence that he had been expelled from Normandy in February, that was enough to provoke a punitive expedition. But if the treaty had lapsed, William too was under no obligation to Malcolm. And although it seems unlikely that in 1089–91, when he was interested primarily in Normandy, he should

---

[112] *GR*, ii, 365–6.
[113] The most entertaining, and often informative, account of Anglo-Scottish affairs in this period is R.L. Graeme Ritchie, *The Normans in Scotland* (1954). See also W.C. Dickinson, *Scotland from the Earliest Times to 1603* (1961), 70 ff.; G.W.S. Barrow, *The Kingdom of the Scots* (1973), 139 ff.; A.A.M. Duncan, *Scotland: the Making of the Kingdom* (1975), 117 ff.; W.E. Kapelle, *The Norman Conquest of the North* (1979).
[114] Above, 37.

have begun to reinforce and extend the French presence in the north by creating new baronies which appeared to threaten Malcolm's kingdom,[115] he was free to do so. Orderic, who was interested in Scottish affairs because of the Anglo-Saxon connexion, but was not very well informed, believed that the cause of the quarrel was Malcolm's refusal to perform his *servitium debitum*,[116] his duty – in its technical sense, military service. If the suggestion is that William had called on Malcolm to take part in his expedition to Normandy, this seems on general grounds unlikely. If it means, however, that Malcolm refused to visit the English court, do homage, and renew the treaties of Abernethy and Falkirk, that is quite possible.

The one other obvious cause of Malcolm's expedition was the apparent weakness of the English defences. The absence of all the royal family from the kingdom; the disgrace of Odo of Bayeux and the eclipse, perhaps exile, of Geoffrey of Coutances, two of the greatest military commanders; the death of the highly respected Lanfranc; the removal of the bishop of Durham and perhaps the earl of Northumberland;[117] and the departure with the king of many of the Midland and Yorkshire barons gave every promise of an easy success. Nor had Malcolm entirely miscalculated. He was to achieve his immediate aims. But by disturbing the *status quo* he hazarded the future.

A vivid description of the panic caused by Malcolm's invasion is given in one of the miracle stories of St Cuthbert.[118] Men fled to the woods and mountains as the Scottish army swept through Northumberland, and when it crossed the Tyne, bypassing the stronghold at Newcastle, the tenants of the church of Durham took refuge as usual in the city with their household goods and flocks and herds, which they penned in the cemetery. An English army raised by the local barons from the young knights (*juvenes*) of the area moved to the city's help, and for a time the walled town lay trapped between the two forces.[119] The congestion in the heat of summer, the presence of large numbers of women and children, and the shortage of food produced heart-rending sights and sounds. Horses were seen biting each other's tails and many animals died. An appeal, however, to St Cuthbert, the tutelary saint, worked a miracle, for at dawn next day the Scottish army was no longer to be seen, whereupon the English forces likewise broke camp and went home. The monks and people had been spared the threat posed by foe

[115] As suggested by Kapelle, *op. cit.*, 146 ff. For these creations, see below, 297–8.
[116] OV, iv, 268.
[117] Above, 167–9.
[118] Simeon, *Opera*, ii, 338–41.
[119] But, according to Simeon, *HR*, ii, 221, Malcolm halted at Chester-le-Street. For this local English army, see also *ASC*, *s.a.*, 169.

and friend alike. And hardly had the blockade been raised when the exiled bishop's officials arrived to take over the city for their pardoned master.[120]

It is possible that it was about this time that the king sent Nigel d'Aubigny, who was the Domesday lord of Cainhoe (Bedfordshire), with other magnates and a strong force of knights to avenge the injury inflicted on him by the king of Scots. The story is told by the twelfth-century author of the *Life and Miracles* of St Oswi, a monk of Tynemouth who could have drawn not only on local tradition but also on Nigel's brother, Richard d'Aubigny, a former monk of Lessay, who was abbot of St Albans, the mother house, from 1097 to 1119.[121] It may be, however, that Nigel accompanied Duncan's expedition in 1094 or Edgar's in 1095 or 1097, although he did not witness charters issued by those pretenders in 1094-5.[122] On Nigel's return to Newcastle after a successful campaign, his forces were short of food and raided the priory in which the local inhabitants had put their stores for safety. The baron, 'who was a good man despite being a vigorous knight', sanctioned this with reluctance; and his kinsman and very dear friend, Nigel de Wast,[123] who completely refrained, was saved from an accidental death by the miraculous intervention of St Oswi, king and martyr. If this episode is correctly placed here, it marks the beginning of Tynemouth's sufferings.

William's own movements before he marched north are uncertain. It is likely that he and Robert went to Windsor, for it was there that the party of monks from St Evroul caught up with them and presented their abbot-elect to the duke.[124] Robert invested the candidate by his pastoral staff, 'as was the custom at that time', and William granted the monks a

---

[120] Kapelle, *op. cit.*, 149, understands the text to mean that the bishop himself appeared at this moment, and so extends the siege until the arrival of the king's army in the autumn. The miracle, however, runs, 'eadem hora . . . suum antistitem de exilio reversum congratulantur. Nam cum, portis reseratis, plebs exitura festinaret, ecce! obvii *officiales episcopi* ingrediuntur, et sui ubique jura ovilis episcopo restituuntur.' The bishop had sent his officials in advance to prepare for his own reception.

[121] *Vita Oswini*, 21-2. The episode immediately precedes the miracle concerning the king's expedition in 1091, but may, of course, be misplaced. Nigel could have been a member of a larger force. For him and his family, see above, 145, and genealogical table, below, 470 no. 11.

[122] Below, 318, 353, 371.

[123] Nigel de Wast in 1086 held of Nigel d'Aubigny, lord of Cainhoe, five manors in Bedfordshire and one in Buckinghamshire: *DB*, i, 214b-c, 151c. An 'Emma, wife of Nigel de Wast', is commemorated in *Liber Vitae of New Minster*, ed. W. de Gray Birch, Hants Record Soc., 5 (1892), 124.

[124] OV, iv, 254. Chibnall notes that this was after the Scottish expedition. As the monks did not get back until 18 December, it is indeed possible that the meeting was delayed; but the narrative gives no hint of a second contretemps, and by December the two brothers were quarrelling.

royal charter confirming all their possessions. The king's participation shows that the condominium was at the time still working. Abbot Roger got back to his monastery on 18 December, not long before Robert's own return to Normandy. In the meantime the two brothers had campaigned in Scotland. Because of this, William was unable to attend the translation of the body of St Augustine carried out at Canterbury by Abbot Guy and Bishop Gundulf of Rochester on 6 September, a ceremony which, according to the hagiographer Goscelin of St Bertin, he had favoured and authorized and had wanted to attend.[125] Instead he called out what the Anglo-Saxon Chronicler called a *scypfyrd* and a *landfyrd*, terms appropriate to the Old-English army and navy. And once more we have no means of knowing exactly who were mobilized. But as the new abbot of Ramsey and all his vassals were excused service on this expedition or possibly that against Carlisle in May 1092,[126] it would seem that part of the feudal army as well as those who had duties under the old law (especially on sea) were summoned. A knight, presumably of the abbey of Bury St Edmunds, which owed a force of forty knights to the royal army, who went on this expedition, dispatched his son, who was being educated as a clerk in the monastery's cell at Binham in Norfolk and was suffering from bad eyesight, to the abbey for a cure; and on 20 November, while he was still absent on campaign, this miraculously happened.[127]

The king had planned the traditional invasion by an army up the Great North Road supported by a fleet sailing up the east coast.[128] By 11 September the army had reached Durham,[129] and the fleet of fifty ships, laden with corn apparently from Wessex, made the mouth of the Tyne before Michaelmas (29 September).[130] As the army had gone on, the sailors, with no one to control them, ravaged around, and even robbed an old woman of the piece of cloth she was weaving. She appealed to St Oswi, whose shrine was in the priory, and he duly punished the miscreants. Next day the fleet, profiting by a favourable wind, reached Coquet Island, some twenty miles north off the mouth of the river of the same name; and in fair weather the ships ran on the rocks, collided with

[125] Goscelin, *De Translatione S. Augustini*, in *ASS*, May, vi, 412–13.

[126] *Regesta*, no. 330. Four associated writs in favour of Ramsey, nos 329–32, and probably 354, are *post* July 1091 (the king's return to England with the bishop of Durham) and *ante* 6 May 1092 (the death of Bishop Remigius of Lincoln).

[127] 'Heremanni archidiaconi miracula S. Eadmundi', *Ungedruckte Anglo-Normannorum Geschichtsquellen*, ed. F. Liebermann, 267–8.

[128] *ASC*, s.a., 169; *GR*, ii, 365–6; Florence, ii, 28–9; OV, iv, 268–70, with dramatic embroideries which add nothing of value to the other accounts.

[129] Below, 294. See also map, below, 350.

[130] *Vita Oswini*, cap. X, 22–4.

each other and were swamped by waves which rose without the help of the wind. The corpses and all the stolen goods were washed up by the tide on the beaches round Tynemouth, and the inhabitants, who had fled to the woods and other fastnesses for fear of both the Scots and the Normans, re-emerged and collected their goods from the sands. William was told of this miracle on his return journey, and he and all his magnates henceforth held St Oswi in great reverence.

Because of the loss of the fleet, the army, moving through an inhospitable country where the sparse population was far from co-operative – the Normans were almost as much enemies as the Scots and almost equally destructive[131] – suffered greatly from a shortage of food and also from the cold, for in October it was very stormy even in the south of England.[132] But it says much for William's determination that he pushed on regardless. When Malcolm advanced into Lothian to meet the threat, there seems to have been no stomach for a fight on either side. Robert acting for William and Edgar for Malcolm had a parley, apparently somewhere between the Tweed and the Firth of Forth, and arranged terms.

Orderic, continuing his probably fanciful reconstruction of this episode,[133] pictures Robert having to argue Malcolm out of his contention that he owed no duty (or military service) to anyone but Robert, to whom, as the Conqueror's eldest son, he had sworn fealty in the past. It is, indeed, possible that the changed circumstances had to be explained to Malcolm and his adjustment to them secured. In the end it was agreed that the relationship between the two kings should be exactly as it was in the Conqueror's time; and the reference back must have been to Falkirk in 1080 and ultimately to Abernethy in 1072. Malcolm became once again the vassal of the English king. If there were ambiguities in both the earlier agreements with regard to the exact scope of the subjection, there is nothing remarkable in that; and obviously there was no further clarification in 1091. Malcolm went to William, became his vassal to the same extent that he had been his father's man, and confirmed the obligation by oath. In other words, he did homage and fealty, but not unconditionally. He was after all a king himself and ruled over a miscellaneous collection of lordships. In return, William promised him all that he had held under his father, which was, according to Florence, twelve villages, with an additional grant of

---

[131] William I's ravaging for provisions in the area (? 1072) is described *ibid.*, cap. VIII, 20–21; cf. also cap. IX, 21–2.

[132] There was storm damage at Winchcombe and London: *GR*, ii, 374–5, Florence, ii, 28–9. The basic *ASC* entry has been lost.

[133] OV, iv, 268–70.

twelve marks of gold (£72 of silver) a year.[134] Robert then reconciled William and Edgar. It cannot be said that William had covered himself with glory, but neither had any 'southerner' since Siward earl of Northumbria, a Scandinavian warrior, had defeated Macbeth in 1054 and prepared the way for Malcolm's success.[135] Nevertheless, he had done as well as his father and should not be judged by higher standards.

It was on 11 September, on the army's outward journey,[136] that William of St Calais re-entered Durham. A charter ascribed to him, which, if based on a genuine parchment, would have been issued when the king returned to the city on his way back, and could be used to show some of the king's companions, has already been discussed in connexion with the alleged witness of Count Henry.[137] Among the witnesses, besides the king and his brothers, are Duncan, Malcolm's eldest son by his first wife, and Edgar Ætheling; Thomas archbishop of York, three bishops, Remigius of Lincoln, Osmund of Salisbury and John of Bath, and three abbots, Guy of St Augustine's, Baldwin of Bury St Edmunds and Stephen of St Mary's, York. Royal officials listed are the chancellor Robert Bloet, the treasurer Ranulf, Robert the dispenser and Gilbert, a steward. Baronial witnesses are Roger earl of Shrewsbury, Hugh earl of Chester, Philip ('the Grammarian', Earl Roger's son), Robert earl of Northumbria and his sheriff Morel,[138] Rogert Bigot,[139] William Peverel,

[134] Scottish historians, following *FWR*, ii, 544, suggest that these vills were places given in 973 to serve as lodgings on the journey to the English court: cf. Duncan, *op. cit.*, 973. If so, the money payments would probably be a maintenance grant for the travelling household. Kapelle, *op. cit.*, 272 n. 115, casts doubt on this interpretation.

[135] See Barlow, *Edward the Confessor*, 201–2.

[136] 3 Id. Sept.: Simeon, *HR*, ii, 218, interpolating Florence; *De Injusta Vexatione*, 195 (after a correction to the punctuation). These two statements are not, of course, independent. David, *RC*, 214–15, would retain the punctuation of the printed text and take 3 Id. Sept. with year two of the bishop's return (i.e. 1092) as the next item and the date for the destruction of Aldhun's cathedral, although this is not dated to the day and month in the source, *HDE*, ii, 128–9. David substituted 14 Nov. for 11 Sept., calculating three years from the day on which Durham castle was surrendered. Ritchie, *op. cit.*, 58, and Offler, *op. cit.*, 50, follow suit. The argument, however, is perverse. In the first place most of the entries in the conclusion to *De Injusta Vexatione*, 195, start with the year. Then, on what date was the bishop driven from his see? When besieged in his castle, he made an agreement with the earls on 8 Sept., and presumably left with them shortly afterwards in order to stand trial before 29 Sept. (see above, 84). He never returned to Durham. 11 Sept. would therefore be a likely date for his 'expulsion'. Moreover, that date for his restoration suits better the chronology of the expedition, for the fleet was wrecked off Coquet before Michaelmas (29 Sept.) and Robert sailed for Normandy before Christmas.

[137] Above, 287–8.

[138] He was the earl's nephew and the slayer of Malcolm in 1093: OV, iv, 270.

[139] Roger seems to have been at Sées, with some of his family, on 7 Nov. 1091: *CDF*, no. 659.

Siward Barn and Arnold of Percy. There are some oddities in the list. Although the fabricator should have known the Percy family, the last name is probably a mistake for Alan, whose father, William I, was still alive in 1091.[140] Ranulf the treasurer, presumably Ranulf Flambard given an unusual title, is an improbable member of the expedition. Gilbert the steward is otherwise unknown. Although reasons could be suggested for the presence of some of the rather unlikely companions of the king on this military campaign, overall the list gives the impression of being a collection of names made at a later date in which little trust can be placed.

It does, however, remind us that not only Edgar but also Duncan, Malcolm's eldest son by Ingibiorg, daughter of Thorfinn, earl of the Orkneys and Caithness, was a frequenter of the English royal court. Duncan had been given as a hostage at Abernethy in 1072 and released and knighted by Robert in 1087.[141] As he married about 1090 Octreda, the fourth daughter of his kinsman Gospatric,[142] it looks as though he went from Normandy to Scotland, perhaps more particularly to Cumbria, and that in September-October 1091 he, like Edgar, decided to rejoin William and Robert. Neither can be considered a hostage in a strict legal sense;[143] both were adventurers hoping for an improvement in their fortunes and both were to be used by William and given their opportunity.

The royal party travelled back from Scotland through Mercia to Wessex,[144] possibly to attend a postponed Michaelmas audit at the treasury at Winchester; and within a week or two William and Robert had quarrelled over the implementation of their compact. With the earl of Northumberland either restored to his position or emboldened to raise his head, the English defences had been left fully manned in the north. Bishop and earl could keep an eye on each other (in fact they were soon at loggerheads) and together keep watch on Malcolm. If Wales also had been subdued, the security of the kingdom had been reaffirmed, and Robert may with justification have thought that he and William should now return to the duchy and repeat the measures there, in particular

---

[140] For William de Percy, see below, 367. An Arnold does not seem to occur among the many members of this family who made grants to Whitby priory. Alan is commemorated in Durham's *Liber Vitae*, 51c.

[141] The former fact is inferred from the latter, for which see Florence, ii, 21.

[142] Ritchie, *op. cit.*, 62 n. 3, without a reference. A genealogical chart of 'the sons of Ingibiorg' is on p. 400. *HBC*, 54: Octreda of Dunbar.

[143] *ASC*, s.a. 1093, 170, makes Duncan a hostage at the English court continuously until that year. *GR*, ii, 476, calls him a bastard and has William knight him in 1093-4. Florence, ii, 32, suggests that Duncan was serving William as a knight.

[144] Florence, ii, 29. *ASC*'s belief that Robert sailed from the Isle of Wight lends support.

recover Maine. It was, however, late in the campaigning season; and
neither brother would have thought of waging war over Christmas. A
more immediate quarrel may have been over William's promise to grant
his brother lands and supply him with money. Anyhow, two days before
Christmas Robert sailed from the Isle of Wight and took Edgar with
him. He was not to make the return journey until 1101.

William for his part did not cross to Normandy until February 1094.
He spent the whole of 1092 and 1093 in England, distracted by
ecclesiastical and Scottish affairs and hampered by a severe illness in
1093. Welsh affairs also occupied his time, although he left the military
operations to those of his barons whose business it was. Henry, at
loggerheads with both brothers, established himself at Domfront and
remained in the wings until at the end of 1094 William made overtures
and brought him back on the stage, this time on his side. Although the
king took his English duties seriously, there can be little doubt that his
eyes were still on Normandy and that he was merely biding his time,
waiting for a suitable opportunity and collecting friends. Doubtless he
was also enjoying himself: the appetite of even an ambitious and
bellicose medieval king for business and campaigns can easily be
exaggerated and the long intervals in which he did nothing worthy of
record are often overlooked.

It was a great help to William that the body of advisers and servants
he had recruited at the beginning of his reign continued in being and
had been strengthened by the restoration to favour of William of St
Calais. It is clear that the bishop of Durham was taken back
immediately into the circle closest to the king, but only as one of a team:
he could not recover the primacy he had enjoyed in 1087–8. Moreover,
there was at least one quarrel. After the bishop had left the king's court
at Windsor 'in anger', William temporarily disseized him of Ross, near
Holy Island, probably through the agency of the earl of Northumberland;[145] and the bishop is recorded, although not necessarily correctly,
as having been at the ducal court in Normandy in February 1092 and at
the death-bed and funeral, in company with Odo of Bayeux, of Geoffrey
of Coutances in February 1093.[146] All the same, he was important in the
royal council. Four writs concerned with the succession of Aldwin to
Herbert Losinga as abbot of Ramsey in 1091–2[147] are witnessed by the
bishops of Winchester and Durham, either together or singly, and
Robert Bloet the chancellor. Another, possibly from this time, has the
witness of Hugh of Envermeu, near Dieppe, the brother of the chaplain
Turold, to whom the king gave the bishopric of Bayeux in 1097–8,[148]

[145] Craster, charter no II.
[146] For 1092, see above, 281 n. 76, for 1093, *Gallia Christiana*, xi, instr. 224.
[147] See above, 292 n. 126.
[148] *Regesta*, no. 354, cf. 400.

possibly a new recruit from Normandy. Two royal documents from September 1093 provide the names of the bishops of Durham, Winchester and Rochester, Eudo the steward, Ranulf Flambard, William Peverel, Haimo the steward, Urse of Abetot and Ranulf, Ilger's brother (sheriff of Huntingdon).[149] The keynote is stability. Robert Bloet, formerly his father's clerk, was chancellor from January 1091 until February 1094, in everyday attendance on the king, and his promotion in 1093-4 to a bishopric seems to have been fortuitous.

The king cannot have been completely satisfied with the results of his northern expedition in 1091, for in May of the following year he attacked with a large army the opposite flank.[150] The old kingdom of Cumbria had been under Scottish rule from the beginning of the eleventh century, and the southern part, the district between the Solway and Stainmore, was in the subordinate possession of the great Northumbrian family in which ran the names of Dolfin, Gospatric and Waltheof.[151] The south-east boundary stone, the Rere Cross, five miles north-east of Kirkby Stephen, near the junction of the counties of Cumberland, Westmorland, Northumberland, Durham and Yorkshire, on the Roman road across the Pennines,[152] was well south of Newcastle-on-Tyne and within easy reach of York. William drove out Dolfin and refounded Carlisle as an English borough. He restored the town, which he settled with English families and their farm stock sent up from the south, built a castle which he garrisoned, appointed a sheriff and put his conquest under the spiritual jurisdiction of the bishop of Durham and his archdeacon.[153]

This was the beginning of one of William's most important achievements – his restoration of the historical frontier with Scotland. One effect of the Norman Conquest had been the loss of control over the north of England, largely because the Normans had insufficient manpower to make settlements north of the Ribble in Lancashire and the Wansbeck in Northumberland. Under the Conqueror, the great mountainous salient from the north, the Pennine Chain, was gradually ringed, especially on the east, with castleries, so that Newcastle-on-Tyne,

[149] *Ibid.*, nos 336-7.

[150] *ASC, s.a.*, 169; Florence, ii, 30, with the information that the city had remained deserted until destroyed by the Danes two hundred years before. The annal is omitted by *GR* and ignored by OV. Barrow, *op. cit.*, 142 ff.; Kapelle, *op. cit.*, 150 ff.

[151] There is controversy over both the identity of the ruler, Dolfin, and the political status of Cumbria. Kapelle, *op. cit.*, 151-2, does not believe that he was the eldest son of Earl Gospatric or that he was subordinate to the Scottish king: Malcolm therefore was not much concerned. But whoever Dolfin may have been, and whatever may have been his relationship to the king of Scots, Malcolm was bound to be concerned by this English encroachment.

[152] Ritchie, *op. cit.*, 50 n. 2, for a description.

[153] *Regesta*, nos 463, 478.

founded by Robert in 1080, was defended in great depth.[154] After the conquest of Carlisle and the death of Malcolm in the following year, there began an English advance towards the Liddel and Tweed which had permanent political effects. William granted the lordship of Carlisle or Cumberland, which also became an episcopal diocese in 1133, to Ranulf le Meschin of Bricquessart, son of Ranulf *vicomte* of Bayeux, and Margaret, sister of Hugh of Avranches, earl of Chester.[155] Ranulf junior was the third husband of the heiress Lucy, who carried the honour of Bolingbroke to her husbands in turn, and in 1120 he also inherited the earldom of Chester. In the meantime, however, he established himself firmly in Cumberland.[156] He enfeoffed his brother William with Irthington and made his sister's husband, Robert of Trevers, lord of Burgh-by-Sands. The latter and Liddel Strength were the new marcher lordships against Scotland. Possibly also at this time, or a little earlier, the king gave the area south of the Lake District, which became known as the barony of Kendal (Westmorland), to his steward, Ivo Taillebois, the first husband of Lucy of Bolingbroke, who died about 1094.[157] He was making perfectly sure that his kingdom should extend in the north-west to the Solway Firth and the Liddel.

On the east flank of the Pennines, William created a barony at Skipton in Craven (West Riding of Yorkshire) for Robert de Rumilly, and the honour of Barnard Castle in upper Teesdale (Durham) and the barony of Bywell in the Tyne valley (Northumberland) for Guy of Balliol. The first holder of the honour of Mitford on the Wansbeck in Northumberland was John, probably a kinsman of Guy.[158] Although the effective frontier was still on the Tyne, Newcastle had been given closer support, and the earl of Northumberland could with confidence operate beyond.

Shortly after the conquest of Carlisle, however, the king suffered an unexpected setback. At the beginning of March 1093 he was north of Bristol at Alveston, a royal manor which had once belonged to Harold, intending more likely to take the Aust ferry to South Wales or set up his headquarters at Gloucester than to intervene again in Scotland, when he fell ill.[159] He managed to travel the twenty-five miles north to Gloucester, where there was a castle, a great abbey and medical help,

[154] Kapelle, *op. cit.*, 142 ff.; G.W.S. Barrow, 'The pattern of lordship and feudal settlement in Cumbria', *Journal of Medieval History*, i (1975), 117.

[155] Sanders, *Baronies*, 32, 18.

[156] For these enfeoffments, see *ibid.*, 124 (and 115); 23; 129.

[157] *Ibid.*, 56. The date is between 1086, when the estates were in the king's hands, and Ivo's death.

[158] *Ibid.*, 142; 25; 131. Kapelle, *op. cit.*, 148. Loyd, *Families*, 87, calls Robert of Rumilly 'Rainfray'.

[159] *ASC, s.a.*, 170; Florence, ii, 30, *DB*, i, 163a; Eadmer, *HN*, 30 ff., *VA*, 64; OV, iv, 176.

9a. Colchester castle, the keep. (See here, 96.)

9b. Old Montgomery castle, Hen Dolmen. (See here, 320, 354.)

10. Westminster Hall. (See here, 371–2, 399 ff.)

but for a time he got worse. Although he does not appear to have been quite at death's door on Sunday 6 March when Anselm abbot of Bec was forcibly invested with Canterbury at his bedside,[160] it seems that he was confined to his chamber for the whole of Lent (2 March–17 April).[161] No one says what his sickness was. Disorders of the stomach and bowels, caused by poor hygiene, bad food and over-eating and drinking were common and could be fatal. Clearly the court and the king himself believed at first that his life was in danger, and it was rumoured that he was dead.

It was also thought by everyone, including the patient, that God was punishing him for his sins; and the courtiers warned him that he would go to Hell unless he repented and made amends. William was terrified and eager to follow the advice which the bishops and barons proffered, and which Anselm later confirmed and elaborated. His acts of atonement are of great interest because they show which of his governmental practices were considered the most unjust and sinful. His private sins were taken care of by Anselm's requirement that he should make a full confession and promise that if he survived he would completely mend his ways.[162] His public offences were corrected not only by his solemn promise that he would live all the rest of his life in mercy and justice but also by two formal acts: he appointed the bishops his sureties before God that he would carry out his promises, and this undertaking was placed on an altar; and, secondly, he authorized writs to be issued which gave administrative effect to his pledges. His engagements were a sort of elaboration of his coronation promises and formed a charter of liberties which most chroniclers took care to record.[163] He would protect and defend the church and no longer practise simony. He would abolish unjust laws, establish good ones, see that they were observed, and set on foot a strict judicial inquiry into all illegalities in order to deter wrong-doers. Some of these phrases have a long history.[164] And as an earnest of the new era he ordered all his prisoners to be released, all his debts remitted and all offences against him to be pardoned. If these instructions were actually sent out, they would have gone to the sheriffs and the treasury officials. He also filled the two vacant bishoprics which were 'in demesne', at farm.[165] Besides

[160] HN, 32 7, VA, 65. Now that Anselm has come into the story, Eadmer becomes an additional and most useful source of information. Everything which concerns his master is described in great detail.

[161] Florence, loc. cit. Anselm visited Winchester at Easter (17 Apr.), VA, 65–6, but it does not necessarily follow that the royal court was there.

[162] HN, 31; GP, 80; OV, iv, 176.

[163] HN, 31–2; ASC, s.a., 170; Florence, ii, 30–1.

[164] Cf. VEdR, 12–13, on Edward the Confessor's engagements.

[165] For royal custodies, see above, 233 ff.

appointing Anselm to Canterbury, he rewarded his chancellor Robert
Bloet with Lincoln. And he gave land to many monasteries.[166] These
concessions can be compared with those in Henry I's coronation
charter.[167]

A crisis of this sort had a long-lasting effect on royal conduct only if the
remedy was difficult to obtain. Henry's loss of his son in *The White Ship*
disaster of 1120 was of that kind. But the promises he made in 1100 were
to rectify what proved to be a temporary weakness; and so it was with
William in 1093. Observers agree that once he recovered from his illness,
he disregarded all his undertakings. 'Who can keep all his promises?' he
had once asked angrily of Lanfranc.[168] Eadmer thought that he even
behaved much worse than before: he was angry with God for inflicting
this illness on him. It seems that the prelates had overplayed their hands,
and William was not one to miss a trick. Be that as it may, the events at
Gloucester show clearly that the king's government was thought
oppressive, especially in its linked judicial and financial operations, and
that the cost of his military campaigns had aroused a resentment which
was potentially dangerous. One strange feature of this episode, however,
is that no one mentions the problem of the succession, so recently
negotiated with Robert. Although the king was believed to be dying, no
suggestion is reported that Robert should be summoned or Henry
informed. Indeed, the consequences of William's death may have
appeared so dreadful that most men may well have hoped that good
might come out of evil in the shape of a chastened and improved ruler.
With the king still only thirty-three, the situation was not irremediable.

No episode in the reign is more carefully described than Anselm's
election to Canterbury, but only from the point of view of the
archbishop and his biographer, the Christ Church monk Eadmer, and
this very considerable bias must always be kept in mind.[169] It was, as
seen by Eadmer, the opening scene in a tragedy, for he noticed only the
resulting injustices done to his hero and the mother church of Britain,
and their great suffering. But the appointment was also a political
mistake on William's part; and if he suffered less, it was only because he

---

[166] According to *ASC* alone, 'but as soon as he was better he took it away again'. Grants
probably in connexion with William's repentance are *Regesta*, no. 339 (Gloucester
abbey), 351 (St Augustine's, Canterbury) and 407 (canons of Lincoln).

[167] *SSC*, 116 ff.

[168] *HN*, 25.

[169] William of Malmesbury's summary of Eadmer in *GP*, 77–105, especially the first
edition, is, if anything, even more hostile to the king. But the anonymous biographer of
the saintly Gundulf, despite the friendship between Anselm and the bishop of Rochester,
is much more cool: *Vita Gundulfi*, in *Anglia Sacra*, ii, 285 ff. Gundulf managed to keep in
with both sides.

had the coarser nature. Indeed, the story of their relationship in the years 1092–7 can be viewed – and doubtless was by the more irreverent courtiers – as a black comedy, the penalty William paid for an uncharacteristic bout of piety which gave him a spiritual father with whom he found it impossible to work. Even the unusual qualities they shared, courage and plain-speaking, exacerbated their relationship. And it was almost entirely William's fault, a rare case of self-deception, induced by an even rarer failure in courage, his fear of death.

It seems also, although Eadmer carefully concealed it, that Anselm too was momentarily deceived by the warm welcome he received initially in England and by William's affability.[170] He should have known better. He knew William and the English scene. Born in 1033 into a noble family from the borders of Burgundy and Lombardy, clever and well educated, he had been a monk of Bec for thirty-three years, having spent fifteen of them as Lanfranc's successor as prior and the last fifteen as abbot, successor to the founder Herlwin.[171] He was beginning to be recognized as a logician and theologian of the very first rank, and, although approaching the age of sixty, was still to produce some metaphysical monographs which, with his other books, have given him a posthumous reputation as the greatest speculative theologian in the West between St Augustine of Hippo and St Thomas Aquinas.[172] Intellectually he was a genius. He wrote fluently and simply in excellent Latin, and probably spoke with equal facility and cogency to the laity in French. He had been known to, and respected by, William I, had visited Lanfranc at Canterbury, and was in a position to learn all that he needed to know about the duties and problems of the English primate and the character of William Rufus. It is obvious that in 1092–4 his eyes were almost completely open: he was conscious of his unsuitability for the archbishopric and was aware of the special problem caused by William's refusal so far to recognize either of the contestants for the Holy See as pope. What both he and Eadmer had to explain after the event was how it was that he allowed himself to get elected.

Eadmer was probably right in seeing Anselm as the innocent victim of a situation from which, given some of his religious attitudes, he was unable to escape.[173] The high-minded, however, are especially vulnerable

---

[170] Anselm, *Letters*, no. 147; *VA*, 64; *GP*, 79.

[171] As Anselm himself explained, *Letters*, no. 156, p. 18.

[172] Cf. Barlow, *EC 1066–1154*, 69–70.

[173] *HN*, 27 ff., *VA*, 63 ff. Sally N. Vaughn, 'St Anselm of Canterbury', *loc. cit.*, reacts strongly against Eadmer's adulation, and, with reference to her 'Anselm of Canterbury, reluctant archbishop', *Albion*, vi, 240–50 argues that Anselm worked deliberately after Lanfranc's death to get Canterbury. In her view Anselm was a superb politician who used 'holy guile' to achieve his ends.

to the charge of cloaked self-interest, and such a suspicion came easily to William. He was not, after all, without experience in these matters; principles can be used, unconsciously as well as consciously, to mask ambition which, however natural, is considered unseemly in certain professions and situations. That Anselm, who had the most tender conscience, occasionally searched out something in his attitude to worldly success of which he was ashamed cannot be doubted. But to see him as a hypocrite, as William in his coarser moments was tempted to do, is unperceptive. It is also to disregard the obligations of office. However humble Anselm might be as a monk, as abbot of Bec and as archbishop of Canterbury he had to maintain the rights of his office and church. Necessary ambition for the metropolitan and primatial see of Great Britain not only put a strain on his monastic humility but also put him in a false position.

In 1092, when Canterbury had been vacant for over three years, Hugh earl of Chester, a great sinner, who wanted to establish a monastery at St Werburgh's, managed to persuade Anselm to visit him and sponsor his foundation. It was also necessary for the abbot to look into the affairs of Bec's estates in England and he wanted to ask the king to reduce their assessment to geld.[174] Eadmer believed that Anselm's reluctance to visit England (which he stresses) was due to his fear that he might be considered for Canterbury; and in the *Vita* he relates that when the abbot arrived at Canterbury on 7 September and some monks and laymen acclaimed him their archbishop, he refused to celebrate the feast of the Nativity of the Virgin there and left abruptly early next morning.[175] His next objective was the royal court, where, after receiving an exceedingly warm welcome from one and all, he took the king aside and rebuked him for his vices. William of Malmesbury thought that the king, who did not want to affront an abbot whom his father and mother had so much respected, merely replied that he could not escape rumours and gossip, but such a holy man as Anselm should not pay them any attention.[176] Whereupon Anselm, probably to William's relief, and without raising the business of his own church, took himself off to Chester.

Apparently he had no more cause for alarm in the following five months, some of which time was spent at Westminster with Abbot Gilbert Crispin, a former monk of Bec;[177] but at the unlocated Christmas court which he attended, some prelates asked the king if he would allow

[174] *GP*, 79.

[175] *VA*, 63–4.

[176] *GP*, 79.

[177] R.W. Southern, 'St Anselm and Gilbert Crispin, abbot of Westminster', *Mediaeval and Renaissance Studies*, iii (1975), 87–8.

prayers to be said in the churches that God would inspire him to appoint a worthy pastor to Canterbury. William, although at first indignant, agreed, remarking characteristically that whatever it was that the church wanted he would doubtless refuse it: indeed, he would do in this matter whatever he liked.[178] Whereupon the bishops persuaded Anselm to devise a prayer which was duly recited in churches throughout the kingdom.

About this time Anselm reported to his monastery that he could not say yet whether his visit had been successful or not. Although the king and the other magnates showed him immeasurable love and honour, William continued to defer giving an answer to his request, and he did not think that he would be home before Lent (2 March 1093).[179] Clearly he was preparing for a protracted stay in England in which he could get down to some devotional and theological work, for he asked that the prayer to St Nicholas that he had written and the answer to the propositions of Roscelin which he had started[180] should be sent to him. Eadmer suggests that William had begun to toy with the idea of making Anselm archbishop.[181] He relates a conversation between the king and one of his barons which took place shortly after Christmas. The baron observed that Anselm was the holiest man they had ever known. He loved nothing save God and had no desire at all for worldly things. 'Not even for the archbishopric of Canterbury?' William jested. 'For that least of all,' answered the baron. At which William remarked that if he had any reason to believe that the abbot would consider taking it he would run joyfully to embrace him.[182] 'But,' he added, 'by the Holy Face of Lucca, not just now. For the present neither he nor anyone else shall be archbishop of Canterbury, apart from me.' It was then that he fell ill. Eadmer saw in this the design of God, even though it was a trap for the saint.

Anselm had been prevented by sickness from helping William I out of this world.[183] In March 1093 he was conveniently near the royal sick-bed at Gloucester and took part in the ministrations. The fateful day was the first Sunday in Lent, 6 March. The penitent king agreed to the bishops' advice that he should make reparation to the church by appointing to Canterbury, and, according to Eadmer, they left the

[178] *GP*, 79, improves this by changing it into more vigorous direct speech: 'Pray what you will; I'll do as I like, for no man's prayer will make me change my mind.'

[179] *Letters*, no. 147.

[180] This developed into the treatise *De Incarnatione Verbi*.

[181] *HN*, 30 ff., *VA*, 64–5; *GP*, 80.

[182] *GP*, 80, turns it into: 'Anselm would put his legs and hands to any use in order to get the archbishopric'; but this, although more characteristic of the king's cynicism, seems to be the opposite of what Eadmer wrote.

[183] *HN*, 24.

choice entirely to him. When he declared that the abbot of Bec was the most worthy of the office, they applauded enthusiastically and hurried Anselm to the bedside to be invested by William. The abbot seems to have been taken by surprise. In all his letters on the subject he stressed the suddenness of the event;[184] and he resisted stubbornly. But he stood completely alone: the Bec monks who were with him were fatalistic; the bishops were determined not to lose this heaven-sent opportunity of getting a primate, and were bewildered by, and then indignant at, Anselm's refusal; and the king had convinced himself that this was the only way in which he could evade death and damnation.

The bishops stressed the abbot's duty to obey the will of God and his obligation to spare the suffering of Canterbury and to reform the irregularities in the English church. William, according to Eadmer, made a most moving entreaty. Almost weeping with sorrow, he exclaimed, 'Oh, Anselm, what are you doing? Why are you delivering me to crucifixion and eternal punishment? Remember, I beg of you, the true friendship which my father and mother had for you and which you always had for them. And in the name of that friendship I entreat you not to allow me, their son, to perish both in body and in soul. I know for sure that I will perish if I die while still in possession of the archbishopric. So help me, lord father, and take it from me.'

William then ordered all to fall at Anselm's feet and beg him to accept. But the abbot threw himself at their feet and begged them to spare him. In the end the courtiers lost patience, pushed and pulled him to the bedside, gave the king a pastoral staff and attempted to prise open Anselm's clenched right hand. But they only managed to pull back his forefinger, using such force that Anselm cried out with pain; and in the end they were reduced to holding the crozier against his closed hand with their own.[185] Eadmer does not mention the episcopal ring. After this semblance of an investiture the assembly shouted, 'Long live the bishop,' and the bishops and clergy struck up the hymn *Te deum laudamus*. They then carried, rather than conducted, him into the nearby church, with Anselm protesting all the way that the election was null and void; and in the church they performed 'the appropriate ceremonies'.

Afterwards Anselm returned to the king's chamber and said, 'I tell you, lord king, that you will not die of this sickness; and therefore I want you to know that you can change what has been done, for I have not accepted, and do not accept, that it is a valid act.' To the bishops and nobles who went with him out of the room he spoke by a parable. They were proposing to yoke an old and feeble sheep with an unbroken bull to

---

[184] Cf. *Letters*, nos 148, 151, 176.
[185] See also Osbern of Canterbury to Anselm, *ibid*., no. 149, p. 7; *GP*, 80 ff.

pull the plough, which as a result would be dragged uncontrollably through the thorns and briers to the great detriment of the sheep, its wool, its milk, and its lambs. The plough, he explained, was the church, which was guided and hauled by the two most distinguished oxen, the king and the archbishop of Canterbury. The one ruled by earthly justice and power, the other by divine learning and instruction. One of the oxen, that is to say Lanfranc, was now dead, but the other, still young, had the ferocity of an untamable bull – and they proposed to yoke him, an old sheep, with that. He then spoke of all the harm which would be caused by that inequality, disasters even worse than those then afflicting the church.

Although, according to Eadmer, William when he recovered his health invalidated all his penitential acts, he allowed the nomination of Anselm to stand, despite all the obstacles which had already emerged and were to continue to appear. It is possible that in the beginning he genuinely liked the abbot; he was affected by his parents' views; it was not the sort of engagement from which he cared to back out; and it is possible that there was almost united pressure on him from the barons and prelates to see this matter through. The long vacancy at Canterbury had become a scandal which all thought should be ended; and the Norman magnates knew a saint when they saw one. Eadmer states that immediately after the 'investiture' on 6 March William ordered Anselm to be invested with the whole archbishopric of Canterbury and added the city of Canterbury, which Lanfranc had held merely as a fief, and the abbey of St Albans, the additions being for the redemption of his soul.[186] Gundulf of Rochester, the friend of both, under whose care the king put him, also believed that the abbot had acquired some of the character of an archbishop. Urging the reluctant monks of Bec to release their head, Gundulf averred that the king, by the advice and at the request of the magnates and also at the petition and through the election of the clergy and people, had granted the government (*gubernatio*) of the church of Canterbury to him, and this doubtless had been procured and ordained by God. They must give him their consent quickly, for the business had gone so far that news of it must already have reached the Holy See.[187] Anselm's own view of the situation was a little different. Although he

[186] *HN*, 37.
[187] Anselm, *Letters*, no. 150. The hostility of the monks to Anselm's departure is seen also in 'De libertate Beccensis monasterii', *loc. cit.*, 636–8. Among the reasons may have been the fact that Anselm's choice as his successor fell on a scion of the local family of Montfort-sur-Risle, who was also related (cousin-once-removed) to Robert count of Meulan and the Beaumonts: *Chronicon Beccense* in *B. Lanfranci Opera Omnia*, ed. L. D'Achery (Paris 1648), app., p. 6; and the likelihood that the archbishop of Rouen would attempt to secure a profession of obedience from the new abbot, and in the circumstances succeed. As it turned out, however, the monks managed to preserve their liberty.

admitted reluctantly that he had been elected, he also maintained that he had not accepted the election; and this allowed him to bargain with the king during the following seven months.

The pressure on him, however, from the bishops and the monks of Christ Church and probably other interested parties was unremitting. The bishops had told him that they would relieve him of all the secular work connected with the office and obey him in all things.[188] Osbern of Canterbury wrote piteous and blackmailing letters on behalf of the cathedral monks.[189] And it may be that at heart the abbot was not quite as reluctant as Eadmer would have us believe. In a letter to the monks of Bec in which he expressed his sorrow at his election, which, he said, was more an act of violence than an election, he nevertheless accepted it as an act of God which he could not resist: he had to obey God's ordinance and judgment.[190] He also worked hard to secure the election of William prior of Poissy as his successor. He even enlisted the king's help in achieving this end.[191] It is understandable that once he had submitted himself irrevocably to God's will, he felt a few twinges of conscience.

In the meantime the external hindrances were one by one removed. William obtained the permission of his brother the duke, the archbishop of Rouen and the monastery of Bec (the last with some difficulty) for Anselm's migration. The other main stumbling blocks were a matter for him alone. In the summer the two met at Rochester.[192] The abbot said that he was still doubtful whether he could accept the archbishopric and stated his terms. First, he must have all the lands of the church of Canterbury exactly as they were at the time of Lanfranc's death and unencumbered by any claims upon them. He must also have justice in respect of all Canterbury lands which Lanfranc had claimed but failed to recover. Second, the king must take him as his principal counsellor, so that, just as he would regard William as his earthly lord and protector, William would have him as his spiritual father and director of his soul. And third, Anselm warned him – lest there be any scandal in the future – that he had already, and still, recognized Urban as pope, whom he knew the king had not yet recognized, and that he wished to continue to be subject to him and pay him due obedience. He would like to have the king's decision on these matters. William called in William bishop of Durham and Robert count of Meulan and asked Anselm to repeat the conditions. After taking his counsellors' advice, he replied that he would restore to Anselm all the Canterbury lands which had been in

[188] *HN*, 33.
[189] Anselm, *Letters*, nos 149, 152.
[190] *Ibid.*, no. 148, cf. 151, 156.
[191] *Ibid.*, nos 156–7, 163–5.
[192] *HN*, p. 39.

Lanfranc's possession at his death, but he could not come to an immediate decision on those estates which he had not possessed. With regard to these and all other matters he would be guided by Anselm as he ought to be. It should be noticed that Eadmer states the third condition in less peremptory terms than the others: none of them was a papalist as yet. On this evidence it cannot be said that Anselm made recognition of Urban II a prerequisite of his acceptance of the office.

Indeed, paradoxically, the main battle was over the Canterbury estates, and if this be thought unworthy of one who was supposed to take no interest in worldly matters, Anselm would not have wanted to appear as one who paid for his promotion at the expense of his church, and it is also possible that he thought that it was here that he could push the king beyond the breaking point and so escape the office. After the consent of the several Norman authorities had been received, William at a court at Windsor asked Anselm to accept the archbishopric, but, with reference to his earlier promise about the estates, asked him to condone, for love of him, some enfeoffments he had made on Canterbury land since Lanfranc's death.[193] Most of the magnates would probably have agreed with the king that this was a trivial matter – the archbishop would still have received service from the fiefs – but Anselm would abate not a jot or tittle of his requirements, and refused. There was a quarrel, and Anselm, according to his biographer, delightedly thought that he had at last escaped the burden. Once again, however, William made promises, which Eadmer does not report in detail, and finally, at a royal court at Winchester in September, Anselm accepted the archbishopric and became the king's vassal, almost certainly doing homage and swearing fealty just as Lanfranc had done, this still being English custom.[194] Whether he was reinvested by the king with ring and staff is not clear. It was an episode which Eadmer chose not to clarify.

From Winchester the archbishop-elect went to Canterbury on 25 September for his enthronement; but the day was probably spoilt for him when Ranulf Flambard personally served a royal writ on him, making him the defendant in some case which Eadmer does not describe beyond remarking that it concerned a matter which pertained more to ecclesiastical than to royal law.[195] Ranulf's main purpose at Canterbury, however, would have been to supervise the handing over of the

---

[193] All the other matters of dispute except this and the recognition of the pope were cut out of the second edition of *GP*, pp. 83–6 and n.

[194] *HN*, p. 41; *GP*, p. 84. Barlow, *EC 1066–1154*, p. 287. William dates a gift, 'on the day after Archbishop Anselm *meus ligius homo factus est*': *Regesta* no. 337. Sally N. Vaughn, *loc. cit.*, p. 282, n. 7, maintains that, although Anselm had been invested with Bec by William I, he had not done homage in return.

[195] *HN*, pp. 41–2.

bishopric after it had been in royal custody for four-and-a-half years and probably under his supervision. It should have come as no surprise to the archbishop, therefore, or even his chaplain, that he would be henceforth closely involved in the temporal affairs of the kingdom. Moreover by this time the die had been cast. Anselm's consecration took place in his cathedral church on 4 December, a ceremony slightly marred by a dispute with York over Canterbury's title, but a disagreement quickly smoothed over and not arising again during William's reign.[196] Anselm then went to rejoin the king at Gloucester for the Christmas celebrations, and was warmly welcomed by William and all the nobles.

If William thought all his troubles over Canterbury were now over, he was soon to discover his delusion. As Anselm had remarked, the two were ill-matched. They had, however, no differences at all on principle. Anselm was old enough to be the king's father, and they were both old-fashioned in their political views. Anselm's parable about the two oxen yoked to the plough states the Gelasian position without even the insistence that the ecclesiastical ox had the greater dignity or responsibility. Indeed, if correctly reported, he gave the lay prince great authority in the church,[197] and, as we have seen, he accepted his nomination and investiture by the king and became his vassal, acts which later, in the changed atmosphere of the triumph of Gregorian ideas, were to cause him some distress.[198] As a monk he welcomed the advocacy and protection of the religiously inclined earthly ruler. Both men, of course, had principles: William was a fanatical upholder of royal rights, and if Anselm could invoke God and mother church, he could appeal to the crown. But it was their character and way of thought which made the behaviour of each incomprehensible to the other.

Anselm was an intellectual of the most uncompromising kind, a trained and eager logician. He analyzed all problems in a rigorous way and did not shrink from the extreme positions into which this pushed him. And his theoretical arguments, often rather divorced from the political scene, could be exasperating to grosser beings. Although as abbot and archbishop he lived very much in the feudal world, and, indeed, loved to use feudal imagery in his parables and 'similitudes', he could be alarmingly innocent. He also had a most scrupulous conscience, a feature of the cloister, which was inconvenient for everyone outside. After his consecration as bishop he wrote to a number of prelates explaining and excusing his behaviour.[199] He thought that some of his

[196] EC 1066–1154, pp. 42–3.

[197] Cf. also Letters, no. 151, to the monks of Bec, in which he refers to the king and duke as 'lords of our church'. EC 1066–1154, pp. 287 ff.

[198] Ibid., p. 301.

[199] Letters, nos. 156, 158–60.

recipients, or other men, were blaming him for cupidity – that he had aspired to the archbishopric through greed. And this he denied. He had been forced into the office against his wishes by the will of God. He had accepted reluctantly and only through fear of God. Such protestations to bishops whose ranks he was joining seem a little lacking in tact, taste and humour. Another attitude which was to cause William offence was his ingrained habit of correcting sin, learnt in his many years as prior and abbot. He had made his intention clear at the interview at Rochester, and William cannot have forgotten their earlier talk about vice at court. The king knew that Anselm would be even more tiresome than Lanfranc, but when in good health he did not care all that much – it was something to joke about with the courtiers.

While Anselm had been making up his mind, William had been demonstrating that he had completely recovered from his illness and had regained his full appetite for adventure. In the summer he went to Dover with the bishop of Durham and the count of Meulan to meet the count of Flanders, and returned by way of Rochester and Windsor once more to Gloucester.[200] Although he does not seem to have intervened physically in South Wales, he must have been keeping an eye on the baronial campaigns.[201] The aftermath of his conquest of Cumbria had also to be faced. In the spring and summer, according to the Anglo-Saxon Chronicler, the ultimate source for the story and the most informative, there were fateful diplomatic exchanges between the two kings.[202] It was Malcolm who took the initiative, and he was seeking a firm peace, which, according to Florence, was also the desire of some of the English magnates. Especially he wanted the terms of their treaty to be carried out. Whereupon William summoned him to Gloucester, sent him hostages, and later dispatched Edgar. The Ætheling was last noticed leaving for Normandy with Robert, and perhaps he was recalled by the king in order to act again as an intermediary.

Malcolm then travelled south. On Thursday 11 August at Durham he joined with the bishop and Prior Turgot in laying the first stones of a new cathedral church,[203] that which still stands in all its barbaric grandeur. William of St Calais must have been involved in the arrangements for the king's visit,[204] and Malcolm, escorted by English officials with every honour, reached Gloucester on 24 August. But William would neither see him nor fulfil the terms of their agreement, whereupon Malcolm

[200] HN, pp. 40–41.
[201] See below, 321 ff.
[202] ASC, s.a., 170; GR, ii, 366; Florence, ii, 31. OV, iv, 270, is very confused.
[203] De Injusta Vexatione, p. 195. See here, pl. 14b.
[204] Cf. the arrangements made for his visit to Gloucester in 1059: Barlow, Edward the Confessor, p. 203.

returned angrily to Scotland. William of Malmesbury thought that he came as an equal and of his own accord. Florence adds that William's behaviour was caused by his excessive pride and overweening power and that he tried to force Malcolm to plead in the royal court and accept the judgment of the English barons alone, whereas Malcolm contended that kings of Scots were obliged to answer kings of England on the frontier and by the judgment of the magnates of both countries. One can almost hear William of St Calais speaking, and there are indeed echoes of his trial in 1088. In this case, when Malcolm came to court under safe-conduct in order to complain about the failure to implement their agreement and possibly air other grievances, William tried to subject a diplomatic issue to a court of law and treat a foreign king like an ordinary baron. The only result was a good deal of ill will.

What no one tells us, unfortunately, is exactly what were Malcolm's grievances. A narrow interpretation of the Anglo-Saxon Chronicle would limit them to the failure to grant the lands and pay the money. But it could be extended to cover additional promises made to Malcolm's envoys. If these had arrived while the king was at death's door, he could have made an ill-considered and later much regretted reply. The sending of hostages, and then Edgar, suggests that at the time William was quite eager to see Malcolm. But why is not obvious: either he was so ill that he wanted to make amends or some vital information is missing. It is easy to bring in here the annexation of Cumbria. It is just possible that this was one of the wrongs William promised to right.[205] And if he held out this inducement to the Scottish envoys in the spring, all that follows is understandable. Malcolm, in a desperate attempt to hold a resuscitated William to his vow, was willing to repeat the journey to Gloucester he had last made thirty-four years before, at the very beginning of his reign and in very different circumstances,[206] only to encounter the full malice of the king's reaction to his recent humiliation.

This, although pure supposition, may well be so. There is also the matter of the removal of Malcolm and Margaret's daughter Edith (later known as Matilda) from a West-Saxon nunnery, probably Wilton, where, together with her sister Mary, she had been living under the direction of her aunt Christina, Margaret and Edgar's sister.[207] Whether

---

[205] Cf. *FWR*, ii, 8–9; Kapelle, *op. cit.*, p. 151.

[206] Barlow, *Edward the Confessor*, pp. 202–3. It occurred at about the time of William Rufus' birth.

[207] Or perhaps they had been with Christina at neighbouring Romsey. For the difficulties over Christina's abbacy, see *HRH*, p. 219; cf. also above, 264. Eadmer, *HN*, p. 123, thought that Edith was at Wilton. It is not known whether Christina was still alive in 1100, but she could well have been. Eleanor Searle's investigation of this case, in 'Women and the legitimization of succession at the Norman Conquest', *Battle III*, pp. 166–9, was published after I had written these pages.

she had been a monastic oblate or had willingly worn the veil became in 1100, when Henry I wished to marry her, a matter of crucial importance. Anselm had to make inquiries, and have witnesses examined, before an ecclesiastical council could pass judgment. Eadmer and Hermann of Tournai claim to give the depositions of Edith and Christina respectively; and the two statements are essentially versions of the same story.[208] Hermann, who had been monk and abbot (1127 c.1137) of Tournai, and claimed to have heard, when a young man, Anselm pronounce judgment in the case and make a pessimistic and true prophecy,[209] when writing a history of his church about 1147 inserted a report of the council into a digression on the history of England occasioned by a reference to the marriage of Matilda of Flanders to William the Conqueror. His main reason for including the council of 1100 was to use Anselm's prophecy, that if Henry insisted on marrying Edith, England would not long rejoice in the children he had of her, as the key to later events, especially those after Henry's death. All the details in his story of most interest to us play no part in that thesis and could hardly have been invented in 1147. Moreover, Eadmer states that Anselm sent the archdeacons of Canterbury and Salisbury to Wilton to check with the nuns whether Edith's deposition was true: and so it was found.[210] A Wilton deposition had, therefore, once been in existence.

Hermann's abbess (unnamed and unlocated, but obviously Christina) declared that the king of Scots (always David instead of Malcolm in this account) had commended his daughter (never named) to her, not that she should become a nun but to be educated in the cloister, and that at the time the events she was about to describe occurred, the girl could have been twelve years old.[211]

One day [she said] I was informed that King William . . . had come to visit the girl, and that he and his knights had already dismounted before the gates and had ordered them to be opened so that they could come in and say their prayers. I was very upset by the news, for I was afraid that the king, who was young and wild and always wanted to do immediately whatever came into his head, might, when he saw how beautiful she was, indecently assault her, especially as he had arrived so unexpectedly and unheralded. So I hid her in a more private room, told the king what the position was, and with her

[208] HN, 121 ff. Hermann, *Liber de Restauratione S. Martini Tornacensis*, in *MGH Scriptores*, xiv, 280.

[209] 'Hec ego adolescens eum dixisse audivi; nunc vero ex magna parte video iam contigisse', *loc. cit.*, 281. R.W. Southern, who discusses the Gunnhildr affair, *St Anselm and his Biographer* (1963), 182 ff., suggests, 190, that Anselm's man, Baldwin of Tournai, may have been Hermann's source.

[210] HN, 123.

[211] *Loc. cit.*, 281.

agreement[212] put a veil on her head so that when the king should see her he would be deterred from an unlawful embrace.

And so it turned out. The king came into the cloister as though he wanted to look at the roses and other flowering shrubs; but as soon as he saw her with our other girls wearing the veil he went out of the cloister and left the church, in this way showing quite clearly that he had come only on her account. Less than a week later her father [again called David] arrived, and when he saw the veil on her head, in a fury tore it off, threw it to the ground and trampled on it. He then took her away with him.

Eadmer in the same context professes to tell Edith's own story.[213] The princess visited the archbishop and denied that she had ever been an oblate or had ever, even once, worn the veil of her own free will. But she could not deny that she had worn it, for when she had been an adolescent and under the strict discipline of her aunt Christina, her aunt had put a black cloth on her head to preserve her chastity from the lust of the Normans who were at that time threatening and setting traps for everyone's chastity. And whenever she threw it off, Christina would punish her with sharp blows and foul language. So she wore it weeping and trembling in the abbess's presence, but, whenever she was out of sight, used to throw it to the ground and crush it under her feet. That is how she wore the veil! What is more, when by chance her father saw her veiled in the way described, he tore it off in a fury, and, while he destroyed it, invoked God's hatred on the person who had put it on her, and said that he had intended her to marry Count Alan rather than spend her life in a nunnery.[214]

King Malcolm's intervention, common to both stories, must have taken place in August 1093, and that Edith left the cloister at about that time is confirmed by a letter Anselm wrote about March 1094 to the diocesan bishop, Osmund of Salisbury, about the affair.[215] Although the daughter of the king of Scots, he wrote, had put off the veil and was living in the world, he had delayed hitherto openly correcting the crime, for he feared she had been pushed into the sin, or encouraged to persevere in it, by the help and encouragement of the king. So when King William was about to cross the sea (February–March 1094), he had raised the matter with him in order to find out how he felt about it. William, as befitted a good king, had told him that it would be all right

[212] *Volente* and *nolente* are, unfortunately, often difficult to distinguish in MSS; but the former probably makes the better sense here – although in the other deposition it is exclusively the latter.

[213] *HN*, 121–2.

[214] '. . . contestans se comiti Alano me potius in uxorem, quam in contubernium sanctimonialium praedestinasse', *ibid.*, 122.

[215] Anselm, *Letters*, no. 177.

by him if she returned to the monastery and that his only responsibility was to provide her with food.[216] So Osmund was to compel her by his pastoral authority to return to her order, and report progress to the archbishop. As Osmund was to act, it is possible that Edith was still within his diocese. Even if she had accompanied her father to Scotland in August 1093, she must have returned south after the death of her parents and the failure of her brothers.[217] She had become, like these, William's pensioner and political tool.

All this evidence is difficult to interpret in the context of 1093 because it was presented in 1100 to prove that Edith had never been a nun. The Eadmer-Edith story suggests, or can be interpreted as meaning, that Malcolm removed his daughter from Wilton because he had seriously considered, and perhaps still intended, that she should marry Count Alan (of Richmond). An alliance with this Breton nobleman would have been advantageous to Malcolm. Alan the Red (Rufus), one of the 'companions' of the Conqueror, was the greatest magnate in the north of England and, as founder of the monastery of St Mary's, York, a man of good reputation.[218] He was also, it would seem, as his heir was his younger brother, Alan the Black (Niger), childless, and perhaps a widower. There were, however, a few stumbling blocks. It would seem unlikely that William would look with favour on so dangerous a marriage. And the prospective groom, although elderly, about this time abducted, likewise from Wilton, the nun Gunnhildr, a daughter of King Harold, who would be about thirty years old, and lived with her until he died soon afterwards. Whereupon the English princess considered marrying Alan Niger. If we could date these escapades we would be in a better position to judge if Edith's marriage to either of the brothers was on the cards in 1093.

The only evidence for Gunnhildr's sexual adventures are two long letters written to her by Anselm.[219] She claimed, according to the archbishop, that she was not bound to her order because she had never

[216] '. . .nec ad se quicquam pertinere, nisi quod ei cibum daret', 61. Cf. similar phrases in connexion with the maintenance of Flemish knights: below, 326.

[217] See below, 317-18.

[218] For his great wealth (he ranked fifth in the baronage), see J.F.A. Mason, 'The "Honour of Richmond" in 1086', *EHR*, lxxviii (1963), 704, and above, 170.

[219] Anselm, *Letters*, nos 168-9, and Schmitt put them, surely correctly, in that chronological order. Southern, however, *loc. cit.*, seems to reverse the order. Anselm titles himself in 168 'dei ordinatione archiepiscopus' and in 169 'vocatus archiepiscopus', the latter the usual style he used until 1095, when 'dei gratia' was often inserted. There is no other internal evidence for the date of either letter, except that they were both written *ante* 1098, when Count Alan Niger died: *Early Yorkshire Charters*, ed. C.T. Clay, iv, *The Honour of Richmond* (1935), 7; and that no. 168 was written before, and 169 after, the death of Alan Rufus, which cannot be dated: see below. For Gunnhildr at Wilton before 1095, see *Vita Wulfstani*, 34.

made a formal profession as a nun before a bishop (Anselm accepted the facts but dismissed them as technicalities) and that a promise made to her of an abbacy had not been honoured. Although Anselm was aware that she was no longer a virgin, and paid some attention to the feature, he strongly urged her to return to the cloister, and, although his second letter is markedly colder than the first, wrote with great tenderness and respect to an errant princess. There seems, unfortunately, no way in which Alan Rufus's death, which is spanned by the letters, or the letters themselves can be precisely dated. There is no firm chronicle or charter date for the death, and both brothers were commemorated on 4 August at St Mary's. It may be that this records the obit of the elder brother, but the Bury St Edmunds date 'about 1093' is not much help, for, if we accept 4 August, 1093 seems to be impossible.[220] Both Anselm's letters were written after his consecration on 4 December 1093. In one of them, almost certainly the first,[221] Gunnhildr is pictured as living in sin with a husband who, Anselm wishfully suggested, was about to despise and repudiate her, and is urged to return to her bridegroom in Christ whom they both have despised and rejected. It is unlikely that Anselm would not have heard by 4 December (and his letter may have been written months later) of Alan's death on 4 August.

Before the second letter was written Alan Rufus had died, Gunnhildr and Anselm had had a meeting and she had also written to the archbishop.[222] Moreover she was involved with Alan Niger (fully named in the letter), whom, Anselm predicted, God would similarly punish with death if the couple got married. The position in August 1093 would seem, therefore, to be that both Alans were alive and that the lord of Richmond might well already have abducted Gunnhildr. If William had connived at, or tolerated, Alan's behaviour and was also opposing his marriage to Edith, Malcolm had every reason to be angry and to remove his daughter from Wilton with some reference to the count. It is unfortunate that Anselm's letter on the subject of Edith's departure from Wilton is so opaque. It is not perfectly clear which king he thought had aided and abetted her, and even if we decide it must have been Malcolm,[223] it is not obvious why, when the two kings had quarrelled,

[220] *Memorials of St Edmund's Abbey*, ed. T. Arnold (Rolls ser., 1890), i, 350. Southern, *loc. cit.*, 187 n., discusses the evidence and accepts 4 August 1093. GEC, x, 785–6, gives this date for Alan Niger's death.

[221] No. 168.

[222] Southern, *loc. cit.*, 186, by taking this letter first, suggests that the meeting had taken place in 1086.

[223] F.S. Schmitt, 'Zur Ueberlieferung der Korrespondenz Anselms von Canterbury: Neue Briefe', *Revue Bénédictine*, xliii (1931), 232 n. 2, thinks that the king, being unidentified, must be William. Southern, *op. cit.*, 183, is of the same view.

the archbishop should have delayed proceedings in the matter or approached William so gingerly. Nor is the import of William's reply – that his only responsibility was the girl's maintenance – of much help. All the same, Anselm's recognition that William had a considerable interest in the girl's fate, and had behaved very well in agreeing that she ought to return to the convent, are signs that he knew more than he put into the letter.

There is still Hermann of Tournai's story to be taken into account; and on this can be based an entirely different view of Malcolm's plans for his daughter. Although the glimpse of William and his escort sauntering in the convent's rose garden one summer day and enjoying the herbaceous borders, while spying on the girls, may cause some surprise, there seems no good reason why the king's visit to Wilton should have been invented. True, it has a bearing on why Edith wore a veil, but in that is no different from Malcolm's visit, which, since it is also mentioned by Eadmer, was undoubtedly recorded in the evidence given in 1100. Moreover William's imagined lust in the Christina story seems merely to have become generalized into 'the lust of the Normans' in the Eadmer-Edith version. The Canterbury monk, when defending Anselm's toleration of Henry's marriage with Edith in the face of much criticism of the archbishop's laxity, may well have thought it wise to suppress the girl's earlier involvement with the king's elder brother. A further impediment to the union could have been lurking in that.[224]

The question remains, in what way had William been involved with Edith? According to Hermann, the king, presumably on his way from Windsor to meet Malcolm at Gloucester, called in at Wilton to inspect the girl. Why, is not explained. But the abbess tricked him into believing that she was a professed nun and he left in a hurry. The use to which the story was put in 1100 may well reveal only a fraction of the truth or be a perversion of it. In the story the abbess was afraid that William was going to do the girl some injury, possibly merely kiss her in an improper way, possibly, as with Alan and Gunnhildr, take her away. So she had to persuade him that the girl was untouchable. The story, however, makes no sense at all outside the peace negotiations between the two kings. It can certainly be fitted into the thesis that Malcolm wished to marry Edith to the count and was prevented by William: the English king called in at Wilton to confirm that the girl was a nun and then used that excuse for refusing his consent. Hence Malcolm's anger at all concerned and his bitter reference to his disappointed hopes.

Nevertheless, Count Alan could well have been out of the running by

---

[224] OV, iv, 272, mentions that William of Warenne (II), earl of Surrey, also was a suitor.

August, and in any case one single enigmatic reference to him may have sent us off on an entirely wrong track. An even more eligible husband for a king's daughter was available, William himself. And it is by no means unlikely that Malcolm had suggested to William in March that their alliance could be cemented by the king's marriage to the girl, and that William, when ill and penitent, had accepted this as another of the sacrifices he had to make. If the undertaking went greatly against his inclinations when he recovered his health, he could have been looking for an excuse for breaking off the engagement, and her status as a nun would have served him very well. Hence the visit to Wilton. And a decision finally taken there to repudiate Edith would also help to explain most of the subsequent events. If so, it was a fateful decision for all parties. For William it meant no marriage and no heir of his body, for Malcolm a violent death, and for Edith an even less predictable future, marriage to Henry I. Edith's sister Mary, who is not mentioned in the context of 1093, married Count Eustace of Boulogne. Had William married Edith he would have become less isolated, both at home and abroad.

In 1093, however, Edith was still only twelve and William thirty-three. It would not have seemed at the time that an irrevocable step had been taken. The king moved in September to Winchester, doubtless for the Michaelmas audit of his revenues and to make a final settlement with Anselm over the archbishopric. The witnesses to two royal charters at this time show the usual governmental circle round the king and typically present when he was at the seat of the treasury.[225] Later in the year an even longer-standing problem was resolved. In 1091, according to Orderic,[226] Robert had given Malcolm of Scots some advice. The situation had changed completely since his father's death. Malcolm would be well advised to submit to William Rufus and become his friend, for he was not only richer and more powerful than Robert but also a closer neighbour. He would find him a kind and generous lord. Malcolm's acceptance of the advice had not, however, brought him much joy, and in the autumn of 1093 he gave vent to his anger at his treatment and raided England for the fifth and last time. On 13 November he was ambushed by Earl Robert of Mowbray and his nephew Morel of Bamburgh close by the River Alne, swollen by the winter rains, and killed together with Edward, the eldest son of his second marriage.[227] Although there was nothing dishonourable in the

[225] Above, 297.

[226] OV, iv, 270.

[227] ASC, s.a. 1093; Florence, ii, 31–2; Simeon, HR, ii, 221–2; OV, iv, 270–2. GR, ii, 309, adds that 'recently' Malcolm's body was translated to Dumfermline by his son Alexander. Gaimar, ll. 6111 ff., states that Geoffrey de Gulevent and Morel were the killers and that also 3,000 Scots were slaughtered.

tactics employed, especially in mobile warfare characterized by destructive raids and all the stratagems used in open but difficult terrain, and Malcolm's depredations in the north had been savage, the modicum of sympathy which the Anglo-Norman chroniclers felt for this survivor from the past, this champion of the Anglo-Saxon cause, prevented them from exulting in his death. Indeed, they brought charges against the victors. The Anglo-Saxon Chronicler claimed that Morel and Malcolm were 'gossips' – God-relatives – that is to say, either the king had been a Godfather to Morel's child or both had been sponsors at some other baptism; and Orderic believed that the Scots had been caught unarmed and that William and his barons were not only saddened by this deed but also ashamed of it. Although Orderic's indignation is based on the misapprehension that the 'murder' took place when Malcolm was returning home under safe-conduct from the royal court, William may well have considered the killing of a king in any circumstances *lèse-majesté*. He may have felt that he had wronged Malcolm, and there was besides more than a whiff of dishonour in the affair. But it was not until almost two years later, and on other grounds, that William was able to vent his wrath on the earl.[228]

The death of Malcolm was nevertheless a godsend. He had been put on the Scottish throne by English power in the hope that he would be a loyal vassal and a friendly neighbour. But his long and successful reign and the change in the direction of English interests which followed the Norman Conquest had allowed him to create an almost independent kingdom on the Anglo-Norman pattern and pursue an expansionist policy not only against the Gaelic-Scandinavian north and west but also against Anglo-Scandinavian Northumbria. At his most ambitious he was heir to Anglian monarchy, Scandinavian colonialism and Scottish imperialism alike. But there were constraints even on Malcolm. Some threat to his power usually lurked in the Gaelic Highlands, and the English court was attractive. It is revealing that he and Margaret should have named their first four sons Edward, Edmund, Æthelred and Edgar, and one of their daughters Edith, after Margaret's illustrious ancestors. And with Malcolm and Edward dead, and Margaret not long surviving them, a Gaelic reaction occurred.[229] Malcolm's brother, Donald Bane, succeeded by the custom of tanistry; some of the late king's English friends were expelled; and all Margaret's sons, except Edmund,

[228] Below, 346 ff.

[229] For the events in Scotland 1093–4, *ASC, s.a.*, 170, 172, is still the basic source, and is followed by *GR*, ii, 476–7, and Florence, ii, 32, 35. Strangely enough, Simeon, *HR*, ii, 222, 224, for the events after Malcolm's death merely copies Florence and adds nothing of his own. OV, iv, 274, is again hopelessly confused. See also Ritchie, *op. cit.*, 60 ff., Duncan, *op. cit.*, 125. Because *ASC* takes the whole story, except for Duncan's death (placed in 1094), under 1093, Kapelle, *op. cit.*, 154 and n. 130, with the help of regnal

the eldest survivor, went south. It was, however, Duncan, Ingibiorg's son, who obtained William's permission to try to dethrone his uncle. He was invested with the kingdom by the English king, swore fealty, and was allowed to recruit Norman and English adventurers, including, no doubt, some of the victims of the revolution. In 1094 he was on his way. Probably at Durham, describing himself as King Malcolm's son and the undoubted king of Scotland by hereditary right, he made a grant of land to the church of St Cuthbert for the soul of his father and on behalf of his brothers, his wife and his children. His brothers (presumably his half-brothers) had agreed to the gift. None of the witnesses is described or can be identified with assurance, but among them are two Edgars and a Malcolm. Duncan is entered in the Durham *Liber Vitae* as a benefactor.[230]

St Cuthbert smiled, however, upon him but for a little while. Although he first defeated Donald and seized the crown, in a second encounter with his rival's adherents many of his supporters were killed and he himself barely escaped with his life. Moreover, he had to promise that never again would he bring Englishmen or Frenchmen into Scotland. Finally, possibly on 12 November, he was ambushed and slain by the mormaer of Mearns, and Donald was restored to the throne, this time in association with Edmund. William's answer was to recognize Edgar, the next senior among the surviving sons of Malcolm and Margaret, as king. He invested him with both Lothian and the kingdom of Scotland and took homage and fealty from him. In 1095 the pretender was in the border area in company with his uncle and protector, Edgar Ætheling.[231] But with Norman affairs now occupying William's attention, Scottish business fell for a few years into the background.

While the Norman kings followed the policy of their English predecessors as regards Scotland, on Wales they significantly increased the pressure.[232] Two main factors account for this. Scotland was remote,

---

lists, would cram all except the death into the period 14 Nov.–25 Dec. 1093. But this is not only obviously quite impossible but also makes no allowance for the chronicler's less rigorous chronological treatment of stories reaching him from a distance. Cf. *FWR*, ii, 32–3.

[230] Charter printed A. Lowrie, *Early Scottish Charters*, no. XII. Authenticity discussed, *Facsimiles*, *s.* pl. VIIIa, and A.A.M. Duncan, 'The Earliest Scottish Charters', *Scottish Historical Review*, xxxvii (1958), 118 ff., where there is a full bibliography. *Liber Vitae*, 2b.

[231] See below, 353.

[232] Lloyd, *History of Wales*, ii, ch. XI, is still the basic secondary authority. An excellent survey of the literature and views since Lloyd is in David Walker, 'The Norman Settlement in Wales', *Battle I*, 131 ff. See also J.G. Edwards, 'The Normans and the Welsh March', *Proc. of the British Academy*, xlii (1956), 155; R.R. Davies, 'Kings, Lords and Liberties in the March of Wales, 1066–1272', *TRHS*, 5th ser., xxix (1979), 41; L.H. Nelson, *The Normans in South Wales, 1070–1171* (Austin & London, 1966).

and the existence of a long-established and relatively stable kingdom of a familiar type, ruled by a king, encouraged ordinary diplomatic and military relations between the two authorities. Secondly, whereas the Conqueror, distrustful of the power formerly wielded by earls such as Siward and Tostig, established none of his closest associates in the north and no one with any likelihood of carving out, by using his own resources, a great lordship of his own, in the west he did the reverse, putting in much stronger men than Ralf of Mantes, Richard fitzScrob and the other 'marcher barons' of Edward the Confessor, a change which more than compensated for his destruction of the great earldom of Mercia. William I's location of Hugh of Avranches at Chester, Roger of Montgomery at Shrewsbury and William fitzOsbern at Hereford was not because he thought that the Welsh menace was greater than the Scottish or because he had not realized that Earls Harold and Tostig had broken the novel Welsh political unity in 1063,[233] but for a number of simpler reasons. In the early years after 1066 he did not look as far as Scotland: it was much too distant and posed no threat to his essential power base, which was well south of the Humber. From the Scots, however much they raided, he had ample defence in depth. But it was otherwise in the west. Some most desirable lands were in close reach not only of Welsh raiders but also of Irish and Scandinavian adventurers operating on the Celtic seas. William was well aware of the need to defend boundaries, and even if he over-reacted here, he erred on the safe side. It is also possible that the three great marcher powers were supposed to look both ways.[234] At the time they were set up, not only was Eadric the Wild disturbing the Welsh marches but also Mercia and Northumbria were far from settled. These three lordships can be regarded as a military salient designed to drive a wedge between two equally hostile regions.

By 1086, however, Mercia had been tamed and the few teeth of the Welsh dragon had been drawn. After the Welsh-Scandinavian Gruffydd ap Cynan ab Iago, king of Gwynedd and Powys, had been captured in 1081, no native prince of much stature remained in that area. And when the geographical and political disunity of Wales as a whole and the many routes open to invaders from the east are considered, the Normans' lack of substantial progress is at first sight surprising. Doubtless the new earls and their vassals initially thought it wise to consolidate their marcher lordships while exploring the possibilities of

---

[233] For the English conquest, see Barlow, *Edward the Confessor*, 204 ff.; Lloyd, *op. cit.*, 357 ff. For this view of William's policy, Walker, *op. cit.*, 132–3.

[234] Cf. J.H. Le Patourel, 'The Norman colonization of Britain', *I Normanni e la loro espansione in Europa nell'alto medioevo*, Centro Italiano di Studi sull'Alto Medioevo, Settimana xvi, (1968), (Spoleto 1969), 425 ff.

expansion,[235] and it is also likely that the king discouraged them from devoting much time and military resources to adventures of little profit to him. He needed their services elsewhere and may have been mistrustful of the creation of independent principalities.

It was in the north that most territory had been gained. Almost all the land between the Rivers Dee and Clwyd, north-west of Radnor and Gresford, was in Norman possession; and on the sea coast Earl Hugh's strenuous cousin, Robert of Rhuddlan, who was paying the king £40 a year for 'North Wales', Gruffydd's confiscated kingdom, had advanced from his castle of Rhuddlan on the Clwyd to the River Conwy, where he had built a castle at Degannwy on the west bank.[236] Rhuddlan with its borough and church had become the rear base, and Robert was intent on both widening the coastal strip in his hands by probing south and extending his lines as far as Anglesey. In contrast, in the centre of Wales there had been less movement. Earl Roger and his vassals had done little more than restore and round off the boundaries of Shropshire, crossing Offa's dyke to found the new Montgomery and advancing a little way beyond the Severn.[237] He or his men had, however, raided West Wales in 1073 and 1074, and were well placed to cut through to the coast again when the opportunity occurred. In the south, both the abeyance of the earldom of Hereford since 1075 and the emergence of a fairly strong Welsh prince, Rhys ap Tewdwr, hindered Norman expansion. Rhys seems to have been recognized by the Conqueror in 1081 as ruler of South Wales, likewise for a rent of £40 a year.[238] The border of Herefordshire ran from a few miles west of Wigmore through Old Radnor and Clifford to Ewias Harold, and so to Monmouth on the Wye. In the coastal strip above the Bristol Channel the frontier was still on the River Usk, but much of the land between the Usk and the Wye had not yet recovered from the warfare in Edward's reign.[239]

Nor did the accession of William Rufus at first help the Norman cause in Wales. In 1088 the southern marchers had joined in the rebellion

[235] For the subinfeudation of the earldom of Shrewsbury, with a glance at Chester, see Mason, 'Roger de Montgomery and his sons', 8–9. Mason suggests that Roger had some difficulty in recruiting men for the settlement of Shropshire.

[236] Lloyd, op. cit., ii, 378 ff.; Walker, loc. cit., 135–6; Domesday Gazetteer, 540–1 and map 6, Cheshire and N.E. Wales.

[237] Lloyd, op. cit., ii, 377–8, 388 ff.; Mason, loc. cit., 3, 8 ff., 12–13; Walker, loc. cit., 138; Domesday Gazetteer, 543–4 and maps 40–1, Shropshire. This heavily wasted Shropshire-Powys border was beginning to recover economically by 1086 and the process continued: P.A. Barker and R.A. Higham, Hen Domen, Montgomery: a timber castle on the Welsh border (Monograph of the Royal Archaeological Institute, 1982). See here, pl. 9b.

[238] DB, i, 179b; Lloyd, op. cit., ii, 393–5.

[239] Lloyd, op. cit., ii, 374–7, 392 ff; Walker, loc. cit., 132; Domesday Gazetteer, 542–3, maps 18, 22, Gloucestershire, Herefordshire.

against him, and Roger of Montgomery's behaviour had been equivocal.[240] Even in the north there was some check to the advance.[241] But suddenly the whole situation changed. The accession of a new king abrogated previous treaty agreements, and William must have required the Welsh princes to visit him at Gloucester or some such border stronghold and do him homage. There is no record that they did so, and the king, as with Scotland, behaved as though he was under no obligation to the native rulers. He seems to have been interested in South Wales. He had probably accompanied his father to St David's in 1081,[242] and, as we have seen, may have made a punitive strike ten years later.[243] The separation of England from Normandy may have encouraged the barons as well as the king to pay more attention to English affairs. And William patronized new men. His friend, Robert fitz-Haimo, the son of the sheriff of Kent, whom he established in Gloucestershire,[244] from his base at Bristol crossed the Usk, built a castle at Cardiff and conquered a coastal strip, later known as the shire fee, with its western boundary on the fortified line of the River Ogwr (Ogmore). His successors turned the Welsh kingdom of Morgannwg into Glamorgan.[245] William fitzBaldwin, the son of the sheriff of Devon, invaded across the Bristol Channel and built a castle at Rhydygors on the River Tywi near Carmarthen.[246] In the valley of the Usk the king established the brothers Hamelin and Winebald from Ballon in Maine, the one at Abergavenny, the other at Caerleon, as the successor to Thurstin fitzRolf. Hamelin's heiress, Emmeline, married Richard fitzCount, a son of the imprisoned earl of Hereford, and so partly rescued a great but ruined Norman dynasty.[247]

Further north another newcomer, Bernard of Neufmarché, a scion of a broken family from the marches of Normandy, conquered the Welsh kingdom of Brycheiniog (Brecknock). A household knight endowed either by the Conqueror after 1086 or by William Rufus with the lands of Alfred of Marlborough and Gilbert fitzTurold in the upper Wye

[240] Above, 70 ff.

[241] When Robert of Rhuddlan returned from 'the siege of Rochester' (see above, 81 and n. 140) he found that King Gruffydd had been ravaging round Rhuddlan: OV, iv, 136. It seems, however, that the chronicler was mistaken about the identity of the ravager: see Lloyd, op. cit., ii, 390 n. 109, and Chibnall, OV, iv, pp. xxiv ff.

[242] Above, 37.

[243] Above, 289.

[244] DNB, xix, 159; Lloyd, op. cit., ii, 402, 439 ff.; Sanders, Baronies, 6; and see above, 93.

[245] Lloyd, op. cit., ii, 439 ff; Walker, loc. cit., 134, 137.

[246] J.H. Round, 'The family of Ballon', Studies in Peerage and Family History (1901), 212 ff. For links across the Bristol Channel, see I.W. Rowlands, 'The making of the March: aspects of the Norman settlement in Dyfed', Battle III, 148–51.

[247] Round, op. cit., 181 ff.

valley in Herefordshire, he had rebelled in 1088, but had been pardoned by the king, probably because he had simply followed his father-in-law, Osbern fitzRichard of Richard's Castle in Herefordshire, the son of Richard fitzScrob of Edward the Confessor's reign. These were marcher barons of the truest kind, for Osbern had married Nest, a daughter of Gruffydd ap Llywelyn, the great Welsh king, and Bernard's wife was named after her mother, although she was also known as Agnes.[248] Bernard established his base and castle at Brecon, at the confluence of the Rivers Usk and Honddu, and it was there that in 1093 Rhys ap Tewdwr was killed in battle. 'From that day,' wrote Florence of Worcester, 'kings ceased to rule in Wales.'[249]

Roger of Montgomery took advantage of these events by sending an army across to the sea, which succeeded in occupying Ceredigion (Cardiganshire) in July 1093, and then wheeled south into Dyfed, which William gave as a barony to Arnulf, Roger's youngest son, who hitherto had held no land in England. Pembroke castle became the *caput* of this new honour, which was soon regarded as an earldom.[250] About the same time a third stranger to the region, but a neighbour of Roger of Montgomery both in Normandy and Sussex, Philip of Briouze, who had supported the king in 1091 in Normandy and after Christmas 1093 succeeded his father William as lord of Bramber, occupied the gap between Bernard and Roger by seizing Radnor and establishing himself at Builth on the upper Wye, an important centre of communications.[251] The march had moved far forward from Shrewsbury, Hereford and Chepstow. In the north, Gwynedd was being overrun. Castles were built in Bangor, Caernarfon and Anglesey, and in 1092 Hervey, a Breton clerk, was appointed bishop of Bangor, the first step towards incorporating the Welsh into the English church.[252]

In this type of small-scale warfare, aimed at conquest and colonization and marked by brutality and trickery on both sides, field commanders were exposed to great risk, and it is noticeable that among the Normans the most eminent men seem to have taken little active part in the fighting.[253] But there were important casualties. In 1093 not only

[248] Lloyd, *op. cit.*, ii, 397–8, cf. 395, 402, 436 ff.; Sanders, *Baronies*, 6–7, 75; Walker, *loc. cit.*, 133–4, 136–7; Barlow, *Edward the Confessor*, 94, 125.

[249] Florence, ii, 31.

[250] Lloyd, *op. cit.*, ii, 400 ff.; Mason, *loc. cit.*, 17–19.

[251] Above, 282. Lloyd, *op cit.*, ii, 402–3; Sanders, *Baronies*, 21, 105, 108; Walker, *loc. cit.*, 141–2. For Philip's later career, see H.E. Salter, *Facsimiles of Early Charters in Oxford muniment rooms* (1929), 3, 5.

[252] Barlow, *EC 1066–1154*, 69.

[253] They were in fact often, perhaps usually, absent from Wales, frequently with the king. For the more important military role of the castellans and honorial barons, see I.W. Rowlands, *loc. cit.*, 145.

Rhys ap Tewdwr was killed but also Robert of Rhuddlan ended his violent life,[254] both, it should be noticed, in chance encounters, as so often happened. On 3 July the Welsh king Gruffydd, probably the son of Cynan released from Hugh of Chester's prison, beached his three ships under the Great Orme, close to Robert's castle at Degannwy, and began to plunder around. Robert was roused from his siesta, hurried to the scene, and from on high saw the raiders under the cliff bundling their booty and captives on to their ships, while waiting for the tide to come in and float them off. In his fury, without bothering to put on his armour or organize a proper attack, with a single companion he slithered down the slope, only to be surrounded and slain. The other knights watched impotently from the top of the cliff as the Welsh cut off Robert's head and fixed it to the mast of a ship, and when they launched boats to go in pursuit, all they recovered was the head, which was tossed into the water to delay the chase. The corpse was first buried in Earl Hugh's new monastery of St Werburgh at Chester and later translated to St Evroul. It seems that William invested Hugh with North Wales in place of the deceased.[255]

The king's involvement in 'the conquest of Wales' cannot be doubted. Although he possibly had less control over Earls Roger and Hugh than his father had had, the events of 1088 had showed that he was not to be trifled with, and it is inconceivable that what looks like a concerted invasion could have taken place without his consent.[256] Some of his own men were involved, and he fully endorsed the result. A fully orchestrated campaign need not have been planned in detail, for the frontier lordships were always on a war footing, and once the movement began all commanders were eager to join in. Each had his prepared lines of advance, and there is a momentum in such offensives. William is noticed at Gloucester in the spring, summer and winter of 1093, and he was surely there in support of the war in south and central Wales. Why such a bellicose knight did not personally take part is an interesting question. He was, of course, seriously ill in the spring. But that is probably not the whole answer. It is just as likely that he considered that he had no proper part to play. Whereas in Scotland there was a king with whom he could deal, in Wales, although the ruling princes were usually given the title of king by the English chroniclers, there was no one at this time who could be compared with even a king of Scots. It may have been agreed by all

---

[254] OV, iv, 140 ff. Chibnall, *ibid.*, xxxiv ff., established this date, rather than 1088, for the death. Walker, *loc. cit.*, 136, agrees.

[255] Lloyd, *op. cit.*, ii, 391-2, quoting Gaimar, ll. 5972-3, 6037; Chibnall, OV, iv, p. xxxvii.

[256] Lloyd, *op. cit.*, ii, 396-7, seemed to think that the penetration of Wales after 1088 was due to William II's laxer control over the marcher barons.

on the English side that the tactical control of the campaigns should be left in the hands of those who were to take the profits and royal power kept in reserve. Neither William I nor William II took any land for himself in Wales, not even a single castle. But William Rufus, by appointing to the bishopric of Bangor, defining spheres of interest and enfeoffing some if not all of the conquerors with their gains, asserted his overall control. Wales was his to give, even if not his to conquer.

There is a story that William boasted that he intended to subjugate Ireland. According to Gerald of Wales, once when the king was at St David's, from where on a clear day you can see the mountains of Ireland, he exclaimed, on taking the view, 'I will make a bridge with my ships to that land and conquer it.' But when this was told to King Muirchertach of Munster (1086–1119), he inquired after some thought, 'Did not the king add to such a threat "God willing"?'; and when he heard that this was not so, he concluded that a man who relied on his own strength alone and confided not in God's, was in no way to be feared.[257] Be that as it may, William in his two years devoted to English affairs had annexed Carlisle and Wales and subdued Scotland. Owing to his continental ambitions, however, the pressure could not be maintained. He was in touch with Robert possibly in February 1092 and undoubtedly in 1093, in connexion with Anselm's promotion to Canterbury,[258] and diplomatic exchanges continued until February 1094, but he seems to have made no real effort either to heal the breach or to prevent its aggravation. Edgar Ætheling was back in England by the summer, and a more important visitor was William, the new count of Eu.[259] This man, a rebel in 1088,[260] had on his recent inheritance of the county reaffirmed his allegiance to Robert, thus seriously compromising the king's position in Normandy, which had largely rested on the loyalty of the dead count, his supporter in 1090–1.[261] Ralf of Mortemer, another of the 1088 rebels, also adhered to the duke at some point in the period 1091–5.[262] And Robert's acceptance of William of Eu's homage, and also of Ralf's if it occurred before 1094, could have been viewed by the king as a violation of the terms of the Treaty of Rouen, giving him a *casus belli*. But, *seductor maximus*, the prince of seducers, he preferred to purchase at great cost the defector's fealty. He regarded Eu as his essential gateway to Upper Normandy.

---

[257] Gerald of Wales, *Itinerarium Kambriae*, ed. J.F. Dimock (Rolls ser.) vi, 109, repeated *De Principis Instructione*, ed. G.F. Warner (Rolls ser.), viii, 290.

[258] See above, 281 n. 76; cf. 296 n. 146. Eudo *dapifer* was with Duke Robert in the autumn of 1093: Anselm, *Letters*, no. 163.

[259] Florence, ii, 33.

[260] See above, 76, 82.

[261] See above, 273 ff.

[262] Ducal charter, Haskins, *NI*, 292.

Also in the summer of 1093 William went with two of his most important advisers to Dover to meet the count of Flanders.[263] Robert I, the Frisian, did not die until 13 October 1093, but it is almost certain that the meeting was with his son and heir, Robert II, who had for some years been associated with his father in the government and was just about to succeed him.[264] The purpose was to reactivate an alliance which had lapsed. According to William of Malmesbury, the Conqueror had suspended his annual payment of 300 marks, started in 1066, when Robert I took the county from their nephew Arnulf. If William Rufus renewed the agreement in 1093 the terms were probably of the same kind as those negotiated also at Dover by Henry I with Robert II on 10 March 1101.[265] In return for 400 marks a year in fee (or, as it can be expressed, a 'money fief'), payable in two equal instalments, one at Michaelmas and the other at Christmas, Robert of Flanders by an oath of fealty assured to the king his personal security and undertook to help him to hold and defend the kingdom of England against all men, saving only the fealty he owed to King Philip of France. The scale of his aid and its cost to his English paymaster, the reservations necessary to protect him from doing wrong to his other lords, the king of France and the Roman emperor, and the exclusion, when relevant, of the count and county of Boulogne, for Eustace had not yet made his peace with the English king, are carefully defined or noted. And the terms deserve careful attention, for they not only define Robert's duties, but also indicate the likely conditions on which William engaged other allies in his wars against his enemies. They have some bearing, as well, in both form and contents, on the treaties made with Robert Curthose and with Malcolm of Scots.

[263] *HN*, 39.

[264] L. Vercauteren-Desmet, 'Etude sur les rapports politiques de l'Angleterre et de la Flandre sous le règne du comte Robert II', *Etudes . . . dédiées . . . à . . . H. Pirenne* (Brussels 1937), 413 ff.

[265] *GR*, ii, 478–9, where it is said that the agreement was easily renewed because Robert II put forward his kinship and William II was an incorrigible spendthrift. Henry I, he thought, was less eager. However that may be, he renewed the treaty as a defence against Robert Curthose and Philip of France at the earliest opportunity after his accession, and the witnesses were his brother's men, Gerard of York, Robert of Lincoln, Robert of Chester, William Giffard the chancellor, Robert of Meulan, Robert fitzHaimo, Eudo *dapifer*, Haimo *dapifer* and William d'Aubigny *pincerna*. The sureties include Robert fitzHaimo, Gilbert fitzRichard, Roger de Nonant, Hugh Maminot (of W. Greenwich), William de Courcy, Miles Crispin, Arnulf of Montgomery and Hugh of Beauchamp. Everything points to a reaffirmation of the old terms, although Henry may have had to pay more for them. The best edition of the treaty is *Diplomatic Documents preserved in the Public Record Office*, i (1101–1272), ed. P. Chaplais (1964), no. 1, cf. 2. The chirograph was written by a scribe of the English royal chancery. For a commentary, see F.-L. Ganshof, R. Van Caenegem, A. Verhulst, 'Note sur le premier Traité Anglo-Flamand de Douvres', *Mélanges dédiés à la Mémoire de Raymond Monier: Mém. de la Soc. d'Histoire du Droit des Pays Flamands, Picards et Wallons*, iv, 245.

Robert could be summoned to come to the king's help in England if Philip of France, or any other people (*gens*) should prepare to invade, or if an English count or other English vassal should so betray him that the king would lose the county or its equivalent. Robert was to appear in person within forty days unless prevented by one of four lawful essoins – sickness, loss of land, or a summons to the army of the king of France or the Roman emperor. If the invader was Philip, he had, of course, a valid essoin; and, in that case, he should first try to dissuade him from invading, then, if unsuccessful, accompany him with the minimum contingent possible. In any event he was to furnish the English king with 1,000 knights ready to sail from Gravelines or Wissant, for whose passage the king had to provide the ships. This force, as long as it was in England, was to be provisioned by the king and indemnified for all losses, in the same way as he treated his own household troops (*familia*). If the king wanted the count's help in Normandy or Maine, Robert should serve the king (unless prevented by the stated essoins) until the king of France should make a judgment – through those of the count's peers who had the right to pass judgment on him – that he should not help the English king. And if Philip then attacked, Robert would join Philip with a contingent of only ten knights. In any case, Robert would provide the king with 1,000 knights in Normandy or 500 in Maine on the conditions mostly as stated in connexion with England. Finally, the two contracting parties each named twelve hostages. These were really guarantors of the treaty, due to pay £100 apiece if either broke the terms and also, if required, go to prison – in the case of the Flemish hostages, in the Tower of London, the fortress from which Ranulf Flambard had just escaped.

William clearly took the treaty of 1093 seriously, for he invoked its terms in the following year.[266] But two years later the count of Flanders (and the count of Boulogne) left on the Crusade, and for the remainder of the reign the compact was of necessity in abeyance.

William held his Christmas court in 1093 for the first time at Gloucester, and among those present were the two archbishops and all the bishops, including Hervey of Bangor, except the old and probably infirm Wulfstan of Worcester and the old and unsociable Osbern fitzOsbern of Exeter. They had probably all travelled with the primate from his consecration at Canterbury, where Worcester and Exeter had likewise been absent. Among the abbots were Gilbert Crispin of Westminster, Thurstin of Glastonbury and the local prelate Serlo. The leading barons were Earl Roger of Montgomery, who had only seven months to live, the Beaumont brothers, Robert of Meulan and Henry of

[266] Below, 333.

Warwick, Eudo the steward and Robert fitzHaimo.[267]

During the ceremonies envoys arrived from the duke to inform his brother that unless he carried out the terms of their treaty, or presented himself at the place where it had been confirmed by oath and justified the delay, he would be branded a faithless perjurer and Robert would repudiate the agreement.[268] William's answer was to take a feudal aid from his vassals in order to pay for an expedition. According to Eadmer, he was collecting and spending enormous sums in preparation for the conquest of Normandy and his callous treatment of Anselm caused the first of their long series of quarrels.[269] The archbishop, before being asked for money, on the advice of friends offered the king £500, with which William was at first satisfied. But later 'evil counsellors' suggested to the king that two, or at least one thousand pounds would be a more appropriate contribution from a vassal to whom he had just granted so great an honour, and that he should refuse the offer. When Anselm heard of this he went to his lord and begged that these first fruits, although small, should not be despised, and promised that they would be followed by others. A little homily on the superiority of freewill offerings over compulsory levies probably added to his offence, for William terminated the audience by exclaiming with an oath, 'You can keep your money. I've got enough of my own. Clear off!'

Anselm recovered from his chagrin by reflecting that, as he expressed it in a letter to Hugh archbishop of Lyons,[270] 'It had happened by the grace of God. For if I had promised nothing or too small a sum the king could have appeared to have had a just cause for anger; but if he had accepted it, I might have suffered great harm and been suspected of simony.' He decided to distribute the £500 to the poor for the redemption of his own soul, possibly for having offered it to the king in the first place, and left the court without having recovered William's favour. He claimed to Archbishop Hugh that from that moment the king seemed to be looking for opportunities to do him harm. Anselm's scruples in this affair are less attractive in the light of his cool and calculating analysis of his action; and his behaviour was probably widely considered not only unworldly and unpractical but also in breach of his feudal duties.

Either before or just after Christmas the king was at Winchester with the archbishop, Bishop Walkelin, Roger Bigot, Hugh of Grandmesnil, Earl Roger of Montgomery and Croc the huntsman. He granted to the collegiate church of Christchurch on the Hampshire coast and its dean,

---

[267] *Regesta*, no. 338, ii, 338a.
[268] *ASC*, s.a. 1094, 171; Florence, MS C, ii, 33-4 n.
[269] *HN*, 43-5; *VA*, 67-9.
[270] Anselm, *Letters*, no. 176.

Ranulf Flambard, and his successors the nearby manor of Affpuddle (Dorset), which in 1086, when worth at least £7 10s a year, was owned by Cerne abbey.[271] In 1093–4 the abbey may have been in the king and Ranulf's custody, but it is strange that Anselm, who, at the king's request, threatened anyone who tried to frustrate the grant with his curse, should have been a party to such apparent spoliation.

When William assembled his forces at Hastings at the beginning of February, inclement weather hindered his sailing for over a month. It had been a particularly hard winter, with great floods soon frozen over and many bridges broken.[272] The sojourn at Hastings started, however, auspiciously enough. On 11 February William had his father's church at neighbouring Battle consecrated by Anselm and seven bishops, and gave as dowry a number of churches from his demesne which had mostly belonged to Earl Godwin and Archbishop Stigand. An indulgence of thirty days' penance was granted to all participants, and the ceremony was followed by the usual banquet. The house chronicler, writing after William's death, believed that the king had had a great love for the abbey, had looked after it well, and had usually paid it an encouraging visit when he was in the area.[273]

On the day after the ceremony William supported Anselm when his right to consecrate Robert Bloet as bishop of Lincoln was challenged by some of the bishops.[274] But the long delay exasperated him, and with Anselm in close attendance he began to feel the full impact of the changes that he himself had made in the church. He lashed out at his former friend Herbert Losinga, bishop of Thetford, for visiting Rome,[275] and he was provoked beyond endurance by his new primate. Anselm, unabashed by the matter of the aid, preached on Ash Wednesday (23 February) against the courtiers' long hair and other degenerate habits, and, if this was not enough, later raised a number of matters with the king, some of which were highly contentious. We know that he discussed amicably the flight of Edith of Scots from Wilton.[276] But in a letter to

[271] *Regesta*, no. 361. As Anselm is styled archbishop, the grant should be after 4 Dec. 1093 and before 2 Feb. 1094. For Affpuddle, see *DB*, iii, 36b i, 77d. The dates of the abbots of Cerne are uncertain.

[272] For the weather, see *GR*, ii, 375, following a lost annal. For the sojourn at Hastings, see *ASC*, *s.a.*, 171; Florence, ii, 33 and n. In *GR*, ii, 376, the king's absence in Normandy is merely mentioned.

[273] *ASC* and Florence, *loc. cit.*; *HN*, 47; *Chron. Battle*, 96–8, 224. Eadmer states that seven of Anselm's suffragans helped him. The king's grant is witnessed by Walkelin of Winchester, Ralf of Chichester, Osmund of Salisbury, John of Bath, William of Durham, Roger (*recte* Ralf) of Coutances and Gundulf of Rochester: *Regesta*, no. 348; *Chron. Battle*, 96.

[274] *HN*, 47. Barlow, *EC 1066–1154*, 39.

[275] See above, 180.

[276] Above, 312–13.

Hugh of Lyons, dispatched shortly after the events,[277] he enumerated those on which he considered he had been ill-treated by the king. He spoke about the need to go to the pope for the pallium (without which he could not properly act as metropolitan); but William asked him not to go as long as he himself recognized no pope, and he could use that as an excuse for the delay. Anselm informed Hugh that, on the advice of the bishops, he had avoided pressing the matter until 'now' in order to avoid unfruitful dissension, and in the hope that God would make it possible for the king to be persuaded to acknowledge the pope. He then asked the king if he could hold a general council, for none had been held during the reign nor for long before, and as a result crimes had multiplied. William answered, according to Eadmer who was in attendance on the archbishop,[278] 'I will deal with these when I want to. It's up to me, not you. But we can discuss this some other time.' Then he added with a laugh, 'And what would you talk about in your council?' To which Anselm replied, 'The most wicked crime of sodomy and unlawful marriages between relatives,' and went on to labour the prevalence and iniquity of sodomy, concluding that only if king and primate attacked it in concert could it be extirpated. William, Eadmer thought, did not like this much, but merely remarked, 'What are you getting out of this?' To which Anselm replied, 'Even if there's nothing in it for me, I hope there's something in it for God and you.' 'That's enough,' William answered; 'I want to hear no more of it.'

Anselm then, in Eadmer's version, raised the matter of the vacant abbeys and asked that William should appoint suitable abbots. This greatly angered the king, who exclaimed, 'What business is it of yours? Aren't they my abbeys? You do what you want with your manors. Why can't I do what I want with my abbeys?' The archbishop explained that they were only his to defend, not ravage. Really they belonged to God and were a provision for God's servants. They were not intended to finance the king's wars; for that he had his own estates and revenues. To this William rejoindered that he found Anselm's words most objectionable: 'Your predecessor would never have dared to talk in this way to my father; and I will do nothing for you.' Anselm told Hugh that the king ended the session by declaring that the archbishop had forfeited his love; to which he had replied, 'I would rather have you angry with me than God angry with you.'

Next day Anselm tried to patch up the quarrel. In his own account he went himself to William and told him that if he had unwittingly offended him in any way he hoped the king would allow him to make amends and then restore his love. William replied that he would do neither unless

[277] *Letters*, no. 176.
[278] *HN*, 48 ff.

Anselm would tell him why he should; and this indicated to the archbishop that he wanted money. But Anselm did not want to give any, lest he should appear thereby to acknowledge a non-existing fault on his part. This so enraged the king that he said things he should not have done and proposed to give away to knights some quite large estates which had been in Lanfranc's peaceful possession during both reigns. This, Anselm remarks bitterly, and, as he harps on the expression, he was clearly quoting William's own words, was 'a sort of arbitrary justice' in respect of lands the king was claiming from him. Anselm then disputed the justice of William's making any claim on the Canterbury estates in view of his earlier undertakings. But what William was maintaining, as appears from Anselm's own explanations, was that some of the land held by the archbishop in demesne was really thegn-land (tenant land) and should be granted out to knights in return for military service. It would seem to be a continuation, and probably an extension, of the dispute which had started at Windsor over the king's enfeoffments of knights on the Canterbury estates.[279]

Anselm informed Hugh that he was determined not to lose any of the rights of the archbishop of Canterbury, for it was a sacred trust. 'The king is the church's protector [advocatus] and I am its custodian [custos].' Anselm suggested that it might even be better for him to divest himself of all the estates, and, like the apostles, exercise the office of a bishop as a pauper, in witness to the injury done to the archbishopric and himself, rather than accept any sort of loss and make restoration impossible. He also had another idea: if he did not visit the pope to get the pallium within a year of consecration he could be justly deprived of the archbishopric, and he would prefer to lose his office than renege on the pope. 'This is how I think, and this is what I want to do, unless you write to me and explain why I should not do it.' Hugh's reply is not extant.

In Eadmer's version Anselm on the second day sent his overtures through the bishops, and William replied, 'I charge him with nothing; but neither will I grant him my favour, for I do not hear any grounds for that.' The bishops understood that as meaning the king did not hear the clink of cash and advised Anselm to pay over the £500 and promise to raise an equal sum from his vassals. Anselm steadfastly refused the advice on various logical and high-minded grounds. He admitted he owed the king fealty (fides) and honour, but should he then dishonour him by buying his favour with filthy lucre as though it was a horse or an ass? Despairingly the bishops begged him at least to give the £500. But most of this, he answered, he had already given to the poor. When William was told of how things stood, he said, 'Yesterday I hated him.

[279] Above, 307.

11. Original capital from Westminster Hall (now in Jewel Tower, near Westminster Abbey). A soldier storming a castle.

12. William Rufus shown on a contemporary Westminster Abbey capital, probably from an arcade in the cloister. Wood-engravings of the lost stone by N. Whittock from lost drawings made by William Capon. The fourth side, 'chopped off' except for the feet of three persons, although drawn by Capon, was not engraved. (See here, 113–14.)

Today I hate him even more. Tell him that from now on I will hate him more and more day by day. No longer will I recognize him as my father and archbishop; and as for his prayers and benedictions, I will spit them back in his face.' Anselm and Eadmer then left the court.

Some of the matters in dispute involved perplexing conflicts of interests and rights which could only be solved with the utmost good will on both sides. And with William proud, rough and clearly in some matters exploiting his rights exorbitantly, and Anselm virtuous, over-scrupulous, pedantically logical and unpractical, a debate developed in which the king, being less intelligent, often appeared petty and childish, and the archbishop priggish and self-righteous. All the same, Eadmer's concentration on the squabbling conceals the desire of both parties to get a settlement on acceptable terms. And the king proved to be the more flexible and resourceful.

In any case, all this was a tiresome complication for William. His one desire was to get to Normandy, and the delay and its consequences were infuriating. His entourage at Hastings in 1094 is even more badly documented than the similar gathering in 1091. Owing to the ceremony at Battle and the other ecclesiastical occasions we know that, as before, the episcopate was present in strength; and, besides the administrative bishops Walkelin of Winchester and William of Durham, Ranulf Flambard was in attendance. There is, however, no authentic record of the laity present, and a writ issued later at Eu is witnessed solely by William (Giffard), the chancellor.[280]

On 19 March William crossed to Normandy.[281] The size and nature of his military forces are unknown, but as his immediate purpose was diplomatic and it was only later that he raised troops for a military campaign, he probably took with him little more than household retainers and those of his baronial companions. First he had a peaceful but fruitless interview with Robert and then went to a meeting of the guarantors of the treaty.[282] Robert of Flanders, performing his duty under the terms of the recent compact, at some point in this year set off to 'help the king of England against the Normans'.[283] On the other side,

---

[280] *Regesta*, no. 348 for 7 bishops: see above, 328 n. 273; no. 348a is a forgery: Eleanor Searle, 'Battle Abbey and exemption: the forged charters', *EHR*, lxxxiii (1968), 456 7. No. 347 for Ranulf Flambard. No. 352, in favour of Chichester cathedral and witnessed by Robert *dispensator* and the Norman baron Richard of Courcy, may be from this period. No. 349 is a Durham confection; cf. the witness lists to the forgeries: Offler, *Durham Episc. Charters*, 19–20, 28–9, 35; *Regesta*, nos 148, 205, 286. Alan of Lincoln and Turald of Papileon are notable witnesses. The writ given at Eu is no. 350.

[281] The fullest account of the year is in *ASC*, s.a., 171–2; Florence, ii, 33–5, and MS C in n. contribute some details. *GR* (see above, 328 n. 272) and OV ignore the events.

[282] Florence, MS C, *loc. cit.* For the location, see above, 281 n. 77.

[283] *CDF*, no. 1325; *Regesta*, no. 360.

Philip of France ordered the celebrated canonist, Bishop Ivo of Chartres, to be at Pontoise or Chaumont with a force of knights on an appointed day, so as to accompany him to a lawsuit (*placitum*) between the king of the English and the count of Normandy; and, as he and Robert were soon to be comrades in arms, this would seem a likely occasion. Ivo, however, refused on three grounds: Philip was under an interdict for his adulterous union with Bertrada; Ivo's household (*casati*) and other knights were either absent or excommunicated for breaches of the peace; and he considered it dangerous for him to venture into the French royal court.[284]

Whether these great men were present at the parley we do not know, but the warrantors declared that William was at fault, whereupon the king refused to accept their verdict and denounced the treaty. He established his headquarters as usual at Eu and set about recruiting allies and soldiers. According to Florence, he enrolled mercenaries and gave or promised vast sums to those Norman barons who would support him against Robert and receive his soldiers in their castles.

He started with a success, raiding south and capturing Helias of Saint-Saëns' castle of Bures-en-Bray, which was garrisoned by Robert. Some of the prisoners he dispatched to England.[285] But no more victories are reported in the north; there was more action in the south. South-east Normandy was either the most disturbed or the best reported sector of the turbulent duchy. The rival depredations of Robert of Bellême and Count Henry since 1092, so abhorrent to Orderic, who had been a dependent of Robert's father in England and at St Evroul suffered from the son's tyranny,[286] were a danger to the integrity of the duchy. In 1092 Robert had tried to transfer Bellême to the lordship of the French king;[287] and Henry acknowledged no lord. A further complication occurred on 27 July 1094 when Robert's father, Earl Roger of Montgomery, died at Shrewsbury and was buried in his new abbey.[288] William cannot have particularly wanted the eldest son, Robert of

---

[284] Letter of Ivo, Migne *PL*, clxii, no. 28. Cf. Fliche, *Philippe I*, 299, for unacceptable views. Philip does not seem to have been publicly excommunicated before the legatine council of Autun of 16 Oct. 1094: Mansi, *Concilia*, xx, 799 ff.; but Ivo may have considered him to be under an interdict since the start of the liaison in 1092. When the brothers met in 1096, although the agreement of the king of France to their arrangement was probably necessary, and the advice of a canon lawyer advisable, the business is not easily viewed as a *placitum*: see below, 363–4.

[285] *ASC, s.a.*, 171; Florence, ii, 34.

[286] See above, 269 ff. OV, iv, 288 ff., takes the story from 1092 to 1094.

[287] M. Prou, *Recueil des Actes de Philippe I roi de France (1059–1108)* (Paris 1908), no. CXXIX.

[288] OV, iii, 148, where in the preceding pages there is a long account of the earl and his family; and iv, 302.

Bellême, who already had his mother's lands, to inherit his father's also; and he gave Roger's English earldom to the second son, Hugh, who had been his father's lieutenant in Wales and spent the rest of his life (1094–8) engaged in Welsh affairs.[289] It is also possible that he promised Montgomery and the Norman honour to the third son, Roger of Poitou, for this warrior is found at Argentan, between Montgomery and Bellême, with a royal garrison of 700 knights and 1,400 squires.[290]

Robert had always supported Robert Curthose against William and it is unlikely that the duke would have opposed his inheritance of Montgomery. It was, therefore, possibly in connexion with Earl Roger's death that in 1094 Duke Robert and Philip of France, operating either from Bellême or Mortagne, attacked north-west towards the valley of the Orne.[291] It was a continuation or resumption of the war which Robert of Bellême had waged in 1090–1 against the Grandmesnil and Courcy lands;[292] and the king and duke had two rapid, but perhaps not very glorious, victories. On the right of the advance, Roger of Poitou surrendered his enormous forces at Argentan, without a fight, to Philip, who put all the captives to ransom and returned home. It looks as though Roger had decided not to stand in his brother's way. Robert then turned west and was opposed by William Peverel with 800 men at 'the castle at Houlme', perhaps Briouze, one of the largest towns in that region.[293] This captain withstood a siege and capitulated presumably only when he was not relieved in the customary period by the king. He does not seem to have completely forfeited William's favour;[294] but Roger of Poitou is not noticed again at the royal court. Robert of Bellême himself is not mentioned in connexion with this campaign, but it was probably as a result of it that he was able to occupy his father's lands. He had surrounded Grandmesnil and Courcy and had become a very great power indeed.

In these circumstances William seems to have been at a loss what to

[289] Mason, 'Roger de Montgomery and his sons', 13–14, 17.

[290] Florence adds the 'twice as many squires' to the ASC entry. It is not clear who was the lord of Argentan at this time. Duke Robert gave it to Robert of Bellême in 1101: OV, v, 308.

[291] ASC, s.a., 171; Florence, ii, 34.

[292] See above, 276.

[293] For Holmetia regio and its strategic importance, see OV, iv, 228. It lay between Domfront and Falaise. Briouze was the caput of Philip of Briouze's honour. FWR, i, 462, however, following Stapleton, expressly rejected this location and identified the place as Le Homme, now L'Isle Marie, at the junction of the Rivers Douve and Merderet, south-east of Valognes in the north of the Cotentin. Le Homme was certainly a ducal castle, probably held by the vicomte of the Cotentin: see Bates, Normandy before 1066, 158, 165–6. But this place would seem to be much too far removed from Argentan.

[294] He witnesses Regesta, no. 397, dateable to 1096–7.

do. In the summer he ordered Ranulf Flambard to raise 20,000 foot soldiers.[295] It is unlikely that so large an army could in fact have been mobilized and transported,[296] but in any case by the time the troops had reached Hastings William had decided not to use them. Ranulf, no doubt to the general relief, collected from each man the 10s which his locality had provided for his maintenance[297] and forwarded it to the king. The men he sent home. The chroniclers recorded that the country was heavily taxed that year: extortionate imposts hit agriculture, resulting in famine and great mortality – so many were sick they could not be cared for and corpses lay unburied for lack of those to bury them.[298] With a military decision impossible while the protagonists were so widely separated, William ravaged Robert's lands,[299] partly, no doubt, to bring in booty and ransoms, partly to draw Robert away from his easy progress in the south-east. In this he was successful, and the duke, once again in company with his royal ally, planned an attack with large armies on Eu itself. But they had only reached Walter Giffard's castle at Longueville-en-Caux, forty kilometres to the south, when Philip abandoned the enterprise 'as a result of intrigue' and the armies were disbanded.[300]

In the meantime, and in the light of the new situation in Lower Normandy, William had summoned Henry and Hugh earl of Chester to join him at Eu.[301] The presence earlier at Hastings of the new bishop of Coutances in his entourage suggests that he was seeking to enlarge or reinforce his influence in the Cotentin. Henry, who is said to have been at Domfront, may have considered his position threatened by the growing power of Robert of Bellême. As he could not have a safe passage through Normandy, the king sent ships for him. The plan was presumably for Henry to make his way westwards to the Cotentin, join up with Hugh, and embark at Cherbourg, the port in William's hands. But for some undisclosed reason, instead of sailing for Eu, they landed at Southampton on 1 November and stayed in England over Christmas, which they spent in London. William, making use of his alliance with

[295] *ASC, s.a.*, 171; Florence, ii, 35. It is the latter who locates the ferry port. Cf. also C.W. Hollister, 'Military obligation in Late-Saxon and Norman England', *Ordinamenti Militari in Occidente nell'Alto Medioevo*, Centro Italiano di Studi sull'Alto Medioevo, Spoleto, Settimana xv, (1967) (Spoleto 1968), i, 179–81.

[296] Cf. Barlow, *Edward the Confessor*, 170–2.

[297] According to *DB*, i, 56c (Berkshire), cf. 64b (Wiltshire), each man should receive from 5 hides 20s for his pay and maintenance for 2 months' service. If the soldier was paid one half of this on his return home, the discrepancy is explained.

[298] *GR*, ii, 376; Florence, ii, 35.

[299] *ASC*, Florence, *loc. cit.*

[300] *Ibid.*

[301] *ASC, loc. cit.*, only.

the count of Flanders, celebrated the first four days of Christmas in the Channel port of Wissant, north of Boulogne, and crossed to England on 29 December.[302] Henry remained with him in England until the spring, and then, furnished with treasure, returned to the duchy to fight on the king's behalf against Robert.[303] Although the Anglo-Saxon Chronicler believed that he did well, he records no incidents and does not indicate in which theatre the count operated.

Eadmer, always a prejudiced observer, considered that in 1094 William had spent an enormous amount of money to no purpose.[304] He must indeed have spent large sums on subsidies, wages, ransoms, military stores and the other expenses of war. The difficulty which faces the modern commentator is ignorance of the king's professed military objectives. Near-contemporary chroniclers, but writing after Henry had dispossessed Robert in 1107, were of the general opinion that William likewise was aiming at taking the duchy from his brother.[305] Although William was a rather different sort of man from Henry and is unlikely to have had such clear objectives and sharply defined and quickly executed plans, wars of succession of this kind were common enough at the time and were sometimes decisive, but usually only after a lengthy and fluctuating struggle. In an age when defence had all the advantages over attack, no one would have expected William to have driven Robert out in the course of a single decisive campaign distinguished by the storming of castles and pitched battles. It would be a war of attrition, decided, if at all, by some accident, some chance military encounter, some sudden turn of the wheel of fortune.

Whatever the king's objective and plans may have been in 1094, his meagre success is obvious. It had been beyond his power to organize his scattered, and probably mostly half-hearted, supporters in Normandy into a military force with a concerted plan of campaign. He had not had the strength to extend his foothold in Upper Normandy southwards to Rouen and the Seine. His position in Lower Normandy had been gravely compromised, and in general he had been proved inferior in resources and prestige to the combined command of Robert and Philip of France. Robert was clearly in a better position at Christmas 1094 than he had been in 1091, when it had looked for a moment as though he might lose Rouen. In short, the duke was regaining the upper hand. But nothing irrevocable had yet happened. William, although he had lost ground in the south, had succeeded in keeping his own sector intact in the north, even enlarged it a little, and he had arranged a sensible

[302] ASC, Florence, loc. cit.
[303] ASC, s.a. 1095, 172 only.
[304] HN, 52.
[305] Eadmer's view: HN, 43; cf. Florence, ii, 34.

reconciliation with Henry. As he approached the age of thirty-five, he was probably still learning how to operate successfully under these frustrating conditions in which ambition usually outran the forces which could be mobilized and effectively applied. Nor should we forget the fun of the game. Neither Robert nor William was in a business run mainly with an eye to material profit.

Chapter 7

THE CONQUERING HERO (1094–1100)

In the years 1094–5 William's fortunes reached their lowest ebb. Not only did he lose ground in Normandy, see his Welsh and Scottish schemes largely undone, and suffer serious inconveniences arising from his rash appointment of Anselm to Canterbury, but also he had to deal with an awkward baronial rebellion. Typically, however, he faced all his difficulties with courage and resource. He was unaffected by visions and portents, and if his lack of imagination made him a rough master and caused him difficulties, it also helped him through perils and defeats.

While he was in Normandy in 1094 there was a general rising of the Welsh against the Norman conquerors.[1] The ease and extent of the conquests and the apparent absence of native princely heroes who could rally the defeated seem to have caused the Normans to take their superiority for granted, a carelessness doubly foolish in view of the likelihood of a popular reaction and the loss of some of their own leaders. In the north, Robert of Rhuddlan had been killed in July 1093, and in 1094 Earl Hugh of Chester was in Normandy, while the interference of Cadwgan ap Bleddyn of Powys and the reappearance of the intrepid Gruffydd ap Cynan provided the Welsh with trusted commanders. Anglesey and the coastal strip west of the Conwy were overrun by the insurgents, and what had appeared one of the securest conquests was completely lost. In the centre, Cheshire, Shropshire and Herefordshire were raided, and although Hugh, the new earl of Shrewsbury, was successful in one encounter, in 1095 he suffered the shame of losing Montgomery itself. In West Wales all of Arnulf's conquests except Pembroke (Gerald of Windsor)[2] and Rhydygors near Carmarthen were reoccupied by the natives, and the latter was abandoned after William fitzBaldwin died in 1096.[3] All these were serious losses and showed that

---

[1] *ASC*, s.a., 171–2; *GR*, ii, 376; Florence, ii, 35. Lloyd, *History of Wales*, ii, 400 ff.

[2] The castellan of Pembroke under Arnulf was the younger son of Walter fitzOther, castellan of Windsor, and became through his marriage to Nest, daughter of Rhys ap Tewdwr, king of Deheubarth, ancestor of the Fitzgeralds. The historian Gerald of Wales was his grandson. See G.H. Orpen, *Ireland under the Normans* (1911), i, 95–7; Sanders, *Baronies*, 116 (Eton); I.W. Rowlands, 'Aspects of the Norman settlement of Dyfed', *Battle III*, 145.

[3] William fitzBaldwin, sheriff of Devon: see genealogical table, no. 10. He was succeeded in the honour of Okehampton and probably the shrievalty by his brother Robert of Meules.

Wales had not been subjugated. But the Normans still held the bases and many of the outposts from which they could once more advance as soon as Welsh fury abated. They had been saved by their castles, and from these, and isolated Pembroke which survived the whole insurrection, they could eventually emerge and take their revenge.[4] In Scotland William Rufus's client king, Duncan II, was killed towards the end of 1094 and Donald Bane restored;[5] but in this theatre his secure bases lay far behind the frontier.

William had returned to England after Christmas probably in order to deal with the Welsh. In January 1095 he travelled west and had reached Gillingham, three miles from Shaftesbury in Dorest, when Anselm joined him.[6] On about 20 January he was some ninety miles to the north at Cricklade in Wiltshire with Robert Losinga, bishop of Hereford, the great mathematician, in attendance,[7] but by 25 February he had moved decisively away from the marches to Rockingham in Northamptonshire, possibly to threaten Robert of Mowbray.[8] If he did make an unsuccessful foray into Wales in this period, as Florence believed[9] – and the Worcester chronicler was well-informed on Welsh affairs – it must have been brief. What frustrated his purpose was a crisis in his relations with Anselm and a baronial conspiracy. At Gillingham, William was faced once more with Anselm's request for permission to go and get a pallium from the pope; and when he asked, 'From which pope?' and Anselm answered, 'Urban,' it was open to him to show that he too could be legalistic and difficult. Everyone knew, Anselm particularly, that no pope had been recognized in England since the death of Gregory VII in 1085. Because neither the Conqueror nor his successor had needed in that period to use the services of Rome, it had suited them well to remain neutral in the schism. Lanfranc, who had not had an easy time under Gregory, was not sorry to escape from papal interference; and Anselm was never an enthusiastic papalist. But if he was to operate as an archbishop – and he intended to relinquish none of Canterbury's rights – he had to get a pallium;[10] and since he had already

[4] For an interesting view of the March, see R.R. Davies, 'Kings, Lords and Liberties in the March of Wales, 1066–1272', *TRHS*, 5th ser., xxix (1979), 41.

[5] Above, 318.

[6] *HN*, 52.

[7] Robert had a visitation from the dead Wulfstan of Worcester, which *Vita Wulfstani*, xliii, 62–3, locates at the royal court, and Florence, ii, 36, at Cricklade.

[8] *HN*, 53 ff.

[9] Florence, ii, 35; soon (*mox*) after the king's return; he also mentions the late autumn expedition. *FWR*, i, 477n., did not believe in the winter campaign.

[10] But it would seem that after his consecration as archbishop he had exercised all the usual metropolitan powers without scruple or hindrance. The opposition in February 1094 to his consecration of Robert Bloet to Lincoln seems to have been on other grounds: *HN*, 47–8; Barlow, *EC 1066–1154*, 38–9.

recognized Urban, his hands were tied. The difficulty had been obvious to everyone from the beginning, but Anselm, and doubtless many others, had probably expected, quite correctly, that, since Urban had been recognized in Italy and France, sooner or later he would be acknowledged in England. There was certainly no party in favour of Wibert of Ravenna, the anti-pope Clement III.[11] The trouble was that no one, apart from Anselm, was in a hurry. And one reason why he made an issue of it was that he did not mind if he lost his office in consequence.

William pointed out at Gillingham that it was his father's custom and his own that no one in the kingdom of England could name the pope without the royal licence, and for Anselm to try to deprive him of this prerogative was as though he was attempting to take away his crown.[12] In return, Anselm correctly affirmed that it was the custom of his predecessors to go to Rome for the pallium, and, moreover, that he had given William full notice of his intentions at Rochester before he had agreed to be made bishop. To this William replied that he could not let him put his obligations to the Roman church before the fealty and obedience he owed him. In this impasse Anselm asked that a council of bishops, abbots and other magnates of the realm should be summoned in order to decide whether it was possible for him, when the reverence and obedience he owed the Holy See were taken into account, to preserve the fealty he owed his earthly lord.

It should be noticed that Anselm fully acknowledged throughout the dispute his duties to both lords, but to William's anger put his duties to the pope first. And since his obligations to Urban predated those to the king, and had been protected by clear and public reservations, he was in a strong legal position. Hence he also declared to William that if the council should decide that his recognition of Urban was incompatible with his being a vassal of the king, he would choose to remain in exile until William should recognize the pope, rather than deny, even for an hour, the obedience he owed to St Peter and his vicar. These last words probably reveal a formula that the royalists had proposed: Anselm should renounce his recognition of Urban and then William would acknowledge him. But the archbishop would not accept the humiliation and infidelity involved.

The proceedings of the council of magnates which was summoned to Rockingham, between Northampton and Stamford, and met at daybreak on Sunday 25 February and on the two following days in the chapel within the castle, were reported in great detail, and in his usual partisan

---

[11] GP, 86 and n., however, claims that the king favoured Wibert and forced the bishops to do likewise.

[12] HN, 52 ff.; VA, 85 ff.

way, by Eadmer, who was present.[13] After the king had conferred in secret with his counsellors, Anselm was allowed to address the meeting. He gave his version of the dispute which had arisen between him and the king at Gillingham and its background, and he pointed out to his audience that it was they who had elected him and put him in this impossible position, and that it was now up to them to get him out of it. 'I regard it,' he said, 'as a most serious matter contemptuously to deny the vicar of St Peter, no less serious to violate the fealty which I have sworn to the king to observe in accordance with God's will [*secundum deum* – an ominous reservation], and equally serious that it should be said that I cannot maintain the one without violating the other.' The bishops, however, led by William of St Calais, who, Eadmer believed, was aiming to succeed Anselm and whose forensic skill is seen in the various royalist proposals, refused his appeal for advice. He was, they replied, much wiser and more holy than they; and they suggested that he should simply accept the king's advice, although they would, if he wished, convey his words to the king.

At the beginning of the second session on the Monday, the bishops reaffirmed their refusal to support their metropolitan against the king and advised him as before, whereupon Anselm appealed from the council to the supreme shepherd, the prince of princes, and the angel of great counsel, to Christ, St Peter and his vicar. The bishops were incensed by this reply and refused to report it back; so Anselm went in person to the king. After a good deal of consternation and confusion, the bishops and some lay magnates declared William's judgment. Anselm was to renounce his obedience to Urban and, when free from this obligation, await in all his actions, as was proper for an archbishop of Canterbury, the decision and order of the lord king. He was to acknowledge that he had committed an offence against the king; and to gain his pardon he must, like a wise man, agree to all those requests the king had previously made. (The reference was probably mainly to the aid and the enfeoffments.) They advised Anselm to accept, but he said it was out of the question and he would like an adjournment until the next day. The bishop of Durham, however, advised William to pronounce a further judgment; and what had started as a conference had turned into a trial (*placitum*). That, perhaps, was only to be expected.

William of St Calais in public session then charged Anselm with polluting the fealty he had sworn to the king and despoiling him of the greatest of his prerogatives, that which made him outstanding among all other kings,[14] and demanded that he re-invest the king with the due

[13] *HN*, 53 ff., *VA*, 85 ff.; *GP*, 87–9. For the date, see M. Rule, *HN*, lxii. *FWR*, i, 491, raises the question of how such an assembly could have been contained in a castle chapel.

[14] His possession of a permanent quasi papal legation: see Barlow, *EC 1066–1154*, 279–80.

dignity of his sovereignty before they discussed an adjournment. Anselm's reply was thought to mean that he could not accept the council's judgment in the matter. But while these exchanges were taking place, the barons and knights began to show that their sympathy now lay with the archbishop. He had been put in an obvious dilemma; he was defending a matter of principle which they could understand; he was not in any ordinary sense a traitor; he was being subjected to a good deal of bullying pressure; and his behaviour was quiet and dignified. Here was a real change from their attitude at the trial of the bishop of Durham in 1088; and it may well be that they cared no more for the bishop as a prosecutor than as a defendant. In the end, on the advice of the bishop, the council was again adjourned to the following day, when, he promised William, he would come up with some new plan.

The plan, according to Eadmer, was to condemn Anselm for *lèse-majesté*, deprive him of his ring and staff, and expel him from the kingdom. If the proposed procedure was correctly reported and seriously intended, it went further than that ventured against William of St Calais in 1088, in that it involved deprivation of office; but it had a precedent in the threat made against Herbert of Thetford in the previous year. The plan, however, miscarried because the barons would have nothing to do with it and the bishops were less than enthusiastic. To the barons William exclaimed, 'If you don't like this, what do you like? I'm not going to have someone equal to me in my kingdom while I'm alive. And if you knew he had such a good case why did you let me start the suit against him? Come on! Give me some advice! Because, by God's face, if you don't do as I want and condemn him, I will condemn you.' To this outburst his close counsellor Robert (and Eadmer is more probably referring to the count of Meulan than Robert fitzHaimo) had to reply that they could not think of any useful advice to give.

William then turned to the thoroughly demoralized bishops. First they said that, as Canterbury's suffragans, they could not sit in judgment on him; then they only half-heartedly obeyed the king's demand that at least they should withdraw obedience and friendship from the archbishop. Finally the barons refused to do even this much: they were not the archbishop's vassals, only his children in Christ, and this they would not deny. When Anselm, in view of the king's enmity which entailed loss of protection, asked for a safe-conduct to a ferry port in order to go into exile, it was William's turn to hesitate, and, on the barons' advice, he allowed the adjournment of the meeting.

When they met again on the Tuesday morning each side realized that it had gone too far and recoiled from the brink. A truce was agreed between king and archbishop to last until 20 May; and it was covenanted that if no final peace should be made by then, William would grant Anselm safe-conduct to the sea.[15] The king must have given some assurances in order to get the truce, raising some hope that a solution acceptable to the archbishop could be found.[16] But Eadmer does not spell it out. The monk may have thought Anselm credulous or even, perhaps, hesitant. He also claims that the king continued to persecute the archbishop. He expelled from the kingdom as trouble-makers Baldwin of Tournai, Anselm's chief adviser, and two of his clerks, had his chamberlain arrested before his very eyes, and had others of his servants condemned by unjust judgments.[17] Anselm waited in patience for his deliverance.

William had indeed made a plan for solving his problems, but, according to Eadmer, kept it secret from Anselm.[18] He immediately dispatched two of his 'craftiest' clerks, Gerard, the former chancellor, and William Warelwast – both future bishops – post-haste to Rome, with instructions, Eadmer thought, to discover which was the lawful pope, for there was general ignorance about this in England at the time. Moreover, they were to obtain from one of them a pallium to be given to the king, not the archbishop, so that William could eject Anselm and bestow the pallium on a new archbishop of his own choice. Even if William shared some of these fanciful ideas, his clerks acted more predictably. They must have, at least conditionally, recognized Urban, perhaps at Cremona, for they returned with his legate, Walter, cardinal bishop of Albano, who carried the desired pallium. The clerks hurried the legate incommunicado through Dover and Canterbury to the royal court at Westminster or Windsor, which they reached before Whitsun (13 May). William learned to his satisfaction that Urban was willing to do a deal with him, partly at Anselm's expense. In particular, in return for recognition, he would grant the king all that he wanted (presumably the royal rights and customs which had been in dispute, even perhaps a legation) for the term of William's life. According to Hugh of Flavigny, who was in the next papal legation to England in the following year (1096), Walter expressly conceded that no papal legate should henceforth be sent to the kingdom except at the king's command. As a result of the concordat, no papal envoy was thereafter received with due honour, while no archbishop, bishop, monk or clerk in England dared to receive or obey papal letters unless the king commanded them to do so.[19] Eadmer adds that William then asked Walter to depose Anselm, and, when the legate refused, felt that he had been completely deceived and

---

[15] *HN*, 70.
[16] Cf. *VA*, 87.
[17] *HN*, 68.
[18] *HN*, 68 ff.; *VA*, 87.
[19] Hugh of Flavigny, *Chronicon*, 475.

that his diplomacy had been a failure. Here, as so often, the monk, by limiting his view to his master, missed the king's considerable success. Moreover, it is by no means certain that William put Anselm's deposition as a major objective. He probably thought archbishops of Canterbury tiresome as a class, and it is unlikely that he consistently disliked Anselm as a person.

Before the truce ran out on 20 May, William ordered the archbishop, who was on his manor of Mortlake for the celebration of Pentecost, to move to Hayes, close to the royal court at Windsor, and then sent most of the English bishops to him. These begged Anselm to offer the king money in order to get his pardon. The archbishop refused and said that, unless he could get the king's peace and cooperation without having to buy it, he would go into exile, as agreed at Rockingham. The bishops then informed him that the legate had brought the pallium, and asked what he would give in return for that. He could at least pay what a journey to Rome would have cost him. But Anselm was intransigent and quite reckless because he was prepared to surrender his office. Suddenly, according to Eadmer, by the advice of the magnates, the king freely restored him to favour and gave him permission to exercise in full his episcopal rights in the kingdom. Whereupon the archbishop went on to Windsor, where he was warmly welcomed at court.

It is only later, in connexion with the new quarrel of 1097, that Eadmer reveals what he had concealed here, the terms on which the final peace was made.[20] On the later occasion William claimed that after the lawsuit at Rockingham, Anselm had sought a reconciliation, and, to obtain it, had promised to observe henceforth the royal usages and laws and defend them faithfully against all men. And Eadmer allows Anselm to agree that he had indeed made that promise, but in this form: he would observe those customs which the king possessed in his kingdom justly and according to God's will (*secundum deum*), and would defend them against all men according to justice and as far as he was able. The king and his barons denied that there had been any reference to God or justice in Anselm's obligation, to which the archbishop had retorted, 'Even if there was no mention of God or justice, as you say, what then? No Christian can accept or defend laws and customs which are known to run counter to God and justice.' More than two years after the event, as so often happens with oral settlements, it could not be decided what precisely had been agreed. Even more remarkable is what the papal curia believed had happened, as transmitted by Hugh of Flavigny: Walter of Albano, seduced by money, had actually ordered Anselm to swear fealty to St Peter and the pope, saving the fealty he owed to his

[20] *HN*, 83 ff.

lord and king.[21] Be that as it may, the terms of the settlement, less reservations explicit or implicit, are clear: in return for William's recognition of Urban, his confirmation of Anselm in his office, and the restoration of his full favour, all without payment, the archbishop had agreed to accept the ancestral royal customs in the future. This had been forced on him by the papal recognition or toleration of them for the time being.

It was a real compromise, and can be compared with that which later Henry I made over investitures. William had had to move a little from the original peace formula – which may have been that Anselm should renounce Urban temporarily so that William could recognize him voluntarily – by himself making a temporary renunciation of his rights and receiving them back only as a limited papal concession. He had also had to reconcile himself to accepting Anselm as archbishop. On the other hand, Anselm and the pope had had to acknowledge the ancestral customs. And since these controlled traffic between England and Rome, the king was left with the full management of the English church that his father had enjoyed. It is likely that some of the royal advisers, abetted perhaps by Walter of Albano, had been seeking to get the royal prerogatives in the English church recognized by the Holy See as a papal legation, such as that shortly to be granted by Urban to Count Roger I of Sicily.[22] But it is doubtful whether William, although he clearly obtained the substance of a legation for life, ever received a formal documentary grant of it. Each side was playing for time. William's behaviour was by no means as unreasonable or tyrannical as Eadmer would have us believe. He too had his problems and scruples. There was no good reason why he should abandon the rights he had inherited from his father and which Lanfranc and most of the other bishops had loyally observed. Two rights had been in conflict, and the royal prerogatives were the better established and the more generally acceptable. No one, it seems, except Anselm, thought that he should give them up.

The qualities of William's diplomacy should also be noticed. He had a habit of pushing disputes to the brink; but it does not seem that he ever went beyond it without being prepared for the consequences. In 1095 it suited him and his advisers to make a settlement with the pope behind Anselm's back, and this turned out to be a wise move. It was to facilitate his acquisition of the duchy of Normandy and it allowed him to disregard the archbishop's attempts to reform the English church and attack the moral evils in the clergy and laity. Anselm learned, as he was to learn again and again, that popes preferred to negotiate with rulers

[21] Hugh of Flavigny, *Chronicon*, 475.

[22] At Capua in June 1098, ironically while Anselm was with the pope: Barlow, *EC 1066–1154*, 279n.

through their own, or the king's, confidential agents and bypass the local man who had little understanding of papal policy and harped on matters of no interest to the curia. He also learned that an archbishop could hold reform councils in England only when he saw eye to eye with the king. No wonder he was subdued between 1095 and 1097.

Only one more matter had to be settled in 1095 in order to achieve perfect peace: the conferment of the pallium.[23] It was suggested to Anselm that he should receive it from the king's hands, but when he refused on the grounds that it was not in the king's but in St Peter's gift, a compromise was quickly reached. The legate was to put the vestment on the high altar of Canterbury cathedral and Anselm should take it from there. This was done on 27 May. In the meantime the bishops of Hereford and Salisbury, Robert of Hereford close to death, had begged Anselm's forgiveness for their behaviour at Rockingham and been absolved. Rochester had never renounced his spiritual lord.[24] William allowed Baldwin of Tournai to rejoin the archbishop. The situation was gradually returning to normal. Some time later in the year, Anselm wrote to the pope to thank him for the pallium and sent him a little gift which he hoped his spiritual master would value more for the good intentions of the sender than for its weight.[25] He also excused himself for not having visited the pope in person, pleading the impossibility of leaving the kingdom at a time when both external and internal enemies threatened the king, his own age and sickness and the dangers of the journey. He protested his grief at his promotion and unsuitability for the office, but he made no written complaint of the king's behaviour.

The king had also as part of his settlement with the pope agreed to resume payment from the bishoprics of Peter's Pence,[26] which had been in abeyance since at least 1085. It is not stated whether it was to be rendered with arrears; but William probably took mischievous pleasure in making the English church pay for the settlement and putting the Roman pontiff and his legate, who remained in England to collect the tax, in an unpopular role. The legend of Roman rapacity was quickly renewed and Anselm was soon reminded of the deviousness of Roman diplomacy. In the late summer of 1095 he received a spiteful letter from the legate, with whom he was already on bad terms, containing charges which, it was admitted, had been made by some of his fellow bishops.[27]

[23] *HN*, 71 ff. For the date see M. Rule, lxii.
[24] *VA*, 86.
[25] Anselm, *Letters*, no. 193.
[26] For this English tribute to Rome, see Barlow, *EC 1000–1066*, 295 ff.
[27] Anselm, *Letters*, no. 192; see also below, 348–9. Sally N. Vaughn, 'St Anselm of Canterbury', *Journal of Medieval History*, i (1975), 290, suggests, most improbably, that the king was behind these charges.

What had caused his suffragans to desert him and why had he failed to bring them to obedience and penitence? How came it that he had allowed himself to be consecrated by schismatic bishops and be invested by, and do homage and fealty to, a schismatic king? Anselm replied calmly, sensibly and persuasively to this outburst, but he must have found the malice of his enemies and the legate alike disquieting and painful. Inevitably he grew closer to the king: one master was usually less onerous than two. On the whole, William gained from the closing of the breach with Anselm and the recognition of Urban as pope. He had secured the warmer support of the church and strengthened his English and international position at a most important juncture in his career.

He could now give his full attention to the baronial plot.[28] The chroniclers attributed the unrest to William's tyranny and excessive taxation; and although his harsh measures would seem to have weighed more heavily on the lower classes than on the magnates, his fiscal exploitation of justice and other feudal rights, his rigorous protection of the royal forest, and the continuing war with Robert doubtless produced enemies among the nobility who could make use of the king's widespread unpopularity. Robert of Mowbray, earl of Northumberland, was the leader of the conspirators. Never one of William's favourites, he had been building up his power nevertheless. Early in 1093, on the death of Bishop Geoffrey of Coutances, he had inherited his uncle's '280 manors', including the honour of Barnstaple,[29] and just before his rebellion he married Matilda, a daughter of Richer of Laigle, a family usually loyal to Robert Curthose, and a niece of Hugh earl of Chester.[30] A monk of St Albans and Tynemouth, partial to the priory's re-founder and patron, described him as the scion of a most ancient and noble family, a tall man and a fine and honourable knight. Orderic, however, used less flattering adjectives: martial, ambitious, haughty, gloomy and secretive.[31] Never entirely secure in the north, and on bad terms with the bishop of Durham, who was again close to the king,[32] he defied William in 1095 in circumstances for which Orderic is the main authority.[33]

[28] *ASC, s.a.* 1095–6, 172–3; *GR*, ii, 372–3; Florence, ii, 38–9; OV, iv, 278–86; Gaimar, ll. 6129–6178.

[29] OV, ii, 266; iv, 50, 278; Sanders, *Baronies*, 104. The twelfth-century honour of Mowbray had little connection in England with its predecessor: D.E. Greenway, *Charters of the Honour of Mowbray, 1107–1191* (1972), xvii ff.

[30] See genealogical table, no. 4.

[31] See above, 167–8.

[32] Among the matters at issue was the ownership of the priory of Tynemouth: see Offler, *Durham Episc. Charters*, 4 ff., and below, 352. *FWR*, ii, 38, suggests that the bishop was involved in the plot.

[33] His circumstantial account is supported in a general way by *GR*'s, 'orta inter eum et regem non modica controversia verborum', p. 372.

Robert and his nephew Morel, either late in 1094 or early in 1095, robbed four large Norwegian trading vessels (*canards*) which entered a North Sea port. William, after receiving the merchants' complaints, ordered the earl to make restitution. On Robert's failure to comply, possibly because he considered that his 'liberty' was being disregarded, William indemnified the merchants out of his own treasury – a typical act of generosity – and summoned Robert to court, probably to both the Easter meeting at Winchester and the Whitsun (13 May) meeting at Windsor[34] and on one other occasion to complete the three summonses necessary to make the earl legally contumacious. The hardening of his attitude since 1088 is shown by his refusal of Robert's request for hostages or a safe-conduct. He would not grant the earl belligerent status: the rebel was simply a traitor, and was sentenced, presumably by judgment of the king's court, to forfeiture of his estates.[35] Geoffrey Gaimar, writing at about the same time as Orderic, believed that there was a northern conspiracy like that in which Earl Walthcof had been involved in 1075, and that one of Robert's vassals whom he had brought up (perhaps Morel) treacherously appealed him of treason.[36] The poet, however, seems to be confusing the first and last scenes of the drama.

Events were indeed to show that Robert was prepared to fight it out, organize a far-flung conspiracy, and possible envisage the king's complete destruction. But since none of his more important allies came to his aid, the list of conspirators is confined to those whom the king punished and those who saved their skins by turning informers; and some reporters of these events believed that not all the victims of the king's wrath were guilty.[37] Besides the earl, William count of Eu and his cousin and steward William of Aldrie, Hugh earl of Shrewsbury and his younger brother Philip the Grammarian, Roger de Lacy of Weobley (Herefordshire), and the king's uncle by marriage, Odo of Champagne, lord of Holderness (Burstwick) in Yorkshire, were also punished. Ernulf (I) of Hesdin, lord of Keevil (Wiltshire) and Kempsford (Gloucestershire),[38] and Stephen of Aumale thought it advisable to go on the Crusade. And Morel and Gilbert fitzRichard of Tonbridge informed on the others.

These barons were not a close family group; and although both Robert of Mowbray and William of Eu were related by marriage to the

---

[34] For both councils, *ASC*; for Windsor, *H.N*, 70.

[35] In a charter issued at the siege of Newcastle in the summer the king referred to the earl's previous forfeiture: *Regesta*, no. 368.

[36] Gaimar, ll. 6129 ff.

[37] See below, 357 9.

[38] Sanders, *Baronies*, 124 5, where, if this is the same man, the date of death should be changed from after 1091 to *c.* 1098 at Antioch: see below, 358.

earl of Chester, Hugh not only, as in 1088, kept clear of the conspiracy but also, according to Orderic, hated his brother-in-law (Eu) because of his ill-treatment of his sister. Nor, although several were, in Normandy as in England, 'northerners', was it a compact geographical association. The one obvious link between Robert of Mowbray, William of Eu, the Montgomery brothers and Gilbert of Tonbridge is that they had been rebels in 1088. In 1095 they either joined up again or were marked down by the king for a belated punishment. Florence believed that the plotters intended to kill William and replace him on the throne with his cousin, Stephen of Aumale, the son of his aunt Adelaide and Odo of Champagne. There could have been talk of this; but Stephen himself does not seem to have moved.

Only through Anselm's movements and actions can we get glimpses of the preliminary stages of William's military dispositions in the face of the plot. The king must have begun as early as the council of Windsor at Whitsun to assemble an army for a campaign in Northumberland. It would be expected that for such an expedition he would have called out the feudal host, or a select part of it, since it was advantageous to have the other barons with him when going against rebels. Thomas archbishop of York and 'other bishops and barons' were in his company at Nottingham.[39] Robert fitzHaimo, Eudo the steward, Peter of Valognes, lord of Benington (Hertfordshire) and sometime sheriff of that county, and Gilbert of Tonbridge are known to have been with him in Northumberland; and it is possible that Edgar Ætheling and Edgar of Scots linked up with him in the north.[40] At some stage the archbishop and the legate rejoined him and accompanied him as far as Nottingham, where William dismissed both, giving Walter of Albano leave to return to Rome and ordering Anselm back to Canterbury.

William entrusted the primate with an important military command. We learn of this not from Eadmer, to whom it must have been most distasteful, but from Anselm's own letters to the papal legate, who was pestering him to go to meet him.[41] According to Anselm, the two bishops had parted, presumably somewhere on their return journey south, 'expecting never to meet again in this land', as Anselm rather testily remarked in his second letter of refusal. And he took a firm line with the legate, who was possibly staying in London while he collected Peter's Pence.[42] It was otiose, he declared, to discuss at this time the reform of the English church, for he knew perfectly well what had to be done and

---

[39] Anselm, *Letters*, nos 191–2, pp. 77, 79.
[40] *Regesta*, nos 363, 366–8, and below, pp. 353–4.
[41] Anselm, *Letters*, nos 191–2.
[42] *ASC*, s.a., 173. Anselm told the legate that he was only free to travel in the direction of the Channel ports.

would get on with it when he could. Besides, with the king and the magnates absent on campaign and himself tethered to Canterbury, the moment was inopportune. Anselm never suggested that the legate should visit him. It is clear that, once he had received the pallium, he regarded the legate's commission as exhausted. For the time being he was much closer to the king than to the legate, with whom personal difficulties had arisen. He was carrying out his military duties puncti-liously, almost, it would seem, with relish.

Anselm reveals in these letters that William had ordered him, first at Nottingham by word of mouth and afterwards at Canterbury by confirmatory writ, that he was to command the defences of his city and of the surrounding area. He was not to leave the place, and, if he received a dispatch from the guards the king had posted on the coast that an invasion had begun, he was, whatever the hour of day or night, to call out all available troops, both cavalry and foot, and send them to repel the invaders. It was as though Anselm had now been girt with the mantle of Lanfranc rather than with the pall of Pope Urban. Anselm further told the legate that they were in daily fear of an invasion through the ports which lay closest to Canterbury (presumably Sandwich and Dover), but unfortunately does not identify the suspected invaders. It would seem that the danger was expected more from Eu or Aumale than from Lower Normandy, for Robert Curthose is more likely to have invaded the south coast. It is indeed interesting that no chronicler thought that the conspirators looked in the direction of Robert or Henry. The former had ceased to attract the English baronage and the latter had not yet gained their esteem. However that may be, William had removed Gilbert of Tonbridge from Kent. The whereabouts of William of Eu, lord of Hastings, are, however, unknown.

The archbishop in his letters seems quite unperturbed by the military command given to him by 'his lord the king'. He denies the legate's suggestion that William had been a schismatic king,[43] and in a letter to Osmund bishop of Salisbury, which may have been repeated to other diocesans, strikes an unexpected patriotic note.[44] He asks the bishop to order prayers to be said throughout his bishopric that God should keep the king in his constant protection and favourably direct all his actions towards a successful end according to his will. 'For the king's prosperity is our prosperity, just as his adversity is likewise ours.' Moreover, prayers were especially needful at that moment, for the land had several neighbours who, typically of bad men faced with the good, envied the king's wisdom and vigour (*prudentia*, *strenuitas*), although they

[43] See above, 345–6.
[44] Anselm, *Letters*, no. 190, p. 76.

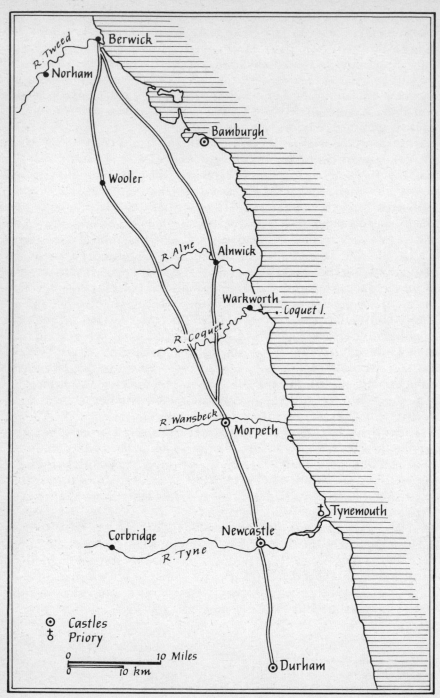

3. The Campaign against Robert of Mowbray (1095)

dissembled their feelings. For Anselm to view the king as a good man and the protector of the land, to whom all Christians and men of good will should rally, even though he may have had the hostile Welsh and Scots principally in mind, was a change indeed.

William with his customary determination marched directly against his main opponent; and Robert of Mowbray tried to hold the whole of his county against him. His unnamed brother was in command of the forces in the south which defended the line of the River Tyne, while he himself with his new wife and his nephew Morel lay in reserve. William could advance with confidence up the Great North Road as far as Durham. His route was then blocked by the castle which Robert Curthose had ordered to be built in 1080 on the north bank of the Tyne to control the first up-stream bridge, and which had passed into Robert of Mowbray's custody with the earldom. The place was on an old Roman site (*Pons Ælius*) and named *Munecaceastre*, Monkchester, presumably because it had belonged to the monastery at Tynemouth down-river. But it was soon called after its new castle, and by the twelfth century Newcastle had become a place-name. In 1095, however, it was so new that its name was uncertain, and the language of the Anglo-Saxon Chronicler and of Florence's Latin version has led to great confusion. According to the former, the king besieged the castle at the mouth of the Tyne, a phrase which Florence expanded to 'the castle of Robert [of Mowbray] situated at the mouth of the River Tyne'. And this has been understood to refer to Tynemouth rather than Newcastle.[45]

Yet there are many reasons for thinking the contrary. There is no evidence, apart from these two texts, that there ever was in the Middle Ages a castle at Tynemouth. Although the priory was on a rocky promontory of great defensive potential, and had a church tower and perhaps a wall or ditch appropriate to a monastery, and although it was regarded as a place of refuge and obviously could have been turned into a useful fortress for the occasion, it could never in this period withstand a

---

[45] 'thone castel aet Tinemuthan', *ASC*; 'castellum praedicti comitis Roberti ad ostium Tinae fluminis situm', Florence; no military details in *GR* or, for this phase, in *OV*. Since the name Newcastle does not appear anywhere in *ASC* or Florence, there is no difficulty in giving that identity to their 'castle at the mouth of the Tyne'. The basic account of the foundation in 1080 is in *HR*, 211: 'castellum novum super flumen Tynae condidit'. It was still only a fortified enclosure without a keep: see R.A. Brown, H.M. Colvin, A.J. Taylor, *The History of the King's Works* (1963), ii, 745 ff.; D.F. Renn, *Norman Castles in Britain* (1968), 245–7. It was usual for a marcher earl and his barons to have custody of the castles of his shire. *FWR*, ii, 46–8, 606 ff., believed that the earl also had a castle at Tynemouth and that the king attacked both. Chibnall, OV, iv, 280 n., is of the same opinion. For the alleged castle at Tynemouth, see C.H. Hunter Blair, 'The early castles of Northumberland', *Archaeologia Æliana*, 4th ser., xxii (1944), 128; Renn, *op. cit.*, 336, who both rely on the words of *ASC* and Florence, quoted at the beginning of this note.

strong attack.[46] Moreover, it had no strategic importance. A glance at the map will show that the earl would have had no reason to fortify it in 1095; and to have put troops in it would have been completely pointless. Newcastle was the fortress he had to hold at any cost. As he did. There are three charters issued by the king in favour of the priory of Tynemouth and St Albans abbey, obviously at the same time, and dated at, or at the siege of, the new castle.[47] The outside dates are Robert's condemnation in the summer of 1095 and the bishop of Durham's death at Christmas. Although there is the complication that by Michaelmas a second new castle had been constructed in Northumberland, this, opposite Bamburgh, was never outside William's control. The charters are also evidence that the priory was not under attack at the same time as Newcastle, for the king is unlikely to have confirmed its privileges without comment while he was trying to force an entry.

William, then, as he followed the main road north from Durham, came up against Newcastle, strongly held by the earl's brother. Typically, he did not try a frontal attack across the river, but, forcing a crossing up-stream, possibly at Corbridge, cut off the garrison's communications with the north and secured the crossing of the Wansbeck by knocking out William of Merlay's little castle at Morpeth, in which were 'most of the earl's best men'.[48] Newcastle surrendered after two months (perhaps July and August), and the earl's brother and the garrisons of both castles were put in prison.[49] William could then advance on Bamburgh, in which the earl and his remaining family took refuge; and he had a stroke of luck on the way, for, as they drew near, Gilbert of Tonbridge threw himself on the king's mercy and confessed that he was privy to a plot to ambush him in the wood they were approaching. He also disclosed the names of the other conspirators.[50]

[46] Its natural strength is frequently stressed in *Vita Oswini*: cf. 11, 22, 25. It was used as a safe deposit and place of refuge when armies were in the neighbourhood, but was plundered in 1072 by William I's troops (above, 293 n. 131) and later by Nigel d'Aubigny's (above, 291). At the end of the campaign in 1095 it could not be held long by the earl: below, 354–5.

[47] 'apud obsidionem novi castri', *Regesta*, no. 366; 'apud obsessionem novi castri', no. 367; 'apud novum castrum', no. 368, Dugdale, *Monasticon*, iii, 313, no. 6. Eudo *dapifer* witnesses all three; P. de Valognes also witnesses the last.

[48] *ASC* starts with the capture of the unnamed *faesten*, translated *munitiuncula* by Florence, and identified by Gaimar, ll. 6151–5. For a plan, see Renn, *op. cit.*, 336. See also Sanders, *Baronies*, 65. Gaimar, misled by *ASC*'s order and confused by the two new castles, omits the siege on the Tyne and makes the king follow Robert to Bamburgh and build a new castle there before taking Morpeth and blockading Bamburgh. *FWR* and Chibnall, *loc. cit.*, identify the *faesten* with Tynemouth.

[49] The duration of the siege of 'Robert's castle' is in Florence only.

[50] OV, iv, 280, where the episode is confusingly located both on the approach to the earldom and just before the siege of Bamburgh.

Bamburgh, an old fortified town surrounded by marshes and pools, was the strongest of the enemy fortresses; and when William realized that the earl was not going to surrender and the castle could not be taken by assault, he had a counter-fortification built which they, presumably the besieged, called *Malveisin*, in the English of the time *Yfel nehhbur* – Bad-neighbour.[51] Orderic believed that Gilbert's disclosures and William's resolution caused the whole league to collapse and left the earl calling frantically from the ramparts to the defectors, now in the royal camp, to remember their promises and come to his aid. But no one moved; and the king had closed the net. On 29 August, 'in the year in which William, son of King William senior [*magnus*], constructed a new castle before Bamburgh against Robert earl of Northumbria', Edgar, William's candidate for the kingdom of Scots, in the presence of what must have been a small army gathered in the cemetery of Norham, a possession of the church of Durham, made a grant of Berwick and some other estates in Lothian to Bishop William and the monks of St Cuthbert.[52] Present were the bishop, Prior Turgot, the reeve of Norham and 'a great multitude of French and English'. The charter was witnessed by Edgar's younger brother, Alexander, who was to reign after him in Scotland (1107-24), David, possibly their brother and successor (1124-53), Edgar Ætheling, Robert de Humet and several other northern barons. Edgar described himself as 'the son of Malcolm king of Scots, holding the whole land of Lothian and the kingdom of Scotland by the grant of my lord William, king of the English, and by inheritance from my father', and declared that he made the grant with the advice of the aforesaid King William, his lord, and his own vassals for the souls of his father and mother, his brothers Duncan and Edward (the one slain in 1094, the other at Alnwick in 1093), and for the salvation of himself and of his predecessors and successors. William confirmed this grant, 'to which he had consented', by writs addressed to Thomas archbishop of York and all his vassals, French, English and Scottish, and witnessed by William his chancellor and the ever-present Robert fitzHaimo.[53] The documents may have been issued from *Malveisin* itself. Edgar had to wait two more years before he could make William Rufus's grant of the Scottish crown effective. But it would seem that in 1095 he, with Edgar Ætheling, Bishop William and the others, was with an army

---

[51] *ASC*, 172; Florence, ii, 38; OV, iv, 282. Orderic provides similar names given by the defenders to siege castles erected by Henry I in 1116 × 18, *Malassis* (Ill-placed) and *Trulla Leporis* (Hare's Form): OV, vi, 186. A useful list of Henry's field-fortifications is given in the index, *s.v. castle*.

[52] A.C. Lowrie, *Early Scottish Charters* (1905), no. XV; A.A.M. Duncan, 'The earliest Scottish Charters', *Scottish Historical Review*, xxxvii (1958), 103 ff.

[53] *Regesta*, nos 364-5 (see also ii, 402); *Facsimiles*, pl. VIII, IX; Duncan, *loc. cit.*

operating to the north of Bamburgh and engaged in preventing Robert of Mowbray from getting aid from Scotland or escaping in that direction.[54]

It was at Bamburgh that William heard that Montgomery had fallen to the Welsh. Leaving a force to continue the siege, he went off to lend a hand to Hugh of Shrewsbury.[55] He raised a new army, and after Michaelmas (29 September) sent detachments to range through Powys and Gwynnedd and rendezvous in Snowdonia at the beginning of November. But as the Welsh took evasive action and could not be provoked to battle, little was achieved except in the way of reconnaissance and the strengthening of the morale of the Anglo-French settlers. Florence, always pessimistic, recorded that the king, as ever, lost many men and horses.

A decision was, however, about to be reached in the north. The chroniclers give a fairly concordant account of the events, with obscurity limited to confusion between the two new castles, *Malveisin* and Newcastle-on-Tyne.[56] Florence, as before, gives the most detail. Robert of Mowbray was informed by the watchman of Newcastle that they would let him in if he came secretly by night. Robert slipped out of Bamburgh with thirty knights under cover of darkness, but was noticed by the garrison of *Malveisin*, who went in pursuit and informed the garrison of Newcastle. So, when he tried to enter Newcastle on the Sunday, he was discovered and fled to the monastery of St Oswin at Tynemouth, some ten miles down-stream.[57] By this time, it seems, the king had returned from Chester; but his personal involvement in the final stages is not vouched for by the chroniclers. The priory was

[54] This event also has a crucial bearing on William of Malmesbury's story, *GP*, 273, that shortly after the bishop of Durham had opposed Anselm (at Rockingham in February 1095), he lost the king's favour, and escaped standing trial in the royal court at Gloucester only by his fatal illness, which occurred there. The suggestion is that the bishop had repeated his treachery of 1088. But not only is the court wrongly placed but the imputation itself is unthinkable, if only because of the chronicler's own belief that since 1091 the bishop had always tried to please the king.

[55] Wightman, *The Lacy Family*, 170–1, suggests that Roger de Lacy, lord of Weobley, was in alliance with the Welsh. Military details in *ASC*, 173, only; cf. Florence, ii, 39. Lloyd, *History of Wales*, ii, 405–6.

[56] *ASC*, 172–3, expanded by Florence, ii, 38–9. No details in *GR*, ii, 372. OV, iv, 282, explains Robert's escape from Bamburgh as provoked by boredom. Some commentators have thought that Robert was the victim of a trick, but it does not seem that Florence's text supports that interpretation. Gaimar, ll. 6164–70, has Robert travel from Bamburgh to Tynemouth in a boat manned by one sailor.

[57] In *Capitula de miraculis et translationibus S. Cuthberti*, Simeon, ii, 346, Robert seems to enter a town, whose geographical strength is described, rather than the monastery, which is not mentioned until the final episode in the church. But none of the sources mentions 'Tynemouth castle' here.

besieged, and on the sixth day Robert was wounded while fighting off an attack. Although all his men were slain or captured, he himself, however, managed to take refuge in the monastic church.[58] But he was dragged from sanctuary and put in custody, and the Durham monks, far from condemning the sacrilege, regarded his capture in the church as St Cuthbert's punishment for having taken it from them and granting it to St Albans.

William then ordered Robert to be conveyed to Bamburgh and no doubt made sure that the discomfiture he had suffered with Odo at Rochester seven years before would not be repeated. The threat to have the captive's eyes put out unless the countess and Morel surrendered the castle was effective; and William took the whole of Northumberland into his hands, appointing no successor to the earldom. The countess he let go free, and Morel disclosed a second list of conspirators, both clerical and lay. William sent Robert to be imprisoned in Windsor castle and ordered all his tenants-in-chief to be at his Christmas court there. He clearly intended to make an example of some of the traitors.

William's Northumbrian campaign was very similar in plan to his Kentish one in 1088: for Tonbridge read Morpeth, for Pevensey Newcastle, and for Rochester Bamburgh. It was, however, conducted without an obvious mistake, or with better luck – his withdrawal to Wales probably encouraged the earl to risk his fatal sortie – and if it can be faulted, it can only be on the grounds of slowness of execution. William never showed any inclination to try to take a major fortification by storm, and he was not a renowned engineer like Robert of Bellême; but his failure to bring his enemies to battle seems caused more by their reluctance than his own, and was typical of the age. Although hardly a creative military theorist and with no special fame for tactical improvements, he had, besides all the qualities of a good fighting commander, an excellent strategic grasp. He never failed to get himself and his forces to his objective, and he was usually right on target.

William did indeed hold his Christmas court at Windsor, perhaps his favourite residence, and on 2 January the bishop of Durham died there. William of St Calais had already been warned of his approaching end by one of his knights, Boso, who had had an alarming vision while lying ill.[59] For three days Boso's spirit had been led by a guide through the purlieus of Heaven and Hell. He had seen two Durham monks stray from the straight and narrow, English and Norman soldiers about to lose

---

[58] According to *ASC*, followed by Florence, it was the men who were in the new castle who besieged Robert, but it is not absolutely clear which this was. Florence puts Robert's capture on the sixth day. In the Miracle of St Cuthbert the siege is for two days, but this may refer to the church alone.

[59] Simeon, *HDE*, i, 130-5.

their lives (presumably in Northumberland), the wives of priests and their doomed consorts, and finally his bishop. In a vast and horrible wilderness stood a tall house made of iron, with a door that was always opening and shutting. Suddenly the bishop stuck out his head and asked Boso where the monk Geoffrey was. 'He should be attending my court,' he said. Geoffrey was the bishop's steward (*procurator*) for the diocese; and the guide said that the bishop and then Geoffrey would soon die.[60] All this Boso, when he was better, told to the prior and bishop.

If the suggestion was that the bishop was too much involved in secular business, he took it to heart and died well. His health began to fail and on Christmas day at Windsor he had a seizure from which he did not recover. Anselm, always magnanimous, took care of his spiritual welfare, and on 1 January the bishop received the last sacraments from Thomas archbishop of York, Walkelin of Winchester and John of Bath, the physician. He said that he wanted to be buried not in the church of St Cuthbert but in the chapter house, where he would be a constant reminder to his monks. He died at daybreak on the next day and was buried on 16 January in the place he had chosen.[61] That he had recovered the king's favour and was once more a valued counsellor and servant is clear, but it is doubtful whether after 1088 there was ever again the same intimacy. It is significant that at the siege of Newcastle, when apparently the bishop was helping his lord against the rebel earl, William should have confirmed ownership of the disputed church of Tynemouth to St Albans,[62] probably because the southern abbey was in royal custody since the death of Abbot Paul in 1093.

The illness and death of the bishop may have made the Christmas court an unsuitable occasion for the trial of the traitors. There would in any case have been the preliminary business of inquiring into the disclosures made by Gilbert of Tonbridge and Morel. On 13 January the court moved to Salisbury,[63] where William of St Calais had been tried in 1088. Perhaps the strength of the fortifications and its seclusion recommended it; perhaps it was the best place for hunting in winter. The judicial procedure followed in the case of the arch-rebel is not specified. According to a recent canon of Urban II's Council of Clermont (November 1095), codifying previous ecclesiastical teaching, 'Anyone

[60] This is the monk who was accused in December 1088 of various 'crimes' in support of the bishop: *De Injusta Vexatione*, 193; and it is probably he who appears in Durham's *Liber Vitae*, inserted after Priors Aldwin and Turgot, 45b.

[61] *ASC*, s.a., dates the death 1 January, and is followed by *HBC*. But the more circumstantial *HDE* seems to be the better witness.

[62] *Regesta*, no. 368. The king had been very angry with the bishops for their poor performance at the trial of Anselm at Rockingham in February.

[63] *ASC*, s.a., 173; *GR*, ii, 372; Florence, ii, 39; OV, iv, 284.

who fled to a church or roadside cross for sanctuary, should, if guilty, be surrendered to justice, saving his life and limbs, or, if innocent, set free.'[64] Although the king, as we know, had little use for canonical rules, he did not in this instance run foul of them. The earl had been condemned in the summer for contumacy and captured in war, and the only step that might have been necessary was to pronounce final judgment. If so, this was a sentence of imprisonment, probably for life; and he remained in prison until he died, some twenty to thirty years later.[65] William permitted no kinsman to inherit. The countess, the unfortunate Matilda of Laigle, was allowed to marry again by the dispensation of Pope Paschal II (after 1099).[66] Morel went abroad and, according to Orderic, eked out a miserable existence.[67]

The chief trial at Salisbury was that of William count of Eu, and this, because of his rank and the punishment meted out, made a great impression on contemporaries. He was appealed by Geoffrey Baynard, an important member of the ministerial nobility, sometime sheriff of Yorkshire, whose brother had been sheriff of Essex and whose family held the honour of Castle Baynard in London.[68] Since Geoffrey would not seem to have been directly involved in the affair, he was probably acting as the king's champion. In the resulting *duellum*, or trial by battle,[69] Geoffrey was the victor, and the vanquished felon was condemned by the king (and his court) to have his eyes put out and then be castrated, a mutilation from which he does not seem to have recovered.[70] He was survived by his widow Helisende, the sister of Hugh of Chester, and their son, Henry, who eventually succeeded to the county. He had also had three children by a concubine.

No one gives an opinion on William of Eu's guilt, possibly because of his previous history, possibly because God had given his verdict. But William of Malmesbury is insistent that the consequent condemnation to death by hanging of the count's cousin and steward, William of Aldrie, was unjust. Florence believed that he was privy to the plot;[71] but for the Malmesbury monk, whose monastery was only a day's ride from

[64] OV, v, 14.

[65] Almost thirty years: OV, iv, 282; twenty years: Gaimar, l. 6175.

[66] OV, iv, 282. She married Nigel d'Aubigny, for whom Henry I created an entirely new honour of Mowbray. Greenway, *op. cit.*, xvii ff. She was repudiated by Nigel, probably because of her childlessness.

[67] OV, iv, 284.

[68] *Gilbert Crispin*, 38–9, for the family.

[69] For this ordeal, see Barlow, *EC 1066–1154*, 163.

[70] Helisende, the widow of a count of Eu, occurs in an anecdote, to be dated 1096, in Guibert of Nogent, *De Vita sua libri tres*, II, v, Migne *PL*, clvi, 903–4. D'Achery in his note guessed that it was Robert's, not William's, widow.

[71] *GR*, ii, 372; Florence, ii, 39. *ASC* makes no comment. OV, rather surprisingly, omits the case.

the two manors, Littleton Pannell and Compton Basset, which the steward held of William of Eu in the centre of Wiltshire, he was not only blameless and honourable and a gossip of the king, but also a man of handsome and noble appearance. He went to the gallows religiously and bravely, protesting his innocence to the end.[72] More fortunate than these was Ernulf of Hesdin, who succeeded in the *duellum*, in which he was represented by a vassal. But he thought it wise to accompany Duke Robert on his Crusade later in the year, and died at Antioch, probably in 1098.[73] Although he had sons, most of his lands seem to have passed with his daughter, Matilda, to Patrick I of Chaworth,[74] perhaps a further punishment of the family. Another who went on the Crusade, possibly for the same reason, was the king's cousin, Stephen of Aumale,[75] mentioned in connexion with the conspiracy but not, apparently, put on trial. He may, of course, have been in Normandy beyond William's grasp. Others sentenced were Odo of Champagne, to disinheritance and, perhaps like Philip of Montgomery, to imprisonment.[76] Philip, like Ernulf and Stephen, went on the Crusade, and, like the former, died at Antioch.[77] Orderic believed that William reproached Philip's brother, Hugh of Shrewsbury, in private and settled for a fine of £3,000.[78] As Hugh would in any case be responsible to the king for a relief in respect of his earldom, his indebtedness must have been immense. But William liked their brother Arnulf, who was made heir to the earldom, for he granted him Odo's lands in Holderness and Lincolnshire,[79] perhaps as compensation for his losses in West Wales. Another punished in 1096 was Roger of Lacy, whose great honour of Weobley William gave to his younger brother, Hugh (I), who had remained loyal.[80] The Anglo-Saxon Chronicler informs us that others of the accused were taken to London and there 'destroyed', perhaps, like William of Eu, mutilated.[81]

Orderic offers some final generalizations and reflections. The king

[72] *DB*, i, 71c–d, cf. 74a. Littleton had been thegnland of the church of Salisbury. Loyd, *Families*, 3, suggests that he may have taken his name from Audrieu, between Bayeux and Caen in the canton Tilly-sur-Seulles. See also Barlow, *EC 1066–1154*, 163.

[73] Chronicle in *Liber Monasterii de Hyda*, ed. E. Edwards (Rolls ser., 1866), 301–2.

[74] Sanders, *Baronies*, 124–5.

[75] David, *RC*, 228.

[76] For Odo, *ASC* and Florence, *loc. cit.* For Philip, Florence only (a good authority here). Philip may already have become a clerk: Mason, 'Roger de Montgomery and his Sons', p. 15 n. 4, with a reference to the absence of his witness to *Regesta*, no. 356. He may, therefore, have been one of the clerks betrayed by Morel: above p. 355.

[77] OV, iv, 302.

[78] OV, iv, 284. Mason, *loc. cit.*, 17–19.

[79] Mason, *loc. cit.*, 17.

[80] OV, *ibid.*; Sanders, *Baronies*, 95; Wightman, *The Lacy Family*, 170 ff. Roger retired to Normandy and was highly favoured by Duke Robert on his return from the Crusade.

[81] 'spillen': cf. *ASC, s.a.* 1124, 'spilde of here aegon and of here stanes'.

had taken the opportunity to punish his enemies and reward his friends. In order to avoid repercussions in Normandy he preferred to take fines from many of the conspirators. Others who had been involved, but lay low and heeded the punishments inflicted on the ring-leaders, on the advice of his counsellors he left alone. (One of these, presumably, was Gilbert of Tonbridge.) The general result was a great strengthening of William's power in the kingdom. Orderic's observations are shrewd. In 1095–6 the king was able to settle scores both new and old. He dealt out heavier punishments with a freer hand than in 1088 and without much of an eye to repercussions. One sign of his confidence was his leaving vacant not only the earldom of Northumberland but also the bishopric of Durham. He feared nothing from Scotland and wanted no more than sheriffs and barons in the northern marches. The detailed history of the confiscations and other judicial penalties imposed in 1096 cannot be written, but, although William would have wanted to share the spoils with his friends,[82] there must also have been vast financial profit to him, for his gifts had usually to be paid for. William of St Calais, too, had performed his last service to his lord, and Ranulf Flambard took over the custody of the bishopric.[83] William was replenishing his depleted treasury in preparation for a new round in his bout with Robert.

In these last two years some important barons and prelates had died. Among the laity the deaths of Roger of Montgomery in 1094 and of the royal steward, Ivo Taillebois, probably in the same year, made the most impression on the royal court. The deaths of Bishops Wulfstan of Worcester (January 1095), Robert of Hereford (June) and William of Durham are equally noteworthy, if only because the three men typify the three main streams of tradition in the post-Conquest English church, the Anglo-Saxon, Lotharingian and French respectively. The king appointed to both the Welsh marcher bishoprics in 1096, without unreasonable delay, and in each case a trusted clerk: Samson, the brother of the archbishop of York, to Worcester, Gerard, his former chancellor and nephew of the bishop of Winchester, to Hereford. Both these had earned their preferment, and Gerard had just carried out an important embassy to Rome.[84] No abbot seems to have been of much importance at court, and William was loath to fill up vacancies. He made a prompt appointment to Battle, his father's foundation, in 1096 of Henry, monk of Bec and prior of Christ Church, Canterbury, possibly on Anselm's advice; but Battle was a special case. Ely, Peterborough, St

[82] Besides the grant of Odo's lands to Arnulf, Robert of Mowbray's honour of Barnstaple passed to Judhel of Totnes, possibly in recompense for Totnes, which William had granted in 1087 to Roger (I) of Nonant: Sanders, *Baronies*, 89, 104.

[83] See above, 237.

[84] *HN*, 68. See above, 342.

Albans and Abingdon were left without pastors, and there was irregularity at St Augustine's, Canterbury, where, after Guy's death in 1093, William appointed a converted knight who was not blessed as abbot until the next reign.[85]

The only deaths which seriously affected the royal administration were those of Ivo Taillebois and William of Durham. Except when the latter had been in exile, both had from the beginning been members of the inner circle of *curiales*, regularly authorizing and witnessing royal writs and charters and clearly much involved in the everyday conduct of affairs. The bishops of Durham and Winchester, as we have previously noted, seem to have been to some extent alternates in a trio completed by Ranulf Flambard, the permanent official. Durham's death left Walkelin of Winchester as the chief justiciar (in the non-technical sense of the term), and probably improved Ranulf Flambard's standing. Walkelin himself died on 3 January 1098, and his place was effectively taken by Ranulf, whom the king appointed to Durham in May 1099.

A handful of writs and charters from 1094–6 afford a good view of the king's counsellors and main servants in that period. Among the bishops, the most frequent witness was Walkelin (8), followed by William of Durham (4), John of Bath (3), Robert Bloet of Lincoln, the former chancellor (2), and Osmund of Salisbury (2).[86] William Giffard, the chancellor, witnesses eight, and Ranulf the chaplain seven.[87] Although Anselm does not appear as a witness, and may have preferred to distance himself from the court, between Whitsun 1095 and Whitsun 1097 he acted occasionally, perhaps in fact continuously, as a royal justiciar.[88] His letter to Bishop Osmund, ordering him to take action on the king's authority and his own, echoes the language used by his predecessor Lanfranc.[89] Eadmer, because he was unwilling to show his hero working in harmony with the king, almost completely ignores that period.[90]

Of the ministerial and familiar baronage, Eudo *dapifer* and Roger Bigot, both with six attestations, are followed by Robert fitzHaimo (5), Urse of Abetot (3), and Robert fitzGerold (of Roumare) and Ivo

[85] See above, 183–4.
[86] Walkelin, *Regesta*, nos 378, 385, 396, 398, 400, 405, 348a, 379a; William, 386, 466, 348a, b; John, 378, 398, 348a; Robert, 400, 406; Osmund, 398, 348a; Ralf of Chichester, 348a; Herbert of Norwich, 348a.
[87] William, nos 386, 396, 399, 400, 405, 410, 377a, 379a; Ranulf, 385, 387, 400, 405, 348b, 377a, 379a.
[88] Cf. above, 348–51.
[89] Anselm, *Letters*, no. 195, cf. 190; Lanfranc, *Letters*, nos 34–6, 53. Cf. F. Barlow, 'A view of Archbishop Lanfranc', *Journ. of Eccles. Hist.*, xvi (1965), 174.
[90] Southern, *VA*, 88n.

Taillebois with two apiece.[91] Earls and counts become almost as rare as abbots in the witness lists. Early in 1095 Count Henry witnessed one of his new lord's charters,[92] but then left for France. Eadmer considered that Robert of Meulan was the king's most trusted baronial adviser; but he too was often abroad. His brother Henry of Warwick appears once.[93] Single appearances of Hugh of Montgomery, Ivo of Grandmesnil, Nigel of Oilli, William Peverel, Roger of Nonant, Robert *dispensator* and Hugh of Envermeu reveal, however, the substantial continuity among the king's baronial servants.[94] This feature, as we shall see, was to persist through the rest of the reign.

On 27 November 1095, while William was finishing his campaign in Northumberland, Pope Urban II preached the sermon in the cathedral church of Clermont Ferrand in the Auvergne which set in motion the expedition against the Saracen occupiers of the Holy Land known later as the First Crusade.[95] At this papal council the Norman church was represented by Bishops Odo of Bayeux, Gilbert of Evreux and Serlo of Sées (Orderic's former abbot), and Hoël of Le Mans was also there.[96] The English church, however, was represented only by Anselm's personal proxy, his friend the Bec monk Boso, who survived with difficulty the rigours of the journey to become in due course the fourth abbot of the Norman monastery.[97] In February 1096 the archbishop of Rouen in a provincial synod disseminated the legislation promulgated at Clermont.[98] Anselm, even if Boso had returned quickly to Canterbury, would have been unable to do the same. The pope, after the

---

[91] Eudo, *Regesta*, nos 386–7, 398, 400, 410, 377a, Roger, 385–6, 398 (Bicet), 400, 466, 348a; Robert fitzHaimo, 386, 405, 407, 377a, 379a; Urse, 387, 377a, 379a; Robert fitzGerold, 377a, 379a; Ivo, 407, 410.

[92] No. 398.

[93] *HN*, 40, 62. For example, Robert witnessed a charter of Robert Curthose dated 15 August 1095, *Regesta*, no. 384. Henry of Warwick, no. 348a.

[94] Hugh, *Regesta*, no. 410; Ivo, 410; Nigel, 410; William 398; Roger, 398; Robert, 388; Hugh, 400.

[95] For the First Crusade, see H. Hagenmeyer, 'Chronologie de la Première Croissade (1094–1100)', *Revue de l'Orient Latin*, vi–viii (1898–1901); R. Grousset, *Histoire des Croissades et du Royaume franc de Jérusalem* (Paris 1934–6); S. Runciman, *A History of the Crusades* (1951–4). The account of it in OV, Bk. IX (v, 2–190), is derived almost entirely from the anonymous *Gesta Francorum*, by way of Baudri of Bourgueil's *Historia Ierosolimitana*. But since he gives it a Norman slant when he can, it is his text which is referred to here.

[96] OV, v, 18; *Hist. Pont. Cen.*, 395.

[97] *Vita Ven. Bosonis* in *Lanfranci Opera*, ed. L. D'Achery (1648), app., 47.

[98] For Clermont, see R. Somerville, *The Councils of Urban II*, vol. i, *Decreta claromontensia*, in *Annuarium historiae conciliorum*, suppl. i (Amsterdam 1972). For Rouen, OV, v, 18–24.

council, in the course of a recruiting campaign in aid of the threatened
Emperor Alexius I Comnenus, reached in February Le Mans, where he
stayed three days with Hoël, and in March moved through Blois and
Touraine. It would seem that Robert Curthose took the Cross in
February, for Urban sent his legate, Abbot Jarento of St-Bénigne at
Dijon, to England before Easter (13 April), partly in order to negotiate a
settlement between the two brothers.[99]

It was just at this time that the great popular movement got under
way which led to a multitude of men, women and children, under the
leadership of a monk, Peter of Achères (the Hermit) and some knights,
to travel by way of Cologne, Hungary and Bulgaria to Cappadocia; and
England contributed to this ill-organized and ill-fated enterprize.[100]
Later in the year Anselm wrote urgently to Osmund bishop of Salisbury
about the abbot of Cerne in Dorset who was urging his monks to go to
Jerusalem and was himself preparing to leave. With his companions he
had bought a boat and had put down 30s on it. Anselm ordered Osmund
on royal authority and his own to inquire into the matter and stop the
abbot or any of his monks from leaving 'before the king's return'. He was
also to make this a general order respecting monks throughout his
diocese and to be good enough on the same authority to order the
bishops of Exeter, Bath and Worcester to make similar prohibitions in
their dioceses. He added at the end that the pope too had prohibited
this.[101]

At Clermont the pope had urged the princes and knights to make
peace among themselves in order to make war on the heathen. No king
went on the Crusade, and this could have been papal policy. Robert
volunteered, according to Orderic, because he was a ruined man,
sickened by the civil war and feuds in the duchy.[102] Like many others he
was attracted by the double lure of adventure and the forgiveness of his
sins. As he had no money for his expenses and wanted only to preserve
his title and safeguard his restoration to the duchy, should he survive, a
'bargain could easily be struck with William. Many crusaders had to sell

[99] Jarento's companion, Hugh of Flavigny, included a report of the mission in his
Chronicon, 474–5. The other business was the king's misgovernment of the English
church: see below, 364–5. Cf. also, Tillmann, *Legaten*, 21–2. It is possible that an,
unfortunately truncated, Bury St Edmunds miracle story, which concerns the saving
from shipwreck on 16 May (1096) of a party travelling from Rome to England, in a ship
laden with more than 64 passengers (presumably only across the English Channel),
refers to this business: 'Heremanni archidiaconi miracula S. Eadmundi', *Ungedruckte
Anglo-Normannorum Geschichtsquellen*, ed. F. Liebermann, 281.

[100] *ASC*, s.a., pp. 173–4; OV, v, 28 ff.

[101] Anselm, *Letters*, no. 195. The editor suggested that the king was in Northumberland
(1095); more likely he had crossed to Normandy (September 1096).

[102] OV, v, 26.

13a. Old Sarum (Wiltshire), cathedral and castle within an old ring-work. (See here, 85, 357.)

13b. Winchester cathedral, north transept, built by Bishop Walkelin. (See here, 388, 429–31.)

14a. Gloucester Abbey (now cathedral), nave, built by Abbot Serlo. (See here, 114–15, 427.)

14b. Durham cathedral, nave, mostly built by Bishop Ranulf Flambard. (See here, 309, 372 n. 146.)

their precious lands cheaply. Godfrey duke of Lower Lorraine, one of the leaders, mortgaged his castle at Bouillon to the bishop of Liège for 7,000 marks of silver.[103] The abbot of Dijon, before he returned to Normandy after Easter, arranged that William should pay Robert 10,000 marks of silver in return for the custody of the duchy for three years.[104] The church in the twelfth century recognized that mortgages could be usurious: the revenues from the land pledged could be concealed usury, or the value of the pledge when foreclosed could be greater than the principal.[105] But it could not be too nice when Crusaders had to raise money for their expenses. Odo of Bayeux granted the church of St Vigor at Bayeux rather surprisingly to the abbot of Dijon; but whether money passed and on what terms is unknown. Robert confirmed this act on 24 May at Bayeux, and Hugh of Flavigny, who had accompanied Jarento and included an account of the mission in his *Chronicle*, wrote the charter.[106]

No official record of the treaty of 1096 between Robert and William has survived, and it is possible that nothing was ever put in writing, for the chroniclers knew only the main conditions and were not completely certain of those. It might be expected that, as in 1091, there were guarantors of the agreement. But the church would have taken responsibility for its enforcement: pilgrims were under its special protection, and when princes and nobles were being urged temporarily to abandon their lands, they needed firm assurance that they would recover them on their return. A wife and children were useful in this connexion, for they could be left behind as regents. Robert, of course, apart from his bastards, lacked such pledges to fortune. He had to make do with his brothers.

The bargain was, like the 1091 treaty, shrewdly negotiated. The lump sum to be paid by William was less than a quarter of his ordinary annual revenue from England;[107] and, although we are ignorant of the ducal income (some of which was already in William's hands), it looks like a

---

[103] OV, v, 16, 208. For smaller bargains, see David, *RC*, app. D.

[104] *GR*, ii, 371, Florence, ii, 40, and OV, v, 26, 208, agree with Hugh of Flavigny on the sum. *Ann. Winton*, ii, 38, gives 6,666 marks (instead of £s) by mistake. The type of transaction is variously described, but all the formulations amount to a sort of mortgage. There is disagreement, however, over the term: 3 years, Hugh and *HN*, 75; 5 years, OV, v, 26, 208; until the duke's repayment of the sum, Torigny, *Interpolation*, 275. Although 5 is the more obvious devisor of 10,000, Hugh and Eadmer should have known. Five is the number of years the duke was absent. What is uncertain is how important the term was. The pledge was not in fact redeemed by Robert in September 1099, but, as it was always in the hands of the mortgagor, a foreclosure at that date may not have been envisaged.

[105] Council of Tours (1163), cap. 2: Mansi, *Concilia*, xxi, 1176; *Dialogus de Scaccario*, 100.

[106] *Regesta*, no. 376; cf. Haskins, *NI*, charter no. 2, p. 285.

[107] See above, 259.

good investment. The arrangement also gave William seizin of the duchy and would facilitate his succession under the terms of the 1091 treaty in case Robert died on the Crusade. On the other hand, ready cash of the order of 10,000 marks was not easy to come by. Indeed, it is difficult to imagine who else in the West but William could have provided such a sum at six months' notice. As for Henry, according to Robert of Torigny, William granted him in return for his complete adherence the counties of Coutances and Bayeux, except for the city of Bayeux and the town of Caen.[108] This was more than he had originally bought from Robert. Moreover, as he was the residuary heir-presumptive of both brothers, his future prospects were much improved by Robert's departure on a hazardous adventure. At the age of twenty-eight, things were beginning to look up. Whether the agreement of the king of France was requested or secured is not known. Although Robert would probably have welcomed it, for the participation of his lord and friend would have been an additional safeguard of his interests, the king had been excommunicated again at the Council of Clermont for refusing to dismiss Bertrada of Montfort, and the papal legate may have considered him incapable at law. Philip's attempt to take Bishop Ivo of Chartres to a lawsuit (*placitum*) between the two brothers, although possibly to be placed here, seems better attributed to 1094.[109]

William had also had to pay something more for the agreement, the entry of a papal legate into the kingdom despite the concordat of the previous year. Urban took advantage of the situation to instruct Abbot Jarento to complain to the king about his treatment of the English church, particularly his keeping bishoprics and abbacies vacant, to condemn simony and the unchastity of clerks, and possibly to re-negotiate the concordat.[110] But William, foreseeing some of the dangers posed by the legate's entry, had sent in advance an envoy to Urban (unnamed, but probably the specialist, William Warelwast), furnished with 10 marks of pure gold (80 oz, worth 15s the oz) in order to defuse the weapon. He welcomed Jarento, with whom he was greatly impressed, with open arms, entertained him suitably at his Easter court, and gave him all kinds of assurances. But he deferred replying to the legate's specific demands while waiting for the return of his own nuncio.

This clerk returned with an equally anonymous papal nephew, the son of Urban's sister, a layman of no rank or education, who offered William a truce in all matters until Christmas, provided he dispatched immediately to the pope, who was about to leave northern France, as

---

[108] Torigny, *Interpolation*, 275.
[109] See above, 332.
[110] Hugh of Flavigny, *Chronicon*, 474–5.

much of Peter's Pence as he could lay his hands on. William imposed this papal truce on Jarento, although, according to the abbot of Dijon, condemning both privately and publicly the pope's supersession of a legate of wide reputation and renown, who was furnished with full documentary credentials, by such an unqualified 'slave', who had not even written authority. And it is not surprising that William, who was learning that he could bribe a pope almost as easily as he could buy lay princes, affected a high moral tone on this occasion. He may even have been genuinely shocked by what Hugh of Dijon called 'the insatiable depths of Roman avarice'. Be that as it may, Jarento left England for Normandy and, as far as we know, the 'truce until Christmas' was quickly transformed into a peace.

William raised the money from his unwilling subjects in the summer, and in September conveyed it to the duchy,[111] probably sixty-seven barrels containing £100 apiece. A charter issued at Hastings before he sailed, granting to Walkelin of Winchester the right to hold an annual three-day fair at St Giles outside the city, may have been a reward for the bishop's efforts in raising the cash and also a douceur for the regency duties he was about to assume. The witnesses are Robert Bloct, bishop of Lincoln, Robert fitzHaimo, Ranulf Flambard, Robert fitzGerold, Roger of Nonant and Urse of Abetot.[112] These six, minus Roger of Nonant, who had crossed with the king in 1091,[113] and Robert fitzGerold, were among William's 'justiciars of England', who, probably with Walkelin, formed the regency council.[114] Another grant made at Hastings, this time in favour of the cathedral monks of Winchester, and witnessed by William the chancellor, Ranulf Flambard, Robert fitz Haimo, Eudo *dapifer*, Robert fitzGerold and Urse, was dated, 'when I set off for Normandy to make an agreement [*concordia*] with my brother, Count Robert, who was about to set off for Jerusalem'.[115] William paid over the money at Rouen;[116] and Robert departed for Constantinople by way of the main pilgrim road to Rome and Norman Italy. He had to leave in haste to cross the Alps before the passes were blocked by snow. Abbot Jarento went with him as far as Pontarlier,[117] which was the point at which he could have turned back to Dijon. Robert's road went on

[111] See above, 246–7. *ASC, s.a.,* 174; Florence, ii, 40; OV, v, 32, 208.

[112] *Regesta,* no. 377.

[113] Above, 279.

[114] *Regesta,* nos 422, 424. See also above, 209.

[115] *Regesta,* ii, 377a. Another royal confirmation, in favour of St Peter's, Gloucester, dated 1096, is witnessed by the chancellor, Bishop Walkelin, Ranulf Flambard, Robert fitzHaimo, Robert of Montfort, Robert fitzGerold and Urse: *ibid.,* 379a.

[116] OV, v, 228. Cf. David, *RC,* 95 n. 31.

[117] Hugh of Flavigny, *Chronicon,* 475.

through the Swiss Jura to Lake Geneva, and through Lausanne, Montreux, Martigny and the Great St Bernard Pass to Aosta. He probably travelled with a light heart.

Robert was one of a party of distinguished princes, his kinsmen and neighbours, and, famous for his prodigality, may well have shared with them his now well-furnished purse.[118] Among his companions were his cousins, Robert count of Flanders and Stephen of Aumale, his brother-in-law Stephen count of Blois and Chartres, and his relation Alan Fergant, duke of Brittany. Hugh II, count of St Pol and Rotrou II of Mortagne, the son of Geoffrey II, count of Perche, were also in this group. Eustace III of Boulogne seems to have been with them at times. Robert took with him his chaplain Arnulf of Chocques, his uncle Odo of Bayeux, and Gilbert bishop of Evreux, nicknamed 'the Crane' (grus) because of his great height.[119] Odo was getting old, but went, according to Orderic, because there was no place for him in the Norman kingdom. He died in Sicily in January or February 1097 and was buried in Palermo cathedral by Gilbert of Evreux.[120] Two out of the seven bishops of Normandy was a more than respectable proportion, but Robert could not attract the baronage to his side. Few members of the great families decided to crusade. Beaumont-Meulan, Tosny-Evreux, Montfort l'Amaury seem to have been unrepresented. Bellême-Montgomery furnished only Philip the Clerk (Grammarian), who had been convicted of complicity in the rebellion of Robert of Mowbray. In June 1099 he was with Robert in the desperate battle outside Antioch.[121] Grandmesnil, however, produced the brothers Ivo, William and Aubrey, the last two then living in Apulia. This couple also tarnished the family's reputation by escaping from the beleaguered city of Antioch by means of a rope and earning the derisive name of 'the furtive funambulists'.[122]

A few of the Norman crusaders had been William's vassals or allies:

[118] Counts of Flanders and Boulogne, ASC; counts of Flanders and Blois, GR, ii, 402. Longer lists in Florence, ii, 39–40; OV, v, 32–4, 58. Full list of his companions in David, RC, app. D.

[119] OV, v, 22.

[120] OV, iv, 118; v, 208, 210.

[121] GR, ii, 460.

[122] Ivo and Aubrey: OV, v, 34; but William and Aubrey escaped from Antioch: 96–8. Neither David nor Chibnall comments on this discrepancy. When OV, iv, 338–40, recounts the careers of these men in connexion with their father's death in 1098, he says that Ivo went twice to Jerusalem and, on the first occasion, suffered great hardships at Antioch; that William, who was based on Apulia and had married Robert Guiscard's daughter, also went to Antioch; and that Aubrey spent some time in Apulia. It is possible, therefore, that Aubrey went with William on the First Crusade. Ivo succeeded his father in his English honour for a time: ibid. He was exiled by Henry I in 1102 and died on his second pilgrimage. See also David, RC, 107 n. 88.

Stephen of Aumale (although he may have played some part in the Mowbray rebellion), Gerard of Gournay and Ivo of Grandmesnil. And two barons travelled from England, the disgraced Ernulf of Hesdin and William of Percy *aux Grenons*, the founder of Whitby priory, whose brother and nephew ruled over it in turn. Both these English crusaders died in the East.[123] Among the pilgrims were the pious and idealistic, the adventurous and irresponsible, and the ruined. The Norman kingdom and duchy provided some of each. A purely English contribution was a fleet operated in the Mediterranean. English ships, perhaps as many as thirty, were noticed in the auxiliary naval squadrons at St Symeon, the port of Antioch, and at Latakia, further south, in the spring and summer of 1098. They may have been part of the fleet which had ferried the crusaders from the south of Italy to Constantinople in the spring of 1097. And a few were still off Jerusalem at Easter 1100, when some Crusaders began to return home.[124] But the stirring events, the acts of heroism and cowardice, were not recorded in the Anglo-Saxon Chronicle. At the end of the annal for 1100 is the mere notice of the safe return from Jerusalem of Robert of Normandy, Robert of Flanders and Eustace of Boulogne. Later in the twelfth century, however, there was more interest in the history of the First Crusade.[125]

William had been left in charge of Normandy. Although he never used the title of duke, he probably did not regard himself merely as a mortgagor. He was a king, his father's heir, and his brother's heir and surrogate. In him for the time being resided all the territorial rights of his dynasty. He had never done homage to the king of France and remained free for the rest of his life from any personal subjection.[126] The situation was not exceptional, and no one, whether the king of France, the pope, other princes or the Norman barons and church, seems to have questioned his authority. The matter was put to the test immediately, according to Orderic.[127] While William and Robert were still together at Rouen in September they were visited by Helias of La Flèche, the

[123] For Ernulf, see above, 347. For William, *Cartularium Abbathiae de Whiteby*, ed. J.C. Atkinson (Surtees Soc., lxix, 1879), i, 2; *HRH*, 78.

[124] Letter of the clergy and people of Lucca, H. Hagenmeyer, *Die Kreuzzugsbriefe aus dem Jahren 1088–1100* (Innsbruck 1901), no. XVII, p. 165, note, p. 359; Letter of Dagobert, patriarch of Jerusalem, *ibid.*, no. XXI, p. 177; Raymond of Agiles, *Historia Francorum*, in *Recueil des Historiens des Croissades* (Acad. des Inscr. ès Belles-Lettres, Paris), *Occ.*, iii, 290; William of Tyre, *ibid.*, i, 310.

[125] There is a long section on the Crusade in *GR*, ii, 390–459, and a whole book (IX) in OV.

[126] Cf. C.W. Hollister, 'Normandy, France and the Anglo-Norman *regnum*', *Speculum*, li (1976), 213–14; Elizabeth M. Hallam, 'The King and the Princes in 11th-century France', *Bulletin of the Institute of Historical Research*, liii (1980), 153–4.

[127] OV, iv, 228–32.

claimant to the county of Maine. He first consulted the duke and then spoke to the king. He explained that he too would like to go on the Crusade and asked William for his peace. But William in his characteristic way replied, 'You can go wherever you like; but before you do, hand over Le Mans and the whole county, for I'm going to have whatever my father held.' When Helias protested that he had a legal right to Maine and would submit it to the judgment of kings, counts and bishops, William rejoindered that he would plead with swords and lances. And when the count declared that in that case he would crusade at home and mark his horse and arms with the Cross, William replied that he had no wish to fight against Crusaders but he intended to recover Le Mans. Clearly Robert left the whole business to William, and Helias accepted that he now had to deal with the king.

William remained in Normandy until Easter 1097. He must have taken homage from those Norman barons who were outside his allegiance and received some acknowledgment of his lordship from the bishops and abbots. Since the recent Council of Rouen had forbidden any priest to become the vassal of a layman, counting it unseemly that the holy hands of a priest should be put between the polluted hands of a secular person,[128] the prelates are unlikely to have done him homage, although they could have sworn fealty. But he was probably more welcome to the church than to the laity. The Council of Rouen had also re-enacted in much detail the Truce of God, an attempt to control warfare and all disorder, and had proclaimed its right to all the possessions and customs it had enjoyed in the time of King William. It would have expected William junior, despite his faults, to be a more acceptable master than Robert, if only because he would maintain better order. A pointer to William's attitude is that one of the first things he did was to buy from Abbot Gilbert and the abbey of Caen the coronation ornaments which his father had bequeathed to the monastery on his death-bed. These are described as the crown he wore on the festivals, his sceptre and rod (*virga*), a cup made out of precious stone (possibly rock crystal), golden candelabra, and all the other things which were used at a coronation.[129] Not only was the purchase an act of piety, it was also an affirmation that he was fully his father's heir and that all aspects of his regality were incorporated in him. These objects had been of no ceremonial use to Robert. William may well have worn them at Caen at Christmas 1096, a public act of great significance.

Orderic, after telling the story about William and Helias of La Flèche, added that William could not in fact give his attention to Maine for two

---

[128] OV, iv, 22.
[129] *Neustria Pia*, 638–9; *Regesta*, no. 397 (below, 372 n. 148).

years since he was involved with the Welsh, the Bretons and the Flemings. These were all border matters. The duke of Brittany and the count of Flanders had, of course, left on the Crusade, and in their cases William may well have promised not only to respect but also to take care of their interests. He had inherited no serious territorial claims or ambitions in either direction, and Norman dukes looked to both for general support and the provision of soldiers. Orderic surprisingly does not mention here William's main frontier interest in Normandy, the valley of the Seine, which was to occupy much of his time and be almost as unlucky for him as it had been for his father. On the whole, as in the past, William was to concentrate his efforts in the north and leave it to others to fight for him in the south. And although the acquisition of Normandy did not make him forget that he was king of England or cause him to neglect his duties in the kingdom, it did drastically change the pattern of his life. Whereas in the first nine years of his reign he had made just two visits, totalling sixteen months, to Normandy, in his remaining four years he spent more than half his time on the Continent.

William spent Christmas in Normandy and intended to hold his Easter court at Winchester. But bad weather detained him until Easter Eve (4 April), when he crossed to Arundel and went on to Windsor.[130] It is unlikely that he visited the kingdom in 1097 solely in order to deal with the Welsh insurgents, although this was a pressing business. The barons who had lost lands during the uprisings of 1094-5 were anxious to recover them, and William, despite his lack of conspicuous success in that difficult terrain, was always ready to lend a hand. In the kingdom at large, feudal troops of the earliest enfeoffments after the Conquest were getting well past their prime and, under English conditions, their successors were often poorly trained and without real fighting experience. Hunting, drill and mimic combat did not produce hardened soldiers. Accordingly, Wales was a most useful training area. The absence of a native prince who could impose respect for his rights and create the appearance of ruling over an organized territorial unit with boundaries which ought to be honoured, licensed the sort of military aggression that had almost disappeared from the rest of the kingdom since about 1070, and, in so unprincipled a form, even from the Norman frontiers. But these features made monastic chroniclers, despite their contempt for the Welsh, entirely unsympathetic to the ethos of the March. And it is likely that those who consistently reported the king's losses and failures were condemning the frontier way of life rather than making a true assessment of the king's objectives and achievement.

In 1096, according to the Anglo-Saxon Chronicler, it was the chief

---

[130] *ASC, s.a.,* 174; cf. Florence, ii, 40. Some time after 28 December 1096: *HN,* 77.

men who ruled the land who sent armies into Wales,[131] and by this he
must have meant the regency council. The expeditions, he thought,
were not only costly and oppressive but also useless. Possibly William
shared this view, for he seems to have invaded Wales twice in 1097, first
between Easter and Whitsun, and secondly after midsummer.[132] He was
once at Hereford, with Bishop Walkelin and Ranulf Flambard in
attendance.[133] From the first expedition he returned, although victorious, highly incensed with Anselm, whom he accused of having
furnished troops who were of the wrong sort and also poorly trained, and
informed him by letter that he would have to answer in the royal court
for the offence.[134] William was also harassed on the campaign by a monk
of St Germer-de-Fly named Richard who had followed him from
Normandy in pursuit of a chasuble which the king had promised the
monastery, and was so importunate that William finally gave him a writ
ordering the abbot of Battle to pay him 10 marks. When Richard
succeeded in collecting the money from the outraged victim, he spent it
on a length of purple cloth which was suitable for the purpose.[135]
William returned to Wales at midsummer for a better planned and more
protracted campaign. He recruited Welsh guides and fully traversed the
country in July. According to Florence he intended to exterminate the
whole male population. But Cadwgan ap Bleddyn organized the
defence and William's probes were indecisive. He ordered that castles
should be built along the border, and withdrew. Even if the main
purpose of the campaign had not been to screen the building operations,
it would seem that William had made as the result of his experiences an
important appreciation of the situation in Wales.[136] War could not be

[131] *ASC*, *s.a.*, 174, alone.

[132] Eadmer, *HN*, 77–8, *VA*, 88, is the sole authority for the earlier expedition, and, in
view of Anselm's embroilment, may well be correct. *ASC*, *s.a.*, 174, describes only the
later expedition, which is carefully dated. Florence, ii, 40–1, who used both *ASC* and
Eadmer, likewise refers only to a single campaign, but which is dated ambiguously 'after
Easter' and referred to confusingly as 'secundo'. It is not surprising, therefore, that some
modern historians, e.g. Lloyd, *History of Wales*, ii, 408, similarly conflate. But it is by no
means unlikely that the king should have made a quick reconnaissance almost
immediately after his return and then undertaken a more carefully planned expedition.
It is possible that Montgomery, if not recaptured in 1095 (see above, 354), was
recovered in this year: it was later in the hands of Robert of Bellême.

[133] Writ dated 'Hereford in Wales', *Regesta*, ii, no. 399a.

[134] Anselm's knights were 'nec convenienter instructi, nec ad bella fuerant pro negotii
qualitate idonei', *HN*, 78; 'male instructi', *VA*, 88. This is not 'badly equipped', as
Southern translates. He also, 88 n. 3, gives the Easter and Whitsun dates for 1095 instead
of 1097. For this quarrel see also *GP*, 91 ff.

[135] See above, 64.

[136] Cf. L.H. Nelson, *The Normans in South Wales, 1070–1171*, 114 ff., where there are
some interesting remarks on booty as the Welsh criterion of success in war.

conducted there in the same way as in Maine or the Vexin: in a
mountainous region there were no obvious military objectives and
battles could not be provoked and nor was there a principality which,
whatever the method employed, could be acquired as a whole. A
permanent frontier position had to be accepted.

It was otherwise in Scotland, and shortly after Michaelmas a more
fruitful expedition was launched against Donald Bane. What exactly
Edgar had been doing since 1095 in pursuit of his claim to the throne, or
William in promoting it, is not clear,[137] but now William sent the young
man back under the protection of his uncle, Edgar Ætheling, who
commanded an army which he was allowed to recruit in England.[138] It
may be that this was the expedition in which Nigel d'Aubigny took
part.[139] Edgar defeated Donald in a fiercely fought battle, drove him out
of the country and established his nephew on the throne as a vassal and
client of the English king in respect of both Lothian and Scotland. He
then prudently withdrew to England with the other invaders, where, no
doubt, suitable rewards awaited them. William of Malmesbury gave
William all credit for the sense of duty which persuaded him, despite the
injuries he had suffered from the father,[140] to come to the rescue of the
suppliant son, and he believed that the friendly relations he established
with the Scottish royal family served as a model for Henry I. Gaimar
pointed out that William did not require Edgar to render any service or
payment for Scotland and promised him a livery of 60s a day whenever
he visited the English court.[141] This was a Norman Conquest in its
mildest form, but a conquest nevertheless;[142] and the profits of William's
magnanimity were reaped fully in Henry I's reign and were not lost
before the realignments that followed the accession of Stephen.

In this year also we first hear of the king's great building works in
London and Westminster: a wall to surround the Tower, the repair or
replacement of London Bridge, which had been damaged by flood
water, and the new hall in the king's palace at Westminster.[143] The
construction of the White Tower had presumably been finished,[144] and
the new rampart was probably to complete its enclosure on the north

[137] See above, 353-4. For the story of Edgar and Ordgar see *FWR*, ii, 114-18.
[138] *ASC, s.a.*, 175; *GR*, ii, 366, 476; Florence, ii, 41.
[139] See above, 291.
[140] *GR*'s 'paternae injuriae' are to be understood in the opposite sense to Terence's
'injury against a father': *Heaut.*, 5, 2, 38.
[141] Gaimar, ll. 6179 ff.
[142] A.A.M. Duncan, 'The earliest Scottish charters', *Scottish Historical Review*, xxxvii
(1958), 125 ff. 'But it is doubtful if we can sustain for much longer the thesis that there
was no Norman Conquest of Scotland' (p. 135).
[143] *ASC, s.a.*
[144] See above, 96.

and west, possibly on the line of the existing curtain from the Bowyer to the Bell Tower,[145] and form a bailey. Westminster Hall, which still stands and is still admired, was probably the greatest of the king's projects.[146] With internal measurements of 240 feet by 67 feet 6 inches, it was at the time perhaps the largest hall in Europe, and, with its necessary auxiliary buildings, was in effect a new palace. The foundations and the masonry remain sound, but the side walls were built with the buttresses four feet out of phase and the stonework was slipshod. This is perhaps evidence of haste. The roof, covered with oak shingles, was probably carried on two internal rows of wooden pillars, but has, of course, been replaced by Richard II's magnificent hammer-beam single-span roof. As the regency council, with its usual ruthless efficiency, employed on these projects the labour services due from the surrounding shires, there was some discontent. We notice that the canons of St Paul's, possibly at the instance of Ranulf Flambard who witnessed the writ, secured the immunity of all their demesne lands from every tax and every type of work, especially those in connexion with London castle, wall, bridge and bailey – as had been granted by the writ of William I; and whatever had been taken from them was to be restored immediately.[147]

A charter which can probably be dated to the king's visit to England in 1097, provides a good list of courtiers. Walkelin of Winchester heads the five bishops, Robert Bloet of Lincoln, John of Bath, Turgis of Avranches and Gerard of Hereford. Hugh earl of Chester is followed by Robert count of Meulan, Robert fitzHaimo, Eudo *dapifer*, Roger Bigot, William Peverel, Robert fitzGerold (of Roumare) and Robert of Montfort. William the chancellor and Ranulf Flambard complete the list.[148] The king's acquisition of the duchy accounts for the presence of the Norman bishop and the Norman representative of the Montfort

---

[145] R.A. Brown, H.M. Colvin, A.J. Taylor, *The History of the King's Works* (1963), ii, 707.

[146] W.R. Lethaby, 'The palace of Westminster in the eleventh and twelfth centuries', *Archaeologia*, lx (1906), 132–41; F. Baines, *Westminster Hall* (H.M. Stationery Office, 1914); *The History of the King's Works*, i, 45–7. For decorative features common to the hall and Durham castle, see G. Zarnecki, 'Romanesque sculpture in Normandy and England in the eleventh century', *Battle I*, 186. The motif of St Eustace and the Stag at Durham points more to Ranulf Flambard than to William of St Calais. For Ranulf's probable indebtedness to Lanfranc's buildings at Canterbury for his geometrically decorated columns in Durham cathedral, see *ibid.*, 170–1. See also here, pls 10, 11, 14b.

[147] *Regesta*, ii, no. 399a (see above, 370 n. 133).

[148] *Regesta*, no. 397. The presence of the Norman bishop and baron makes April–November 1097 more likely than June–September 1096 for its date. The subject matter, too, is more a consequence than an anticipation of a visit to Normandy. Cf. also nos 396, 411, 426, and 389a, issued at London, which contributes the additional name of William Baynard.

(-sur-Risle) family. Also William d'Aubigny, who seems to have been based on Norfolk and was the elder brother of the Nigel who was to have such a spectacular career under Henry I, was still in the royal service.[149]

Meanwhile the breach between the king and his archbishop was widening fast.[150] Probably ever since the expiry of the truce at Christmas 1096 Anselm had been pressing for permission to hold a council for the reformation of morals and the correction of abuses in the church and kingdom, but William had always put him off with the excuse that he was too busy defending himself and the kingdom against his enemies to find time for it. Anselm had thought that William could hardly refuse permission once the Welsh campaign was over, and suspected that the complaint against his knights was trumped up in order to pre-empt his bid. It is as plain as a pikestaff that William was determined that the primate should not hold a reform council. On the evidence of Anselm's remarks to the king and the *acta* of his Westminster synod of 1102,[151] he would have condemned simony and deposed abbots for that and other sins, and, among other inconvenient legislation, taken strong measures against married and unchaste priests, the hereditary succession to benefices, the incestuous marriages of the laity, long hair and, above all, sodomy. It was William's determination to prevent this which led inevitably to Anselm's departure, for, so deeply concerned was the archbishop with the spread of immorality in the kingdom, which he considered that William's example encouraged, that he feared that God would hold him personally responsible if he took no steps to stamp it out. So he came to the despairing conclusion that the only course open to him was to consult the pope.

Accordingly, at the Whitsuntide (1097) court at Windsor, where preparations for his trial were being made, Anselm asked William through intermediaries for permission to go to Rome. The king professed amazement at the request, and answered jokingly, 'No way! I can't believe he has committed such a dreadful sin that he has to go and get special absolution from the pope, or that he is so short of counsellors that he needs to get the pope's advice. I would have thought he could give the pope some advice.' Anselm merely remarked that he would keep on asking until he got permission. William made the conciliatory gesture of dropping the suit against him, but the move was not reciprocated. Anselm left Windsor for his own manor of Hayes, and on the way saved a hare which the boys of his household were chasing with their hounds.[152]

Anselm asked William a second time at a royal council held at an

[149] *Regesta*, no. 412. Sanders, *Baronies*, 70, and *s.v.* See below, genealogical table, no. 11.
[150] *HN*, 78–80; *VA*, 88 ff.; *GP*, 92 ff.
[151] *HN*, 141–4.
[152] *VA*, 89.

unlocated place in August, possibly to discuss Welsh and Scottish affairs, and a third time at a royal court at Winchester in October.[153] William could stand it no longer and allowed the quarrel to come to a head. Secure now in both England and Normandy, he had less need to humour the archbishop. He told him that he was tired of being importuned and that he must pay him a fine, to be assessed by the court, for the offence. When Anselm rejoindered that his request to visit the pope was lawful and he had done nothing wrong, William declared that he would never grant permission and, if the primate went without his leave, he would resume the archbishopric and never allow him to return to it. The next day, 15 October, William sent Bishops Walkelin of Winchester, Robert of Lincoln, Osmund of Salisbury and John of Bath and some nobles, including Robert of Meulan, to Anselm to persuade him to change his mind, and after they had returned to report their failure, and sat discussing the matter with the king, the bishops received a message from Anselm, who was offended by their unduly long absence, ordering them to come and give him, instead of the king, some aid and advice, as they had once sworn to do.

The royalist bishops were being torn and exasperated beyond bearing, and may have made at this point some unbecoming remarks.[154] In any case they would not desert the king for the archbishop. In the end they presented William's ultimatum: since Anselm, by threatening to go to the pope without his permission, was breaking the agreement made after Rockingham, he must either take an oath never again to make an appeal to St Peter or his vicar or leave the king's territory immediately. There then occurred the dispute over the exact terms of the agreement,[155] and Anselm finally declared that the English royal custom in question was contrary to God and justice, and hence completely ineffective as far as he was concerned. He cited the form of the feudal oath of fealty – 'Through the fealty I owe God I will be faithful to you' – in support of his case. And, although he conceded that the time for argument and reason had passed, he could not restrain himself from a further lengthy exposition of the matter as he saw it, only to be interrupted by the impatient king and the count of Meulan with shouts of 'You're giving us a sermon, not a reasoned answer to the problem'.

The king had by now gained the sympathy of the lay nobility as well as the bishops, in contrast to Rockingham, and with the full concurrence of his court ordered Anselm to present himself in eleven days' time at the cross-Channel port (Dover), where a royal servant would tell him what he and his party could take out of the country. The archbishop, by no

[153] HN, 80 ff.
[154] Barlow, EC 1066–1154, 289.
[155] Above, 343–4.

means dispirited by what his biographer considered the king's mean and vindictive behaviour, but instead exhilarated by his unexpected release from the burdens of office, replied that he would nevertheless always work for William's salvation, and offered him his blessing. This William did not refuse, and bent his head for the last time before his disconcerting father in God. Both must have expected that soon the pope would accept the proffered resignation. Anselm was another who rode away from the English king with a light heart, and he managed to remain, despite disappointments, characteristically magnanimous. He soon created a fairly standard catalogue of complaints about his treatment by the king which was remarkably free from private rancour, and made no attempt to use the king's personal vices, true or imagined, in order to create prejudice.

Anselm, equipped as a pilgrim, was at Dover with his fellow monks Eadmer and Baldwin of Tournai on the appointed day, and was met by the royal clerk William Warelwast, whom the king had appointed to supervise their departure.[156] After a fortnight's detention in port owing to unfavourable winds, on 8 November, when their baggage had been examined and found to be free from contraband, they sailed for Wissant. The season was late, there were dangers from brigands and supporters of the anti-pope on the road, and Anselm was elderly and in poor health. The party progressed in easy stages by way of St Omer and the main pilgrim route to Burgundy, and spent Christmas at the great abbey at Cluny, which it reached on 23 December. They then went on to stay with Archbishop Hugh at Lyons.

From there Anselm wrote a relatively short letter to the pope, explaining that it was impossible for him to complete his journey to Rome owing to various impediments (Urban's hold on Lombardy and even Rome was far from secure), and stating his case.[157] He reminded him that he had been forced into the bishopric and, since he had not been allowed to correct abuses, his four-year tenure of the office had been fruitless. He complained especially of the king's treatment of vacant churches, of his spoliation of the estates of Canterbury, particularly by his enfeoffment of knights, and of the unprecedented and grievous services demanded from him. The law of God and the sacred canons, pure justice, were overthrown by arbitrary customs. After explaining the most recent events which had caused him to leave England, he asked to be relieved of the intolerable burden of his office. Urban must have refused his request and urged him to travel on, for the English monks left Lyons for Rome on 16 March 1098. They had to live

[156] HN, 87 ff.; VA, 93 ff.
[157] Letters, no. 206.

on charity because William, as he had threatened, had taken the archbishopric into demesne and invalidated all innovations made by Anselm during his tenancy. He had, however, as Anselm admitted, left the revenues for the maintenance of the cathedral monks intact.[158]

William had intended to leave England for Normandy at the same time as Anselm left for Flanders, but, similarly delayed by bad weather, he and his household did great damage in the Southampton area in which they waited.[159] From the Isle of Wight he issued a writ, witnessed by the chancellor and Urse of Abetot, to Bishops Walkelin and Samson, Ranulf Flambard and the other royal justiciars, apparently in favour of Hervey, the dispossessed bishop of Bangor.[160] According to the Winchester annals, Walkelin and Ranulf had been left as regents,[161] but they obviously had, as usual, several colleagues, and Walkelin had less than two months to live. On 11 November the king at last set sail for the duchy, where he was to stay for seventeen months.[162]

William's extremely ambitious purpose was to demand from Philip of France the 'return' of the French Vexin. Although it is doubtful whether King Henry I had, as later dukes chose to believe, formally ceded this *comté* to Robert I in 1033, ducal influence over it had been strong until the last Valois prince, Simon of Crépy, had abdicated in order to become a monk in 1077.[163] Philip I had then enfeoffed his younger brother, Hugh the Great, with Vermandois and Crépy, and had taken the French Vexin, which had reverted to the royal abbey of St Denis, because of its strategic importance under his own special protection. It was while making a retaliatory raid into the French Vexin that William I was fatally injured; and his dutiful son may always have hoped to be able to take his revenge.[164] In 1092 Philip invested his only legitimate son, Louis (VI, the Fat), who had been educated at St Denis and was then about eleven years old, with the Vexin and the towns of Mantes and Pontoise; and the boy's defence of his apanage was to be described by Abbot Suger, who had entered St Denis as an oblate in 1091, in the first chapter of his biography of his dead friend and patron, written about 1144.[165]

---

[158] *Ibid.*, no. 210.

[159] *ASC, s.a.*

[160] *Regesta*, no. 389.

[161] *Ann. Winton.*, ii, 39.

[162] Martinmas (11 November) *ASC*, 175; about the feast of St Andrew (30 November), Florence, ii, 41.

[163] See above, 5–6, 31. For the alleged grant of the Vexin to Robert I in 1033, see Bates, *Normandy before 1066*, 71.

[164] See above, 40.

[165] A. Luchaire, *Louis VI le Gros: Annales de sa vie et de son règne* (Paris 1890), xi ff. Suger, *Vie de Louis VI le Gros*, ed. H. Waquet (Paris 1929, 1964), v ff.

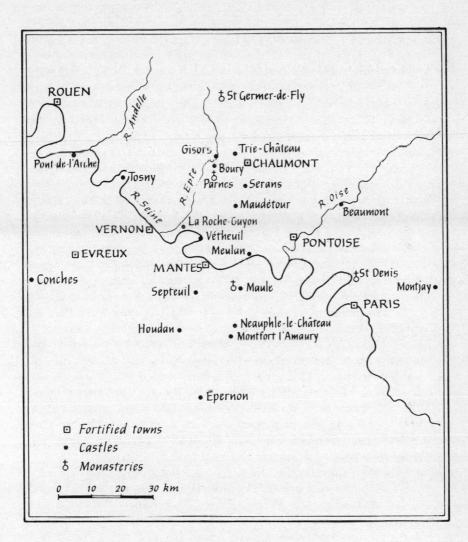

4. The French Vexin 1097–1099

It was probably Hugh the Great's departure on the Crusade in 1096 and the growing political impotence of the French king since his 'marriage' to Bertrada of Montfort which tempted William to act. Hugh left his sons Ralf and Henry in charge of his lands and married his daughter Isabel to Robert count of Meulan. Someone was interested in preventing this alliance, for Bishop Ivo of Chartres prohibited it on the grounds of consanguinity;[166] but if it was intended to secure Robert's adherence to the Capetian cause, it would seem to have failed. Suger, recollecting these events almost half a century later, emphasized William's wealth, military experience, vaulting ambition and tenacity. Many people thought that he was aiming at the French throne, and indeed, with Philip having only one undoubtedly legitimate son (for his children by Bertrada were of doubtful standing), he could have entertained hopes of that.[167] It should also be noted that William was, through his mother, a great-grandson of Robert II of France and, through the second marriage of Louis VI's maternal grandmother, Gertrude of Saxony, to Robert I count of Flanders, William Rufus's uncle, further related to the French royal family. But Suger, no doubt expressing more the views of the 1140s than of the 1090s, observed that it was contrary to natural law for the French to be subject to the English and vice versa, and that inevitably William's ambition came to nought. William would not have cared for that denial of his French nationality.

Suger's anachronism is shown by the fact that the only detailed account of the Vexin wars of 1097–8 and 1098–9 is given by Orderic.[168] St Evroul had a special interest in the Vexin, for it possessed two dependent priories, one south of Meulan at Maule,[169] the other in the north at Parnes, near Chaumont,[170] both founded and subsequently supported by the local nobility. Orderic was, therefore, an expert on the landed families and politics of the region, and no great partisan of the king in this affair. In contrast, these wars are completely omitted from the Anglo-Saxon Chronicle and so from all the English histories. Now that William had become ruler of Normandy and consequently less of an English resident, the islanders seem to have lost interest in his French adventures. It is also possible that as duke he made far less use of English soldiers. His experiences in Wales may have convinced him that they were mostly of inferior quality. It was Suger's opinion that with English money he recruited knights abroad – and in very great numbers.[171]

---

[166] OV, v, 30; Ivo of Chartres, *Letters*, no. 45, col. 57.
[167] Suger, 10.
[168] OV, v, 212 ff.
[169] OV, iii, 170 ff.
[170] OV, ii, 132, 150 ff. The abbey also had an estate at 'Heudicourt' in the same area.
[171] Suger, 8.

Orderic thought that he was so warlike that even if he had been faced by Julius Caesar and the Roman legions he would not have hesitated to join battle. The monk also believed that he laid formal claim to the three chief fortified towns in the French Vexin Chaumont, Mantes and Pontoise – and that only when King Philip refused to surrender them did he invade across the Epte, probably in November. Such punctiliousness would have been expected of him.

William had made preparations by buying the support of some of the barons: Orderic mentions Robert of Meulan (who is oddly placed in the category of mercenary allies) and Guy of La Roche-Guyon, with his castles at La Roche and Véthcuil on the Seine between the Epte, the effective Norman frontier, and Mantes. There is also some evidence that he tried to curry favour with the monasteries of the region. His hesitant generosity to St Germer-de-Fly has already been noticed.[172] But although through bribery he had opened the Seine valley from the Norman bases of Vernon and Evreux and could put pressure on Mantes, Chaumont was screened by a line of castles in the valley of the Epte – Boury, Trie-Château, Serans and Maudétour; and Pontoise, which blocked the road to Paris, lay well to the rear.

Orderic and Suger agree that it was the local nobility which in general stood firm against the Normans. The monk of St Evroul thought that Louis was too inexperienced to make much of a contribution. The abbot of St Denis describes his hero as darting into Berry, Auvergne and Burgundy, as needs be, and then returning to the defence of the Vexin. He opposed William's 10,000 knights with his own 300–500.[173] There is here, of course, the usual exaggeration and distortion. Orderic lists William's captains. Robert of Bellême was the most distinguished of his knights (or, probably, his commander-in-chief).[174] The other counts in his army were his brother Henry, William of Evreux, Hugh of Chester and Walter Giffard, earl of Buckingham. Suger contributes the name of Simon of St Liz, earl of Huntingdon and Northampton *jure uxoris*. Both also list some of the distinguished combatants captured in the wars, and we see that among the leaders in William's army only Simon of St Liz and Hugh of Chester (and he was usually operating in Normandy) had significant English interests.

In the winter of 1097–8 William can have done little more than reconnoitre and lay the foundations of a castle at Gisors, for in February

[172] Above, 370. Cf. Chibnall, OV, v, 212 n. 6.

[173] Suger, 8.

[174] Fliche, *Philippe I*, 303–4, doubts whether Robert was present as he was involved in Maine, but there was time for at least a visit to the Vexin. It is not certain exactly what OV meant by *magister militum* – 'master of the cavalry/knights'. Possibilities are cavalry commander, perhaps with the advance guard, or acting constable, i.e. deputy commander-in-chief.

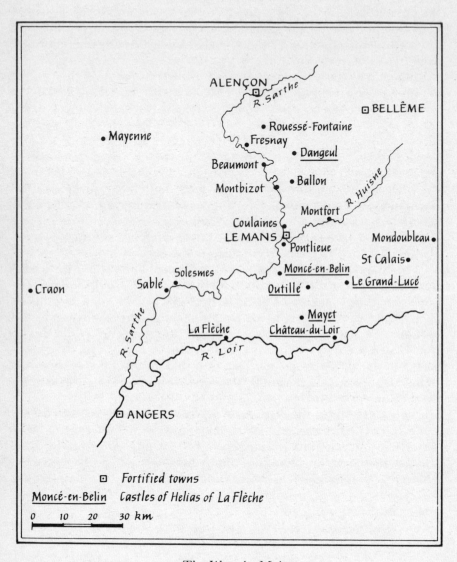

ALENÇON

□ BELLÊME

• Mayenne

• Rouessé-Fontaine

Fresnay

Dangeul

Beaumont

Ballon

Montbizot

Montfort

Coulaines

Mondoubleau

LE MANS

Pontlieue

St Calais

Solesmes

Moncé-en-Belin

Sablé

Outillé

Le Grand-Lucé

Craon

Mayet

La Flèche

Château-du-Loir

R. Sarthe

R. Huisne

R. Loir

□ ANGERS

□ Fortified towns

Moncé-en-Belin Castles of Helias of La Flèche

0   10   20   30 km

5. The Wars in Maine

he went off with Robert of Bellême to help him in Maine. The new castle, situated on the manor which Robert Curthose had granted to King Philip in 1089,[175] was sited and designed by Robert of Bellême and was intended to confront the great fortress of Chaumont and its satellites. Orderic noted the importance of Gisors in his own day; Robert of Torigny records how Henry I made it with towers and walls impregnable; and it remained one of the principal border strongholds until the loss of Normandy by John. The only fighting described by Orderic is skirmishing in this area, no doubt connected with the building of the castle. William had to defend the site and workers and needed to keep the opposing castellans occupied. The hostile captains are identified as Otmund of Chaumont, the son of Robert 'the eloquent'; Walbert of Boury and his brother Richard; Godfrey and Peter, the sons of Herbert of Serans, also known as *pincerna*, the butler; and Robert of Maudétour. Of these men, at least the Chaumont and Serans families were associated with Parnes and were benefactors of St Evroul.[176] Orderic speaks highly of their patriotism and military prowess. On one occasion they captured Theobald Pain of Gisors, on whose land the castle was being built, Walter of Amfreville and Gerold of Envermeu. On another, while the king's headquarters troops were ravaging round Chaumont, the French captured Gilbert of Laigle and the English Pain of Montjay-la-Tour, a lord from Claye, situated between Paris and Meaux.[177] Both Orderic and Suger agree on the military and economic importance of the ransoms. The French could not afford to pay them, and William kept his prisoners captive for some time and released them only when they agreed to do him homage, serve in his army and swear never again to fight against him.[178] But he promptly redeemed his own knights, and the revenue enabled the French castellans to continue fighting.

In February 1098 William abandoned the Vexin war in order to go with Robert of Bellême to Maine. Orderic gives a copious account of these events which occurred at no great distance from his abbey, and when his facts can be checked by the biographies of the bishops of Le Mans, the only other important source,[179] they pass muster. But he was a

---

[175] Above, 273. See also Torigny, *Interpolation*, 275.

[176] OV, v, 214–16. For Robert and Otmund of Chaumont see also ii, 154, iv, 50; for Herbert of Serans and his sons, ii, 132, 152. The men of Parnes hoped that St Evroul would protect them against Norman marauders: ii, 154.

[177] OV, v, 217. Suger, 10, confirms Pain of Gisors, Pain of Montjay and Gilbert of Laigle. Other names supplied by Suger, 8–10, are, captured by the French, Simon (of St Liz), and, by the English, Matthew of Beaumont-sur-Oise and Simon de Montfort.

[178] But see the case of Nivard of Septeuil, below, 394.

[179] OV, v, 232 ff.; *Act. Pont. Cen.*, 400 ff. Gaimar devotes ll. 5784–5974 to the king's four expeditions to Maine, which he conflates, and produces scarcely a detail which can be trusted. Cf. also R. Latouche, 'La commune du Mans (1070)', *Mélanges Louis Halphen* (Paris 1951), 377.

deeply prejudiced observer. He hated Robert of Bellême and admired Helias of La Flèche,[180] and was inclined to assign to William the role of a fairly honest broker between the two, although frequently misled by Robert's bad advice. Robert, he thought, used his influence over the king solely in his own interests and to the detriment of his lord's. He had important estates and castles in Maine and an expansionist policy,[181] and he drew William away solely in order to advance his own schemes. Orderic also claims that the king was dragged from the Vexin very much against his will; but here prejudice seems to have misled him. Robert was William's natural, indeed indispensable, ally in Maine. Helias had recently constructed a castle at Dangeul in the north-east of the county to give additional protection to the valley of the Sarthe and more cover to Le Mans and to check Robert's advance from Bellême, and William had every reason to help Robert destroy this new threat to them both. Moreover, William was eager to punish the cathedral church of Le Mans for its insubordination. Two general considerations must also be borne in mind. William greatly valued Robert's abilities as a commander and engineer and was rarely successful in his continental wars without his assistance. He evidently felt no jealousy or fear of him and found him a congenial brother-in-arms. In his characteristically generous way he was always eager to reward him for his services. If Robert had helped him at Gisors, he would have wanted to repay the debt. Moreover, it is difficult to believe that this brief diversion from the Vexin had much influence on the outcome of the war in that theatre. In wars which consisted largely in attacks on castles and sieges there were often long periods when the commander-in-chief could more profitably give his attention elsewhere. William's dash to Maine was not unlike his swoop into Wales from Northumberland in 1095.

In the long struggle between Normandy and Anjou for the control of Maine, the northerners had lost much ground since the Conqueror's death. This small county, originally organized around the important fortified Gallo-Roman city of Le Mans, by the end of the eleventh century contained three separate, and usually discordant, political elements – the feudal aristocracy, the citizens of Le Mans and the bishop and clergy of the city. Few of the barons seem to have been much attracted to Norman rule, and in the south, bordering on Touraine and Anjou, there was unremitting hostility to it. The citizens of Le Mans had created a commune in 1070, one of the first in France, and in defence of their interests and privileges opposed 'tyranny' of every sort, whether feudal, episcopal, comital or ducal-royal. The city was an important road-centre, linked with Caen, via Sées and Falaise, but, more

---

[180] Cf. OV, v, 232.
[181] OV, v, 234, lists Robert's nine *castra* in Maine.

importantly, with northern France, Ponthieu and Flanders, via Chartres and Paris, and with Angers and Tours in the south; and it does not
seem that the citizens saw any advantage in a special relationship with
Normandy. Nevertheless, because of their suffering during the anarchy,
by 1099 some of them, perhaps a majority, had come to think that the
best hope of orderly government lay in William's undisputed rule.[182] On
the other hand, William's relations with the church deteriorated. In
1065–7 the master of the cathedral school, Arnold, nephew of the
previous schoolmaster who had migrated from the Norman Avranchin,
was elected bishop, doubtless through Duke William's influence, and
the next two bishops, Hoël (1083–96) and Hildebert (1096–1125), were
likewise elected out of the chapter. Arnold and Hoël were strong
supporters of the Norman connexion, and the latter did his best to
restrain the baronial independence movement and the emergence of
Helias of La Flèche as count, under the lordship of Fulk the Surly, count
of Anjou. But this alliance was based on no fundamental or permanent
identity of interests. The lives of these three bishops were written by an
anonymous member of the cathedral chapter who admired them all,
although the last completely reversed the political policy of the others.[183]
The biographer viewed their actions entirely in the light of the changing
interests of the church of Le Mans: he was both a patriot and also a
believer in the freedom and independence of his church.

In these circumstances William Rufus's only chance of recruiting
popular support lay in the appeal of his generosity and magnanimity to
the nobles and in being able to convince the citizens and bishop that he
would provide better government in the county and city than would
either a local magnate, such as Helias of La Flèche, or the count of
Anjou. And although it was just such a reputation which brought him
undoubted success in Normandy, he could not establish it in Maine. His
alliance with Robert of Bellême cast doubt on the promise of good
government, and he could never dispel the appearance of being merely
an invader and military conqueror that arose from the lack of general
support for his cause. Bishop Hoël died on 29 July 1096, just before
William took over the government of the duchy, and the cathedral
chapter, taking advantage of the situation, had elected as his successor
its archdeacon, Hildebert of Lavardin, the most famous Latin poet of his
time.[184] Hildebert was, however, opposed by the dean, Geoffrey, a

---

[182] The anti-Norman biographer of Bishop Hildebert admits that the citizens' support
for Helias became uncertain after his capture in 1098: see below, 386–8, 403 ff.

[183] *Act. Pont. Cen.*, cxxxvii f., 374 ff.

[184] *Ibid.*, 399–400. For a critique of OV's account, see Chibnall's notes to OV, v,
234–8. For the charges against Hildebert, see Ivo of Chartres, *Letters*, no. 277. For
Hildebert, see *inter alios*, P. von Moos, *Hildebert von Lavardin, 1056–1133* (Pariser
historische Studien, 3, Stuttgart 1965).

Breton by birth and a Norman supporter, who claimed to have been excluded from the election and with his supporters continued to oppose Hildebert until elected to the archbishopric of Rouen in 1111. He was accused by his enemies of having had many concubines and swarms of children when archdeacon. Nevertheless, he seems to have won a swift victory and to have been consecrated bishop by the archbishop of Tours in the abbey of St Vincent, outside the walls of Le Mans, on Christmas day 1096.[185] He also came to terms with Helias, who originally had been another of his opponents. Hildebert, who finished his career as archbishop of Tours, was anti-Norman either from the start or as a result of William's interference. He was attracted to Tours rather than to Rouen and had close connexions with the distinguished canon lawyer, Ivo bishop of Chartres. He also sometimes attended the court of the count of Anjou.

The War of February–April 1098 was fought round Dangeul.[186] According to Orderic, Robert said to the king that February was a suitable time for a surprise attack because the garrison was lulled into a false sense of security by the winter rains and William's campaign in the Vexin, and was widely dispersed. But in fact they could not keep their approach secret, and Helias called out the local militias and posted contingents wherever the road crossed a river, went through a gap or entered a wood. Delayed and harassed by these tactics, William authorized Robert to prepare for a full-scale campaign at his cost, and returned to Rouen. Robert strengthened the defences of his castles by adding walls and turrets and digging deep ditches round them, and recruited a large force of soldiers as garrisons. On 28 April Helias raided from Ballon into Robert's territory, and while returning in the afternoon took seven knights with him on a detour in the vicinity of Dangeul. There he was ambushed by Robert in a wood, and the whole party, including his standard-bearer, Hervey of Montfort, was captured, except for one or two who escaped and carried the bad news to Ballon. Robert surrendered Helias to William at Rouen, and the king put him in honourable captivity at Bayeux. Orderic contrasts William's generous behaviour to knightly prisoners of war with Robert of Bellême's unspeakable cruelty.[187] Fulk of Anjou reacted to this disaster by

---

[185] The date was established by A. Dieudonné, *Hildebert de Lavardin . . . sa vie, ses lettres* (Paris, Mamers, 1898), 8–9 (nos 5, 9), 110. Hildebert was consecrated on 25 December, and the year is determined by his witnessing an instrument issued at the Council of Saintes, held by the papal legate Amatus archbishop of Bourges, apparently in March 1097: Mansi, *Concilia*, xx, 931–2, where 6 Non. March 1096 must be 1097 n.s., a date which is also recorded. Episcopal instruments dated 20 June 1097 are noticed by Dieudonné, 8, nos 6–7.

[186] OV, v, 232–8. This *bellum gravissimum* receives only a mention in *Act. Pont. Cen.*, 400.

[187] OV, v, 238, cf. 234.

occupying Le Mans and leaving in charge his son, Geoffrey, whom he had betrothed to Helias's daughter, Eremburge.[188]

The capture of Helias and Fulk's intervention changed the whole scene, and Orderic is probably right in thinking that William held a great council of his barons at Rouen to advise him what to do. The choice lay between prosecuting the war in the Vexin or exploiting the position in Maine. He could hardly do both at the same time, and the choice was difficult. Acquisition of the Vexin was probably closer to William's heart, but Maine offered more hope of a quick success. The barons advocated war in the south and promised their aid. In May William sent out the summonses to his army and invited volunteers from France, Burgundy, Flanders and Brittany. In June he marched through Sées[189] and the Norman border town of Alençon into Maine and advanced on Le Mans in easy stages on a line two or three miles to the east of the modern main road, camping the first night at Rouessé-Fontaine ten miles from Alençon, covering the thirteen miles to Montbizot on the Sarthe on the second day, and, on the third, another ten miles to Coulaines, an episcopal estate a mile-and-a-half north-west of the city.[190] Giles of Sully, an aged French nobleman of great distinction and experience, who had been educated in the household of Henry I of France, thought that William's army numbered some 50,000 men and that he had never seen its equal north of the Alps.[191] It included archers and crossbowmen and, since Robert of Bellême was either with the king or near at hand, there was probably a unit of engineers.

As William progressed, the leaderless barons and castellans of the northern region, who may, in the last resort, have preferred William to Fulk, came to terms with him, probably a truce until he should return from Le Mans. This would enable them, if the king took the city, to submit with the remainder without loss of honour. Those who made a truce were the *vicomte*, Ralf V of Beaumont-sur-Sarthe, Geoffrey of Mayenne, and Rotrou of Montfort. Later Pain of Mondoubleau surrendered the castle in Ballon,[192] which William entrusted to Robert of Bellême, no doubt as his first share of the spoils, and furnished with a defence force of more than 300 knights.

[188] OV, v, 242; *Act. Pont. Cen.*, 400. After Geoffrey's death, Eremburge married his brother, Fulk V of Anjou: OV, v, 228, 306 and n. 3.

[189] Gaimar, l. 5784.

[190] Bishop Hoël had built a new church (of St Nicholas) and a bourg at Coulaines: *Act. Pont. Cen.*, 394.

[191] OV, v, 240–2. Gaimar, ll. 5841–53, estimates the king's household knights at 1,700 and those summoned by writ at 3,000. Robert of Bellême, he thought, had 1,000 knights: ll. 5878, 5890. These are, as usual, conventional figures, but more realistic than some.

[192] Pain had been forced to surrender his fortress to Duke Robert in 1088: see above, 268–9.

The main military task was the capture of Le Mans, which was garrisoned by Angevin troops and also defended by the commune with the tacit support of the bishop.[193] William had managed to organize a party of supporters among the citizens, but was disconcerted when a citizen army came out to engage his advance guard and succeeded in holding it up for a whole day.[194] He then settled down to a siege,[195] posting archers on all the approach roads and ravaging the surrounding area, especially the episcopal estates. It was, however, the besiegers who suffered worst. The old harvest was exhausted, and the new, when not destroyed, was not yet ripe. Oats for the horses reached 10s the sester.[196] William had to lead his troops back to Normandy and order them to reassemble after the harvest. Once he had turned his back, Fulk attempted to recover Ballon.[197] But while he and his army one day about eight o'clock (tierce) were sitting carelessly at breakfast in their tents, beggars from the town who had been collecting alms reported the opportunity to the garrison, who charged out and captured four important Angevin castellans and about 140 other knights.

Whereas the capture of Helias had not opened the gates of Le Mans for William, the taking of Fulk's men did the trick, for he was now able to use both princes against the citizens and bishop. He reached Ballon in the third week of July, and when he entered the town the Angevin captives called out to him, 'Noble king, please let us out.' William immediately ordered them to be released on parole and given a good dinner with his own men in the courtyard. When some of his barons objected on the grounds that the prisoners would find it easy to escape, he censured their harshness and declared that never would he believe that a true knight would break his word, for, if he did, he would incur contempt and be for ever barred from society. It was words like these – always matched by deeds – which explain William's popularity with the army and among all those who admired the military code of behaviour he observed.

Meanwhile Fulk had re-entered Le Mans, where his troops were still holding the forts. He was now ready to do a deal with the English king; and it was this which forced the hands of the others. The biographer of

---

[193] OV, v, 242 ff.; *Act. Pont. Cen.*, 400 ff.

[194] William's recruitment of 'traitorous' citizens in *Act. Pont. Cen.* only; urban militia, *ibid.*; Fulk's knights in OV.

[195] The siege only in OV. According to *Act. Pont. Cen.*, 401, William, feeling that he had been deceived by the citizens, abandoned Coulaines and retreated, apparently to Normandy, that very same evening.

[196] The Le Mans penny was of less value than its English equivalent. In 1085–6 there was such a dearth in Le Mans that a sextary of wheat sold for 7s: *ibid.*, 385.

[197] Events at Ballon only in OV.

Bishop Hildebert believed – and he should have known – that Helias feared that Fulk and William were about to make a settlement which would completely disregard his own interests and leave him in perpetual imprisonment.[100] He, therefore, asked permission of William for Hildebert and some of the leading citizens to visit him in prison in order that he might persuade them to surrender the city to William in return for his release. This they agreed to do, for neither the commune nor the church wanted to be under the direct rule of the count of Anjou and the release of Helias would give them a possible champion who might once again be able to stand up to William. Fulk had little choice but to fall into line.[199] The two rulers agreed that Le Mans and all the other towns which William the Conqueror had possessed should be returned to his son, and that all the prisoners should be exchanged. What we are not told specifically is the juridical or titular status of either Helias or William under the terms of the treaty. Although Orderic was under the impression that Helias was being deprived not only of the county but also of his comital title,[200] he does not seem to ascribe to William much interest in the latter. Since the king was not using the title of duke, this is quite possible: he may have been content to hold the city and other towns from Fulk and effectively join the county to Normandy without bothering too much about legal definitions. After all, he himself was only in a caretaker position. As for Fulk, he had found the war unrewarding and was ready to leave it to Helias, in any capacity, to make life difficult for William. Hence the exact titles and status of the parties may have been left undefined.

Once the treaty had been concluded, William ordered his *magister militum*, Robert of Montfort (-sur-Risle), with 700 picked knights to take over from the Angevin garrison of Le Mans and occupy the fortifications, including the Royal Tower with its flanking towers of Mont-Barbet and Petit-Mont-Barbet all constructed by the Conqueror after his capture of the city in 1063.[201] When this had been done, the royal standard was raised with full ceremonial from the main tower. Everything seems to have been carried out in an orderly fashion. William himself entered the city on the morrow with a thousand fine knights and was met with welcoming processions of the citizens and of the clergy, led by the bishop, who conducted him into the cathedral church. William issued laws, perhaps a confirmation of the city's liberties together with regulations concerned with the change of ownership, and came into full possession of the place. Orderic, despite

[198] *Act. Pont. Cen.*, 401.
[199] Terms of the treaty only in OV, v, 246.
[200] See below, 390–1.
[201] *GND*, 130; OV, *Interpolation*, 184; OV, iv, 150; v, 246, 304–6.

his admiration for Helias, clearly took pride in this Norman achievement. And so did the king. He wanted to emulate his father's ceremonial takeover of the city in 1063,[202] and behaved with the utmost correctness and most conspicuous magnanimity. His triumphal entry, meticulously planned and executed and adorned with elaborate and significant ceremonial, raised his dignity to a new level. Like the mighty Tamburlaine, he thought it passing brave to be a king and ride in triumph through Persepolis. No ruler in the West, except the emperor of Germany, could have done better. This, after his acquisition of England, was his first real conquest. His efforts were being rewarded at last, and already, no doubt, he was thinking of the prizes to come.

He seems to have stayed in the city no longer than was needed to make arrangements for its safe-keeping and future government. He appointed as governors of the city principally William count of Evreux and Gilbert of Laigle, ransomed after his capture at Chaumont, and as warden of the castle Walter of Rouen, Ansger's son.[203] It will be noticed that he relied exclusively on Norman magnates who had been loyal to his brother, and seems to have made no attempt to bring in his own men. Next he received the submission of all the barons of the county, including the *vicomte* Ralf of Beaumont, Geoffrey of Mayenne and Robert the Burgundian, the younger, lord of Craon and Sablé, whose father had just left on Crusade. He then made tracks for Normandy, where he was under an obligation to set Helias free.

While William had been on campaign on the frontiers of Normandy, two important deaths had occurred in the kingdom. On 3 January 1098 his faithful minister, Bishop Walkelin of Winchester, had died in his cathedral city, worn out, the local annalist believed, by the king's remorseless demands for money. A requisition for £200, which arrived as he was celebrating mass on Christmas day, dealt the final blow.[204] Among the earliest of the Conqueror's appointments, this former canon of Rouen, strategically placed at the seat of the royal treasury, a shrewd administrator, a great builder and benefactor to his church, worldly but not scandalously unseemly, completely loyal to his royal masters, had been a strong buttress to their government. He also earned an extremely laudatory epitaph from his saintly prior, Godfrey of Cambrai:[205]

---

[202] For which see also *GG*, 90–2.

[203] OV, v, 254, mentions also Clarembald of Lusores (? Lisores); cf. *Regesta*, no. 440. Walter fitzAnger was a founder-benefactor of Bermondsey priory: *Regesta*, no. 398. William fitzAnger had been a supporter of William in Rouen in 1090: see above, 275.

[204] *Ann. Winton.*, ii, 39. See also above, 257.

[205] Wright, *Satirical Poets*, ii, 154.

Sound judgment, love of virtue, sweet eloquence,
  These, father Walkelin, were always yours.
Teacher of the young, corrector of the old,
  A shepherd ruling both by leading the way,
You were a staff for the lame, a guiding light for the blind;
  You carried the sick and raised those who had fallen down.
Controller of wealth, you gave it joyfully away;
  And while you fed the many you starved yourself.
You were the mouth of the people, the king's privy ear,
  Setting king and subjects and you yourself at peace.
January the third snatched you away,
  And the indivisible triad lifts you above the stars.

The second, and even more fateful, death had occurred in far distant Wales about the time that William received the surrender of Le Mans – the slaying of Robert of Bellême's younger brother, Hugh of Montgomery, earl of Shrewsbury. The Anglo-Saxon Chronicler, increasingly laconic, reports only that the earl was killed in Anglesey by Vikings and that his brother Robert was appointed by the king to succeed him,[206] but other writers contribute a good deal of information. Welsh sources indicate that Earls Hugh of Chester and Hugh of Montgomery made a joint expedition into North Wales in order to recover their losses west of the Conwy, and, using Welsh allies and guides, reached the Menai Strait. The Welsh leaders, Gruffydd ap Cynan and Cadwgan ap Bleddyn, had recruited Irish-Norse auxiliaries from Ireland (the latter had been born and brought up in Dublin), and withdrew with their troops to Anglesey. But the mercenaries changed sides, the earls crossed the strait, and the Welsh princes fled to Ireland.[207]

According to Florence, the earls killed a number of Welsh on Anglesey and barbarously mutilated others. Among their atrocities was the dragging of an aged priest named Cenred, who had been advising the defenders, from his church, then castrating him, tearing out one of his eyes and cutting off his tongue.[208] All the chroniclers agree that it was while the earls were ravaging that Magnus Barefoot, king of Norway, arrived at the strait with a small fleet. He had been making a tour of the island parts of his empire, including the Orkneys, Hebrides and the Isle of Man, but whether he had strayed into Anglo-Welsh waters out of curiosity, on reconnaissance or with hostile intent is not clear. William of

[206] *ASC*, *s.a.*, 175. OV, v, 218 ff., professed to know much more about the background to Magnus's expedition, but is not to be trusted.
[207] Lloyd, *History of Wales*, ii, 408–10.
[208] Florence, ii, 41–2.

Malmesbury believed that he had with him Harold, son of Harold the
former king of England, and was intending to invade the kingdom.[209] Be
that as it may, his attempt to land was intercepted accidentally by the
two earls and repulsed; but in the skirmish, exactly a week after the
cruelty to the priest, Hugh of Montgomery was killed by a missile, a
spear or arrow, propelled from one of the ships. According to Norse
court poetry it was Magnus himself who shot the arrow which struck
Hugh in the eye as he rode proudly in the foaming waters of the rising
tide dressed in full armour.[210] Orderic records that the corpse was
recovered when the tide went out, and seventeen days later was buried
in the cloister of the earl's monastery at Shrewsbury. Hugh, he thought,
was the only one of the sons of Mabel of Talvas to have been a nice man.

Magnus sailed away. The Norman expedition was called off. In the
following year Gruffydd and Cadwgan returned from Ireland.
Although it is possible that William Rufus responded by granting Hugh
of Chester North Wales,[211] for the time being, it seems, the Marchers
were prepared to abandon their more distant ambitions and concentrate on the consolidation of what they had retained and recovered.
At what point William recognized Robert of Bellême instead of Arnulf
as Hugh's heir is uncertain. The news must have reached the king by the
time he returned from Le Mans to Rouen. On 27 August Arnulf,
described as a man of great worth and highly esteemed, granted the
church of St Nicholas at Pembroke and other lands to St Martin's, Sées,
for the souls of his father Roger and his brother Hugh, 'who was slain in
that year'.[212] It looks as though he was with William in Normandy.
Orderic relates that Robert offered the king £3,000 sterling for the
earldom and for four years terrorized the Welsh.[213] This would take us
back to 1099, not 1098.

The matter is, however, best considered in connexion with William's
treatment of Helias of La Flèche. To the meeting of these two men at
Rouen Orderic devotes his last dramatic reconstruction of the reign.[214]
The black and hirsute count humbly approached the king and begged
that he should be restored to the title of count and serve in the king's
household until he should deserve to be restored to the city and towns of

---

[209] *GR*, ii, 376.

[210] *Icelandic Sagas*, ed. G. Vigfusson, trans. G.W. Dasent (Rolls ser. 1887–94), i, 69–70,
iii, 70–71. The earls are distinguished as (Chester) *digri*, the fat, and (Shrewsbury) *pruthi*,
the proud. For *digri*, cf. also *VEdR*, 21: 'Siwardus dux Northumbrorum, Danica lingua
"Digara", hoc est fortis, nuncupatus'. Hugh was called in French *vras*, equivalent to 'le
gros': GEC, iii, 164.

[211] See below, 401.

[212] *CDF*, no. 666.

[213] OV, v, 224.

[214] OV, v, 246–8.

Maine. (He would then, presumably, hold them of the English king, who would hold them of the count of Anjou. But Orderic is vague at this point: he was probably thinking of the situation later when Helias was the vassal and ally of Henry I.) The king generously agreed; but then Robert of Meulan, fearing a rival among the king's counsellors and casting suspicion on Helias's motives and good faith, dissuaded him. When Helias discovered that William had changed his mind and could not be over-persuaded, he declared his intention to recover his lost honour and possessions by all the means in his power and asked for a safe-conduct back to Maine. The king, enraged, granted him his safe return, and exclaimed, 'Be off, and you can do your damnedest against me.'

For once Orderic is outclassed by William of Malmesbury, who gives an even more elaborate version of the meeting, which, however, he assigns to the king's intervention in Maine in the following year; and he is so much a stranger to the continental scene that the great and noble count appears as a certain Helias, the man responsible for the disturbances.[215] The king, on meeting his prisoner, exclaimed, 'I've got you, sir!' To which Helias replied, 'Only by a fluke! And if I can escape I know what I'm going to do.' 'You do? You clown you. You do?' the king shouted, grabbing hold of him and stuttering with rage. 'Do you think I care what you would do? Go away! Get out! Sod off! You can do whatever you like. And, by the Face of Lucca, if next time you're the winner, I shan't be asking for something back for this.' The Malmesbury monk gives this anecdote as another example of William's greatness of soul, and adds that a reader of Lucan (*Pharsalia*, ii, 51-5) might well think that the king had modelled himself on Julius Caesar. But in fact he had never had the interest or the time to learn his letters, and such deeds and words flowed rather from the natural warmth of his disposition and the courage he had nurtured. Indeed, if our religion allowed us to believe such things, we could think that just as the soul of Euphorbus was said long ago to have transmigrated into Pythagoras of Samos,[216] so the soul of Julius Caesar was incarnated in King William.

So Helias was released, and the story of the interview went the rounds. He returned to his possessions in the south of the county, his patrimonial town of La Flèche on the River Loir and his wife's strongholds of Château-du-Loir, Mayet, Outillé, Le Grand-Lucé and Moncé-en-

---

[215] *GR*, ii, 373-4. The editor, William Stubbs, confused him with the sailor who conveyed the king across the Channel in the storm, and indexed him, ii, 629, as 'the sailor who mutinied against William Rufus'. Gaimar, ll. 5925 ff., gives a third version, which differs from the others in that the king remains throughout in a very good humour. Wace also tells the story, ll. 9977 ff., and follows *GR* in dating the capture summer 1099.

[216] Horace, *Carm.*, 1, 28, 9 ff.

Belin. With a wide and firm base on the Loir and friendly Anjou, they pointed towards Le Mans. His first task was to put his fortresses in order, and he kept the peace until Easter (1099).[217] Even if William rewarded Robert with the earldom of Shrewsbury at this time, the freeing of Helias made it necessary for his rival to keep an eye on him from Ballon and Bellême. He is not mentioned as taking part in the resumed war in the Vexin and is found at Ballon in May 1099.[218] He would seem to have been William's viceroy in Maine. In any case, William is unlikely to have allowed him to go to Shrewsbury while he himself stayed on the Continent. It was there that he needed his services.

He had, however, possibly while in Maine, acquired a new ally, William count of Poitou (VII) and duke of Aquitaine (IX), an important nobleman, one of the earliest known troubadours, and a poet of great distinction. Although this alliance between the king and a prince from the Languedoc, seven years his junior and a notorious womanizer, may seem at first sight surprising, there were connexions and some common interests.[219] They had recently become related by marriage. In 1094 the duke had married, secondly, Philippia, the widow of Sancho Ramirez, king of Navarre and Aragon, and heiress of William IV, count of Toulouse, who had died probably in 1093 in the Holy Land. She was also, through her mother Emma, a daughter of Robert count of Mortain, William Rufus's second (half) cousin. By July 1098 the duke had enforced her claim to Toulouse against her 'intruding' cousin, Bertrand, and by the autumn or winter had joined the king in Normandy. It is possible that Philippia had some claim also on the honour of Mortain,[220] or simply that the duke wished to pay court to one of his wife's most important relatives, a childless king whose ambitions ran parallel to his own. Neither was on good terms with their common neighbour, Fulk of Anjou (the duke had repudiated Ermengarde, Fulk's daughter, whom he had married in 1089), and both were quite independent of Philip of France. It is also possible that the duke was already wondering whether the English king would provide him with the means, as he had helped Robert Curthose, to play a part in the war against the heathen.[221]

[217] OV, v, 248–50; *Act. Pont. Cen.*, 401.

[218] OV, v, 254.

[219] For the political history and genealogies, see C. de Vic and J.J. Vaissete, *Histoire Générale de Languedoc*, ii (1733), 272 ff., note XL, pp. 621 ff. A. Richard, *Histoire des Comtes de Poitou, 778–1204* (Paris 1903), 394 ff., seems merely to rewrite and sometimes reinterpret the earlier work.

[220] She seems to have been proud of her Norman descent. In a document of 1114 she styles herself 'Philippia daughter of Emma': de Vic and Vaissete, preuves, no. CCCLXVI; and after her marriage to William IX she was sometimes called Matilda.

[221] For Toulouse and William IX's crusading and financial schemes, see below, 416 ff.

William Rufus was in this period indefatigable, and by September 1098 had already reassembled his army at Conches in order to launch a major invasion of the French Vexin. Orderic seems to describe two phases of the war which lasted until the following Easter. In the first, the king crossed the Seine and ravaged the Vexin as far as Pontoise, and then, having protected his rear, invested Chaumont.[222] The castellan of Pontoise would seem to have been Walter Tirel, lord of Poix, who later joined the king and was generally thought to have been his accidental slayer in 1100.[223] In the second phase of the hostilities, king and duke campaigned south of the Seine and tried to break through the screen of castles which protected Paris on the south-west.

It has been suggested that Suger described only the war of 1097–8 and omitted that of 1098–9 because Louis had quarrelled with his father and was no longer in command.[224] But the abbot's remarks are so generalized that he cannot be said to describe any particular period of a war which, he mentions, lasted for more than three years;[225] and two of the French losses he notices, Simon of Montfort and Matthew of Beaumont-sur-Oise, are more likely to have occurred in the second part than in the first. It may be that Louis was knighted by Guy I, count of Ponthieu (Robert of Bellême's father-in-law), on 24 May 1098,[226] while William was preoccupied with Maine, that this was done against the wishes of King Philip and the Bertrada of Montfort faction, and that Louis took refuge in Flanders and the country of his repudiated mother. But William's invasion south of the Seine was outside his apanage and directed at the territory of the lord of Montfort l'Amaury and his vassals, who were, of course, Bertrada's kith and kin.[227] Suger had every reason to blur the story of this war.

Orderic dates William's entry into France shortly after 27 September,[228] and, because of the priory of Parnes, is able to tell a rather mythical-sounding story of how the defenders of Chaumont directed their arrows and lances not at the attacking knights but at their chargers, and were able to kill more than 700 extremely valuable horses. But even with dismounted troops William seems to have been unable to take a single castle. On 12 November, probably in this year, he was at

[222] OV, v, 216–18. If he set out from Conches he might be expected to have advanced via Evreux and the three castles he held on the Seine between the Epte and the Oise; but OV, v, 218, mentions in passing the crossing of the Epte.
[223] OV, v, 288, for his office; see further below, 407.
[224] Luchaire, *Louis VI*, xv, xx–xxiii.
[225] Suger, 12.
[226] Letter of Guy of Ponthieu to Guy bishop of Arras, printed Migne *PL*, clxii, 664, no. 44.
[227] See genealogical table, no. 8.
[228] OV, v, 216.

Pont-de-l'Arche,[229] south of Rouen, perhaps in the process of switching the direction of his attack. In the joint campaign south of the Seine, king and duke had an initial success, for the French outposts, Houdan and Septeuil, were surrendered to them, and their castellans, Amaury (III) of Montfort, the Young, and Nivard, joined their army.[230] But the main defences of Paris held firm. Amaury's half-brother, Simon (II), the Young, defended Montfort and Epernon, Simon (I), the Elder, their father, held Neauphle, while Peter de Maule and his sons survived in their castle. Here, too, Orderic had a good source of information.

The exile of Anselm may also have done William some harm. To the king's great annoyance, Nivard of Septeuil was able to persuade his diocesan bishop, Ivo of Chartres, to release him from the undertaking (*fiduciae*) and oaths he had taken to his captor. William wrote a letter of protest in which he asked the bishop on what grounds he had given the absolution, since all Christians should observe towards other Christians the undertakings and oaths they had entered into. There may well have been irony in this phrase; but the bishop replied politely, if also firmly and coolly.[231] He offered greetings and service (but not, we note, 'faithful service') to the glorious king of the English, whose letter he admitted was temperate and bore the imprint of 'a gentle and wise man' ('mansueti et prudentis hominis ingenium'), which could have been reciprocal irony. Throughout, Ivo referred to his 'humble self' and to the king as 'your excellency' or 'your sublimity'. He accepted the king's proposition, but only if the oaths were lawful or not unlawful. In this case Nivard had testified to him that the oaths he had made to William ran counter to the oaths he had made previously to his natural and lawful lords from whose hands he had received his hereditary fiefs, and he could not observe the later oaths without violating the former. Whereupon Ivo had advised him that he should do penance for having entered into the later commitments and observe the previous ones. The bishop then cited to William a number of canonical texts in support of his view, and claimed that they showed that whereas lawful and licit oaths should be observed, illicit oaths should be avoided, or, when made, dissolved with penance. It was, therefore, his duty to give such advice to his errant and ailing parishioner. Such an opinion no doubt confirmed William in his view that non-feudal bishops were tricksters.

[229] For writs issued here, see above, 210.

[230] Suger, 10, mentions the capture by the English of Simon de Montfort. Waquet identifies him as Simon II, although OV, v, 218, maintains that this Simon preserved his castles unharmed. Simon *senex*, who held Neauphle, is identified by Luchaire, p. xx, as Simon I of Montfort; but Chibnall, OV, v, 218, would make him Simon of Neauphle, who appears as a witness to royal charters. There is obviously some confusion here. If Orderic is right about Houdan, Suger's Simon of Montfort is probably a mistake for Amaury II.

[231] Ivo of Chartres, *Letters*, no. 71.

15a. Loading military stores, including hauberks, helmets, swords and lances (Bayeux Tapestry). (See here, 277.)

15b. Ships of the period, horses and shields (Bayeux Tapestry). (See here, 277.)

16a. Earl Harold riding to Bosham with hawk and hounds (Bayeux Tapestry). (See here, 121, 128.)

16b. Ready for action: an armed knight, holding a pennon of command, with his warhorse (*dextrarius*) and groom (Bayeux Tapestry). (See here, 284, 393.)

When in the duchy the king did not spend all his time on campaign, but there are not many documents which illustrate his administrative activities.[232] Private warfare, however, seems to have ceased – the Crusade and the frontier wars gave the barons other employment – and it can be assumed that after nine disorderly years, orderly government had returned. William's secretariat certainly produced crisper instruments than Robert's. The record of one lawsuit heard in the royal court has survived. It was probably in the winter of 1097–8 or the autumn of 1098 that at Foucarmont, situated between Aumale and Eu, William heard a case between the monks of Saumur (on the Loire) and Philip of Briouze, lord of Bramber in Sussex and of Radnor in Wales, which concerned churches and rights in Sussex claimed by both Saumur and Fécamp abbeys. Robert count of Meulan gave evidence for Fécamp, which won the case, and the judges *ex parte regis* were the same Robert, Eudo the steward, William Giffard the chancellor, William Warelwast (probably just about to leave for Rome)[233] and William fitzOger. Among the abbot of Fécamp's suite were Roger Baynard, Philip of Briouze, Roger fitzGerold, Geoffrey Martel, Odo fitzAnger and William Malconduit, all well-known persons. It is recorded that, to implement the verdict, the king sent sealed letters to his justices in England.[234] A writ, unfortunately copied without witnesses, addressed to Ralf bishop of Chichester (because it concerned Sussex), Ranulf Flambard, Haimo the steward and Urse of Abetot answers the description.[235] If this writ reveals some of the regency dispositions in England, nothing similar informs us about what arrangements William made for the government of the duchy after his departure in 1099. He may simply have relied on the bishops and *vicomtes* to keep things going and inform him of anything he needed to know.

In the spring of 1099 William made a truce with the French and returned to England.[236] The Vexin war was an anticlimax after the conquest of Maine. In a longer campaign William had not achieved his chief object and, since he was prevented by death from reopening the war, he was effectively defeated. But, although neither reporter of the fighting was sympathetic to his cause, both thought that in general he did quite well. They were fully aware of the enormous advantages

---

[232] Cf. *Regesta*, no. 425.

[233] Below, 398.

[234] *Regesta*, no. 423. See also below, 407. Moreover, on 13 January 1103 at Salisbury, in the presence of the king and queen, William III, abbot of Fécamp, and Philip of Briouze made a concordat *re* 18 burgesses of Steyning (Sussex), whom Philip's father, William, had taken away from the abbey and whom the abbot, in the presence of King William, the previous king (probably Rufus), had recovered by the judgment of the king and barons: *Cartae Antiquae* (Pipe Roll Soc., xxxiii, 1960), no. 544.

[235] *Regesta*, no. 424. See above, 209.

[236] OV, v, 218; Suger, 12: 'subsedit', which Waquet translates, 'il perdit courage'.

enjoyed by the defence over attack. The fortified towns and castles were not easy prey, and, if resolutely defended, could usually survive the duration of a single campaign. Unless they fell to surprise or some mischance, they had to be blockaded into surrender. And there was no glory in that. Also, the more a commander was renowned for his courage, generosity to his troops and greed for reputation – as William was[237] – the more difficult he found it to provoke a pitched battle. In 1097–9 William was opposed by no general of any standing or authority. Philip kept away and Louis made only fleeting appearances. William was able to carry war almost to the gates of Paris without meeting more than skirmishing forces commanded by the local nobles and castellans, and when he broke off the war to campaign in Maine, the French made no attempt to attack him in the rear. Yet Chaumont, Mantes and Pontoise remained intact and the French had lost hardly any territory – they may even have recouped the damage suffered by their lands through the ransoms and other spoils of war. William's only material gain was the new and important castle of Gisors.

Nevertheless, it is possible that he was poised to achieve great things. Poitiers was for the taking; the kingdom of France could be kept distantly in view. William of Malmesbury thought that he had so much courage that he dared accept whatever opportunity his rule offered him.[238] At thirty-eight he was of the same age as his father when he won a kingdom on Senlac field. He had accumulated considerable military experience as a commander under a variety of conditions, and should have learnt something from working with Robert of Bellême and William of Aquitaine. Moreover in Normandy he could find that indispensable requirement for success in war, battle-hardened soldiers, troops obviously far superior to those he could call up in England; and after three campaigns based on the duchy he would have knocked into shape a seasoned army capable of realizing many of his objects. In April 1099 he was manifestly a successful general, and the Vexin could wait its turn. Geoffrey of Monmouth, who towards the end of Henry I's reign created a history of Britain, modelled his King Arthur in part on William Rufus; and Geoffrey Gaimar in his turn borrowed from Arthur in order to embellish his picture of William.[239] Never, he thought, was a

[237] 'usui militiae aptus, laudis avarus famaeque petitor', Suger, 6, drawing on Horace and Lucan.

[238] *GR*, ii, 379: 'quodlibet sibi regnum promittere auderet'; cf. 'si tibi regnum permittant homines', Horace, *Sat.*, I, 3, 123–4.

[239] J.S.P. Tatlock, *The Legendary History of Britain* (1950), 271, 308–10, where it is possible that Rufus should have been given an even more prominent part than his father; cf. also J.O. Prestwich, 'The military household of the Norman kings', *EHR*, xcvi (1981), 33.

king more loved or honoured by his people than William. Throughout France the barons feared him as a lion; there was not a man this side of Poitiers whom he did not compel, through the grandeur of his nobility, to bow down before him; and if he had lived longer he would have gone to Rome to claim the ancient rights to that country which Brennus and Belinus had held.[240] William was a second Arthur. No praise could have been higher.

A generation later, John of Salisbury, when advocating in his *Policraticus* the value of military training for kings, included William's campaigns against Maine in a series of notable 'recent' examples of outstanding feats of arms. The other heroes were Brennus, Cnut, Henry I and Henry II. Although John admitted that William was not very religious and had persecuted the saints, notably St Anselm, he chose to put him as a soldier above his father and in the most distinguished company, both mythical and historical, that he could muster.[241]

Although William's treatment of Anselm was reprehensible in the eyes of some, he was conducting that business too with considerable success. The archiepiscopal estates were contributing heavily to the war chest, and the king was able to prevent diplomatic repercussions. Anselm had eventually reached Rome towards the end of April 1098 and had lodged for ten days with the pope in the Lateran palace.[242] Both wrote letters to William, which have not survived, the pope ordering him to release all the archbishop's possessions in England and reinvest him with them. In return William sent letters, also lost,[243] and gifts to various rulers, including the duke of Apulia, stating his case against Anselm. It is in this context that Eadmer inserted in his *History* the stories of William and the Jews of Rouen and the English poachers, for which he does not vouch, but which were intended to harm the king's reputation.[244] Anselm travelled around, sometimes with the pope, and was revered, we are told,[245] even by the duke of Apulia's Muslim soldiers. He attended the papal council of Bari in October, where William's behaviour was discussed and the cardinals advised that if the king remained obdurate after three summonses he should be excommunicated. But Anselm interceded for the king and the matter was left to diplomacy.

[240] Gaimar, ll. 5924–5, 5965–74. Brennus was the Gallic king who in legend captured Rome in the fourth century BC; Belinus was the mythical builder of the Roman roads in Britain: *ibid.*, ll. 4376–7, epilogue, ll. 182, 255, 276. Gaimar took both men from Geoffrey of Monmouth's *Historia Regum Britanniae*: cf. Tatlock, *op. cit.*, index, *s.v.*

[241] *Policraticus*, VI, xvii–xviii, (ed. Webb) ii, 612 ff.

[242] *HN*, 96 ff.; *VA*, 105 ff.

[243] According to *GP*, 97, William replied that Anselm should remain with the pope.

[244] See above, 110 ff.

[245] *VA*, 110–12.

Just before Christmas 1098 the messenger who had taken the letters to
William in Normandy or Maine returned to Rome and reported that
while the king had grudgingly accepted Urban's, he had utterly refused
to touch Anselm's. Moreover, when the king had discovered that the
messenger was a vassal of Anselm he had sworn by God's Face,that if he
was not out of the country right quick he would have his eyes torn out in
a flash. On this man's heels arrived the royal nuncio, William
Warelwast, who must have been dispatched in the course of the Vexin
campaign. According to Eadmer, the gist of the king's answer was that
he was amazed that the pope should order him to return Anselm's
possessions, when he had warned the archbishop that if he left the
kingdom he would confiscate them. When the pope asked if there were
no other charges against Anselm, and the clerk replied 'no', Urban
expressed his amazement at both the king's action and his justification.
'Absolutely unheard of! And you have come all this way to bring that
answer? Be off at once, and, on behalf of St Peter, order the king to
reinvest Anselm immediately and completely if he does not want to be
excommunicated. And let him do this before the council I shall celebrate
in Rome in the third week of Easter [1099], otherwise I will excommunicate him then.' William Warelwast listened patiently to this tirade
uttered in the presence of Anselm and Eadmer, and then remarked
coolly that before he left he would like to have a private audience with
the pope. He stayed in Rome for some days, distributing gifts and
rallying support for the king. Urban was most insecure in the city owing
to the activities of the supporters of the anti-pope and in no position to
throw away English financial subsidies. The upshot was the granting on
Christmas day 1098 of a truce until the following Michaelmas (29
September).

By Christmas Anselm and his party had realized that Urban would do
nothing inconvenient on their behalf – that he too was governed by
expediency – and they wished to return to Lyons. But Urban insisted
that they should remain until the Easter synod. There the pope
restrained the bishop of Lucca, who tried to raise Anselm's case, and the
archbishop had to draw what comfort he could from the customary
general excommunication of all adversaries of Holy Church, including,
on this occasion, those guilty of lay investiture and (a problem for
Anselm's conscience) those who had become the vassals of laymen in
return for ecclesiastical honours. The statement that it was disgusting
beyond measure that hands sanctified and devoted to the holiest of
purposes should be placed in subjection between hands defiled night and
day by obscene contacts and stained by rapine and the unjust spilling of
blood must have caused Anselm much pain.[246] The day after the

[246] *HN*, 114. Eadmer did not repeat the clause about homage in *VA*, 115.

conclusion of the synod, Anselm left for Lyons, and settled down there as Archbishop Hugh's suffragan and vicar-general, being convinced that he would never be able to return to England while William Rufus was alive.[247] In a letter to the next pope, Paschal II, written at the end of 1099 or the beginning of 1100, Anselm answered the question, 'put by some rather unintelligent people', why he himself had not excommunicated the king. There were two good reasons: it was improper for him to be both accuser and judge, and in any case the king would simply disregard and make fun of the sentence.[248]

At Easter 1099 William crossed to England, but by what route is uncertain, for he is next found, three weeks later on 1 May, at Brampton, presumably the royal manor near Huntingdon which was used as a hunting lodge. There he issued a writ in favour of the monks of Christ Church, Canterbury, witnessed by the triumvirate, Ranulf Flambard, Haimo the steward and Urse of Abetot,[249] who had been acting as justiciars during his absence and were doubtless rendering an account of their stewardship and advising him on English affairs. William had probably travelled north in order to meet Edgar king of Scots and conduct him to the Whitsun court at London.[250] Although Edgar's appearance on the scene is barely noticed, it may have had some important consequences. He is said to have carried the sword before William at the crown-wearing ceremony in Westminster abbey on 29 May,[251] a precedent for his brother David's service at Henry I's crown-wearings. He may well, therefore, have come south in order to return thanks to William for helping him to obtain the throne and to demonstrate publicly his vassalage. The two kings would have discussed northern affairs, and the almost immediate appointment of Ranulf Flambard as bishop of Durham could have been one of the results. Edgar may also have brought with him, or come to visit, his sister Edith. If he was looking for a marriage alliance with the English royal family, his eventual success may have lain in an unexpected quarter, for it was to Henry that less than eighteen months later Edith was married in Westminster abbey.

The Whitsun court in 1099 was a very grand affair. This time it was for the lord of Scotland and the conqueror of Maine that the *laudes* rang

---

[247] *GP*, 103, relates that the anti-pope Wibert had sent an artist to Rome to paint Anselm's portrait, so that he could be recognized in any disguise and captured *en route* for Lyons.

[248] Anselm, *Letters*, no. 210, p. 107.

[249] *Facsimiles*, no. VI, where dated and fully discussed; *Regesta*, no. 418. *DB*, i, 203c, for the place.

[250] For which see *ASC*, s.a., 175; Florence, ii, 44.

[251] *Ann. Wint.*, ii, 40.

out in the abbey;[252] and the royal martyrs invoked to aid him, St Edmund of East Anglia, St Hermenegild of Spain and St Oswald of Northumbria, and the martyred soldiers invoked to aid the other nobles and the army, St Maurice of the Thebean legion, St George and the imperial guardee St Sebastian, might well have admired at least his martial qualities. Afterwards William held his feast for the first time in his new hall at Westminster and, it was said,[253] when he first saw it and others praised its great size, he exclaimed that it was not big enough by half for him. One charter issued at Westminster at Whitsun lists some of the most important courtiers present: the archbishop of York, Bishops Robert of Lincoln, Maurice of London, Gundulf of Rochester, John of Bath, Gerard of Hereford, Samson of Worcester and Robert of Chester, and the nobles Henry, the king's brother, Robert count of Meulan, Robert fitzHaimo and Roger Bigot.[254]

Geoffrey Gaimar gives a long, rambling and mostly mythological account of this great occasion, which had obviously passed into legend by 1140.[255] As Henry I became increasingly niggardly with his celebrations, Gaimar was harking back to the good old days. The poet describes the king hearing mass 'in his house'[256] after the start of the banquet, or at least after the reception of the guests, but what he has to say sounds like a legendary account of the crown-wearing in the abbey. Present were the kings of Wales, who had the duty of carrying the swords and wanted to claim the right (Gaimar is still harping on Arthur's court), but the Normans would not concede it, and four earls[257] carried them before the king. Earl Hugh of Chester, however, threw down his sword, saying he was not a serjeant. This led to one of those plays which were so popular in romance and must have had some correspondence with courtly behaviour. The king laughed at this prank and invited the earl instead to carry his golden rod and share his rule. Hugh answered that, at his lower level, he would be honoured to bear some of the king's burdens and would always serve him as a faithful vassal. So he held the rod until the reading of the Gospel, when he returned it to the king.

---

[252] The Canterbury *Laudes regiae*, which H.E.J. Cowdrey thinks were in use at this time: 'The Anglo-Norman Laudes Regiae', *Viator*, xii (1981), 40–1, 62 ff.; printed, 72 ff. Hermenegild seems an outsider in this company; but the number of royal martyrs was limited and there were political considerations.

[253] HH, 231. Cf. *GR*, ii, 374, 'William's great house in London'.

[254] *Regesta*, ii, no. 414a.

[255] Gaimar, ll. 6975 ff.

[256] 'estage'. *Estagium* could also, apparently, mean an upper storey: see my note in *Winton Domesday*, 35.

[257] Gaimar was probably not thinking of historical characters. We know, however, that the king's brother and Robert of Meulan were present at court. Other possibles are Henry of Warwick, William of Warenne, Walter Giffard, Simon of St Liz and Arnulf of Pembroke, besides Hugh of Chester.

William was so pleased by the earl's words that he granted him and his heirs the office of bearing the rod and also gave them North Wales.[258] The earl often jested to his familiars at his own court about this profitable exchange of the sword for the rod. And, Gaimar thought, such deeds and the king's bounty would be talked of for ever. There were also moral lessons to be learnt from the society of the king and his barons, especially of how men rise today and fall tomorrow.

The feast should have followed the coronation. Gaimar remembered it as a rich and splendid occasion, owing something to Geoffrey of Monmouth's inventions, attended by many kings, dukes and counts. Three hundred ushers or doorkeepers, who held important and honourable offices at court and were in receipt of fees and liveries, were dressed in vair or gris or some imported cloth and carried wands to keep the throng at bay. It was they who conducted the barons up the steps in the hall and prevented any page[259] from approaching them except on their order. They also conducted the servants who carried the messes, the meat and drink, from the kitchen and other departments, in order to safeguard the silver vessels and defend the victuals from the hands of the greedy.

It was at this assembly also that 'Giffard the Poitevin' appeared with his thirty squires, all with shaven heads, to be dubbed knight, and there was much cropping of locks at court.[260] The king held his feast 'like a baron', displaying his riches, distributing largesse and dubbing gentlemen knights. All London was resplendent. No feast could have been richer.

Although we need believe few of the details, Gaimar probably catches much of the spirit of these celebrations. And one certain recipient of the king's bounty, a man noticed elsewhere by the poet but not on this occasion, was Ranulf Flambard. For more than ten years the chaplain had toiled in the king's service, his indispensable financial agent, his completely loyal man of affairs. Since the death of Walkelin of Winchester just over a year before, he had probably been acting as chief justiciar. It was he, with his fellow justiciars, who had been raising the money for the king's campaigns and had superintended the building of the great hall and the other works in London. William in his gratitude allowed Ranulf to buy for £1,000 the bishopric of Durham which had been in the chaplain's custody since the death of William of St Calais at Christmas 1095.[261] And we can well believe that Ranulf was not only

[258] Wales was, of course, the scene of Hugh's recent discomfiture. This is an early reference to a dispute over coronation privileges.

[259] 'garçon': page, squire, or groom.

[260] See above, 105-6.

[261] ASC, s.a., 175; GP, 274 and n.; Florence, ii, 44; OV, v, 204, 250, where there is some confusion. Barlow, EC 1066-1154, 72.

making a good investment for himself and his family but also buying the place in society for which he had qualified. Anselm's exile was no hindrance to his promotion, for Durham was in the province of York; and Ranulf got Thomas to perform the ceremony at St Paul's, London, where the chaplain was well connected, on 5 June.[262] Anselm was amazed and scandalized by the appointment.[263] But even he in time came to terms with the unjust ups and downs of fortune's wheel which God seemed in his wisdom to allow.

William had to perform one more deed of derring-do before he could settle down to enjoy the holiday he well deserved. He had barely reached the New Forest in June after the Whitsun celebrations when a messenger from Robert of Bellême named Amalchis caught up with him. The courier had probably crossed to Wight or Southampton and had been directed to Clarendon in Wiltshire, south-east of Salisbury, some twenty miles distant. Gaimar seized on this occasion.[264] The messenger found the king at Brockenhurst, 'the *caput* of the New Forest', sitting at dinner, and, after telling him that Le Mans was besieged and that gallows were set up daily on which to hang knights, serjeants and burgesses, handed him a letter. The king hastily broke the seal and handed the parchment to Ranulf Flambard to read.[265] It confirmed what the messenger had said. What they had to tell was that Helias, who had restarted hostilities at Easter, had now entered Le Mans.[266] The count had rallied his supporters in the south and had remained popular in the city. Marching north with a large army, he had been engaged in the south-eastern suburb of Pontlieue by a contingent drawn from the garrison and citizens, but had forced his way across the River Huisne and had managed to get some of his troops, who were mixed up with the routed defenders, through the gates of the city. The Norman garrison, however, had succeeded in reaching the security of the tower and the other fortifications, where they had ample stores of food. When Helias had entered the city to the cheers of the populace, Walter fitzAnger, the castellan, had ordered his artillery to hurl molten metal, prepared by the smiths, on to the roofs of the houses, and with an east wind blowing, the

[262] Dated by Simeon, *HDE*, 138, *HR*, 230. A writ of privilege for St Paul's, witnessed by Bishop Ranulf, William Giffard the chancellor and Haimo *dapifer*, may be Ranulf's gift to the minster: *Regesta*, no. 415, cf. also 484. It is interesting to note that a royal writ addressed to Haimo *dapifer*, issued at Westminster and witnessed by R. the bishop, was sent *per Fulch'* the chaplain, presumably Ranulf's brother: *ibid.*, no. 464.

[263] Anselm, *Letters*, no. 214, pp. 112–13.

[264] Gaimar, ll. 5797 ff.; cf. Wace, ll. 9873 ff.

[265] 'Li reis le prist, tost le fruissat, / Ranulf Flambard le bref baillat', ll. 5817–18. Cf. Tristan, 103, 106. William issued a writ at Brockenhurst in favour of St Paul's, London, which Ranulf witnessed as bishop of Durham: *Regesta*, ii, no. 484a.

[266] OV, v, 254–60; *Act. Pont. Cen.*, 402 ff.

whole city had gone up in flames. The forts were still holding out against Helias's attacks, which were receiving less than enthusiastic support from the populace; and Robert of Bellême had taken up position at Ballon. They required immediate relief.

The king responded in a way which caught the imagination of contemporaries, and the story had become an epic by the time that Eadmer, William of Malmesbury, Orderic and Gaimar wrote. But the underlying facts are plain. In the more dramatic versions, William, on hearing the news, turned his horse and made for the coast. He rejected the advice that he should first summon an army. 'Let's see who'll follow me,' he cried. 'Do you think I shan't have men? If I know my lads they'll fly to me even through raging seas.' In stormy weather with a few companions he reached the coast and found the wind contrary and the sea rough. But he forced a reluctant ship's captain to take them across, joking that never had he heard of a king lost by wreck at sea. 'Cast off, sailor. You'll find that the wind and sea will soon do all I want.'[267] Guided through the storm by God, according to Orderic, he reached at dawn the port of Touques,[268] where he was greeted by a crowd of curious locals, and, jumping on to a priest's mare, he made for Bonneville, an important ducal residence up-stream. From there he sent out orders to assemble an army.

Once he had troops, he marched into Maine, with Robert of Montfort once more his *princeps militiae*.[269] As he approached Le Mans, Helias retreated towards his strongholds in the south. William passed straight through the burnt-out city and camped outside, across the River Huisne. Most of the citizens had followed Helias out of the city, and those who remained were cruelly punished by the Norman soldiers. But the bishop's biographer had a good word to say for the king: had he not generously and nobly restrained the rapacity of the ferocious plunderers, Le Mans would for certain have been utterly destroyed.[270] William then went in pursuit of the enemy.[271] Helias, as he fell back, set Vaux-en-Belin

[267] The king's words to the shipmaster are given by *GR*, ii, 373 (the version translated here); and, probably not independently, by Gaimar, ll. 5835–8, and Wace, ll. 9843 ff., who puts the scene at Southampton; Torigny, *Interpolation*, 276; and the *Chronicle of St Martin of Tours*, in *RHF*, xii, 64. Strangely enough, they were omitted by OV. Eadmer was aware of the story: *HN*, 116–17, and below, 407.

[268] Barfleur, according to Gaimar, l. 5840, Wace, l. 9859.

[269] Wace, ll. 9873 ff., puts Robert of Bellême in his army, but this is probably a confusion and the excuse for an anecdote. He also has the rather good story that there were two rivers named *Cul* and *Con* on the way from Alençon to Le Mans, and William insisted on making a détour in order to enter them. He mentions a bourg called *La Fesse* in connexion with the fighting; but this may be another of his jokes.

[270] *Act. Pont. Cen.*, 402. For the ravaging, see also Wace, ll. 9889 ff.

[271] OV, v, 256–60, is the sole early authority for this campaign south of Le Mans.

and Outillé on fire; but Robert of Montfort with an advance guard of 500 knights managed to put out the fire at Vaux and restore it to use. Possibly Le Grand-Lucé also was captured. Helias ordered his men to make a stand at Mayet, which covered his castles on the Loir. William came up to it on a Friday and ordered an assault on the following day. But while the soldiers were arming for the attack, the king, on the advice of his staff, ostensibly because of the reverence due to Sunday, called it off, and gave the garrison a truce until Monday. Both forces used the respite to make preparations, the defenders to improve their shelter against missiles, the attackers to gather material for filling in the ditch and constructing a bridge over it on poles as far as the pallisade. But when the assault was launched, the garrison threw down cauldrons of burning charcoal on to the infilling and set it on fire; and while the king watched this disaster, a stone thrown from a tower hit a knight standing next to him on the head and dashed out his brains. At once shouts and laughter rang out from the tower: 'Fresh meat for the king! Take it to the cookhouse and serve it up for his dinner.'[272]

William, with the utmost reluctance, accepted the advice that Mayet could not be taken by storm. His assault troops had no protection against the counter-measures of a brave garrison holding a strongly fortified place. There was no point in advancing on Château-du-Loir, where Helias had his headquarters. So at dawn on Tuesday he pulled out his troops and sent them back to Le Grand-Lucé while he ravaged the countryside, tearing up the vines, cutting down the orchards and smashing the walls and hedges. Orderic reports all this with complacency.[273] It was a normal feature of warfare. It not only hurt the enemy in his pocket but also impeded him from resuming the war. William then returned to Le Mans and paid off his army.[274]

He also dealt with the bishop, who seems to have been full of excuses, but whom he correctly judged to be hostile. According to Hildebert's biographer, some of the canons who had been opposed to his election accused him of complicity in Helias's occupation of the city.[275] The king, who had suffered from the trickery of Odo of Bayeux at Rochester and William of St Calais at Durham, lent a ready ear to the charge. It was also alleged that the transeptal towers of the yet unfinished cathedral church, the towers that Bishop Arnold had begun and Hoël had completed,[276] had been involved in the fighting. The northern tower

---

[272] Wace, ll. 9919 ff., attributes the failure of the siege to a joking and mischievous order of the 'false baron' Robert of Bellême that horses and peasants as well as other material should be thrown into the ditch, which caused most of the army to desert.

[273] It is also described by Wace, ll. 9965 ff.

[274] 'tribes': OV, v, 260.

[275] *Act. Pont. Cen.*, 402–3.

[276] *Ibid.*, 383.

was in the north-east corner of the ancient ramparts and abutted on the wall,[277] and Helias could have used it for his artillery when bombarding the forts. William, according to Hildebert, moved 'by the delation of wicked men and their imaginary conjectures', decided to put the bishop on trial. But the proposed procedure, Hildebert complained to Ivo of Chartres, was unlawful. Although he was prepared to offer lawful purgation, the king was insisting that he should undergo the ordeal of hot iron. What, Hildebert inquired of Ivo, should he do? Should he prove his innocence and recover the king's favour by submitting to the ordeal, or should he accept the penalties of refusal? Ivo replied that the ordeal of hot iron was sanctioned neither by ecclesiastical custom nor by canonical authority in ecclesiastical cases. He was in fact opposed to ordeals in general. Hildebert must not agree to the procedure and must suffer the consequences.[278]

Fortified by Ivo's advice, Hildebert, like William of St Calais in 1088, refused an unlawful trial, whereupon the king offered him a further choice. He could either order the tower's demolition or accompany him into exile in England, where, the bishop feared, he might well be forced to stand trial. All the same, Hildebert chose the latter course, and was for long highly indignant at his treatment. To excuse himself from attendance at a legatine council summoned to Poitiers for November 1100, Hildebert listed his various misfortunes.[279] In the last three years and more, Le Mans had been briefly under the power of six rulers,[280] all of whom had entered by force and oppressed the inhabitants; and not only his city but also his extramural estates had been destroyed. He had, moreover, suffered especially from the savage tyranny of the English king, who had required him, in order to placate his wrath, to raze the

---

[277] See Dieudonné, *Hildebert de Lavardin*, 56, with references to archaeological literature, and 57 n. The demolition of the north transeptal tower and the walls took place much later.

[278] Ivo of Chartres, *Letters*, no. 74.

[279] Hildebert, *Letters*, Migne *PL*, clxxi, II, 8, col. 215. To John and Benedict, legates of Pope Paschal II (after 13 August 1099). The council was called to deal with Philip of France's union with Bertrada of Montfort, and the bishop may not have been over-anxious to attend: hence exaggerated excuses. For the legate's activities, see Hugh of Flavigny, *Chronicon*, 488 ff.; Mansi *Concilia*, xx, 1117. Hildebert in fact left for Rome about 20 November: Dieudonné, *op. cit.*, 111.

[280] 'consules', explained by the editor, Bourassé, as *scabini*, but the more classical word for *comes*, count. Dieudonné, *op. cit.*, 53 n., believed that it could stand for any political master, and would include William among the *consules*. As Hildebert says that the troubles started before the completed triennium (i.e. his own rule, Jan. 1097–Nov. 1100), he may possibly be referring to Robert Curthose, Hugh of Este, Helias, Fulk of Anjou, Geoffrey Martel and William Rufus. But he treats the king, whom he probably did not view as a count, separately, and he could have been counting some of the others more than once or including in his total other temporary 'tyrants'.

towers of his cathedral church, and, on his refusal, had forced him to cross the sea so as to be judged by a foreign court.

In a poem written after his return from exile in 1100 Hildebert speaks of a winter's journey,[281] so, if we make allowance for his exaggeration, it is likely that he crossed with the king at Michaelmas 1099. It was, he wrote, while he was at great risk defending the laws of justice that this new tyrant, the equal of Fortune herself in his fickleness and deceit, the destroyer of the rights of the Manceaux and the defender of all vices, a man who had brought nothing but shame on to the heads of his ancestors,[282] had expelled him from his native country and exposed him to the perils of the deep. While they were still far from port, a southerly gale had blown up and lashed the ship. The captain had turned pale in the fear that he was going to provide food for the fishes, and they had escaped only when the vessel, stripped of its poop, had been driven on to the shore. This terrifying experience was not quickly forgotten by the land-lubber. He was later to remind Anselm that visitors to England had to test the mercy of the sea and wind, and in another poem remarked that, 'The shipwrecked man fears even the calmest sea.'[283] But the rough crossing seems in fact to have been the worst he suffered during this episode.[284]

William could deal rigorously with the bishop of Le Mans because he had once again become his own master in the church. Urban II had died on 29 July, and Rainer, a Benedictine monk, cardinal-priest of San Clemente, was elected on 13 August as Paschal II. The news would have reached the king in the course of September, just before the truce he had made with Urban expired. William is supposed to have exclaimed on receiving the news, 'God rot him who cares a damn for that', but then asked what sort of man the new pope was. When told that in some ways he was rather like Anselm, he replied, 'If so, by God's Face, he's not worth much. But in any case, he's out on his own now, for, by this and that, this time I'm not going to be under his papacy. I'm free again, and I'm going to do whatever I like.'[285] It does not seem that William, or indeed the English church, recognized Paschal before the king's death a year later. Wibert (Clement III) was still alive, and William had every excuse to delay a decision.

[281] Poem, no. 22, ed. A.B. Scott (Teubner): Migne *PL*, clxxi, no. 75, col. 1418.

[282] Hildebert does not seem, however, to have been a great admirer of William I, whose relations with St Hugh of Cluny he omitted from the life of the saint he was commissioned to write in 1121–2: F. Barlow, 'The Canonization and the early Lives of Hugh I, abbot of Cluny', *Analecta Bollandiana*, xcviii (1980), 331, 'William I's relations with Cluny', *JEH*, xxxii (1981), 131 ff.

[283] Migne *PL*, clxxi, cols 216, 1420.

[284] See below, 441 ff.

[285] *HN*, 115–16, *VA*, 122.

Before William returned to England at the end of September 1099, he had perhaps a month for dealing with Norman affairs. He was involved once more in the case between the abbeys of Saumur and Fécamp, and at Lillebonne addressed a writ on the subject, witnessed by Robert of Meulan, to Ranulf, now bishop of Durham, Haimo the steward and Urse of Abetot.[286] If he visited Gisors and inspected the Vexin sector, no one reported it; but it may have been at this time that he was joined by Walter Tirel III, lord of Poix and castellan of Pontoise. Poix, on the road from Aumale to Amiens, was a communications centre of great importance; but Walter's connexion with the Vexin made him of even more interest to William. This distinguished knight had married into the Anglo-Norman baronage, taking as wife Adelaide, daughter of Richard fitzGilbert of Clare and Rohese, daughter of Walter Giffard earl of Buckingham.[287] With Adelaide he received as *maritagium* Langham in Essex.[288] He was, therefore, one of those international nobles with the widest connexions who moved easily from one princely court to another.[289] It was thought that by the summer of 1100 he was one of William's closest friends, always in his company.[290]

Eadmer, when noticing the king's death, reflected on the events since his illness in 1093 and the profane remark he had made to Bishop Gundulf.[291] William had had so much success in repressing and conquering his enemies, in acquiring lands and in pursuing pleasure that it seemed as though fortune indeed smiled upon him. Even the winds and the sea itself seemed to be his subjects. Eadmer was telling the absolute truth in relating that whenever the king wanted to cross from England to Normandy, or return according to his caprice, as soon as he approached the sea, any storm, even the frequent savage tempest, subsided and offered him a calm passage. He was so fortunate in everything that it was as though God had made this answer to him: 'If, as you say, in return for evil I shall never have good from you, I will at least see if, in return for good from me, I can have good from you. And so I will grant you everything that you think good.' But, Eadmer concludes, as those who were familiar with William maintain, as a result of his success he never rose from, or retired to, bed without having become a worse man than he had been before. And such trifling with God could not continue for ever.[292]

---

[286] *Regesta*, no. 416. See above, 210.
[287] J.H. Round, 'Walter Tirel and his wife', *FE*, 468.
[288] *DB*, ii, 41.
[289] Walter, or his father, witnessed a charter of Philip of France dated 1091: *CDF*, no. 3.
[290] See below, 420 ff.
[291] *HN*, 39. This was suppressed in the second edition of *GP*, 83 and n.
[292] *HN*, 116–17.

Chapter 8

DEATH IN THE AFTERNOON (1100)

William Rufus had not returned to England in September 1099 in order to die, but to rest and plan new schemes, new conquests. Because of his precarious tenure of the duchy, England remained his base and, perhaps, his home. As the children of the conquerors and settlers reached middle age, they accepted the kingdom as their domicile. They had the ambivalent attitude of most immigrants, combining pride in their ethnic roots with a day-to-day acceptance of another tradition. William of Malmesbury, who in his Histories exemplifies both the dichotomy and its adjustment, placed the England of his day rather ambiguously between the most civilized nations and the outlandish areas of Christendom. After Urban II had preached his great sermon at Clermont, he wrote, the desire to go to Jerusalem seized not only the Mediterranean provinces but also Christians in the remotest islands and the most barbarous nations. The Welsh gave up hunting their forests, the Scots the society of their fleas, the Danes their continuous drinking and the Norwegians gorging with fish.[1] The English, however, he passes discreetly by.

The England of 1099–1100, some quarter of a century before the Malmesbury monk wrote his Histories, was an even more dubious place. It had in fact taken little part in the First Crusade. Archbishop Anselm was an exile in some of the holiest places, and it was while he was the victim of a tyrant that he wrote his last and perhaps most important theological work, *Cur Deus homo*, a study of the Atonement.[2] He was not a strident or even particularly active publisher of his wrongs – he was no Thomas Becket – but his presence at Cluny, Lyons and the papal court was a reproach to the rulers of the kingdom.[3] Hugh of Flavigny, who had accompanied Jarento on the papal mission to England in 1096 shortly after the Council of Clermont, was unfavourably impressed by the kingdom, partly, no doubt, because he believed that their main purpose, the reform of the church, had been frustrated by the crafty king. It was, in his view, the sort of place where the most dreadful things were wont to

[1] *GR*, ii, 399.
[2] The work, which was probably started in England, was finished in 1098 at Liberi near Capua: R.W. Southern, *St Anselm and his Biographer*, 77 ff.
[3] See above, 397–9.

happen; and when noticing in his rather chaotic chronicle the king's death under the year 1099, he entered some of the enormities.[4]

He thought that William was a worldly man, addicted to carnal pleasures and pride, and having no fear of God; but he admitted that if he had not been so ungodly and puffed up with the pomp of kingship, he would have been of a truly royal disposition. Far worse was Gerard, the royal clerk just then appointed bishop of Hereford and soon to go to York. He had lived a depraved life ever since childhood and was completely unfitted for episcopal office. At York he planned to make all his vassals, friends and servants communicants of the devil. He ordered his chamberlain to bring him a pig, and the servant, when told to withdraw, was so suspicious that he hid and spied on the archbishop. He overheard Gerard talking to an invisible devil – uttering unspeakable words – and then saw him, on the devil's instructions, carry the pig through the lavatories and 'worship' it. When the chamberlain was recalled, he was ordered to invite a large number of guests to a feast, and from that pig make sufficient *hors d'oeuvres* for the whole company, so that it would be certain that all would partake of it. But the servant buried it in the ground and prepared another one for the banquet; and when he was betrayed to his master by the devil, he managed to fight off with his sword those sent to arrest him and escape on horseback to Henry I's court, where he told the whole story. Hugh of Flavigny, however, left England before the archbishop was brought to trial. If this was not bad enough, Gerard's brother, Peter, another royal chaplain, confessed to having been impregnated by a man, and died of the monstrous growth. Denied Christian burial, he was interred outside the cemetery, like an ass.

Hugh, besides repeating some of the 'marvels' which were supposed to have presaged William's death, contributed an interesting story of his own about the packs of watchdogs in London, that 'large and populous city'. Very short in the body and extremely fierce, these animals congregated at night around St Paul's and were a great danger to pedestrians, especially if they were infirm, alone or without a stick. The situation became so bad that the citizens complained of it three times in the folk-moot (which met at St Paul's Cross);[5] and, when an edict that everyone should shut up their dogs at night failed to satisfy them, it was decreed that on a certain day all the dogs should be killed. But the night before the appointed day they disappeared, all 4,000 of them, no one knew where to, perhaps into the sea, and not one of them was ever seen

[4] Hugh of Flavigny, *Chronicon*, 495–7.

[5] 'in banno placito suo', more likely the folk-moot, which met three times a year at the very setting of the story, than the husting. For these courts, see C.N.L. Brooke and G. Keir, *London 800–1216* (1975), 249.

again. It is noticeable that the abbot, although a credulous scandal-monger, had nothing unpleasant to say about Robert Curthose, Odo of Bayeux or Rouen. The duke and his uncle were Crusaders. And it may be thought that the king did well to protect the English church from such scurrilous investigators.

The church, however, was not noticeably grateful. In the three financial years 1097–1100, William paid for his wars not only by his severe levies of geld and military service and the exploitation of justice but also by doubling the previous yield from ecclesiastical custodies.[6] Monastic writers found this particularly hateful, especially when the king was thought neither to love the church nor to walk in the paths of righteousness. The Anglo-Saxon Chronicler on the occasion of William's death stressed his ferocity to his neighbours and his own people alike, and introduced none of those grudging admissions which had softened a little his father's hostile obituary. In 1100 there must have been in some circles a feeling of oppression; but if William had continued on his victorious way the unrest is unlikely to have posed a threat to his security. Nor at this time is he likely to have feared treachery. Monks did not assassinate, and the length of service and loyalty of the royal servants is a conspicuous feature of the reign. Even the most hostile moralists admitted that he was popular with his cronies and hangers-on.

Nothing, however, not even prosperity, softened his attitude towards Anselm. It is unlikely that he was under any pressure from the English and Norman barons and prelates to recall him and he paid no heed to foreign bishops. Urban, apparently, was still at the time of his death waiting for an answer from him on the subject. But while William was in Maine in the summer of 1099, he sent the abbot of St Calais on a mission to Hugh of Lyons. Even if he approached Hugh as the primate of the archbishop of Tours in the case of the bishop of Le Mans, the only reply which has been preserved, written towards the end of August, refers exclusively to Anselm.[7] Hugh, one of the greatest 'Gregorian' prelates, a man completely outside William's power, wrote him a letter of extraordinary deference, moderation and tact. To the most victorious king of the English he sent devoted prayers and faithful service. He thanked William for his letter and magnificent gifts. He wrote not as a legate of the Holy See or as one in authority (*magister*), not to upbraid or refute, but as an old and devoted friend, and only to supplicate on behalf of the holy church of God.

The exile of Anselm, he believed, was much to be deplored. Referring to William as 'your majesty' or 'your serenity', he observed that

---

[6] *ASC*, s.a. 1100, and see above, 233 ff., especially 237 ff.

[7] J.P. Gilson, 'Two letters addressed to William Rufus', *EHR*, xii (1897), 290. Hugh's letter was preserved among those of Ivo of Chartres.

although the king had for the management of his kingdom many loyal counsellors, he had fewer for the salvation of his soul, since too many of them loved his wealth (*tua*) rather than his person. In the circumstances he would like to suggest a few things pertinent to the king's salvation and honour. William should consider how small a victory it was, if one at all, to banish a bishop from his see, and how little secular glory it brought in comparison with the many victories he had won over foreign (*barbarus*) nations, and when all who lived in the kingdoms subject to him could be sent into exile merely by his word or nod. This was not making war on the kings of the land or the princes of the people, but provoking to anger him through whom kings reign and through whom William had become conqueror of the nations. He implored William to allow himself to be conquered by him by whose permission he was wont to conquer others. And Hugh developed this last theme at some length, appealing to the king's magnanimity, now that Urban II was dead and pressure from that quarter had ceased, to recall Anselm as an act of charity and for fear only of God, so that he should be one of those to whom it would be said at the Last Judgment, 'What you have done unto one of the least of mine, you have done it unto me' (cf. *Matthew* 25: 40).

The tone of the letter must have pleased William, but he could have made no satisfactory reply, for Anselm remained in exile.[8] Hildebert of Le Mans, in exile in England, did rather better, however, probably because he was more unscrupulous. Although he seems to have had little to complain of beyond the stormy crossing, he did his best to injure the king's reputation and shorten his life.[9] His biographer states that William renewed his demand that the bishop should dismantle the towers of his cathedral, even offering as a douceur a large amount of gold and silver for the making of a new shrine for St Julian, whom Bishop Hoël, in the presence of the archbishop of Tours, had translated to a new tomb on 17 October 1093, the occasion of the dedication of the new church.[10] It is clear that William regarded the towers not merely as a symbolic threat to his authority but as a real danger to his security in the city. Hildebert, however, avoided 'everlasting shame' by fobbing the king off with an ingratiating reply: 'In our country there are no craftsmen capable of carrying out such an important commission. A major and costly project of this kind should be directed by the king himself, for in his kingdom flourish marvellous workmen who produce

---

[8] Anselm informed Paschal about Christmas 1099 that the archbishop of Lyons had received one unsatisfactory approach from William and was expecting the nuncio to return with an improved offer: Anselm, *Letters*, no. 210.

[9] See above, 404 ff. and *Act. Pont. Cen.*, 403–4.

[10] *Act. Pont. Cen.*, 394.

wonderful carvings.'[11] He also asked for time in which to consider the matter and consult his chapter, and, as appears from the sequel, undertook to get its consent. William granted permission and allowed him to return to his see, with hands by no means empty. The bishop took back two precious bells, a fine cope of rich material, two silver basins and some other ornaments, all of which still adorned the church at the time the biographer was writing. Although we are not told who was the benefactor, it would be surprising if it were not the king.

Hildebert also, to judge by the recipients of his poems and letters in the following years, made a number of friends in England, including Ranulf Flambard, Clarembald, a physician and canon at Exeter, William Giffard the chancellor, later bishop of Winchester, Robert Bloet, bishop of Lincoln, and the celebrated poets Reginald of Canterbury and Muriel of Wilton.[12] He became, too, such an admirer of Edith of Scots, Henry I's queen, that he may also have met her, or heard much of her, at Wilton.[13] Hildebert regarded himself, however, as an innocent victim of William's tyranny. Basically he was a prince bishop, but in Gregorian dress, who manoeuvred to keep himself and his church free from secular domination. In the period 1096–1100 he seems to have regarded the rule of Helias of La Flèche as the least of the possible evils, but later he accepted, perhaps even welcomed, Helias's subjection to Henry I.

Towards William he was rancorous and deceitful. It looks as though he was allowed to return to Le Mans after Easter, for he reported to William the proceedings of a diocesan synod he had held at Whitsun.[14] His letter, therefore, may be dated to the latter part of May 1100. Hildebert informed 'his most dear lord, by the grace of God king of the

[11] It was not, however, an implausible answer. In the autumn of 1092, after the earthquake of November 1091, Bishop Geoffrey of Coutances, aware that he was approaching his death, sent to England for the plumber *Brismetus*, clearly an Englishman, and had him re-lead all the outlets (*discessiones*) of the church, repair the towers and apse (*capitium*) and re-erect an even larger golden weathercock than the one which had been destroyed: *Gallia Christiana*, xi, instr. 223.

[12] For Hildebert's correspondents, see P. von Moos, *Hildebert von Lavardin*, 17 ff. Clarembald 'von Exham' (Dieudonné's 'canon d'Exham', p. 149) is, of course, the canon of Exeter cathedral, for whom see Frances Rose-Troup, 'Clarembald and the miracles of Exeter', *Exeter Vignettes* (Univ. Coll. of the S.W. of England monograph, no. 7, 1942), 9. For Reginald of Canterbury, see F. Liebermann, 'Reginald von Canterbury', *Neues Archiv der Gesellschaft für ältere deutsche Geschichtskunde*, xiii (1888), 549. For Muriel, cf. Barlow, *EC 1066–1154*, 219.

[13] For Edith, see above, 310 ff. Her movements between 1093 and 1100 are not clear, but the number of adulatory poems addressed to her by Hildebert suggests a personal relationship.

[14] Printed Gilson, *loc. cit.* Hildebert refers to the alms which the priests had brought to the mother church – presumably the Pentecostal offerings.

English' that he had told the assembled clergy that the king had promised a most precious receptacle (*vas*) for the body of St Julian in return for the 'humbling' of the tower of the church, and that he had warmly enjoined them to teach their parishioners how profitably the king was providing for their[15] church and how much damage, both to the church and to them and him, had arisen from that tower. But this injunction had raised such a storm and scandal that about five hundred priests had got up and left, taking away their alms and saying that if he, whose duty it was to protect the house of God, should destroy it and set such a bad example to others, they would render him no obedience and the church of Le Mans no revenue. Hildebert could produce witnesses to prove that he had done his best to overcome the opposition, and, since his episcopal authority would be at an end if he were to be seen as the destroyer of his church, he begged the king to change the sentence. Completely impotent, he awaited the king's orders, which he would carry out to the best of his ability, and never would he renounce the fealty he owed him.

Although there may well have been an element of deceit in the bishop's conduct, there is undoubtedly a note of anxiety, almost anguish, in his letter. It was no easy game he was playing. And we learn from the biography that the continuing threat to his cathedral towers, the destruction of his property and the dispersal of the chapter caused him to pray to God for relief from William's tyranny. And God heard his prayers and answered with the king's unexpected death in the forest.[16] This was undoubtedly fortunate for Hildebert, because William did not care to be duped by bishops.

The king wanted to stabilize the situation in Maine, all the more because of his negotiations with William of Aquitaine and the impending return of Robert from the Crusade. The duke of Normandy, after taking part in the battle of Ascalon on 12 August 1099, spent twelve months on the way back.[17] The chronology of Robert's journey is uncertain, but even if he did not reach Sicily until 1100, it was there that he relaxed after the hardships of the long and arduous expedition. He evidently was in no hurry to return to Normandy. He needed a rest; the emperor had rewarded him well as he passed through Constantinople; his arrival in the duchy would create all sorts of problems; and he fell deeply in love.[18] The girl, praised on all sides for her virtue and beauty, was Sibyl, the daughter of Geoffrey of Conversano, lord of Brindisi in Apulia, who was a grandson of Tancred of Hauteville, and so a nephew

[15] *ecclesiae vestrae* in printed text.
[16] *Act. Pont. Cen.*, 403–4.
[17] OV, v, 170 ff.
[18] *adamo*, the strongest in the series from *diligo*.

of Roger I, count of Sicily, and a cousin once removed of Roger, duke of Apulia and Calabria. The marriage was potentially of the utmost importance for the Anglo-Norman realm, for it gave Robert influential relations, the hope of a lineage (a son, William, was born at Rouen on 25 October 1102),[19] and a large marriage-portion in the form of treasure which he sold in order to raise the cash with which, Orderic believed, he intended to redeem his duchy.

William celebrated Christmas 1099 at Gloucester, perhaps keeping an eye on Wales, and Easter (1 April) 1100 at Winchester, watching over the treasury.[20] News of the Crusader's progress home must have travelled faster than the traveller himself. The king would have known at Christmas that his brother had started back, and by Easter may even have heard of the marriage or its possibility. He was allowed plenty of time to consider all the implications. Although Orderic was of the opinion that the king intended to resist Robert's return,[21] this is not supported by all the evidence. It is clear that Robert in his happy-go-lucky way expected to recover the duchy and that his wife's family were banking on it. He had sown his wild oats of various varieties and had now, at long last, taken the decisive step expected of an eldest son. He was, although probably far from enthusiastically, prepared to shoulder the burdens of the head of a family. His reception in Normandy in late August or early September 1100 would have been only a little less enthusiastic had William still been alive and prepared to resist him. He had always been on good terms with the majority of the Norman barons, and with his reputation enhanced by the stories of his exploits on Crusade, he could hardly have been stopped. Even the church, which had always viewed him with distaste, could not have opposed the return of a Crusader.

William's behaviour, too, is for the most part congruent with an intention to come to some sort of terms with his brother. Although he was still taking his ducal duties seriously as late as the autumn of 1099, it is noticeable that he then abandoned his enterprises. Had he intended to dispute Robert's restoration, he would surely have been engaged in the following year in rallying in person baronial support and probably in coming to terms with the Capetians and Angevins. Instead, both he and Henry gave themselves up to the pleasures of hunting in England. Some important Norman magnates, besides Henry, for example Robert of Meulan and William of Breteuil, were with him in the kingdom, and, as he died about a month before Robert reappeared, he would have had

[19] C.W. Hollister, 'The Anglo-Norman civil war: 1101', *EHR*, lxxxviii (1973), 330.
[20] *ASC*, s.a., 176.
[21] See below, 416. C.W. Hollister, 'The strange death of William Rufus', *Speculum*, xlviii (1973), 44–5, argues strongly that William intended to keep Robert out.

plenty of time in which to cross to Normandy before his arrival; and this could well have been his intention. But such evidence as there is does not point to a prepared policy of absolute hostility. What is more likely is that he intended to bargain with Robert for a larger share of the duchy than he had possessed in 1096. Although he was a man of honour in some spheres, he was not above sharp practice in regard to treaty obligations. In 1092 he had taken Carlisle despite his peace with Malcolm, and in 1094 had been convicted of breaking his agreement with Robert. Neither of those infractions, however, was flagrant, and he had an arguable defence in both cases. It is more than likely that he had always expected that, even if Robert should survive the adventure, the duke would return, if not penniless, at least, as usual, short of cash, and that this belief was little shaken even by stories of Robert's two strokes of good fortune. There was plenty of time on the road between Apulia and Normandy for the dissipation of a fortune; and if he could not produce the 10,000 marks some new bargain would have to be struck. Even in the unlikely circumstances of Robert being able to repay the full loan on the nail, William could still have prevaricated.

Some modern commentators have thought that Robert's return would even have threatened William's position in England.[22] It is true that the duke had acquired not only greater military experience and reputation but also a stronger ambition and sense of purpose: in 1101 he at last invaded the kingdom in order to press his claim. And it is possible to imagine that the harshness of William's government might have tempted more barons than before to change sides. But, as has already been remarked, William's rule did not press unduly heavily on the nobility. The events of 1088 and 1095 could not have offered much encouragement to Robert; and in 1101 he attracted no greater support than before, because William's supporters almost to a man championed Henry.[23] William in the year of his death is unlikely to have feared that he might be dispossessed by either of his brothers; and to imagine that he was in serious danger is to place too much reliance on the views of hostile monks, such as Eadmer, who were simply wishful thinkers, deluded by their hopes.

In considering William's attitude, Henry's presence at his court should also be noticed. The youngest brother was undoubtedly the hardest, least scrupulous and most devious of the three. He already had estates and castles in Normandy and would not have contemplated giving them up. Robert's return with a bride and the promise of an heir

[22] R.W. Southern, *The place of Henry I in English history* (Raleigh Lecture on History, British Academy, 1962), 153; C.W. Hollister, 'Magnates and *Curiales* in early Norman England', *Viator*, viii (1977), 77.

[23] Hollister, *ibid.*

threatened also his long-term prospects, for even if the Treaty of Rouen of 1091, which regulated the succession between the two elder brothers, had been abrogated in 1093, Robert's paramount claims to the patrimony remained. Henry, therefore, may have been in even more of a predicament than William, for, although he stood a better chance as William's heir, if he were to remain in England he could easily lose his only landed possessions. That he stayed with William probably shows that he expected the king to make some deal with Robert which would take account of his interests too. Indeed, the younger brothers must surely have discussed their plans and been at the time in close alliance. William could have bought Henry's support by making him his heir. But Henry would certainly have gone over to Robert if ever it seemed to him advantageous so to do. In later years he would even make an alliance with Anjou in order to safeguard his dynasty. In 1100 he was prepared for anything – as events were to prove. His behaviour was probably simply and instinctively opportunistic.

There is also the question of William and Poitou. William of Malmesbury knew the story that William of Aquitaine wanted to imitate Robert and pawn some part of his lands to the English king in order to pay for an expedition to Jerusalem, and that Rufus, when asked on the day before his death where he intended to spend Christmas, replied, 'Poitiers'.[24] Orderic's version is both longer and probably more fanciful. The duke wanted to crusade with 300,000 men from Aquitaine and Gascony and other western regions. He therefore decided to pledge the duchy of Aquitaine and all his lands to Rufus in return for a great sum of money, and sent an embassy to him. Rufus agreed readily and ordered a large fleet and a great force of knights to be assembled in England, so that he could cross to the Continent, prevent Robert from entering Normandy, purchase the duchy of Aquitaine and, after conquering all who stood in his way, extend his empire to the Garonne.[25] By June the ships were being fitted out, and the king with the great treasure he had amassed was waiting near the Solent for the preparations to be completed.[26]

William of Aquitaine had in fact made a similar arrangement with a claimant to the city and county of Toulouse; and four recent changes of ruler in that county are worth consideration, for they not only further illustrate the effect of lengthy pilgrimages on the succession to principalities but also help us to judge how serious the duke was in his

[24] GR, ii, 379. Poitiers also occurs in Wace's view of the king's achievements: see above, 396–7.
[25] OV, v, 280.
[26] OV, v, 285.

negotiations with the English king.[27] William IV, count of Toulouse, Albigeois and Quercy, passed his dominions to his younger brother, Raymond IV, count of St Gilles, in 1088 when he left for the Holy Land, thus reuniting the partitioned county. But in 1096 Raymond, when he joined the First Crusade with his third wife and their infant son, handed over the city and county of Toulouse to one of his elder sons, Bertrand, count of St Gilles. It is possible that both Raymond, until the end of 1093, when William IV died, and Bertrand were, like William Rufus in Normandy, mortgagees, administrators or *locum tenentes* for their absent kinsmen, although Raymond in 1088 styled himself count of Toulouse, duke of Narbonne and marquis of Provence, and Bertrand, while his father was still alive, called himself count of Toulouse, Rouergue and Albigeois.[28] Obviously their status was open to different interpretations. In any case, William of Aquitaine claimed Toulouse in the right of his wife Philippia, William IV's heiress, and in 1098 captured the city. But before departing on his Crusade he returned the county to his wife's cousin. By June 1100 Bertrand was again in possession,[29] and in March 1101 the duke left for Jerusalem.

The Anglo-Norman chroniclers William of Malmesbury, Robert of Torigny and William of Newburgh give some account of these affairs, the first because of Raymond's distinguished part in the First Crusade, the other two, although probably not independently, because William IX's cession of Toulouse to Bertrand had some bearing on King Henry II's claim to Toulouse in the right of his wife, the duchess of Aquitaine.[30] The Malmesbury monk, in an account of Raymond which is full of errors, states that he had bought Toulouse from his elder brother, but does not explain what arrangements he made with his son. Robert of Torigny, when describing Henry's Toulouse expedition in 1159, explains that the county was in the possession of the then count of St Gilles because William IX had pledged (*invadio*) the city to his wife's uncle, Raymond count of St Gilles, in return for money to be spent on the Crusade; and William of Newburgh likewise thought that there had

---

[27] C. de Vic and J.J. Vaissete, *Histoire Générale de Languedoc*, ii (1733), 272 ff., notes XL, XLI, XLIV. C. Higounet, 'Un grand chapitre de l'histoire du XIIe siècle: la rivalité des maisons de Toulouse et de la Barcelone pour la prépondérance méridionale', *Mélanges Louis Halphen* (Paris 1951), 313–14. Again, A. Richard, *Histoire des Comtes de Poitou*, adds little or nothing. See above, 392.

[28] de Vic and Vaissete, *op. cit.*, 272, 297.

[29] *Ibid.*, 328. Richard, 427 n., thinks that Bertrand was acting as count by December 1099.

[30] *GR*, ii, 455 ff. Robert of Torigny, *Chronica*, in *Chronicles of Stephen, Henry II and Richard I*, ed R. Howlett (Rolls ser. 1884–9), iv, 201–2. William of Newburgh, *ibid.*, i, 121–2, tells a similar, but less detailed, story in his *Historia* in the same context. This is presumably derivative.

been a mortgage. Robert, however, we notice, was mistaken over the identity of the mortgagee, although Bertrand could have been considered his absent father's representative; and the precise nature of the bargains struck in 1088, 1096 and 1100 cannot be established with any assurance from such remote and inaccurate sources, the only ones that are available. Doubtless on each occasion money changed hands or was promised, but Henry II's apologists had an interest in describing William IX as a mortgagor and Bertrand as a mortgagee.[31] More important perhaps in the context of William Rufus's affairs than the exact nature of the transaction is its date: the bargain between the duke and Bertrand had been completed by June 1100, perhaps even six months earlier. This does not prove that the negotiations with William Rufus had broken down – discussions with both princes must have been going on at the same time. Rather it shows that the duke was indeed prepared to 'sell off' an outlying county in order to raise money, and it lends support to the chroniclers' opinion that he had discussed such a scheme with the English king.

It is most unlikely, however, that the proposed pledge or object of sale was the whole duchy of Aquitaine. The duke had a wife and children to represent his interests (the wife being the king's relation); and he would surely never have proposed more than the county of Poitou, with its southern boundary on the River Sèvres, even in negotiations which may always have remained a little in the air. The practical difficulties of administering as much as Poitou from Normandy or England were enormous, for there was no easy access to the county by land or sea. Separated from Normandy by Anjou and Touraine, William had either to get a close alliance with Fulk the Surly or to force a passage through his dominions; and neither of these courses seems feasible. Moreover, as Orderic probably realized, with Robert restored to Normandy, Poitou became even more remote. Granted that there were many scattered lordships in France at this time, that the king and duke had managed to organize a joint campaign in the Vexin in 1098–9, and that in the thirteenth and fourteenth centuries Gascony was successfully joined to England by sea communications, the administration of Poitou from England would, nevertheless, seem to have been beyond the capabilities of the royal government in 1100.

The possible outcome of these negotiations cannot be predicted, and their existence provides only an enigmatic clue to the king's intentions as regards Normandy. He could have been intending to take a new principality in pledge either in order to replace the redeemed Norman duchy or, as Orderic believed, to add to his existing empire. The truth

[31] de Vic and Vaissete, *op. cit.*, 327–8, 622b–623.

may be that at the time of his death he was still keeping all his options open. Even as late as August 1100, the situation was still fluid. William was probably aware that Raymond and Bertrand had kept possession of Toulouse because of the absence of kinsmen on Crusade and despite the claims of other relatives, and although Poitou may have seemed almost as remote as Ireland, the Normans were acquiring new principalities in the most far-away places. It was a period of high adventure, and perhaps William Rufus wanted to rival Robert Curthose in his exploits. All we can say, then, is that he died when full of great schemes, which, in the nature of things, would not all have come to term.

It is probably because of the king's death that so few events, apart from marvels, are recorded after the expedition to Maine. Osmund bishop of Salisbury, a bishop of some stature, even if not much loved or outstandingly important in the royal council, died at the beginning of December 1099, and the see was, of course – and perforce – left vacant. On 9 January William was at Salisbury, perhaps making arrangements for the custody; and the fact that he chose this moment to confirm, in a writ witnessed by William the chancellor, Robert count of Meulan and Robert fitzHaimo, that he had decided in favour of Ranulf bishop of Durham in his dispute with Alan of Percy over some lands in Yorkshire,[32] may indicate that Ranulf was on hand at least to advise. After spending Easter at Winchester, William moved to Westminster for Whitsun,[33] but seems to have returned to the New Forest area for the summer. Although the itinerary has few fixed points, it does support Orderic's view that the king was prepared to cross to Normandy at short notice. In May occurred a hunting fatality which has some bearing on the king's own death. Richard, a bastard son of Duke Robert, was, like his namesake and uncle some thirty years before,[34] killed in the New Forest.[35] According to Orderic, who, as usual, knew more than the other chroniclers, Richard was one of a party of royal knights hunting deer with bows and arrows, and was struck accidentally and killed instantly by an arrow aimed at a beast by one of his companions. The unfortunate archer immediately fled to the Cluniac priory of Lewes where he became a monk, seeking both to expiate the sin of homicide and to avoid the vengeance which would have been exacted by the victim's kinsmen and friends. Orderic thought Richard a promising young man with a bright future, and seems to hint that he was of some dynastic importance. But no one suggests that there was anything sinister about his death.

[32] *Regesta*, no. 427, ii, 406.
[33] *ASC*, s.a.
[34] See above, 13 and n. 37.
[35] *GR*, ii, 333; Florence, ii, 45; OV, v, 282.

On Thursday 2 August William was at his hunting lodge in the New Forest. This was probably Brockenhurst; but exactly where he met his death is uncertain.[36] Nor was the king's entourage on that day recorded: it is unlikely that anyone wanted to be associated with the tragedy. Certainly in attendance were his brother Henry, Robert fitzHaimo and Walter Tirel, and probably William of Breteuil. And it is likely that several of the eleven magnates who witnessed Henry's charter issued three days later at his coronation had accompanied him from Winchester:[37] William Giffard, who had already been promised the see of Winchester, Gerard bishop of Hereford, Henry earl of Warwick, Simon earl of Northampton, Walter Giffard (possibly earl of Buckingham), Robert of Montfort, a constable, Roger Bigot and Eudo *dapifer*. As regards the remaining three, Robert fitzHaimo has already been counted; Maurice bishop of London, who performed the coronation, is unlikely to have been at the hunt; and the last witness, Robert Malet, a chamberlain, is making a documentary reappearance.[38] If we also take into account the witnesses to Henry's letter inviting Anselm to return to England,[39] we can perhaps add the clerk William Warelwast, the expert on the subject, and Haimo *dapifer*. Other members of the hunting party, we are told, scattered. The reticence of the chroniclers is impenetrable.

No one would have been surprised that William was engaged in hunting at the beginning of August, for the fat season, 'grease-time', for red deer stags started on the feast of St Peter's Chains (1 August), and in six weeks' time, at the feast of the Exaltation of the Holy Cross (14 September), hunting for stags would cease.[40] Moreover, such a keen hunter would have been expected to rise before dawn so that the hunting party could move off at first light, as was the general custom.[41] Many chroniclers describe the circumstances in which William died on 2 August 1100, and for those who thought about them, it was the late start which was the most unusual feature. Most writers, of course, merely repeated or embroidered the previous accounts with which they were familiar.

[36] The earliest reporters give the impression that William was killed in a wood near his base. Later, two widely separated places had some local support. Leland in the 1530s offered the lost 'Througham', for which see *DB*, i, 51a–c, 'Tru(c)ham'. A very ancient and extensive settlement, it seems to be represented now by Beaulieu, omitted from *DB*. On the other hand, the 'Rufus Stone' was set up in 1745 near Canterton to mark a site traditional since Charles II's visit to the Forest. The former, in particular the area west of Beaulieu River, seems the more likely. I owe most of this information to the kindness of the local historian. Arthur Lloyd.

[37] *SSC*, 119; cf. *GR*, ii, 470–1.

[38] See above, 151.

[39] *SSC*, 120.

[40] *The Master of Game*, appendix, *s.v.* 'Grease-time, Seasons of Hunting'.

[41] Edward of York, *ibid.*, *passim*, assumes that the hunt begins at dawn.

Stripped of portents, which will be discussed later, the events of that day seem well attested and hardly controversial. The earliest and most succinct account is in the Anglo-Saxon Chronicle: 'In the morning after Lammas King William when hunting was shot by an arrow by one of his own men.'[42] Those writing fifteen to thirty years later could add little except the place, the name of the killer and sometimes a brief explanation of how the accident occurred. Eadmer recalls in both his works their receipt of the news at the monastery of La Chaise-Dieu in Auvergne, where they were staying, having left Lyons on 5 August, no doubt to avoid the heat.[43] Just after a terrible thunderstorm, two of their fellow monks arrived with the momentous tidings: the king had gone hunting in the morning in a wood and had been pierced through the heart by an arrow. Anselm had burst into tears, and when the others expressed their astonishment, had said in a voice broken by sobs that he would have given anything for it to have been him rather than the king who had died in the body. Eadmer was, of course, implying that the saint would have stood a better chance of a spiritual life thereafter. In the *History*, he gave the news from England in a little more detail. After lunching in the morning, William went out to hunt in a wood, was struck by an arrow in the heart, died immediately, impenitent and unshriven, and was soon forsaken by everyone. Some say that the arrow was shot, rather more are of the opinion that the king stumbled and fell on it. But there was no point in trying to clarify the matter: the death was simply the just judgment of God. The name of the alleged slayer must have been current when Eadmer wrote, and he undoubtedly knew of, and had probably met, Walter Tirel, count of Poix.[44] But he most likely suppressed the name and favoured the alternative explanation because Walter was a benefactor of Bec and well-disposed towards Anselm.

William of Malmesbury, who used both the Chronicle and Eadmer, writing in 1118–25 had his own considerable contributions to make to the story.[45] At Malmesbury in Wiltshire he was not all that far from where the event occurred. According to him, a warning vision told by a foreign monk to Robert fitzHaimo before dawn caused the courtiers to dissuade William from going hunting before lunch, so he spent the morning in serious business, 'spewing out the flatulence of his fierce temper, for it was said he had dined and wined rather more generously than usual the previous day'. However, after lunch he went into the wood with a few companions, of whom the most intimate was Walter Tirel, a visitor from France attracted by the king's bounty. After the

[42] *ASC*, s.a. The chronicler used *fla* for the weapon, an ambiguous word which could stand for any missile; *s.a.* 1083 he used the more specific *arewa*.
[43] *HN*, 116, 118; *VA*, 125 6.
[44] *VA*, 27–8.
[45] *GR*, ii, 377–9.

company had dispersed in a haphazard way, as was usual when hunting,[46] Walter remained alone with the king. The sun was already low in the sky when William shot at a stag crossing in front of him. But he did not inflict a mortal wound, and, shielding his eyes from the sun with his hand, was watching it run on, when Walter, seeing the king otherwise engaged, thought himself free to bring down a second stag which at that moment happened to appear. Unwittingly and involuntarily,[47] he hit the king in the chest with his arrow.[48] William uttered not a single word, but, breaking off the shaft of the arrow which protruded from his body, fell on the wound and hastened his death. Walter rushed up, but when he saw that the king was dead, jumped on his horse and made off at speed. He was not, however, pursued because some men preferred to close their eyes, others commiserated with the unfortunate man, and all had more pressing things to do. William of Malmesbury seems to reconcile the two ways in which the king was thought to have died mentioned by Eadmer, and produced a lively and likely, although not necessarily true, story. He is the first chronicler to name the killer, and the only obvious omission from his version, apart from the location, which he may have taken for granted, is how it was that Walter managed accidentally to hit the king, although this too he may have regarded as self-evident.

Florence of Worcester takes us little further: he merely says that William was the victim of rash shooting by Walter Tirel in the New Forest;[49] and it was left to Orderic, who was either using all the others or a source which lay also behind the Malmesbury account, to purvey about 1135 the last detailed version which can have any claim to be based on first- or second-hand evidence.[50] After a morning meal[51] with his parasites, the king was sitting and joking with his men while he put on his boots in preparation for going hunting, when a blacksmith arrived with six arrows.[52] William praised the workmanship and

[46] Correcting the printed text's *per moram venationis* to *morem*. OV, v, 290, in a linked passage, has *rite*: see below, 423 n. 55.

[47] *inscius et impotens*, p. 378. The second adjective is unusual.

[48] *lethalis arundo*, Virg. *Aen.*, 4, 73, a common collocation, used also of the arrow which killed Harold at Hastings: Baudri de Bourgueil, poem CXCVI, l. 463.

[49] Florence, ii, 45: *incaute*.

[50] OV, v, 288–90.

[51] *prandium*, not *cena*: the mid-day, not the evening, meal.

[52] *catapulta*. There has been some discussion whether the hunters were using crossbows and bolts or ordinary bows and arrows. *FWR*, ii, 329, understands *catapulta* as quarrels. The literary sources provide a variety of words for the fatal missile, and clearly were, as usual in such cases (cf. above, 390: the killing of Hugh of Montgomery), indulging in elegant variation. There is much to be said for the view that they all (being well acquainted with the sport) assumed the use of bows and arrows and felt free to give stylish renderings.

accepted them gladly, and, ignorant of things to come, kept four for himself and gave the others to Walter Tirel, whom Orderic identifies correctly and praises as an important baron and fine soldier. 'It is only right,' William remarked, 'that the deadliest shot should get the sharpest arrows.' Later, when the household servants were grouped round the king, all engaged in idle talk, a monk arrived from Gloucester with a letter from Abbot Serlo in which he described a monk's vision that God intended the king's death as punishment for his treatment of the church. William broke into jeering laughter at the news, and said mockingly to Walter, 'You do justice in this matter.'[53] The knight replied, 'I will, indeed, my lord.' William went on to ridicule the abbot's credulity and folly in paying attention to the dreams of snoring monks, and exclaimed, 'Does he take me for an Englishman? Let them put off their journeys and business because some old woman has sneezed[54] or had a dream! Not me!'

William then mounted his horse and galloped into the wood with his brother Henry, William of Breteuil and others; and they all, as usual, scattered and chose their stands.[55] After the king and Walter had taken their place with a few companions (presumably servants) in a glade, and with bows at the ready waited for their prey, a deer came running between them. William stepped back and Walter let fly. The arrow passed over the animal, just grazing its hide, and fatally wounded the king, who was standing directly opposite. William fell to the ground and died instantly. Amid the general confusion, Henry made tracks for Winchester and Walter hurried to the coast and crossed to France in order to avoid the vengeance which some wanted to take on him.

Orderic tells the story well, but it is doubtful whether he contributes any historical fact unknown to his predecessors. Basically he tells a moral story: God had condemned the king to death because of his impiety, and the heedless man not only disregarded every warning but also unwittingly made remarks which foretold his doom in detail. The irony is quite effective. Moreover, his explanation of how Walter managed to hit the

[53] Perhaps it should be translated more boldly: 'You, Walter, carry out this just sentence.' Chibnall's note, echoing FWR, ii, 330 n., 'it is not clear what Orderic believed the significance to be', is surprising: Walter was to be God's executioner.

[54] Both FWR, ii, 330, and Chibnall, OV, v, 289, translate sternutatio as 'snore'.

[55] 'et venatores per diversa rite loca dispersa sunt', p. 290; dispersi would improve the text. Venatores usually has the meaning of huntsmen, that is to say, servants, and is so translated by Chibnall. But the passage is connected with GR, ii, 378, where 'ceteris . . . dispersis' undoubtedly means that it was the royal party — the 'Henricus comes . . . et Guillelmus de Britolio aliique illustres' of OV – which was dispersed. Although the meaning of the common source (if OV was not using GR) cannot be elicited by textual analysis, the story is concerned with the courtiers and it is their dispersal which is of importance. It would seem, therefore, that GR is to be preferred to OV.

king, although it makes sense, is probably imaginary. The king surely, as
William of Malmesbury recognized, had the right to the first shot; but
perhaps Orderic implies that William, by stepping back, conceded the
privilege to his guest.

The accounts already considered seem to lie behind all other notices
and reconstructions of the king's death,[56] but two later contributions
must be taken into account. Abbot Suger of St Denis, in his Life of Louis
VI, written in the 1140s, and John of Salisbury, in his Life of St Anselm,
eliminate Walter Tirel. The abbot states that, although some men
alleged that it was the noble count who had shot the arrow, he himself
could vouch that he had often heard Walter, at a time when he had
nothing to hope or fear, affirm on the solemnest of oaths that on the fatal
day he neither went into that part of the wood where the king hunted
nor even caught sight of him in the wood. Responsibility for the death
lay, Suger concluded, with the power of God.[57] John of Salisbury, who
was no doubt acquainted with Suger's book, when rewriting Eadmer's
Life of Anselm in the 1160s in the hope of the archbishop's canonization,
remarks that William, like a second Julian the Apostate, was killed by an
arrow to the relief of Anselm, a second Basil. And in both cases the
identity of the slayer remained uncertain. Walter Tirel, who was blamed
by many for William's death, since he was a close friend and almost his
only companion in the enclosure,[58] proclaimed on his death-bed,
invoking God's judgment on his soul, that he was innocent of the deed.
Many men say that it was the king himself who dispatched the fatal dart;
and it was this that Walter, although he was not believed, constantly
asserted. But really, John concludes, whoever did it was only carrying
out the orders of God, who felt pity for the sufferings of his church.[59]

The truth of the matter cannot be established. It seems to have been
commonly believed that Walter Tirel was the man, and a reported
denial from a good, but sometimes hazy or inaccurate, source is not
conclusive. Walter may only have denied criminal intent; and this was
universally accepted. The lord of Poix, like the English king, was a man
of honour. He could well have been the unknowing agent of the
avenging God, but he was not the tool, conscious or unconscious, of an
earthly prince. The lack of malicious purpose would not have saved him
from a blood feud or a charge of homicide, but since it seems that he was
neither punished nor rewarded by Henry I – the manor of Langham

---

[56] For these, see *FWR*, ii, 657 ff.
[57] Suger (ed. Waquet), 12.
[58] *indago ferarum*: John envisaged that the hunting was in a deer-hay or stable: see
above, 129 ff.
[59] *Vita S. Anselmi*, Migne *PL*, cxcix, 1031. John, when denouncing hunting in his
Policraticus, does not mention William Rufus by name: see above, 120.

passed in due course to his son, Hugh[60] – this issue also is uncertain. Even his pilgrimage to Jerusalem, on which he died,[61] can be variously explained.

It is clear that there is only one story, and that this, even with the minor variations introduced by the several retailers, is no more than a bare outline. The king, contrary to his usual custom, did not go hunting at dawn but waited until after the midday meal: perhaps he had a hangover or was detained by important business; possibly he was held up by warnings of danger to his person. The method of hunting envisaged, but never explicitly described, by those who wanted to explain how the accident occurred, was shooting dismounted from butts or trysts at animals driven by the huntsmen through the glades in the wood where the royal party was stationed, split up into small groups at some distance from one another.[62] The king was killed accidentally; but since his companion, Walter Tirel, fled, apparently without offering an explanation, and those in attendance may not have seen what happened, the precise circumstances remained a mystery. And, as it was long before the age when writers constructed ingenious plots, no one looked further than the obvious suspect, and no one considered who benefited by the death. There are no dark hints of earthly crime in the accounts already discussed. When such an evident sinner perished, there was no need at all to look beyond the avenging hand of God.

It has been left to modern historians to hint that a baronial conspiracy, perhaps led by the 'Clares', in the interest of Count Henry, had contrived William's death.[63] But there is not a shred of good evidence and the theory merely avoids the obvious. Hunting accidents were, after all, not uncommon. The deaths of the king's brother and nephew have already been noticed. On Christmas eve 1143, Miles of Gloucester, the new earl of Hereford, was likewise shot in the breast by a companion knight and died immediately before he could confess his sins.

[60] Round, *FE*, 468, 470–1.

[61] OV, v, 294.

[62] For this type of hunting (the stable), see above, 130–2. See further, F. Barlow, 'Hunting in the Middle Ages', *Transactions of the Devonshire Association*, cxiii (1981), 7–8.

[63] Round, *FE*, 472. It is Round's *obita dicta* after placing Walter Tirel within the Clare family circle which gave firmer form to this long-running innuendo. Cf. also *FWR*, ii, 325–7. C.W. Hollister, however, 'The strange death of William Rufus', *loc. cit.*, 687 ff., very sensibly demolishes the several strands in the case one by one. In particular he points out that this was for Henry the least favourable moment for William's death. Emma Mason, 'William Rufus: myth and reality', *Journal of Medieval History*, iii (1977), 18 n. 1, goes as far as to say, 'Most writers on this period (except Hollister) believe that William II was murdered either on the orders of his brother or by dissidents who supposed that their interests would be better served with Henry on the throne.'

His death is described in words which echo those used of Rufus's.[64]

What was unusual was the killing of a king, and this was a highly fraught event: the denunciations of William's moral and political behaviour, inserted at this point in most chronicles, were surely intended to dissipate the guilt in which the whole of society was involved. Florence and Orderic believed that the 'depopulation' of Hampshire for the making of the New Forest contributed to God's anger, and the former thought that William was killed on the spot where formerly a church had stood – by which he may have meant Brockenhurst.[65] Both Florence and Hugh of Flavigny associated the bad weather and various unusual natural phenomena from which the reign suffered with the king's death.[66] Moreover, the several portents described helped to transfer the blame to the king himself, for he irreverently refused to take heed of repeated warnings. The Anglo-Saxon Chronicle tells only of the spring in Berkshire which bubbled up with blood. William of Malmesbury, closer to the scene, knew that it was at Hampstead (Marshall or Norris) and flowed for fifteen days, Florence that it was at Finchamstead and flowed for three weeks.[67] A strange feature of this story is that the Chronicle also reported the same phenomenon two years earlier in 1098. It may have been a usual or intermittent occurrence which could be cited when required. According to Hugh of Flavigny, almost everyone in the island went to see the marvel. He himself, however, when he returned to England, apparently in 1101, and the spring flowed once more with blood, did not go to have a look.[68] William of Malmesbury also introduced the portent of how the devil appeared in person to men in forests and waste places, and spoke to them. In Florence's version the men approached were Normans and the speech was of the king, Ranulf Flambard and other persons.[69]

Eadmer, in exile with Anselm at Lyons and Cluny, heard of many signs and visions which had occurred in England and foretold the king's death as punishment for his treatment of the archbishop – doubtless correspondents passed on such cheering news that came their way – but he relates only the revelation of St Hugh, abbot of Cluny, made on 30

[64] 'dum cervis insidiaretur, a comite pectus sagitta transfixus sine mora interiit'; 'sine confessionis verbo, sine poenitentiae fructu . . . sagitattus interiit'; 'dum . . . cervis insidiaretur, a milite, sagittam imprudenter in cervum dirigente, pectus transforatus, sine poenitentiae fructu miserabiliter occubuit': *Gesta Stephani*, ed. K.R. Potter and R.H.C. Davis (1976), 24, 148, 160.

[65] Florence, ii, 45; OV, v, 282–4. The Winchester annalist reported, *s.a.* 1094, that William had turned 30 cemeteries into pasture: *Ann. Winton.*, ii, 38.

[66] Florence, ii, 45; *Chronicon*, 495–7.

[67] *ASC, s.a.*; *GR*, ii, 376; Florence, ii, 45–6.

[68] *Chronicon*, 497.

[69] *GR*, ii, 376; Florence, ii, 46.

July 1100, just three days before the fatal accident. During a conversation in the daughter nunnery of Marcigny, Hugh affirmed to Anselm that during the previous night the king had been arraigned before the throne of God, judged and condemned to hell. The startled audience was, however, too disturbed to ask him how he knew.[70] Such wishful thinking must have been common in ecclesiastical circles which feared or hated the king.

William of Malmesbury quoted Eadmer's story and added two further premonitions of the king's approaching end. William Rufus himself had a warning dream the night before his death. He dreamt that he was being bled,[71] and that his blood spurted so far into the heavens as to blot out the sun and change day into night. Waking up, he called on the Blessed Virgin Mary, and ordered a light to be brought in and his chamberlains to stay with him. He could not get back to sleep for a long time. Then, just before dawn, a foreign monk told Robert fitzHaimo, who was in attendance on the king, a horrible dream he had just had about their master. He had seen William entering a church and in his usual proud and insolent way glaring disdainfully at all those present. He had then seized the crucifix in his teeth and gnawed its arms and almost bitten off the legs. The crucifix had suffered this for a time, but then kicked its assailant to the floor; and from the mouth of the king as he fell issued such a great flame that the billowing smoke almost licked the stars. When Robert hastened to tell this to the king, William laughed uproariously and said, 'He is a monk, and to get money dreams like a monk. Give him 100s.'[72] The story, of course, illustrates not only William's profanity but also his extravagance.

Orderic gives only one example of the many terrifying visions involving the king which he thought frequently occurred at this time in the abbeys and bishoprics. His instance took place at St Peter's, Gloucester, where the new church built by Abbot Serlo, previously a canon of Avranches and then monk of Mont St Michel, had been dedicated on 15 July.[73] One of the monks, a good man of high reputation, saw in a dream the Lord Jesus, sitting on his throne in Heaven, and humbly approached in supplication by a radiant virgin. 'Lord Jesus Christ, the saviour of mankind, for whom you shed your precious blood on the Cross, look mercifully, we beseech you, on your people who groan under the yoke of William. Avenger of all wickedness,

---

[70] VA, 122–4. The story also occurs in the several lives of St Hugh: F. Barlow, 'The canonization and the early Lives of Hugh I, abbot of Cluny', Analecta Bollandiana, xcviii (1980), 330, 332, G. 22.

[71] The blood-letting (minutio) undertaken for health or medical reasons.

[72] GR, ii, 377–8.

[73] Florence, ii, 44. See here, pl. 14a.

most just of all judges, deliver me, I pray you, from William and set me free from his hands, for he does all that he can to pollute me and afflicts me savagely.' To which the Lord replied, 'Be patient, and wait a little while, for before long I will exact from him the full penalty.' The monk understood the vision to mean that the church's complaints against the depredations, unnatural vice and other intolerable crimes of the king and his servants had effectively reached the ears of the Lord, and that William's end was nigh. This vision Abbot Serlo communicated to the king in a letter which arrived, as we have seen, just as he was about to go to his death.[74]

Orderic also gives an account of the sermon preached to the people in Gloucester abbey on the festival of St Peter's Chains (1 August), that is to say on the day before William's death, by Fulchered abbot of Shrewsbury, a former monk of Sées. Fulchered denounced the deadly sins which were corroding England's moral fibre, particularly pride, lust and avarice. But, he promised, the revolution was at hand; the rule of the sodomites was coming to an end; the Lord God was about to appear and punish the public enemies of his bride (the church). 'For behold,' he continued, 'the bow of divine wrath is drawn against the sinners, and the arrow swift to wound has been taken from the quiver. Soon now it will strike; and the wise man will correct his life so as to avoid the blow.'[75] The words of this vivid sermon were inevitably, after the event, considered prophetic, although William himself had been allowed short shrift for repentance.

Gloucester abbey seems to have been particularly involved in the prophesying and could also have popularized the miraculous well in Berkshire, which was only some fifty miles away. This hostile activity is a little surprising. The king was later remembered in the house as a benefactor and several of his barons, including Robert fitzHaimo, had been generous with their gifts.[76] Serlo, we notice, took steps to warn him of the danger. But since 1093 the king had been a frequent visitor, and it is possible that the cost of entertaining the court had been burdensome. Moreover, the monks had been given plenty of opportunity to observe the corruption of the courtiers, and the most recent visit, at Christmas 1099, may, for reasons unknown, have made a special impression upon them. Thus both anxiety for the state of William's soul and resentment at the intrusion of his worldliness could account for the visions with which some of the brethren were afflicted.

In one respect the omens and predictions reported by the chroniclers give a completely false idea of the immediate reaction to the king's

[74] OV, v, 284 ff.; above, 423.
[75] OV, v, 286–8.
[76] See above, 114–15.

death. The event had been hoped for by some, but, with William only forty and obviously full of vigour, it was not expected. Indeed, it came as a complete surprise and threw everything into disorder. With no long fatal illness, as with Edward the Confessor and William the Conqueror, men were entirely unprepared. William of Malmesbury was probably correct in thinking that those present neither went in pursuit of Walter Tirel nor took proper care of the corpse because the king's government had suddenly collapsed, bringing an end to law and order: it was every man for himself. Some of those in the hunting party went off to fortify their castles and look after their possessions, some to search for booty. Others turned their thoughts to the problem of succession. A few peasants, or perhaps inferior royal servants (accounts differ)[77] conveyed the body, which bled copiously all the way, on a horse-drawn waggon – like a wild boar pierced with spears[78] – to Winchester. It was buried the following morning, Friday 3 August, in the Old Minster under the tower, in the presence of a good number of magnates but with little show of grief.[79] As the see was vacant, the prior, Godfrey of Cambrai, the poet so much admired by William of Malmesbury,[80] was in charge. So stern a moralist may well have allowed only minimal rites. He certainly composed no historical epigram on Rufus's death.

Orderic, who often when describing William's deeds of chivalry reveals his admiration, when it came to the death and burial was surprisingly more hostile and less charitable than William of Malmesbury. According to him, only monks and clergy and the poorer citizens went out to meet the corpse. The doctors of theology and prelates also declared that the king, because of his filthy life and shameful death, could not be absolved from his sins by the church. Church bells which rang for the poorest of the poor, and even harlots, were silent for him. No alms were distributed to the needy from his rich treasury for the soul of the avaricious owner. The adulterer was mourned only by mercenary soldiers and prostitutes, both male and female, who had lost their paymaster.[81] Orderic may give the truer picture. Although Henry and his adherents must still have been in the city on the morning of the

[77] *rustici,* *GR*, ii, 379; *clientuli quidam,* OV, v, 292. Orderic's is the vaguer description. See also the next note.

[78] OV, *ibid.* According to *The Master of Game*, 188, it was the duty of the Master Forester or Parker to warn in advance the sheriff to produce sufficient carts for the conveyance of the carcases from where the deer were slain to the curée (where the bag was laid out and the final ceremonies of the hunt took place): see appendix, *s.v.* 'Curée'. If the carts were requisitioned, they would be driven by *rustici*.

[79] *ASC, s.a.;* *GR*, ii, 379; Florence, ii, 45; OV, v, 292.

[80] Cf. Barlow, *EC 1066–1154,* 77.

[81] 'nebulones [*glossed* lecatores] ac vulgaria scorta'. None of the words is specific: OV, v, 292.

funeral, indeed, it is generally thought that they did not leave for London until the following day (4 August), they may easily have neglected this duty. Henry, who had absented himself from his father's death-bed, though probably not from his burial, in order to withdraw his inheritance from the treasury and put it in safe-keeping, had even greater distractions in 1100.

William had, like many in that violent age, died without having the immediate opportunity to repent and confess his sins; and in the case of so obvious a sinner the circumstances certainly increased the chances that he would go to hell.[82] Moreover, if Orderic can be believed, the prelates refused him post-mortem absolution on the grounds that he had paid no heed to the church's teaching when alive, and his executors hastened his descent by having no prayers or masses said for the good of his soul. Prior Godfrey could have been responsible for such severity. We learn from William of Malmesbury that there were people who said that it was wrong that one who had been lustful and licentious all his life and had died without the last sacraments should be buried in such a sacred place, and attributed the collapse of the tower in 1107 to that outrage. In later editions, however, the chronicler expressly refrained from reporting idle talk on the subject, for he conceded that, owing to the instability of the structure, it could have fallen down even if the king had not been buried there.[83]

Both William of Malmesbury and Orderic had a weakness for the sensational, and when we reflect that the dead king's chancellor, his constant companion during the last six-and-a-half years, was immediately nominated bishop of Winchester and in 1129 was succeeded by the royal nephew, Henry of Blois, we may think that no deliberate injury would have been done to William's grave in the twelfth century. The history of the royal coffin and its contents, placed originally in the centre of the choir beneath the tower, and presumably partly at least below ground, is reassuringly obscure, and there is no reason to doubt that it survived the disaster of 1107. It must have remained substantially intact until about 1525, when Bishop Fox, after erecting stone screens on each side of the presbytery, placed six mortuary chests upon them containing the relics of various ancient kings, queens and bishops, including those of William Rufus, which he had collected while making improvements in the choir and presbytery.

By 1683, however, a coffin of oolitic stone covered with a coped slab of purbeck marble, devoid of symbols and uninscribed, which stood before

[82] But, since it was a common happening, not all theologians were rigorous: cf. also Barlow, *EC 1066–1154*, 268.

[83] *GR*, ii, 379 and n. The high water-table at Winchester makes the building of tall structures most difficult.

the high altar in the choir, but had already once been moved, was known as Rufus's Tomb. This, as well as the mortuary chests, had been rifled by Cromwell's men in 1642, and was reopened on 27 August 1868, preparatory to its removal to its present position in the presbytery. On the first occasion some objects, including fragments of cloth of gold, a large gold ring and a small silver chalice, were found within, on the second the greater part of a damaged and much disturbed skeleton of a man, 5′ 8″ or more tall, and various other objects were discovered in what was, no doubt, a much more thorough investigation of the dust and debris. The new finds raised the separate questions of whether this was indeed the royal coffin and the royal skeleton; and there were differing opinions from the start. One archaeologist, who had not been invited to the opening of the tomb, held that neither was possible.[84] However, a medical doctor and antiquarian, who had been present, believed the contrary.[85] The bones, he thought, covered by dust, had been missed by Fox in 1525 and by the marauders in 1642, and the chalice was simply an erratic; moreover, the fragments of a wooden shaft and iron head were the remains of the very arrow which had caused the king's death. Although, according to current archaeological views, the marble grave slab is more likely to be from the late than the early twelfth century, there can be no certain answers to the two questions.

Whatever may have happened in modern times to the king's remains, in 1100 he had not been refused Christian burial or denied the succour of the faithful. He could hardly have been held responsible for the failure to distribute his wealth in alms: that meanness, if true, has to be laid at his brother Henry's door. Nor is it likely, despite the moralists, that all his former friends and servants were uncharitable.[86] The haste with which barons, prelates and ministers rallied to Henry or Robert is not evidence that they preferred either to their dead lord. William's obit was remembered on 31 July or 1 August at Durham cathedral, presumably through the action of Ranulf Flambard, who was granted by God plenty of time in which to regret the good old days, and in Normandy at Lire on

[84] J.G. Joyce, in *Proceedings of the Soc. of Antiquaries*, 2nd ser., iv (1867–70), 242; *Archaeologia*, xlii, pt 2 (1870), 309–21. But on the earlier occasion, if correctly reported, he was inclined to think that the tomb was William's.

[85] F.W. Richards, in *Proceedings of the Soc. of Antiquaries, loc. cit.*, 293–8; *William Rufus' Tomb* (publ. by Hampshire Chronicle, 1868).

[86] For example, before 1104 Aline, wife of Roger of Ivry, Domesday lord of Beckley (Oxon), granted to St Peter's, Gloucester, land for the soul of King William and for her own: *Regesta*, no. 1006. On the other hand, in 1112 Robert of Meulan pointedly omitted him from a grant to Bec for the souls of William I and Matilda, Henry I and Matilda and their children, his own parents, his wife and their children, and his brother Henry and his wife and children: no. 1004.

29 July or 1 August and at Mont St Michel on 3 August,[87] surprisingly careless recordings of such a memorable event.

Nor was William's soul completely forgotten by his younger brother and Henry's family. When the next king made a grant to St Mary's, York, he remembered the souls of his father and mother and of his brother William, and when granting land to Cluny stated that it was for the souls of King William his father, Queen Matilda his mother, King William his brother, Matilda his queen and William his son. Even the Empress Matilda made a grant to St Benet of Hulme for the souls of King Henry her father, William her grandfather, William her uncle and all her relations.[88] And it is unlikely that Henry fitzEmpress saw much to blame in William's conduct. One of Henry's courtiers, Walter Map, called William Rufus, for expelling Anselm, 'the worst of kings', and even attributed to him the devastation of the countryside in order to create the New Forest – on the advice of Walter Tirel.[89] But neither of these alleged crimes would have cut much ice with the Angevin. William had taken his due, and distinguished, place in the unfolding catalogue of English kings.[90]

[87] *Liber Vitae*, 2b. Obituaries, 144, 151. William (I) is correctly commemorated on 5 Id. September in both obituaries, 145, 151. *RHF*, xxiii, 473, 579. William I and Henry I are more generally commemorated.

[88] *Cartae Antiquae* (Pipe Roll Soc., xxxiii, 1960), nos 505, 609, 442; cf. *Regesta*, ii, nos 538, 554, 569. It would seem that Henry I, whenever he made a grant in free alms, included William explicitly or implicitly among the souls to be prayed for.

[89] *De Nugis Curialium*, V, vi, ed. T. Wright (Camden Soc., 1850), 222–3.

[90] For his posthumous reputation, see T. Callahan Jr, 'The making of a monster: the historical image of William Rufus', *Journal of Medieval History*, vii (1981), 175.

EPILOGUE

The importance of the reign of William Rufus is that it prevented the reign of Robert Curthose and also assured the reign of Henry I. The English barons and prelates made their choice freely and deliberately in 1097–8 and 1100–1. They could have had Robert for king if they had wanted him strongly enough, but they were in something of a quandary. They did not regard William or Henry as having quite the same weight as their father. It was difficult to match his outstanding military achievements, and in a way Robert, with his Crusading adventures, came closest to them, but they recognized in both the younger brothers the same seriousness of purpose, a sense of responsibility, that Robert lacked.

If Robert had succeeded to the united Norman kingdom in 1088 or 1101, the results would not necessarily have been catastrophic – the medieval state could survive a great deal of misrule or un-rule – but they would certainly have been different. Normandy under Robert and later England under Stephen give us some idea of what could have happened. Dependent regions and frontier areas would have been lost. The magnates, both lay and clerical, would have gained their liberties, their freedom, and as a result have quarrelled among themselves and even found their own government undermined by an equal intractability on the part of their vassals and subordinates. There would have been a general devolution of authority and a good deal of disorder. But, under medieval conditions, local communities could usually endure, if not always thrive, in this situation. In Stephen's reign a great monastic revival was not hampered by the lax royal government, and trade seems to have flourished. Monasteries and other churches were seldom seriously injured by warring barons; urban communes and guilds could be formed when seigneurial authority was weak. Moreover, the pattern of Norman lordship in England meant that the kingdom could not easily break up into a congeries of semi-independent counties. The barons had to find some *modus vivendi* among themselves to replace royal authority. It also seems that in England a period of disorder always conditioned the aristocracy to look for a strong ruler who would remedy the ills from which it had suffered during the interregnum.

The reign of William Rufus, therefore, saved England, and eventually

Normandy, from mild or ineffective royal government. This has almost invariably since the eighteenth century been regarded as a good thing. Historians have usually admired strong and centralizing rulers and despised weak and ineffectual kings, such as Stephen and Edward II. The only concession made is to allow that armed reaction to tyrants was a useful brake which prevented strong rule from hardening into despotism and maintained the golden mean. But it is possible to hold that in Stephen's reign the several orders or estates in England enjoyed for a time the liberties to which they aspired after the oppression of the earlier Norman kings, and that as a result there was more satisfaction in the country than before. And although it can be countered that a strong king kept the disorderly and exploitive barons and prelates under restraint to the benefit of the lower orders, it is a thesis equally difficult to prove. The king indeed tended to protect merchants and Jews so that he could be their sole exploiter, but he shared the interests of the nobility and would rarely intervene between a lord and his villeins.

Leaving such political judgments aside, it must be accepted that the rule of William Rufus ensured the continuity of the type of government that his father had established, namely the Old-English polity, modified and stiffened by French practices and ruthless direction. Although the replacement of the eldest son also contributed to the destruction or weakening of some of the highest nobility, which, through its natural conservatism, tended to be partial to the firstborn, in all other ways it favoured continuity, for it was Robert who was the erratic son. We have noticed the substantial continuity within the baronage and royal household, the unchanged policy with regard to ecclesiastical appointments, the *pietas* of the new king towards the memory of his father and mother. William's aim was the *renovatio imperii Normannorum*, the renewal of the Norman empire, and as mortgagee of the duchy he took care of it as though it were his very own. It was the property of his race, his *gens*, and of his family. Although he died unmarried, it cannot be said with certainty that he intended never to provide for the succession; and there was always the prolific Henry lurking somewhere in the wings. It is Henry who is the great disappointment as a dynast. Not only did this great lover of women produce no satisfactory heir, he handed over the Norman realm to the hated Angevins, and also by his dynastic shifts and despotic rule provoked a reaction which looked for a time as though it would undo all his ambitions.

Although Henry in 1100 in his immediate weakness had to renounce some of his dead brother's 'illegal' practices, he was soon able to reintroduce them. William, therefore, in his government had not yet reached the point of exerting on his subjects an intolerable pressure, one which could have provoked a successful rebellion. He passed on an efficiently administered, even perhaps a well-governed kingdom to his successor. He had made Scotland once more a client state and had begun the reconquest of Wales. He had recovered Maine for Robert. Only in the Vexin had he failed, and that problem had also defeated his father. In truth, the French Vexin was too near Paris to be an easy prey

If he failed also to earn the title of 'the Good' – he could hardly have borne 'the Great', for *magnus* rarely meant more than the senior king, and so was the preserve of the Conqueror – he was in excellent company.[1] Since the chroniclers and annalists were clerks, and almost every king was in his different way offensive to some clerical ambition, they all received notices which contained an element of censure. If the memorials had been written in the households of the nobles, there would usually have been less blame. William offended the church because the cost of his wars fell heavily on the monasteries and because he was a sinner. The problem is, by what standards should he be judged? Obviously not according to those of an Anselm. And the chroniclers were even more biased than the primate. The Anglo-Saxon Chronicler, Eadmer, William of Malmesbury and Orderic were relatively humble monks. Besides which, the first two were native Englishmen and the others of mixed blood. Orderic, if not William, sided with the conquered. As the king was not only an 'oppressor' of the church but also, as a Norman, by definition an oppressor of the English, an unprejudiced account of his life and deeds is hardly to be expected from these writers. His dues and taxes, they considered, not only oppressed the church but also the cultivators of the soil, who were, of course, English

One of the most hostile interpretations of his life and death is to be found in Orderic. At the end of Book XII, written towards the close of Henry I's reign, he quotes from Geoffrey of Monmouth part of Merlin's prophecy, 'there shall follow two dragons, one of which will be snuffed out by the dart of envy while the other will return under the shadow of a (mighty) name'; and this he interprets as 'two lustful and savage lords, William Rufus killed by an arrow when hunting and Duke Robert dying deprived of his title in prison'. These were followed by the Lion of Justice, who was, of course, Henry, 'a ruler richer and more powerful than any who had reigned in England before him'.[2]

The laity always thought that priests shaved them too close, especially on the death-bed: their standards were impossible for a gentleman to observe, and the proofs of contrition they demanded from the dying were too heavy for his family to bear.[3] We must as far as possible judge the king by the standards of the nobility; and there are some pointers.

[1] Rufus is called both *junior* and *minor* in *Hist. mon. Gloucest.*, i, 68, 102, 109, 115.
[2] OV, vi, 384, 386–8; cf. Lucan, *Pharsalia*, I, 135.
[3] Cf. *William, earl of Pembroke, Knight-Marshal of the King's House: L'Histoire de Guillaume le maréchal*, ed. P. Meyer (Soc. de l'Hist. de France, Paris 1891–1901), ll. 18,476–19,502.

William was a soldier-king, who was always followed in peace and war by his barons. Those who rebelled against him, in 1088 as in 1095, have little to recommend them and display no signs of superior standards or ideals. To have been killed by a friend was one of Fate's dirtiest tricks. His private life, however, owing to the lack of hard evidence, has to remain something of a mystery. We cannot tell if Robert fitzHaimo, his constant friend, was a lover, another Piers Gaveston or Buckingham. We cannot establish what exactly brought Walter Tirel into his privy company on 2 August 1100. We know nothing of the characters of these men or of most others who were in daily contact with him beyond the obvious fact that they too were soldiers and must have shared some of the king's interests. Only Ranulf Flambard comes out clearly, and, even as portrayed by his detractors, is by no means unattractive. William liked intelligent and witty men; he was not simply a brute. All these courtiers, we may think, shared courage, magnanimity and what was beginning to be regarded as chivalry, the ethos of the noble cavalry officer.

William's reputation has at all times been higher than the strictly historical record warrants. He reigned at a time when European kingship had fallen to a low ebb. Philip of France and the Emperor Henry IV did little that was warmly acclaimed and both incurred the ban of the church. Alfonso VI of León-Castile operated in a world of his own and was surpassed in fame by his general, el Cid. In the Slav and Celtic fringes and in Scandinavia the rulers were beyond the pale. There was no proper king of Italy. Jerusalem was liberated by the princes, not the kings, of Christendom. In such royal company as existed, it was not too difficult to cut a dash. But that is probably not the whole explanation. William Rufus's historical reputation suggests that the recorded facts do not properly convey his qualities and superiority, his slightly diabolical charisma, and that only through the partial untruth of anecdotage can his true stature as man and king be measured. It is the collection of his sayings which brings him out distinctly, words recounted by chroniclers against their better judgment, *dicta* of which they half disapproved, half marvelled at. Here we have the blunt, rough commander, but shrewd and sometimes generous, always capable of emotion, even the gift of tears; always a gentleman, and that, despite the limitations, in no pejorative sense; always close to the popular image of a king.

It is unlikely that his homosexuality was held much against him in military circles. It was common enough and fitted easily into the life of the camp and, in the field, into the comradeship of soldiers-in-arms. Not even the chroniclers suggested that William had low-born or unworthy favourites or was manipulated by creatures. If there were catamites at court, they were in the same *galère* as harlots. It was a vice for Anselm and no doubt others to deplore. But it does not seem to have worried unduly the other bishops, almost all of whom are found regularly at court. The ambience was unedifying, but apparently less so than Robert's scandalous household; and Henry I's 'puritanical' court had features offensive to moralists. Unlike Philip of France and the German emperors, William was never under the ban of the church. He committed no public enormities.

William was, as Eadmer recognized, up to the final unexpected tragedy exceptionally fortunate, so indulged and privileged by God that even the winds and the waves were at his command. In 1100, men thought that he was on the verge of some even more splendid triumphs; the greatest churchmen wrote deferentially to him; the duke of Aquitaine courted his favour. And it was the ignoble, arbitrary and uncharacteristically unfortunate accident which finally destroyed his reputation in the eyes of the pious clergy, for it could only be explained by the judgment of God on William's and his father's sins. God, driven beyond forbearance, had at last stretched the bow, and the arrow had flown straight into the king's heart. Thus perished the tyrant. The luck had run out. The irony is that, as William had shown in 1093, he was capable of making a good end. He may have feared both men and God too little, but he had a great fear of the death that comes by stealth in the shape of disease. He did not then count the cost of the penance – only after he had recovered. If Eadmer's merciful and indulgent God had given him instead another twenty years of life, we may be sure that his works of piety would have earned him some relief from the censure of the chroniclers.

In the event, Eadmer and those of like mind were not to be cheated. William was struck down when defenceless, impenitent, unshriven, irredeemable. The saints had been avenged. It was the more noble Anselm who wept at the tragedy of the event, at the precipitate death of a sinner. In 1106, Abbot Hugh of Cluny, a nobleman and a friend of the great, wrote to Philip of France, who had consulted him about becoming a monk, that the lamentable and deplorable deaths of the king's contemporaries and neighbours, William king of the English and the Emperor Henry IV, should indeed terrify him, the former killed instantaneously by a single arrow, not in battle, but in a wood.[4] Clearly Hugh thought that the ignobility of the occasion contributed to its horror. He, and no doubt Anselm, had the magnanimity to think that William would have preferred to die like Hugh of Montgomery amid the deadly hail of battle. To deprive a hero of a hero's death was the most terrible punishment that God could inflict.

[4] Migne *PL*, clix, 930.

APPENDICES

THE ROYAL ITINERARY

SELECT BIBLIOGRAPHY

GENEALOGICAL TABLES

INDEX

Appendix A

THE CHILDREN OF WILLIAM I AND MATILDA

The exact composition of this family and the dates of the children's births cannot be established with certainty.[1] The chroniclers usually give the names of the sons and daughters in separate lists,[2] and whereas there is general agreement on the names of the boys and their seniority, there is confusion over the girls. These were less in the public eye and the names themselves were not so plain. Although it is certain that *Adela* and *(H)adala* are the same person, and likely that *Adeliza* and *Adelidis* are merely variants of another name and can both be translated 'Adelaide', the series is less distinct than *Robertus, Ricardus, Guillelmus* and *Henricus.*

Orderic Vitalis lists the children in Volumes III, IV and V of his *Historia Ecclesiastica*; and a fourth catalogue, which has a St Evroul provenance, and a series interpolated by Robert of Torigny about 1139 into William of Jumièges are also most likely derived from Orderic's work.[3] The variations in these five lists therefore only reveal the St Evroul monk's uncertainty or carelessness. Common to almost all these lists are the four girls with whom Orderic started in Book III, which was written during the decade before 1123–4: Adeliza and Constance, Cecily (*Cecilia*) and Hadala; and he put them in pairs probably to imply that the first couple was senior to the second. Robert of Torigny listed the same four, but presented them as though they were born in the following order: Cecily, Constance, Adeledis and Adela, a conflict with Orderic over the age of Cecily. Meanwhile in Book IV, which was written shortly after III, probably in 1125, Orderic had introduced the complication of Agatha. He now offered Agatha and Constance, Adeliza, and Adela and Cecily. By substituting Agatha for Adeliza he was forced to insert the latter on her own. In Book V, written after 1127, the order is Agatha, Adelidis, Constance and Adela. Here Agatha has replaced Cecily. The final St Evroul list, Agatha and Adeliza, Constance, Adela and Cecily, is just another variant. We should notice that in all these associated lists Matilda, an undoubted daughter of the marriage, is omitted and that Agatha is known only to Orderic.[4]

[1] The problem has been considered in *FNC*, iii, app. O, and Douglas, *WC*, app. C.
[2] The model is probably Einhard, *Vita Karoli*, cap. 18.
[3] OV, ii, 104, 224; iii, 114; iv, 351; *GND*, 316 ff. For the date of Torigny's interpolations, see E.M.C. van Houts, 'The *Gesta Normannorum Ducum*', *Battle III*, 109–10, 113.
[4] For another case of his making a slip and then elaborating it, see above, 19 n. 65.

One further list of daughters remains to be considered. The mortuary roll of Matilda, first abbess of Holy Trinity, Caen, but not a daughter of the duke, as Delisle believed, was probably composed after her death in 1113 by her coadjutor and successor, Cecily, a genuine daughter. The obituary notice asks for prayers also for Queen Matilda, their founder, and for her daughters, Adilidis, Matilda and Constance.[5] These three were therefore dead, and as they were presented as princesses, distinct from the deceased nuns, the omission of Agatha is evidence that either she was still alive or she was an invention of Orderic. Even if it be thought that she could have been overlooked by Cecily because she was, according to Orderic, buried at Bayeux, it should be noticed that the cathedral too disregarded her in 1113.[6] On the other hand, the daughter Matilda is confirmed by an entry in Domesday Book, where Geoffrey, the chamberlain of the king's daughter, is entered as holding Hatch Warren in Hampshire of the king for the service which he performed (*fecit*) for his daughter Matilda.[7] It may be that she was dead by 1086.

The problem of Agatha is bound up with the stories of the contracts of marriage into which one or more of the elder daughters entered. William of Poitiers, who was in the best position to know the truth but was no more accurate than Orderic,[8] informs us that a daughter, unfortunately not named, and not necessarily always the same one, was betrothed to Herbert count of Maine (before 9 March 1062), Earl Harold of Wessex (before 1066) and one of two Spanish royal brothers.[9] William of Malmesbury, writing in 1118–25, names and correctly identifies Cecily, Constance and Adela, and adds that he has forgotten the names of two others, but one was betrothed to Harold and died before reaching marriageable age, and the other, although promised in marriage to Alfonso king of Galicia, obtained from God death as a virgin.[10] When Orderic between 1109 and 1113, at about the same time as he started work on *Historia Ecclesiastica*, interpolated William of Jumièges, he named Adeliza as the daughter whom the duke affianced to Harold;[11] and about 1139 Robert of Torigny copied him.[12] But in

[5] *Rouleaux des Morts du IXe au XVe siècle*, ed. Léopold Delisle (Soc. de l'Hist. de France, 1866), no. 36, 181–2.

[6] *Ibid.*, tit. 5, 185.

[7] *DB*, i, 49b: where *filiae regis* is interlined after *camerarius*, as an identification.

[8] For William's life and historical sources, see Davis, 'William of Poitiers', 71 ff. William was born at Préaux, where his sister became abbess of St-Léger, and Davis suggests that his father was a tenant of the Beaumont family.

[9] *GG*, 88, 230, 142.

[10] *GR*, ii, 333.

[11] *GND*, 191. Cf. also Chibnall, OV, ii, xiv n. OV's interpolations in *GND* have been shown by E. M. C. van Houts, *loc. cit.*, 109 and 'Quelques remarques sur les interpolations attribuées à Orderic Vital . . .', *Rev. d'histoire des Textes*, viii (1978), 213–22, to have been started before 1109 and finished after 1113.

[12] *GND*, 318.

Book V of *Historia Ecclesiastica* Orderic changed his mind and attributed both this and the Spanish betrothal to Agatha: after Harold's death she was sent to marry Amfurcius king of Galicia; but she had loved only Harold and God mercifully released her from this odious contract; her virgin body was brought back from Spain and buried in Bayeux cathedral. He adds, no doubt to complete the change, that Adelidis became a nun when she reached marriageable age and died under the protection of Roger of Beaumont,[13] which should mean at the nunnery of St-Léger at Préaux. Roger himself became a monk at St Peter's, Préaux, about 1090, and died some years later. Meanwhile in Book IV Orderic remarked in passing that William had offered to marry one of his daughters to Edwin earl of Mercia, and it was the king's failure to honour the promise which led to Edwin's revolt in 1068.[14]

An anonymous life of Simon of Crépy, count of Amiens-Valois-Vexin (1074–7), who had been brought up by the duke, takes the story even further. In 1077, after Simon's engagement to Judith of Auvergne had fallen through, the king summoned the young man to him and offered him a daughter who was at the time being sought in marriage by Anfursus king of the Spains and Robert (Guiscard) prince of Apulia. Simon declined, giving the excuse that he was related to her mother, but really because he intended to become a monk.[15] There are, however, severe chronological difficulties in these stories. Whoever the Spanish suitor or suitors may have been – and Anglo-Norman writers had a very confused knowledge of Spanish history – any betrothal to a daughter of William would seem a possibility only between the death of Ferdinand I of Castile and León in 1065 and the marriage of the last surviving son, Alfonso VI, in 1074.[16] But a girl who died in or before 1074 could not have been offered to Simon in 1077. Perhaps her tragic death in Spain is merely a romantic story. Certainly William of Poitiers, who did not lay down his pen before 1077, gives no indication that the girl he had in mind in connexion with Spain was no longer alive. The difficulty caused by Robert Guiscard's appearance as a suitor can, however, best be solved by simply dismissing the story as impossible. From 1058 until at least September 1080,[17] five years before his death, he was married to Sigelgaita, princess of Salerno, and, unless he intended to repudiate her, just as he had her predecessor, he was not free to marry during those years. Nevertheless, it is by no means unlikely that William regarded Simon from the time he looked like inheriting land, or once he had succeeded his father (1074), as a possible and desirable son-in-law.

[13] OV, iii, 114.

[14] OV, ii, 214–16.

[15] *Vita B. Simonis*, cols 1215 16.

[16] Foreville, *GG*, 142 n.; Chibnall, OV, iii, 114 n. If it was the same girl who was offered to Earl Edwin, the betrothal is to be dated *post* 1067.

[17] Gregory VII, *Register*, VIII, 8 (ed. Caspar, 527).

The only certainty among so much uncertainty is that it was believed that one or more of the elder daughters was offered or sought in marriage several times and that among the suitors were Spanish princes. The problem of whether we are concerned with one or two daughters, and which they were, cannot be solved with assurance. Cecily, Constance and Adela can presumably be ruled out as they did not die young virgins. This leaves Adelaide, Agatha and Matilda. The last seems too obscure to have been involved. Orderic by Book V has a coherent account of Agatha and Adelaide which makes the former the fiancée and the latter a nun. All the same it does not inspire complete confidence. Whereas the existence of Adelaide is independently attested, Agatha, to whom so much is attributed, has a name inexplicable in the family and is unknown to anyone but Orderic. On balance the probability is that Adelaide was the much betrothed daughter and was involved in all the schemes from Herbert of Maine to a king of Spain, and even perhaps to Simon of Crépy.

Another reference to an unnamed daughter is in a poem which Baudri abbot of Bourgueil in Touraine addressed to Cecily, apparently when she was a nun but not abbess of Caen, i.e. between 1075 and 1113; but the date is unlikely to be later than 1107 when Baudri became archbishop of Dol and almost stopped writing poetry.[18] He hears that Cecily has with her (detinere) a sister whose name he has forgotten, but to whom he sends greetings. 'She was of Bayeux and then of Anjou.' These places do not help. There was no nunnery at Bayeux: indeed, the only nunnery in the diocese was Cecily's at Caen. Baudri presumably met her in Anjou, and Fontevrault was a famous house on the Loire, south-east of Angers; but nothing falls into place. Finally, a daughter of the king who in the time of Abbot William of Fécamp (1078–1107) was maintaining a dumb boy at her expense at the abbey,[19] was probably Cecily.

There seem, therefore, to have been four sons, Robert, Richard, William Rufus and Henry (1086), in that order, and at least five daughters, Adelaide, Constance, Cecily, Adela and Matilda, in an uncertain order. Cecily's early religious career is well dated. According to Holy Trinity's pancarte, the duke and duchess gave her to the nunnery, with the approval of Archbishop Maurilius, when the church was dedicated on 18 June 1066.[20] According to the Annals of St Evroul, repeated by Orderic, the king gave his daughter to be consecrated by Archbishop John at Easter 1075.[21] If we are concerned with the oblation

[18] Baudri de Bourgueil, no. CXCVIII, 255.
[19] L'abbé Sauvage, 'Des Miracles advenus en l'église de Fécamp', Soc. de l'Hist. de Normandie, Mélanges 2 (Rouen 1893), 28.
[20] Fauroux, Recueil, no. 231, p. 446.
[21] OV, iii, 8–10.

and then the consecration it would seem that Cecily was born in 1058–9, which is the traditional date for the foundation of Holy Trinity. This would make her close to William Rufus, who, if he was over forty in 1100,[22] was born in 1060 or earlier.

We can do little more than work backwards and forwards from this point. Older than William were Richard and Robert. Adela was generally considered the youngest daughter. The date of her marriage to the count of Blois is uncertain, but is usually given as 1080.[23] She died after 1135, probably in 1137, as a nun at Marcigny-sur-Loire. A likely date for her birth would be 1064 or earlier. Constance, generally regarded as one of the elder daughters, married in 1086. A birthdate of about 1062 would be possible. Cecily placed Matilda between Adelaide and Constance.

A hypothetical conflated list would be: Robert (c.1053–1134), Richard (c.1055–1069 × 74), Adelaide (c.1057–?), Cecily (1058 × 59–1127), William Rufus (c.1060–1100), Matilda (c.1061–? *ante* 1086), Constance (c.1062–90), Adela (c.1064–?1137) and Henry (1068–1135). These dates do not conflict with any known facts.

[22] See above, 3.
[23] But M. Bur, 'Les Comtes de Champagne et la "Normanitas": semiologie d'un tombeau', *Battle III*, 25, without citing references, dates it probably 1084.

WILLIAM II's SHERIFFS

Abbreviations used: * taken over from William I; Morris, *Med. Eng. Sheriff*; Farrer, 'The sheriffs of Lincolnshire and Yorkshire, 1066–1130', *EHR*, xxx (1915), 277; *R.* = *Regesta*.

County	Sheriff	Reference
Bedfordshire	? Hugh of Buckland	*R.* nos 395, 471; Morris, 52 n.
Berkshire	Gilbert of Bretteville	*R.* no. 359; *Chron. Abingdon*, ii, 26, 159; *De Injusta Vexatione*, 191–2
	Hugh of Buckland	*R.* no. 528; *Chron. Abingdon*, ii, 43
Buckinghamshire	Hugh of Beauchamp	*R.* nos 314b, 370; Morris, 48 n.
Cambridge	? *Picot	Morris, 48 n.
Carlisle	William fitzTheodoric	*R.* no. 463
	G. (? the same)	*R.* no. 478
Cornwall	Warin	*R.* no. 378
Derbyshire	? Henry de Ferrers or William Peverel	*R.* no. 337
Devonshire	*Baldwin fitzGilbert	*DB*
	William fitzBaldwin	*R.* nos 378, 401
	? Robert fitzBaldwin	
	Richard fitzBaldwin	Round, *FE*, 330 n. 37
Dorset	(Aiulf)	*R.* no. 204
Essex	*Peter de Valognes	*R.* nos 426b, 436, 442, 471; Morris, 48 n.
	? Swegn of Essex	*R.* no. 429a
	? Hugh of Buckland (1100)	*R.* no. 519, and *see* Hertfordshire
Gloucestershire	*Durand	*DB*
	Walter de Pîtres	*R.* nos 400, 411, 554
Hampshire	*? Hugh de Port	Morris, 47 n.
	Durand (1096)	*R.* no. 377, 377a, 483a
Hertfordshire	*Peter de Valognes	*R.* no. 314b, 335a; Morris, 48 n.
	Hugh of Buckland (1100)	*R.* no. 488; Liebermann, *TRHS*, n.s. viii (1894), 40

Huntingdonshire	Ranulf, bro. of Ilger	R. nos 321, 329, 413, 447, 462, 477
Isle of Wight	W.	R. no. 412d
Kent	*Haimo dapifer	R. nos 304, 340, 351, 355, 372, 458, 516
Leicester	*? Hugh of Grandmesnil	Morris, 49 n.
	? Ivo of Grandmesnil	
Lincolnshire	? Turold	R. nos 283, 333, 335
	? Ivo Taillebois	R. no. 406
	N.	R. nos 305, 468a
	Osbert the clerk	R. nos 374, 407, 467, 469–70, 504; Farrer, 277–80
London	R. Delpare/de Parc	R. nos 444, 444a
	? Ralf de Marcy	R. nos 389a, 399a
Middlesex	Hugh of Buckland	R. no. 471; cf. Gilbert Crispin, 138, no. 12
Norfolk	Hermer de Ferrers	R. nos 291, 392, 461
	Humphrey the chamberlain	R. nos 373, 385a, 395
	(Roger Bigot, Christmas 1100)	R. no. 508
Northamptonshire	*William de Cahagnes	R. nos 288b, 383, 476; Morris, 49 n.
Northumberland	Robert Picot	R. no. 367
Nottinghamshire	? Turold/Earnwig	R. nos 333, 335, 337
	(Richard fitzGodse, Christmas 1100)	R. no. 502
Oxfordshire	Peter	R. nos 390, 466
	(William, 1100)	R. no. 527
Somerset	? William de Mohun (1086)	Morris, 48 n.
	Aiulf the chamberlain	R. nos 315, 326, 457; Morris, 47 n.
	William Capra	R. nos 362, 386a
Staffordshire	N.	R. no. 456
Suffolk	Godric dapifer	R. nos 291, 392, 461
	(Roger Bigot, Christmas 1100)	R. no. 509
Surrey	? O.	Morris, 49 n.
Sussex	? E. fitzAnger	R. no. 460
	? Hugh of Buckland	R. no. 416
Warwickshire	? Robert d'Oilli (1086)	Morris, 47 n.
	William fitzCorbucio	R. no. 388
Wiltshire	Walter Hosatus	R. no. 290a, 494
	*Edward of Salisbury	Morris, 47 n.
	O (? mistake for E)	R. no. 417

Worcester	*Urse of Abetot	*R.* nos 388, 429, 488; Morris, 47 n.
Yorkshire	Ralf Pagnell	*De Injusta Vexatione,* 172 ff.; Farrer, 282–4
	Erneis de Burun	*R.* no. 403, cf. 226; *De Injusta Vexatione,* 192
	Geoffrey Baynard	*R.* nos 338, 344, 421, 431; Morris, 48 n.
	H.	*R.* no. 412
	Bertram de Verdun	*R.* no. 427, 494

THE ROYAL ITINERARY

Date	Place	Reference
1087		
7/8 September	Rouen	53 ff.
	? Touques	
	? Hampshire/Sussex coast	
	Winchester	
26 September	Westminster (coronation)	57
	Winchester	63 ff.
Christmas	London	66
1088		
February/March	? Dover	75 ff.
	? Hastings	
Easter (16 April)	London	77 ff.
April	Tonbridge	
	Rochester	
May–June	siege of Pevensey	
June–July	siege of Rochester	
2 November	Salisbury	85
	Berkshire	89
Christmas	? London	89
1089		
1090		
? Spring	Winchester	273
Christmas	Westminster	276
1091		
27 January–2 February	Dover/Hastings	276 ff.
February	Normandy	280 ff.
	Eu	
	Rouen	
March	Avranches	284
18 July	Caen	287
	England	287–8
	? Wales	289
	Windsor	291
11 September	Durham	292
	? north of Berwick	293
? October	Mercia	295

? November	Wessex (? Winchester)	295
1092		
? Summer	Carlisle	297
Christmas	? Westminster	302–3
1093		
Before 6 March	Alveston (Glos)	298
	Gloucester	298 ff.
Summer	Dover	309, 325
	Rochester	306–7
	Windsor	309
	Wilton	311–12
24 August	Gloucester	309–10
Before 25 September	Winchester	307
Christmas	Gloucester	308, 326–7; *R.* no. 338a
1094		
? January	? Winchester	327
Early February	Hastings	328
11 February	Battle	328; *R.* no. 348a
19 March	Normandy	331
	Rouen	
	Eu	
	Bures-en-Bray	332
October	? Eu	334
Christmas	Wissant	335
1095		
January	England	
	Gillingham (Dorset)	338
c. 20 January	Cricklade (Wilts)	
	? Wales	
25–27 February	Rockingham (Northants)	
Before 13 May	? Westminster	342
13 May	Windsor	342; *R.* no. 362
? June	Nottingham	348
	Newcastle	351 ff.
	? Corbridge	
	Morpeth	
? July–August	siege of Newcastle	*R.* nos. 366–8
	Bamburgh	353
	Wales	354
	? Newcastle, Tynemouth	354–5
	? Bamburgh	
Christmas	Windsor	355
1096		
2 January	Windsor	355
13 January	Salisbury	356 ff.; ? *R.* no. 396

September	Hastings	365; *R.* nos. 377, 377a
	Normandy	
	Rouen	365
Christmas	Normandy	368
1097		
4 April	Arundel	369
	Windsor	369
	Wales	370
	Hereford in Wales	*R.* no. 399a
Whitsun (24 May)	Windsor	373
July	Wales	370
14–15 October	Winchester	374
	Southampton area	376
	Isle of Wight	376; *R.* no. 389
11 November	Normandy	376
Winter	Gisors	379–81
	French Vexin	
1098		
February–March	Maine	381–4
	Rouen	384
June	Sées	385
	Alençon	
	Rouessé-Fontaine (Maine)	
	Montbizot	
	Coulaines	
	siege of Le Mans	386
	Normandy	386
After mid-July	Ballon (Maine)	386
	Le Mans	387
	Normandy	388
27 September	Conches	393
	French Vexin	393
	outside Pontoise	
	siege of Chaumont	
12 November	Pont-de-l'Arche	393–4; *R.* nos 412b, 473, 480
28 December	Rouen	*R.* no. 412a
1099		
	Houdan	394
	Septeuil	
	Normandy	
Easter (10 April)	England	395, 399
1 May	Brampton (? Hunts)	399; *R.* no. 418
Whitsun (29 May)	London/Westminster	399; *R.* no. 414a
June	New Forest (Hants)	402
6 July	Brockenhurst	402; *R.* nos 484–a
	? Southampton/Portsmouth	402–3

	Normandy	
	Touques	403
	Bonneville	
	Maine	403
	Le Mans	
	Le Grand-Lucé	
	siege of Mayet	404
	Le Mans	404
	Normandy	
	Lillebonne	407; *R.* no. 416
September	England	408
Christmas	Gloucester	414
1100		
9 January	Salisbury	419; *R.* no. 427
Easter (1 April)	Winchester	414; *R.* no. 429
Whitsun (20 May)	Westminster	419; ? *R.* no. 464
Summer	New Forest	419
2 August	death in forest	420
3 August	burial at Winchester	429
(5 August	coronation of Henry I)	

SELECT BIBLIOGRAPHY

The lists which follow are not to be regarded as a full bibliography for the history of William Rufus and his times. They serve to give further precision to the citations in the footnotes of this book and to give some indication of the author's indebtedness to other scholars. The conventional division into Primary Sources and Secondary Authorities is not entirely satisfactory, for most editions of texts are of a mixed nature: and that feature explains some of the apparent inconsistencies in the listing here.

I. PRIMARY SOURCES

ABINGDON, *Chronicon Monasterii de Abingdon*, ed. J. Stevenson, (Rolls ser., 1858).

Acta Lanfranci, in *Anglo-Saxon Chronicle* (text), ed. J. Earle (*q.v.*).

Acta Sanctorum, ed. J. Bollandus, G. Henschenius, etc., 1734 ff.

Actus Pontificum Cenomannis in urbe degentium, ed. G. Busson and A. Ledru, Archives historiques du Maine, 2 (Le Mans 1901).

ALEXANDER NECKAM, *De naturis Rerum*, ed. T. Wright (Rolls ser., 1863).

Anglo-Latin Satirical Poets and Epigrammatists of the Twelfth Century, ed. T. Wright (Rolls ser., 1872).

Anglo-Saxon Chronicle, text, *Two of the Saxon Chronicles parallel*, ed. J. Earle (1865); *The Peterborough Chronicle, 1070–1154*, ed. C. Clark (2nd edn 1970); trans. D Whitelock with D.C. Douglas and S.I. Tucker, in *English Historical Documents*, *1042–1189*, ii, ed. D.C. Douglas and G.W. Greenaway (2nd edn 1981), and independently (1961).

Annales de Wintonia, in *Annales Monastici* (*q.v.*), ii.

Annales Monastici, ed. H.R. Luard (Rolls ser., 1864–9).

ANSELM, *S. Anselmi Opera Omnia*, ed. F.S. Schmitt (1946–52).

ARNULF, *The Letters of Arnulf of Lisieux*, ed. F. Barlow, Royal Hist. Soc., Camden, 3rd ser., lxi (1939).

Asser's Life of King Alfred, ed. W.H. Stevenson (1904).

BARLOW, F., BIDDLE, M., VON FEILITZEN, O., KEENE, D.J., *Winchester in the Early Middle Ages*, Winchester Studies, ed. Biddle, I (1976).

BATTLE, *The Chronicle of Battle Abbey*, ed. and trans. E. Searle, (Oxford Med. Texts, 1980).

BAUDRI DE BOURGUEIL, *Les oeuvres poétiques de Baudri de Bourgueil*, ed. P. Abrahams (Paris 1926).

BEROUL, *The Romance of Tristan*: text, ed. A. Ewert (1967); trans. A.S. Fedrick (1970).

BISHOP, T.A.M., and CHAPLAIS, P., *Facsimiles of English Royal Writs to A.D. 1100* (Galbraith *Festschrift*, 1957).

BOUQUET, M., *Recueil des Historiens des Gaules et de la France* (Paris 1738–1876).

BOURIENNE, V., *Antiquus cartularius ecclesiae Baiocensis ou Livre Noir* (Rouen 1907–8).

Brevis Relatio, in J.A. Giles, *Scriptores* (*q.v.*).

Cartae Antiquae, Pipe Roll Soc., new ser., xxxiii (1960).

Cartularium Abbathiae de Whiteby, ed. J.C. Atkinson, Surtees Soc., lxix (1879).

Chronica Guillelmi Thorne . . . de gestibus abbatum S. Augustini Cantuariae, in R. Twysden, *Historiae Anglicanae Scriptores X* (1652).

Chronicle of St Martin of Tours, in Bouquet (*q.v.*), xii.

Chronicon Beccense in B. *Lanfranci Opera Omnia*, ed. L. D'Achery (Paris 1648).

Chronicon monasterii de Hida, in *Liber monasterii de Hyda* (*q.v.*).

CLAY, C.T., *Early Yorkshire Charters*, iv: *The Honour of Richmond* (1935).

Constitutio Domus Regis, in *Dialogus de Scaccario* (*q.v.*).

COWDREY, H.E.J., 'The Anglo-Norman Laudes Regiae', *Viator*, xii (1981).

CRASTER, H.H.E., 'A contemporary record of the pontificate of Ranulf Flambard', *Archaeologia Æliana*, 4th ser., vii (1930).

De Injusta Vexatione, in Symeon of Durham (*q.v.*), i.

De Libertate Beccensis monasterii, in J. Mabillon, *Annales Ordinis S. Benedicti*, v (Paris 1713).

De Obitu Willelmi, in William of Jumièges (*q.v.*).

Dialogus de Scaccario, ed. and trans. C. Johnson (1950).

Diplomatic Documents preserved in the Public Record Office, i (1101–1272), ed. P. Chaplais (1964).

Domesday Book, seu liber censualis . . ., ed. A. Farley, (Record Commission, 1783).

DUGDALE, W., *Monasticon Anglicanum*, ed. J. Caley, H. Ellis and B. Bandinel (1817–30).

DUNCAN, A.A.M., 'The earliest Scottish charters', *Scottish Historical Review*, xxxvii (1958).

EADMER, *Historia Novorum in Anglia*, ed. M. Rule (Rolls ser., 1884).

——, *Vita Anselmi: The Life of St Anselm by Eadmer*, ed. and trans. R.W. Southern (1962).

EINHARD, *Vita Karoli Magni*, ed. and trans. L. Halphen (Paris, 3rd edn, 1947).

ENGELS, L., 'De obitu Willelmi ducis Normannorum regisque Anglorum: Texte, valeur, et origine', in *Mélanges offerts à Mlle Christine Morhmann* (nouveau recueil, Utrecht-Antwerp 1973).

FLORENCE OF WORCESTER, *Chronicon ex Chronicis*, ed. B. Thorpe (Eng. Hist. Soc. 1848–9).

GAIMAR, GEOFFREY, *Lestorie des Engles*, ed. T.D. Hardy and C.T. Martin (Rolls ser., 1888–9).

GALBRAITH, V.H., 'Royal Charters to Winchester', *EHR*, xxv (1920).

Gallia Christiana in provinciis ecclesiasticis distributa, xi, ed. monks of St Maur (Paris 1759).

GERALD OF WALES, *De Principis Instructione Liber*, ed. G.F. Warner (Rolls ser., 1891).

——, *Itinerarium Kambriae*, ed. J.F. Dimock (Rolls ser., 1868).

Gesta abbatum monasterii S. Albani, ed. H.T. Riley (Rolls ser., 1867).

Gesta Stephani, ed. K.R. Potter and R.H.C. Davis (1976).

GILES, J.A., *Scriptores Rerum Gestarum Willelmi Conquestoris* (Caxton Soc., 1845).

GILES OF PARIS, *Vita S. Hugonis*, ed. A. L'Huillier (Solesmes 1888); ed. H.E.J. Cowdrey, *Studi Gregoriani*, xi (1978).

GILSON, J.P., 'Two Letters addressed to William Rufus', *EHR*, xii (1897).

GOSCELIN OF ST BERTIN, *De Translatione S. Augustini*, in *Acta Sanctorum* (*q.v.*), May, vi.

GREENWAY, D.E., *Charters of the Honour of Mowbray* (1972).

GREGORY VII, *Registrum*, ed. E. Caspar, *MGH Epist. Select.*, 2, 1/2 (Berlin 1955).

GUIBERT OF NOGENT, *De Vita sua libri tres*, in Migne *PL*, clvi.

HAGENMEYER, H., *Die Kreuzzugsbriefe aus dem Jahren 1088–1100* (Innsbruck 1901).

HEARNE, T., *Textus Roffensis* (1720).

Hemingi Chartularium ecclesiae Wigorniensis, ed. T. Hearne (1723).

HENRY OF HUNTINGDON, *Historia Anglorum*, ed. T. Arnold (Rolls ser., 1879).

HERBERT LOSINGA: *Epistolae Herberti de Losinga, Osberti de Clara, et Elmeri*, ed. R. Anstruther (Brussels 1846).

Heremanni archidiaconi miracula S. Eadmundi, in *Ungedruckte Anglo-normannische Geschichtsquellen*, ed. F. Liebermann (Strasbourg 1879).

HERMAN, *De Miraculis S. Mariae Laudunensis*, in Migne *PL*, clvi.

HERMANN OF TOURNAI, *Liber de Restauratione S. Martini Tornacensis*, in *Monumenta Germanniae Historica, Script.*, xiv.

HILDEBERT OF LAVARDIN, *Letters*, in Migne *PL*, clxxi.

——, *Carmina Minora*, ed. A.B. Scott (Teubner) (Leipzig 1969).

——, *Vita S. Hugonis*, in Migne *PL*, clviii.

Historia Dunelmensis Ecclesiae, see Symeon of Durham.

Historia et cartularium monasterii Gloucestriae, ed. W.H. Hart, (Rolls ser., 1863–7).

Historia Regum, see Symeon of Durham.

HOLTZMANN, W., *Papsturkunden in England* (1930–52).

Hugh of Flavigny, *Chronicon*, ed. G.H. Pertz, *MGH. Script.*, viii.

Hugh the Chantor: the History of the church of York, 1066–1127, ed. and trans. C. Johnson (1961).

Icelandic Sagas, ed. G. Vigfusson, trans. G.W. Dasent (Rolls ser., 1887–94).

IVO OF CHARTRES, *Opera*, in Migne *PL*, clxii.

JOHN OF SALISBURY: *The Letters of John of Salisbury*, i, ed. W.J. Millor, H.E. Butler, C.N.L. Brooke (1955); ii, ed. Millor and Brooke (1979).

——, *Policraticus*, ed. C.C.J. Webb (1909).

——, *Vita S. Anselmi*, in Migne *PL*, cxcix.

LANFRANC: *The Letters of Lanfranc archbishop of Canterbury*, ed. and trans. H. Clover and M. Gibson (1979).

Leges Henrici Primi, ed. L.J. Downer (1972).

Liber Eliensis, ed. E.O. Blake, Royal Hist. Soc., Camden, 3rd ser., xcii (1962).

Liber monasterii de Hyda, ed. E. Edwards (Rolls ser., 1866).

Liber Vitae ecclesiae Dunelmensis, ed. W.H. Stevenson, Surtees Soc., xiii (1841).

Liber Vitae . . . of the New Minster and Hyde Abbey, ed. W. de Gray Birch, Hants Record Soc., v (1892).

LIEBERMANN, F., *Die Gesetze der Angelsachsen* (Halle 1903).

——, 'Reginald von Canterbury', *Neues Archiv der Gesellschaft für ältere deutsche Geschichtskunde*, xiii (1888).

LOWRIE, A., *Early Scottish Charters* (1905).

LUCHAIRE, A., *Louis VI le Gros: Annales de sa Vie et de son Règne* (Paris 1890).

MACK, R.P., *R.P. Mack Collection*, Sylloge of Coins of the British Isles, British Academy, xx (1973).

MANSI, J.D., *Sacrorum Conciliorum nova et amplissima Collectio* (repr. Graz 1960–1).

Memorials of St Edmund's Abbey, ed. T. Arnold (Rolls ser., 1890–6).

Miracles of St Cuthbert, see Symeon of Durham.

MUSSET, L., *Les Actes de Guillaume le Conquérant et de la Reine Mathilde pour les abbayes Caennaises*, Mém. de la Soc. des Antiquaires de Normandie, Caen, xxxvii (1967).

Neustria Pia seu de omnibus et singulis abbatiis et prioratibus totius Normanniae, ed. A. du Monstier (Rouen 1663).

OFFLER, H.S., *Durham Episcopal Charters, 1071–1152*, Surtees Soc., clxxix (1968).

ORDERIC VITALIS: *Orderici Vitalis ecclesiasticae historiae libri tredecim*, ed. A. le Prévost, Soc. de l'Histoire de France (Paris 1838–55); *The Ecclesiastical History of Orderic Vitalis*, ed. and trans. M. Chibnall (1969–81).

Pipe Roll of 31 Henry I, ed. J. Hunter (1833; 1929).

PROU, M., *Recueil des Actes de Philippe I roi de France, 1059–1108* (Paris 1908).

RAYMOND OF AGILES, *Historia Francorum*, in *Recueil des Historiens des Croisades*, Acad. des Inscr. ès Belles-Lettres, Paris, *Occ.*, iii (1866).

Recueil des Actes des ducs de Normandie, 911–1066, ed. M. Fauroux, Mém. Soc. Antiquaires de Normandie, Caen, xxxi (1961).

Regesta Regum Anglo-Normannorum, 1066–1154, i, ed. H.W.C. Davis and R.J. Whitwell (1913); ii, ed. Davis, C. Johnson and H.A. Cronne (1956).

Registrum Antiquissimum of the cathedral church of Lincoln, ed. C.W. Foster, Lincoln Record Soc., xxvii (1931).

ROBINSON, J.A., *Gilbert Crispin abbot of Westminster* (1911).

Rouleaux des Morts du IXe au XVe siècle, ed. L. Delisle, Soc. de l'Hist. de France (1866)

ROUND, J. H., *Calendar of Documents preserved in France* (1899).

SALTER, H.E., 'A dated charter of Henry I', *EHR*, xxvi (1911).
——, *Facsimiles of Early Charters in Oxford muniment rooms* (1929).
SAUVAGE, L'ABBÉ, 'Des Miracles advenus en l'église de Fécamp', *Soc. de l'Hist. de Normandie*, Mélanges 2 (Rouen 1893).
Sir Gawain and the Green Knight, trans. B. Stone (1959).
SOMERVILLE, R., *The Councils of Urban II*, i, *Decreta claromontensia*, in *Annuarium historiae Conciliorum*, suppl. i (Amsterdam 1972).
Song of Roland, trans. D.L. Sayers (1957).
STUBBS, W., *Select Charters and other Illustrations of English Constitutional History*, 9th edn, revised by H.W.C. Davis (1921).
SUDENDORF, H., *Berengarius Turonensis* (Hamburg and Gotha 1850).
SUGER, *Vie de Louis VI le Gros*, ed. and trans. H. Waquet (Paris 1929, 1964).
SYMEON OF DURHAM, *Historical Works*, ed. T. Arnold (Rolls ser., 1882-5).

THE ASTRONOMER, *Vita Hlodowici Imperatoris*, ed. G.H. Pertz, *MGH Script.*, ii (1829).
The Black Book of St Augustine's, ed. G.J. Turner and H.E. Salter (1924).
The Life of Christina of Markyate, ed. and trans. C.H. Talbot (1959).
The Master of Game by Edward, second duke of York, ed. W.A. and F. Baillie-Grohman (1909).
The Prose Salernitan Questions, ed. B. Lawn (1979).
TORIGNY, ROBERT OF, *Chronica*, in *Chronicles of Stephen, Henry II, and Richard I*, ed. R. Howlett (Rolls ser., iv, 1890).
——, *Interpolations*, in William of Jumièges (*q.v.*).
TURNER, D.H., *The Claudius Pontificals*, Henry Bradshaw Soc., xcvii (1971).

Vita Ædwardi Regis, ed. F. Barlow (1962).
Vita S. Godrici, ed. J. Stevenson, Surtees Soc., xx (1847).
Vita Gundulfi, in *Anglia Sacra*, ed. H. Wharton, ii (1691).
Vita Oswini, in *Miscellanea Biographia*, ed. J. Raine, Surtees Soc., viii (1838).
Vita B. Simonis, in Migne *PL*, clvi.
Vita Wulfstani of William of Malmesbury, ed. R.R. Darlington, Royal Hist. Soc., Camden, xl (1928).

WACE: *Le Roman de Rou de Wace*, ii-iii, ed. A.J. Holden (Paris 1971-3).
WALTER MAP, *De Nugis Curialium*, ed. T. Wright (Camden Soc., 1850).
WILKINS, D., *Concilia M. Britanniae et Hiberniae, 446-1717* (1737).
WILLIAM OF JUMIÈGES: *Guillaume de Jumièges: Gesta Normannorum Ducum*, ed. J. Marx, Soc. de l'Histoire de Normandie (1914).
WILLIAM OF MALMESBURY, *De Gestis Pontificum Anglorum*, ed. N.E.S.A. Hamilton (Rolls ser., 1870).
——, *De Gestis Regum Anglorum*, ed. W. Stubbs (Rolls ser., 1887-9).
——, *Historia Novella*, ed. and trans. K.R. Potter (1955).
WILLIAM OF NEWBURGH: *Guillelmi Neubrigensis Historia*, ed. T. Hearne (1719).
——, *Historia Rerum Anglicarum*, in *Chronicles of Stephen, Henry II, and Richard I*, ed. R. Howlett (Rolls ser., i, 1884).

William, earl of Pembroke, Knight-Marshal of the King's House: L'Histoire de Guillaume le Maréchal, ed. P. Meyer, Soc. de l'Hist. de France (Paris 1891–1901).

WILLIAM OF POITIERS: *Guillaume de Poitiers: Histoire de Guillaume le Conquérant*, ed. R. Foreville (Paris 1952).

II. SECONDARY AUTHORITIES

BAINES, F., *Westminster Hall* (HMSO, 1914).

BARKER, P.A. and HIGHAM, R.A., *Hen Dolmen, Montgomery: a Timber Castle on the Welsh Border*, Monograph of the Royal Arch. Institute (1982).

BARLOW, F., *Durham Jurisdictional Peculiars* (1950).

——, *William I and the Norman Conquest* (1965).

——, 'A view of Archbishop Lanfranc', *JEH*, xvi (1965).

——, 'Edward the Confessor's early life, character and attitudes', *EHR*, lxxx (1965).

——, *The English Church, 1000–1066* (2nd edn, 1979).

——, *The English Church, 1066–1154* (1979).

——, *Edward the Confessor* (2nd edn, 1979).

——, 'The Canonization and the early Lives of Hugh I, abbot of Cluny', *Analecta Bollandiana*, xcviii (1980).

——, 'William I's relations with Cluny', *JEH*, xxxii (1981).

——, 'Hunting in the Middle Ages', *Transactions of the Devonshire Association*, cxiii (1981).

BARRON, O., 'Our oldest families: X. The Berkeleys', *The Ancestor*, viii (1904).

BARROW, G.W.S., *The Kingdom of the Scots* (1973).

——, 'The pattern of lordship and feudal settlement in Cumbria', *Journ. of Medieval History*, i (1975).

BATES, D.R., Odo bishop of Bayeux, 1049–97' (unpublished Exeter PhD thesis, 1970).

——, 'The character and career of Odo, bishop of Bayeux', *Speculum*, l (1975).

——, 'The land pleas of William I's reign: Penenden Heath revisited', *Bull. of the Inst. of Hist. Research*, li, no. 123 (1978).

——, 'The origins of the Justiciarship', *Battle IV* (1982).

——, *Normandy before 1066* (1982).

Battle: Proceedings of the Battle Conference on Anglo-Norman Studies, ed. R.A. Brown, I–IV (1978–82).

BECKERMAN, J.S., 'Succession in Normandy, 1087, and in England, 1066: the role of testamentary custom', *Speculum*, xlvii (1972).

BLAIR, C.H. HUNTER, 'The early castles of Northumberland', *Archaeologia Æliana*, 4th ser., xxii (1944).

BÖHMER, H., *Kirche und Staat in England und in der Normandie im XI. und XII. Jahrhundert* (Leipzig 1899).

BOUCHARD, C.C., 'Consanguinity and noble marriages in the tenth and eleventh centuries', *Speculum*, lvi (1981).

BOUSSARD, J., 'La seigneurie de Bellême aux Xᵉ et XIᵉ siècles', *Mélanges . . . Louis Halphen (q.v.)*.

——, 'Le comté de Mortain au XIe siècle', *Le Moyen Age*, lviii (1952).

BROOKE, C.N.I., 'The composition of the chapter of St Paul's, 1086–1163', *Cambridge Hist. Journal*, x (1951).

——, and G. KEIR, *London 800–1216* (1975).

BROOKE, G.C., *English Coins* (1932).

BROWN, R.A., *Rochester Castle* (HMSO, 1969).

——, H.M. COLVIN, A.J. TAYLOR, *The History of the King's Works*, ii (1963).

BULLOUGH, V., and CAMPBELL, C., 'Female longevity and diet in the Middle Ages', *Speculum*, lv (1980).

BUR, M., 'Les comtes de Champagne et la "Normanitas": semiologie d'un tombeau', *Battle III* (1980).

CALLAHAN, T. JR., 'The Making of a Monster: the historical image of William Rufus', *Journ. of Med. Hist.*, vii (1981).

CARY, G., *The Medieval Alexander* (1956).

CHIBNALL, M., 'Feudal society in Orderic Vitalis', *Battle I* (1978).

CHURCHILL, I.J., *Canterbury Administration* (1933).

CLARK, C., 'Women's names in post-Conquest England: observations and speculations', *Speculum*, liii (1978).

CORBETT, W.J., 'The development of the duchy of Normandy and the Norman Conquest of England', *Cambridge Medieval History*, v (1926).

COX, J.C., *The Royal Forests of England* (1905).

CRONNE, H.A., 'The office of Local Justiciar in England under the Norman kings', *Univ. of Birmingham Hist. Journal*, vi (1958).

DAVID, C.W., *Robert Curthose, duke of Normandy* (Cambridge, Mass., 1920).

——, 'The claims of Henry I to be called learned', *Anniversary Essays in Mediaeval History by students of C.H. Haskins* (Boston and New York 1929).

DAVIES, R.R., 'Kings, Lords and Liberties in the March of Wales, 1066–1272', *Trans. Royal Hist. Soc.*, 5th ser., xxix (1979).

DAVIS, H.W.C., *England under the Normans and Angevins* (1905, 1924).

DAVIS, R.H.C., 'William of Jumièges, Robert Curthose and the Norman succession', *EHR*, xcv (1980).

——, 'William of Poitiers and his History of William the Conqueror', in *The Writing of History in the Middle Ages* (Southern *Festschrift*, 1981).

DHONT, J., *Etudes sur la naissance des principautés territoriales en France, IXe–Xe siècle* (Bruges 1948).

DICKINSON, W.C., *Scotland from the earliest times to 1603* (1961).

Dictionary of Medieval Latin from British Sources, prepared by R.E. Latham (1975).

Dictionary of National Biography, ed. L. Stephen (1885–1900).

DIEUDONNÉ, A., *Hildebert de Lavardin . . . sa Vie, ses Lettres* (Paris, Mamers, 1898).

Domesday Gazetteer, compiled by H.C. Darby and G.R. Versey (1975).

DOUGLAS, D.C., *The Domesday Monachorum of Christ Church Canterbury*, (1944).

——, 'The earliest Norman counts', *EHR*, lxi (1946).

——, 'Les évêques de Normandie, 1035–1066', *Annales de Normandie*, iii (1953).

——, *William the Conqueror* (1964).

DUBY, G., 'Dans la France du Nord-Ouest au XIIe siècle: les "jeunes" dans la société aristocratique', *Annales E.S.C.*, xix (1964).

——, 'Les Origines de la Chevalerie', *Ordinamenti Militari in Occidente nell' Alto Medioevo*, Centro Italiano di Studi sull'Alto Medioevo, Spoleto, Settimana xv, 1967 (Spoleto 1968), ii.

——, 'Le mariage dans la sociéte du haut moyen âge,' *Il matrimonio nella società altomedievale*, Centro Italiano di Studi sull'Alto Medioevo, Spoleto, Settimana xxiv, 1976 (Spoleto 1977).

DUNCAN, A.A.M., *Scotland: the Making of the Kingdom* (1975).

DUNCOMBE, G.R., 'Feudal tenure in eleventh-century England: the Norman Conquest of Kent' (unpublished Exeter MA thesis, 1967).

EDWARDS, J.G., 'The Normans and the Welsh March', *Proc. of the British Academy*, xlii (1956).

EVANS, G.R., 'Schools and Scholars: the study of the abacus in English schools, c.980–c.1150', *EHR*, xciv (1979).

EYTON, R.W., *A Key to Domesday . . . Dorset Survey* (1878).

FARRER, W., 'The sheriffs of Lincolnshire and Yorkshire, 1066–1130', *EHR*, xxx (1915).

——. *Honors and Knights' Fees* (1923–5).

FEUCHÈRE, P., 'Essai sur l'évolution territoriale des principautés françaises, X^e–XIIIe siècle: étude de géographie historique', *Le Moyen Age*, lviii (1952).

——, 'Une tentative manquée de concentration territoriale entre Somme et Seine: la principauté d'Amiens-Valois au XIe siècle', *Le Moyen Age*, lx (1954).

FINBERG, H.P.R., 'The early history of Werrington', *EHR*, lix (1944).

——, *Lucerna* (1964).

FINN, R. WELLDON, *The Domesday Inquest and the Making of Domesday Book* (1962).

——, *An Introduction to Domesday Book* (1963).

——, *Domesday Studies: The Liber Exoniensis* (1964).

——, *The Eastern Counties* (1967).

——, *The Norman Conquest and its Effect on the Economy, 1066–86* (1971).

FLICHE, A., *Le Règne de Philippe I, roi de France, 1060–1108* (Paris 1912).

FLORI, J., 'Les origines de l'adoubement chevaleresque: étude des remises d'armes et du vocabulaire qui les exprime dans les sources historiques latines jusqu'au début du XIIIe siècle', *Traditio*, xxxv (1979).

FOREVILLE, R. and J. LECLERCQ, 'Un débat sur le sacerdoce des moines au XIIe siècle', *Analecta Monastica*, 4th ser., iv, *Studia Anselmiana*, xli (Rome 1957).

FOWLER, J.T., 'An account of excavations made on the site of the chapter house of Durham cathedral in 1874', *Archaeologia*, xlv. pt.2 (1880).

FOX, L., 'The Honor and earldom of Leicester', *EHR*, xxxiv (1939).

FREEMAN, E.A., *The History of the Norman Conquest of England*, i, ii, (2nd edn, 1870); iii–v (1st edn, 1869–75).

——, *The Reign of William Rufus* (1882).

GALBRAITH, V.H., 'Girard the Chancellor', *EHR*, xlvi (1931).
——, *The Literacy of the Medieval English Kings*, Raleigh Lecture on History (British Academy, 1935)
——, *The Making of Domesday Book* (1961).
——, *Domesday Book* (1974).
——, *Domesday Book, its Place in Administrative History* (1974).
G.E.C [OKAYNE], *The Complete Peerage of England, Scotland, Ireland, Great Britain and the United Kingdom*, (rev. edn, 1910–59).
GENICOT, L., 'Recent research on the medieval nobility', in T. Reuter, *The Medieval Nobility* (1978).
GIBSON, M., *Lanfranc of Bec* (1978).
GOLDING, B., 'The coming of the Cluniacs', *Battle III* (1981).
GREEN, J.A., 'William Rufus, Henry I and the royal demesne', *History*, lxiv (1979).
——, 'The last century of Danegeld', *EHR*, xcvi (1981).
GRIERSON, P., 'L'origine des comtés d'Amiens, Valois, et Vexin', *Le Moyen Age*, xlix (1939).
——, 'Sterling', in *Anglo-Saxon Coins*, Stenton *Festschrift*, ed. R.H.M. Dolley (1961).
GRINNELL-MILNE, D., *The Killing of William Rufus* (1968).
GROUSSET, R., *Histoire des Croisades et du Royaume Franc de Jérusalem* (Paris 1934–6).

HAGENMEYER, H., 'Chronologie de la Première Croisade, 1094–1100', *Revue de l'Orient Latin*, vi–viii (1898–1901).
HALL, E. and SWEENEY, J.R., 'The "licentia de nam" of the abbess of Montivilliers and the origins of the port of Harfleur', *Bulletin of the Institute of Hist. Research*, lii (1979).
HALLAM, E.M., 'The king and the princes in 11th-century France', *Bulletin of the Institute of Hist. Research*, liii (1980).
HALPHEN, L., *Le comté d'Anjou au XIe siècle* (Paris 1906).
Handbook of British Chronology, ed. F.M. Powicke and E.B. Fryde (2nd edn, 1961).
HART, C., 'The hidation of Huntingdonshire', *Proc. of the Cambridge Antiqu. Soc.*, lxi (1968).
——, *The hidation of Northamptonshire*, Leicester Univ. Occas. Papers, 2nd ser., iii (1970).
——, *The hidation of Cambridgeshire*, ibid., vi (1974).
HARVEY, S., 'Royal revenue and Domesday terminology', *Ec. Hist. Rev.*, 2nd ser., xx (1967).
——, 'Domesday Book and its predecessors', *EHR*, lxxxvi (1971).
——, 'Domesday Book and Anglo-Norman governance', *Trans. Royal Hist. Soc.*, 5th ser., xxv (1975).
——, 'Recent Domesday Studies', *EHR*, xcv (1980).
HASKINS, C.H., 'The abacus and the king's curia', *EHR*, xxvii (1912).
——, *Norman Institutions* (New York 1918, 1967).

HAUCK, K., 'The literature of house and kindred', in T. Reuter, *The Medieval Nobility* (1978).

Heads of Religious Houses, England and Wales, 942–1216, ed. D. Knowles, C.N.L. Brooke, V. London (1972).

HIGOUNET, C., 'Un grand chapitre d'histoire du XIIe siècle: la rivalité des maisons de Toulouse et de la Barcelone pour la prépondérance méridionale', *Mélanges . . . Louis Halphen (q.v.)*.

HOLDSWORTH, W.S., *A History of English Law* (1923–72).

HOLLISTER, C.W., 'Military obligation in Late-Saxon and Norman England', *Ordinamenti Militari in Occidente nell'Alto Medioevo*, Centro Italiano di Studi sull'Alto Medioevo, Spoleto, Settimana xv, 1967 (Spoleto 1968), i.

——, 'The Anglo-Norman civil war: 1101', *EHR*, lxxxviii (1973).

——, 'The strange death of William Rufus', *Speculum*, xlviii (1973).

——, 'Normandy, France and the Anglo-Norman *regnum*', *Speculum*, li (1976).

——, 'Magnates and *Curiales* in early Norman England', *Viator*, viii (1977).

——, 'Henry I and the Anglo-Norman Magnates', *Battle II* (1980).

HOLT, J.C., 'Politics and property in early medieval England', *Past and Present*, lvii (1972).

HOSKINS, W.G., 'The Highland zone in Domesday Book', *Provincial England* (1965).

HOWELL, M., *Regalian Right in Medieval England* (1962).

JÄSCHKE, K.-U., *Wilhelm der Eroberer, sein doppelter Herrschaftsantritt im Jahre 1066* (Sigmaringen 1977).

John le Neve: Fasti Ecclesiae Anglicanae, 1066–1300, compiled by D.E. Greenway, I, *St Paul's London* (1968).

JOLLIFFE, J.E.A., *Angevin Kingship* (1955).

KAPELLE, W.E., *The Norman Conquest of the North* (1979).

KENDRICK, T.D. and TONNOCHY, A.B., 'Flambard's Crozier', *The Antiquaries Journal*, xviii (1938).

KENT, J.P.C., 'From Roman Britain to Saxon England', *Anglo-Saxon Coins*, Stenton *Festschrift* (1961).

KEYNES, S., *The Diplomas of King Æthelred the Unready* (1980).

KIENAST, W., *Der Herzogstitel in Frankreich und Deutschland, 9. bis 12. Jahrhundert* (Munich and Vienna 1968).

KNOWLES, D., *The Monastic Order in England* (1940, 1963).

LATOUCHE, R., *Histoire du comté du Maine pendant le Xe et le XIe siècle* (Paris 1910).

——, 'La Commune du Mans, 1070', *Mélanges . . . Louis Halphen (q.v.)*.

LEMARIGNIER, J.F., *Recherches sur l'hommage en marche et les frontières féodales* (Lille 1945).

LE PATOUREL, J.H., 'Geoffrey of Montbray, bishop of Coutances, 1049–93', *EHR*, lix (1944).

——, 'The Norman colonization of Britain', *I Normanni e la loro espansione in Europa nell'alto medioevo*, Centro Italiano di Studi sull'Alto Medioevo, Spoleto, Settimana xvi, 1968 (Spoleto 1969).

——, 'The Norman succession, 996–1135', *EHR*, lxxxvi (1971).

——, *Normandy and England, 1066–1144*, The Stenton Lecture, 1970 (Reading University, 1971).

——, 'Norman kings or Norman "king-dukes"?', in *Droit privé et institutions régionales: études historiques offertes à Jean Yver* (Rouen 1976).

——, *The Norman Empire* (1976).

LETHABY, W.R., 'The palace of Westminster in the eleventh and twelfth centuries', *Archaeologia*, lx (1906).

LLOYD, J.E., *A History of Wales*, ii (3rd edn, 1939).

LOYD, L.C., *The Origins of some Anglo-Norman families*, ed. C.T. Clay and D.C. Douglas, Harleian Soc., ciii (1951).

LOYN, H.R., 'Domesday Book', *Battle I* (1979).

MAITLAND, F.W., *Domesday Book and Beyond* (1897; reprinted 1960).

MASON, E., 'William Rufus: myth and reality', *Journ. of Med. Hist.*, iii (1977).

——, 'Magnates, Curiales and the Wheel of Fortune', *Battle II* (1980).

MASON, J.F.A., 'The "Honour of Richmond" in 1086', *EHR*, lxxviii (1963).

——, 'Roger de Montgomery and his sons', *Trans. Royal Hist. Soc.*, 5th ser., xiii (1963).

——, 'The Rapes of Sussex and the Norman Conquest', *Sussex Arch. Coll.*, cii (1964).

Mélanges d'Histoire du Moyen Age dédiés à la mémoire de Louis Halphen (Paris 1951).

MOOS, P. VON, *Hildebert von Lavardin, 1056–1133*, Pariser historische Studien, iii (Stuttgart 1965).

MORRIS, W.A., *The Medieval English Sheriff to 1300* (1927).

MORTIMER, R., 'The beginnings of the honour of Clare', *Battle III* (1981).

NELSON, L.H., *The Normans in South Wales, 1070–1171* (Austin and London 1966).

OFFLER, H.S., 'Rannulph Flambard as bishop of Durham', *Durham Univ. Journal*, lxiv (1971).

ORPEN, G.H., *Ireland under the Normans* (1911).

PACAUT, M., *Louis VII et son Royaume* (Paris 1964).

PETIT DUTAILLIS, C., *Studies and Notes supplementary to Stubbs' Constitutional History*, ii (1915).

POOLE, A.L., *From Domesday Book to Magna Carta* (1951).

POOLE, R.L., *The Exchequer in the Twelfth Century* (1912).

PRESTWICH, J.O., 'War and Finance in the Anglo-Norman State', *Trans. Royal Hist. Soc.*, 5th ser., iv (1954).

——, 'The Military Household of the Norman Kings', *EHR*, xcvi (1981).

RACKHAM, O., *Ancient Woodland* (1980).

RAMSAY, J.H., *A History of the Revenues of the Kings of England, 1066–1399* (1925).

REEDY, W.T. JR, 'The Origins of the General Eyre in the Reign of Henry I', *Speculum*, xli (1966).

RENN, D.F., *Norman Castles in Britain* (1968).

REUTER, T., *The Medieval Nobility; Europe in the Middle Ages, Selected Studies*, xiv (1978).

RICHARD, A., *Histoire des Comtes de Poitou, 778–1204* (Paris 1903).

RICHARDSON, H.G., 'The coronation in medieval England: the evolution of the office and the oath', *Traditio*, xvi (1960).

RICHARDSON, H.G., and SAYLES, G.O., *The Governance of Medieval England* (1963)

RITCHIE, R.L.G., *The Normans in Scotland* (1954).

ROSENTHAL, J.T., 'The education of the early Capetians', *Traditio*, xxv (1969).

ROSE-TROUP, F., 'Clarembald and the Miracles of Exeter', *Exeter Vignettes*, Univ. College of the S.W. of England monograph, vii (1942).

ROUND, J.H., *Geoffrey de Mandeville* (1892).

——, *Feudal England* (1895).

——, 'Bernard the king's scribe', *EHR*, xiv (1899).

——, *Studies in Peerage and Family History* (1901).

——, 'The origins of the Fitzgeralds', *The Ancestor*, i (1902).

——, *The King's Serjeants and Officers of State* (1911).

——, *Family Origins* (1930).

ROWLANDS, I.W., 'The making of the March: aspects of the Norman settlement in Dyfed', *Battle III* (1981).

RUNCIMAN, S., *A History of the Crusades* (1951–4).

SALTMAN, A., *Theobald archbishop of Canterbury* (1956).

SANDERS, I.J., *Feudal military service in England* (1956).

——, *English Baronies . . . 1086–1327* (1960).

SCHMID, K., 'The structure of the nobility in the earlier Middle Ages', in T. Reuter, *The Medieval Nobility* (1978).

SCHMITT, F.S., 'Zur Ueberlieferung der Korrespondenz Anselms von Canterbury: Neue Briefe', *Revue Bénédictine*, xliii (1931).

SCHNITH, K., 'Normannentum und Mönchtum bei Ordericus Vitalis', in *Secundum Regulam Vivere: Festschrift für P. Norbert Backmund, O. Praem.* (Windberg 1978).

——, 'Die Wende der englischen Geschichte im 11. Jahrhundert', *Historisches Jahrbuch*, lxxvi (1966).

SEARLE, E., 'Battle Abbey and Exemption: the forged charters', *EHR*, lxxxiii (1968).

SEARLE, E., 'Women and the legitimization of succession at the Norman Conquest', *Battle III* (1981).

SOUTHERN, R.W., 'The place of Henry I in English history', *Proc. of the British Academy*, xlviii (1962–3).

——, *St Anselm and his Biographer* (1963).

——, *Medieval Humanism and other Studies* (1970).

——, 'St Anselm and Gilbert Crispin, abbot of Westminster', *Mediaeval and Renaissance Studies*, iii (1975).

STENTON, D.M., 'Roger of Salisbury Regni Angliae Procurator', *EHR*, xxxix (1924).

STENTON, F.M., *The First Century of English Feudalism, 1066–1166* (1932).

——, 'The road system of medieval England', *Ec. Hist. Rev.*, vii (1936–7).

STUBBS, W., Introduction to *Gesta Regis Henrici Secundi Benedicti Abbatis*, Rolls ser., ii (1867).

TATLOCK, J.S.P., *The Legendary History of Britain* (1950).

TILLMANN, H., *Die päpstlichen Legaten in England bis zur Beendigung der Legation Gualas, 1218* (Bonn 1926).

TURNER, G.J., 'The Sheriff's Farm', *Trans. Royal Hist. Soc.*, n.s. xii (1898).

VAN HOUTS, E.M.C., 'Quelques remarques sur les Interpolations attribuées à Orderic Vital . . .', *Rev. d'histoire des Textes*, viii (1978).

——, 'The *Gesta Normannorum Ducum*', *Battle III* (1980).

VAUGHN, S.N., 'St Anselm of Canterbury: the philosopher saint as politician', *Journ. of Med. Hist.*, i (1975).

VERCAUTEREN-DESMET, L., 'Etude sur les rapports politiques de l'Angleterre et de la Flandre sous le règne du comte Robert II', *Etudes . . . dediées . . . à . . . H. Pirenne* (Brussels 1937).

VIC, C. DE and VAISSETE, J.J., *Histoire Générale de Languedoc*, ii (Toulouse 1733).

Victoria History of the counties of England (1900 etc.).

VINOGRADOFF, P., *English Society in the Eleventh Century* (1908).

WALKER, D., 'The Norman Settlement in Wales', *Battle I* (1979).

WATSON, A.M., 'Back to Gold – and Silver', *Ec. Hist. Rev.*, 2nd ser., xx (1967).

WERNER, K.F., 'Kingdom and principality in twelfth-century France', in T. Reuter, *The Medieval Nobility* (1978).

——, 'Noble families in Charlemagne's kingdom', in T. Reuter, *The Medieval Nobility* (1978).

WEST, F.J., *The Justiciarship in England, 1066–1232* (1966).

WHITE, G.H., 'The Household of the Norman Kings', *Trans. Royal Hist. Soc.*, 4th ser., xxx (1948).

WIGHTMAN, W.E., *The Lacy Family in England and Normandy, 1066–1194* (1966).

WILLIAMS, A., 'Land and power in the 11th century: the estates of Harold Godwineson', *Battle III* (1981).

WOLFFE, B.P., *The Royal Demesne in English History* (1971).

WYON, A.B., and A., *The Great Seals of England* (1887).

ZARNECKI, G., 'Romanesque sculpture in Normandy and England in the eleventh century', *Battle I* (1979).

GENEALOGICAL TABLES

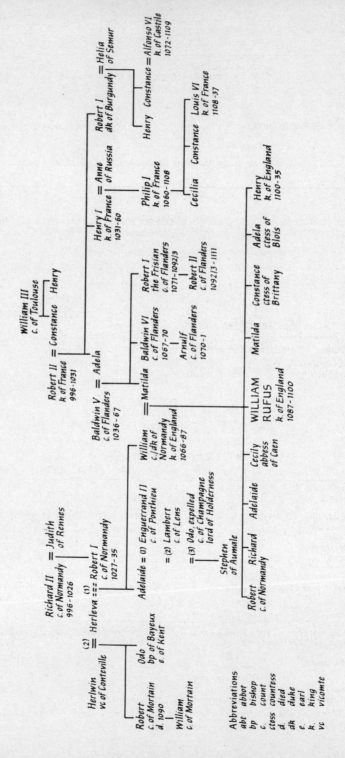

1. William Rufus and his relations

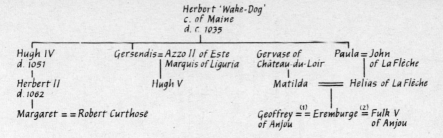

Herbert 'Wake-Dog'
c. of Maine
d. c. 1035

| Hugh IV d. 1051 | Gersendis = Azzo II of Este Marquis of Liguria | Gervase of Château-du-Loir | Paula = John of La Flèche |

Herbert II
d. 1062

Hugh V

Matilda ═══ Helias of La Flèche

Margaret = = Robert Curthose

Geoffrey =(1) = Eremburge (2)= Fulk V
of Anjou   of Anjou

2. Counts of Maine

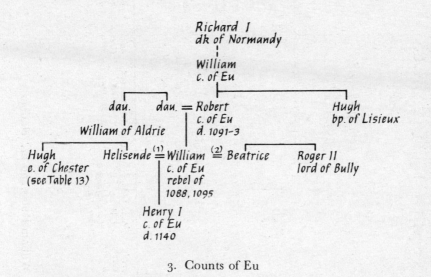

Richard I
dk of Normandy

William
c. of Eu

dau.   dau. = Robert   Hugh
              c. of Eu   bp. of Lisieux
William of Aldrie d. 1091-3

Hugh   Helisende (1)═ William (2)═ Beatrice   Roger II
c. of Chester   c. of Eu   lord of Bully
(see Table 13)   rebel of
                               1088, 1095

              Henry I
              c. of Eu
              d. 1140

3. Counts of Eu

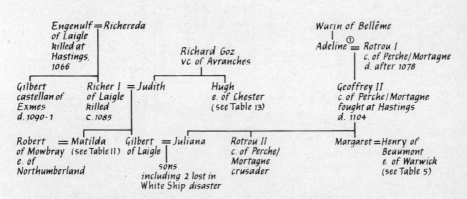

| Engenulf = Richereda of Laigle killed at Hastings, 1066 | | Richard Goz vc of Avranches | | Warin of Bellême Adeline ① = Rotrou I c. of Perche/Mortagne d. after 1078 |

Gilbert   Richer I = Judith   Hugh   Geoffrey II
castellan of   of Laigle   e. of Chester   c. of Perche/Mortagne
Exmes   killed   (see Table 13)   fought at Hastings
d. 1090-1   c. 1085   d. 1104

Robert = Matilda   Gilbert = Juliana   Rotrou II   Margaret = Henry of
of Mowbray (see Table 11) of Laigle   c. of Perche/   Beaumont
e. of   Mortagne   e. of Warwick
Northumberland   sons   crusader   (see Table 5)
                   including 2 lost in
                   White Ship disaster

4. Counts of Perche/Mortagne and the lords of L'Aigle

1. This relationship is, however, denied by J. Boussard, 'La seigneurie de Bellême aux Xe et XIe siècles', *Mélanges Louis Halphen* (Paris 1951), 45–6.

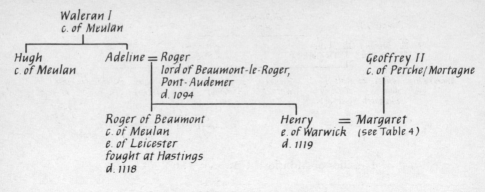

5. Counts of Meulan, lords of Beaumont

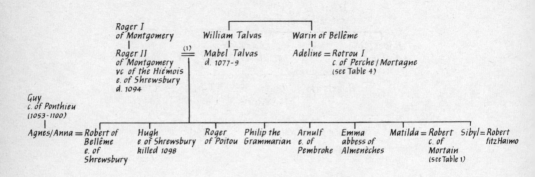

6. Lords of Bellême-Montgomery

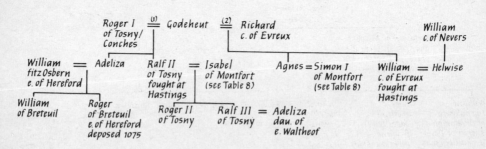

7. Counts of Evreux and lords of Tosny/Conches and of Breteuil

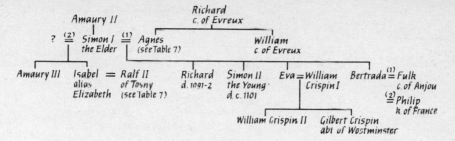

8. Families of Montfort (l'Amaury) and of Crispin

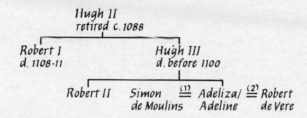

9. Lords of Montfort (-sur-Risle)

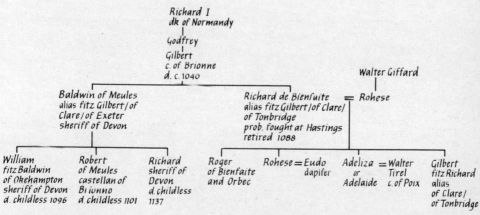

10. Family of 'Clare'

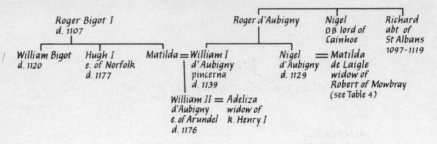

11. Families of Bigot and d'Aubigny

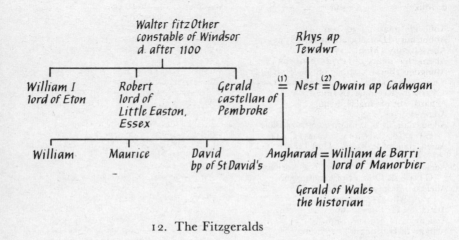

12. The Fitzgeralds

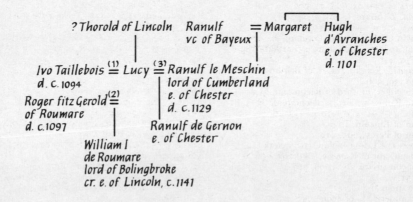

13. Lucy of Bolingbroke's husbands:
    Ivo Taillebois, Roger fitzGerold, Ranulf le Meschin

INDEX

Persons are indexed under their first name